P9-APN-181

CRIMINAL
LAW

Examples and Explanations

Editorial Advisory Board
 Aspen Publishers, Inc.
Legal Education Division

Richard A. Epstein
James Parker Hall Distinguished Service Professor of Law
University of Chicago

E. Allan Farnsworth
Alfred McCormack Professor of Law
Columbia University

Ronald J. Gilson
Charles J. Meyers Professor of Law and Business
Stanford University
Marc and Eva Stern Professor of Law and Business
Columbia University

Geoffrey C. Hazard, Jr.
Trustee Professor of Law
University of Pennsylvania

James E. Krier
Earl Warren DeLano Professor of Law
University of Michigan

Elizabeth Warren
Leo Gottlieb Professor of Law
Harvard University

Bernard Wolfman
Fessenden Professor of Law
Harvard University

CRIMINAL LAW

Examples and Explanations
Second Edition

Richard G. Singer
Distinguished Professor of Law
Rutgers, The State University of
New Jersey School of Law

John Q. La Fond
Edward A. Smith/Missouri Chair in
Law, the Constitution, and Society
University of Missouri-Kansas City
School of Law

ASPEN LAW & BUSINESS
A Division of Aspen Publishers, Inc.
Gaithersburg   New York

Copyright © 2001 by John Q. La Fond and Richard G. Singer

All rights reserved. No part of this publication may be repro-
duced or transmitted in any form or by any means, electronic
or mechanical, including photocopy, recording, or any information storage and retrieval system, without permission in writing
from the publisher. Requests for permission to make copies of
any part of this publication should be mailed to:

Permissions
Aspen Law & Business
1185 Avenue of the Americas
New York, NY 10036

Printed in the United States of America

1 2 3 4 5 6 7 8 9 0

Library of Congress Cataloging-in-Publication Data

Singer, Richard G.
  Criminal law : examples and explanations / Richard G.
Singer, John Q. La Fond. — 2nd ed.
    p. cm. — (Examples & explanations series)
  Includes index.
  ISBN 0-7355-2013-5
    1. Criminal law — United States — Outlines, syllabi, etc.
I. La Fond, John Q. II. Title.   III. Series.

KF9219.3 .S54 2001
345.73 — dc21

                              00-053579

About Aspen Law & Business
Legal Education Division

With a dedication to preserving and strengthening the long-standing tradition of publishing excellence in legal education, Aspen Law & Business continues to provide the highest quality teaching and learning resources for today's law school community. Careful development, meticulous editing, and an unmatched responsiveness to the evolving needs of today's discerning educators combine in the creation of our outstanding casebooks, coursebooks, textbooks, and study aids.

ASPEN LAW & BUSINESS
A Division of Aspen Publishers, Inc.
A Wolters Kluwer Company
www.aspenpublishers.com

To Karen: For the laughter, and the love
—R.G.S.

To my mother, Dorothy Quinn La Fond
—J.Q.L.

Summary of Contents

Contents

Preface

Criminal law forces us to confront the most important moral dilemmas of our times. More than most law school courses, criminal law engages our emotions as well as our intellects. This book will encourage that engagement. Many of our examples are taken from current topics of intense public debate such as euthanasia, abortion, rape, and black rage. But the underlying normative challenge of the criminal law — justifying the coercive use of state power against individuals — transcends particular controversies. Indeed, this debate has challenged great thinkers of the past like Plato, Socrates, Aquinas, and Kant. And it will certainly challenge us and future generations. This text keeps that tension in sharp and continuous focus.

This book seeks to help students master a broad range of criminal law doctrines. But it does not merely present a collection of "rules." It also explains and analyzes those doctrines and the problems they generate in a cohesive and comprehensive way. Where there are ambiguities — either theoretical or practical — we discuss them. Not to do so would mislead students and trivialize the criminal law. By recognizing how complex the tapestry is and how interwoven are its various threads students can appreciate the rich nuances of its doctrine and policy. This book examines that complexity, while remaining easy to read and to understand. Its sole purpose is to help students learn.

We were attracted to the format of the *Examples and Explanations* series long before we began work on this book. The format fits the typical law school classroom experience by posing challenging problems first (without answers of course!), followed by proposed solutions. We also enjoyed the humor evident in some other volumes in this series. Learning is serious business — but no business is so serious that it cannot be approached with an occasional smile. We have tried to sprinkle humor generously throughout the book.

From all reports, students have found the First Edition of this book very helpful not only for mastering criminal law, but also for learning what is expected of them on law school exams. We are pleased that the First Edition was successful. We have maintained the same basic approach, but we have thoroughly updated the Second Edition. New material has been added on important and current topics like sexual predator laws, stalking statutes, and the Federal Sentencing Guidelines. Examples drawn from newspaper headlines, such as the Columbine High School massacre and high-tech computer crimes, will interest and challenge you. We think that you will enjoy this book and that it will help you, as it has evidently helped many other students, to succeed in your criminal law course.

Finally, a plea for your help. This book can only be successful in helping students if the authors know what works—and what doesn't. We are anxious for your comments—negative and positive—on the piece, either on specific topics or hypotheticals, or generally. Please write us at our email addresses and give us your criticisms and comments. We can't promise we'll respond directly, but we can promise that we'll consider every point as we move toward a third edition.

rsinger@crab.rutgers.edu
lafondj@umkc.edu

To all who read this book, we hope you learn from it and enjoy it.

Richard G. Singer
John Q. La Fond

February 2001

Acknowledgments

This book bears the name of its "authors." But it required the hard work, assistance, and sacrifice of many people. Our students contributed helpful comments on many of the examples in this book, thereby saving future students the foibles found in earlier versions. Research assistants, particularly Laura Anglin, Jenifer Hanlon, Tara Manley, and Anne-Marie Sargent at Seattle University School of Law, and Seawn Hersini and Katherine Schoofs at the University of Missouri-Kansas City School of Law, made significant contributions to the manuscript. Moral support was provided by our respective Deans — Roger Dennis, Jim Bond, and Burnele Powell. The tedious and frustrating job of reading our scribbles and making sense of them fell to wonderful and indefatigable secretaries: Noreen Slease at Seattle University, Norma Karn at the University of Missouri-Kansas City School of Law, and Mary Ann Purvenas at Rutgers University. We wish especially to thank our respective spouses, Karen Garfing and Evelyn La Fond, for their continuing tolerance and patient support.

We wish to thank the following copyright holder who kindly granted permission to reprint excerpts from the following material:

Model Penal Code and Commentaries, Copyright © 1985 by The American Law Institute. Reprinted with permission.

1

The Sources and Limitations of the Criminal Law

Overview

Ever since Cain slew Abel (if not since Adam and Eve ate the apple), societies have had to deal with those whose acts seem "wrong." A conclusion that an act is wrong may be simply innate.[1] Some wrongs, however, seem worse than others. Thus, breaking a promise or tripping someone seems wrong, but homicide, rape, maiming, and so on seem "really" wrong. If a general consensus arises that specific acts are "really" wrong, there will be laws against such acts. Some acts will be criminally punished, while others, deemed by a legislature to be less serious, will be handled by civil parts of the legal system. This book focuses on how some behavior is defined and punished as "criminal."

American criminal law has three main sources: (1) the common law, (2) statutory law, and (3) constitutional law. Of these, the most important is statutory law, since it is now accepted that it is unconstitutional to punish someone unless his conduct was previously proscribed by the legislature. Nevertheless, criminal statutes are interpreted in light of an 800-year history of common law principles and against more modern constraints imposed by constitutional doctrines. The criminal law is yet further limited: Since most of criminal law consists of statutes, courts have established maxims of statu-

---

1. G. Fletcher, Rethinking Criminal Law 115-118 (1978).

1

tory interpretation, some rooted in the Constitution, others not. Of these, the most important are examined at pages 9-10, including the void for vagueness doctrine and the rule of lenity.

Finally, this chapter explores, if only briefly, the procedural limitation that requires the prosecution to persuade a jury beyond a reasonable doubt that the defendant is guilty. Just as important as the standard and its articulation are the reasons why the Supreme Court has held this standard to be required by the Constitution.

Sources of Criminal Law

The Common Law as a Source of Criminal Law

Early English custom condemned as felonies seven offenses: mayhem, homicide, rape, larceny, burglary, arson, and robbery. All other offenses were misdemeanors. These classifications became known as the common law because they were commonly shared.[2]

The term "common law" is usually employed to refer solely to judge-made law, typically in the areas of torts and contracts. However, legislatures early became interested in defining crimes; therefore, in the context of criminal law, the term "common law" incorporates both statutes and judge-made law as well as judicial interpretations of statutes. The power of courts to "create" crimes existed until well into the nineteenth century and in some rare instances continues even today.

Initially, English law treated all injuries, except homicide, as inflicting private harms that could be compensated. If the injured party accepted compensation, the defendant could not also be criminally sanctioned. After the Norman Conquest, however, the new kings, unhappy with leaving such decisions in private hands, sought to establish their power over crimes by punishing these actors. Although this divergence between torts (compensable acts) and crimes (punishable acts) began more than 800 years ago, and took centuries to complete, even today many acts that constitute crimes also often constitute torts. Therefore, it is still helpful to compare the common law rules of tort, in which compensation to the plaintiff is the major concern, with the common law rules of crimes, in which punishment of the defendant is the sole concern. Keep these comparisons in mind as you read through this book.

---

2. Because it was an evolutionary process, however, there is no "starting point" to the common law, although Hale has urged 1192, the date of the ascension of Richard I to the throne of England, as the "best" starting date. Hale, The History of the Common Law in England (3rd ed. 1739).

Legislative Sources

When tort and crime procedures (and remedies) divided, the role of the legislature was enhanced. The English Parliament codified the common law of crimes and — slowly at first, then rapidly — enlarged the list of felonies beyond the initial seven. In the United States, legislative dominance in defining crimes through statutes has continued, on the ground that the protection of citizens was too important to leave to the gradual development by judges of the common law.

In political theory, legislatures should be at least predominantly, if not exclusively, the source of criminal law in a democracy. To the extent that criminal law reflects moral sentiments of the community, the legislature, as the most democratically elected institution, should prevail. Courts, which are usually appointed, should be subordinate to the representative body; even where judges are elected, they are not as frequently reviewed by the populace.

Statutes, however, can be ambiguous. Statutes are usually written not one provision at a time but address many issues that are considered in a relatively short time. It would be unrealistic to expect legislatures to focus on the precise questions that litigation may pinpoint. Moreover, no matter how carefully written, statutes are in English, a notoriously ambiguous and opaque language. Thus, judicial interpretation of statutes is inevitable.

The interplay between the common law (developed by courts) and statutes (developed by legislatures) is dynamic. American courts can no longer "create" crimes, as their English forebears did in earlier times (see Chapter 10 (theft) and Chapter 13 (conspiracy)). There is also agreement that there can be no crime unless there is a statute prohibiting the conduct.[3] Still, courts can construe statutes either broadly or narrowly, thus effectively broadening or narrowing the reach of the statutory criminal law.

The Model Penal Code as a Source of Criminal Law

In our federal system each state is free within constitutional limits to develop its own common and statutory law. Consequently, state and federal legislatures have enacted differing statutes, and the courts have interpreted English common law principles differently. As a result, American criminal law, while sharing a common basis, is quite diverse. Prior to 1960, it was difficult to speak of "the criminal law of the United States."

In 1962 the American Law Institute (ALI), a private organization comprised of leading lawyers, judges, and scholars, adopted the Model Penal Code (MPC), intended as legislation for states to adopt or reject. Since its

---

3. S. Pomorski, American Common Law and the Principle Nulla Crimen Sine Lege (1975).

promulgation in 1962, the MPC has been adopted in whole or in part by legislatures in over 35 states. Because of that general acceptance, no survey of current criminal law could omit the MPC. This book compares the doctrines of the MPC with the previous doctrines of law. Those earlier doctrines, whether statutory or common, are referred to together here as the "common law." Be warned, however—our comparison is with the MPC *as adopted by the ALI*. No state has adopted the MPC precisely as proposed by the ALI, and many jurisdictions (most importantly, the federal Code and that of California) still have not adopted the MPC in any way. Thus, while it may be generally true that the MPC is "American law," any specific provision may not be "the law" in a particular jurisdiction. Still, even in jurisdictions that have not enacted the MPC, courts sometimes look to it for guidance because it is thought to embody neutral and carefully constructed approaches to criminal law doctrine.

Constitutional Sources and Limits

Many decisions you will read in your constitutional law class are criminal law cases. In this sense, many constitutional guarantees in the Bill of Rights *directly* limit legislative policy. Thus, under the First Amendment, Congress and state legislatures may not pass *any* law (including a criminal law) that restricts freedom of speech, religion, or the press. In addition to these well-recognized constitutional rights, decisions of the last 30 years have recognized a "right of privacy" that legislatures may not infringe. It was under this theory that the Supreme Court decided the famous case of *Roe v. Wade*, 410 U.S. 113 (1973). Although procedurally that case was a civil matter, it held that states could not criminally punish persons performing or undergoing abortions. Similarly, *Bowers v. Hardwick*, 478 U.S. 186 (1986), was a civil suit to enjoin enforcement of a criminal statute. There, however, the court held that the right to privacy did not forbid states to punish criminally homosexual sodomy.

The precise contours of these rights, including the right to privacy, are not clear. Nonetheless, each of these constitutional rights reminds us that the criminal law is not merely a means of punishment—the doctrines of the criminal law also protect those whose conduct does not fall directly within its clear meaning.

One final point—none of these doctrines necessarily answers the question of the *wisdom* of criminalizing certain behavior. Conflicts about so-called "victimless" crimes are one example. Another is the use of the criminal law in attempts to improve undesirable behavior—for example, punishing drug addict mothers for "delivering" the drug to their unborn fetuses. See *Johnson v. State*, 602 So. 2d 1288 (Fla. 1992).

The basic doctrines of the common law of crimes are sometimes said to be so "essential" to the proper exercise of governmental authority that it is suggested that at least some set *constitutional* limits to legislature power in this arena. Thus, some state courts have held that criminal statutes that do not require the prosecution to demonstrate that the defendant committed a voluntary act or had a guilty mind (which were predicates of all common law crimes) violate constitutional limits. Although such holdings are rare, the tacit presence of this constitutional prohibition strongly influences the way in which courts interpret and apply statutes. Courts seeking to avoid deciding whether an ambiguous statute is constitutional may apply the doctrine of lenity or the requirement of fair notice (discussed below).

While it is true that only legislatures can define crimes, the legislative power is more restricted in the criminal arena than in other areas, in which courts give much greater deference to legislative judgments. Whether that is due to the unique sanctions that criminal law carries (see Chapter 2 on punishment) is not clear. However, recognizing the interplay of these three sources—common law, statutes, and constitutional precepts—is essential to understanding American criminal law.

Limitations on the Criminal Law

Law-abiding people should not have to guess at whether there is a criminal law forbidding their conduct or, if there is, what that law means. Likewise, the police, who enforce the law, should not have the power to decide what behavior the law covers. Finally, both trial and appellate courts need to know what the law is in order to apply it fairly and consistently in numerous cases.

Several doctrines, including the principle of legality, the constitutional doctrine of "void for vagueness," and the rule of lenity, address these concerns. The principle of legality provides that before individuals can be convicted and punished for engaging in such conduct, it must be legislatively prohibited. The constitutional doctrine of void for vagueness requires the criminal law to be sufficiently clear so that individuals of ordinary ability can understand what their legal obligations are. The rule of lenity requires a court to construe criminal statutes strictly, resolving doubt in favor of the defendant.

The Principle of Legality
The Common Law in England

The common law method of formulating new crimes virtually stopped in the mid-nineteenth century and most (though not all) American legislatures have now expressly abolished common law crimes.[4] Nonetheless, Eng-

---

4. 3 J. Stephen, A History of the Criminal Law of England 359-360 (1883).

lish judges still occasionally apply common law crimes to novel situations that are not expressly covered by a criminal statute.

Thus, in *Shaw v. Director of Prosecutions*,[5] the defendant published a "Ladies Directory" of prostitutes, which contained their names, pictures, addresses, telephone numbers, and other customer information. Prostitution itself was not a crime, but soliciting in public was. The House of Lords upheld the defendant's conviction for "conspiracy to corrupt public morals" even though there was no criminal statute forbidding the publication of such a directory. Viscount Simonds concluded that courts retained:

> residual power to enforce the supreme and fundamental purpose of the law, to conserve not only the safety and order but also the moral welfare of the State. . . . [I]t is their duty to guard against attacks which may be the more insidious because they are novel and unprepared for. . . . Such occasions will be rare, for Parliament has not been slow to legislate when attention has been sufficiently aroused. But gaps remain and will always remain since no one can foresee every way in which the wickedness of man may disrupt the order of society.[6]

The Common Law in the United States

The early colonists brought with them the common law of England and its statutes, both civil and criminal.[7] Thus, most states had common law crimes. A number of states enacted comprehensive statutory criminal codes in the nineteenth century. In some states common law crimes were virtually displaced by specific statutory declaration; in others, the common law was preserved.

The Strengths and Weaknesses of Common Law Crimes

Common law crimes have some strengths. As Viscount Simonds observed, they ensure that the criminal law is always available to punish harmful conduct even if the legislature failed to anticipate its occurrence by enacting an applicable criminal statute. They also discourage the imaginative exploitation of loopholes in the criminal laws, which may cause great harm. Common law crimes provide flexibility, which permits adjustment to new and unanticipated situations.

Common law crimes, however, also have serious weaknesses. First, un-

---

5. House of Lords, [1962] A.C. 220.

6. Id.

7. See Hall, The Common Law: An Account of Its Reception in the United States, 4 Vand. L. Rev. 791 (1951).

less there is a clear precedential case available, an individual could not know beforehand if her contemplated conduct is lawful or criminal. Only when a court decides after the fact, using analogies or cases from other jurisdictions, would a defendant learn whether she had committed a crime. Even someone trying to obey the law must act at her own peril. The defendant in *Shaw* found himself in this position. Faced with such uncertainty, many individuals may play it safe and avoid engaging in conduct that would not be declared criminal and that may be socially useful.

Second, under a common law system the limits on governmental authority are not clear. The criminal law is a restriction on individual liberty, but it is also a restriction on governmental authority. Unless the law draws a clear boundary between permissible and impermissible behavior, the government can more easily use the awesome power of the criminal law to convict and incarcerate individuals it considers its enemies for behavior that may have actually been innocent.[8]

The absence of a clear set of rules embodied in criminal statutes thus creates uncertainty in predicting the future. It also weakens the moral justifications for conviction and punishment and diminishes the restraints on government.

Contemporary Law

Today, most jurisdictions have enacted comprehensive modern criminal statutes. This clear preference for a statutory criminal law reflects a collective sense of justice that individuals are entitled to the protection afforded by clearly announced rules that both protect individual autonomy and limit governmental authority. Fair warning is an essential part of the American criminal justice system.

The principle of legality is an important part of American criminal law today, a principle expressed in the often-cited Latin maxim: "*Nullum crimen, nulla poena, sine lege*" ("There is no crime without law, no punishment without law"). Today, a defendant cannot be convicted of a crime unless the legislature has enacted in advance a statutory definition of the offense.[9]

Providing prior notice of illegality by statute also supports the reasons for convicting and punishing lawbreakers. Utilitarians would concede that an individual must be able to know what conduct is forbidden and the consequences of breaking the law before deterrence can be effective. Most retributivists conclude that the fundamental purpose of punishment is to blame those who choose to do wrong. Unless adequate notice of criminal behavior

---

8. Pomorski, supra note 3; Jeffries, Legality, Vagueness, and the Construction of Penal Statutes, 71 Va. L. Rev. 189 note 15 (1985).

9. H. H. Packer, The Limits of the Criminal Sanction (1968).

is provided, it is difficult to argue that the defendant has "chosen" to commit a wrongful act. Moral condemnation and punishment without such notice are indefensible.

Ex Post Facto

The Constitution expressly forbids both Congress and state legislatures from passing ex post facto criminal laws.[10] Legislatures cannot enact criminal statutes that criminalize acts that were innocent when done or that increase the severity of the crime or the punishment after the fact. Such laws are a form of retroactive criminalization. This constitutional restraint ensures that the legislature give fair warning of criminal conduct and its consequences.[11]

The ex post facto prohibition is expressly limited to legislatures. Nonetheless, American courts today are sensitive to the basic unfairness created by unforeseen judicial interpretations of criminal statutes that expand their reach and, in effect, retroactively criminalize behavior or aggravate the severity of the crime or its punishment. Concern that due process prohibits such judicial construction of criminal statutes and respect for the separation of powers have influenced courts to avoid such interpretations.[12]

A good example of this cautious judicial approach is *Keeler v. Superior Court*.[13] The defendant was charged with murder under California law after he intentionally shoved his knee into the abdomen of his former wife, who was in an advanced state of pregnancy, and said: "I am going to stomp it [the unborn fetus] out of you." The fetus was delivered stillborn with a fractured head.

The majority, rejecting the prosecution's argument that the statute should be interpreted in light of changing medical technology, interpreted the phrase "human being" as used in the California murder statute as having the common law meaning of "born alive," which was the generally understood meaning of "human being" when the statute was enacted first in 1850 and reenacted in 1872. The majority decided that a court should not expand the reach of a criminal statute to conduct beyond that intended by the legislature. In its view, to do so might violate the separation of powers by judicially rewriting a law enacted by the legislature, thus usurping the legislature's law-making authority.

Interpreting the phrase "human being" to include a viable fetus might also violate due process, according to the majority. Providing a new judicial definition of this material element of murder was constitutionally impermis-

---

10. U.S. Const. art. I, §9 (federal) and §10 (state).

11. *Calder v. Bull,* 3 U.S. (3 Dall.) 386 (1798); *Bouie v. City of Columbia,* 378 U.S. 347 (1964).

12. *Bouie,* 378 U.S. 347.

13. 2 Cal. 3d 619 (1970).

sible. Under the applicable law in effect when the defendant struck his wife, he had only committed an assault (or possibly an abortion). Deciding after-the-fact that his conduct actually constituted murder would be an exercise in retroactively increasing the severity of the defendant's crime and its penalty.

Subsequent to this decision, the California legislature amended the state murder statute to include the unlawful killing of a "fetus."[14] This amended statute would punish as murder what Keeler did.

The Rule of Lenity

This concern for improper judicial expansion of a statutory definition of crime is also reflected in the rule of lenity. English courts originally developed this principle to restrict capital punishment in response to the increasing number of felonies punishable by death.[15] Today, many courts still use this rule of strict judicial construction that requires courts to "construe a penal statute as favorably to the defendant as its language and the circumstances of its application may reasonably permit."[16] Simply put, any ambiguity in the statutory language should be resolved in the defendant's favor.

The Model Penal Code, however, did not adopt the rule of lenity. Instead, it requires that criminal statutes be "construed according to the fair import of their terms." In cases involving ambiguous language, however, it directs courts to construe statutory language to further both the general purposes of the criminal law and the specific purposes of the statute under consideration.[17]

Void for Vagueness

The United States Supreme Court has consistently struck down criminal laws that are so vague that ordinary people could not reasonably determine their meaning and application from the language of the statute[18] or which confer excessive discretion on law enforcement authorities to arrest or prosecute[19] or on judges and juries to determine what conduct is prohibited.[20] The "void for vagueness" doctrine is based on the due process clauses of the Fifth Amendment when a federal statute is involved, and on the Fourteenth

---

14. 1970 Cal. Laws ch. 1311, §1.

15. Jeffries, supra note 8, at 198.

16. *Keeler,* 2 Cal. 3d at 631.

17. Model Penal Code §1.02(3). Providing "fair warning" of criminal conduct is one of the general purposes of the MPC. §1.02(d).

18. *Connally v. General Constr. Co.,* 269 U.S. 385 (1926).

19. *Papachristou v. City of Jacksonville,* 405 U.S. 156 (1972).

20. *Giaccio v. Pennsylvania,* 382 U.S. 399 (1966).

Amendment when a state statute is involved. It helps ensure that the American criminal law implements the principle of legality.[21]

The doctrine ensures that criminal statutes provide fair notice of what behavior is forbidden. If an ordinary citizen cannot determine what a criminal statute forbids, then its actual meaning cannot be known until a court explains the law. This, in turn, requires the judiciary rather than the legislature to define the elements of the crime retroactively. The vagueness doctrine also prevents police from arbitrarily choosing which persons they will arrest. Finally, it helps ensure a consistent and equal application of the criminal law.

For the most part, void for vagueness does not preclude the legislature from passing a criminal law to accomplish a legitimate law enforcement goal. It simply requires the legislature to use clear and focused language. Of course, it is not always clear when a law is too indefinite so as to be unconstitutional. Courts are more likely to strike down laws as unconstitutionally vague when they are very general in scope, are overly broad or too readily reach innocent behavior (especially if the First Amendment is involved), and confer very broad discretion on police officers to arrest whom they choose (especially if racial discrimination appears to be involved).[22] Thus, in *Papachristou v. City of Jacksonville*, the Supreme Court struck down a broadly worded vagrancy ordinance because it gave the police "unfettered discretion" to decide whom to arrest. Justice Douglas noted: "The rule of law, evenly applied to minorities as well as majorities, to the poor as well as the rich, is the great mucilage that holds society together."[23]

However, courts usually uphold a statute against a vagueness challenge if it would alert the common person that there is a reasonable risk that his conduct would violate the law. As Justice Holmes said in *Nash v. United States*, "the law is full of instances where a man's fate depends on his estimating rightly, that is, as the jury subsequently estimates it, some matter of degree."[24] Finally, a court can construe the statute more narrowly so that, as interpreted by the court, it is not unconstitutionally vague.[25]

The Burden of Proof

A final "limit" on the criminal law's reach is the procedural protections afforded a criminal defendant. In this book, we discuss only one[26]—the high standard of proof required in criminal cases.

---

21. Packer, supra note 9, at 93. But see Jeffries, supra note 8, at 200-201.
22. *Papachristou*, 405 U.S. 156; *Kolender v. Lawson*, 461 U.S. 352 (1983).
23. *Papachristou*, 405 U.S. at 171.
24. 229 U.S. 373, 377 (1912).
25. *Winters v. New York*, 333 U.S. 507 (1948).
26. See R. Bloom & M. Brodin, Criminal Procedure: Examples and Explanations (2d ed. 1996), for a discussion of many others.

In virtually all legal proceedings, the person who wishes to change the status quo must demonstrate that there is good reason for doing so. Thus, she must carry the burden of proof that some legal harm has been inflicted, and that some legal remedy should be provided. In most lawsuits, the standard by which this proof must be established is articulated as a "preponderance" of the evidence. In a few suits, the standard is "clear and convincing," which is assumed to be "more than" a mere preponderance. In 1972 the United States Supreme Court confirmed in *In re Winship*[27] what had been the rule in the United States for over two centuries: In a criminal case the prosecution has the burden of proof, and the standard of proof is beyond a reasonable doubt (BRD). The Court gave two reasons for this requirement: (1) defendants *might* face loss of liberty if convicted; (2) defendants would *certainly* be stigmatized as having committed immoral acts. In later cases, the Court made clear that *both* of these factors must be present to require this level of proof. In civil commitment cases, where there is a potential loss of liberty but no stigmatization as a criminal, for example, the standard is "clear and convincing," not BRD.[28]

It is fairly easy to quantify the preponderance standard: 50.01 percent of the probabilities. And "clear and convincing" is "somewhat more" (70 percent?). But how much is "beyond a reasonable doubt"? In *United States v. Fatico,* 458 F. Supp. 388 (S.D.N.Y. 1978), a United States district court judge polled his colleagues and found that they "quantified" BRD as low as 76 percent and as high as 95 percent.

Nor can words better capture the heart of the standard. Since *Winship,* the Court has continuously questioned attempts to explicate more fully the purport of the words. In *Sandoval v. California* and *Victor v. Nebraska,* 511 U.S. 1 (1994), the Court upheld instructions that defined reasonable doubt as "not a mere possible doubt, because everything relating to human affairs and depending on moral evidence is open to some possible or imaginary doubt" or as requiring proof beyond a "moral certainty" and an "actual and substantial doubt." The Court's opinions, however, were clear that the Justices were troubled by *any* attempt to define the term. Indeed, it has been suggested that trial judges should *never* try to do so.[29]

The reason for this high standard is to avoid erroneous convictions because of the harsh consequences — certainty of stigmatization and possible loss of freedom — that attend a conviction.

Recently, because of changes in how defendants are sentenced, courts have grappled with what facts the prosecutor must prove [as elements of the crime] beyond a reasonable doubt to a *jury,* and what facts the prosecutor must prove [to determine the sentence] to a *judge* by a lesser standard. This

---

27. 397 U.S. 358 (1972).

28. *Addington v. Texas,* 449 U.S. 418 (1979).

29. Note, 108 Harv. L. Rev. 1955 (1995).

is a heated area of debate because considering a fact as part of sentencing may lessen the prosecutor's burden of proof significantly as well as allow the use of evidence that would otherwise not be admissible at trial. For example, if a statute proclaims that "having a dog" is a crime punishable by a $500 fine, but that if the dog is unlicensed the penalty is $5,000, the prosecutor may argue that the *crime* is having a dog, and that the lack of a license merely increases the sentence for that crime. Adopting the prosecutor's view might be seen as weakening Winship's protection, while rejecting that view might interfere with attempts to rationalize the sentencing process.

EXAMPLES

1. Tarrance promotes "rave" concerts in San Francisco. These concerts are one-time events featuring rock bands and are put on in secret locations on short notice. The promoters often sell drugs at these happenings.

    Tarrance receives anonymous calls from the producers detailing their plans to put on an all-night "Techno-Funk" rave concert and also to sell XTC, an illegal designer drug. They tell Tarrance the date and location of the concert and hire him to print up catchy flyers advertising the event and the directions to the secret location. He is also hired to find friends who will pass out flyers to individuals who might be interested in attending the concert.

    Tarrance knows that XTC is often sold at rave concerts, but he has never been to a rave concert, does not sell drugs, and has never taken XTC. He is hired only to promote the concert.

    A teenager passing out flyers is stopped and questioned by the police. She tells the police that Tarrance hired her to pass out the flyers. The police obtain a warrant and search Tarrance's home. They find no drugs or drug paraphernalia; they find only a printing press and the printed flyers.

    A creative prosecutor charges Tarrance with "advertising an event at which drugs will be sold," even though there is no statute defining this offense. Can Tarrance be convicted on this charge?

2. Benton, a convicted felon, is arrested after he is caught buying a gun that has been transported across state lines. The prosecutor initially charges him with violating Title IV of the Omnibus Crime Control Act, which prohibits a convicted felon from buying a gun that has been transported in interstate commerce and provides a maximum penalty of two years in prison.

    Unfortunately for Benton, the prosecutor does some additional research and discovers that the Safe Streets Act of 1968, using the same language as Title IV, proscribes the very same conduct but provides a maximum sentence of *seven* years. The prosecutor amends the charge, dropping the Title IV charge and adding the Safe Streets charge, hoping to obtain a longer prison term.

The defense counsel moves to dismiss the prosecution, claiming the statutes are void for vagueness because the law does not clearly set forth the penalty for this offense. What result?

3. Gabriela is an attorney for Scussy Scum, who has been charged in Las Vegas with solicitation to commit murder in a high profile case. After the grand jury indicts Scussy, Gabriela holds a press conference where she states that the police fabricated stories and tampered with evidence in this case, and that these practices have become "all too common in Nevada."

    Two weeks later Gabriela is charged with violating a criminal statute that forbids a lawyer to speak about a pending case in ways that "a reasonable lawyer should know would have a substantial likelihood of materially prejudicing an adjudicative proceeding." Section (b) of the law provides that a lawyer "may state without elaboration . . . the general nature of the . . . defense." Statements by an attorney are permitted under this section even though they may "materially prejudice" the case.

    Gabriela claims she reasonably believed she could speak generally about her client's defense because of the language in section (b). She claims that the statute is constitutionally void for vagueness because attorneys, the group targeted by the law, must guess at it meaning. What result?

4. Defendant is charged with having an unlicensed weapon, which carries a ten-year sentence. A state statute provides that if a prosecutor proves to the judge, by a preponderance of the evidence, that the *purpose* of having the weapon was to intimidate people on the basis of race, the sentence may be doubled. Is the second statute constitutional?

EXPLANATIONS

1. At one time many American jurisdictions recognized "common law crimes," thereby allowing prosecutors to charge new crimes even though there was no statute specifically forbidding the defendant's conduct. If the evidence established that the defendant had injured social interests generally protected by the law, judges and juries were allowed to determine the criminality of the defendant's behavior based on the evidence presented.

    In such a common law jurisdiction the court might well conclude that Tarrance had committed a crime because his behavior helped other individuals violate a specific statute that forbids selling drugs. This approach provides the criminal law with sufficient flexibility to meet new and unanticipated dangers. It also discourages creative criminals from taking advantage of the legislature's failure to pass a criminal law that prohibits such harmful behavior.

Today, however, virtually every American jurisdiction has abolished common law crimes and, instead, requires the legislature to pass laws that specifically state what conduct is criminal and what punishment can be imposed. This provides individuals with adequate notice of what they can and cannot do and avoids retroactive punishment. It also ensures that prosecutors and juries are not making law, thereby preserving the important role of the legislature in our constitutional system of separated powers.

Tarrance will not be convicted of the charged offense because there is no law that criminalizes his conduct — promoting concerts. He did not attend the concert nor did he supply or sell drugs there. If the legislature wishes to prohibit the act of promoting events at which drugs will be sold, it must enact a law specifically making such conduct criminal. This principle of legality will help ensure that the legislature has thought about the problem and also will limit police and prosecutorial discretion. More important, it will provide sufficient guidance to individuals about what conduct can expose them to criminal responsibility.

2. The void for vagueness doctrine also applies to punishment. At first glance Benton's case seems to be one of unacceptable ambiguity. Two different laws provide different punishments for the very same offense. Can Benton successfully argue that these laws are void for vagueness because the statutes do not clearly set forth what penalty can be imposed for this offense?

In *United States v. Batchelder*, 442 U.S. 114 (1979), the Supreme Court held that two similar criminal statutes were *not* unconstitutionally vague. Each statute clearly set forth the conduct proscribed and the punishment authorized. The Court then concluded that two different statutes prohibiting the same conduct but providing two different penalties create no more uncertainty than does a single statute authorizing alternative penalties. These laws provide Benton with adequate notice of the range of punishment that can be imposed for his conduct and impose a reasonable limit on sentencing discretion.

3. The court might well find this statute void for vagueness. The "safe harbor" provision of section (b), which allows attorneys to describe the "*general* nature" of the defense "without *elaboration*," may mislead them into believing that they cannot be prosecuted for publicly discussing possible defenses even if they should reasonably know that the discussion might "materially prejudic[e] an adjudicative proceeding."

Gentile v. State Bar of Nevada, 501 U.S. 1030 (1991), involved a Nevada supreme court rule (uncannily similar to the criminal statute in our example) that governed what lawyers may say about a case outside a judicial proceeding.

The United States Supreme Court concluded that the Nevada rule failed to provide "fair notice to those to whom [it] is directed," and that a lawyer would have to guess at whether section (b) protected his discussion of his client's defenses. Section (b) was not sufficiently clear because the terms "general" and "elaboration" are classic terms of degree, which in this context have no settled usage or traditional legal interpretation. As a result, section (b) does not provide sufficient guidance for lawyers trying to fit within its "safe harbor." The Court held that the court rule as applied in Mr. Gentile's case was void for vagueness.[30]

A statute can be constitutionally void on its face or as applied in a specific case. The standards are the same in each instance. The statute must (1) give adequate notice of what conduct is forbidden and (2) provide adequate enforcement standards. There is a difference between the two instances. A statute that is unconstitutionally vague *on its face* does not satisfy this two-part test for *any* conduct. A statute that is vague *as applied* does not satisfy the two-part test when applied to *specific conduct*. However, there is some conduct to which the statute can readily be applied without violating the test. In our example the statute would be considered impermissibly vague when applied to what Gabriela actually did.

4.   This case was recently decided by the United States Supreme Court, which held that all factors which increased the maximum sentence must be proved to a jury beyond a reasonable doubt. *Apprendi v. New Jersey,* —U.S.—(June 26, 2000). It is highly likely that this decision will reach other instances of "sentence enhancements."

---

30. Though agreeing that courts may adopt ethical rules that regulate what lawyers can say publicly about pending cases, the Court was also concerned that the rule as applied in this case could impermissibly infringe on Mr. Gentile's First Amendment right to criticize public officials.

2

The Purposes
of Punishment

Overview

Why do we punish? Why isn't requiring a defendant to pay damages to his victim "enough"? These are hardly new questions; philosophers have debated them for millennia. This chapter explores some of the answers they have given, upon which modern criminal law is founded. The two usual answers—utilitarianism and retributivism—are explored, and these answers are assessed in the examples within the context of current legislative efforts to broaden the reach of the criminal law.

Defining Punishment

In general discussions we often use the term "punishment" as the equivalent of any suffering or loss that a person endures. Thus, if *A* has recklessly killed his beloved child in a hunting accident, we may be loathe to prosecute him criminally because "he has been punished enough." That usage of the term "punishment," however, is both inadequate and inaccurate in the law (and in philosophy as well). Punishment is suffering *purposely* inflicted *by the state* because one of its laws was violated.

Thus, when Carol negligently injures Alice, compelling Carol to compensate Alice, while causing loss to Carol, is not punishment.[1] Punishment,

---

1. Zedner, Reparation and Retribution: Are They Reconcilable?, 57 Mod. L. Rev. 228 (1994); Barnett, Getting Even: Restitution, Preventive Detention, and the Tort/Crime Distinction, 76 B.U.L. Rev. 157 (1996).

instead, connotes a *blaming*, a *stigmatizing*, of the perpetrator as a choosing agent.

In the criminal system it is often said that the individual victim is not relevant, and that the victim is the state.[2] Compensating Alice, therefore, does not compensate the victim of the criminal act, the state. Instead, the state *punishes* the offender—purposely inflicts discomfort upon her—*because* she has broken the law. In fact, no individual "victim" is required. Consider statutes punishing bribery, failure to pay taxes, or drug use.

The Purposes of Punishment

As we saw in Chapter 1, criminal law and tort law were once joined in the same proceeding. Even today most acts that constitute crimes also constitute torts. Thus, if Charlie purposely hits Doug with a baseball bat, Charlie will have to pay Doug for the injuries for the tort of battery. Why, then, also punish Charlie criminally? What does criminal punishment add to the goals of the legal system?

Traditionally, two different responses are given to this question. One suggests that punishment serves *utilitarian* ends, such as (a) deterring persons who might be thinking about committing crimes, (b) incapacitating those who if released are likely to commit additional serious and violent crimes, or (c) rehabilitating those who have already committed offenses. The other explanation of criminal punishment (*retribution*), argues that persons who have committed crimes have acted immorally and must be punished to atone for the immoral action.

These two basic philosophies of punishment theory have clashed for centuries. Each has strong proponents, but each has significant weaknesses; supporters select one over the other more on faith than proof.

Utilitarianism

The basic premise of utilitarian explanations of punishment is that punishment is itself an evil because it deliberately inflicts harm on a human being. Therefore, we should hurt criminals only if some "good" is achieved by this act. That "good reason" is found in various social benefits to the law-abiding—primarily reduction of future crimes—that are said to result from punishing criminals.

---

2. There is a growing recognition that the individual victim should not be barred from some parts of the criminal process — e.g., at sentencing. Indeed, there have been attempts to enact a constitutional amendment explicating "victims' rights." This movement, however, is highly controversial.

Deterrence

Deterrence theory posits that punishment of a criminal (*D*) reduces future crime in two ways: (1) *D* can decide not to commit future crimes or (2) other persons, contemplating committing crimes and learning of the threatened punishment, will decide not to do so. The first of these is *specific deterrence*, the second *general deterrence*.

Both specific and general deterrence are based on the ability of the law to threaten potential *D*s with a serious enough penalty to dissuade them from acting. The pain threatened must be greater than the pleasure that *D* thinks he will attain by committing the crime. The premise is that criminals balance these pleasures and pains; indeed, Jeremy Bentham, the founder of utilitarianism, called this the "felicific calculus." As he put it: "[I]n matters of importance every one calculates."[3]

We all experience deterrence in our daily lives. When we contemplate speeding, we may consider both the possibility of being caught and the penalty that may be assessed if we are captured. If Joan never speeds because she fears a ticket, this is general deterrence. If, just as Bob decides to speed, he sees a police car and does not speed, he demonstrates specific deterrence.

However, what works in one setting may be less effective in another. There are simply too many variables to measure accurately the actual deterrent effect of a threatened punishment. For example, if the legislature increases the penalty for burglary, and the rate of burglaries thereafter decreases (assuming that we are relatively sure of that), it is very difficult to prove that the threat of increased punishment *caused* the decline. After all, all the burglars may have already been put in jail, or (if unemployment is related to crime) the unemployment rate might have dramatically decreased, making fewer people "turn to" crime. After examining all the studies on this subject, the National Research Council of the National Academy of Sciences concluded that we "cannot yet assert that the evidence warrants an affirmative conclusion regarding deterrence."[4]

To be effective, deterrence requires that *D* receive *notice* of the threat of punishments. However, how members of society learn of the possible punishments threatened if they violate the criminal law is uncertain. Obviously, few citizens read the statute books to determine the possible punishments. Most of us probably learn simply by experience that crimes are "bad," and that some crimes are "worse" than others. We also sense that "worse" crimes are punished more severely than others.

The theory of deterrence requires not only that *D* hears the threat of

---

3. Principles of Penal Law, in J. Bentham's Works 396, 402 (J. Bowring ed., 1843).
4. Deterrence and Incapacitation: Estimating the Effects of Criminal Sanctions on Crime Rates (1978). See also Law Reform Commission of Canada, Fear of Punishment (1976).

the criminal law, but that he hears it *accurately*. Thus, if the law threatens a punishment of five years, but *D* believes the punishment is only three years, he will be less deterred than he should be. (On the other hand, if he believes that the punishment will be ten years, he will be overdeterred.)

A more sophisticated version of providing notice assumes that there are "target" groups who are more likely to commit certain kinds of crimes. Consequently, it is more important to ensure that they hear the threat than that the general public hear it. Thus, for example, to deter embezzlement, we might ensure that bank tellers or others entrusted with large amounts of funds are expressly and continuously reminded of the penalties associated with that crime.

In addition to being public, the threat must be *credible*. This requires two further suppositions: (1) *D* thinks he will be captured; (2) *D* believes that, if captured, he will be punished as threatened.

Most criminologists believe that the *certainty of capture*, even if punishment is small, deters much more than severity of punishment.[5] Unfortunately, both theory and practice undermine both hopes: Current FBI statistics indicate that police "clear" (believe they have found the guilty party) in only a small percentage of most crimes. For example, in 1998, police "cleared" 69 percent of murders and 59 percent of rapes, but only 19 percent of larceny-thefts, 28 percent of robberies, and 14 percent of burglaries.[6]

Furthermore, every criminal, even if he knows that the capture rate is high "in general," believes that *he* is smart enough to avoid capture. If that were not the case, he would not commit the crime. Bentham's "felicific calculus" requires that the defendant accept the possibility of capture, but most actual criminals do not do so.[7] Indeed, critics of the deterrence theory point out that when pickpockets were publicly hanged, many pockets were picked at the public executions, thus suggesting that the pickpockets did not expect to be caught (since the severity of the penalty, if caught, was obvious).

Even when defendants are captured, these same FBI data show that most persons are prosecuted for and convicted of less serious offenses than those for which they were "cleared." Assuming for the moment that the police clearance rate is accurate, this means that many persons who actually commit crime A are punished for a less serious crime B; unless the threatened

---

5. See Fear of Punishment, supra n.4, at vi.

6. These figures, of course, relate to "reported" crimes. There is wide consensus among experts that the reported crime figures are substantially below actual crime figures, except possibly for homicide. Estimates based on victimization studies suggest that only one-third to one-half of all rapes are reported, and that anywhere between one-third to four-fifths of all property crimes are unreported.

7. A 1996 study of nearly 500 armed robbers showed that 83 percent of them believed affirmatively that they would not be caught. R. Erickson, Armed Robbers and Their Crimes 38, 39, 89 (1996). This was true even though 48 percent had been previously imprisoned. An unspecified additional percentage had been caught and put in jail or on probation.

punishment for B is (almost) as severe as that for A, the threatened punishment for A has become irrelevant.[8] Thus, such practices as pretrial diversion, plea bargaining, early release on parole, and so on, all undercut the deterrent impact of the threatened punishment. These realities are exacerbated by the fact that the persons most likely to avoid punishment for crime A are those who know how to manipulate "the system." Paradoxically, the professional criminal may well be more able to obtain a lesser sentence than the first-time offender.

The deterrence theory requires that the defendant actually "calculate" the possible pains and pleasures involved in the criminal act and possible punishment. Critics of the theory, however, argue that many crimes are *not* crimes of calculation. Indeed, current analysis argues that deterrence theory is most applicable in white collar crimes, which often take long periods of planning, followed by long periods of implementation, and that "street crimes," such as muggings and burglaries, are far less amenable to the deterrence calculus. Yet most current concerns about crime focus on street crime rather than white collar crime.

Finally, though the evidence is slim, several studies have concluded that peer pressure and the threat of losing position and friendships have much more effect on a potential criminal than does the threatened criminal penalty.[9]

None of these criticisms necessarily demonstrates the invalidity of the deterrence model. Most likely, criminal punishment achieves some "general prevention" and "educates" us to both the threat and the morality of the criminal law as we grow up.[10]

Note that it is the *threat,* and not the actual punishment, that brings about deterrence. Under utilitarian theory, if it were possible to threaten punishment but never impose it and yet achieve the same amount of deterrence, punishment itself would be unnecessary. Thus, if Professor Wing convinces her students that she lowers grades on the basis of poor class performance — even if she never does — she may obtain better participation in class. And if Ezekial performs badly, Professor Wing may merely have to *appear* to note his poor behavior in her class notes in order to increase preparation.

---

8. This, of course, is true only if *D knows* of these facts. To the extent that he overestimates either the possibility of capture or the possibility that the threatened punishment will actually be imposed, he is "overdeterred."

9. F. Zimring & G. Hawkins, Deterrence (1973).

10. Even here, however, there are cavils. What of the person who "grows up" in a "criminal" milieu? Can he be deterred? Suppose that, in his sub-culture, capture and punishment are *not* seen as stigmatizing but are approved? These issues are now being raised in the area of "rotten social background" or "cultural defense." See Chapter 17.

Incapacitation[11]

A second utilitarian explanation of why we punish is that those who commit criminal acts have rejected important social norms and have thereby demonstrated their willingness to continue to do so in the future. Thus, for the good of those who abide by the law, these offenders must be prevented (incapacitated) from reoffending.

Incapacitationists must either (1) punish for lengthy periods of time every person committing the same crime equally, or (2) assume that they can accurately identify those who are most likely to reoffend and impose on them lengthy periods of incarceration. This latter premise partially explains the establishment of parole boards, which are theoretically composed of experts who can determine when an offender has "learned his lesson" and no longer needs incapacitation.

Opponents of incapacitation pose several objections. First, they assert it is not possible to predict accurately who will recidivate. Thus, if incapacitation is to reduce the crime rate, many offenders must be incarcerated at very high cost for long periods of time. Assume, for example, that statistics indicate that 10 percent of all burglars actually commit 80 percent of all burglaries. Out of a group of 100, unless we can identify the 10 high repeaters, we must incapacitate for long terms 90 who will not "seriously" recidivate. Some argue that this is too high a price to pay both economically and morally.

Supporters of incapacitation respond by saying that it *is* possible to predict some kinds of recidivism within "acceptable" limits. Furthermore, they suggest, if there *is* overprediction, and some offenders are kept unnecessarily long, the pain imposed on them is outweighed by the pain not imposed on those putative innocent victims of the ten who would be "improperly" released.

A major critique of incapacitationist theory is that it ignores the so-called "replacement" phenomenon in crime. Many criminal activities are "market" driven. If there is a demand for contraband goods (drugs, prostitution, stolen TVs), someone will supply them. Thus, when one supplier of goods is convicted and incapacitated, another supplier will replace him. While it may be true that when Aloysius is incarcerated, he will not push drugs on the corner, it is still likely, given no reduced demand, that someone else will.[12] Whether crimes of violence, rape, homicide, or robbery follow this same pattern is less clear. Some criminologists argue that even these crimes have "markets," in the sense that the arrest of one burglar or robber simply widens the possibilities for those who have not been arrested. If so, incapacitating

---

11. For a thorough study of this view, see F. Zimring & G. Hawkins, Incapacitation (1995).

12. This is also true, of course, if *A* is part of a gang, which will continue without him. If *A* is replaced by *B*, we may paradoxically have created a new criminal, *B*.

one burglar will result in no reduction of the overall crime rate for that offense.

Rehabilitation

Between 1800 and 1975, American jurisdictions seemed dominated by a third utilitarian theory, rehabilitation. This theory holds that offenders can be "changed" into nonoffenders if given proper "treatment." That idea emanated from the Quakers who, in the first decade after the American Revolution (and as a reaction to the widespread use of capital punishment for virtually all felonies), invented the penitentiary, where a criminal would become "penitent" by reading the Bible and renounce further criminality.

During its ascendancy, rehabilitation took several different modes. Between (roughly) 1800 to 1870, crime was seen as a "social" disease generated by conditions in the industrial cities. Hence, many prisons were built in places remote from those cities. From 1870 to 1900, crime was analogized to a medical disease, and the proper "care" would cure the offender. Parole boards, consisting of experts who could best detect whether a defendant was cured, would release the offender when he was no longer in need of treatment. In a subsequent wave from 1900 to 1940, criminality was seen as inherited. Many states provided for the sterilization of criminals to avoid crime by their progeny.[13] Finally, between 1940 to 1975, crime was seen primarily as a symptom of psychological disturbance; psychiatrists were added to parole boards, and "behavior modification" programs blossomed in prisons.

Each of these models resulted in other changes in the criminal justice system. The rehabilitationist theory (like an incapacitationist one) required an indeterminate sentence for each criminal because the "symptoms" and cure would differ with each individual. Similarly, judges would require "presentence reports," which would inform them of the social background of the defendant, the likelihood that he needed rehabilitation, and for how long. Indeterminate sentencing was adopted in virtually every state.[14]

---

13. In *Skinner v. Oklahoma*, 316 U.S. 535 (1942), the Supreme Court invalidated an Oklahoma statute that provided for the sterilization of some thieves, but not all, on the grounds of *equal protection*, since the Court found no basis for distinguishing among thieves. There was no suggestion that the penalty itself would be unconstitutional (although that view might hold sway in today's Court).

14. Prior to 1976, California adopted the most indeterminate adult system in which many crimes were punished by "0-life." The most indeterminate system, of course, was the juvenile justice system, which was also seen as the most "rehabilitative" in nature. Juveniles would be sentenced to totally indeterminate terms (capped only by reaching their majority) without regard to the crime at all. Thus, assuming a majority age of 21, a 17-year-old would receive essentially a four-year term for an offense for which a 12-year-old would receive a nine-year term.

Critics of rehabilitationist theory generally argued that there was no evidence that "treatment" during punishment worked. No data showed that persons put in treatment programs while in prison were less likely to recidivate.[15] This skepticism was strongly supported by a landmark paper in the mid-1970s that, after reviewing studies of scores of such programs, was interpreted as concluding that "nothing works."[16] In fact, that was not the conclusion of the piece, as its author thereafter recognized,[17] but by that time, it was too late. The "nothing works" message had been generally accepted by legislatures around the country.

Empirical Critiques

Each of the utilitarian theories claims to reduce the crime rate, either through deterrence, incapacitation, or rehabilitation. When, as in the rehabilitation study cited above, the efficacy of the practice is questioned by empirical studies, the validity of the theory is similarly questioned. This may be unfair, since there are so many other variable factors that affect the crime rate (including, for example, the reporting rate) that have nothing to do with any of the theories. Moreover, much of the data may be soft. Assertions about the incapacitative effect, for example, often rely on self-reports by prison inmates concerning how many crimes they "really" committed before being captured. Therefore, the very claims about reducing crime rates that make the utilitarian theories attractive also tend to make them susceptible to empirical attacks. (The retributive theory, discussed below, is not subject to the same critique, since it explicitly rejects any claims of real-world effect.)

Normative Critiques

In addition to the practical questions that confront utilitarian theory, there is a separate issue: Is it fair? Retributivists argue that utilitarians are willing to use the defendant as a "pawn" for purposes other than fair punishment. It is sometimes suggested that utilitarians would even be willing to punish a person they know is innocent, if they could hide that fact from the "target population."

The great philosopher H.L.A. Hart attempted to reconcile these problems by suggesting that the "General Justifying Aim" of the criminal law

---

15. Whether this is due to the inadequacy of resources devoted to rehabilitative programs or to some notion that criminality is "inborn" is unimportant to these critics.

16. Martinson, What Works? Questions and Answers About Prison Reform, 35 Pub. Interest 22 (1975).

17. Martinson, New Findings, New Views: A Note of Caution Regarding Sentencing Reform, 7 Hofstra L. Rev. 243 (1979).

could be utilitarian, but that the "General Distributive Aim" could be re-tributivist.[18] That is, we would punish only those who, by committing crimes, deserved punishment, but we would punish them with utilitarian, rather than retributivist, goals in mind. Even if one accepts Hart's accommodation, it does not fully meet the critique made by Immanuel Kant of any utilitarian theory. Kant argued that the "categorical imperative" of morality forbade treating a human being for any social purpose whatever. Utilitarians, he argued, did exactly that, thereby ignoring the difference between civil law (which is utilitarian) and criminal law (which he asserted was based on moral judgments).

Retribution

The alternative major explanation for punishment is *retribution*. Retribution argues that persons who choose to do wrong (i.e., criminal) acts *deserve* punishment, and that it should be imposed on them even if it serves no utilitarian purpose. Indeed, there is an argument accepted by many retributivists that punishment *must* be imposed because the offender deserves to be treated as a moral agent who has earned punishment by his crime. Failure to impose such punishment refuses to recognize this capacity. Thus, there is a "right to punishment."

Unlike utilitarianism, which looks to effects in the future to justify the imposition of punishment, retributivism looks backward to the *past* act that the criminal chose to commit. Retributive theory restricts punishment only to those who have made moral, willing choices; it would not allow the state to punish those who, such as the mentally ill or the duressed, had no (or little) choice. Nor would retribution allow *criminal* confinement based on prediction of *future* acts.

Most retributivists focus on the ability of the defendant to "choose" at the time of the crime. In the past two decades, however, a variation of retributivism has emerged that suggests that we can and should punish persons because of their *character*— as exemplified by their choices. This school of thought argues that if a "criminal" act is not "in character" for the defendant, then she should not be punished at all, or as much, as would be a "real" criminal.[19]

When the theory of retribution is pressed, however, many of its supporters seem to explain it by referring to the need to reaffirm society's mores,

---

18. Punishment and Responsibility (1968).

19. Pillsbury, The Meaning of Deserved Punishment: An Essay on Choice, Character, and Responsibility, 67 Ind. L.J. 719 (1992); Sendor, The Relevance of Conduct and Character to Guilt and Punishment, 10 Notre Dame J.L. Ethics & Pub. Poly. 99 (1996); Kahan & Nussbaum, Two Concepts of Emotion in the Criminal Law, 96 Colum. L. Rev. 269 (1996).

which seems like a utilitarian objective. Another weakness in the retributive theory is its difficulty in explaining how punishing the criminal "makes up for" the injury that D inflicted on society. Some argue that D has obtained an unfair advantage through his crime, and that only by punishing him can that advantage be balanced. But that claim surely is not clear: If D has stolen $100 from Z, and D has been captured and the $100 returned, it would seem that Z is already back in the status quo ante. One response to this is to suggest that Z's psychological state has been affected in a way that requires that D be punished, but to some this seems like vengeance. Another response is that the rest of society, possible future victims of D, are put in psychological fear and need reassurance that D will not commit more crimes. However, this sounds like incapacitation, which retributive theory expressly rejects as a basis for punishment.

Yet another criticism of retributivism is its ambiguity. Retributive schemes of punishment require proportionality. While the *lex talionis* (an earlier version of retribution) established the notion of "an eye for an eye," retributivists point out that their theory is also one of limits. No *more* than one eye for one eye is allowed, even if total blindness would deter (or incapacitate) more offenders. Perhaps such a proportionality was possible when most crimes (and punishments) were corporal in nature, but when a society refuses to use certain methods of punishment — death, torture, maiming—even if the defendant used them, the concept is difficult to apply. Moreover, determining the "proportionate" length of imprisonment for theft or for bribery or, for that matter, the purposeful infliction of the loss of an eye — known as the problem of *cardinality* — is surely difficult if not impossible.

Furthermore, proportionality requires *ordinality,* ranking crimes according to their seriousness. Again, there seems to be no objective basis for at least some ordinal rankings.

Moreover, notions of proportionality are extremely fluid. When retributivists argue that one should be punished "for the crime," the seriousness of the crime is in the eyes of the beholder. If A wishes to impose more punishment than would B, there is no obvious way to resolve that dispute except to say that one of these punishments "feels" wrong. Thus, capital punishment for jaywalking may "feel" disproportionate, but articulating why that is true is more difficult. In recent years, the United States Supreme Court has confronted several challenges, based on an alleged constitutional doctrine of proportionality, to punishments of life imprisonment for (1) three-time bad check passers, *Solem v. Helm,* 463 U.S. 277 (1984), and (2) one-time possessors of significant amounts of drugs. *Harmelin v. Michigan,* 501 U.S. 957 (1991). The Court appears to have decided that there was a requirement of proportionality. However, the Court also held that life imprisonment for these offenses was not disproportionate, provided there was a possibility of parole after some length of time (12 years in one instance). *Rummell v. Estelle*, 455 U.S. 263 (1980).

In addition to these concerns, critics argue that the theory validates hatred. Indeed, one major advocate of retributivism once said it was morally right for the public to hate criminals.[20] That view is often taken to justify vengeance. Phrases such as "an eye for an eye" seem to suggest not only that the anger raised by a crime is acceptable (which it may be), but that any actions taken as a result of that anger are also acceptable (which a retributivist would reject).

Finally, in an era when utilitarianism is the dominant philosophy in many areas of public policy, retributivists awkwardly face the utilitarian question of "Why punish unless some good comes out of it?" To those who adopt utilitarianism in other arenas, the response that "Because it's right to do so" sounds strange.

In the past two decades retributivism has experienced a resurgence, in part because of the empirical uncertainties of utilitarian claims, and in part because of the inherent attractiveness of a normative approach to punishment.

The Relationship of the Theories

Proper analysis of criminal law doctrines requires that we keep these various theories of punishment separate and assess doctrines according to each of these theories. In practice, however, the theories frequently reach the same result. A deterrence theorist would support a claim of self-defense because persons who are, or who believe themselves to be, under imminent attack cannot be deterred from defending themselves, and because allowing such a response might deter future aggressors (see Chapter 16). A retributivist would agree that the claim should be recognized, but on the grounds that an actor is not morally blameworthy for taking action to prevent injury to himself. A rehabilitationist would probably conclude that he is in no need of treatment, since he acted (ex hypothesis) as most persons would act. And an incapacitationist would not need to incarcerate a self-defender since he will use deadly force only in such situations. Thus, all four support a claim of "self-defense" but for different reasons.

It is when this harmony does not occur that the criminal law must choose among those conflicting purposes. A deterrence theory might support a claim of insanity because the insane cannot be deterred, and a retributivist would argue that the insane person is not blameworthy because he is not a freely choosing agent. However, the incapacitationist and the rehabilitationist

---

20. J. Stephen, A History of the Criminal Law 81 (1883).

might well want to confine the insane actor to prevent future harm to others or to have the opportunity to treat him. Therefore, whether we recognize a claim may depend on what we see as the purpose of the criminal law.

The Importance of Sentencing[21]

The theories of punishment outlined above obviously have their impact not only on doctrines of the substantive criminal law but on sentencing as well. Far too often, courses in criminal law ignore the sentencing process. While we cannot here discuss that process in any detail, it is critical for students to recognize the way in which sentencing schemes can undo the doctrines of substantive criminal law.

Much of the course in criminal law is spent in differentiating one crime, or one level of crime, from another. Thus, for example, criminal law usually treats persons who "purposely" commit some act as different from (and hence deserving of more punishment than) persons who commit the same act "recklessly" or "negligently." However, if the sentencing scheme in a particular jurisdiction allows both to be punished equally, the distinctions drawn by the criminal law are undermined. For example, substantive doctrine distinguishes between a premeditated killing (Melinda wants to kill Bill, lies in wait for Bill, puts the gun to Bill's head, and pulls the trigger six times) and a reckless killing (Constance, while twirling a loaded gun, drops it; it discharges and kills Dudley). The first of these is called first-degree murder, the second manslaughter. However, suppose the sentencing system provides that either killer can be sentenced to zero to life. If a judge sentences Melinda to 5 years and Constance to 20 years, the doctrinal differences that are debated in criminal law courses become less important (one might say meaningless) to Constance. Conversely, to the extent that sentencing systems provide for no overlap between similar crimes (in the example above, 0-15 for manslaughter and 20-life for first-degree murder), they reinforce the distinctions drawn by the substantive criminal law.

Many jurisdictions have established sentencing guidelines that purport to limit judicial discretion in sentencing. The United States Supreme Court has upheld such limitation against constitutional attack. *United States v. Mistretta,* 488 U.S. 361 (1989). See also *Koon v. United States,* 518 U.S. 81

---

21. We have here chosen to focus on sentencing discretion because it most obviously undercuts criminal law doctrine. However, at every stage of the criminal justice system, discretionary decisions can have this effect. Thus, if police do not arrest, prosecutors do not prosecute, or fact finders do not convict obviously guilty persons, the substantive law is frustrated. After conviction and sentencing, if parole boards release offenders "too early," they arguably undermine the intended legislative effect of the statute.

(1996). It is not clear, however, that these guidelines were intended to, or will, lessen the tension between goals of the criminal law and those of sentencing policy. Uniformity in enforcing sentences imposed primarily for the purpose of incapacitation, for example, will not reduce the conflict if the goal of the substantive criminal law is seen as deterrence, or retribution, or rehabilitation.

The sentencing system should reflect the theories of punishment as much as the substantive criminal law. Thus, suppose that the reason substantive criminal law distinguishes between murderers and manslaughterers is that it endorses retributivism. It may turn out that Melinda really regrets her act, whereas Constance is not at all sorry that the gun discharged and would commit the same reckless act again if given the chance. Under an incapacitationist sentencing scheme, Melinda *should* receive a lighter sentence than Constance, but under the retributivist criminal law, Constance should receive less punishment than Melinda. This would seem to require that the substantive criminal law and the sentencing schemes be based on the same theories. If those two processes are based on different theories, a significant conflict can arise that undermines each part of the system.

The relative disappearance of rehabilitation as a goal of punishment has resulted in the disappearance — or the reduction — of indeterminacy in sentencing. In the last two decades, at least half the states have adopted some form of restrictions on such discretion. Mandatory minimum sentences are one example. Sentencing guidelines, usually established by sentencing commissions, are another. These approaches do not necessarily avoid the clash between theories we have outlined above. Commissions can still use a different basis for setting sentences than did the legislature in establishing definitions of crimes.

"Civil" v. "Punitive"

The Difference Between "Criminal" and "Civil" Confinement

Our constitutional system provides vigorous protection for individual liberty. Thus, under the criminal law a person can lose his liberty only *after* the government proves beyond a reasonable doubt that he has committed a crime. But our system also allows the government, in limited situations, to take away an individual's freedom to *prevent* him from committing a harmful act. The government may civilly commit someone to a mental health facility to prevent such harm and to treat him if it can prove that he suffers from a *mental condition* that *causes* him to be *dangerous*. These laws are "civil" because they do not further either retribution or deterrence. Instead, they are intended to incapacitate and treat mentally disturbed and dangerous individuals who do not respond to the threat of criminal punishment. Every state has an involuntary civil commitment law.

A Contemporary Example: Sexual Predator Laws

Since 1990 at least 15 states have also enacted "sexual predator laws." They allow the government to civilly commit sex offenders about to be released from prison if it can prove they suffer from a "personality disorder" or "mental abnormality" that makes them likely to commit another serious sex crime. Commitment is to a secure mental health facility for an indefinite period. The government must provide treatment and periodically review their condition to see if they can be released. The Supreme Court upheld the constitutionality of these laws in *Kansas v. Hendricks*, 521 U.S. 346 (1997), provided the government can prove the person suffers from a condition that makes it "difficult, if not, impossible for the person to control their dangerous behavior." The mental condition that causes loss of volitional control need not be recognized by mental health professionals.

The Court set forth criteria for determining when laws that deprive a person of their liberty to prevent crime should be considered "civil" rather than "punitive" and, thus, not violate either the constitutional prohibitions against ex post facto or double jeopardy:

> Where the State has 'disavowed any punitive intent;' limited confinement to a small segment of particularly dangerous individuals; provided strict procedural safeguards; directed that confined persons be segregated from the general prison population and afforded the same status as others who have been civilly committed; recommended treatment if such is possible; and permitted immediate release upon a showing that the individual is no longer dangerous or mentally impaired. . . . [*Hendricks* at 368-369.]

Supporters claim these laws are necessary to prevent dangerous sex offenders from committing another serious sex crime after they are released from prison. Critics argue they allow unconstitutional preventive detention under the guise of 'civil commitment' and cannot in theory be limited in their reach.[22]

EXAMPLES

1. A number of towns in the United States have adopted ordinances holding parents criminally liable for the acts of their children. What are the theoretical arguments for and against such provisions?

---

22. See Special Theme: Sex Offenders: Scientific, Legal, and Policy Perspectives, Winick and La Fond (eds.), 3 Psychol., Pub. Pol., & L. 1 (1998).

2. Congress and many state legislatures have adopted "three strikes and you're out" statutes, which provide that a person convicted three times of a felony (sometimes limited to violent felonies, sometimes not) must be sentenced to mandatory terms of life imprisonment. What are the theoretical bases for such provisions, and what are the critiques?

3. Recent developments in genetics have suggested that some violent conduct may be greatly influenced by genes. On the basis of such preliminary suggestions, some social critics have proposed testing all six-year-old children to determine if their genetic makeup or behavior suggests that they are likely to commit violent criminal acts. If the finding is affirmative, they would confine and (if possible) treat such persons. What theories support such a proposal?

4. State X provides a term of 0-20 years for burglary. Sentencing guidelines, which are very strict in the state, require a sentence of no more than 5 years for the "usual" burglar. If, however, the offender is proven to be a "patterned sex offender," the judge must impose the maximum term of 20 years. What are the theoretical bases for this statute?

5. Kim has been convicted of aggravated assault of his wife with a weapon for a second time and is about to be released from jail. The prosecutor has filed a petition to send him to a mental health facility as a "dangerous violent person" under a recently enacted law that authorizes involuntary civil commitment for any person "convicted of a crime of violence against the person who suffers from a personality disorder or mental abnormality that makes him likely to commit another serious assault." A mental health professional will testify that Kim suffers from an "antisocial personality disorder," a recognized mental disorder, which is based in part on a history of "irritability and aggressiveness, as indicated by repeated physical fights or assaults." Otherwise, the law is identical to the one upheld in *Kansas v. Hendricks*. Is this law constitutional?

6. Most states have adopted "Megan's Laws," statutes requiring that communities be warned of prisoners about to be released to that community who have been convicted of sexually abusing children. What theories of punishment do these law embody?

EXPLANATIONS

1. Most retributivists would find such a statute repugnant because the parent has not, by their definition, committed any morally blameworthy act. Utilitarians, however, might support some versions of these ordinances: The threat of imprisonment might coerce parents to supervise more closely their children. This would result in fewer juvenile crimes and thus less pain to the entire populace. (Some utilitarians might argue, however, that parents might *oversupervise*, thereby becoming disutilitarian.) A rehabilitationist might similarly argue that the parent needs

"training" in how to supervise a child. An incapacitationist, however, would find it hard to support this approach, since the incarceration of the parent might mean less supervision of the child.

Some retributivists, and most utilitarians, might conclude that although the parent has not affirmatively committed a criminal act, the failure to properly supervise may be morally blameworthy. This would be particularly cogent if the provision were restricted (as is tort liability) to parents who were on notice that their child had committed, or was likely to commit, criminal acts. If negligence can be a proper basis for criminal liability (see Chapter 4 infra), such negligence may be blameworthy.

2. Retributivists would oppose such statutes, since the punishment proposed is, by definition, in excess of that required *for this crime*. Deterrence theorists might argue that such statutes are desirable because the mandatory nature of the penalty might deter felons from engaging in even "minor" crimes. (Of course, since "major" crimes would already carry long penalties, the issue for the deterrent theorist is whether the life sentence carries sufficient "marginal deterrence.") The primary explanation for such statutes is, of course, incapacitationist: the confinement of all such offenders ensures they would not offend again in society. This, however, raises several empirical issues: (1) are we "over-incapacitating," in the sense that not all three-time felons will continue to commit future crimes?; (2) can we accurately predict those who will recidivate a fourth time? Experts disagree on the accuracy with which such predictions can be made, although there is general agreement that accuracy increases with an increase in the number of prior felonies. Additionally, there is the question of whether the economic cost of lifelong incarceration is outweighed by the hoped-for reduction in crime in the community. This is a normative, not an empirical, question.

3. No theory of *criminal* liability supports incarceration in this manner. There is no deterrence to be gained since, by hypothesis, the defendant's conduct is caused by noncognitive facts (his genes). Similarly, unless therapy can be effective treatment, there is no rehabilitative support for confinement. And the retributivist would strongly reject the argument that the child is responsible for his genetic makeup. Only an incapacitationist approach supports such a proposal. However, this kind of confinement, if allowed at all, would surely not have to be "criminal" in nature. The child *may* be dangerous, but since she has done nothing yet to demonstrate that, civil incapacitation would serve society just as well. Indeed, since "criminal" confinement requires more procedural safeguards and hence more chance of not confining the child, it would be burdensome and hence counter-utilitarian. There are other, perhaps determinative, arguments against such a project because the prediction

of future behavior, even if highly accurate, would not be entirely certain. In a society that favors freedom, we have to run risks rather than incarcerate the child before she has injured anyone. However, these arguments go generally to the moral desirability (and possible constitutionality) of such a proposal, not its link to criminal law generally.

4. How can burglary be sexually motivated? Burglary is defined as the "breaking and entering of (a place) with the intent to commit a felony therein." In one case decided under such a statute, the court found that the presence of a condom in the defendant's pocket was sufficient to warrant finding that his motivation for the break-in was sexual in nature. *State* v. *Christie,* 506 N.W.2d 253 (Minn. 1993). The question here is why sexual motivation justifies the quadrupling of the normal sentence. Again, incapacitationists would argue that sexually motivated offenders might be less deterrable than others, and therefore more in need of long-term incarceration. Rehabilitationists might agree. Retributivists would argue that the sentence is disproportionate to the harm actually inflicted, since the legislature has determined that 5 years, not 20, is the appropriate penalty for non-sexually-motivated burglary, and the defendant's motive is irrelevant.

5. The answer to this question depends on whether the court concludes the "dangerous violent person" law is "civil" or "punitive." Under *Hendricks* a court would probably uphold the law, provided it meets the requirements set forth in that case. The state must prove that Kim suffers from a mental condition that so impairs his ability to control himself that he is likely to commit another assault. It must also provide treatment, periodically review his condition, and release him when he no longer suffers from this condition *or* is not dangerous.

   Why do you think states would enact a civil commitment law that can only be used *after* the person serves his full prison term? To provide needed treatment? To extend incapacitation after the state's authority to confine someone under the criminal law has ended? Other good reasons?

   Should an individual be considered both *criminally* responsible and punished for his conduct and then *civilly* committed to a mental health institution for care and treatment because of a mental condition that it defined in large part by the same criminal acts? (You might want to reconsider this example after you have read The Insanity Defense in Chapter 17.)

6. The explosion of such laws is clearly due to a hope that future crimes will be prevented, a utilitarian concern. But is such a requirement "punishment"? Under long-standing doctrine, an imposition is criminal punishment only if intended to be such. Although some courts initially disagreed, the unanimous consensus now is that the legislative purpose

was not to punish the offender, but to prevent crimes, or find the perpetrator of new crimes. Thus, these statutory requirements were not punishment. Since these challenges were brought under the ex post facto clause, which prohibits only ex post facto *punishments,* these courts concluded that the legislation was constitutional even as applied to sex offenders who had served their criminal prison terms.

3

Actus Reus

Overview

The criminal law needs a practical and consistent method to describe the behavior for which its special power of arrest, conviction, and punishment may be used. Simply put, it needs a basic architecture to define crime. Although they may differ on their reasons, most utilitarians and retributivists agree on the basic elements of a crime.

Voluntary Act. Subject to some exceptions we will discuss shortly, the criminal law only punishes voluntary action; it does not punish inaction or mere thinking. The "voluntary act" element of a crime is usually called the *actus reus.*

Many utilitarians would argue that involuntary behavior should not be criminalized because it cannot be deterred. Retributivists would claim that an individual who did not choose to do a wrongful act does not deserve punishment. Moreover, other systems of care and control, such as involuntary hospitalization, are used for individuals perceived to pose an ongoing threat of harm by involuntary acts.

There are good reasons why the criminal law does not punish thoughts without action. First, it is extremely difficult to tell what a person is thinking, let alone whether he will act on those thoughts by committing a crime. Second, without this limitation, perhaps most of us would be subject to the reach of the criminal law because we fantasize about committing a crime at one time or another!

Omission and Legal Duty. The criminal law generally punishes an individual only for the affirmative harm he himself inflicts; it does not punish for failing to prevent harm caused by others or by natural forces. (Note, however, that speaking words is usually considered an act rather than "mere thoughts" in the criminal law.)

In limited cases, however, the failure to act—usually called an *omission*—may be a crime if the defendant had a *legal duty* to act. Of course, the defendant must have been capable of doing the legally required act because "the law cannot hope . . . to stimulate action that cannot physically be performed."[1]

Sometimes a criminal statute explicitly requires an individual to act. A common example is the federal statute requiring most people to file an income tax return. Failure to file the return is considered a voluntary act rather than an omission because the statute specifically defines the failure to file as the prohibited "voluntary act."[2]

Mental State. Some type of mental state or attitude is usually (though not always) necessary for the commission of a crime. Strict liability crimes do not require a mental state *(mens rea)*. (See Chapter 6.) This requirement reflects a community consensus that the attitude with which the actor did a voluntary act is important in determining whether to punish and, if so, how severely. Generally, the mental state component of crime requires some degree of intentionality or carelessness. At common law the mental state was called "mens rea"; the Model Penal Code calls it "culpability." We will discuss mental states more fully in Chapter 4.

Prosecutors often use the defendant's conduct or actus reus as their primary evidence in proving the defendant's mental state. This makes sense because human conduct is generally the product of mental processes. Moreover, an individual's behavior is usually easier to establish than her internal thought processes.

Summary. The definitional components of crime are straightforward. Most crimes consist of an actus reus and a mens rea. Both must occur together. In limited cases an omission or failure to act, together with a legal duty, may also be a crime.

The Common Law

Crime requires either a voluntary physical act or an omission when there is a legal duty to act.

Voluntary Act

A voluntary act is a movement of the human body that is, in some minimal sense, willed or directed by the actor. A straightforward example is

---

1. Model Penal Code and Commentaries 214-215 (1985).

2. In the real world we think of a failure to file as an omission because the taxpayer has not done what he was supposed to do.

when a professional killer deliberately points a loaded pistol at his victim's head and pulls the trigger.

A voluntary act can also be the result of habit or even inadvertence as long as the individual *could* have behaved differently. Driving to the child care center to pick up your child even though your spouse told you the child did not need a ride qualifies as a voluntary act. This is the case even though you made the trip purely out of habit or while you were daydreaming.

Involuntary acts are those over which the individual had no conscious control. These may include acts done while unconscious or sleepwalking or acts resulting from physical causes such as an epileptic seizure. They also may include bodily movements caused by being struck by another person or object. If *A* pushes *B* off the dock, *B*'s plunge into the water is not a voluntary act. There is controversy over whether some behavior, such as that occurring while one is hypnotized, is voluntary or involuntary.

Usually, a voluntary act is essential for criminal responsibility—even for strict liability crimes that do not require any mental state (see Chapter 6). However, not all of the behavior must be voluntary before criminal responsibility attaches. As long as there is at least *one voluntary act* in the defendant's course of conduct, he may be criminally responsible. For example, in *People v. Decina*, 2 N.Y.2d 133, 138 N.E.2d 799 (1956), the defendant, knowing he was subject to epileptic seizures, nonetheless voluntarily drove a car and subsequently killed four people when he lost control of the car during an epileptic seizure. He was convicted of negligent vehicular homicide even though the actual "act" that killed was itself "involuntary" because it occurred during a seizure. The *earlier* voluntary act of getting into the car and driving it satisfies the voluntary act element of the crime.

Sometimes people do harmful acts because they are threatened with death or serious injury or to avoid a greater harm or because of serious mental impairment. Though these acts are often done under a great deal of pressure, the criminal law usually considers them "voluntary." Whether someone will be punished in such cases usually depends on whether a defense based on justification or excuse is available. (See Chapters 15-17.)

Omission and Legal Duty

Though usually concerned with preventing individuals from doing affirmative harm to others, the criminal law is occasionally used to motivate individuals to perform obligations imposed on them by other laws. The threat of criminal punishment may provide this extra motivation. Thus, the failure of a person to act when he is under a legal obligation arising from civil law also satisfies the actus reus requirement for crime.

The legal duty may be based on (1) *relationship* (e.g., a parent must provide food, shelter, and clothing to a child); (2) *statute* (e.g., many states have a law that requires medical providers and others to report suspected child abuse); (3*) contract to provide care* (e.g., nursing homes often enter into a contract to provide medical services to residents); (4) *voluntary assumption of care that isolates the individual* (e.g., taking a sick person into one's home may result in a duty to provide care); (5) *creation of peril* (e.g., someone who pushes another who cannot swim into a deep lake must take reasonable steps to rescue him); (6) *duty to control the conduct of another* (e.g., a business executive may have a duty to prevent the company chauffeur from speeding); and (7) *duty of a landowner* (e.g., a theater owner has a duty to provide reasonable emergency exits for his patrons). Limiting *criminal* liability to cases where the *civil* law imposes a legal duty at least provides "notice" to individuals that they are legally required to act and fail to perform that duty at their peril.

Generally, a defendant must know the facts from which the duty to act has arisen. However, he may not avoid criminal responsibility by claiming he was unaware that a legal duty to act arose from those facts. Thus, a nursing home operator who entered into a contract to care for elderly patients cannot claim he did not know he had a legal duty to provide them with care. Nor can he claim he did not know that he could be held criminally liable for breaching that duty by failing to provide such care. Such a claim is, in reality, a defense based on ignorance of the law and is not a valid defense. (See Chapter 5).

Several recent cases have confronted the question of whether a parent can be criminally punished for failing to prevent someone else from abusing a child in situations where the parent also feared violence at the hands of the abuser. Some courts have found mothers, who knew of ongoing sexual abuse of their young daughters by a father, stepfather, or boyfriend, guilty of child abuse for failing to take steps reasonably calculated to prevent the abuse. See, e.g., *Commonwealth v. Cardwell*, 515 A.2d 311 (Pa. Super. 1986). Some courts, however, have reached a contrary conclusion. See, e.g., *Knox v. Commonwealth*, 735 S.W.2d 711 (Ky. 1987). Most courts conclude that a parent does have a legal duty to act, and that failure to prevent the abuse can result in criminal responsibility.

Moral Duty

In general our society expects people to do the right thing, which includes fulfilling their moral duties. Moral duties are those obligations that, according to our basic sense of right and wrong, people should live up to. However, the criminal law does not impose responsibility for failure to live up to a moral duty to act unless it is embodied in a civil law duty. Though we may hope or even expect our fellow citizens to be "good Samaritans" and prevent serious harm to others when they can do so at little or no risk to themselves, the criminal law generally does not impose this affirmative obligation.

Several arguments can be made in favor of this approach. They include a preference for personal autonomy and "laissez-faire" government. Law should only prevent individuals from affirmatively harming others; it should not compel citizens to help one another, especially when resources are limited. Moreover, requiring assistance may cause overreaction that could overwhelm or even harm the victim. Finally, the "slippery slope" argument asks where we should draw the line.

Some states, however, have enacted "good Samaritan" statutes that make it a criminal offense to refuse to help those known to be in serious peril when aid could be provided without danger.[3] This approach may strengthen a sense of community, make society safer, and prevent serious harm with little or no cost to the rescuer. It may also bring the law into closer conformity with our sense of moral decency and send a message encouraging cooperation rather than isolation.

Possession

Many criminal statutes forbid possession of specified items, such as laws punishing the possession of burglar tools or of illegal drugs. In a sense this type of law does not require the defendant to "do" anything. Rather, mere possession—or the failure to terminate possession once the defendant learns of the item's presence—is sufficient. Nonetheless, these statutes comply with the requirement of a voluntary act because they are generally construed as requiring active or constructive knowledge on the defendant's part of the nature of the item he has under his control or custody. Thus, knowingly taking or keeping a forbidden item is a voluntary act.

Frequently, courts conclude that an individual or several individuals had "constructive possession" of forbidden items even though they did not individually exercise physical dominion and control over the items. Instead, courts often base their conclusion on the proximity of these individuals to the items or their ability to reduce an object to control and dominion.

The Model Penal Code

Voluntary Act

The MPC defines an "act" or "action" as "a bodily movement whether *voluntary* or *involuntary*." MPC §1.13(2). It also provides that a person is not guilty of a crime under the MPC unless "his liability is based on conduct that includes a voluntary act or the omission to perform an act of which he

---

3. See, e.g., Vt. Stat. Ann. tit. 12, §519.

is physically capable." MPC §2.01(1). However, the MPC does not define a "voluntary act." The Commentaries suggest that it is essentially behavior that is "within the control of the actor."[4]

In addition, MPC §2.01(a) describes certain types of action that are *not* voluntary acts. These include "(a) a reflex or convulsion; (b) a bodily movement during unconsciousness or sleep; (c) conduct during hypnosis or resulting from hypnotic suggestions; and (d) a bodily movement that otherwise is not the product of the effort or determination of the actor, either conscious or habitual."

Section 1.02(1) makes it clear that only the individual's *own* conduct will support criminal responsibility. Section 1.05 speaks of "conduct" that can "constitute an offense."

Omission and Legal Duty

Like the common law, the MPC permits an omission or failure to act to satisfy the conduct element of a crime in two different types of cases: (1) when the statute defining the offense expressly states that failure to act is a crime, or (2) the defendant has a duty to act imposed by civil law. MPC §2.01(3)(a) and (b). Failure to file an income tax return is an example of the first type; the law expressly states that such failure to act is a crime. A parent's failure to provide necessary food, shelter, and clothing to her child is an example of the second type because most states have laws that require parents to do this.

Though not entirely clear from the text, the MPC effectively requires a voluntary act — or an omission and legal duty — for criminal responsibility.

A More Precise Definition for Actus Reus

The MPC also provides a more thorough analytic framework for the actus reus component of a crime. It breaks it down into three separate components — conduct, circumstance, and result — called "material elements." MPC §1.13(9)(i), (ii), and (iii). These components or material elements describe more precisely what the defendant did. They are the basic building blocks for defining each crime and for assessing blame and imposing appropriate punishment.

Conduct is the physical behavior of the defendant. Driving a car or shooting a gun, for example, would be considered conduct under the MPC.

A *circumstance* is an objective fact or condition that exists in the real world when the defendant engages in conduct. Many criminal statutes include circumstances in the definition of the crime. For example, if a defendant

---

4. Model Penal Code and Commentaries 215 (1985).

enters a residence at night to steal something inside, the fact that his conduct occurred "at night" is a circumstance that describes what he did with more precision. If the burglary statute so requires, the prosecution will have to prove that the defendant entered a residence "at night."

A *result* is the consequence or outcome caused by the defendant's conduct. If a defendant points a loaded pistol at another human being, pulls the trigger, and causes a bullet to strike and kill him, the death of that human being is the result of defendant's conduct.

Possession

The MPC explains when possession is an act or conduct. This provision applies when someone takes possession of an item — illegal drugs, for example. If the defendant knows that he is accepting custody of illegal drugs, then his "possession" is clearly a voluntary act under the MPC and he can be convicted of illegally possessing drugs.

What about someone who initially does not realize that he has drugs in his control but subsequently realizes that he does? The MPC states that the person's possession is sufficient for criminal responsibility if, after becoming aware of the fact that he has drugs in his control, he does not terminate his possession within a sufficient period. His failure to act (i.e., terminate possession) is an omission in face of the legal duty to do so.

EXAMPLES

1.   Elizabeth, jealous that her boyfriend Bob was also dating Connie:

1a. drove her car directly at Connie while Connie was crossing the street, hoping to kill her while making it look like an accident. Her car struck and killed Connie.

1b. took a gun she knew was loaded over to Connie's apartment and waved it at Connie, yelling that Connie had better not see Bob again or else. The gun discharged and killed Connie.

1c. while driving her car, failed to see Connie crossing the street in a pedestrian crosswalk because Elizabeth was totally distracted by her own jealous rage.

1d. while driving her car, suffered a heart attack for the first time in her life and lost consciousness. Unfortunately, her car struck and killed Connie while Elizabeth was unconscious.

1e. while driving her car, started to feel drowsy. Rather than pull over, Elizabeth continued driving. Soon thereafter, Elizabeth fell asleep at the wheel and her car struck and killed Connie.

1f. while driving her car, started to feel drowsy. Pulling her car over to the curb, Elizabeth took a nap so she would not fall asleep while driving.

She left the motor running to provide heat because it was so cold outside. Awaking suddenly from a deep sleep, Elizabeth's hand struck the automatic gear shift, putting the car into drive. Unfortunately, the car struck and killed Connie.

2. Jack is a highly respected golf pro. While on an airplane flight to California to play in the U.S. Open, Jack started to act very strangely, taking off his clothes and speaking incoherently. He then broke into the plane's cockpit and wrestled with the co-pilot, trying to grab the controls and yelling, "I'm going to kill you." Several passengers helped the co-pilot subdue and restrain Jack. After his arrest, doctors discovered that Jack was suffering from encephalitis, a viral infection of the brain that can cause confusion, altered consciousness, fever, and other symptoms. The disease is transmitted by mosquitoes and can be controlled by medication if the person knows he has it.

3. Michael, a grade school teacher, noticed that Bernie, a 7-year-old boy in his second grade class, frequently came to school with a black eye, choke marks, and other readily visible signs of physical abuse. A state law requires school teachers to report to the police when they observe visible indications of child abuse in one of their students or be subject to discharge from their job; however, Michael did not report Bernie's situation. After several months of observing Bernie's physical condition, Michael noted that Bernie did not come to school one day. The police found Bernie dead, the victim of ongoing child abuse.

4. Anthony, a school teacher in the same state as Michael, was watching television in his apartment late one evening. Suddenly, he heard screams from the apartment located directly across from his, separated by a narrow alley. Anthony looked out and through an open window saw a man brutally beating a 7-year-old child. Though he thought about calling 911, the police emergency number, Anthony did not want to get involved. He returned to finish the movie he was watching. The child died from the beating which, as Anthony could tell from the noise, continued for another two hours.

5. Patricia wore her black leather jacket to school. During recess she accidentally put on a similar looking jacket that, unknown to her, had a gun in its pocket.
   a. Just as Patricia finished putting on the jacket, a school security officer noticed the gun protruding from the jacket Patricia was wearing. He took Patricia immediately to the principal's office where the gun was removed. Patricia was charged with possession of a gun on school premises, a strict liability offense that has no mens rea element.
   b. Feeling a hard object in her pocket, Patricia put her hand into the pocket and found a pistol. For the next ten minutes she walked around the school looking for someone who might have put her coat on by mistake so they could exchange jackets. A school security

officer noticed the gun protruding from the jacket Patricia was wearing. He took Patricia immediately to the principal's office where the gun was removed. Patricia was charged with criminal possession of a gun on school premises, a strict liability offense that has no mens rea element.

EXPLANATIONS

1a. Elizabeth's driving the car directly at Connie is a voluntary act. She moved her hands on the wheel and pressed her foot on the gas pedal so that the car would collide with Connie. She consciously directed her body to engage in behavior that constitutes a "voluntary act."

1b. Elizabeth's waving a loaded gun at Connie is a voluntary act that satisfies the criminal law's requirement of an actus reus. The fact that the gun discharged "accidentally" (i.e., arguably without any mental determination on Elizabeth's part) does not preclude criminal responsibility for a homicide charge. A voluntary act is not rendered involuntary simply because it may include an involuntary act or because it had unintended consequences.

1c. Elizabeth's driving her car is still a voluntary act for the same reasons described in 1a. The fact that the car struck Connie because Elizabeth inadvertently did not see her does not alter the essential nature of Elizabeth's driving as a voluntary act.

1d. Because Elizabeth lost consciousness as a result of an unforeseeable heart attack, her behavior during this time period is not considered a voluntary act. She did not in any sense control the vehicle and her physical incapacity to change or alter her conduct make this an "involuntary act" as far as the criminal law is concerned.

1e. Though Elizabeth was sleeping when her car struck and killed Connie and was not itself a voluntary act, Elizabeth has still engaged in a voluntary act by driving even though she was tired. Thus, this aspect of her behavior satisfies the criminal law's general requirement of at least one voluntary act in the course of conduct before criminal responsibility can attach.

1f. This is a tough call. Elizabeth may have been in an unconscious state when her hand engaged the gear shift of the car. The prosecutor would argue that this case is like the case in 1e above; that is, Elizabeth engaged in a voluntary act when she went to sleep leaving the car engine running. The defense would argue that the relevant course of conduct is Elizabeth's "act" of engaging the gear shift while sleeping; consequently, there is no act that can satisfy the criminal law's insistence on a voluntary act. It is not clear how this case would come out.

2. Jack did not commit a crime if he did not perform a "voluntary act." The viral infection may have physically affected his brain and seriously

impaired Jack's ability to engage in volitional and conscious behavior. Because he may have acted in a fugue state without any memory of the incident, Jack's conduct may not satisfy the actus reus requirement for committing a crime — even though his behavior seemed conscious and rational to other passengers. Note that the prosecution must prove a voluntary act beyond a reasonable doubt and that, without such proof, a defendant cannot be convicted of *any* crime, even a strict liability offense (see Chapter 6). If Jack was aware of his illness and could have prevented the symptoms by taking medication, he may be responsible based on his earlier "omission" (failure to take medication) and his duty to do so. This example is based on a real case.[5]

3.   Michael's failure to report to the police the apparent signs of physical abuse in Bernie's case violates a legal duty imposed on him by statute. His omission (failure to report) plus breach of civil duty satisfies the criminal law's requirement of an actus reus. Consequently, Michael could be charged with homicide for failing to prevent Bernie's death.

4.   Most individuals would probably conclude that Anthony had a moral duty to call the police since he readily could have done so without any peril to himself, and such action might well have saved the life of a very young and vulnerable child. However, the reporting law in this state only requires a teacher to report observable signs of child abuse if one of his students is involved. It does not impose a general duty to report *any* sign of child abuse. Consequently, Anthony is under no civil law duty to act in such a situation, and he cannot be punished for his omission by the criminal law.

5a. In the first example Patricia does not know or have reason to know that the jacket she has mistakenly put on has a weapon in it. Thus, in most states her physical possession is not a voluntary act, and she cannot be convicted of the charged offense.

5b. The second example is more difficult. Though Patricia does not know there is a gun in the jacket when she first puts it on, she soon realizes that a weapon is located in the jacket pocket. At this point Patricia is under a legal duty to terminate her possession within a reasonable time; failure to do so may lead to a possession charge. Patricia would argue that she was trying to terminate her possession by attempting to locate the original owner. The prosecution may argue that Patricia should have immediately removed the jacket or gone to school authorities to turn in the weapon. A conviction on these facts is possible.[6]

---

5. See "Illness cited in cockpit attack," Kansas City Star, June 19, 2000, p. B-1.
6. See *In the Matter of Ronnie L.,* 121 Misc. 2d 271, 463 N.Y.S.2d 732 (1983).

4

The Doctrines of Mens Rea

Overview

As we saw in Chapter 2, criminal law is distinguished from all other fields of law because of the sanctions it can impose: loss of liberty and moral stigmatization. We regularly incarcerate, or otherwise deprive of freedom, persons who are not morally blameworthy — the mentally ill, the addicted, the fatally contagious, and so on. However, only criminal punishment declares that defendants are to blame for their acts; the essence of the judgment is not that they should be incarcerated for our sakes, but that they deserve punishment because they have chosen freely to violate the criminal law. Such a free choice appears to require that they *knew* what they were doing, and were aware, or risked, that it was morally blameworthy. For centuries, the law has captured this notion of free will and knowledge by looking for "mens rea" — Latin for "guilty mind." This chapter is concerned with the basic definitions of mens rea.

Until 1900 or so many different terms were used to describe states of mind that seemed to reflect aspects of moral blame. However, behind each of these statutory terms stood the larger backdrop of mens rea itself: the broader notion of looking for a truly "immoral" person. We will refer to that notion as *traditional mens rea*. In the past century however the term "mens rea" has lost much of that moral connotation and has come to mean merely the mental state required by statute. We will call this *statutory mens rea*. Unfortunately, neither courts nor commentators differentiate consistently in their use of these concepts.

This chapter explores various aspects of mens rea: (1) defining the relevant mental states; (2) investigating the relation of mens rea to motive; and (3) interpreting statutes that use mens rea words. Succeeding Chapters 5 and 6 continue this exploration in the specific contexts of mistake and strict liability.

The Concepts of Mens Rea

Criminal law is not tort law. While that may seem obvious, the point is critical to understanding the central importance of mens rea to criminal law. Because tort law also deals with conduct that often results in physical injury, and because, historically, criminal and tort causes of action were joined in the same proceeding, it is helpful to contrast the two systems of law. In tort, an objective standard ("the reasonable person") is used to assess the actions of the defendant because the prime aim is to compensate the innocent plaintiff. Criminal law, however, has other concerns. Under most of the four theories of punishment discussed in Chapter 2, the defendant's mental state is critical in determining whether to punish him. A utilitarian who seeks to rehabilitate the defendant needs to know whether the defendant *needs* "treatment," which means that he must know whether the defendant was contemplating the injury at the time he acted. If so, then the defendant needs to be trained to avoid such injuries; if not, he needs to be trained to be aware of possible injuries. Similarly, only persons who are *thinking about* the possible penalties will be deterred.

It might appear that an incapacitationist might think mental state is not relevant. If the defendant is dangerous, she should be locked up without regard to her mental state. However, the criminal process and criminal incarceration are a costly business. If we are only interested in confinement, we can use the less costly and less burdensome civil process. If the criminal process is to be relevant to an incapacitationist, it must be because the defendant will continue to be dangerous because her mind is dangerous.

The notion of blame, however, fits most easily in the retributivist's theory. To a retributivist, a person is morally culpable, and therefore properly subject to punishment, only if she had a "real choice" in her conduct and knowingly exercised her free will to execute that choice. As Justice Jackson put it in a frequently repeated observation:

> The contention that an injury can amount to a crime only when inflicted by intention is no provincial or transient notion. It is as universal and persistent in mature systems of law as belief in freedom of the human will and a consequent ability and duty of the normal individual to choose between good and evil. A relation between some mental element and punishment for a harmful act is almost as instinctive as a child's "But I didn't mean to . . . ." Unqualified acceptance

of this doctrine by English common law . . . was indicated by Black-stone's sweeping statement that to constitute any crime there must first be a "vicious will."[1]

"Traditional" and "Statutory" Mens Rea

Clearly heavily influenced by religious notions of sin, the criminal law as early as the thirteenth century encapsulated the need for a "vicious will" in the Latin term "mens rea." This view that a defendant could be punished only if he were a "sinner" influenced the common law and created a broad view of mens rea, the *traditional mens rea* concept described earlier. Between that time and the middle of this century, both common law courts and legislatures used a dizzying variety of adverbs in an attempt to capture the notion of general malevolence and blameworthiness at the heart of the original Latin term. These adverbs included "feloniously," "unlawfully," "maliciously," "corruptly," "fraudulently," "spitefully," and "willfully." The Model Penal Code found that there were 76 terms in federal statutes alone that were used to describe mens rea.[2] This abundance of terms might have been amusing except that, under the principles of legality (see Chapter 1), courts faced with this wide variety of legislative terms felt compelled to conclude that there must be differences among *each* of them.[3] Explaining the nuances between 76 different terms challenged the creative limits of the courts' ingenuity. As courts focused on the statutory words, however, the moral content of "mens rea" became diluted. Thus, for example, a court might ask only whether a defendant "intentionally" carried a white powder, which turned out to be a drug, rather than asking whether the defendant "intentionally" carried a white powder that he knew to be a drug. This is what we mean by *"statutory mens rea"* — applying the "mens rea" term "intentionally" only to the conduct, and not asking whether the defendant knew his conduct was immoral.

The distinction between traditional and statutory mens rea can work either to the benefit or detriment of a person charged with crime. If reck-lessness, for example, is morally blameworthy, a reckless defendant who is

---

1. *Morrissette v. United States,* 342 U.S. 246 (1952).

2. Model Penal Code §2.02, commentary at 230 n. 3 (1980).

3. Thus, in *Rex v. Davis,* 168 Eng. Rep. 378 (1788), a statute prohibited "wilfully and maliciously" shooting, but the indictment charged that the defendant "unlaw-fully, maliciously, and feloniously" shot. The indictment was ruled invalid because "wilfully" must mean something different than "unlawfully and feloniously." There was certainly no doubt that the indictment charged the defendant with having *traditional* mens rea, but that was insufficient: There was a requirement that the prosecution prove *statutory* mens rea as well. Today, there is a dispute as to whether proving statutory mens rea is *sufficient,* or whether a prosecutor must also prove traditional mens rea.

charged with "intentionally" doing *x* would be convicted under traditional, but acquitted under statutory, notions of mens rea. On the other hand, if "intentionally doing *x*" means only that the defendant must intend the consequence and not the result (see Chapters 5 and 6), then a nonblameworthy actor who intentionally does an act that turns out to result in *x* might be found guilty under the statute.

Specific Kinds of Mens Rea

In an attempt to define mens rea, courts divided (and combined) the legislative terms into three major concepts: (1) intent; (2) knowledge; (3) recklessness.

Intent

In General. A person who *intends* harm is clearly a proper subject for punishment under any theory of punishment. He is dangerous, in need of rehabilitation, and a morally culpable actor. Moreover, to the extent that deterrence works at all, it is also likely that his punishment can deter others like him. It is the defendant's subjective malevolence, not the likelihood or result, that determines his liability. Suppose, for example, that Hector wants to kill Achilles and, with this purpose in mind, aims at him a feather that is unlikely to harm him in any way. The feather, however, hits Achilles in a vital spot and, wonder of wonders, Achilles dies. If Hector had not wanted to kill Achilles, this would be a tragic accident, and probably Hector would not be punished at all. Should Hector be able to claim that he did not intentionally kill Achilles because the physical facts made it unlikely, almost fantastic? The common law answer to this was no; if Hector really wanted to kill Achilles, the fact that he did so by what would ordinarily be ineffective means was irrelevant. If Hector intended the death, and the death occurred, Hector was liable for intentional homicide.[4]

However, it is not that easy. We must distinguish between *intending the conduct* and *intending the result*. Suppose that Peter Pumpkin has intentionally pulled the trigger of a gun, and a bullet from the gun has killed Lucretia. If Peter is charged with "intentionally killing a person," he may admit he pulled the trigger intentionally (intended the conduct) but still respond that he is not guilty of the offense for several reasons:

1. He did not intend to shoot the gun (e.g., he thought it was empty).
2. He did intend to shoot the gun, but he did not intend the bullet to hit

---

4. Of course, this hypothetical rests mostly in the minds of law professors: Imagine that someone sees Hector aim a feather at Achilles, and Achilles dies. Unless Hector admits his intent, no one, including the witness, is likely to deduce Hector's actual mens rea.

anyone (e.g., he was aiming at a tree and did not know Lucretia was in the tree).

3. He did intend to shoot the gun but meant to hit not Lucretia but the Joker, who was assaulting him.

4. He did intend to shoot the gun and to hit Lucretia, but earnestly hoped that this would not kill her (e.g., he was trying to *wound* her in the heart).

Can one characterize Peter's mens rea as intentional? We will leave Cases 1 and 2 for Chapter 5, which treats the subject of mistake. However, in Cases 3 and 4 there is at least *some* intention on Peter's part to inflict harm. How should the law resolve these cases?

Transferred Intent: Case 3. The third case incorporates a fiction borrowed from tort law, transferred intent. Here, the conclusion is that the intent follows the bullet. Transferred intent, however, is limited to results that create *the same type of harm* as was actually intended. Thus, if Mary throws a stone at Jim and hits John, the intent is said to transfer, and Mary will be convicted of intentionally hitting John. If, however, the stone misses Jim and breaks a plate glass window behind him, the intent is not transferred. *Pembliton v. Regina,* 12 Cox C.C. 607 (1874).

Some commentators argue that the doctrine is not necessary: Mary intended to assault a human being and she did just that. However, suppose that the actually injured party is not just "a" human being but a "specially protected" human being — the King, the Pope, a federal judge — for whose intentional assault the penalty is enhanced. Should Mary pay the extra penalty? At least arguably, no. Mary threw the stone intentionally, but did not hit the Pope intentionally; Mary should be punished for *attempting* to hit Jim and for negligently or recklessly assaulting the Pope. The transferred intent analysis ignores Jim as a victim, and concentrates all its attention on punishing Mary for hitting the Pope.[5]

Oblique Intent: Case 4. Most courts deal with Case 4 by treating the defendant *as though* he had intended the actual result. Some courts explain this by using the term "oblique" intent. The defendant didn't really "intend" the result, but knew that if he acted, the result was practically certain to happen *if* he achieved his actual goal. In other cases, the courts simply have said that if someone knew that the result was almost certain to occur, even if the defendant did not in fact want it to happen, the defendant would be deemed to have intended it. Thus, if Captain America seeks to destroy a Nazi munitions factory to slow down the war effort, but the munitions factory is located so as to make inevitable the deaths of scores of children in an

---

5. One might find an echo here of the "greater crimes" theory. See Chapter 6. Since Mary was willing to engage in some criminality, she should be required to take the risk that her actual crime is greater than she expected it to be.

adjoining school, the Captain may well be found to have intended their deaths, even if he desperately prayed that they would all be safe. (Note: Captain America may have a claim of necessity, which we will discuss in Chapter 16; the question here is whether he will be deemed to have "intended" the deaths.)

The policy behind the doctrine of oblique intent is fairly clear: The defendant is almost as morally blameworthy, or as much in need of rehabilitation or incapacitation, as the defendant who *actually* intended to kill the person he shot. This explanation can also explain the transferred intent doctrine, which held Mary guilty of intending to hit John, but it will not explain her acquittal when she breaks the window. If anything, she is *more* morally culpable (and in need of rehabilitation or incapacitation) than a person who actually intends to break a window. Only adherence to the *statutory* meaning of mens rea and the view that this outcome is mandated by the principle of legality can explain that result.

An example may help. In *Regina v. Cunningham,* 41 Crim. App. 155 (Ct. Crim. App. 1957), the defendant tore a gas meter off the wall of a house. The gas escaped, and *V* was nearly poisoned. Defendant was charged with "unlawfully and maliciously" causing *V* to inhale the gas, to which he responded that he had absolutely no intent that she inhale the gas. Indeed, he didn't know the gas would escape. The trial judge instructed the jury that it would be sufficient for conviction if they were persuaded that the defendant had acted "wickedly." The defendant's conviction was reversed on appeal because, although he intended to remove the gas meter (and thus commit theft), he did not intend (even obliquely or by transfer) to hurt *V* in any way. In the terminology we are using here, the trial court instructed the jury that if the defendant had traditional mens rea (just plain wickedness), that was enough. But the appellate court held that that was not enough; the defendant had to have statutory mens rea as well.[6]

"Specific" and "General" Intent: An Island of Confusion in an Ocean of Chaos. Every student must try to learn the difference between *specific* intent and *general* intent, although all criminal law scholars (and many courts) believe the distinction to be totally meaningless and unrelievedly befuddling. As one authority puts it, "In confusing circularity, a general intent offense can be said to be any crime that requires *mens rea* and that has no special or specific intent required."[7]

Often, the legislature will help out by using the phrase "with intent to" when designating a specific intent offense. Thus:

----

6. *Cunningham* is often interpreted as saying that whether the defendant has traditional mens rea is irrelevant, but that is not the holding. The holding is that traditional mens rea is not sufficient; whether it is necessary is not raised by the case.

7. The reason for the creation of this distinction we will keep shrouded in mystery for the moment; if you want a preview, see Chapter 16 (defenses); 17 (intoxication); and 5 (mistake of fact).

1. Assault is a general intent crime, *People v. Hood*, 1 Cal. 3d 444 (1969); assault *with intent to rape* is a specific intent crime.
2. Breaking and entering is a general intent crime; breaking and entering *with intent to commit a felony* therein is a specific intent crime.
3. Burning down your house is a general intent crime; burning down your house *with the intent to obtain insurance* thereon is a specific intent crime.

Often, but not always. And therein lies the rub. While the presence of "with intent to" almost always indicates that a crime is a specific intent crime, the absence of that phrase does not necessarily indicate that it is a general intent crime. Moreover, the same conduct can often be described (and charged) as *either* a general or specific intent offense. For example:

1. Aggravated assault (a general intent offense) may also be described as assault with intent to kill or maim (specific intent).
2. Burglary is defined by common law as a breaking and entering (usually a dwelling house) with intent to commit a felony therein (and therefore a specific intent offense). However, aggravated (or second-degree) trespassing *can* be defined to reach the same conduct without using the magic words "with intent to."

Virtually no one — courts, commentators, defendants — thinks the specific-general intent distinction is very helpful. Only prosecutors, whose charging discretion is enhanced by these differences, seem to support the idea. However, courts sometimes candidly acknowledge that they will (re)define an offense as general or specific intent because of the effect of other doctrines on the charge. See *People* v. *Hood*, supra.

"Willfully" and "Knowingly." In many modern codes "oblique intention" is now called "knowingly." Knowingly, while close to intentionality, is not intentionality. The defendant need not intend a result; she need only know that the result is very likely. Thus, Captain America has probably "knowingly" killed those children, though he mightily regrets it. (Again, Cap may have an explanation of necessity, so don't despair.) In inchoate crimes (see Chapters 12 to 14) and in accessorial liability (Chapter 14), which are said to be "specific intent" crimes, a person who knows that a crime *might* occur, but does not intend that the crime occur, is not guilty. On the other hand, "knowingly" sometimes means *less* than meets the eye. Thus, if Tom is handed a glassine envelope of white powder, and told to sell it to Helen for $100 a gram, and says he will do it, "just don't tell me what it is," he is treated as though he knew that the substance was cocaine. He is said to have made himself "willfully blind" to the facts.

Many statutes and common law crimes used the term "willfully." However, "willfully" was often interpreted to mean "by one's will," which, as discussed in Chapter 3, would reduce that term to mean only that the defendant acted in a voluntary way. This was too narrow a reading. Other courts required that the prosecution prove the defendant "knew" what the consequences of his action were likely to be.

Recklessness

The *Cunningham* decision discussed above is known for its holding that "recklessness" is required for criminal mens rea. Recklessness is not a concept familiar to tort law, and therefore perhaps not even to law students who have struggled through torts. Recklessness stands between intent on one side and criminal negligence on the other. It is usually defined as a *conscious decision to ignore a risk, of which the defendant is aware,* that a "bad" result will occur or that a fact is present. The essence of recklessness, therefore, is that the defendant *knows* injury is being risked but proceeds anyway.[8]

Not every risk, of course, is to be condemned. In everything we do — driving a car, walking down the steps, hitting a golf ball — we knowingly take risks that serious bodily injury or death might ensue. However, these risks are acceptable because they are outweighed by the social good that occurs: commerce, autonomy, pleasure. Only if the social good does not outweigh the possible harm (e.g., speeding, walking down steps while carrying a loaded gun, hitting a ball with persons standing only ten feet in front of the ball) do we say that the risk is unacceptable. Determining both recklessness and negligence entails this kind of weighing. The difference between negligence and recklessness is not that there is a risk, but that in recklessness the defendant actually recognizes the risk but proceeds. In negligence the defendant should have foreseen the risk but did not.

Caveat. The term "recklessness" is often misused in general language and occasionally in court decisions as well. As used in the criminal law, and particularly in the Model Penal Code, recklessness requires that the defendant recognize that there is a particular risk and *subjectively choose to disregard that risk.* Thus, as with negligence (remember *Palsgraf* from your torts class?), there is no such thing as recklessness in the air. If LeeAnn drives 90 miles an hour on a crowded city street, she may be acting *dangerously* but cannot be accurately described as driving *recklessly* with regard to the risk of death or serious injury unless she *actually, subjectively recognized* and shrugged off that risk. If LeeAnn did not consider the possibility of death, and she kills someone in such a situation, it would be incorrect to say that she killed recklessly. Again, it is important to distinguish between being reckless as to the conduct and as to the result. Do not be misled on exams (or in other contexts either).

Although there must be "a" risk of the result occurring, there is no minimum level of probability that must be met before a risk will render a defendant potentially liable. For example, assume that Peter Pumpkin is put

---

8. If the defendant does not know that there is such a risk, then the defendant is not reckless but at worst criminally negligent.

in a room with 10,000 guns and told that one is loaded. He selects one at random, aims it directly at Lucretia's head, and pulls the trigger. If death results, Peter is reckless with regard to that result, even if, statistically, the chances of the gun firing were very, very small.

Some courts and commentators have suggested that a balancing test should be used to define recklessness. Thus, if the resulting harm is severe, a minimum degree of recklessness may be required; if, however, the resulting harm is less serious, the same defendant may not be found reckless. Thus, Peter may be a reckless murderer, but it is possible to argue that he is not guilty of "recklessly" discharging the gun in public. This kind of analysis again suggests the fact-sensitivity of law, and particularly criminal law.

Negligence as a Predicate for Criminal Liability

If there is some dispute about the meaning of the three previous levels of mens rea, there is a hurricane of disagreement, both among the courts and the commentators, on both the meaning and desirability of criminalizing negligent behavior.

A person who is negligent has not subjectively foreseen even the remotest possibility that harm may occur. This is the distinguishing factor between negligence and recklessness. Should persons who are merely negligent be punished as criminals?

Surprisingly, the different theories of punishment are divided on this question. Some retributivists argue that a person who has not paid attention to a risk has not chosen to create that risk and therefore is not morally culpable. Other retributivists (the "character" school), however, argue that a person who has the capacity to be non-negligent but fails to use that capacity *is* morally blameworthy, either because he has not used his capacity at the time of the event, or because he has not honed his skills and character better in the past to allow him to have perceived the risk when it arose.

Utilitarians are no more united on this issue. Some argue that punishing negligent defendants may encourage others to become more careful, thereby deterring future criminal harms. Others, however, argue that persons rarely act without believing that they *are* acting rationally and reasonably, and that they will not teach themselves to be more than what they believe is reasonable. Therefore, there will be no educative (deterrent) effect, and the punishment of the negligent actor will have no beneficial effect in the real world. To this argument the first school responds that, since *criminal* negligence as defined punishes only minimal care (something not even the *very* stupid would do), such punishment *may* marginally affect the behavior of some defendants.

Finally, some utilitarians argue that nefarious evildoers falsely claim they were "merely negligent" in the hopes of duping the fact finder. This argument, however, proves too much. At its most extreme, it would require strict liability for all harms, since *any* requirement of proof of mens rea, or excuse, or even actus reus could be abused by a duplicitous defendant.

Defining Criminal Negligence. Common law in very limited circumstances allowed criminal negligence as the basis of some liability. But what does the term mean? The basic definition can be easily stated: Mere tort negligence is insufficient to ground criminal liability; the negligence must be "criminal." This is obviously not helpful, so try these definitions:

1. "That degree of negligence or carelessness which is denominated as gross, and which constitutes such a departure from what would be the conduct of an ordinarily careful and prudent man . . . as to furnish evidence of that indifference to consequences which in some offenses takes the place of criminal intent." *Fitzgerald v. State*, 112 Ala. 34, 20 So. 966 (1896).
2. "Negligence, to be criminal, must be reckless and wanton." *State v. Weiner*, 41 N.J. 21, 194 A.2d 467 (1964).

As these (not very helpful) "definitions" illustrate, many courts invoke words that are so close to recklessness as to make criminal negligence indistinguishable from that concept. Some decisions even talk about advertent negligence, a notion that is even harder to explain than jumbo shrimp.

Analytically, one might try to explain the concept of degrees of negligence in various ways. It could require (1) a subjective recognition of the harm, and/or (2) a risk of only some, very serious, harm (see below) and/or (3) a statistically greater risk of harm. While we might find the defendant tortiously liable if the risk were 40 percent, we would find her criminally liable only if the risk were 70 percent because *virtually every person,* not merely the average person, would see the risk. The cases seem to endorse something like this latter view: Only if the defendant's failure to recognize the risk was "really outrageous" or "really stupid" should he be convicted. We could refer to this as the "really stupid reasonable person" test.

There is also some question about whether criminal negligence applies to most offenses. Most cases defining criminal negligence (including the two quoted above) involved charges of homicide, usually of murder. More modern cases, involving charges of nonhomicidal acts, have allowed conviction on the basis of "tort" negligence.

For example, in *United States v. Garrett*, 984 F.2d 1402 (5th Cir. 1993), the defendant was charged with attempting to board an airplane with a concealed weapon. She claimed that she had forgotten that the gun was in her purse. Moreover, she had been late in getting dressed that morning and had hastily picked up a purse that she used only infrequently. The court held that a jury could convict her if they found her mistake to be tortiously (civilly) negligent.

Some courts have carried the confusion even further. For example, in *State v. Santillanes,* 115 N.M. 215, 849 P.2d 358 (1993), the court interpreted a statute allowing conviction if the defendant were "negligent" as requiring "more than" mere tortious negligence but less than "criminal negligence" as defined by the Model Penal Code.

Other states have also allowed tort negligence to be sufficient for criminal liability in such areas as child abuse and neglect. Some state legislatures have enacted statutes dealing with very specific and discrete behavior and results — for example, negligent operation of a vehicle resulting in death, which is treated less seriously than other types of homicide.

These developments in applying tortious negligence to criminal liability are relatively new and are not yet clearly settled. Given the new endorsement by the United States Supreme Court of the traditional mens rea requirements (see pages 92-93), the future of this movement is uncertain.

Subjectivity vs. Objectivity. As every torts student knows, adoption of an objective standard is hardly the end of the question. Even in torts, where the prime objective is compensation to innocent plaintiffs injured by unreasonable defendants, the question constantly arises as to what characteristics of the defendant are relevant in the test of the reasonably prudent person (RPP). Characteristics that increase the defendant's duty of care — higher degrees of expertise, training, or learning—are routinely added to the RPP (e.g., the reasonable brain surgeon). There are also relevant characteristics that lower the possible level of care. In torts, age (the children's rule) and long-term or permanent physical characteristics (e.g., blindness, deafness) are frequently added to the RPP standard.[9] It should not be surprising, therefore, that wherever the RPP test is used in criminal law, these kinds of characteristics are easily incorporated. Because the criminal law focuses much more on the actual subjective blameworthiness of the defendant, however, the impetus to further "subjectivize" the objective reasonable person test is strong, indeed virtually irresistible. We will explore these issues in more depth when we deal with specific defensive claims, but it may be helpful now to suggest at least some of the holdings of recent vintage on this question. The RPP

1. reads police gazettes and has been the victim of a mugging; his doorman has recently been viciously mugged. *People v. Goetz,* 68 N.Y.2d 96, 497 N.E.2d 41 (1986).
2. is a glue sniffer. *R. v. Morhal,* [1995] 3 All E.R. 659.
3. has been socially acculturated to use only deadly force to repel nondeadly force. *State v. Wanrow,* 88 Wash. 2d 221, 559 P.2d 548 (1977).

---

9. On the other hand, in tort law, the defendant's mental illness or insanity is irrelevant, whereas in criminal law insanity is a full excuse (see Chapter 17).

4. can be provoked by the crying of a small infant to kill that infant. *R. v. Doughty*, [1986] 83 Cr. App. R. 319.
5. is pregnant. *D.P.P. v. Camplin*, [1978] 2 All E.R. 168 (dictum).

Given this trend toward increasingly subjectivizing the RPP, there is now substantial debate whether the concept of objective criminal negligence using a tort standard is sensible.

Proving Mens Rea

The first three kinds of mens rea (intent, knowledge, and recklessness) require that the state prove the defendant's actual mental state with regard to facts and result. But how can the state prove that? Other fields of law have concluded that it is simply too hard and too costly to prove what was actually in the defendant's mind.[10] However, criminal law does focus on individual blameworthiness as a basis for punishing.

Can we ever know what someone else is thinking? Some philosophers and psychiatrists argue that we never even know what *we* are thinking.[11] How, then, are we to determine whether the defendant in a criminal case had the requisite mens rea for conviction?

The answer is *inference*. We can only infer, primarily from the defendant's conduct and words and secondarily from other facts that help us assess those inferences, what the defendant was thinking. Perhaps because we recognize the fallibility of such inferences we require that the jury be persuaded beyond a reasonable doubt that the inference of mens rea is a reasonable one to draw in this case.[12]

Again, an example may be helpful. Peter Pumpkin, who shot Lucretia, claims that he did not know the gun was loaded. If Peter is proven to be an expert gun handler, we may begin to doubt his denial. If the evidence also shows that Peter spent ten minutes looking at the weapon before he fired it, we may find further reason to reject his claim. And if more evidence shows that Peter actually loaded the gun, we may think the case clinched. *But be careful.* Peter may claim that he thought the items he placed in the gun were

---

10. In *Vaughan v. Menlove*, 132 Eng. Rep. 490 (1837), for example, the court explicitly rejected a subjective standard of negligence because it would require "measuring the feet" of every defendant. Thus, tort law uses an objective fictitious person to assess the defendant's liability and does not actually care what was actually going on in *this* defendant's mind.

11. See I. Buford, Essays on Other Minds (1970); Comment, Motive, Crimes and Other Minds, 142 U. Pa. L. Rev. 2071 (1995).

12. Prior to the twentieth century, defendants were generally prohibited from testifying in their own behalf. The common law, seeking some way in which to allow the prosecutor to establish mens rea, and particularly intent, established a "presumption" that a person "intends the natural and probable consequences of his act."

blanks, and he may show us the box, marked "blanks," that he used. Much of our decision will depend on Peter's credibility, should he choose to testify. If we believe Peter about other items, we are more likely to infer that he is telling the truth about this item as well. However, inference is our best, perhaps our only, guide.

As discussed below, considering the defendant's motive complicates matters. If Robin Hood intentionally robs the Sheriff (statutory mens rea), the fact that his motive for doing so is to give the proceeds to the poor (arguably a morally good reason, and thus denying "traditional" moral blameworthiness) is irrelevant to his guilt. But the argument can be easily overstated. If the statute explicitly requires a "specific intent" (robbing with the intent to become wealthy), Robin's motive become relevant. Similarly, if Bartholomew has put a knife to Lorraine's throat and taken her into a dark alley, at which point he is arrested, his liability may well depend on the charge. If he is charged with "assault with intent to rape," he may well respond that his motive was not to rape but to rob her (the reverse will also work). If he is believed, he has not committed the crime. Of course, he is still guilty of assault (a general intent crime). Similarly, if he is charged with attempted rape or attempted robbery, his "motive" (specific intent) in taking Lorraine into the alley will be critical to his liability. (See Chapter 12.)

Motive and Mens Rea[13]

Euthanasia raises most directly the difference between the two kinds of mens rea in dealing with motive. A person who (often with the victim's consent) intentionally disconnects life-prolonging devices or kills with a shotgun at point-blank range for the sole purpose of relieving that person's suffering certainly has statutory mens rea. However, is he blameworthy? Does he have traditional mens rea? Motive suggests he does not have traditional mens rea. Yet most courts today would exclude evidence of such a motive.

Motive is admissible to bolster the prosecutor's case, since from motive the jury may well infer mens rea. For example, Gertrude, who has just run over Jillian with her car claims she did not see Jillian. So far as we initially know, they are total strangers. Charged with purposely killing Jillian, Gertrude is likely to be acquitted. We simply can't see why Gertrude would purposely kill the victim, even if the external evidence suggests that (1) it was a bright and sunny day; (2) Gertrude traveled over 500 feet before she hit Jillian, who was on the sidewalk; (3) Gertrude never hit the brakes. However, if we discover that Jillian is having an affair with Gertrude's

---

13. Gardner, The Mens Rea Enigma: Observations on the Role of Motive in the Criminal Law Past and Present, 1993 Utah L. Rev. 635.

husband, or that Gertrude stood to inherit from Jillian, or that Jillian was blocking Gertrude's advancement in her field, we might *now* be willing to infer that Gertrude purposely killed Jillian, *because she had a motive for doing so.* It is the lack of apparent motive that spurs Hitchcock's great film, *Strangers on a Train,* where strangers agree to "swap murders" in the belief that the police will not suspect them of "motiveless" crimes.

If motive is not relevant to the determination of guilt, it may be relevant at the time of sentencing. Even if Robin Hood and Smokey the Rat are both robbers, we may tend to think Robin deserves less punishment. Similarly, bad motive may seem to warrant increased punishment. Assault alone may be a crime. If it is motivated by racial animosity, we may consider it worthy of more punishment.

Motive and Defenses

If motive means the reason why the defendant acted with the requisite statutory mens rea, the criminal law sometimes does consider motive, but it has cloaked this consideration by calling some motives "defenses." Thus, if Hillary claims that she purposely killed Andrew because Andrew had fired four shots at her, or that she purposely stole the painting because Andrew had a gun trained on her (or on her son), these *reasons* (motives) are relevant under standard criminal law doctrine because they constitute defenses (self-defense and duress, respectively). We will explore the rules as to those defenses in Chapter 16, but it is useful, even now, to at least recognize that there are motives that the criminal law does consider.

Contemporaneity, Prior Fault, and Time Frames

It is frequently said that a defendant is liable only if the actus reus and the mens rea coincide. Like many other truisms of the law, this is true only if it is understood properly. If not, it can prove to be a trap for the unwary. So beware.

A defendant is not liable if at one point in time (T) she has formed the requisite mens rea upon which she does not act but, at a later time (T2) when that mens rea is not present, the harm that she had envisioned occurs. For example, Carmen, in a blue funk, decided to kill her toreador lover, Chuck, by shooting him the next time he brought her a rose. However, as (his) luck would have it, Chuck stops bringing Carmen roses, and the thought disappears. Two weeks later, choking in daffodils, but fully reconciled with Chuck, Carmen is taking pot shots at a tree in the backyard. You guessed it: Chuck walks out from behind the tree (carrying a rose yet), and the next bullet accidentally terminates his breathing. Quite obviously, Carmen is not guilty of purposely killing Chuck, even though she has killed him (actus reus) and she has previously intended to kill him (mens rea). To explain this result, the common law courts said that the mens rea and actus reus must coincide.

But take a different case. Chiquita decides to kill her lover, Clancy, for exactly the same reasons that energized Carmen. She gets a vial of arsenic and pours the contents into Clancy's sugar bowl. She knows that, sometime within the next three weeks, Clancy will use the sugar. Immediately after this event, Chiquita leaves the house and is trampled by a rogue elephant. She goes into a coma and is kept alive only by a respirator; no part of her body is acting voluntarily. (See Chapter 3.) Sure enough, two weeks later, with Chiquita in the coma, Clancy takes the poison and dies. Miraculously, Chiquita awakes from her coma ten seconds after his death and shouts out: "Someone warn Clancy. I don't want him to die." If Chiquita is prosecuted for murder, she will raise the doctrine of contemporaneity. At the moment Clancy died, she was not acting at all; the actus reus (Clancy's death) and the mens rea (purpose to kill) did not coincide. Nice try, Chiquita. The *relevant* actus reus here is not Clancy's death, but Chiquita's *act* of putting the poison in the sugar bowl although the *result* occurred much later. When *that* actus reus occurred, Chiquita did have the requisite mens rea.

One way of conceptualizing this analysis is to say that we can move the time frame back to see if, at some relevant time, the defendant, with the requisite mens rea, acted in a way that ultimately caused the harm. Consider *People v. Decina,* discussed in Chapter 3. At the time his car hit the four school children (the time of the harm), Decina was suffering an epileptic seizure, and neither acting voluntarily nor entertaining a mens of any kind. However, by moving the time frame back to before the seizure (indeed, perhaps to the time he entered the car and turned on the ignition), the court found both an act (beginning to drive) and a mens rea (criminal negligence or recklessness as to the possibility that he would have a seizure, lose control of the car, and cause death or serious injury).

In looking for prior fault or asking whether the defendant has created the conditions of his own excuse, we must accurately identify the mental state at the time of the relevant act. Suppose, for example, that Melissa recklessly becomes intoxicated, is later involved in an automobile accident, and charged with intentionally running a red light. If, at the time of running the light, Melissa has no mind at all, her liability should be for recklessly, rather than intentionally, creating a situation (by drinking) where she might later run a red light (not even for recklessly running the light). Failure to observe this requirement results in overcharging the defendant. The reluctance of legislatures to create new crimes that more accurately reflect the actual blameworthiness of the defendant at the time of the *act* results in more liability than the defendant deserves for the *harm* inflicted. We will see this phenomenon in a number of doctrines. Stay alert.

Statutory Interpretation and Mens Rea

Principles of Statutory Construction

Because modern criminal law consists of interpreting statutes, it is important to have some grasp of general rules of statutory construction and how they apply to criminal cases. Writers and courts debate whether the "maxims" of statutory interpretation are meaningful, not only in criminal law but in law generally.[14] We will not enter that debate here. Instead, we assume the general usefulness of such maxims, particularly in interpreting criminal statutes, where the policies of lenity and legality attain constitutional, or quasi-constitutional, status (see Chapter 1). Similarly, many of the rules of interpreting criminal statutes are generated by the substantive policy positions of the criminal law. For example, under the common law mens rea is presumed to be required to be proved, even if the legislature has not explicitly required a mens rea. This specific result could be seen as an application of the maxim that *penal statutes are to be construed narrowly and against the state.*

Other maxims dealing with legislative silence are also important in construing criminal statutes. If, for example, a statute does not require an element of proof that the common law did require, courts would probably apply the general maxim that *statutes in derogation of the common law are to be construed narrowly.*

Furthermore, the general rule of *in pari materia*—statutes dealing with similar subjects should be construed similarly—often have particular impact. Consider the following statutes:

A.   Whoever sells cocaine shall be fined $1,000.
B.   Whoever knowingly sells heroin shall be fined $1,000.

Can a person violate statute A without "knowing" that he is selling cocaine? The two statutes *seem* to deal with the same basic evil, the sale of drugs. Since statute B requires "knowingly," statute A might be similarly construed. On the other hand, since statute B tells us that the legislature has articulated

---

14. K. Llewellyn, The Common Law Tradition (1960) (maxims of statutory interpretation can conceivably be manipulated to include or exclude anything).

a requirement of "knowingly" on occasion, should we infer that its failure to do so in statute A means that the omission was purposeful?

The argument that the two are to be read in pari materia because they deal with drugs is strengthened by the fact that the punishments are identical. However, suppose that statute B prohibited knowingly selling poisoned food (or stolen pencils) and specified the same fine of $1,000. It would then be harder to use the *in pari materia* approach because drugs and pencils (or even poisoned food) might not be seen as the same "matter." On the other hand, if the punishment is the same, that might be the same "matter." Or suppose that the punishment for selling heroin, in statute B, is raised to five years. Now it might be argued that statute A does not require proof of knowledge, because knowledge must be proved only if the punishment is "very" severe.

Another maxim of statutory construction tells us to read the statute in its "plain meaning." At great tension with this general philosophical approach are at least two legal principles: (1) restraining the reach of the legislature into the lives of citizens; (2) requiring the legislature to speak clearly, particularly when freedom is at stake. This latter guideline is known in criminal contexts as the "rule of lenity." As noted in Chapter 1, this rule holds that if the legislature has not clearly spoken, the statute's ambiguities should be construed against the legislature and in favor of the defendant (and the defendant's freedom).

Thus, if the legislature enacts a statute that incorporates a mens rea word, there is a strong argument that the mens rea word applies to every "material element" of the crime. In the following statute, we begin with the general proposition that "knowingly" applies to "bald eagle" as well as "kills":

Whoever knowingly kills a bald eagle commits a crime.

But what if the statute has no mens rea word in it? Suppose, that is, the statute reads:

Whoever kills a bald eagle commits a crime.

The statute does not expressly require a mens rea: A person who chops down a tree that kills a bald eagle that has come to rest near the tree only seconds before it falls is within the "plain words" of the statute. If the courts are not to "rewrite" the statute, it should be applied to this defendant or even to the defendant who took every measure possible to ensure that there would be no bald eagles in the vicinity when the tree fell.

Courts confronting such a statute are faced with a dilemma. The plain words of the statute do not require a mens rea. Does the omission of a mens rea word reflect a firm legislative decision to impose strict liability? Should we assume that the legislature *intended* to omit mens rea? Or should we assume that the omission was a mere oversight? (Or, only somewhat more impishly, that the statute was drafted on a Friday, when everyone was tired and wanted to get home for the weekend?)

The problem is that to argue about what the legislature *could* have done is sterile: Just as it *could* have written in the word "knowingly," it *could* just as easily have said, "Anyone who kills a bald eagle, whether or not they know, suspect, or could have known it was a bald eagle, is guilty of an offense."[15]

In the end, the legislative intent argument leads us nowhere unless we have a starting point. Some courts have provided that starting point by asserting that the legislative intent to do away with mens rea must be "patently" clear.[16] Other courts begin at the other end, with the "plain meaning" rule. Again, the lack of a legislatively declared rule of interpretation leaves the courts rudderless. They therefore use other guides to try to fight their way out of this morass.

The above remarks should be regarded as an introduction to the problems of interpreting statutes generally, and not solely those in the criminal law. General rules of interpretations may or may not be applicable to the exotic field you are about to enter. However, it won't hurt to keep those rules in mind.

Element Analysis

Little Red Riding Hood has been instructed by her mother to deliver a package to her grandmother. Red, who had been planning a round of golf, is not pleased. As she is walking through the woods, she comes across a great bonfire. Herman is standing there and shouting "No more books" as he throws volume after volume of Charles Dickens on the fire. Angry that she cannot play golf, Red throws the package into the fire and watches it burn. It turns out that the package contains a first edition of Hogan on Golf. Red is charged under a statute that punishes anyone who "purposely hides, destroys, or mars a book." Is Little Red guilty under this statute?

If the prosecutor has only to prove that Red purposely destroyed the *package*, that hurdle is easily cleared: Red obviously purposely destroyed whatever were the contents of the package. But does the prosecutor have to prove that Red knew the package contained a "book"? This problem raises the issue of how far down the statute the mens rea word ("purposely") goes. Prescient lawyers call this the "traveling" question.

The first approach to this problem must be grammatical. "Purposely" is an adverb; "book" is a noun. Since adverbs modify only verbs, "purposely"

---

15. For example, the New Jersey "drug-free school zone" statute expressly provides: "It shall be no defense . . . that the actor was unaware that the prohibited conduct took place while or within 1000 feet of any school property." New Jersey Stat Ann. 2C: 35-7.

16. *People v. Hager*, 476 N.Y.S.2d 442 (Nassau Cty. Ct. 1989).

cannot apply directly to the word "book" in the statute. A number of common law decisions therefore concluded that Red would be guilty of the crime, even though she did not know that it was a book she was destroying, since she "purposely" destroyed.[17]

However, this result seems wrong. The legislature was not concerned with persons who purposely destroyed *packages*, only with persons who purposely destroyed *books*. No one would condone what Red did and she might be sent to bed without supper, but the issue here is not *only* whether she has acted in an immoral way (traditional mens rea) but whether she has also acted in a way proscribed by the statute (statutory mens rea). Whether traditional mens rea is always necessary, statutory mens rea *is* necessary to meet the principle of legality. To use our earlier terms, Red may have been *reckless* or *negligent* (even criminally negligent) as to what was in the package. If the legislature had prohibited recklessly or negligently destroying books, Red might (given further facts, such as the shape of the package or her ability to feel the contents) be guilty of one of those offenses. However, she was not acting "purposely" with regard to the result of a destroyed book, and is therefore not guilty under the statute. Moreover, to punish Red for purposely destroying the book would mean that she should be treated as being equally bad as Herman, who was well aware that the items he was throwing on the bonfire were books.

The common law's response to this dilemma was to create a separate set of doctrines dealing with mistake. We shall investigate those doctrines in the next chapter. Here, however, we focus on the impact of mistake solely as one of statutory interpretation, apart from the independent question of the law of mistake. One method of resolving this question would be to define in general terms what a particular mens rea word such as "purposely" *means* with regard to each of the words in the statute. For example, we could say that a person acts "purposely" with regard to the "book" in the statute only if she knows that the book exists. This approach of applying a statutory mens rea word to every significant part of the statute is now called *element analysis*.

A recent United States Supreme Court decision appears to have adopted element analysis in interpreting federal statutes. In *X-Citement Video v. United States*, 513 U.S. 64 (1994), the defendant distributed a pornographic film whose cast included minors. A federal statute punished anyone who "knowingly ships" such a film involving the "use of a minor." The Court held that the word "knowingly" modified not only the verb "ships" but the phrase "use of a minor." Thus, a defendant who knows that he is shipping a film, and even knows that what he is shipping is a sexually explicit film, is not guilty of this offense unless he *also* knows that the film includes a minor.

---

17. *Cotterill v. Penn*, 1 K.B. 53 (1936).

Note that unless this approach to statutory interpretation is adopted (or an additional set of rules created), the statute essentially establishes strict liability (see Chapter 6) for the element of "minor" (or "book" in Little Red Riding Hood's case.) It is possible to restrict *X-Citement Video's* holding to the specific statute involved because there was a First Amendment issue in the background. However, a fair reading of the case suggests that the Court will apply element analysis to all federal statutes.

The "Default Position"

Suppose that Red Riding Hood had been prosecuted under a statute punishing "anyone who destroys a book." This statute, unlike the first one, contains no mens rea word at all. The possibility that the legislature intended to impose strict liability, perhaps both with regard to the word "destroys" and with regard to the word "book," cannot be ignored and will be discussed below in Chapter 6. However, in light of the general position of the criminal law requiring mens rea, let us here assume that the statute should be interpreted as requiring a mens rea. When mens rea was used in its "traditional" sense, the problem was perhaps less evident. The basic question then was whether Red had acted in a blameworthy way. This revived the debate as to whether negligence could amount to blameworthiness (see above), but beyond that the courts did not need to go. Any level of blameworthiness would suffice. As the principle of legality took hold, however, and statutory mens rea became ascendant, courts could no longer ask merely whether the defendant was blameworthy. They had to decide as well which of the statutory mens rea words would apply. Traditional mens rea, even if necessary, was no longer a sufficient condition for liability. Since there were scores of statutory mens rea words from which to choose, this was a daunting task.

Most courts adopted the view that criminal punishment should not be imposed unless the defendant was at least reckless (actually foresaw a possibility of criminal harm) and went ahead anyway. In a recent decision, the United States Supreme Court has gone beyond that. It now appears to have adopted the view that in interpreting federal statutes that are silent on the mens rea issue, it will begin with the presumption that the defendant must act *knowingly* as to each element of the statute. The case, *United States v. Staples,* 511 U.S. 600 (1994), involved a defendant who was charged with failing to inform the federal government that he owned a specific rifle. Federal law did not require that all gun owners register all guns with the government; only owners of "firearms which shoot, or can be readily restored to shoot, automatically" had to register them. The statute contained no mens rea word at all. The defendant acknowledged that he owned a rifle that in fact could shoot automatically but contended that he was unaware the gun had been altered to fire automatically. The Court concluded not only that some mens rea would be required, but that the level of mens rea required was "knowingly." *Staples* is an important decision regarding strict liability, and we will discuss it in that context as well. But it is important here because it appears to adopt "knowingly" as the default position—if Congress does not specify recklessness (or some lower standard of mens rea), federal courts should construe such a criminal statute to require actual knowledge of the facts. This is not merely a statutory interpretation point; the decision carries significant moral weight as well because it appears to adopt the subjectivist view.

The Model Penal Code

Perhaps the greatest contribution that the Model Penal Code has made is in the area of defining mens rea and providing rules for statutory interpretation. The Code:

1. adopts element analysis (indeed, the Code really invented the idea);
2. reduces statutory mens rea culpability to four states;
3. adopts subjective liability (recklessness) as the default position.

Furthermore, the Code provides helpful definitions for the culpability levels and when and how element analysis works.

Element Analysis
Elements and Material Elements

The Code first establishes a general approach to statutory interpretation by concluding that most words in a statute are "elements" of the statute. It then concludes that these can be divided into "simple" elements and "material" elements. Under §1.13 of the Code, simple elements are those terms related "exclusively" to items such as venue, jurisdiction, or the statute of limitations, and therefore "unconnected with the harm or evil, incident to conduct, sought to be prevented by the law defining the offense."

Under this approach we must first decide what evil the legislature was trying to prevent when it passed the statute. The Code itself gives no specific guidance in this task, but common sense helps us. Take the following statute: "Whoever kills a bald eagle commits a crime." It is fairly apparent that the evil here is improperly reducing the number of bald eagles in the community. The legislature does not care *how* they are killed—by arrow, shotgun, poison, or strangulation. Had the concern been to reduce excessive *shooting* of birds, the legislation would probably have punished "Whoever shoots (and kills) a bald eagle." Moreover, the concern is protecting bald eagles and *only* bald eagles; it is not preservation of endangered bird species. If the defendant kills a condor, the harm that the legislature sought to prevent does not occur: the number of endangered birds may be reduced but not the number of bald eagles. Moreover, the legislature is not concerned (in this statute) with the death of other kinds of eagles. Similarly, the concern is with the *death* of such a bird. If the defendant merely wounds or maims a bald eagle, that concern is not involved. We can therefore conclude that the legislature had in mind the evil of (1) killing (2) bald eagles. These are therefore "material" elements.

Some statutes may be more difficult. A statute that punishes any person "who discharges a gun in public" may be concerned with (1) loud noises in public places; (2) possible endangerment of persons in public. The statute is unclear, particularly since in either interpretation it is drastically underinclusive. Usual approaches to statutory interpretation may assist but not always; we and the courts will just have to try to interpret statutes as legislatures wanted them interpreted (wouldn't it be nice if the legislature were a bit more sensitive to these problems?).

Kinds of Material Elements

Conduct and Result. The Code divides "material elements" into (a) conduct; (b) attendant circumstance; (c) result. It defines neither result nor attendant circumstance, though it does define conduct in §1.13(5). Again, common sense is usually a helpful guide. Consider once more the Red Riding Hood case. That statute penalized anyone who "purposely destroys a book." Intuition tells us that "destroys" is a material element. The legislature was not concerned with people who leafed through books, nor with those who damaged books. However, is "destroys" a word describing (1) conduct or (2) result? The answer is both. Indeed, many verbs in the English language (*kill, touch, hide*) describe both conduct and the result of that conduct.

Attendant Circumstance. However, it is not enough that Red destroyed the package. Under the statute, she must destroy a *book*. Clearly, "book" is a material element; the legislature was not concerned with the destruction of computers, wild birds, or furniture. Whether it was concerned with newspapers, magazines, or software would be a different and more difficult question, but one involving the definition of "book," not whether "book" is a material element. "Book" is neither conduct nor result. If, therefore, it is a material element, "book" becomes an attendant circumstance, almost by default. Indeed, it would be possible in most instances to equate the term "attendant circumstance" with statutory "factual elements."

Levels of Culpability

Section 2.02 of the Code establishes four levels of culpability:

1. purposely
2. knowingly

3. recklessly
4. criminally negligently

Purposely. This mens rea word in the Code is roughly the equivalent of "intentionally" under the common law. The Code requires that the defendant "be aware or hope or believe" an attendant circumstance is true, and that he entertain a "conscious object" to achieve the proscribed result. The Code also retains two of the subsidiary doctrines of the common law of intent. Transferred intent is retained as a matter of causation (§2.03(2) & (3)). Similarly, the Code occasionally talks in terms of a crime being committed only if an act is done "with the purpose of" achieving a result, a rough analog to specific intent.

Knowingly. This Code term is essentially the equivalent of "oblique intention" under the common law. The defendant acts knowingly if he knows that the result, although one he does not consciously seek to cause, is "practically certain to occur," should he continue his present course of action. The Code has a specific provision that equates "willfully" with "knowingly." See §2.02(8). This eliminates the term "willfully" from statutory usage.

The Code also defines and adopts the general notion of willful blindness. Section 2.02(7) provides that a person acts "knowingly" with respect to a material element if he is "aware of a high probability of its existence." Commentators have argued about whether this is broader or narrower than the common law notion of willful blindness.

Recklessly. As with the common law, the Code provides that the defendant is reckless only if he *actually foresees* that a harm may occur. Thus, subjective liability is continued. There is, however, one major possible problem with the Code's approach to recklessness. The Code requires that the risk that the defendant foresees (and thereafter consciously disregards) be "substantial and unjustifiable." The latter term is understandable, and it clearly puts on the prosecution the burden of proof as to lack of justification. (See Chapter 15.) The difficulty, however, is in the apparent requirement that the risk be *substantial.* Taken literally, this requirement might lead to a different result in the hypothetical, discussed above, where Peter Pumpkin takes the one loaded gun out of 10,000 and kills his wife. We there concluded that Peter was reckless. However, a chance of .001 is not really "substantial." To avoid the absurd result that Peter is not reckless as to death under the Code's definition therefore requires that the word "substantial" be read as qualitative ("of real importance") rather than merely quantitative ("highly probable").

Negligence. Section 2.02(2)(d) of the Code proposes criminal negligence as a possible predicate for criminal liability — that is, not tort but criminal (or wanton or culpable) negligence, as understood under the common law. However, the Code in fact only allows criminal negligence in one crime, homicide, in which case the penalty is less than that for manslaughter (which is usually the level of punishment for negligent homicide in common law jurisdictions). Thus, while appearing to embrace negligence as a basis of liability generally, the Code really uses this approach as a way of mitigating punishment for those who might otherwise be convicted of manslaughter. (See Chapter 8.)

Mens Rea and Material Elements

Now comes the Code's monumental achievement. The Code merges its definitions of culpability with its establishment of material elements, and provides that *every material element in every statute must be modified by one of the mental culpability states* (§2.02). This simple but elegant move solves many of the dilemmas we have confronted in the earlier sections of this chapter. The result is best shown graphically in Table 1.

Let's take the case of Little Red Riding Hood, who is charged with "purposely destroying a book." Since the statutorily stated mens rea is "purposely," and since "book" is an attendant circumstance material element, the state must show that Red either was "aware of the existence of such circumstance or believe[d] or hope[d]" that it exists — i.e.— that the package contained a book. We have already posited that Red did *not* know, or even suspect, that the package contained a book. Thus, she does not meet the Code's requirement and is not guilty of the crime charged. Herman, on the other hand, *did* know that he was burning a book. Assuming that it was his conscious object to cause the destruction of the book, he is guilty under the statute.

Suppose, instead, that Little Red was charged under a different statute, punishing anyone who "recklessly" destroyed a book. Here the analysis is the same: "Book" is an attendant circumstance material element. Under the recklessness provision, Red is guilty if she "consciously disregards a substantial and unjustifiable risk" that the item she is destroying is a book. That disregard must involve "a gross deviation from the standard of conduct that a law-abiding person would observe" in Red's situation. So if Red manipulated the package and it felt like a book, or she saw that an attached sales receipt was from a bookstore, she might be found guilty of violating this statute. Note that the difference between her possible liability under "knowingly" and "recklessly" depends on the degree of probability that Red recognizes that the item might be a book. If she is aware of a high probability that the package contains a book, she is "willfully blind" under §2.02(7) of the Code and hence acts "knowingly." If, on the other hand, she is aware of a substantial (but not highly probable) risk that the package contains a book, she is reckless, and not knowing, with regard to that material element.

In the Red Riding Hood statute, "purposely," is the only mens rea word articulated in the statute, and thus modifies all the material elements in the

Table 1. Mens Rea and the Model Penal Code

Culpability Level	Conduct	Attendant Circumstances	Result
Purposely	Defendant's conscious object is to engage in such conduct.	Defendant is aware or hopes or believes circumstances exist.	Defendant's conscious object is to cause *this* result.
Knowingly	Defendant is aware his conduct is of this nature.	Defendant is aware the circumstances exist.	Defendant is aware that the result is practically certain.
Recklessly	Defendant consciously disregards a substantial and unjustifiable risk that he is engaging in this proscribed conduct.	Defendant consciously disregards a substantial and unjustifiable risk that the proscribed circumstances exist.	Defendant consciously disregards a substantial and unjustifiable risk that the result will occur.
	The disregard involves a gross deviation from the standard of conduct that a law-abiding person would observe, considering defendant's purpose and the circumstances known to him.		
Negligently	"grossly" fails to recognize a substantial and unjustifiable risk he is engaging in this conduct.	"grossly" fails to recognize an unjustifiable risk that the proscribed circumstances exist.	"grossly" fails to recognize a substantial and unjustifiable risk that the result will occur.
	The failure to recognize the risk, given defendant's purpose and the circumstances known to him, involves a gross deviation from the standard of care a reasonable person would observe.		

statute. But the legislature may require different mental states with regard to different material elements in a statute. Thus: "Whoever, while purposely destroying a package, recklessly destroys a book, is guilty of a crime." Here, purposely requires that the defendant *know* (or hope) that it is a package, but merely be reckless as to whether it contains a book. If the statute read "Whoever, while destroying a package, recklessly destroys a book," the defendant obviously must be reckless as to whether a book is involved. But what is the mens rea as to whether a package is involved? This involves the default position.

The Default Position Under the Code

The Code establishes recklessness as the default provision of mens rea. Section 2.02(3) provides that if there is no mens rea stated in the statute, the element is proved if a person acts purposely, knowingly, or recklessly with respect thereto. In our cocaine statute, for example, there is no mens rea stated. Thus, the prosecution will be successful only if it proves the defendant was reckless (or worse) with regard to the item being cocaine. In the case suggested above, the government would have to prove that Red was reckless as to a package being involved (and as to whether she was destroying it) *not* because reckless is used somewhere in the statute, but because the default provision applies.

The Code's position on default does two things (at least). First, it rejects the view, apparently adopted by the United States Supreme Court in *Staples*, supra, as a matter of interpreting federal criminal statutes, that "knowingly" is the presumed mens rea requirement. Thus, the Code seems to adopt a lower standard of culpability than did *Staples*. Second, the Code rejects, at least as a presumptive matter, imposing criminal liability on the basis of civil tort negligence. (The Code itself allows such liability only in the case of homicide, and then only where the negligence is "criminal.") Thus, all criminal liability is *presumed* to be based on subjective moral culpability. Unless the legislature expressly allows criminal negligence as a predicate for criminal liability, the statute will be interpreted as requiring subjective culpability.

Subjectivity vs. Objectivity

The Model Penal Code seeks to restore subjectivity to much of the criminal law. Although this will be more fully discussed in other chapters, it can be generally said that the Code provides more room for excuses and more possibility for exculpation and focuses more on the defendant's subjective state of mind than did the common law of the nineteenth century (but not necessarily that of the seventeenth or eighteenth centuries). For example, the Code allows *any* mistake to negate criminal liability (see

§2.04(1)), where some states required a mistake to be reasonable (see Chapter 5). The Code is not "fully" subjective, however; on several key points, it adopts the view of (a) the "reasonably prudent person" (b) "in the actor's situation." The former phrase points to an objective standard while the latter points toward subjectivity. The Code's emphasis on the subjective state of mind and personal characteristics contrasts sharply with the nineteenth century's movement toward objective standards. This theme will be mentioned throughout this book.

It would be too much to say that the Code solves the issues of interpretation raised earlier in this chapter. However, it gives more guidance and more serious consideration to these problems than any other tool we know. Moreover, since the Code has been adopted in a majority of states, and has influenced common law courts even when the legislature has not adopted the Code, it may now be suggested that element analysis is part of the American law of crimes.

EXAMPLES

1. One day in October, Napoleon, an avid hunter, goes to the nearby woods, which are in Smith County, to pursue rabbit. Unknown to him, his trek takes him across the county line into Jones County. As (good) luck would have it, he spots a rabbit and kills it with a single shot. As (bad) luck would have it, however, as he goes to pick it up, Odie, the friendly game warden, arrests him and charges him under a statute prohibiting anyone from "knowingly killing a rabbit in Jones County"; killing a rabbit is not illegal in Smith County. What result?

2. Lucy was angry at Ricky for his obsession (as she saw it) with golf paraphernalia. He had "mashies" and "niblicks" and "feather balls" all over the house. One night, when Ricky was out, Lucy collected all the clubs, took them outside, and began wrapping them around a tree. As she did so, the head of one of the clubs flew off and went through her neighbor's window, killing her good friend Ethel. Has Lucy intentionally killed Ethel?

3a. Napoleon, having paid his penalty to society, goes hunting again. This time, he knows that he's in Jones County, but he is after deer, which are legal game in Jones. An animal scurries across the path (it is nighttime) and Nappy, in a quick instant, shoots. Dead hare again. He is prosecuted for knowingly killing that rascally rabbit.

3b. Same facts, except that the charge is "recklessly" killing the rabbit.

3c. Same facts as 3a, but this time the statute prohibits "negligently" killing a rabbit.

3d. Same facts as 3a, except that it is a child who is killed. Is Nappy guilty of any form of homicide ("purposely," "knowingly," "recklessly," or "negligently" killing a human being)?

4. Barney goes into FAO Schwarz to buy toy dinosaurs for his children. He pays for the toys with a VISA credit card. Unknown to Barney, the card has expired. He is prosecuted under a statute that punishes anyone who "purposely uses an expired credit card to obtain goods or services."

5a. Jacob is a devout Snaker. His religion teaches him that no bite of a snake will be harmful, much less deadly, if the handler of the snake has true belief in God. Jacob does. He therefore takes his six-month-old son to church one day and, handling the snakes himself, allows them to bite the boy three times. The boy dies. Assume that a statute penalizes, in varying degrees, anyone who "intentionally, purposely, knowingly, maliciously, or recklessly" causes the death of another. Of which of these crimes, if any, is Jacob guilty?

5b. Same facts. The statute penalizes anyone who "causes the death" of another person.

6. Diana, in full view of 600 people, picks up a gun and carefully and deliberately loads it with bullets from a box plainly marked "deadly ammunition." She then walks over to Charles, who is studying pictures of his newest polo ponies, and, holding the gun to Charles' temple, pulls the trigger, shouting, "And that's for Camilla, you bastard." Charles dies. Has Diana "purposely" killed Charles?

7. Cary is driving his new Rolls Royce one night at ten miles per hour *under* the speed limit. He is keeping a careful watch on the road. Suddenly a child runs out in front of the car, only 100 yards ahead. Cary presses his foot to the brakes, but there is no response. Desperately, he screams at the child and veers his car hard to the left, applying the emergency brake at the same time. Nothing works. The child is killed. Cary is prosecuted for "reckless homicide." What result?

8. Helen, a burglar, has decided to burglarize a warehouse. She has "cased" the place for three weeks and is sure that everyone leaves by 10 p.m. On the night in question, she double-checks the parking lot and waits until 2 a.m., just in case anyone has stayed late. She then breaks in to the building by smashing a window and jumping through. As she lands, her foot hits the windpipe of Harry, a homeless person who has sneaked in through the back door and is sleeping there. Harry dies. Has Helen killed Harry "purposely, knowingly, recklessly, or negligently"?

EXPLANATIONS

1. Napoleon may have found his Waterloo. He obviously knew he was killing a rabbit. He did not know, however, that he had wandered into nearby Jones County. As a general matter, many common law courts

concluded that a mens rea word modified only the verb, thereby imposing strict liability (so far as mens rea is concerned) as to the remaining
parts of the statute. *Caveat:* No one doubts that "Jones County" is an
element of the offense, and the prosecution must prove beyond a
reasonable doubt that the killing occurred there (see Chapter 1). The
issue here is whether the prosecutor must also prove beyond a reasonable
doubt a relevant mens rea (here "knowingly") with regard to that
element.

The Model Penal Code will probably provide the same result but
for a different reason. It requires culpability with regard to any "material" element but not with regard to a mere "element." The Code's
distinction, however, is stated in the negative: A material element is an
element that "does not relate exclusively to the statute of limitations,
jurisdiction, venue or any other matter similarly unconnected with (i)
the harm or evil incident to conduct, sought to be prevented by the law
defining the offense." This would seem to mean that only if the prosecution can show that "Jones County" is "exclusively" related to jurisdiction is it not a "material element"; if she cannot carry that burden,
then the item *is* a material element, and mens rea must apply.

However, how does one determine that? One position is that
nothing can relate "exclusively" to jurisdiction, venue, and so on — that
by prohibiting rabbit killing only in Jones County, the legislature was
after an evil unique to Jones County, and therefore that the location is
"incident to the conduct sought to be prevented by the law defining
the offense." This argument, however appealing, is certainly wrong, for
it would make the Code's attempted distinction meaningless. Thus, one
must conclude that "Jones County" (which certainly sounds like it is
solely related to jurisdiction) is not a *material* element, but only an
element, and mens rea does not apply to that element. As long as
Napoleon knew he was killing, and that what he was killing was a rabbit,
he's a gone goose.

2. This is an easy one. No. Even the doctrine of "transferred intent" applied
    only "inside" a particular crime (e.g., property damage, homicide).
    Here, Lucy intended to destroy property, not people. The Model Penal
    Code reaches the same conclusion on a causation analysis. See Chap-
    ter 3.

3a. Even under the common law, Napoleon has a better chance here, and
    he'll clearly be exculpated under the Model Penal Code. Although, as
    indicated above, many common law courts stopped the mens rea word
    after the verb, a separate doctrine of "mistake" developed. That doctrine
    was, essentially, that a reasonable mistake would exonerate. See Chap-
    ter 5. We would therefore have to inquire whether Napoleon's mistake
    was reasonable: Did the animal "look" like a rabbit, would one know

that there were likely to be rabbits around, how long did Napoleon have to decide whether to shoot, would a reasonable person have waited longer, and so on.

Under the Model Penal Code, the answer is easy. "Rabbit" is clearly an attendant circumstance material element. Thus, under a statute requiring "knowingly," the Code allows conviction *only* if the defendant "was aware" that the attendant circumstance existed. Since Nappy was not "aware" that the animal was a rabbit, he is not guilty. Reasonableness is not at this point a relevant consideration.

3b.   Again, we have to know what was going on in Nappy's mind. Regardless of the factual circumstances that might have alerted a "reasonable man" to the possibility that a hare would cross his path, was the defendant himself, with all his foibles, weaknesses, and incapacities, actually aware of a risk? If not, he was not reckless under either the common law or the MPC.

Caveat: The problems of proof go both ways here. If the prosecutor shows that the area was infested with rabbits, that there was only one deer, that deer are much larger than rabbits, that Nappy had plenty of time to see the animal, and so on, the jury might not credit Nappy's statements as to his ignorance. However, they cannot convict him on the basis of what a reasonably prudent person (RPP) would have figured out; they must be convinced that he really knew the risk.

3c.   Here, the problem is the same under the common law and the Code: Does "negligently" require tortious or criminal negligence? Most courts required "criminal" negligence, but in most instances those decisions involved homicides (of people, not rabbits). Moreover, since only "reasonable" mistakes of fact exculpated when there was no mens rea word (see below), many courts concluded that "tortious negligence" could suffice here. Under the Code the resolution of this question is clear: Nappy's acts must constitute a "gross" departure from the conduct of an RPP. Mere tortious negligence is insufficient. Of course, trying to distinguish between "tort" and "gross" negligence is not easy, but the prosecutor could try. In addition to the facts suggested in 3b, the prosecutor would try to prove, for example, that the papers were full of stories about the influx of rabbits, that rabbits are easy to spot because of their white tails, and so on.

3d.   Almost certainly not. Nappy clearly intended the death of what he shot, but he did not hope or believe that it was a child nor was he aware that it was. On the question of recklessness or negligence, we would have to explore the possibility that a child would be out, at night, in the middle of a forest without a parent. This risk seems so unlikely that its disregard is neither reckless nor negligent.

4. Barney seems like a nice enough chap, but he may well have violated this statute under the common law. The first question, of course, is whether Barney "purposely used" the credit card. This seems fairly straightforward: Barney used what he knew to be a credit card and therefore "purposely" used it. But is that sufficient for liability? Or must Barney's "intent" be to use an "expired" credit card? How far down the statute does the word "purposely" run? Many common law courts would conclude that "purposely" does not modify "expired" or even "credit card"; as long as Barney "intentionally used" something that was in fact a credit card, and that was in fact expired, that would have been enough. His mens rea as to what it was, or whether it was expired, would have been irrelevant. Moreover, if "purposely" modifies "expired," what does "purposely" mean? Would it require that Barney intended to cause the card to be expired? Or would it require that he know that it was expired? Or that he know that it "might be" expired? Common law courts wrestled with these statutory interpretation problems and came to different conclusions.

    Under the Model Penal Code, the answer is easy. The mens rea word modifies every material element of the statute. Obviously, it is material that the card be "expired." If it were *not* expired, there would be no harm (assuming, for example, it was not stolen). Under §2.02(1), "purposely" modifies every material element. Since "expired" is not a result (at least not of Barney's conduct), it must be an "attendant circumstance" material element. And, by §2.02(a)(ii), Barney must "be aware of the existence of such circumstances or . . . believe or hope that they exist." Unless Barney knows or hopes the card is "expired," he is home free.

    What result if the statute prohibited "feloniously" or "wantonly" or "maliciously" using an expired credit card?

5a. Surprise. Under the Model Penal Code, Jacob is not guilty of any of these crimes. Each of these mens rea words requires, with regard to the result element of death, that the defendant either "consciously desire death," "know that it is practically certain," or "consciously disregard a substantial . . . risk" that death will occur. None of these describes Jacob's mental state with regard to death. Jacob honestly believed that there was no risk to his son. Therefore, he did not "consciously disregard" any such risk.

    Under the common law, the question is closer because Jacob did "intend" that the snakes bite the boy. However, at least in homicide cases, the courts looked beyond the "statutory mens rea" and often inquired about the "traditional mens rea" issue of moral culpability. From his own viewpoint, certainly, Jacob is not "morally culpable." That may mean that he did not have the requisite mens rea. See the discussion of homicide in Chapter 8. See also *People v. Strong*, 37 N.Y.2d 568, 338 N.E.2d 602 (1975).

5b. More difficult at first blush. Clearly, Jacob "caused" his son's death. However, common law courts, certainly when faced with a severe punishment (possibly execution), would usually read into a statute like this some level of mens rea. Almost certainly they would have required at least recklessness. *Staples,* discussed in the text, adopted "knowingly" as the position in a nonhomicidal (federal) case. Even if recklessness were the requisite mens rea, Jacob is not guilty, since that mens rea requires subjective awareness of the risk. The result under the Code is the same. Section 2.02(3) establishes recklessness as the "default" position in such statutes. Since, as discussed above, Jacob did not consciously disregard the risk of death for his son, he was not reckless.

This is an unsettling result. Obviously, Jacob is a dangerous person, at least to his own children. Is there nothing the law can do? There is, in fact, much that the "law" can do. Jacob might be civilly committed for mental illness (assuming the jurisdiction has the properly drawn statutes, and Jacob fits within them). The state could also take away Jacob's other children. Very frequently the undoubted need of society often persuades courts or legislatures to "find" some crime of which Jacob could be convicted, rather than rely on processes of civil commitment, confinement, quarantine, reeducation, and so on. See, e.g., *State v. Williams*, 4 Wash. App. 908, 484 P.2d 167 (1971).

There is one crime of which Jacob is almost surely guilty (aside from child abuse). If "negligent" homicide were punished in the state, and negligence were measured by an objective, rather than a subjective, standard, Jacob would almost certainly fall within that statute.

6. Not necessarily. One's first inclination, of course, is to assume that Diana knows the bullets are real, and to infer from her words that we know what is going on in her mind. If, however, Diana and Charles are actors in a play (hence the 600 people), we might well conclude, in the absence of other information, that Diana (as she claims) didn't know the gun was loaded, and that she did, and said, what the script required. We can never be sure what another person is thinking. We can only infer from their actions and from other facts.

Suppose, for example, that we were to discover that, in addition to being thespians, Diana and Charles were long-standing competitors in art collecting, and that only moments before the play began, Diana had discovered that Charles had destroyed all of her Picassos. Or that Diana and Charles were brother and sister, and that Diana had just learned that their ailing mother had left everything to Charles, but if Charles died first, then the entire $100,000,000 estate would go to Diana. From these facts about motive we might begin to reevaluate our first inference (and our willingness to believe Diana) and draw others.

7. It depends. At the time of the injury, Cary is anything but reckless. However, if his brakes fail because he has consistently refused to have them adjusted, and they have been slowly deteriorating, then his prior fault (indeed, his getting into and driving the car that night, if he took cognizance of that risk) could render him liable. Remember that the principle of contemporaneity does not require that the mens rea coincide with the *harm*, but with the *act* that causes the harm. (Of course, if the evidence shows that even if the brakes had been in superb condition, the child would have been killed, then Cary's negligent act is not a cause in fact of the death.)

8. Helen is surely not guilty of any kind of homicide that requires a mens rea. Her care that there be no one present demonstrates that she did not even consider that there was a risk, much less consciously disregard such a risk, that injury, much less death, could result from the burglary. She took every precaution that injury would not happen. Moreover, given all the circumstances, it is hard to say that she was "negligent" or criminally negligent *with regard to the risk of death*. *Caveat.* In Chapter 8, we will discuss Helen's possible liability under the felony murder doctrine, which does not require mens rea of any kind as to a death occurring during a felony.

5

Mistake

Overview

We all make mistakes—even criminals. However, suppose someone who thinks that what he is doing is legal turns out to be mistaken, and the act is a crime. Is he guilty? The common law answered this question as it often does: "It depends." Consider a *factual* mistake. If Angelica thinks the white powder in her vial is salt though it is really cocaine, she is not guilty of transporting cocaine. However, consider a *legal* mistake. Arthur has been told by a lawyer that he may, without a permit, dump what he knows to be toluene. The advice turns out to be a misinterpretation of the environmental statutes. Such a mistake would never exculpate. This tension between legal and factual mistakes and the exceptions to these general rules create ulcers in law students—not to mention in clients.

Mistake and Ignorance of Law

Perhaps no rule of criminal law is better known than the doctrine *"ignorantia lexis non exusat"*— "ignorance of the law is no excuse." Thus, in the example in the Overview, even if Arthur has gone to five lawyers, four priests, three government officials in charge of pollution control, and read the statute books himself, he is still liable if the advice he has received has been erroneous. See *United States v. Traxler*, 847 F. Supp. 492 (S.D. Miss. 1994). He will be convicted and punished as though he were just as culpable as Dave, who dumped toluene in the river knowing it was illegal.

Supporters of the rule argue that people *should* know the law and not act until they do. They argue, further, that anyone could claim reliance on the advice of others, and that this would either be too hard to prove or generate collusion between defendants and others, who would claim to have given such advice. A more recent argument sustaining part of the doctrine is that persons who are, or should be, aware that their conduct might be regulated have a "duty to inquire" about the law and are morally blameworthy for failing to ascertain its reach.

Opponents of the doctrine contend that failure to know every statute and administrative regulation, and the interpretation of every statute and administrative regulation, does not reflect moral blameworthiness. (Indeed, if it did, every lawyer, indeed every judge on every court, should beware.) A person who is truly ignorant or mistaken about whether his conduct is unlawful, particularly one who has actively and fairly sought to determine the law, is neither morally culpable (in the "traditional" sense of mens rea) nor purposeful or reckless about breaking the law (in the "statutory" sense of that term).

The opponents are right—the rule is seriously flawed, both in its origins and its application. Its historical roots are extraordinarily weak; it was first supported by Blackstone (circa 1766), but his two supported cites turned out to be erroneous. Still, the rule has been repeated in numerous cases in the last two centuries. As one attempt to provide theoretical explanation for the rule was refuted, other reasons were given to continue its vitality.

The rule is sometimes rephrased as saying that everyone is conclusively presumed to know the law. When Blackstone wrote, such a view was at least plausible. A claim that one did not know that rape, murder, robbery, or mayhem was illegal (or immoral) would hardly be taken seriously. (Not even embezzlement was a crime until 1801, and many activities that we now consider criminal were either legal or merely tortious or violations of contract.) Yet the rule continues to be followed today, when criminal law applies to many new areas of activities and encompasses literally hundreds of thousands of administrative regulations as well.[1] If this explanation of the rule were tested against modern methods of assessing presumptions,[2] it would be clearly unconstitutional.

The argument that the claim of ignorance is too easily made and too

---

1. E.g., *United States v. Freeman,* 535 F.2d 1251 (4th Cir. 1976) (ignorance of any rule in the Federal Register is irrelevant). See also *United States v. Freed,* 401 U.S. 601 (1971); *United States* v. *International Minerals and Chemical Corp.,* 402 U.S. 558 (1971). In each of the last two there was no conviction at the point the United States Supreme Court heard the case; the holding in each case was that the prosecutor need not allege in the indictment knowledge of the law, which leaves open the possibility that the defendant could raise ignorance; who then would carry the burden of persuasion was not discussed. The language of each opinion, however, certainly leaves the impression that ignorance of the law is still irrelevant. *Cheek* and *Ratzlaf,* more recent cases discussed in the text below, may narrow the implications of these two decisions.

2. See Chapter 15.

difficult to refute was rejected by Justice Holmes, who pointed out that that concern was present for virtually all defensive claims. To the extent that it was easier to make than some of those other claims, the law could place on the defendant the burden of persuasion. O.W. Holmes, The Common Law (1881).

Holmes proffered another support for the rule, however—that we wish to encourage people to learn what the criminal law is. Moreover, as a true utilitarian, he argued that it is occasionally necessary to sacrifice the morally innocent person to achieve the better good of establishing an incentive for learning the law. However, the doctrine has been applied even where the defendant has actively sought legal advice from various sources, including court opinions, judges, prosecuting attorneys, and lawyers.

Similarly unsuccessful has been the argument that, even if ignorance of the *criminal* law should not excuse (in order to encourage persons to learn what the criminal law is), ignorance (or mistake) as to other laws, which are then incorporated into the criminal law, should excuse.[3] Suppose the criminal law prohibits blocking public roads, and Yehudi knows that he is blocking a road but he believes the road to be private. Unknown to him, the road has become "public" under condemnation just a few hours before. Yehudi should not be punished, the argument goes, because he has learned what the criminal law prohibits. His mistake is about condemnation law, not criminal law.

The rule has been subject to a number of "exceptions," many of which overlap. Thus, it is sometimes said that ignorance or mistake of law is relevant whenever it "negates" the statutory mens rea. Another exception to the rule is that mistake is relevant when the charge is one of specific intent. In fact, however, these "two" exceptions are often two ways of articulating the same exception.

Until very recently the rule has reigned virtually unchallenged. However, the Model Penal Code and several recent United States Supreme Court cases discussed below suggest that future decisions may be more open to changing the rule, at least in some contexts.

Ignorance of the Law

We can distinguish between a defendant who does not know that a particular act is even arguably criminal and a defendant who knows that there

---

3. Yet another argument supporting the doctrine emerged in the 1940s. Professor Jerome Hall argued that to allow a defendant to exculpate himself by simply claiming his interpretation of a law would negate the law and elevate that defendant to the status of lawmaker. J. Hall, General Principles of the Criminal Law (2d ed. 1961). This, too, was quickly rejected, by showing that the law did not change; however, as with all other successful defendants, these wrongdoers would not be punished because their wrongful acts were not morally blameworthy.

is a law generally applying to his area of activity, but believes that the law does not cover his particular act. The first is *ignorance* of the law; the second, *mistake*.

The few reported decisions of ignorance of the law usually involve aliens to a particular culture[4] and epitomize the injunction, "When in Rome (or at least a common law country) do as the Romans do." Thus, in *In the Matter of Etienne Barronet and Edmund Allain*, 118 Eng. Rep. 337 (1852), the defendants, Frenchmen who had taken political asylum in England, acted as seconds in a duel fought on English soil. Dueling was not merely legal in France; participation was a "matter of honor." The defendants were unaware that dueling was illegal in England. The court declared their ignorance of the law to be irrelevant.

A very recent decision by the Ninth Circuit suggests that this rigor is still in force. In *United States v. Moncini*, 882 F.2d 401 (9th Cir. 1989), the defendant, who lived in Italy and who was interested in pornographic pictures, was contacted by an undercover FBI agent in the United States and induced (but not entrapped) to send such pictures to the agent. When the defendant arrived in the United States for unrelated business, he was arrested and charged with "using the mails to send child pornography." He contended that since dissemination of such materials was not a crime in Italy, he should be excused in the United States as well. The court rejected his claim of ignorance of the law.[5]

A more recent opinion of the United States Supreme Court *may* suggest a slight movement away from this doctrine, at least in interpretation of federal statutes. In *Ratzlaf v. United States*, 510 U.S. 135 (1994), the defendant owed a gambling casino in Reno, Nevada, over $100,000. When he tried to pay off most of this debt in cash, he was informed that if he paid the entire amount in one lump sum, the casino would have to report this to the United States government under anti-money-laundering statutes. The casino did not tell Ratzlaf that another federal statute made it illegal to "willfully" structure a monetary transaction so as to avoid the reporting requirement. For reasons

---

4. *Star Trek* fans will recall that in both the original series and in *The Next Generation* the issue of ignorance is raised. In *Star Trek*, a crew member, while visiting a planet for recreation, picks a flower; this turns out to be a capital offense in that culture, and he is accordingly tried for that crime. In *Next Generation*, Wesley Crusher inadvertently enters an area that, under the law of the planet, is forbidden. He too is tried capitally. In both episodes, the Captain (Kirk or Gerard) persuades the rulers that the doctrine is too harsh. Fortunately for the crewmen, they never landed in a jurisdiction governed by the common law.

5. The court did note that even in Italy the kinds of photographs involved, while not illegal, were regulated, thereby putting the defendant on notice to inquire about the laws of other jurisdictions to which he might send such pictures. Although not critical to its holding, the court's position at least attempts to portray the defendant as reckless and hence morally blameworthy in this regard.

known only to Ratzlaf, he did not wish the government to know of his transactions. The casino thereupon offered to drive him in a limousine to a number of banks in the town, at each of which he could obtain a cashier's check for an amount under $10,000, in which case neither the casino nor the bank would have a duty to report the transaction. Ratzlaf agreed that he had willfully structured his transactions so as to avoid reporting, but argued that he did not know that this was prohibited. The trial judge instructed the jury that this ignorance was irrelevant, as long as Ratzlaf in fact "willfully structured" the transaction. The Supreme Court reversed, holding that his ignorance of the legal duty not to structure the transaction made his act "nonwillful" under the statute. It is at least possible, therefore, that courts may be rethinking the doctrine of ignorance.[6]

Mistake of Law

Far more common are cases where a defendant suspects that his activity may be subject to government, even criminal, regulation, but concludes, either on his own or as the result of advice that he has sought, that his actions are not criminal. In all of these cases the defendant has sought to discover what the law is, as Holmes hoped. Yet in virtually none is he exculpated. Thus, for example, a minister charged with erecting an illegal sign in his front yard was precluded from presenting evidence that he sought, and relied on, advice from a county attorney that the sign was acceptable. *State v. Hopkins*, 193 Md. 489 (1959). Similarly, a restauranteur who relied on the judgment of a municipal court (given in another proceeding) that the device he was installing was not a "gambling device" within the meaning of the criminal law was held liable for his mistake of law. *State v. Striggles*, 202 Iowa 1318 (1926). And a fisherman was precluded from introducing evidence that he had obtained advice from both an attorney and a commissioner of fishing licenses that his method of fishing for smelts was not illegal. *State v. Huff*, 89 Me. 521 (1897).

Similarly, reliance on a lawyer's advice was unacceptable under the

---

6. Two other ignorance cases should be mentioned here. In *Lambert v. California*, 355 U.S. 255 (1957), the Court held that constitutional due process was denied a defendant who was precluded from introducing evidence that she was unaware of a city ordinance requiring her, as an ex-felon, to register her presence with the city. Some commentators thought that the decision would lead to a series of constitutional challenges to the entire "ignorantia lex" rule, but it has been restricted to cases involving (a) ignorance of (b) a local ordinance (c) imposing a duty to act (in contrast to imposing a prohibition against acting). It has become, as Mr. Justice Frankfurter predicted in his dissent in the case, a "derelict upon the waters of the law." In *Bryan v. United States*, 524 U.S. 184 (1998), the Court, in dictum, referred to *Cheek* and *Ratzlaf* as involving "highly technical statutes." This suggests that the Court might narrowly construe their effect in the future.

common law. In *Staley v. State,* 89 Neb. 701 (1911), the defendant and his cousin, both of whom lived in Nebraska, wanted to marry but knew that their marriage was illegal under Nebraska law. They then were married in Iowa, which did not prohibit marriages between cousins. When they returned to Nebraska, the county prosecutor told the defendant that he would be prosecuted for fornication if he continued living with his cousin. The defendant then went to three attorneys, each of whom informed him that the Iowa marriage was indeed not valid in Nebraska. Consequently, the defendant left his cousin. A year later, he married another woman in Nebraska and was then prosecuted for bigamy. It turned out that the Iowa marriage *was* valid in Nebraska, and that he was therefore still married to his cousin when he "remarried." On the basis of "ignorantia lex," the defendant was precluded from presenting any evidence of the legal advice given him by the three lawyers or by the county prosecutor concerning the validity of his marriage to his cousin.

Thus, under common law, the defendant's mistake of law was usually held to be irrelevant to his guilt. A recent decision from the United States Supreme Court, however, casts doubt on this rule. In *United States v. Cheek,* 498 U.S. 112 (1991), the court held that even an *unreasonable* mistake of law could negate liability. Cheek, an airline pilot, was repeatedly told that his wages constituted "income" for purposes of the federal income tax laws. However, he was also told by anti-income tax zealots, and by lawyers who agreed with them, that this was *not* the proper interpretation of the tax laws. He was also told (notwithstanding numerous court decisions to the contrary) that the income tax law, as well as the amendment that allowed it, was itself unconstitutional. He claimed he honestly relied on this advice, but the trial court instructed the jurors that unless his reliance was reasonable, they could not consider it. In reversing Cheek's conviction for "willfully" failing to file tax returns and pay taxes, the Supreme Court concluded that the jury should have been instructed that *any* reliance, however unreasonable, on *any* advice would exculpate.[7]

Like *Ratzlaf, Cheek* might be restricted to cases involving statutes that contain the word "willfully." Or it might be restricted to tax cases or other areas of "complex" law. However, there is much in the Supreme Court opinion that would make such restrictions doubtful, and *Ratzlaf* certainly suggests that the Court does not so limit *Cheek.*[8]

---

7. The *Cheek* decision was muddled by the Court's conclusion that, while Congress intended ignorance of tax law to negate liability, it did not intend ignorance or mistake of *constitutional* law to do so. One could easily argue, of course, that constitutional law is even murkier than tax law.

8. On retrial, a jury that was instructed that any belief actually held by Cheek would negate his criminality nevertheless convicted him, apparently concluding that he did not actually believe the advice he received. See 3 F.3d 1057 (7th Cir. 1993).

Exceptions to the Rule
"Specific Intent" Crimes

Common law courts carved out minor exceptions to the harsh rule of "ignorantia lex." One was the rule that any mistake of law, no matter how unreasonable, would be a valid "defense" to a specific intent crime. Larceny is a "specific intent" crime (see Chapter 10). If Abraham believes, however unreasonably, that by law he is the owner of Esau's car and proceeds to take it "back," Abraham is not guilty of larceny because larceny requires that one intend to take the property of "another." Since Abraham thinks that he is the owner of the car, he has not "intentionally" taken property he knows to be another's.

It may well be that Abraham is not morally culpable, given his belief, and therefore should not be punished. However, as we have already seen, the distinction between a "specific intent" and a "general intent" crime is ephemeral at best. To make Abraham's criminal liability hang on the precise words of the statute or of the common law definition is highly debatable. Both *Ratzlaf* and *Cheek* involved statutes that expressly required that the defendant act "willfully." Under the common law, this level of mens rea requires "specific intent." While these cases *may* therefore be interpreted merely as reiterations of the doctrine that mistake of law may "negate" a specific intent, a close reading of either decision belies that impression, and the two taken together do not support such a view.

Non-Criminal Law Mistake

Commentators have suggested another possible "exception" to the "ignorantia lex" doctrine. If the defendant is mistaken (or ignorant) not as to the criminal law, but as to a part of the civil law that is incorporated in the criminal law, they contend that the doctrine should not apply. Here, the reason for the rule (enhancing knowledge of the criminal law) does not apply. Suppose that Abraham, in the car problem above, believes the law requires ten months to possess adversely a chattel, but the time period is really one year. His mistake then is not one of criminal law. He knows there is a law against *larceny*, but he believes that, as a result of *property law doctrine*, the car is his.

Staley is an even more attractive case for this exception. Staley knew that there was a criminal law against bigamy. He also knew that under Nebraska domestic relations law, cousins could not marry. His mistake, and that of the three attorneys he consulted and the county prosecutor who threatened him, was one of *federal constitutional law*. They all failed to understand that under the full faith and credit clause of the United States Constitution, Nebraska had to honor a marriage that is valid where it was performed.[9] While it may be desirable that citizens know the criminal law, and perhaps even the domestic relations law of the state, it seems unduly optimistic to think that we can encourage every citizen to become a constitutional law scholar.

The Model Penal Code

Retention of the "Ignorantia Lex" Doctrine

The Code retains the basic doctrine. Section 2.02(9) expressly provides that "neither knowledge nor recklessness or negligence as to whether conduct constitutes an offense or as to the existence, meaning or application of the law determining the elements of an offense is an element of such offense unless the definitions of the offense or the Code so provides." There is one exception to the "no ignorance" position of the Code. If the statute or regulation in question "has not been published or otherwise reasonably made available" to the defendant, the claim is allowed. See §2.04(3)(a).

The "Reasonable Reliance" Approach to Mistake

In General. On the other hand, the Code takes a significant, though cautious, step to protect defendants who "reasonably" rely on advice as to the legality of their proposed conduct. Section 2.04(3) provides that a defendant has a defense[10] to a charge if he can show that he has acted "in reasonable reliance" on:

> (b) an official statement of the law, afterwards determined to be invalid or erroneous, contained in (i) a statute or other enactment; (ii) a judicial decision, opinion or judgment; (iii) an administrative order or grant of permission; or (iv) an official interpretation of the public officer or body charged by the law with responsibility for the interpretation, administration or enforcement of the law defining the offense.

Notice that this provision helps persons in Striggles' position because it allows reliance on *any* judicial opinion. And it probably helps Hopkins, if the county attorney falls within the words of subsection (iv). But Staley's reliance

---

9. See, e.g., *Williams v. North Carolina*, 317 U.S. 287 (1942); *Davis v. Davis*, 305 U.S. 32 (1938); *Loughran v. Loughran*, 292 U.S. 216 (1934).

10. Reasonable reliance is indeed a "defense," which the defendant has to prove by a preponderance of the evidence. See §2.04(4). This stands in stark contrast to most of the rest of the Code, which puts on the prosecution the burden of disproving defensive claims, including all justifications and excuses, once properly raised. See §§1.12 and 1.13. This topic is discussed in more detail in Chapter 15.

on his lawyers is not relevant even under the Code, for reasons we will explore in a moment.

First, however, let us assess the general purpose of this provision. Surely in a maze of government bureaucracy, citizens have come to rely on all levels of government bureaucrats to help them stay within the law. The Code provides some amelioration of the common law rule in light of this reality, but *only* if the defendant relies on persons whose *official tasks* involve statutory interpretation or enforcement. This seems unduly narrow.

Consider Butch, who goes to his local zoning ordinance office to get advice about building an addition to his house. Jocelyn, an employee there, tells him, incorrectly, that he needs no permit for it. She's wrong, and he is prosecuted. If Butch *knew* that Jocelyn was not so authorized, his reliance on her advice might be unreasonable. However, few citizens would be likely even to raise the question of whether the person behind the desk who gives them the answer to their question fits the statutory definition: to consumers, persons working in a government office are probably fungible.[11] And even if they asked, could they be sure that they have gotten "the right one"? Furthermore, is *any* prosecutor sufficient under subsection (iv), or must the interpretation come from "the" county prosecutor? Laymen are unlikely to make such a distinction. Also, the reliance must be on "an *official* interpretation" by that office. What makes the interpretation "official"? The Code and Commentary are silent. Surely, however, any reliance by a citizen on the word of a governmental official who works in the relevant office or *appears* authorized should be sufficient to exonerate.

Reasonable Reliance and Lawyers. The Code confirms the rule, exemplified by *Staley*, that reliance on a lawyer's advice is not a defense. Supporters of this position argue collusion may occur between a lawyer and his client. However, this is a dubious explanation: some government employees, like some lawyers, may collude with clients. But the Code does not blanketly prohibit reliance on their advice.

A better explanation, perhaps, is not that lawyers are too ready to break the law, but that they are trained to assist the client to obtain what she wants. Lawyers, some argue, will be too tempted, unconsciously, to give the "desired" advice. And certainly law students know that there are at least two possible interpretations and arguments to every legal question. Thus, to be not snide but realistic, it may be that *no* reliance on the word of an attorney is "reasonable."

New Jersey, however, allows *any* reasonable reliance, including on the advice of an attorney, as a defense. N.J. Stat. §2C: 2-4d (1994). (Perhaps because New Jersey has more lawyers per capita than any other state in the country, it is impossible *there* to avoid advice from a lawyer.)

---

11. See Cremer, The Ironies of Law Reform: A History of Reliance on Officials as a Defense in American Criminal Law, 14 Cal. W.L. Rev. 48 (1978).

Does the Code really change everything? Does it change anything? The fear that the Code's reasonable reliance doctrine would exculpate too many defendants seems overdrawn. Mr. Ratzlaf would be worse off under the Code than under the United States Supreme Court decision. He relied on no "official interpretation," and his claim of ignorance of the law is not explicitly recognized in the statute (unless one interprets willfulness as a "specific intent" word). Moreover, it is quite possible that many of the defendants in the other cases summarized above would still be found liable under a "reasonable reliance" doctrine.

Mistake of Fact

Reasonableness and Specific Intent

In stark contrast to the doctrine of mistake of law, the common law acquits persons who, because of mistakes of *fact*, commit what turn out to be crimes. Thus, Little Red Riding Hood (remember her? if not, see Chapter 4) would have been held not guilty of "knowingly" destroying a book, because she had made a "mistake of fact" (i.e., she didn't know she was burning a *book*). Although most statutes were silent as to mistake, the common law courts created a whole doctrine of mistake, which held that some mistakes of fact "negated" mens rea.[12]

The reasons for not finding Red guilty seem obvious: a retributivist would not convict her because she is not morally blameworthy; and because people will not be deterred from doing what they believe to be innocent acts, there is no utilitarian need to punish either. The one possible exception to this last statement has created much uncertainty in the law of mistake of fact, and involves the question, already discussed, whether negligence is a proper basis for criminal liability.

Prior to the nineteenth century, if Red honestly believed that she was not burning a book, the "reasonableness" of her belief was irrelevant: Red

---

12. The metaphor that mistake of fact (or other relevant claim by the defendant) "negates" mens rea is misleading and can have significant practical importance. The mere wording of the concept suggests that the defendant "had" mens rea (i.e., that her mens *was* "rea") but that somehow the "mistake of fact" (or other claim) "threw the reus part out of her mens." Obviously, this is not true. If the jury believes that the defendant was mistaken, it will conclude that she never harbored a mens rea of any kind. More accurate, though still somewhat tricky, is the explanation that we assume *not* that the defendant *had* mens rea, but that the prosecutor's evidence raises an *inference of mens rea that is negated by the defendant's claim*. The inference of blameworthiness effectively "disappears" when the jury believes the defendant's claim that she was harboring a mistaken view of the world. But even then, the metaphor could lead, and has led, to the conclusion that a defendant can be required to carry the burden of proof on defensive claims because (after all) the mens rea has been shown to be present.

was exculpated.[13] Within the last 150 years, however, this view has changed dramatically.

The creation in the nineteenth century of the doctrine of specific intent (see Chapters 4 and 17) created an almost irresistible urge to use it in cases other than homicide. Just as this was occurring, the move toward using the "reasonable person" as a standard in both tort and crimes was beginning. Perhaps not surprisingly, the courts merged the two doctrines: unreasonable people, who made unreasonable mistakes, would not as a usual matter be acquitted; only reasonable mistakes would now acquit. However, if the defendant were charged with a "specific intent" crime, the legislature had effectively indicated that only the "really" bad (not merely the unreasonable) should be convicted. Thus, in these crimes an unreasonable mistake, if honestly held, became a relevant claim.

As in other areas of the law, the invocation of a term such as "reasonable" only begins the inquiry: What does it mean? As discussed in Chapter 4, when the crime is defined as "negligently" doing X, the criminal law required more than a showing that the defendant was "merely" (tortiously) negligent; he had to be "criminally" negligent. By analogy, if the criminal law wanted to punish only the "really negligent" defendant, then even an "unreasonable" mistake, unless truly outrageous and one that "everyone" (certainly not just the reasonable person) would have avoided, should exculpate. Unfortunately, however, the courts rarely addressed that question, choosing instead to leave the definition to the jury. If the jury, unguided, interprets "unreasonable" to mean "tortious" negligence, then the focus of the criminal law on the "criminally" negligently culpable has been lost.

As in some other areas of the law, the view here is "all or nothing." If the defendant makes a reasonable mistake, she is exculpated. However, if she makes an honest, but unreasonable, mistake, she is punished for the crime as though she had made no mistake at all. Thus, if Paul sells what he knows to be cocaine, he will be punished for doing so. If Hermione honestly though unreasonably believes the white powder she is possessing is salt, but it turns out to be cocaine, then (if her mistake must be reasonable) she is convicted of possessing cocaine and assumedly punished as much as Paul. Those who oppose the requirement that the mistake be reasonable argue that the unreasonably mistaken person is significantly less culpable than the knowing actor and, if convicted at all, should be punished less.

Knowledge and Willful Blindness

In the Red Riding Hood hypothetical, we assumed that Herman *knew* that he was burning a book. And in Red's case, we have concluded that if

---

13. See Singer, The Resurgence of Mens Rea II: Honest but Unreasonable Mistake of Fact in Self-Defense, 28 B.C.L. Rev. 459 (1987).

she did not "know" it was a book, we would exculpate. However, suppose the defendant strongly suspects a fact but purposely avoids actually "knowing"? For example, suppose that Red knew that her grandmother loved books, that her mother had just bought a book for the grandmother the day before, and that the package was "big enough" for a book. Red doesn't actually "know" that it's a book inside the package; it could be a box that "feels like" a book. Can Red claim a mistake of fact or lack of knowledge?

The common law's commonsense answer was no. Red has made herself "willfully blind" to the facts and should be treated as though she knew the facts. This fiction allows us to punish Red on the ground that anyone confronted with facts that should alert them to the "relevant" facts is as morally blameworthy as someone who actually knew. In essence, it establishes a duty to inquire when the facts are highly suspicious. Because this is a fiction, however, the idea of willful blindness, while generally accepted in every jurisdiction, has been severely criticized by many commentators as vague and unfair.[14]

Mistake of Legal Fact

A defendant's liability for a mistake (reasonable or unreasonable) thus depends on whether that mistake is characterized as one of fact or law. The doctrinal difficulties become even more complex when the defendant's mistake is one of "legal fact" — a word or phrase that is defined by law in a strange way. As a general matter, "we all know" what a man, or a table, or an umbrella is. But be careful. The law can, for various purposes, define a word to mean something other than its usual meaning. And there are many "facts" in our lexicon that depend, in whole or in part, on the implicit incorporation of a legal norm.

For example, "we all know" whether a person is a "female" or a "male." But do we? The definition of that term may depend on the context. Years ago, a male professional tennis player underwent a sex change operation. There was then a dispute as to whether she could play in women's tournaments. Was she a female? The Lawn Tennis Association said yes. However, that same person may not be a "female" for purposes of inheriting money ("I leave all my money to be divided among my female descendants"). Similarly, "we all know" whether a person is "married" or "single." However, that status is not a "natural" one. It depends solely on a legal norm—whether

---

14. *United States v. Jewell*, 532 F.2d 697 (9th Cir. 1976); J.L. Edwards, Mens Rea in Statutory Offenses (1955); Perkins, "Knowledge" as a Mens Rea Requirement, 29 Hastings L.Q. 953 (1978); Williams, The Theory of Excuses, 1982 Crim. L. Rev. 157-159.

the ceremony (or the divorce) followed specific legal requirements. Consider as well:

1. Whether a person is "Caucasian" or "Negro" was explicitly a matter of legal definition in this country during the Jim Crow days of the nineteenth century.
2. Whether the gun that Staples (see Chapter 4) owned was a "firearm" was purely a matter of legal definition; as the dissenters argued, no one would have even questioned whether the AR14 was a "firearm" in the usual meaning of that term.
3. Whether property is "stolen" or not usually depends on a legal definition.
4. Whether a liquid is "intoxicating" or a "hazardous waste" may depend not on our common experience with the particular liquid but on a legal (almost chemical) definition.

These examples could be multiplied endlessly, but the point here is how these issues affect the mistake doctrine. Suppose that I snub the tennis player and am prosecuted for snubbing a "female"? My liability may well depend on how the question is characterized rather than on my culpability as such. If it is viewed as a *legal* mistake, no amount of reasonableness on my part will exculpate. If it is viewed as a *factual* mistake, however, reasonableness may exculpate.

Model Penal Code

The Code's approach to mistake of fact is straightforward. Section 2.04(1) provides that "ignorance or mistake as to a matter of fact . . . is a defense if: (a) [it] negatives the purpose, knowledge, belief, recklessness or negligence required to establish a material element of the offense." A reference back to Chapter 4, and especially to the chart on page 69, will show that as to crimes committed purposely, knowingly, or recklessly, the defendant must *know* either that a fact (attendant circumstance) exists, or that there is a substantial probability that it exists. Definitionally, a defendant who honestly, no matter how unreasonably, believes that the fact does not exist (the white powder is not cocaine, but salt) does not know the contrary. Thus, at least for these three states of mind, any mistake "negatives" the requisite mental state. In cases of "negligence," however, a mistake as to fact that is a "gross deviation" from what a reasonable person would understand will suffice for liability. Remember, again, that the Code recognizes negligence only as a predicate for homicide.

The Code also retains willful blindness. See §2.02(7).

A Note on the Future of Mistake

The doctrines regarding mistake of both fact and law, however, seem to be changing. The Model Penal Code is one harbinger, but common law courts on their own have increasingly reverted to the nineteenth century view of the impact of mistake. In a highly controversial decision in 1976, the House of Lords held that any honest mistake, no matter how unreasonable and outrageous, by the defendant that the victim consented, would be a defense to a charge of rape. *Regina v. Morgan,* 2 All Eng. Rep. 347 (1975). *Morgan* was vigorously opposed by those who disagreed with its views of the crime of rape; those questions are discussed below in Chapter 9, but its more important legacy was to reinvigorate the view that only subjectively culpable defendants should be punished. Wells, Swatting the "Subjectivist Bug," 1982 Crim. L. Rev. 209.

Throughout this chapter and Chapter 4, we have referred to four recent United States Supreme Court cases[15] that seem to portend changes at least in the way in which the Court approaches issues of mistake in federal statutes. It is possible to state narrowly the holding of each of these four cases. *Ratzlaf* and *Cheek,* each dealing with legal mistake, involved a statute that proscribed a mens rea of "willfulness." This is a form of "specific intent" mental state, and the cases might be limited to such statutes.

Similarly, *X-Citement Video* trod near First Amendment issues; had the shipment been of contraband cigarettes rather than reading matter, it is possible that the Court would not have allowed the mens rea word to travel all the way down the statute, thus holding the defendant liable for his mistake. And although *Staples* could be read as endorsing a requirement of knowledge in all federal statutes, thus establishing mistake as a defensive claim in all such instances, it could also be read as a case where the government conceded that, if mens rea were required at all, the proper level would be knowledge.

But a fair reading of these cases, individually and collectively, suggests that this is too narrow a view.[16] In each of these four cases, and in the precedent upon which each relied, the Court exhibited a newfound concern with "innocently" mistaken behavior. In each case, the Court declared that a holding against the defendant would mean that potentially thousands of innocent persons could be made criminals. And in each, the Court rejected the argument that the defendant was "nefarious" in his acts or his motivations.

---

15. *Ratzlaf v. United States, Staples v. United States, Cheek v. United States,* and *X-Citement Video v. United States.*

16. Pilcher, Ignorance, Discretion and the Fairness of Notice: Confronting "Apparent Innocence" in the Criminal Law, 33 Am. Crim. L. Rev. 1 (1995); Michaels, Constitutional Innocence, 112 Harv. L. Rev. 829 (1999); Wiley, The New Federal Defense: Not Guilty by Reason of Blamelessness, 85 Va. L. Rev. 1021 (1999).

Just as important for the purposes of this chapter, the Court seemed to see no difference between *legal* and *factual* mistake; the "innocence" rationale was enunciated in each case. It is, of course, too early to be sure whether these cases are indications of future decisions or merely isolated instances. But if you like to gamble, bet that they will be followed again.

EXAMPLES

1a. Sylvester manufactures widgets. As a side effect of the manufacturing process, he creates "crud," a messy looking but otherwise apparently innocuous substance. For years, Sylvester has simply put the "crud" in a barrel with other trash and had it carted off to the local dump. Unknown to Sylvester, the Environmental Protection Agency, after years of internal debate, has just issued a regulation that lists "crud" as a substance that must be disposed of according to specific procedures. Weeks after publication of this new rule, Sylvester puts some of the "crud" into his garbage can and is prosecuted for "willfully disposing in an improper manner of a substance designated by the EPA. . . ."

1b. Same facts, except that the statute omits the word "willfully."

1c. Same facts as in 1a, except that Sylvester has kept apprised of the regulations, which require only that crud A (with a specific percentage (20 percent) of toluene) be disposed of as required; crud B is not covered. Sylvester is not sure, however, whether the substance he has is crud A or crud B. He calls in his chemist, who tells him that the material is not crud A. The chemist's conclusion, alternatively (1) is wrong because the material contains 24 percent toluene, but he believes that only material containing more than 30 percent toluene is crud A; (2) is wrong because his analysis shows that the material Sylvester has contains less than 20 percent toluene, and therefore is not crud A.

1d. Same as facts in 1a, except that, rather than ask his chemist, Sylvester takes a sample of the crud down to the local EPA and leaves it with Aloysius Angst, whose title is "Deputy Director," for assessment. A week later, Sly calls the EPA and asks Angst whether his crud is covered. Angst tells him it is not covered. Consider, alternatively, that (1) Angst's conclusion is based on a misunderstanding of the regulation; (2) Angst's conclusion is based on an erroneous assessment of the toluene content of the material.

2. Julio, a guard at a federal prison, is charged, in state court, for carrying a weapon in violation of a state law. He argues that the state statute allows "peace officers" to carry a weapon, and that he carried the weapon in reliance upon the wording of the statute. If Julio is not, as a matter of statutory interpretation, a "peace officer" within the meaning of the statute, is he guilty of the crime?

3. Jack, while driving, observes a police officer engaged in what Jack assesses as erratic and reckless chase of another car, which then crashes. Jack pulls up behind both cars, and indicates his concern at the speed of both cars. At that point, the police officer threatens Jack. Fearful of confronting the officer, Jack uses his car phone and contacts the nearest police station, asking whether he can leave the scene of this accident, and report to the police station. The receptionist says he may. If the receptionist is wrong, and Jack is prosecuted for leaving the scene of an accident, can Jack claim mistake of law?

4a. Joan is prosecuted for "knowingly killing a homing pigeon." She seeks to introduce evidence that she believed the bird was a bald eagle. She concedes that her mistake was unreasonable. Should the evidence be admitted?

4b. Same facts, but the charge is "killing a homing pigeon."

These examples demonstrate the link between common law doctrines of mistake and current definitions of mens rea. In addition, a statute such as the one in 2b would raise questions of strict liability, discussed in Chapter 6. You must keep the interrelationship of Chapters 4, 5, and 6 in mind whenever confronting a mens rea problem, be it of statutory interpretation or common law liability.

EXPLANATIONS

1a. Under the common law, Sylvester would be convicted. His ignorance of the regulation would be no defense. After *Cheek* and *Ratzlaf,* however, the result is not clear. If this were a federal regulation, then those cases dealing with a statute that also established "willfulness" as the mens rea would interpret that word as essentially requiring a "specific intent." This would seem to require that the government prove that Sylvester *knew* that he had a duty to dispose of crud in a particular way. Since those decisions are not based on the Constitution, however, they do not necessarily affect the interpretation of state statutes. Thus, the usual ignorantia lex rule might apply, and Sylvester would be convicted. The Model Penal Code would reach the same result as the states. Under §2.02(9), ignorance of the law is irrelevant, where the statute establishes knowledge, recklessness, or negligence as the mens rea. The implication, not expressed in the Code, is that ignorance might be relevant if the statutory mens rea were purpose. Because that is not the case here, Sylvester's ignorance, however reasonable, is irrelevant.

1b. If *Cheek* and *Ratzlaf* are limited to statutes involving the word "willfully," then it would appear that Sylvester is off to the hoosegow. However, if the cases apply to "complex" regulatory schemes, Sylvester still might be exculpated. Under the Model Penal Code, assuming that the statute does not establish a strict liability offense (see Chapter 6), the requisite mens rea under §2.02(3) is either recklessly, knowingly, or purposely (see Chapter 4). Since, by operation of §2.02(9), ignorance of the law is irrelevant unless purposely is the requisite mens rea (and perhaps not even then), Sylvester will have no defense of ignorance of law.

Note that the entire difference depends on the legislature's use of the word "willfully," and the assumption that the presence or absence of this mens rea word was intended to change dramatically the defendant's liability, even though his behavior is exactly the same.

1c. These variations raise the question of the relation of mistake of law and mistake of fact. In (1), Sylvester's "mistake" is one of law, derivative of the chemist's mistake of law. Since the mistake really involves a definitional error (what is the legal meaning of "crud"), it can be characterized as a mistake of legal fact. Under earlier common law views, this would not have been relevant; Sylvester's error would be seen as one of law, and it would be irrelevant. Under *Staples*, however, the mistake might be exculpatory. *Staples* requires that the government show that the defendant knew every "fact" that gave rise to his legal obligation. Since the definition of crud A is a "legal fact," one could argue that *Staples* gives Sylvester a plausible claim of mistake. If the statute requires "willfulness," then *Cheek* and *Ratzlaf* arguably affect the case as well and allow Sylvester's claim that he did not know of the duty to dispose. On the other hand, Sylvester's reliance on his own employee might be unreasonable per se, since employees are likely to tell the boss what he wants to hear.

In (2), Sylvester's claim comes closer to a mistake of fact. *He* knows that he must dispose properly of anything that contains more than 20 percent toluene and is told that this substance does not contain that percentage of toluene. Again, assuming no strict liability issue (see Chapter 6), he may have a mistake of fact (or a mistake of "legal fact") here; his action looks reasonable, and most people would (or could) rely on a chemist for this information.

1d. Things are getting complicated. Sylvester has now removed the objection (possible in 1c) that reliance on an employee *cannot* be reasonable. In either alternative of 1d, Sylvester appears to be relying on the conclusion of an outside, objective person. However (at least as far as the facts given are concerned), it is not clear that he *asks* Angst the basis of the conclusion that he is not covered by the regulation. Whether Sylvester's reliance on Angst's advice is therefore reasonable may be critical, unless the statute is interpreted to require "specific intent," in which case even an unreasonable mistake would exculpate. As with our earlier example, Sylvester's mistake in alternative (1) appears to be one of "law" and not of "fact." Again, under the common law, assuming no "specific intent" such as "willfulness," Sylvester's reliance on Angst, however reasonable, will be irrelevant. Under the Model Penal Code, however, "reasonable reliance" on an "official interpretation" of the statute by someone "charged by law with responsibility for the interpretation, administration or enforcement of the law" is allowed as a claim. Does Angst's telephonic approval constitute an "interpretation"? If so, is it "official"? Is *he* a proper person upon whom Sylvester can rely? The Code's commentary is not helpful on these points, and there is sparse case law interpreting these provisions.

As to alternative (2), our earlier analysis would seem to stand. The debate over this mistake of "legal fact" would be whether the "mistake of fact" or the "mistake of law" doctrine applied. If the former, then any reasonable mistake would exonerate, even in a statute not requiring specific intent. If the latter, then no mistake, no matter how reasonable, would exonerate *except* in a statute requiring specific intent. The relation can be shown as follows:

	Statute Requires Specific Intent	Statute Requires General Intent
Reasonable Mistake of Law	Exonerates	Guilty
Unreasonable Mistake of Law	Exonerates	Guilty
Reasonable Mistake of Fact	Exonerates	Exonerates
Unreasonable Mistake of Fact	Exonerates	Guilty

2. Held, in *People v. Marrero,* 69 N.Y.2d 382 (1987): Julio is guilty, both under the common law and under the state's version of the Model Penal Code. The opinion, which is scathingly criticized in Comment, 54 Brooklyn L. Rev. 229 (1988), rejected any weakening of the ignorantia lex rule because "Any broader view fosters lawlessness."

3. Under the common law, no reliance on the word of anyone, no matter how reasonable or honest, was allowed. Moreover, even under the Model Penal Code, the telephone receptionist is not a person "charged with interpreting or enforcing" the law, and therefore her word — even if affirmed by a higher level police officer — would be insufficient. See *State v. Castro,* 81 Haw. 147 (1996).

4a. Under common law, unless "knowingly" is interpreted as a specific intent requirement, Joan's evidence is irrelevant, since only reasonable mistakes "negate" "general intent" crimes. Under modern criminal law, "knowingly" is likely to be interpreted as a specific intent requirement. This is particularly true after *Staples* and *X-Citement Video.* Thus, her mistake, even though unreasonable, will exonerate. This result, of course, should be reached even without deeming the statute one requiring "specific intent." It seems clear that Joan, whatever her faults, is not the evil malefactor — purposeful killer of homing pigeons — that the legislature is after. Perhaps she should be required to wear glasses or take bird recognition courses, but sending her to prison is unlikely to achieve any goal, including deterrence.

Under the Model Penal Code, Joan must be "aware" that the bird was a pigeon (as required by the word "knowingly"). Since her actual belief contradicts that requirement, the evidence is admissible.

4b. Under the Code, "recklessness" is the default position when the statute contains no mens rea word (see Chapter 4). Since recklessness requires that Joan be aware of the risk that the bird could be a pigeon, the evidence should be admitted. Under the common law, the evidence appears inadmissible, since there is no statutory mens rea. But under the separate doctrine of mistake of fact, Joan's mistake would be relevant if unreasonable. Since she concedes it is not reasonable, Joan is heading for the big house. Under the tetralogy of United States Supreme Court cases discussed above, however, "knowingly" may be an implied term of the statute, in which case the answer follows that in 4a.

6

Strict Liability

Overview

Notwithstanding the law's general insistence on a mens rea, in a very few instances courts interpret statutes as allowing criminal liability to be imposed even though the defendant has not had *any* mens rea (even tortious negligence) with regard to one or more material elements of the offense. (See Chapter 4 for a discussion of "elements analysis.") That liability is said to be *strict*. A common example is a statute that makes it a crime to sell alcohol to a minor. Most courts would require that the government prove that the defendant knew he was selling liquor; a mistake of fact that the item sold was water would usually exonerate.[1] If there is strict liability in such a statute, it is with respect to the material element of the customer's age.

Suppose that Gregori, a bartender, makes it a practice to "card" every new customer. In walks Herbert. Gregori asks for identification as to age, and Herbert produces a driver's license and a union card, each of which shows him to be 24. Since such documents can be easily forged, reliance on them might not be deemed reasonable by a court or a jury. But *assume* that Herbert looks 24, and that Gregori has acted reasonably. Under a strict liability approach Gregori's reasonableness is irrelevant. If Herbert turns out to be under the proper age, Gregori is guilty. Now suppose that Gregori, having been stung (not to mention convicted) once, takes "supercare" the next time. When Isaiah comes in, Gregori asks for his driver's license, his

---

1. See Singer, The Resurgence of Mens Rea III: The Rise and Fall of Strict Liability, 30 B.C.L. Rev. 337 (1989). The mistake must be one of *fact*. If the mistake is one of legal fact (see Chapter 5), the situation is less clear. If the defendant knows he is selling cider but wrongly believes it is not "alcoholic," he may be held liable, since this may be seen as a mistake of law by some courts. Also, some courts, particularly with regard to liquor or drugs, have held that no mistake, however reasonable, as to these two items will exculpate.

university or union ID, his birth certificate, and a notarized letter from his parents, whose signature Gregori has obtained in advance, all attesting to Isaiah being over the legal drinking age. If Gregori serves him, and Isaiah is underage, TOO BAD. Gregori is still liable. Wait — it gets worse. Suppose that in the Isaiah example, the documents were not forged, and that EVERY-ONE (including Isaiah's parents) was wrong about his birth date. Even then, Gregori is liable. When the courts say *NO* mens rea — not even tort negli-gence — is required, they mean it.

One further distinction must be drawn. There are many other areas of the criminal law, felony murder (discussed in Chapter 8) and mistake of law (discussed in Chapter 5) among them, where the common law has, for decades if not centuries, imposed liability without regard to mens rea as to one or more elements of the crime. Yet they are not generally referred to as strict liability crimes. Perhaps they are better thought of as strict liability "doctrines."

This is a short overview of common law doctrine. However, §2.05 of the Model Penal Code precludes any penalty of imprisonment, even of one day, unless the prosecution proves at least some mens rea with regard to every element of the offense. That is, it essentially rejects strict criminal liability.

The Reach of Strict Criminal Liability

Strict criminal liability was only established during the second half of the nineteenth century. Early cases in which some courts upheld strict criminal liability usually involved either sexual acts (e.g., adultery, bigamy, and statu-tory rape) or the protection of minors (serving or selling alcohol; allowing minors to be present during gambling, billiards, or other such act). Thus, a defendant who remarried, believing that he was divorced or that his earlier wife was dead, was guilty of bigamy if his belief, no matter how reasonable, turned out to be erroneous. Similarly, if a defendant had intercourse with a female whom he reasonably believed to be over a stated statutory age, he was guilty of rape if his partner turned out to be younger than the statute allowed.[2] Similar results occurred in cases involving the possession of or the serving of liquor.

The courts here relied on two main premises: (1) legislatures were unrestrained in their ability to proscribe conduct and did not have to require

---

2. This is so-called "statutory rape." Note that the defendant must still have mens rea as to the conduct element (intercourse) and the result as well as to the gender element. His liability is strict only with regard to the age element. See *People v. Hernandez,* 61 Cal. 2d 529 (1964). Seventeen states now allow a reasonable mistake as to age to avoid liability. See *Garnett v. State,* 632 A.2d 792 (Md. 1993); Annot., 8 A.L.R.3d 1100.

mens rea (a jurisprudential philosophy known as legal positivism); (2) there was a compelling need to protect society against such injury, and it was too hard to prove mens rea.

During the first half of this century, some courts applied these decisions to newly enacted "welfare" statutes, such as those prohibiting (1) the sale of oleomargarine; (2) the possession or sale of alcohol generally (during Prohibition); and (3) the sale of adulterated food. In the last half of this century, prosecutors have argued (not surprisingly, since their burden is eased) that statutes not specifying a mens rea should be construed as establishing strict criminal liability in numerous new settings. Courts have usually resisted these attempts and have increasingly emphasized the need for mens rea in virtually all criminal prosecutions.

Decisions in the United States Supreme Court have been equivocal. In *United States v. Dotterweich*, 320 U.S. 277 (1943), the Court used language that clearly endorsed the principle of strict liability in the shipping or sale of adulterated food contrary to the Food and Drug Administration Act. In this case, the "adulteration" involved an innocent misrepresentation of the contents of the item. There was no actual threat to the safety or health of anyone who consumed the item. The actual holding of the case, however, was very narrow. The defendant argued that the statute was aimed solely at corporate liability and not at individuals. The Court held that the word "person" did include individuals, and that a human being could be a "person" within the meaning of the statute.

Much more recent, and even more ambiguous, is *United States v. Park*, 421 U.S. 658 (1975). Park was the president of a national food chain, one of whose warehouses in Baltimore inadequately protected against rodent infestation, causing some of the food in the warehouse to become "adulterated." Park did not know of the actual contamination before he was notified of it by the Food and Drug Administration; he then ordered his subordinates to clean up the warehouse. When this was not done, the FDA prosecuted him for possessing adulterated food for sale. The trial judge instructed the jurors that they could convict Park if they found that he was in a position of power to avoid the adulteration even if he was unaware of its existence.

The Court upheld the conviction, finding that the jury instruction was not critically misleading. Both the holding and much of the language in the opinion seem to support strict criminal liability. However, the facts demonstrated that the persons to whom Park delegated the cleanup of the Baltimore warehouse had previously allowed a warehouse in Philadelphia to become similarly contaminated. As the Supreme Court put it, "[Defendant] was on notice that he could not rely on his system of delegation to subordinates to prevent or correct insanitary conditions of [the] warehouses, and . . . he must have been aware of the deficiencies of this system before the Baltimore violations were discovered." 421 U.S. at 678. This language suggests that Park was either willfully blind, reckless, or negligent. It emphasizes that

Park's moral culpability lay not in his ignorance of the facts in the Baltimore warehouse, but in his *knowing* reliance on people who he knew had previously been unable to keep his warehouses clean.

Legislative Intent, Positivism, and Democracy

The issue of strict liability is almost always one initially of statutory interpretation: The legislature has not included a mens rea word. Of course, it is possible that the legislature's omission is inadvertent, in which case the court will quickly read in a mens rea (see *Staples,* in Chapter 4, as an example). But suppose the court concludes that the legislature really intended to allow conviction without mens rea of any kind, with regard to one or more elements of the offense. Should the court follow the legislature's wishes? On the one hand, mens rea is the defining point of the criminal law. On the other, in a democracy legislatures are dominant because they are the most frequently elected bodies and hence assumedly the most representative of the feelings of the people. Courts, whether their members are elected or appointed and whether for a short period or for life, are the least democratic of the branches of government. If all laws, including criminal laws, are to reflect the will of the people, then courts should be reluctant to overturn what they perceive as legislative prerogatives.[3]

This preference for judicial acquiescence in the decisions of democratically elected institutions, often equated with what is called "legal positivism," was especially significant in the nineteenth and early twentieth centuries. Courts at that time would read statutes that had no mens rea word "plainly" and assume that the legislature wished to impose strict criminal liability.

This legal postivistic position was undermined substantially by several decisions in the United States Supreme Court, including the very influential opinion in *Morissette v. United States,* 342 U.S. 246 (1952). In that case, Justice Jackson declared that where a statute criminalized behavior that "looked like" a felony under the common law, the statute would be interpreted as requiring the mens rea that the felony had required. As a rule of statutory construction, this is helpful. However, the opinion in *Morissette* went beyond merely establishing such a rule and created a general presumption against strict liability that all statutes should be read to require mens rea.

---

3. This is a very simplistic statement of the enormously complex question of the scope of judicial review in a democracy, which we cannot treat here. See, e.g., A. Bickel, The Least Dangerous Branch: The Supreme Court at the Bar of Politics (1962); J. Ely, Democracy and Distrust: A Theory of Judicial Review (1980).

Definitions and Indicia of Strict Liability

Faced with the impasse of conflicting maxims of legislative interpretation, how does a court (or, more to the point, a student) tell whether a statute should be construed as one involving strict liability? The courts have established several guideposts, but they are hard to read and often point in different directions. Good luck!

Public Welfare Offenses

In his classic article discussing strict liability decisions, Professor Sayre used the term "public welfare offenses" to describe these kinds of crimes. Sayre, Public Welfare Offenses, 33 Colum. L. Rev. 55 (1933). At first blush, the phrase seems fairly understandable: It appears to refer to instances where the "public" rather than a single individual is endangered. Justice Frankfurter added significantly to this view in his opinion in *United States v. Dotterweich*, 320 U.S. 377 (1943), in which he suggested that something like strict liability was permissible in instances where the public could not protect itself. Thus, he declared:

> Congress has preferred to place [any hardship] upon those who have at least the opportunity of informing themselves of the existence of conditions imposed for the protection of consumers before sharing in illicit commerce, rather than throw the hazard on the innocent public, *who are totally helpless* [320 U.S. at 285 (emphasis added)].

The facts in *Dotterweich*, which involved the sale of mislabeled drugs, would seem to involve such helplessness. However, the earlier cases, which concerned the possession of contraband, sexual activity, and protection of minors, do not seem easily to fit this definition.

There are other problems with this test for strict liability. It is certainly true that individuals are usually unable to protect themselves against the dangers lurking in a can of soup. But are they any more able to protect themselves against death from a gunshot as they walk down the street? If inability of the victim to protect herself is the criterion, we should equally punish even a non-negligent shooter, although he had no mens rea at all. And even if a consumer is unable to check the fish he buys to determine if it is undersize, some would argue that this is no reason to punish on a strict liability basis the truck driver who transported the fish. See *State v. Williams*, 94 Ohio App. 249 (1952).

Moreover, one philosophical explanation of all crimes, including homicide, rape, theft, and burglary, as well as food adulteration and serving alcohol to minors, is that the real victim is the "state" (the public) and not the actual individual who is injured. The "public welfare" explanation of strict liability may differentiate among offenses depending on how many persons are endangered. However, this seems unhelpful as well. A terrorist destroying the World Trade Center endangers at least as many lives as a company executive who fails to protect against salmonella in his packaged food. Yet the terrorist is seen as perpetrating a "real" crime that requires proof of mens rea, while the manufacturer of the food product is not. The number of victims, actual or potential, seems not to be a useful criterion here.

Finally, the kinds of cases in which the courts have employed the "public welfare offense" language do not always fit even the "public endangerment" thesis expounded by Justice Frankfurter. Thus, some courts have imposed strict liability for persons who kill migratory birds or endangered species. While these are important interests to protect, it is hard to see how the public is "endangered" or even "affected" by these crimes in a way distinct from the way in which it is affected by other, non-strict-liability, crimes. Indeed, there is a very plausible argument that one of the major harms created by "real" crimes is public insecurity. The mugger injures not only his actual victim, but all those who, fearful of being mugged, remain in their homes, "prisoners" of the mugger. Von Hirsch & Jarburg, Gauging Criminal Harm: A Living Standard Analysis, 11 Oxford J. Legal Stud. 2 (1991). The argument that the public is more endangered in "public welfare offenses" than in non-strict-liability offenses is, at best, tenuous.

Mala in Se ("Real") vs. Mala Prohibita ("Unreal"?) Crimes

When lawyers don't understand what they're doing, they often try to make it seem more defensible by clothing it in Latin. (Does "res ipsa loquitur" ring a bell?) Courts appear to have taken the same approach in this arena. In seeking to determine which crimes can be made strict liability and those that cannot, courts have invented the terms (respectively) of *malum prohibitum* and *malum in se*. The reference is to crimes that are "merely" prohibited by statute and those that are both prohibited by statute and that are "in their nature" bad. Initially, this distinction seems confusing. As we discussed in Chapter 1, the principle of legality requires that *all* crimes now be statutory: Actions are criminal only because the legislature has prohibited them by statute. How can we formally distinguish between two statutes, one that punishes burglary and one that punishes a parking violation? On the other hand, the distinction seems to reflect common sense. Parking in violation of a statute or ordinance (malum prohibitum) doesn't "really" seem bad; burglary (malum in se) does.

Some courts have expanded on these Latin phrases by explaining that if the offense was punishable under common law, it is a "real crime" (malum in se), while if the offense is a "new" crime, it is not a "real" crime (malum prohibitum). If the latter, the defendant can be convicted without proof of a mens rea with regard to every element of the offense.

Again, there is a surface plausibility to this distinction. Those acts that all societies regard as heinous—rape, homicide, theft—must require a mens rea, or they are not "really" crimes at all ("killing" is different than "homicide"). The grain of truth here, however, undermines the central point. If something isn't "really" a crime, then why use criminal sanctions to indicate displeasure? Such an approach does little to help us determine whether some "new" crimes, which seem as serious or as evil as the "old" ones, should be strict liability offenses. For example, burying toxic wastes or discharging particulates into the air was not, as a general matter, a common law offense. However, today these acts seem highly obnoxious and at least as life-threatening as burglary. Morals and perceptions of dangers change over time. There is a possibility that the "malum in se" notion freezes the criminal law, or at least that part of it requiring mens rea, in the amber of the nineteenth century (or earlier).

Finally, many would argue that to say that malum prohibitum acts are wrong simply because they are prohibited is virtually meaningless. Most statutory rules[4] seek to prevent some real harm from occurring. Parking by a fire hydrant would normally not be "wrong," except that it endangers lives by blocking firefighters' access to water. Carrying or selling cocaine is not "wrong," except that the legislature has made a judgment that cocaine involves a public danger. Indeed, had the legislature not made that judgment, the statute would potentially run afoul of the principle of legality discussed in Chapter 1. Thus, *all* statutory rules appear to prevent some "real" harm and are not merely the whim of a legislature.

"Regulatory" or "Police" Offense

Much the same points can be raised with regard to "regulatory offense" or "police offense," terms often used by courts seeking to explain the imposition of strict liability. The notion here was that these rules were not "real" crimes, but only "regulations" to be enforced by "regulatory" agencies. Perhaps when the only sanctions were fines, this distinction was meaningful. Today, however, in a governmental system suffused with many regulatory agencies, the phrase seems less limiting. Moreover, many regulatory offenses carry very severe penalties, which was not the case with traffic or regulatory violations in earlier decades.

---

4. Some statutory rules do not have any moral basis. Thus, for example, it is imperative that we all drive on the same side of the road. Whether that is the right- or left-hand side is morally neutral, as long as we all follow the same rule once established.

The Litmus Test of Available Punishments

Professor Sayre, after reviewing the above attempts to distinguish strict liability offenses from others, concluded that there was only one rational distinction:

> The real distinction depends on the nature of the penalty involved and the character of the offense. If the penalty is a serious one, particularly if it involves imprisonment . . . [strict liability is improper]. But if the maximum penalty consists in no more than a light fine, and if the character of the offense is such that infraction involves wide-spread public injury [strict liability may be proper].[5]

Sayre's suggestion has been adopted by at least one state[6] and by the Model Penal Code. However, other courts have upheld strict criminal liability where the penalty is very significant, sometimes up to ten years' imprisonment. See, e.g., *United States v. Freed*, 401 U.S. 601 (1971) (dictum). In *Staples v. United States*, 511 U.S. 600 (1994), the United States Supreme Court explicitly rejected the intensity or duration of punishment as "the" litmus test of strict criminal liability, choosing instead to consider it as but one (albeit a very important one) of a list of factors in making such a determination.[7]

Innocent Actors

In the *Staples* case, the Court reinvigorated another criterion to the strict criminal liability analysis by declaring that strict criminal liability would be inappropriate if it criminalized ostensibly innocuous conduct.[8] The Court

---

5. The Present Significance of *Mens Rea* in Criminal Law, Harvard Legal Essays 399, 408 (1934).

6. *Commonwealth v. Koczwara*, 397 Pa. 575 (1959).

7. "(W)here, as here, dispensing with *mens rea* would require the defendant to have knowledge only of traditionally lawful conduct, a severe penalty is a further factor tending to suggest that Congress did not intend to eliminate a *mens rea* requirement. In such a case, the usual presumption that a defendant must know the facts that make his conduct illegal should apply." 511 U.S. at 624.

8. "The government protests that guns, unlike food stamps, but like grenades and narcotics, are potentially harmful devices. Under this view, it seems that *Liparota*'s concern for criminalizing ostensibly innocuous conduct is inapplicable whenever an item is sufficiently dangerous, that is, dangerousness alone should alert an individual to probable regulation and justify treating a statute that regulates the dangerous device as dispensing with *mens rea*. But that an item is "dangerous," in some general sense, does not necessarily suggest, as the Government seems to assume, that it is not also entirely innocent. Even dangerous items can, in some cases, be so commonplace and generally available that we would not consider them to alert individuals to the likelihood of strict regulation." *Staples*, 511 U.S. at 619-620.

pointed to two cases to demonstrate the difference. In *United States v. Liparota*, 471 U.S. 429 (1985), the Court had decided against strict liability in a case involving a restaurant owner who had accepted food stamps in a way that, unknown to him, violated federal law. On the other hand, the Court had upheld an indictment against a possessor of hand grenades, even though the indictment did not allege that he knew the grenades were unregistered, because "innocent" persons do not possess hand grenades. *United States v. Freed*, 401 U.S. 601 (1971).

Again, this criterion initially seems relatively easy to apply. Most people do not possess what they know to be hand grenades unless they have nefarious schemes; many people deal in food stamps without intending to commit a crime. To impose strict liability with regard to food stamps might expose tens of thousands of morally innocent persons to criminal liability and punishment.

The distinction, however, seems less obvious when applied to other strict liability items. Thousands of persons transport, deliver, trade, or sell canned food every day, yet *Dotterweich* seems to impose strict liability on all of them if the food in the can is adulterated. Similarly, thousands of persons hunt every day, yet many cases would seem to allow the imposition of strict liability on hunters who accidentally, and even non-negligently, kill a migratory bird or endangered animal.

One possible trouble with the test, therefore, is that it may be too fact-specific and dependent on the description of the factual setting: How many persons who hunt in this way, with this kind of weapon, in this area, under these circumstances, etc. (ad nauseam) are "innocent"? Many persons — manufacturers, truckers, wholesalers, retailers — handle soup cans (where botulism is a strong possibility). Are they all "innocent" within the meaning of *Staples*?

The facts of *Staples* itself show the difficulty. Staples was prosecuted for "possessing" a "machine gun" that had not been properly registered with the federal government. Federal regulations defined a "machine gun" as any weapon capable of firing more than once without recocking. Staples' rifle fit this description because it had been altered (by whom was never shown) to allow such firing. Staples claimed that he did not *know* the gun was capable of this firing. The majority in the Supreme Court held that this knowledge was essential because there were many innocent persons who owned "fire-arms" who would be subject to strict liability if it were applied in this case. The dissent argued, however, that the defendant owned not merely a "gun" but a "machine gun," and that no one possessing a rifle that had been altered to allow multiple firings could be deemed "innocent."

The *Staples* Court's solicitude of innocent parties is, of course, salutary. But it presupposes a test of innocence that is precisely the point at question. Eventually, the *Staples* opinion may prove less helpful than the Court had hoped it would be.

Strict vs. Vicarious Liability

Strict liability must be distinguished from vicarious liability. In a case involving only vicarious liability, *someone* (usually the person who actually met the conduct element of the offense) has entertained the requisite mens rea; the issue is whether the defendant should be held responsible for that person's acts and mental states. Differently stated, the issue is whether the actus reus element of the crime should be *imputed* from the actual actor to the *putative* actor, our defendant. The answer is easy if the defendant has *told*, or encouraged, the actor to act as he did; we call this accomplice liability, and it is discussed in Chapter 14. Thus, if *A* tells *B* to shoot *C*, *A* is responsible for *B*'s shooting of *C*, even if *A* never held the gun and even if *A* was not present at the shooting. Suppose, however, that the defendant's connection is less direct than that. The classic case involves a bartender who *knowingly* serves a minor: Should the owner be held liable, even though the owner was not present and perhaps even admonished the bartender against such sales? However one resolves that question, there is mens rea present; the bartender knew the minority of the customer. Though it is true that the employer is morally innocent, and that as to him the liability is in some sense strict, at least there is someone present who has acted in a morally blameworthy fashion.

At least two state courts have held that vicarious liability violates the due process clause of their *state* constitutions. *Davis v. City of Peachtree City*, 251 Ga. 219, 304 S.E.2d 701 (1983); *State v. Guminga*, 395 N.W.2d 344 (Minn. 1986). In each case it was unclear whether the bartender knew the age of the minor, but each court's opinion seems to bar conviction unless the owner personally knew the purchaser's age.

One must distinguish the more difficult case, the one that raises all the policy issues in this area. It involves the bartender who does everything humanly possible to ensure that the customer is over the drinking age (recall the Gregori/Isaiah hypothetical at the outset of this chapter). If his customer now turns out to be one day under that age, should the bartender be held liable? If he is, *strict liability* holds. If the *owner* is held on the basis of the bartender's acts, *strict vicarious liability* operates. Before concluding that a case imposes strict liability, be sure that it is not "only" one of vicarious liability.

Policy Analysis: Arguments For and Against Strict Liability

Proponents of strict liability contend that strict liability is acceptable where (1) the need for deterrence is great and the ability to prove mens rea is difficult (e.g., food adulteration); (2) the penalty is small and the number of cases large (e.g., parking violations); (3) there is no stigma attached to the conviction.

Each of these arguments, taken separately, seems unable to carry the day. Strict liability obviously clashes dramatically with the view that mens rea is a bedrock of criminal liability. If one believes that persons who are not at least criminally negligent are "morally innocent," then strict liability means punishing the morally innocent. Moreover mens rea is always difficult to prove. Although it is difficult for the prosecution to prove that the defendant knew that the milk was less than 2 percent cream, it is equally difficult to prove that the defendant "purposed" death in a homicide case. Indeed, to the extent that we are seeking to control serious crime, the "difficulty of proof" argument would seem to support abolishing the requirement of mens rea entirely.

Nor is court backlog a persuasive reason. Having too many cases is always a problem, and there are far too many "real" crimes today. Moreover, as we have seen, the Supreme Court has recently opined that the larger the number of potential defendants, the *less strong* the argument for strict liability becomes because of the danger of ensnaring truly innocent parties.

Finally, opponents argue that stigma may well be in the eye of the beholder. As summarized by one panel of dissenting judges in a recent case:

> We undermine the foundation of criminal law when we . . . vitiate the requirement of a criminal state of knowledge and intention as to make felons of the morally innocent.[9]

Some supporters of strict liability argue further that strict liability is necessary to prevent truly malevolent actors from fooling juries or escaping conviction because of proof problems.[10] This concern, however, would exclude all instances that would allow exoneration of a defendant.

Finally, proponents of strict liability argue that many such crimes involve regulated activities into which defendants voluntarily enter (e.g., banking, food manufacturing, waste management), and therefore it is not unfair to require them to take the risk of strict liability since the defendants knew of this risk when they undertook the activity. Furthermore, the argument goes, the government regulates this activity because it is potentially harmful to society, and the risks to the public at large outweigh the risk that a truly innocent defendant will be criminalized.[11]

---

9. *United States v. Weitzenhoff*, 35 F.3d 1275, 1299 (9th Cir. 1993).

10. E.g., Alexander, Reconsidering the Relationship Among Voluntary Acts, Strict Liability and Negligence in Crime, Culpability and Remedy 84, 88 (E. Paul, F. Miller & J. Paul eds., 1990).

11. The argument somewhat begs the question of whether there should be strict liability by assuming that the acquiescence of the defendant answers the question.

The sum of the arguments for strict criminal liability in a very few cases cannot be easily dismissed. If strict liability were indeed limited, opposition to the concept might dissipate. For example, Professor Perkins has called for the adoption of a "civil offense." Perkins, The Civil Offense, 100 U. Pa. L. Rev. 8323 (1952). Even the Model Penal Code accepts strict criminal liability where loss of freedom is not a possible sanction.

Despite those contentions, strict liability seems inherently unfair, even to many who enforce such provisions. Empirical studies show rather conclusively that agencies do not enforce these regulations on a strict liability basis, but give the defendants frequent and constant notice of known or suspected violations before bringing criminal charges. Richardson, Strict Liability for Regulatory Crime: The Empirical Record, 1987 Crim. L. Rev. 295.

In addition to this empirical evidence, juries themselves may well nullify strict liability when confronted with actual defendants. Thus, some may argue that the debate over strict criminal liability is a tempest in a very small teapot indeed, but this may not be so. First, juries *do* listen to instructions and follow them (see *Park*, supra, and the frequent state court opinions involving strict liability). Second, there is surely something unsettling about a system that must rely on jury nullification or executive discretion in order to achieve justice. Third, reliance on jury nullification could indicate a willingness to accept *any* rule, however undesirable, on the grounds that it will not be followed. Finally, to the extent that strict liability (or any other legal doctrine) fails to comport with the community's moral norms, it may bring the entire system into disrepute.

Alternatives to Strict Liability

The strongest argument against strict liability is that it authorizes the criminalization of the morally innocent. Opponents also point out that no other country embraces strict liability, either rejecting it entirely or adopting one of several options. If compromise were necessary, they posit, the following alternatives could be explored. For example, one could

1.   adopt the Model Penal Code approach, discussed infra, which restricts such liability only to fines and precludes loss of freedom as a sanction. If deterrence seems necessary, the legislature could add a crime of "recklessness" and severely increase the penalty.
2.   require the state to prove negligence.
3.   permit the state to prove its prima facie case on the basis of strict liability,

---

Suppose the government were to notify every car owner that, by virtue of using the public roads, he "consented" to a search at random of his car or his house. Would that consent be valid?

but then allow the defendant to avoid conviction by proving that he was not negligent (usually in a tortious sense). Canada and many other Commonwealth countries have taken this path. *Regina v. City of Sault Ste. Marie,* 85 D.C.R.3d 161 (1978).

"Greater Crime" Theory

Some instances of the imposition of strict liability are more readily understood. If *A* does not know he possesses cocaine at all, throwing him in prison seems unfair. Suppose, however, that *B* knows that he possesses cocaine (or even that he possesses a controlled dangerous substance) but is unaware of the quantity involved. If the statute provides for stiffer penalties depending on the amount of cocaine possessed, it does not seem intuitively unfair to impose on *B* the larger penalty. *B*, after all, is not an innocent party to begin with; he is engaging in a crime and he knows it. Similarly, if *C* purposely punches *D* in the nose, *C* knows he is committing a criminal assault. If it turns out that *D* is a police officer, and a statute penalizes assaults on police officers more severely, it is arguably acceptable to impose on *C* the higher penalty.

This general approach has been termed the "greater crime" theory (though sometimes called, in the bizarre way that law professors have of making the obvious more difficult, the "lesser crime" theory). In such instances the defendant knows (or is acting recklessly with regard to the risk that) he is committing a crime, and is held for the greater offense, even though he did not know (or was not reckless with regard to) the elements that made the crime "greater." In many instances there is no serious injustice done to *D*. For example, *D* may say to *V*, "Give me what's in the box," expecting to find only several hundred dollars. *D* may not suspect that *V* is in fact carrying the Hope Diamond; however, if the state punishes thefts netting more than $1,000,000 more severely, *D* is arguably not unjustly hurt. After all, he was at least reckless to the possibility that *V*, randomly chosen, had more than $1,000,000 on him. [Note, however, that this is not a good analogy to the "thin-skulled plaintiff" rule in torts, since our object there is to compensate the plaintiff. Here, the question is how severely we will punish *D*, even if *V* gets the Hope Diamond back.]

However, there are serious problems with the "greater crime" approach. First, suppose that *D* is not reckless or even criminally negligent with regard to a specific element. For example, suppose that *D* purposely punches *V* in the nose, but that *V* is a hemophiliac and dies. If *D* is charged for the death (see Chapter 8), *D* is actually being held "strictly liable" for the element of death. Or suppose that *D*, having been given a vial of cocaine, learns upon arrest that there is crack at the bottom of the vial, for which the penalty is much higher. If *D* is held to "knowingly possess" crack, even though he has attempted to learn the true facts, he may be punished too severely for his mens rea.

This latter point demonstrates (a la Professor Sayre) the need to assess the element of *penalty* involved in the crime for which we seek to punish *D*. A good example may be found in current statutes prohibiting the sale of drugs in or near school property. A defendant who knowingly sells cocaine anywhere, for example, may be sentenced to a specific sentence (let us say five years). But if he commits that same act near a school property,[12] without knowing that fact, and without being negligent as to that fact, in many states and under the federal statute his sentence may be substantially increased, sometimes doubled. 21 U.S.C. §860. The case law thus far seems to treat "school property" as a strict liability element, but this doubling of sentence seems disproportionate to the added fact.[13]

A second problem with the "greater crime" theory is that it can lead to other, even more expansive, notions. Thus, in the classic case of *Regina v. Prince*, 80 All Eng. L. Rep. 881 (1875), the defendant and his girlfriend, Annie Phillips, ran off to Leeds. When prosecuted for taking a girl under the age of 16 from her parents without their consent, Prince argued that he believed Ms. Phillips was over 16. The jury found this belief to be reasonable. Nevertheless, a majority of the judges subscribed to two theories that went beyond the "greater crime" to uphold Prince's conviction. They would hold the defendant guilty if he knew either (1) that he was committing a possible tort, and therefore should take the risk that he was committing a crime ("greater legal wrong" theory); or (2) that he was committing an immoral (though not necessarily illegal) act, and therefore should take the risk that he was committing a crime ("greater moral wrong" theory). Some would argue that each of these approaches expands the net of criminality far beyond what theories of deterrence or retribution would allow.

Constitutionality

Although the United States Supreme Court has frequently talked about strict liability crimes, a careful reading of the decisions demonstrates that the Court has never actually rendered a holding on whether such offenses are

---

12. What constitutes school property varies from state to state. In some states, this term is limited to buildings used primarily for education. In others, it may include all property owned by the school board, even if used for totally noneducational purposes. Additionally, some statutes encompass school buses, so that the school zone is constantly changing (at least during those hours when the buses are running).

13. This is particularly true in jurisdictions that impose strict liability when the crime occurred at night, or during vacations, when the possibility of children being involved in any way seems no greater in school yards than at any other place.

constitutionally permissible. This is due in large part to the fact that virtually all of the cases concern federal statutes, and therefore are technically decisions involving statutory construction rather than constitutional limitations. The Court also has frequently indicated its refusal to become enmeshed in deciding the constitutional implications of the mens rea doctrine. Finally, the procedural posture of some of the cases has frequently been such that no "holding" on the issue is necessary. Thus, for example, in each of three of the leading cases, *United States v. Balint*, 258 U.S. 250 (1922); *United States v. International Minerals and Chemical Corp.*, 402 U.S. 558 (1971); and *United States v. Freed*, supra, the lower court dismissed an indictment that had not alleged knowledge on the part of the defendant. Each case held that such an allegation is not necessary, but no decision states what should be done when the defendant raises the issue at trial.[14]

Similarly, the opinions whose language strongly supports a "presumption" that all statutes require mens rea, as well as the opinion in *Morrissette*, ultimately avoid the constitutional issue by construing the statute to require mens rea. Even in the most recent of these opinions, *Staples v. United States*, the Court explicitly acknowledged in dictum in a footnote[15] the possibility of strict criminal liability.

The only case *holding* that a conviction dispensing with mens rea is unconstitutional is *Lambert v. California*, 355 U.S. 255 (1957). The Court held that the conviction of an ex-felon for not registering with the police in Los Angeles, as required by a city ordinance, violated the Fifth and Fourteenth Amendments because there was no showing that the defendant knew, or should have known, of a duty to register. That decision, however, has been a "derelict on the waters of the law," precisely as Justice Frankfurter, in dissent, predicted. There may be several reasons for the failure of *Lambert* to start a flood of anti-strict-liability decisions. First, it involved a city ordinance rather than a state statute. It is one thing to require defendants to be familiar with state statutes; it is a burden of a different order to require them to be familiar with every ordinance of every city in which they happen to find themselves (see Chapter 5). Second, the ordinance imposed a duty to register rather than imposing a duty *not* to do something. The common law has always been wary of imposing duties to act (see Chapter 3).

On the other hand, the Court in *Leland v. Oregon*, 343 U.S. 790 (1952),

---

14. There are many other issues, insanity being the most obvious, that the prosecution need not allege, but upon which the state may have to carry the burden of proof beyond a reasonable doubt once defendants raise them. See Chapter 15.

15. "[I]f Congress thinks it necessary to reduce the Government's burden at trial to ensure proper enforcement of the Act, it remains free to amend §5861(d) by explicitly eliminating a *mens rea* requirement." *Staples*, 511 U.S. at 1802. See also *Bouie v. City of Columbia*, 378 U.S. 347 (1964).

held that Oregon's statute placing on the defendant the burden of proof that he was not sane did not violate due process. That opinion at least raises the possibility that mens rea is not a constitutional prerequisite for liability *if* one believes that the insanity claim raises a mens rea issue.

In short, the United States Supreme Court has given mixed signals on the constitutional significance of mens rea and its counterpart, "strict liability." There has been much eloquent language repeated in several recent decisions about the crucial role that mens rea plays in all criminal charges. However, there is also some language, usually in the earlier decisions, that both supports the concept of strict liability and in some instances endorses the application of strict liability in particular areas.

The Model Penal Code

The Model Penal Code takes what it calls a "frontal attack" on strict criminal liability. Section 2.05 provides expressly that culpability is not required *only* with regard to "[o]ffenses which constitute violations." "Violation" is, under the Code, a term of art meaning an act for which imprisonment, even for a day, is not an available sentence (§1.04(5)). This, of course, follows precisely the line that Professor Sayre proposed in his article some 70 years ago.

However, the Code's attack does not end there. Even where the defendant is charged with a violation, a court may still interpret a statute to require mens rea if the court determines that requiring the state to prove mens rea is "consistent with effective enforcement of the law defining the offense" (§2.05(1)(a)).

There is only one exception to §2.05. If the statute in question appears in a "non-Code" title of the laws, strict liability may still apply. Section 2.05(1)(b) was meant to protect preexisting statutory provisions that had been interpreted to impose strict liability. The Code's general rules of interpretation, particularly those in §2.05(1), were expected to apply to all statutes enacted after the Code was adopted. Even in preexisting statutes, the Code permits conviction without mens rea only if "a legislative purpose to impose (such) liability . . . plainly appears." Courts have found such a "plain purpose" where statutes are ambiguous or even where a fair reading suggests a legislative intent to adopt mens rea. This is understandable with regard to statutes written before the Code was adopted in a particular state, since the legislature passing that statute did not anticipate such a rule of construction.

The Code also rejects the "greater crime" theory. Section 2.04(2) provides that mistake is not a defense "if the defendant would be guilty of another offense had the situation been as he supposed." *However,* the next sentence provides that "In such case . . . the . . . mistake . . . shall reduce the grade and degree of the offense of which he may be convicted to those of the offense of which he would be guilty had the situation been as he supposed." In short, in the Hope Diamond case discussed above, *D*'s mistake as to the attendant circumstance would reduce his liability to that of petty larceny.

A Recap and a Methodology

How, after all this, can one begin to assess a statute to decide if it even arguably imposes strict liability? Under the Model Penal Code, the answer is fairly straightforward: If imprisonment is possible, the statute cannot impose strict liability. Even under common law there are some helpful guides:

1. If the statute contains a mens rea word, then it is likely that the mens rea word modifies all material elements of the offense. (See *X-Citement Video*, Chapter 4, supra.)
2. If the statute does *not* contain any mens rea word, then:
   a. If it prohibits something like a common law crime, it is probably not strict liability (*Morissette*, supra).
   b. If it carries a severe penalty (usually more than one year of imprisonment, but this is very shaky), it is probably not strict liability.
   c. If it involves a complex regulatory scheme, it may be strict liability as long as (a) and (b) are not true, and possibly even if they are. (Boy, was that some help!)
   d. If the defendant would have been guilty of a crime even under the facts as he supposed, many states will impose strict liability on the "greater crime" theory.

Remember that these are only guidelines. If state legislatures declared expressly when an offense is strict liability, most of *these* questions would be answered, and we would be left only with the (easy?) issues of fairness and constitutionality. Good luck in the woods.

EXAMPLES

1. Chris parks his car, puts sufficient money in the meter for one hour, and walks into a meeting. Later, noting that his watch indicates that he has eight minutes left, he leaves the meeting and returns to put more money in the meter, only to find a meter reader writing him a parking ticket for overtime parking. The meter reflects a violation. Unknown to him, Chris' watch stopped three times for a period of four minutes each during the hour, although on each occasion the watch began running again. The offense is punishable by a fine of $50. Is Chris guilty of overparking?

2. Bjorn is driving his van through a 60 m.p.h. zone. He sets his cruise control at 58 and takes his foot off the pedal. The control malfunctions, and the car's speed slowly rises to 72. It sticks there, and Bjorn carefully darts in and out of traffic, honking his horn as he goes. He finally pulls over and pulls out the ignition key, stripping the gears and causing $6,000 damage to his van. At that point a friendly state trooper points out to Bjorn that haste makes tickets as well as waste. The maximum penalty for speeding is $500. The maximum penalty for reckless driving is 30 days' imprisonment. Is Bjorn guilty of both these offenses? Of either?

3a. Jack is a cook at Burger Prince. Jill is the cashier. A customer purchases from Jill a burger that was cooked by Jack and becomes ill. It is determined that the meat that Jack used contained bacteria that were not destroyed by the cooking process, although a properly working stove would have killed them. Neither Jack nor Jill is responsible, as a matter of employee functions, for cleaning the stove. Jack and Jill are prosecuted under a statute that prohibits the "manufacture or selling of dangerous food." The penalty is up to two years in jail. What result?

3b. Jack and Jill's supervisor, John Schmidlap, is also charged with selling adulterated food. Is John guilty?

4. Michael, a fruit stand operator and scrap iron collector, goes hunting. He discovers in an open field some metal cylinders that were apparently abandoned. In broad daylight, and with no attempt to hide what he is doing, he loads them on his truck and crushes them. It turns out that they are spent bomb casings, and the property on which they were found is a range owned by the Air Force. Michael is indicted under a statute that provides that "Whoever embezzles, steals, purloins, or knowingly converts to his use . . . any thing of value of the United States" is subject to a ten-year prison sentence. What result?

5. Emily purchases a white powder in a small glassine envelope from a friend. She is told and believes (reasonably) that it is sugar. GUESS WHAT.

6. Striker, a star pitcher for the local baseball team, is also a leading cocaine pusher. He has arranged to meet his latest purchaser near a movie theater in a section of town with which he is not familiar. As the sale goes down, he is arrested and charged with "knowingly selling cocaine within 1,000 feet of a school property." Some 900 feet away, hidden by trees, a railroad trestle, and an interstate highway, is a warehouse owned by the Board of Education and used to store books. The penalty for knowingly selling cocaine (a different statute) is five years. The penalty for this statute is twenty years. Striker argues that he did not know, and could not reasonably have known, that he was near school property.

7. Marty purchases a box, which he believes contains stolen gems worth

$500. He gives it to his girlfriend, hoping to surprise her. She opens it in his presence. But it explodes, killing her; Marty was handed the wrong box. Since Marty *knowingly* received stolen property, can he be convicted of *knowingly* killing his girlfriend?

8. Mary, seeking to rent an apartment in a very tight market, falsely tells the realtor that she works for the Defense Department. Unknown to her, the realtor is an FBI agent. Mary is prosecuted for knowingly providing false information to a federal employee. What result?

EXPLANATIONS

1. This is the prototypical strict liability offense. Whether Chris knew that he was overparked or not, he will be found liable. The penalty is low, and it is at least plausible that there are too many such offenses to allow or require a prosecutor to prove, and a court to inquire about, the defendant's actual state of mind. It is also unlikely that there is any moral stigma to such an offense. (But in a world where people kill for parking spaces, who knows?) The Model Penal Code would agree, since there is no imprisonment possible.

2. Even assuming that the malfunction of the cruise control is not his fault, Bjorn is likely to be found strictly liable of speeding, primarily on the flood-of-cases rationale, but also due to the potential harm involved. This will be true even if Bjorn just had his car, including the cruise control, checked and serviced ten minutes before the event. Tough luck, Bjorn. Next time don't be so decadent. If he is charged with reckless driving, Bjorn's best argument is that he was not *driving*, not that he was not speeding.

   The Model Penal Code would allow strict liability if the charge is speeding. However, Bjorn would not be guilty of the reckless driving charge. At that point, the state would have to prove recklessness, which under the Code requires a subjective awareness of the risk of committing the crime (in this case speeding).

   Note: This is a real case. *State v. Baker,* 571 P.2d 65 (Kan. App. 1977). However, the court's analysis in *Baker* is not technically based on strict liability. It distinguished two earlier decisions in which drivers involved in accidents because of failing brakes and failing throttles were not held strictly liable on the grounds that those items were "essential" to the operation of a car, whereas a cruise control was not.

3a. Unless the court reads a mens rea requirement into the statute (see Chapter 4) or they are in an MPC state, Jack and Jill should pack for Statesville now. Food and other health offenses are frequently deemed "public welfare offenses," allowing strict liability unless the statute expresses a mens rea even if imprisonment is possible. Again, the rationale is that the public generally is endangered and cannot protect itself. If the two were charged, on the other hand, with "reckless" sale of dangerous food, they might have a good claim. They will stay home in an MPC state, which precludes imprisonment without mens rea.

3b. Jack and Jill will have a cellmate, John. Even if John wasn't present in the building, he may be held on a vicarious strict liability basis, even if the punishment is incarceration (except in an MPC state or those states that have held vicarious liability involving imprisonment to be unconstitutional). Burger Prince will pay a fine but can't be incarcerated (actually, it could be incapacitated, but we won't get into that here).

4. This is *Morrissette v. United States*, 342 U.S. 246 (1952), in which the Court interpreted the statute as requiring mens rea on the rationale that the offense was "similar to" the common law crime of larceny, which had required mens rea. Therefore, Michael should be allowed to argue that he had a mistake of fact (possibly of legal fact). The Court so held in *Morrissette*, hinting that to do otherwise would raise serious constitutional questions. Remember that this is the opinion in which Justice Jackson so eloquently lauded the requirement of mens rea.

5. The answer to this example depends, incredibly enough, on *when* the event occurred. Prior to 1970 or so, virtually every state, following the Uniform Narcotic Drug Act suggested in 1932 by the Conference of National Commissioners on Uniform State Laws, held that drug crimes, including possession or sale, could be prosecuted on a strict liability basis. The defendant's belief, no matter how reasonable, about the nature of the item was irrelevant. In 1970 the Commissioners revised their view and required mens rea. Within 15 years, every state had followed this lead, either legislatively or judicially. Whether this had to do with possible increased punishments, or a sense that drug deals were now "mala in se" rather than "mala prohibitum" (assuming we know what that distinction means), or for some other reason is unclear. So Emily stays home, even under the common law.

6. This is an example of the "greater crime" theory. Drug sale, after all, is a crime by itself. Many states, following the example of the federal government, have passed "drug-free school zone" statutes such as the one involved in this example. These statutes vary in form. Some, such as the one here, are "free-standing" crimes. Others, including the federal statute, build on a preexisting statute that bans drug sales, and declare that any sale that occurs near a school yard doubles the maximum penalty. With the latter, the argument that "school property" is not a material element of the crime, but merely a "sentencing enhancer," is plausible. Under the statute as presented in this example, however, it is much more likely that a court would, or at least should, find it to be a "material element" of the crime, thus requiring the state to prove mens rea with regard to the proximity of school property. Some courts,

however, have simply ignored this distinction and held that there is no mens rea requirement as to that element. On the precise issue, several states, including New Jersey, have expressly declared in a statute that lack of knowledge that the event occurred near school property is irrelevant as to guilt. Again, whether one agrees with that result or not, at least these legislatures have directly addressed the question, thereby avoiding the difficult statutory interpretation issue.

The question of constitutionality and proportionality, however, still remain.

It looks like Striker will be pitching for the state prison team for the next few years.

7. This tests the limits of the "greater crime" doctrine. Almost surely, the courts would hold that Marty is not guilty of knowing homicide, even though he was engaged in a crime when his girlfriend was killed. A good example may be *Regina v. Faulkner*, 13 Cox C.C. 550 (1877). Faulkner, a sailor, went down to the hatch to steal some rum. He lit a match to see what he was doing, the rum caught fire, and the ship burned. His conviction of maliciously burning the ship was reversed on appeal, the court rejecting what it called a "very broad" claim by the prosecutor that anyone involved in any crime should be held liable for any greater crime that happens to ensue. On the other hand, the felony murder doctrine (see Chapter 8) comes very close to adopting such a view.

8. Believe it or not, under both the common law and the MPC, it is likely that Mary will be on her way to prison. This is a variation of *United States v. Bakhtiari*, 913 F.2d 1053 (2d Cir. 1990), which actually has much more bizarre facts than the example. Some courts would explain that "federal employee" here is not a "material" element, but only a "jurisdictional" element of the offense, and no mens rea is required. If this is a valid argument, the Model Penal Code would agree. Other courts might consider this an example of the "greater moral wrong" theory, while still others might consider a mistake (or ignorance) as to the legal status of the realtor a legal mistake, and hence governed by ignorantia lex.

7

Causation

Overview

Some crimes require the prosecution to prove that the defendant caused a particular result. Proving this fact is usually not difficult. However, challenging issues of causation sometimes occur in the criminal law, most frequently in homicide cases because homicide requires the prosecutor to prove the defendant caused the death of another human being. (See Chapter 8.)

Causation often can be established by showing that the defendant's action directly brought about the resulting harm. In most cases causation is simply a question of physical occurrence. Did the defendant initiate physical forces that, according to the laws of nature, led to a particular result?

Establishing that the defendant's conduct caused the proscribed result ordinarily is not difficult. If a professional killer shoots the victim in the head and the victim dies, a pathologist can conduct an autopsy and then testify at trial that the bullet fired by the defendant brought about the victim's death by producing massive injury to the victim's brain. Because the defendant produced the victim's death in exactly the manner he intended, there is no controversy about his criminal responsibility for causing death. Likewise, when a defendant engages in risky conduct that brings about death in exactly the way his conduct made probable, proving that the defendant's conduct caused the prohibited result is not hard. The actor is rightly blamed for the predictable consequences of natural events that he intentionally set in motion.

However, as in all human experience, the unusual or unexpected sometimes happens. What if the defendant did not intend or anticipate the harm, or the harm occurs in an improbable manner? Is she criminally responsible for that harm? Judges, juries, and especially law students have difficulty determining when the criminal law will conclude the defendant has "caused" the harm and when she did not. In such cases, what started out as a simple inquiry into what caused a physical occurrence often requires a moral judgment as well.

The analytic tools developed by the criminal law to resolve difficult causation issues are not always clear or easy to apply. This doctrinal difficulty is prompted, in part, by the ongoing debate concerning the relevance of harm in determining and grading criminal responsibility.[1]

Utilitarians are less concerned with the occurrence of harm than some retributivists. Some utilitarians argue that the defendant's *attitude* toward harm — not the *causation* of harm — is critical in determining whether he needs to be punished. They point out that whether harm occurs is often a matter of luck or skill and that the dangerousness of the individual is the same regardless of what harm his conduct actually causes.[2]

Some retributivists, on the other hand, argue that humans intuitively feel that the harm done is an important element in determining criminal responsibility and setting an appropriate punishment.[3] This particular retributive theory requires that individuals be punished only for harm they caused. Otherwise, punishment is disconnected from a moral concept of just deserts.

The Rationale of Causation

A primary goal of the criminal law is to prevent harm. Individuals may be punished for the harm they cause, provided other necessary elements like mens rea are satisfied. However, there must be a connection between someone's conduct and the resulting harm sufficient to justify the infliction of punishment.

The causation requirement limits criminal responsibility to those individuals whose conduct has been essential in bringing about harm. Individuals would be unable to plan their lives or to ensure freedom from government interference if they could be punished for harms they did not cause. To punish in such cases would be arbitrary and unrelated to fundamental notions of personal guilt.

---

1. The moral debate over the relevance of harm to criminal responsibility also occurs in attempt. See Chapter 12.

2. Schulhofer, Harm and Punishment: A Critique of Emphasis on the Results of Conduct in the Criminal Law, 122 U. Pa. L. Rev. 1497, 1514-1516 (1974); Alexander, Crime and Culpability, 5 J. Contemp. Legal Issues 1 (1994).

3. M. Dan-Cohen, Causation, 1 Encyclopedia of Crime and Justice 165-166 (S. Kadish ed., 1983); Crocker, A Retributive Theory of Criminal Causation, 5 J. Contemp. Legal Issues 65 (1994). But see H.L.A. Hart & A.M. Honore, Causation in the Law 395 (2d ed. 1985).

One approach to determining causation in the criminal law is analogous to how a scientist might examine cause and effect in the physical world. The scientist might examine the natural forces that brought about the harm and determine whether the defendant's act played an essential part in physically causing the harm. Another approach focuses on the defendant's moral culpability; that is, did she act with the intention or contemplation that she might cause harm? If not, *should* she have contemplated the harm?

The former approach stresses the mechanisms by which harm occurs in the real world. The latter approach focuses more on the defendant's attitude toward the occurrence of harm.

Causation is also an important element of tort liability. An individual who commits a tort may be required to pay compensation only for the damage he has caused. However, the goals of tort law are different from criminal law goals. Tort law seeks in part to distribute the risk of harm to those most able to bear the cost as well as to those who benefit from the activity that produced the harm. Moreover, negligent conduct is usually sufficient for the imposition of liability in tort. Thus, the concept of causation in tort is quite broad so that these goals can be more easily accomplished.

Criminal law punishment, on the other hand, is aimed both at deterring and at "paying back" intentional or risky harmful conduct. Thus, the concept of causation in criminal law may be more narrow.

There is an ongoing debate in criminal law on whether tort law concepts of causation should become part and parcel of what criminal law requires or whether criminal law should have a more narrow concept of causation. Needless to say, this debate has not been resolved.

The Elements of Causation

The Common Law

Responsibility for Causing Harm

As in tort, to be held criminally responsible for causing a proscribed harm under the common law, the defendant's conduct must have been both the "cause in fact" and the "proximate cause" of the harm.

Cause in Fact

Cause in fact is "but for" causation. If the harm would *not* have occurred *unless* the defendant had engaged in the conduct, there is "cause in fact." This inquiry is essentially one of fact. Was the defendant's conduct necessary or a substantial factor for the harm to occur? Frequently, the analysis will conclude that the defendant's conduct started a chain of events that eventually resulted in the proscribed harm. Put simply, "but for" defendant's conduct, this chain of events would never have begun and the harm would not have occurred.

Cause in fact ("but for" causation) is required before an individual can be convicted of a crime that requires him to *cause* a result. Without it the harm that has occurred cannot be linked to the defendant's behavior. After all, the harm may have happened even if the defendant had done nothing. To punish someone in these circumstances is arbitrary and unfair because it is not based on what the defendant did. Thus, "but for" causation must be established whenever causation is necessary for criminal responsibility. However, as we shall soon see, cause in fact is not enough for criminal responsibility under either the common law or the Model Penal Code.

Omission as a Cause

Though the rule raises interesting philosophical questions, an omission can also satisfy the legal requirement of causation.[4] This is so even though it is difficult to think of "doing nothing" as bringing about a result. In reality, an omission fails to interrupt other forces already at work and, as a consequence of the defendant's not intervening, a harm that was avoidable occurs.

Concurrent Causation

Concurrent causation is the one situation when the cause in fact requirement does *not* have to be met. It occurs when *two* independent causes in fact occur at the same time, and *either* of them would have caused the result by itself.

If two gang members intentionally shoot a victim at the same time with the intent to kill him and each of their bullets inflict a mortal wound, *each* has been the cause of *V*'s death. This is true even though the victim would have died had either of the defendants not intentionally shot the victim. This is a case of concurrent causation: Each defendant's conduct is considered the "cause in fact" because both acted with the intention of killing the victim and the conduct of either would have been effective in bringing about the proscribed result. The criminal law does not excuse the intentionally harmful conduct of one actor just because another actor also caused the same harm.

People v. Arzon, 92 Misc. 2d 739, 401 N.Y.S.2d 156 (1978), is a close case of concurrent causation. Defendant (*D*) started a fire on the fifth floor

---

4. See Leavens, A Causation Approach to Criminal Omissions, 76 Cal. L. Rev. 547 (1988).

of an abandoned building to keep warm. Firefighters responded to fight the fire. Meanwhile, another fire started independently by *B* on the second floor trapped the firefighters. Overcome by smoke from the first and second fires, *V*, a firefighter, sustained injuries from which he died. Has *D* caused the death of *V*? In all likelihood, *V* would not have died had someone else not set the second-story fire. Nonetheless, *D*'s fire satisfied the "but for" requirement. If *D* had not set the chain of events in motion, *V* would not have died. Moreover, the court could point to *D*'s conduct—starting the fire—as one component of the forces that caused the firefighter's death.

Direct Cause

Direct causation occurs when the defendant's act is the only causal agent in bringing about the harm. There is no other causally connected act.

In most criminal law cases the defendant's conduct *is* the only cause of harm and, therefore, is also the *direct cause* of the harm. No one else even partially helps produce the harm. In the case of our professional killer discussed earlier, the defendant's intentional act of shooting the victim in the head is the only act necessary to bring about death.

Direct causation always satisfies the requirement of proximate cause. The defendant is the sole causal agent, and he brought about the harm in precisely the manner intended or made likely.

Proximate Cause

Is the defendant criminally responsible when another actor or event (called an "intervening cause" since it generally occurs *after* the defendant has engaged in his conduct, but *before* the harm results) plays a causal role in bringing about the harm?

Proximate cause is the doctrine the criminal law generally uses to decide when the defendant *should* be held criminally responsible for causing harm even though an intervening cause helped bring about the harm. Proximate cause is satisfied if the intervening cause was (1) intended or reasonably foreseeable and (2) not too remote or accidental as to fairly hold the defendant responsible. There can be more than one proximate cause of a particular harm. (Note, however, that some jurisdictions require direct causation for criminal responsibility because proximate causation is considered too broad.)

Proximate cause questions cannot be answered solely by the physical sciences; thus, they are not "facts" that can be uncovered by scientifically examining cause and effect in the real world. Instead, their answers will depend to a large extent on public policy and the value judgments made by judges and juries about a defendant's moral culpability and their intuitive sense of justice in a particular case.

Dependent Intervening Cause. A dependent intervening cause is one that was intended or reasonably foreseeable by the defendant, or sufficiently related to his conduct, to impose criminal responsibility for causing the harm. Characterizing the intervening cause as *dependent* results in a finding that the defendant *proximately caused* the harm. In more simple terms, the fact that another causal agent contributed to the result will not relieve the defendant of responsibility.

If a defendant forces a woman into a car and states that he is going to rape her, and she subsequently leaps out of the moving car and seriously injures herself, her conduct will be considered a dependent intervening cause because human experience shows that victims will take serious risks in trying to escape from their captors. Thus, the defendant has proximately caused her injuries.

Independent Intervening Cause. Occasionally, however, another actor or event causes the harm in such an unexpected or unusual manner that the defendant will not be held criminally responsible for causing it. This is so even though the defendant's conduct set in motion the chain of events that produced the harm, thereby satisfying "but for" causation.

To find that the intervening cause is *independent,* the fact finder must conclude that (1) the harm was not intended by the defendant or was not reasonably foreseeable, or (2) that it is simply unfair and unjust to hold him responsible for the harm that has occurred. Put more simply, the direct cause of the harm was sufficiently fortuitous or coincidental in its occurrence and unconnected to the defendant's conduct so as to make it unjust to punish him for causing that harm.

A finding of *independent* intervening causation breaks the chain of events that the defendant started and results in a finding of no proximate cause. It thus prevents his being convicted of any crime that requires the prosecution to prove the defendant *caused* the harm. (Note: Some courts and commentators as well as the Restatement of Torts call this *superseding causation.*)

Consider a case in which the defendant inflicts a minor wound on a victim, and afterwards the victim is driven by a friend to a doctor's office for some stitches. While sitting in a waiting room, a disgruntled patient enters the doctor's office and opens fire with a gun, killing the victim. The defendant's initial assault satisfies the "cause in fact" requirement. But for his conduct, the victim would not have been at the doctor's office at that particular moment. However, the killing by the former patient is really a coincidence; it is just bad luck that the assault victim became a murder victim. Even though the defendant initiated the sequence of events that eventually resulted in the homicide, the death was not foreseeable nor made more likely by the defendant's act. Thus, the disgruntled patient who fired the fatal shots would be considered an *independent intervening cause,* and the defendant would not be considered the "proximate cause" of death.

For a visual summary of proximate causation, see Table 2.

Table 2. Proximate Causation

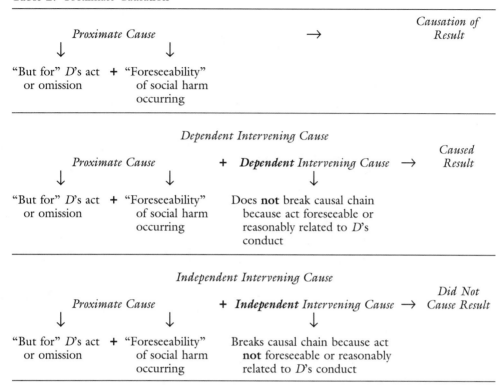

Proximate Cause		→	Causation of Result
↓	↓		
"But for" D's act or omission	+ "Foreseeability" of social harm occurring		

Dependent Intervening Cause

Proximate Cause		+ **Dependent** Intervening Cause	→	Caused Result
↓	↓	↓		
"But for" D's act or omission	+ "Foreseeability" of social harm occurring	Does **not** break causal chain because act foreseeable or reasonably related to D's conduct		

Independent Intervening Cause

Proximate Cause		+ **Independent** Intervening Cause	→	Did Not Cause Result
↓	↓	↓		
"But for" D's act or omission	+ "Foreseeability" of social harm occurring	Breaks causal chain because act **not** foreseeable or reasonably related to D's conduct		

Judicial Rules of Thumb for Finding Dependent Intervening Causation. As noted at the outset, the definitions of proximate cause and intervening cause do not provide much help in analysis because they require both a factual inquiry and a moral judgment. As a result, courts often use rules of thumb to justify their conclusion that the defendant *should* be held liable in a particular case. There are some generalizations from the case law that may be useful.

Harm Intended or Risked Versus the Manner in Which It Occurs. If a defendant intended a particular harm or created a risk that a particular harm would occur but it occurs in a manner different than intended or expected, courts generally will find the intervening cause to be dependent, provided the specific causal mechanism was not entirely unexpected or coincidental.

This principle is illustrated in *People v. Kibbe*, 35 N.Y.2d 407, 321 N.E.2d 773 (1974). Late in the evening two defendants robbed a near-sighted and very intoxicated victim on a cold winter night in upstate New York where heavy snow had fallen. They left him without his glasses near the side of a road surrounded by steep snowbanks. The victim, unable to see clearly and somewhat immobile, sat down in the middle of the roadway. Soon a truck driver, who was speeding, struck and killed the victim. The defendants argued that they did not cause the victim's death. They claimed that either the defendant—by putting himself in such obvious peril of being hit by a vehicle—or the truck driver—who could not brake in time because he was speeding—were independent supervening causes.

The New York Court of Appeals disagreed with the defendants. It concluded that the defendants, in committing armed robbery and leaving their intoxicated victim in these harsh and perilous conditions, could anticipate that he would seek help by moving onto the road, especially because he had trouble seeing and walking. Nor was it unusual for drivers to be driving over the speed limit at that hour.

In this case defendants surely knew they created a strong possibility that the victim might die from exposure to the cold. They might even have anticipated his being struck by a vehicle while walking alongside the road. However, it is unlikely they anticipated, or should have anticipated, the particular manner in which the defendant was killed because most people, even if drunk and unable to see or walk well, do not sit in the middle of a highway. Though conceding that it was somewhat unusual for someone to sit down in the middle of the road, the court concluded that the victim's *death* was foreseeable, even though the *particular manner* in which it occurred may not have been. Only if the victim had died in a manner that was not related to what the defendants did—perhaps by having a meteor fall on him because *that* would be a matter of pure chance — would the court probably find an independent intervening cause.

Preexisting Conditions and Negligent Medical Treatment. Most jurisdictions will consider the victim's preexisting medical condition as a *dependent* intervening cause. Thus, in *People v. Stamp,* 2 Cal. App. 3d 203, 82 Cal. Rptr. 598 (1969), the court found the defendant had proximately caused the victim's death during the commission of an armed robbery when the 60-year-old victim, who was extremely overweight and had a history of heart disease, died during the robbery.[5]

Likewise, subsequent negligent medical treatment is usually considered a dependent intervening cause even though it contributes to the victim's death.[6] We expect medical care to be furnished to individuals who have been assaulted. Because medical aid is so likely and because the possibility of negligent medical aid is a fact of life, the criminal law considers this intervening cause *dependent*. It is foreseeable and sufficiently related to what the defendant did. Consequently, negligent medical care usually does not break the causal chain of events set in motion by the defendant, and proximate causation will be found.

Foreseeable Human Action. Action taken in response to the danger created by the defendant is also considered foreseeable. Thus, persons in

---

5. See also *State v. McKeiver,* 89 N.J. Super. 52, 213 A.2d 320 (1965).
6. See e.g., *Hall v. State,* 199 Ind. 592, 159 N.E. 420 (1928).

danger will try to escape and others will try to rescue them. The police will also try to apprehend criminals.

Defendants who create peril to human life should realize that their conduct elicits precisely this kind of human response. They should not be surprised if harm occurs as a result of what they did. Consequently, an actor will be held responsible even if another person, including the victim, a would-be rescuer, or a police officer, actually brings about the harm. Increasingly, courts are holding fleeing criminals responsible for the death of police officers giving chase even when the conduct of the pursuing police officer is itself extremely reckless and, therefore, arguably unexpected.[7]

Contributing Cause. Occasionally, a defendant will hasten the death of a victim who is already suffering from a mortal wound inflicted by another. Or the victim himself, suffering from a mortal wound, will hasten his own death by inflicting another mortal wound.[8] Most courts do not allow the individual who inflicted the initial mortal injury to avoid responsibility by claiming that the subsequent voluntary act of another human being was an intervening independent cause. They conclude instead that *both* acts (i.e., those of the initial actor and of the subsequent actor) caused the harm. This situation is often called a case of contributing causation because both acts are effective in bringing about the harm. It can also be considered a case of "concurrent causation." (See pages 124-125.)

Judicial Rules of Thumb for Finding Independent Intervening Causation. Not surprisingly, courts also use judicial rules of thumb to support their conclusion that the defendant *should not* be held responsible in a particular case.

Grossly Negligent or Reckless Medical Treatment. If a physician provides grossly negligent or reckless medical treatment, a finding of *independent* intervening causation is likely, cutting off the defendant's responsibility for causing death.[9] The logic in such cases is that the defendant's conduct set in motion a chain of events that would normally not result in the victim's death. Death was actually caused by extremely poor medical treatment, which is a very unusual event. Consequently, the grossly negligent treatment, rather than the defendant's initial conduct, will be considered the cause of death.

Irresponsible Human Agent. As we will see in the discussion of accomplice liability in Chapter 14, the criminal law generally does not look beyond the last human actor for a causal explanation of events. Because every human being is presumed to have free will, the last actor is considered capable of deciding whether to engage in conduct intended to cause harm.

---

7. See, e.g., *People v. Acosta,* 284 Cal. Rptr. 117 (1991).

8. See, e.g., *People v. Lewis,* 124 Cal. 551, 57 P. 470 (1889).

9. See, e.g., *Regina v. Cheshire,* 3 All E. R. 670 (1991).

Suppose, however, that a defendant engages in conduct, such as continuous rape and other assaultive behavior, that renders another human being so distraught that she cannot make rational decisions; if she were to intentionally take poison that contributes to her death, the defendant may be held responsible for causing her death.[10] (This approach is very similar to how the law attributes the act of an innocent agent to the principal. See Chapter 14.)

In *Stephenson v. State*, 205 Ind. 141, 179 N.E. 633 (1932), the defendant held the victim prisoner against her will for several days and committed various sexual assaults on her. The victim consumed a poisonous substance in an attempt to commit suicide. Subsequently, she died from several causes, including the self-administered poison. The court held the defendant responsible for the victim's death, rejecting his argument that, in taking poison, the victim was an intervening independent cause. It concluded that the victim's becoming irresponsible was a "natural and probable result" of defendant's conduct.

Unforeseeable Human Action. Courts will generally find intervening causation to be *independent* when a person subsequently acts in a very unusual or unlikely manner. A defendant who swindles retired people out of their life savings will probably not be found guilty of homicide if one of the victims, distraught by his financial losses, commits suicide. Based on human experience, the law will generally assume that most fraud victims, even though suffering severe financial and psychological harm, would not take their lives as a consequence of being so victimized.

Identifying the Specific Causal Mechanism. Some cases hold that the defendant cannot be held responsible for causing a harm if the specific causal mechanism cannot be identified. Thus, in *People v. Warner-Lambert*, 51 N.Y.2d 295, 414 N.E.2d 660 (1980), the defendant knowingly used two explosive ingredients in its manufacturing process and had been warned that high concentrations of these chemicals were creating dangerous conditions in its factory. Several employees were killed after an explosion occurred in the factory. The corporation and several of its officers and employees were convicted of second-degree manslaughter. The prosecution could prove that defendant had knowingly created the dangerous conditions. It could not establish the specific mechanism that triggered the explosion.

The court of appeals concluded that cause in fact ("but for" causation) was insufficient to hold the defendants responsible. Though this case seems wrongly decided, one can argue that, without knowledge of what exactly triggered the explosion, it is impossible to know if the manner in which the harm came about should have been within the defendant's contemplation. Thus, it is possible (though highly unlikely) that a burglar entered the factory

---

10. See, e.g., *People v. Roberts,* 2 Cal. 4th 271, 826 P.2d 274 (1992).

late at night and deliberately sparked the explosion. Of course, it is more likely that the explosion occurred in precisely the way the defendants knew it might.

The cases go both ways on this question. However, the prosecution's case is stronger if it can show the precise manner in which the harm occurred. This will then enable the fact finders to conclude that the defendant should have foreseen that this particular causal mechanism could occur.

Contributory Negligence and Proximate Causation

Conduct by a victim that would be considered contributory negligence in a tort case does not prevent a finding that the defendant was the proximate cause of the victim's death. Thus, if *A* engages in a high-speed drag race with *B*, who dies in a car crash during the race, *A* can be prosecuted for proximately causing *B*'s death even though *B*'s survivors could not successfully sue *A* in tort because *B*'s own act of driving was contributory negligence.

The Model Penal Code
Responsibility for Causing Harm

The Model Penal Code dramatically revises the role of causation in assessing criminal responsibility. In effect, the MPC transforms much of the analysis of causation into an inquiry about the defendant's culpability.

"But For" Causation

To be held criminally responsible for causing a proscribed harm, the MPC requires the prosecution to establish "but for" causation (cause in fact under the common law approach) and any other specific causal requirement "imposed by the Code or the law defining the offense."[11] Causation is not established under the MPC if the harm would have occurred without the defendant's conduct. Additional analysis is required only when the result that occurs is different from the result intended or contemplated. Consequently, in most cases it is very easy for the prosecution to establish causation necessary for criminal responsibility under the MPC.

---

11. MPC §2.03(1)(a) and (b). Section 1(a) and (b) provides:

> (1) Conduct is the cause of a result when: (a) it is an antecedent but for which the result in question would not have occurred; and (b) the relationship between the conduct and result satisfies any additional causal requirements imposed by the Code or by the law defining the defense.

Other Causation, Concurrent Causation, and Transferred Intent

The MPC allows legislatures to impose traditional causal elements in a statute if they wish,[12] but it does not directly address "concurrent causation." Common law cases of "transferred intent" are treated by the MPC as cases of causation, requiring causation analysis; that is, did the defendant *cause* the result? This question arises only if the result that occurs is *not* within the purpose or contemplation of the actor.

Culpability as to Result

The MPC focuses on the defendant's culpability toward the result.[13] It compares what *actually* happened with what the defendant *thought* or *should have thought* would happen. When results different from what the defendant intended, contemplated, or should have contemplated occur, subsections (2)(a) and (2)(b) (purposefully or knowingly) or (3)(a) or (3)(b) (recklessly or negligently) are applied, depending on the culpability required for conviction.

Section 2(a). Purposefully and Knowingly. If the actual result differs from what the actor purposed or knew would occur, then he is *not* responsible for the actual result unless (i) a *different person* or *property* was harmed, or (ii) the defendant actually caused a *lesser* harm than contemplated.[14] In either of these two situations the defendant *is* responsible for the actual harm he causes.

The MPC approach in holding the defendant responsible for injuring a different person or property than he intended or contemplated is just like the common law's use of "transferred intent." If *D* shoots at *A* and hits *B*, then the MPC treats *D* as having caused *B*'s injury. Likewise, if *D* sets out to burn down *A*'s house by use of an incendiary device and instead only

---

12. MPC §2.03(1)(b). In most jurisdictions the "law defining the offense" will require "proximate causation."

13. To refresh your memory on culpability, see Chapter 4.

14. Section 2.03(2)(a) of the MPC is difficult to read. It provides in part that the actual harm or injury is not within the purpose or contemplation of the actor unless the "injury or harm designed or contemplated would have been *more serious* or *more extensive* than that caused." The effect of this language is to make the actor responsible for an injury or harm that he causes, provided it is *not* as serious or extensive as that he designed or contemplated. Put another way, the actor is not held responsible for causing a more serious injury than the one he intended or contemplated. To punish in such a situation would impose disproportionately more punishment than his culpability deserved.

produces some charring of *B*'s house, then *D* has caused the harm to *B*'s house. (Note that the defendant must cause a harm equal to, or less than, the harm he intended or contemplated.)

Section 2(b). Under this section, even though the same kind of injury occurred as the actor intended or contemplated, he will not be held responsible if unusual and unexpected causal mechanisms actually caused the harm. Thus, the jury must decide whether the actual causal agent is "not too remote or accidental in its occurrence to have a just bearing" on the actor's liability or the severity of the offense.

The approach in subsection (b) lets the fact finder conclude that the mechanism that caused the harm is simply too coincidental or unexpected to impose liability. It is a very open-ended approach, inviting subjective judgments about moral culpability, chance, desert, and whatever else the fact finder considers relevant. Thus, if the victim in the *Kibbe* case discussed above was killed in a random drive-by shooting, a jury might conclude that the defendants should not be held responsible for causing the harm.

Recklessly or Negligently. Section 2.03(3) of the MPC uses the same approach here for these culpability requirements as described above for purposefully and knowingly in §2.03(2).

Again, the MPC compares the harm that actually occurred with the harm risked by the actor and asks the same questions. A person is responsible for the harm that actually occurs if the harm simply involves injury to a different person or property or was less serious than the harm risked. Likewise, if the harm that occurs is the same kind as the harm risked, the actor is responsible unless it is "too remote or accidental in its occurrence" to fairly blame the actor.

Strict Liability. Section 2.03(4) sets forth how causation is analyzed in a strict liability offense that contains a result element. The actual result must be a "probable consequence of the actor's conduct."

EXAMPLES

1. Roberta, angry at Raoul and wanting to kill him, pointed a loaded pistol at his head while Raoul was asleep and pulled the trigger. The gun discharged, killing Raoul. Did Roberta cause Raoul's death?

2. Charlie enters a hotel room to steal valuables left behind by the guests. Unfortunately, Edna is still in the room and sees Charlie. Charlie hits her over the head with a heavy object, intending to kill her because she can identify him. Charlie leaves Edna lying in a pool of blood. A maid discovers Edna, who is then rushed to the hospital. Edna, still uncon-

scious, is diagnosed as having suffered serious brain damage. Did Charlie cause Edna's death in the following examples?

2a. Dr. Able skillfully performs complicated and risky brain surgery, reasonably concluding that otherwise Edna will surely die within a few days. Despite the surgery, Edna dies from excessive bleeding resulting from the surgery.

2b. Edna would have survived if Dr. Inept had not provided negligent medical treatment.

2c. Edna would have survived if Dr. Hopeless had not provided grossly negligent medical treatment.

2d. Edna, still unconscious, is fed intravenously while connected to a respirator that mechanically breathes for her. Dr. Choice, after consultation with Edna's family, (i) stops the respirator and Edna dies ten minutes later; (ii) stops the intravenous nutrition and hydration and Edna dies 13 days later.

3. While driving along the highway with Tara in the passenger seat, Jennifer spotted Bob, her fiance, several car lengths ahead of her. She speeded up to wave at him. Bob, recognizing Jennifer in the car behind him, waited until she almost caught up to him and then sped away. Jennifer then increased her speed so she could catch up to Bob once more. Again, Bob, laughing, waited until Jennifer almost caught up and then increased his speed even more. This game of "cat and mouse" continued until suddenly Jennifer, traveling well above the speed limit, lost control and hit a tree. Tara died instantly. Jennifer and Bob are both charged with homicide. Did Bob cause Tara's death?

4. Kim tried to kill his wife, Juang, by pushing her off a high cliff while hiking in the mountains. The fall did not kill Juang. Instead, it left her a paraplegic confined to a wheelchair and with a great deal of uncontrollable and unbearable pain in her upper torso. Kim was convicted of attempted murder and sentenced to a prison term.

   Six months later Juang, realizing she would never walk again and that her excruciating pain would be a constant companion for the rest of her life, committed suicide. Did Kim cause Juang's suicide?

5. Jack and Jill are drinking heavily at Jill's apartment. They decide to take some heroin. Jack drives downtown and buys some heroin from Buster, his usual supplier. Jack brings the heroin back to Jill's place. He fixes himself a bag, injects it, and then fixes a bag for Jill. Jill injects the heroin into her arm. After 15 seconds Jill loses consciousness and collapses on the floor. Jack calls paramedics immediately, but Jill dies before they arrive.

The coroner determines a heroin overdose and Jill's drinking as the cause of death. Could the prosecutor argue that Jack caused Jill's death?

6. Martin was desperate for money. One night he deliberately set fire to a large abandoned warehouse he owned in order to collect the fire insurance. The fire department responded and started to fight the fire.

   Sven, a firefighter, wearing a breathing apparatus with a 30-minute tank of oxygen, entered the burning building without a buddy. When the alarm signaled that Sven had only five minutes of oxygen left in his tank, Sven disregarded it and stayed to fight the fire. Almost five minutes later, Sven died from suffocation. Fighting a fire "solo" (without a buddy) and failing to immediately leave a fire when the warning signal sounds on the oxygen tank are both serious violations of department regulations. Should the judge instruct the jury that Martin could not have caused Sven's death?

7. Nyguen walked into the bank, pulled a gun, and told the teller to put money in a bank bag. Betty did this while triggering a silent alarm. Seeing a police car pull up in front of the bank, Nyguen grabbed Betty by the arm, pointed his gun at her head, and used her as a shield while leaving the bank from a rear exit. A police sharpshooter, stationed in the alley, saw Nyguen leaving the bank with Betty in front of him and his gun pointed at her head. Taking very careful aim at Nyguen, the sharpshooter waited for a clear shot and fired. Unfortunately, Nyguen turned at the same moment. The bullet struck and killed Betty instantly. Is there a viable theory that the prosecutor can use to hold Nyguen responsible for Betty's death?

8. Hal, tired of living, jumped off the top of a 15-story office building. Just as Hal was passing by the twelfth floor, Julia, angry that her boyfriend, Chet, was leaving her, fired a pistol at him intending to kill Chet. Fortunately, Chet moved and the bullet missed him. Unfortunately, it went through the window of the twelfth-floor apartment, killing Hal instantly in mid-flight. The prosecutor has filed a murder charge against Julia. Is she guilty?
   a. What if Cindy had pushed Hall off the building, intending to kill him, after he told her their relationship was over? Who killed Hal? Cindy? Julia?

9. Alberto is madly in love with Adelaide, who is married to Francesco. Alberto correctly believes that Adelaide (who does not believe in divorce) does not love Francesco and would marry him if Francesco were dead.

   Alberto knows that Luca, who is married to Maria, is an extremely jealous and violent husband. Luca has been convicted of assault on several occasions both for beating Maria for alleged "flirting" and for beating the men he erroneously thought were making advances toward Maria.

Hoping that Luca will kill Francesco, Alberto anonymously calls Luca and tells him that Francesco has been having a secret affair with Maria for several months. Alberto provides false dates, descriptions, and locations to make his story convincing. Alberto then flies to Kansas.

The day after receiving the anonymous telephone call, Luca, believing Alberto's tales of spousal infidelity, finds Francesco sitting in a cafe and kills him with a single shot to the head. Luca then returns home and

a. kills Maria.

b. kills himself.

10. Joe Camel, president of Federated Tobacco, recently testified before a Congressional committee that cigarette smoking is not addictive and that there is no evidence scientifically establishing that smoking causes cancer.

Rusty Lunchpail, a lifelong smoker of cigarettes made by Federated, died recently of lung cancer. On his deathbed Rusty swore in a video-taped deposition that he knew cigarette smoking was harmful to his health, but that he could not break the habit.

Billy Jackson, a crusading prosecutor from Mississippi, has indicted Federated and Joe Camel, as its president, for murder in connection with the death of Rusty Lunchpail. Billy can prove that the United States Surgeon General has publicly warned that smoking cigarettes is harmful to human health and that nicotine, a primary ingredient in cigarette tobacco, does create a physiological craving for its continued consumption. He also has a witness who will testify that Federated carefully monitored the amount of nicotine in its cigarettes and always blended in sufficient amounts of nicotine-rich tobacco to ensure that its cigarettes contained at least a specified amount of nicotine. Finally, he can prove that Joe Camel knew nicotine was addictive.

11. Roberta, angry at Raoul and wanting to kill him, pointed a loaded pistol at his head while Raoul was asleep and pulled the trigger. The gun jams and does not fire. Raoul wakes up and grabs the gun from Roberta before she can pull the trigger again.

EXPLANATIONS

1. In firing a loaded pistol at the head of another human being, Roberta intended to cause a particular result, Raoul's death. In a homicide prosecution the prosecutor should easily establish causation as required by the law. Roberta's conduct was the cause in fact and direct cause of Raoul's death. The very same harm she intended to bring about occurred in exactly the manner Roberta intended.

2a. Under the common law Charlie's conduct satisfies both cause in fact and proximate cause. Hitting Edna with a heavy object satisfies cause in fact; but for this conduct, Edna would be alive. It was also foreseeable that Edna's death was a natural and probable result of Charlie's conduct.

True, Edna died as a direct result of Dr. Able's skillful and high-risk surgery. However, only such surgery might interrupt the fatal causal forces that Charlie had previously set in motion. Thus, such invasive medical treatment was a likely and a natural result of the chain of events put in motion by Charlie. The surgery will therefore be considered a dependent intervening cause, and Charlie will be held responsible for proximately causing Edna's death.

The MPC would also find Charlie responsible. The actual result, Edna's death, is the same as that intended or contemplated. Although the operation was the immediate and direct cause of Edna's death, it is highly likely that medical professionals will undertake high-risk surgery to avoid the harm Charlie's actions will otherwise cause. Thus, the surgery is not too remote or accidental to have a just bearing on Charlie's guilt.

2b. Charlie's conduct satisfies "but for" causation. Edna's injury and subsequent medical treatment would not have occurred unless Charlie had struck her. However, there is an intervening cause — the negligent treatment provided by Dr. Inept.

In most jurisdictions negligent medical treatment is considered foreseeable and the natural and probable result of the actor's harmful conduct. Thus, it is a *dependent* intervening cause that does *not* defeat a finding of proximate cause. Charlie would be found to have caused Edna's death in most jurisdictions and could be convicted of a homicide charge.

The outcome under the MPC is not clear. Charlie's conduct satisfies its "but for" causation requirement. The jury would then have to decide whether the actual mechanism of death, Dr. Inept's negligent medical care, was "too remote or accidental" to convict Charlie.

2c. The initial analysis here is the same as in Example 2b. *Grossly negligent* medical treatment is generally not considered foreseeable or the natural and probable result of the defendant's conduct. Such a deviation from the standard of medical competency is unusual as a matter of human experience. Thus, it is an *independent* intervening cause that precludes a finding of proximate causation for Charlie.

Under the MPC there is a strong case for concluding that the grossly negligent medical treatment provided by Dr. Hopeless is too remote or accidental to fairly hold Charlie responsible. This will be a value judgment that the fact finder will have to make.

2d. (i) Charlie will argue that Dr. Choice was an independent intervening cause that was the direct cause of Edna's death. Charlie will claim that it was the act of disconnecting the respirator that caused Edna's death and, therefore, he cannot be convicted of a homicide charge because he did not cause the victim's death.

Some courts have determined that a physician is under no civil duty to provide extraordinary medical care (such as a respirator or other high-technology assistance) to prevent a patient dying from natural causes. Dr. Choice's disconnecting the respirator is not, therefore, the cause of Edna's death. Not interrupting fatal forces already at work does not generate criminal responsibility if there is no independent civil duty to do so. Charlie would be convicted of a homicide charge.

(ii) The analysis here is essentially the same as that in (i) above. The only difference is that Dr. Choice did not provide nutrition and hydration. Some jurisdictions classify these services as ordinary medical treatment that a physician has a legal duty to provide to an ill patient. If that is the case here, then Dr. Choice is criminally responsible for failing to provide these basic needs. Charlie has a stronger argument that Edna died from an independent intervening cause.

The prosecutor might then argue that *both* Charlie and Dr. Choice caused Edna's death. If she is successful, Charlie and Dr. Choice would both be concurrent causes, and each could be held criminally responsible for causing this death (but probably for different degrees of homicide).

3. At common law Jennifer is both the cause in fact and the proximate cause of Tara's death. Jennifer can easily be convicted of vehicular homicide.

The MPC would reach the same conclusion. Jennifer's driving is the "but for" cause of Tara's death. The analysis then turns to the culpability required under the relevant statute. Most vehicular homicide statutes require recklessness. The prosecutor should be able to prove that, while driving the car, Jennifer acted with conscious disregard toward a substantial and unjustifiable risk of a fatal car accident. Moreover, the victim was the very same person whom she put at risk and the actual result, Tara's death, was the very same risk that she contemplated.

Bob, by initiating and continuing to play car tag, satisfies the common law's cause in fact requirement. He might argue that Jennifer's driving is the only cause in fact; had she not driven recklessly, the accident would not have happened. Nonetheless, his conduct will probably be found also to have been a proximate cause of Tara's death. (Remember that there can be more than one proximate cause.) Thus, *both* Jennifer and Bob have legally caused Tara's death.

Jennifer's response to Bob's game of car tag is foreseeable because Bob knew she would continue to speed to catch him. Thus, it was foreseeable that either he or Jennifer might lose control of their respective vehicles and cause someone's death. Note that the foreseeability analysis here does not depend on what Bob subjectively expected or contemplated. Rather, it depends on what human experience indicates can happen. At common law proximate causation is not dependent on the actor's subjective awareness of risk or probable consequences.

Under the MPC Bob's driving satisfies the "but for" requirement of §2.03(1)(a). The analysis then focuses on the culpability required in the relevant statute. The prosecutor could establish that Bob acted with conscious disregard toward a substantial and unjustifiable risk that either he or Jennifer might lose control of their respective cars, resulting in a fatal accident. The actual outcome is the same as the contemplated outcome, and the result is not "too remote or accidental" as to justly blame Bob.

4.   Should the criminal law consider Juang a responsible moral agent who has caused her own death, thereby relieving Kim of any responsibility? Or is Kim responsible for Juang's taking her own life because he has rendered her irresponsible?

Normally, the law does not look beyond the last human agent in determining causation, particularly in suicide cases. Because life is precious, the law assumes that individuals will not take their own life. Only if the human agent is irresponsible or innocent is causation attributed to someone else. *Stephenson v. State*, 205 Ind. 141, 179 N.E. 633 (1932).

A prosecutor might persuade a jury that Kim's intentional conduct had done so much physical and psychological damage to Juang that, under the common law, she was rendered irresponsible. If successful, the prosecutor will have established that Kim proximately caused Juang's death, and the jury may convict Kim of a homicide charge.

Under the MPC Kim's conduct satisfies the "but for" requirement. Thus, the analysis turns to culpability. The actual harm here, Juang's death, is the same as that Kim intended. But is the result or method "too remote or accidental in its occurrence" to convict Kim? Kim intended Juang to die, but he did not anticipate or intend the actual manner of her death. That does not necessarily mean, however, that it is "too remote or accidental."

The prosecutor will argue that Kim realized Juang would suffer serious physical harm as a result of his conduct, and that disability, pain, and suffering were a likely consequence of a plunge from a high cliff. Thus, the causal connection between Kim's conduct and Juang's resulting physical and mental condition is sufficiently close and probable that Kim should be held responsible. It will be a close call for the jury to decide.

5.   The prosecutor will argue that Jack proximately caused Jill's death, claiming that Jill would not have died had Jack not started this chain of events by obtaining the heroin and giving it to Jill and that it was

foreseeable that the heroin could substantially and materially contribute to Jill's death.

Jack will respond that Jill killed herself, arguing that she was a responsible moral agent who committed the last act necessary to bring about her death. Thus, she is an independent intervening cause. Jack will also argue that she alone caused her own intoxication; thus, he did not cause her to be in this condition.

The prosecutor will reply that Jill's self-injection was intended or contemplated by Jack and was a foreseeable consequence of his buying heroin and bringing it back to Jill. She will also point out that Jack knew that Jill had been drinking when he gave her the heroin, and it is foreseeable that alcohol makes heroin use more risky.

This case could go either way. Some jurisdictions would find proximate causation on these facts and hold Jack responsible.[15] Others would consider Jill a responsible agent who caused her own death.

The Model Penal Code's "but for" causation is satisfied by Jack's purchasing the heroin and giving it to Jill. The actual result is the same result as that contemplated, though obviously not intended. The jury would have to decide if Jill's death from the heroin and alcohol consumption is too remote or accidental in its occurrence to hold Jack responsible. Because the MPC only requires "but for" causation, it would permit (though not require) a jury to convict Jack in this situation.

6. In charging Martin with felony murder (see Chapter 8), the prosecutor will argue that an arsonist creates a risk that a firefighter may die fighting the fire. Thus, this particular harm is, or should be, within Martin's contemplation and occurred during the course of the victim doing his job. Martin's setting the fire was the proximate cause of Sven's death.

Martin will respond that he did not proximately cause Sven's death. Sven should be considered an independent intervening cause of his own death because Sven would not have died if he had complied with the department's regulations. By disregarding two separate regulations, Sven acted negligently, or even with gross negligence, and such negligence by a professional firefighter is simply not foreseeable.

The court will probably conclude that an arsonist has no right to expect that a fire will be fought carefully, and that any negligence by a firefighter that contributes to his death does not preclude a finding of proximate causation.

Under the MPC Martin's conduct satisfies cause in fact. Though the MPC does not provide for felony murder, in analyzing causation the Code asks whether the causal agency for this harm is "too remote or

---

15. See, e.g., *State v. Wassil*, 233 Conn. 174, 658 A.2d 548 (1995).

accidental" in its occurrence to have a "just bearing" on Martin's responsibility. A jury could go either way in this case. It might find no causation here if it concluded that Sven acted in a very unprofessional and reckless manner. Or, angered by the death of a public servant in the course of his duties, the jury might want to blame Martin and, in order to achieve this goal, find that Martin did cause Sven's death and thus convict him of some form of homicide. Ultimately, causation in this case is a value judgment to be determined by the fact finder.

7. Nyguen would not be liable under a felony murder theory in most jurisdictions because neither he nor another co-felon killed an innocent person during the commission of a felony. (See Chapter 8.) Causation theory, however, would allow a conviction of Nyguen for proximately causing the death of Betty even though she was killed by a police officer trying to rescue her.

  By using Betty as a human shield, Nyguen satisfies cause in fact; but for his act, she would not have been killed. Moreover, by using her as a shield, Nyguen put Betty in harm's way. It was foreseeable that a police officer would try to rescue her from this dangerous situation by using deadly force against Nyguen. By keeping Betty so close to him while threatening her with imminent death, Nyguen started a chain of events, the natural and probable consequence of which was her accidental death.

  This example demonstrates how conduct that manifests extreme indifference to the value of human life that proximately causes the death of either a felon or an innocent person can generate responsibility for homicide. For a good example of this approach, see *Taylor v. Superior Court*, 3 Cal. 3d 578, 477 P.2d 131 (1970).

  Under MPC §210.2(1)(b) the prosecutor could argue that, in using Betty as a shield, Nyguen committed murder "recklessly under circumstances manifesting extreme indifference to the value of human life." To satisfy causation, she would prove that Nyguen's act was the "but for" cause of Betty's death and that, because the police often use deadly force to rescue hostages, the result was contemplated by Nyguen. Note that the MPC requires the prosecutor to prove culpability with respect to result in this example.

8a. Hal would have died in a few seconds ("splat") and he certainly would have been the direct cause of his own death in that event. Nonetheless, Julia has *directly* caused Hal's death because it was her shot that actually ended his life. Thus, under the common law her intent to kill Chet is "transferred" to Hal (See Chapter 4) and she can be convicted of intentional homicide. Even though the chance of Julia's shot hitting anyone else (let alone killing anyone else) other than Chet was a million in one, her actions satisfy the common law's causation requirement.

Under the MPC a jury could conclude that Julia has caused Hal's death because her errant shot caused the death of a "different" person than she intended. Because Julia has brought about a harm *equal to* the one she intended (the death of a human being), conviction and punishment would not be disproportionate to the harm she intended to cause. However, the MPC would also allow the jury to conclude that she did not cause Hal's death. The jury might decide that the causal mechanism of his death (Julia's shooting at Chet and killing Hal) was "too remote or accidental" to have a "just bearing" on her liability. What are the odds of anyone dying in this manner? And yet, Julia surely intended to kill someone. Should attitude or harm be more important? How would you vote as a juror?

8b. Cindy would argue that Julia is the "direct" cause of Hal's death. Furthermore, she would argue that the manner in which Hal died was absolutely unforeseeable and accidental. Thus, Julia was the *independent* intervening cause and Cindy can only be convicted of attempted murder.

The prosecutor would argue that this is a case of *concurrent* causation and that both Cindy and Julia caused Hal's death. He will argue that either Cindy's or Julia's conduct would have caused Hal's death and that Julia's conduct merely hastened an inevitable result set in motion by Cindy. Thus, this must be a case of two *independent* causal agents who must bear joint responsibility for causing Hal's death. The prosecutor probably has the better argument. Cindy intended to cause Hal's death. She should not escape responsibility simply because the particular harm she intended came about in such a bizarre and unexpected manner. But, it is a close call!

Under the MPC Cindy is a "but-for" cause of Hal's death; Hal would not have been in Judy's line of fire had Cindy not pushed him off the building. But was Judy's errant shot "too remote or accidental in its occurrence to have a just bearing" on Cindy's responsibility? One suspects that a jury would not let Cindy, the primary actor who set out to kill Hal, off the hook just because Judy was trying to kill someone else and did the job for her.

9. Alberto has acted with the premeditated intent to cause the death of Francesco. Thus, he satisfies the mens rea requirement of first-degree homicide. However, has he caused Francsesco's death? After all, Luca shot and killed Francesco; Alberto didn't.

Under the common law Alberto is the cause in fact of Francesco's death. If Alberto had not called Luca and lied to him about Maria's infidelity, Luca would not have killed Francesco. However, should the law look beyond the direct cause of Francesco's death, Luca, the last human actor and moral agent, to establish causation? Alberto might be held criminally responsible for proximately causing the death of Francesco. The prosecutor would argue that Luca's killing Francesco was the "natural and probable consequence" of Alberto's conduct. Because the intervening act of Luca was foreseeable (that is why Alberto lied to Luca), it does not break the chain of causal connection between the original act of Alberto and the subsequent harm.

If Alberto is found to have proximately caused Francesco's death, Alberto might argue that Luca acted in the heat of passion and, consequently, Luca could only be convicted of manslaughter. Alberto would then claim that *accomplice* liability limits his responsibility to the same crime committed by Luca, his principal. Depending on the law of complicity in this jurisdiction, that argument might succeed.[16] As a matter of *causation*, however, the question is simply whether Luca's intervening act was foreseeable; if it was, then it is a *dependent* intervening cause that does not preclude Alberto being held responsible.

Under MPC analysis Alberto may also have caused Francesco's death. Under §2.03 Alberto satisfies the "but for" requirement of subsection (1)(a). Under subsection (2)(a) the result that occurred is exactly the same as that purposed by Alberto. Thus, Alberto has caused the result.

(a) *The Death of Maria.* Alberto did not intend to cause Maria's death. Nonetheless, Alberto might be convicted of at least manslaughter. Because he knew that Luca was extremely jealous and violent where Maria was concerned, a strong argument can be made that he acted recklessly (with gross and callous disregard of the risk that Luca might also kill Maria) or negligently (he should have known of the substantial and unjustifiable risk that Luca might kill Maria). These mental states satisfy the respective mens rea requirements of manslaughter.

But has Alberto *caused* Maria's death? The prosecutor would argue that, because Alberto knew Luca had jealously assaulted Maria in the past, it was even more foreseeable that Luca might harm Maria rather than her alleged lover. Luca's act would then be a *dependent* intervening cause, which will not defeat a finding of proximate causation.

Under the MPC this is a more difficult problem. Alberto did not intend or contemplate Maria's death. However, is this a case in which the harm that occurred is different from the harm intended? Not really; after all, Francesco is dead. That harm is the same as that intended. Thus, Maria's death is not a case of "transferred intent," and §2.03(2)(a) probably does not apply. More likely, §2.03(b) applies. Maria's death is the same kind of harm as that intended by Alberto and, because Alberto knew of Luca's past jealous violence against Maria, Luca's killing Maria

---

16. For complicity, see Chapter 14.

is not "too remote or accidental in its occurrence to have a just bearing" on Alberto's liability.

(b) *The Death of Luca.* Luca's suicide, on the other hand, will probably be seen as an *independent* intervening causation that breaks the chain of causal connection between Alberto's conduct and this resulting harm. Alberto did not intend to kill Luca nor was the risk that Luca might kill himself foreseeable. Nothing in Luca's history indicated he might turn his jealous rage against himself.

The analysis under the MPC is the same as that for Maria's death in (a) above. However, because Alberto had no basis for anticipating that Luca might take his own life, a jury would probably conclude that the harm *is* "too remote or accidental in its occurrence" to hold Alberto liable. This would essentially be a value judgment for the jury to make.

10. Billy Jackson will argue that selling cigarettes to Rusty was the cause in fact and the proximate cause of his death. Billy will claim that Joe Camel knew cigarettes are dangerous to human health and that many smokers cannot break their "habit."

Joe will respond that the available evidence does not establish that lung cancer is a foreseeable result of smoking cigarettes. Moreover, Joe will maintain that Rusty was forewarned about any possible health risk and that, consequently, Rusty's decision to smoke and to continue smoking broke any causal chain that Federated may have put in motion by selling cigarettes.

This is a hard case. If the jury finds that lung cancer is a natural and probable result of smoking cigarettes and that nicotine is physically addictive, making it difficult for individuals to discontinue smoking, it might find that Federated and its president caused Rusty's death and return a homicide verdict.

In *Commonwealth v. Feinberg*, 433 Pa. 558, 253 A.2d 636 (1969), the defendant, who stocked and sold regular strength sterno (which contains methanol) to alcoholics on skid row, was convicted of 32 counts of manslaughter after selling industrial strength sterno, which contains a much higher percentage of methanol, to customers who then drank the product. The Pennsylvania Supreme Court held that the voluntary acts of the victims, though considered contributory negligence in a tort action, were not independent supervening causes in the criminal case.

11. Roberta has acted with the same mens rea as in Example 1, yet she has not caused Raoul's death. Roberta could be convicted of attempted murder, probably in the first degree. However, why should she be punished less severely than in Example 1? She acted with the same state of mind and took the last step she could to bring about the result. The fact that she did not actually kill Raoul was fortuitous. Only luck saved her from causing his death.

Some would argue that causing harm should not be an important consideration in determining the severity of punishment. Rather, the defendant's attitude toward causing harm and her conduct designed to bring it about should be the primary considerations. Others argue that the public is rightly angered by the fact that harm has occurred and that more severe punishment should be imposed in such cases.

8

Homicide

Overview

Homicide is defined by the common law as the unjustified and unexcused killing of a human being. Prior to the Model Penal Code, most American jurisdictions divided homicide into two major categories, *murder* or *manslaughter*, and then subdivided these categories to reflect differences in available punishments. Murder was divided into *first degree* (for which a defendant could be executed and *second degree* (which did not carry the death penalty). Manslaughter was viewed as a less serious killing and was not initially divided into degrees. However, over the years many states divided manslaughter into *voluntary* (or first degree) and *involuntary* (or second degree) manslaughter.

Human Being

The definition of homicide includes the killing of a "human being." This term was once self-evident, but current medical technology now raises questions about both the beginning and end points of life's temporal spectrum.

When Does Life Begin?

Death comes to fetuses just as it does to full-born persons. Most courts, reluctantly, have held that a viable fetus, even if the obvious target of a purposefully homicidal act, is not a "human being" within the meaning of the homicide statute. *Keeler v. Superior Court,* 2 Cal. 3d 619 (1970). But see *Commonwealth v. Cass*, 392 Mass. 700 (1984). A rarer question is whether a fetus, even at the moment of birth, qualifies as a "human being." Thus, in *People v. Chavez*, 77 Cal. App. 2d 621, 176 P.2d 92 (1947), *D* delivered her baby into a toilet bowl where it drowned. *D* testified that the baby did not cry, and that she did not tie its umbilical cord. The court held that the fetus became a "human being" after the child passed through the birth canal and took a breath; it was irrelevant that the baby may have been dead by the time the process was finished.[1]

These cases, though rare, raise serious questions about the degree to which the criminal law should broaden its net to capture persons who seem as evil and malevolent as persons already captured by the "normal rules." Against this goal is the general belief that criminal statutes should be construed narrowly, in order to avoid judicial expansion of legislative determinations of the proper scope of the criminal law. In the absence of legislative action, courts usually read the statutes narrowly. Legislatures, reacting to these decisions, have either broadened the definition of "person" to include fetuses or created a separate offense called "feticide," as did California after *Keeler*. Cal. Penal Code §187.

When Does Life End?

At the other end of life's path is the question of whether the victim of an unlawful act was "dead" (and hence no longer a "human being") before the defendant acted. In past centuries, death was assessed practically. The majority rule was that a "human being" ceases to exist once the heart stops functioning. The majority of states today, however, now define death as "brain death," although there are various definitions of this event.

Cause and Death

A related question arises as to whether a defendant's act "causes" death, particularly if the actual cessation of breathing is due to the intervention of a third party. Most of these causation issues were discussed in Chapter 3, but one aspect must be addressed here. In earlier days, when victims tended to die soon after an assault, the common law established a rule that any death that did not occur within a "year and a day" of the assault was not "caused" by the assault. In all likelihood this was medically correct. If the victim could survive for more than a year, it was at least arguable that something else

---

1. The question sometimes arises in nondeath cases. Thus, in *Johnson v. State*, 602 So. 2d 1288 (Fla. 1992), the mother, who was addicted to cocaine, was charged with delivering the drug through the umbilical cord to a "human being," her newly born child, in the 90 seconds between the time the child was "born" and the time the cord was severed.

(extraneous disease, incompetent medical assistance) had in fact caused the death. In such ambiguous circumstances, the better rule is to favor the defendant and find that the defendant's act did not cause the death. Modern medical technology, however, has again created problems. We can now extend, sometimes by years or decades, the "life" of a person who, in other times, clearly would have "died" at an earlier date. Courts confronted with cases of this kind have properly abolished the year-and-a-day rule as inconsistent with modern technology. The state of Washington, for example, has legislatively adopted a "three years and a day" rule as a compromise position.

Murder

"Original" Murder: Killing with "Malice Aforethought"

The common law and statutes of fourteenth-century England originally defined "murder" as a killing with "malice prepense (aforethought)." The words meant precisely what they suggested in ordinary English: an intentional, preplanned, deliberate killing, motivated by ill will (malice) toward the victim. Over a period of several centuries, however, judges redefined the term "malice aforethought" to encompass not only these calculated killings (often labeled "express" malice), but also those that resulted from extremely reckless or wanton conduct (often labeled "implied," "universal," or "constructive" malice). In this way the courts substantially broadened the legislature's net for "murderers." By the mid-nineteenth century, the term "malice aforethought" had come to mean in England any killing with

> (a) intention to cause the death of, or grievous bodily harm to, any person. . . .
> (b) knowledge that the act which causes death will probably cause the death of, or grievous bodily harm to, some person . . . although such knowledge is accompanied by indifference or by a wish that it may not be caused. . . .[2]

Thus, the term "malice aforethought" acquired a much broader meaning. It was no longer limited to ill will toward the victim or preplanned killings, as Parliament originally intended; it had been broadly "reinterpreted" by the courts to have little, if anything, to do with either malice or aforethought.

Part (a) of the definition above seems obvious as to why such persons might be labeled as serious offenders. People who *intend* to kill are arguably the "worst" killers and most deserving of the death penalty. Part (b) of the

---

2. J. Stephen, A Digest of the Criminal Law 161-162 (1887).

definition is less evident; not everyone who sets out to severely hurt someone by, for example, stabbing them in the arm, intends death. Perhaps in past centuries, when serious bodily harm often led to death because of inadequate medical treatment, an intent to kill could be inferred from any intent to inflict serious harm. That inference is less sound today.

The common law developed a set of romantic terms to describe the second kind of killings done with "malice aforethought," sometimes called *implied malice*. Persons who, though not intending to kill, nevertheless acted in a way that they knew created a very high risk of death, and not caring whether death occurred or not, were said to act with a "depraved and malignant mind" or to have a "heart regardless of social duty and fatally bent on mischief." Such, for example, was the case of a defendant who, for no apparent reason, fired a rifle into a train, killing (by mere fortuity) a trainman. Under this approach someone who knowingly creates a great risk of death generally, and actually kills someone, can be found to have acted with "malice aforethought" toward the victim.

In sum, both those who *wanted* to kill and those who engaged in very dangerous conduct that they actually foresaw almost surely would (and did) result in death could be convicted of murder with "malice aforethought."

Presumed Malice

Proving the mental state of the defendant is extraordinarily difficult, even if one can compel the defendant to testify. Prior to the end of the nineteenth century, criminal defendants were not allowed to testify in court (even if they wanted to), and current constitutional prohibitions preclude the prosecutor from compelling the defendant to testify. The common law therefore established several "presumptions" with regard to malice. Of these, two are of interest here. The first was that a person is "presumed" to intend the "natural and probable consequences of his act." The other was that a killing committed with a deadly weapon (defined as a weapon calculated to or likely to produce death or great bodily injury) was presumed to have been committed with malice. Although some courts today continue to rely on these doctrines, the better view is that these are not "presumptions" at all but merely permissive inferences, which the jury may use or disregard at its discretion. See *Bantum v. State*, 85 A.2d 741 (Del. 1952). See also Chapter 15.

Gradations of Murder

"First-Degree" Murder

After the American Revolution, many state legislatures, aware that English courts had expanded the meaning of "malice aforethought" to include those who, while not intending death, created a great risk of death, responded by dividing "murder" into two "degrees." These statutes provided the death penalty only for "first-degree" murders — that is, only those "murders"[3] that were "premeditated, willful and deliberate."[4] In so doing, state legislatures clearly intended to recapture the original meaning of "malice aforethought," that is, killings committed by individuals who (1) thought about killing their victim (premeditated), (2) brooded over it for some significant period of time (deliberated), and (3) then killed willfully.

As in England, however, many American courts quickly thwarted this ameliorative legislation by construing the term "premeditation" to encompass even split-second decisionmaking. Thus, in *State v. Arata,* 56 Wash. 185, 105 P. 227 (1909), the court declared that

> the law knows no specific time; if a man reflects upon the act a *moment antecedent* to the act, it is sufficient; the time for deliberation and premeditation need not be long. . . . [Emphasis added.]

Many courts upheld jury verdicts finding premeditation to occur in a matter of seconds even though the legislature probably did not intend to include such killings within the meaning of "premeditation." As a consequence, the death-eligible group of killers was once again judicially broadened. In recent years, an increasing number of courts, rejecting this expansion, has required a "reasonable period of time" to find premeditation or deliberation. In the well-known case of *People v. Anderson,* 447 P.2d 942 (Cal. 1968), the court listed three elements tending to show the requisite premeditation and deliberation — (1) planning activity, (2) motive, and (3) manner of killing — which would combine to establish that the defendant acted with a preconceived design. This is very close to the fourteenth-century view of what "malice prepense" meant.

This struggle between the judiciary and the legislature over which killers should be death-eligible is neither surprising nor difficult to explain. While the legislature must define general categories of offenders eligible for the death penalty, courts encounter specific instances where the defendant, though perhaps not fitting within the precise words of the legislation, falls

---

3. Some state statutes used the word "killing" rather than "murder." Although it was probably inadvertent, the distinction was relatively unimportant in most instances. However, in *People v. Aaron,* 409 Mich. 672 (1980), the court seized on this semantic difference to abolish judicially the doctrine of felony murder. See pages 149-156.

4. The first such statute was enacted in Pennsylvania in 1794 and was quickly followed by other states. The statutes also defined as first-degree murder killings by "lying in wait, torture, and poison." The first of these is virtually taken verbatim from the fourteenth-century statute first establishing malice prepense as the critical distinction for murder. All three types of killing require premeditation. It is difficult (though not impossible) to conceive of an intended *poisoning* that was not premeditated. And it is only slightly less possible to think of an *intentional* death by torture that does not require preplanning. One might conclude, therefore, that these phrases are superfluous, if not redundant.

within its spirit. As the court said about the defendant described above who, for no apparent reason, shot into a passing train:

> That man who can coolly shoot into a moving train . . . in which are persons guiltless of any wrongdoing toward him . . . is, if possible worse than the man who . . . waylays and kills his personal enemy.[5]

Confronted with persons they considered "as morally bad" (or as dangerous) as the killers clearly falling within the legislatively defined group, courts frequently construed the statute's words to meet their views. Because they could not expressly *say* they were "adding" a new category, they merely "redefined" the terms to encompass killers they saw as equally blameworthy (and dangerous).

"Second-Degree" Murder

The statutory division of murder into two "degrees" meant that second-degree murder became the "default" position. If a killing was murder (committed within the broadened notion of "malice aforethought") and was not premeditated, it was second degree. These killings were not capitally punishable, although they might result in a sentence of life imprisonment.

To determine under a statute dividing murder into two degrees whether a murder was first- or second-degree requires three steps:

1. Was the killing a "murder" (was it done with malice aforethought)?
2. If so, was it "premeditated, deliberate and willful"?
3. If yes, it was first-degree murder; if not, second-degree.

The Model Penal Code Approach

The Model Penal Code essentially agrees with the policy views of the nineteenth-century courts that no single set of general words describing an actor's state of mind can adequately encompass all the factors that should go into deciding whether to execute a particular killer.[6] Section 210 of the Code abolishes the distinction between first- and second-degree murder. Instead,

---

5. *Banks v. State*, 85 Tex. Crim. 165 (1917).

6. Although the Code provides that all "murderers" may be eligible for the death penalty, that penalty is not imposed on all murderers. Instead, the Code establishes a procedural scheme that requires specific findings on a list of "aggravating" *and* "mitigating" circumstances that must be considered in determining whether the killer should be sentenced to death. The aggravating factors, taken together, are intended to cover most of the killings that motivated earlier courts to interpret broadly the words ("premeditation and deliberation") of the earlier statutes, while not forbidding the death penalty because any single factor is missing. The list of mitigating factors is intended to cover most of those cases where a jury would usually decide that the defendant is not so blameworthy as to be sentenced to death. Because of several decisions by the United States Supreme Court on the constitutionality of the death

it characterizes as "death eligible" all killers who cause the death of another human being

1. purposely;
2. knowingly; or
3. recklessly under circumstances manifesting extreme indifference to the value of human life.

These words closely parallel the notions enunciated in the common law. Any "premeditated and deliberate" homicide would fit within the Code's definition of "purpose" or "knowing." The Code's third category can encompass those killers said to have a "malignant heart." On the other hand, the Code does not explicitly include the "intent to inflict serious bodily injury" category of murder (unless such intent can be said to imply recklessness under "extreme circumstances"). It is critical to remember that the Code's definition of "reckless" would require that the defendant *subjectively recognize* the risk of death. Even if the defendant is reckless, the death must *also* occur under "circumstances manifesting extreme indifference." If this is not true, and the defendant is "merely" reckless, the death is manslaughter, not murder. (See below.)

Some Further Thoughts

The common law's preoccupation with mens rea as "the" dividing line in grading homicides is not the only approach that could have been chosen. One might, for example, distinguish, even among premeditators, depending on (a) the victim;[7] (b) the method of killing; or (c) whether it was done for hire. Thus, a torturer of a two-year-old child or a premeditated killer of a police officer might well be seen as "worse" than a poisoner of a fifty-year-old man even though both killings are premeditated murder. Similarly, one could conclude that a reckless killer of an infant is more culpable or dangerous than one who poisons an adult who happens to be his worst enemy. The Code allows some of these factors to be considered in sentencing.

Although historically the availability of the death penalty was thought to require gradations among offenders, even some countries that have abolished the penalty have consciously decided to retain the label "murderer" because of its association with the "worst" kind of killer.[8] The argument is

---

penalty, a significant number of states that have the death penalty have adopted a procedure similar to that recommended by the Code.

7. The word "murder" actually stems from a fine (the "murdrum") imposed by the first Norman kings of England upon a town if the town refused to disclose the murderer of a Norman. If the victim was proven to be a Saxon, however, no fine was imposed. Thus, "the worst kind of killing" was initially designated by victim rather than by mens rea.

8. N. Cameron & S. France, The Bill in Context, in Essays on Criminal Law in New Zealand 1, 4-5 (1990).

that criminal law does and should make moral distinctions among offenders, and that simply calling all criminal killings "homicide" would weaken the law's moral status.

EXAMPLES

1. Karen learns that her worst enemy, Rick, is coming to town in two days. She buys a gun and decides to kill Rick as he steps off the train. Two days later, she takes the gun with her to the station, loads it there, and walks up to Rick and shoots him at point-blank range in the head five times, killing him instantly. What level of homicide?

2. Karen has watched her brother, Rick, die slowly and painfully from cancer over the last six months. Totally distraught, she buys a gun and decides to kill Rick. Two days later, she walks into the hospital room, deceives a nurse into leaving the room, and then shoots Rick at point-blank range in the head five times, killing him instantly. What level of homicide?

3. Geraldo is waiting for a bus one day when he sees a four-year-old boy nearby, walking on the sidewalk. He instantly pushes the boy off the sidewalk into the path of an oncoming car (which Geraldo saw), killing him. Is this murder? What level?

4. John and Evelyn have a heated dispute over John's excessive golfing, an issue that has divided their marriage for years. After five hours, John, more in frustration than anything, reaches into his golf bag and pulls out a five iron. After ten seconds, he swings it once at Evelyn and hits her in the head, killing her instantly. Is this murder?

5. Widgets Inc. manufactures widgets. A side-product of the process is "gooey," which is extremely toxic and has been declared by the state Environmental Protection Agency to be a hazardous waste. Daniel, vice president of Widgets, knows of gooey's characteristics but, needing money, decides to dispose of the gooey by dumping it into a nearby river and pocket the money that is otherwise earmarked for disposal processes. Six months later, Billy, age 5, dies from swimming in the river; an expert will testify that gooey, still present in the river, caused Billy's death. Dan is charged with Billy's death. What result?

6. Reba, aware that she is "drunk," nevertheless attempts to drive home. She weaves across a median and collides with another car head on, killing two occupants. Of what level of murder, if any, is she guilty?

7. Jack is a telephone operator for 911 Emergency Services. He agrees with Fast and Speedy Ambulance Service that he will divert at least 20 calls a day to them, for $50 a call. This arrangement continues for two months, with no ill effects. One day, Jack receives a call from Joseph Johnson, who screams over the phone: "My wife is having trouble

breathing. Please get down here soon!!" Jack obtains basic information, and concludes that the situation is not as bad as Johnson believes. Rather than calling the nearest ambulance, Jack diverts the call to Fast and Speedy who this time isn't. Johnson's wife dies. Assuming that the prosecutor can establish causation, of what crime is Jack guilty, if any?

EXPLANATIONS

1. Karen intended to kill, and thus under the common law has "malice aforethought" and a "depraved mind" (not to mention heart). She is thus guilty of at least second-degree murder. Because she has planned the killing, this is the paradigm case of first-degree murder. The jury may readily find that she premeditated the event, deliberated and mulled it over, and then willfully killed. She is thus guilty not merely of murder but of first-degree murder. Under the Model Penal Code, Karen has acted "purposely" and is therefore guilty of murder.

2. This case is intended to be almost precisely the same as that in Example 1 to illustrate a point: The "premeditation" formula sometimes is *over*-inclusive as well as *under*-inclusive in assessing moral blame. *This* Karen is a good example of someone who thought for a long period of time about taking life before acting and thus "premeditated." Under the common law she would be found guilty of first-degree murder and of murder under the Model Penal Code. But Karen's premeditation does not indicate that she is a "wicked" or "depraved" person. On the contrary, she has tried to do the right thing (as she saw it) and has, arguably, acted from the best of motives. (See Chapter 4.) There is something jarring about treating her as equally "culpable" or equally "bad" as Karen in Example 1, no matter how one feels about euthanasia as a general matter. We will explore and explain this tension at various points in the book, especially in the materials on "new excuses" (Chapter 17). However, as the law now stands, Karen is a first-degree murderer and may be executed.

3. It is unlikely that the legislature intended such a killing to fall within the term "premeditated." Indeed, it is precisely because this term fails to capture such killers that nineteenth-century American courts often declared that juries could conclude that a person premeditated "in an instant." See, e.g., *People v. Waters*, 118 Mich. App. 176 (1982), in which the defendant, a youth armed with a gun, became annoyed with the victim's husband. He fired his gun into the victim's car once and then within five seconds, but with both hands on the pistol, fired the gun a second time, killing the victim. The trial court found premeditation, which was upheld on appeal.

    Caveat: Merely because the jury *could* find premeditation does not mean it must. And mere time alone, in the absence of other factors, may not be sufficient even to allow a jury finding of premeditation. Thus, in *State v. Bingham*, 105 Wash. 2d 820 (1986), the defendant spent five minutes strangling his victim. The (very divided) court, however, said that there was no other evidence of premeditation, and that "time alone," without more, would not support such a finding.

As already noted, the Model Penal Code eliminates the concept of "premeditation" precisely because of these ambiguities. The Code's formulation is significantly more helpful here. A jury could easily find "purpose" or "recklessness under circumstances manifesting extreme indifference to the value of human life." Whether the death penalty would then be imposed would depend on a series of factors rather than merely one.

4. This is a difficult case. Under the common law, a jury could find that John intended to kill or seriously injure Evelyn, or that he "thought about the risks involved and went ahead anyway," thereby demonstrating a "depraved heart." He therefore has "malice aforethought" and is guilty of common law murder. But did he premeditate so as to be guilty of "first-degree murder" under American statutes? As in Example 3, John's ten seconds is probably sufficient time to allow a jury to find not merely intent but premeditation. In a similar case, a Pennsylvania court found the defendant guilty of first-degree murder and sentenced him to life in prison. *Commonwealth v. Carroll*, 412 Pa. 525 (1963).

    Under the Model Penal Code, "premeditation" is not the key. The jury could easily find "purpose" and thus render the defendant eligible for the death penalty. And they could even more readily find that John was "reckless under circumstances manifesting extreme indifference to the value of human life." Who said golf was not a dangerous sport?

5. Clearly, Daniel is not guilty of first-degree murder under the common law. He did not intend, much less premeditate, the death of anyone. Whether he had a "depraved heart" is less clear. He knew of "some" risk, perhaps even a substantial risk, that someone might be injured. However, that might not qualify as actually foreseeing that death might "probably" result.

    Under the MPC, the result is likely to be the same. Even assuming that there was a "substantial risk" of death, it is not obvious that Daniel foresaw the risk as substantial and therefore "consciously disregarded" it. However, if this part of the Code's test were met, since Daniel was aware that the substance was potentially dangerous to human life, he could be found to have acted under circumstances "manifesting extreme indifference to human life" as required by §210 of the Code.

    Alternatively, under the common law "felony murder" doctrine,

Daniel might be found guilty of murder if his failure to follow EPA disposal methods qualified as a felony. See the next section.

6. This would almost certainly not have qualified as "depraved heart" murder under earlier views. However, an increasing number of courts, outraged by the number of highway fatalities caused by drunk drivers, have allowed second-degree murder charges to go to the jury, at least where it can be shown that the defendant was "excessively" drunk and had been warned and cautioned about his driving. See, e.g., *Pears v. State*, 672 P.2d 903 (Alaska App. 1983).

7. Is this common law murder? Does Jack have "malice aforethought,"—a mind "disregardful of social duty"? Under the Model Penal Code terms, is the risk "substantial" enough to warrant imposition of liability for murder? Under either regime, this is surely a jury question, and a jury could conclude that Jack must have considered the fact that he is involved in a business that literally involves life and death decisions, and must have considered the risk that something like this would happen.

Felony Murder

Introduction

Although murder in the common law generally required "malice aforethought," two kinds of slaying were labeled murder even without such a mens rea. One, the killing of an officer in resisting arrest, will not be discussed in these materials. The other is an infamous rule called the "felony murder" rule. Of dubious origin, the felony murder rule, as usually stated at its broadest possible form, declares:

any death occurring during the course of a felony is murder

The rule in this broad form has been called "a monstrous doctrine," 3 J. Stephen, History of the Criminal Law of England 75 (1883). The doctrine imposes liability (and perhaps capital punishment) for murder whether a felon kills intentionally, recklessly, negligently, or even non-negligently. It is in fact a form of strict liability.

One explanation for this harsh rule is the notion of "transferred intent" —the defendant's intent to engage in the felony is "transferred" to the death. This use of the transferred intent doctrine, however, is problematic at best, since it usually refers to transferring an established intent from one victim to another (A intends to kill B, but the bullet misses and kills C, A's closest friend). Perhaps when all felonies were capitally punishable, transferring one's intent to commit one capital felony to another capital felony might have made some sense. This explanation, however, is no longer applicable, since the penalty for all non-homicidal felonies is less than death.

The primary philosophical explanation given for the rule is that it will deter felonies. However, even Justice Holmes, a prime believer in deterrence, declared that threatening to hang at random one chicken thief out of every thousand would carry more deterrence and be just as sensible. O. Holmes, The Common Law 58 (1881). Moreover, it is difficult to understand how such a rule "deters" negligent homicides which, by definition, the defendant is not contemplating.

Restrictions on the Doctrine: "Cause" Questions

Most courts have shared the view that the doctrine is too broad and have found ways to limit its application.

As originally understood, the felony murder doctrine applied to "any" death that "occurred" during the felony. This obviously clashed with notions of causation (discussed in detail in Chapter 7), and the courts battled mightily with these questions in the last half of the 20th century. The cases arise where, while *D* is committing a felony (e.g., a robbery), the actual victim is killed by someone other than the *D* or his accomplice. Thus, in the classic cases, *D* and *C* attempt to hold up a grocery store and

1. *V* (the intended robbery victim) or *P* (a police officer responding to the crime) kills *D*'s accomplice, *C*;
2. *V* or *P* kills an innocent bystander (*IB*);
3. *D* grabs *IB* and uses her as a "shield," during which *V* or *P* kills *IB*.

Obviously, *D* is "a" cause of the death: "But for" the attempted robbery, *C* or *IB* would be alive. However, not even tort law rests liability on mere but-for causation. There is always the issue of proximate cause. In the context of felony murder, the courts have used different approaches, although ultimately the results are similar. In most states, *D* is liable only in Case 3, and possibly not even then, under the felony murder theory.

The "Proximate Cause" Theory

As indicated in Chapter 7, courts have wrestled with whether criminal liability should *ever* be predicated on tort causation concepts. Although some courts attempted to apply the tort notion of "proximate cause" to the situations discussed here, that effort has proven largely frustrating and unfruitful for several reasons. First, the elusive quality of "foreseeability" raises serious questions itself. Second, the use of an objective standard in assessing criminal *guilt* seems undesirable. In a famous series of decisions,[9] the Pennsylvania Supreme Court first adopted and then rejected the "proximate cause" approach, although it is still used in some jurisdictions.

The "In Furtherance" or "Agency" Theory

Courts have also required that the killing be "in furtherance" of the felony. See, e.g., *People v. Washington*, 402 P.2d 130 (Cal. 1965). This obviously eliminates Case 1, where D's accomplice is killed, thus making the felony more difficult to accomplish. A similar notion is the "agency theory," which draws its theoretical base from accomplice doctrine (discussed in Chapter 14). A person is responsible only for his own actions or those who are acting with him in the felony and who are, therefore, his "agents." If C had killed *IB*, D would be liable because C is D's agent. But neither V nor P is D's agent. Although these two approaches usually come to the same conclusion, there is some possibility of a conflict in strange situations. Thus, if *IB* or V shoots an officer who is about to thwart the robbery, the killing may in fact further the criminal purpose, although *IB* is obviously not D and C's agent. The most obvious way around this tension is to say that while *IB*'s acts *did* further the crime, they were not *intended* to be "in furtherance thereof."

In other states, the result may depend on who fired the first shot. This may be a rational result on the basis of cause. After all, one who starts a gun battle may anticipate the likelihood that others will return fire and misaim. However, that explanation would also hold if V fires first: Store owners may reasonably react without waiting to see if they are killed.

Justified vs. Excused Killings

Still other courts have argued that D should not be liable for C's death because the policeman or the robbery victim was justified in killing C. D is liable, however, for the death of *IB* or V because that death is not justifiable but excusable. (See Chapter 15.) Thus, since C's death is *desirable*, D should not be held liable for it. But the death of *IB* or V is not *desirable*, and D should be held accountable.

This is a misunderstanding of the distinction between excuse and justification approaches. An act is justified depending not on its results but on the circumstances under which it occurred. Thus, when V shoots at D but hits *IB*, it is V's *act* of shooting, not the result, that is either justified or

---

9. *Commonwealth v. Almeida*, 362 Pa. 596 (1949); *Commonwealth v. Redline*, 391 Pa. 486 (1958); *Commonwealth ex rel. Smith v. Meyers*, 438 Pa. 218 (1970).

excused, not the result. Whether the bullet hits *IB, C, D,* or *X* should be irrelevant.

The Shield Cases: Exception to an Exception to an Exception

However the courts decide these cases, they all agree that in the "shield" case (Case 3 above), *D* is liable. Thus, in *State v. Canola,* 73 N.J. 206 (1977), the court, while holding that *D* could not be liable for the death of a co-felon by the intended victim of a robbery, declared in dictum that the result would be different if the deceased were used as a shield. Although this result can be easily explained on a "risk-generating" theory of mens rea (see below), the court did not attempt to so rationalize the result.

The Mens Rea Approach

Most persons whose "inherently dangerous" felonies result in unintended deaths can nevertheless be found to have acted with a "depraved heart" or (in MPC terms) "recklessly under circumstances manifesting extreme indifference to the value of human life." That is certainly true in most armed robberies, for example, where a jury might well find that a defendant not only should have been, but was, aware that putative victims of such crimes may respond with force, including deadly force, rather than submit, and undertook that risk when committing the crime.

Other Restrictions

In addition to resolving the issues of causation, American courts by the middle of the twentieth century had established other restrictions on the felony murder doctrine as well:

1. The killing must be done "during" the felony.
2. Neither person-endangering felonies nor "non-dangerous" felonies can be the basis of a felony murder charge.

Duration of the Felony: Time Matters

The felony murder rule applies while a defendant is attempting a crime or escaping from the scene. Though courts have grappled with how long an "escape" may take, it is clear that a death occurring days after the felony takes place is not covered by the felony murder rule. Courts have often spoken of the felony "coming to rest" or the defendant having obtained "temporary respite" or having found a "safe haven."

Thus, if *A* robs a store and, while exiting the store, pushes *VI,* who dies from the fall, the death is said to occur "during" the felony. If, however, *A* returns to his house, sits an hour, and then, hearing the police come to the front door, runs through the back door, pushing *V2*, who dies from the fall, the death does not occur "during" the felony, and the homicide is not felony murder.

Limitations on the Predicate Felony

Two limitations are placed upon which felonies can be the basis of the doctrine.

(1) "Merger" (or "Independent Felonious Purpose") Doctrine. This doctrine states that the *predicate felony must not be one involving personal injury* but have a purpose other than inflicting harm. The explanation for this limitation is easier to understand than to apply. If, for example, manslaughter could be used as a basis for the felony murder rule, there would be no more manslaughter convictions, since every such death would become a felony murder. The application of this doctrine becomes more difficult when the underlying felonies are less clearly life-threatening. Most courts agree that if the underlying felony is assault or mayhem, the merger occurs. Thus, in *People v. Smith*, 678 P.2d 886 (Cal. 1984), the court held that a mother who intentionally beat her child could not be held for the resulting unintended death *under the felony murder doctrine*.[10] In more difficult cases, the courts have been divided. Thus, California holds that if *D* breaks into a building with the precise purpose of assaulting *V*, the resulting burglary cannot be the predicate of a felony murder charge. *People v. Sears*, 2 Cal. 3d 180 (1970). Most states disagree. However, only a few jurisdictions refuse to acknowledge the limitation at all.

(2) "Inherently Dangerous Felony" Rule. By far the most important limitation, and very difficult to apply, is the "inherently dangerous felony" rule, which states that the felony can only be used as the basis of a conviction if the defendant was engaged in a felony that created serious risk of death. This limitation has two variations.

1. "dangerous" as defined *in the abstract* by the statute;
2. "dangerous" *as perpetrated*.

The first of these approaches looks only at how the felony in question is perpetrated "in most cases." If, most of the time, it is not dangerous to human life, then it is not considered dangerous "in the abstract," even if, on occasion, a defendant does commit it so as to endanger life. An infamous

---

10. This does *not* mean that the mother could not be convicted of "depraved heart" murder.

case is *People v. Phillips,* 64 Cal. 574, 414 P.2d 353 (1966), in which a chiropractor, knowing that his 8-year-old patient was dying of cancer of the eye, continued to deceive her parents that he could cure her. Upon her death, he was charged with (1) grand larceny and (2) felony murder. The Supreme Court of California held that only felonies "inherently dangerous in the abstract" could be used for this doctrine and that grand larceny "in the abstract" is not a dangerous felony. It could therefore not be the basis of a charge of felony murder.

This approach has several problems. First, since there is no evidence at trial to determine how a felony is perpetrated "normally," judges may guess at the way in which "this crime" is usually perpetrated. Second, it can create major difficulties when the legislature combines multiple offenses in one statute. Thus, for example, in *People v. Patterson,* 49 Cal. 3d 15 (1984), the defendant furnished cocaine to a friend, who died of an overdose. Defendant's act violated a statute that prohibited "selling, transporting, administering or furnishing" nearly one hundred different dangerous controlled substances, including marijuana, heroin, and cocaine. The court had to decide what "the felony" was: (1) all 400 (or so) of these acts; (2) each specific kind of conduct with respect to all the listed drugs; (3) all acts with respect to a specific drug; (4) each act with regard to each drug. The court chose the last approach and asked, in the case, whether *furnishing cocaine* was an inherently dangerous felony in the abstract.[11]

The court then had to face the further problem of deciding what test should be used in deciding this question. The court rejected a standard that would have found the crime "inherently dangerous" if there were a "substantial likelihood" of death. Instead, the court selected a test requiring a "high probability" of death. The dissent argued (almost surely correctly) that if the majority's test is to be based on statistical probabilities, it essentially nullified the doctrine, since *no* felony carries with it the "high probability" of death as a side result.[12]

The alternative approach asks whether the felony was dangerous "as

---

11. Some states have chosen a different route. For example, New Jersey provides that a person who dispenses any controlled drug "[i]s strictly liable for a death which results from the injection, inhalation or ingestion" of the drug. N.J.S.A. 2C:35-9 (upheld in *State v. Maldonado,* 137 N.J. 536 (1994)).

12. The drafters of the Model Penal Code cited statistics showing that .59 percent of all robberies, .35 percent of rapes, .0036 percent of burglaries, and .019 percent of auto thefts resulted in homicides. More recent statistics support these data. In 1975, for example, New Jersey statistics found that .41 percent of robberies resulted in death. The United States Department of Justice Bureau of Justice Statistics for 1994 show that of all violent crimes, only 20 percent resulted in any injury at all, and that only 1 percent of all victims required any hospitalization. In 1992, less than a third of robbery victims were injured, and only 3 percent required medical treatment. See Moran, FBI Scare Tactics, *New York Times,* May 7, 1996, at A23.

perpetrated." Thus, in *Phillips,* supra, the defendant clearly perpetrated the felony of grand larceny in a way to endanger the life of his patient, even if grand larceny usually does not endanger life. However, this approach makes the felony murder doctrine virtually superfluous. If the jurors find that the defendant perpetrated the felony in question in a dangerous way, they can surely find that he was aware of this risk and acted recklessly and with a depraved heart. Such a finding establishes mens rea by itself and makes the felony murder rule unnecessary. Indeed, in *Phillips,* the defendant was reconvicted on retrial solely on the basis of depraved heart murder.

These two limitations together, or separately, narrowly restrict (some would say essentially abolish) the felony murder doctrine. When a defendant engages in a felony that is "dangerous in the abstract" (such as armed robbery or rape or burglary), a jury could easily find that he was reckless (or had a malignant heart) with regard to the risk of death. *People v. Wilson,* 1 Cal. 3d 431 (1969). And even if the felony is not one "dangerous in the abstract" but only "as perpetrated," the jury may well find the requisite mens rea for murder, as it did in the retrial of *Phillips.* See also *People v. Washington,* 62 Cal. 2d 777 (1965).

No jurisdiction follows every limitation, and there is an endless variety of mixing these limitations together. However, if they were all joined in a specific jurisdiction, there would be little left of the doctrine.

In sum, the courts have generally been critical of the doctrine, and many limit its application to cases where the mens rea for murder could be found in any event. Only in the truly rare cases involving inherently dangerous felonies carried out in a nondangerous way is the full impact of the doctrine likely to be put to the test.

Despite the virtually unanimous criticism by legal scholars, and the willingness of courts to invent limitations upon its reach, however, the felony murder rule is still viable in all but a few states. A few legislatures have repealed it by statute, and one court[13] has judicially abandoned it. Even the Model Penal Code version (see below) has only been adopted by a few jurisdictions. The tenacity of the doctrine probably has several explanations. First, there *is* an intuition that persons engaged in felonies, particularly very risky felonies, should be held responsible if they commit a greater harm than they anticipated. See the discussion of the "greater crimes" theory in Chapter 6. Second, we are willing to place on the prosecution the burden of proving mens rea with regard to death when the defendant has not shown himself to be "criminal" or "evil" in some other way. We recognize that an erroneous conclusion would imprison a totally innocent person. However, when the defendant has already demonstrated a mens rea of ignoring the mores and laws, we are less willing to cede that benefit of the doubt. See gen-

---

13. *People v. Aaron,* 409 Mich. 672 (1980).

erally Tomkovicz, The Endurance of the Felony-Murder Rule: A Study of the Forces That Shape Our Criminal Law, 31 Wash. & Lee L. Rev. 1429 (1994).

Statutory Felony Murder: The Interplay of Courts and Legislatures

The picture is even more complex. In the United States, where murders are divided into "degrees," legislatures have typically listed a number of felonies that can serve as the predicate for "first-degree" murder. These usually include rape, kidnapping, robbery, arson, and burglary. Individual state statutes may include others as well. But what of "other" felony murders? Under the common law (and by inference therefore in most states), these are "murders." By default, since they are not included in the statutory provision, they are "second-degree" murders.

Several difficult questions are raised by these facts. As suggested, the courts in many states have declared that certain felonies, even though listed in the "first-degree" statutory provision, *cannot* serve as the predicate for a murder conviction (much less a first-degree murder conviction) because those crimes either (1) are not inherently dangerous in the abstract or (2) have no independent felonious purpose other than physical harm. Do such holdings violate, or at least jeopardize, separation of powers?

Another way of looking at this question is to try to define the constitutional limits on a state legislature's ability to define crimes. Could a state legislature, for example, declare that any homicide occurring during jaywalking would be capitally punished? Additionally, in recent years, numerous attacks have been leveled at the doctrine on the ground that the felony murder doctrine generally, and most specifically with regard to the statutory version, establishes a presumption of mens rea, which is at least arguably violative of the due process clause. See Chapter 15. Courts have rejected these arguments but have pointed out that the felonies to which the doctrine is generally restricted are all (or nearly all) ones that could lead to a conclusion of mens rea in any event. Were the legislature expressly to apply the doctrine to an unquestionably non-inherently-dangerous, non-person-endangering felony without the other limiting doctrines as well, the courts might confront a different, and more testing, constitutional problem.

The Model Penal Code Approach

In accord with most judicial and academic criticism, the Model Penal Code severely limits the doctrine, allowing its application only in cases involving robbery, rape, arson, burglary, kidnapping, or felonious escape. Even then, the Code raises only a *presumption* that the defendant was murderously reckless with regard to the possibility of death. That presumption is rebuttable by the defendant. Under the Code, once a defendant produces sufficient evidence to raise an issue on which there is a presumption, the prosecution must then prove the presumed fact (mens rea) beyond a reasonable doubt. It is fair to say that the Code effectively abolishes the doctrine in the vast majority of cases. Most legislatures that have otherwise adopted the MPC have rejected its view here.

England, the originator of the rule, statutorily abolished it in 1957. Eng. Homicide Act, 1957, 5&6 Eliz. 2, c.11, §11. State legislatures, while not following the Code on this question, have also limited the doctrine. See, e.g., N.Y. Penal Law §125.25(3), which has been adopted by several states.[14]

EXAMPLES

1a. Ashley walks into Mom and Pop's grocery with a gun and says "Give me your money." Pop refuses, and she shoots him six times at point-blank range. She is charged with murder. Is it?

1b. On her way to the grocery store, but several blocks before she gets there, Ashley trips and falls, the gun discharging and killing a pedestrian. Is this murder?

1c. Ashley attempts the hold-up, but Pop shoots first, killing Zuzu, a customer in the store. Murder?

1d. Pop shoots at Ashley and misses, whereupon Ashley takes Zuzu hostage, using her as a shield. Thereafter, (a) Pop or (b) a police officer responding to the call shoots at Ashley, killing Zuzu instead. Murder by Ashley? By Pop or the officer?

2. Russ, a bank teller, decides one day to embezzle $50,000 from the bank. As he walks out of the bank with the money in his briefcase, he non-negligently slips on a bank pen left on the floor by some customer and falls into Jezebel, the bank guard, whose gun discharges, killing her. Is Russ guilty of any level of homicide?

3. Helen, a burglar, has decided to burglarize a warehouse. She has "cased" the place for three weeks and is sure that everyone leaves by 10 p.m. On the night in question, she double-checks the parking lot and waits

---

14. That statute provides that the defendant may plead an affirmative defense in a felony murder case if he can prove that he "(a) did not commit the homicidal act or in any way solicit, request, command, importune, cause or aid the commission thereof; and (b) was not armed with a deadly weapon, or any instrument, article or substance readily capable of causing death or serious physical injury and of a sort not ordinarily carried in public places by law abiding persons; and (c) had no reasonable ground to believe that any other participant was armed with such a weapon, instrument, article or substance; and (d) had no reasonable ground to believe that any other participant intended to engage in conduct likely to result in death or serious physical injury."

until 2 a.m., just in case anyone has stayed late. She then breaks into the building by smashing a window and jumping through. As she lands, her foot hits the windpipe of Harry, a homeless person who has sneaked in through the back door and is sleeping there. Harry dies. She is charged with murder. What result?

4. Zeke, a cocaine dealer, sells Gonzo, one of his regular purchasers, enough cocaine for six days. Gonzo takes the cocaine home and, in a fit of depression or pique, consumes all six days' supply in one hit and dies. Will Zeke be guilty of murder?

5. Charles Keater perpetrates a massive securities fraud on thousands of people, inducing them to invest millions of dollars in areas he knows are speculative at best and fraudulent at worst. Two of these investors, having lost their life savings in this scam, commit suicide. Is Keater a murderer?

6a. Larry burns down his house for the insurance money. Hortense, a firefighter called to the scene, is killed while fighting the fire. Has Larry murdered Hortense?

6b. Same facts, except that Hortense's actions are negligent.

7. Jethro, envious of Pete's new Picasso, douses it with gasoline and sets it afire. The fire spreads, and Patricia, Jethro's wife, is killed in the fire. Jethro is charged with felony murder under a statute that defines destruction of property as a felony, committed by "exploding, shredding, or otherwise disposing of or damaging, personal property." What result?

8. Dave sees an SUV sitting outside a convenience store, with the motor running. He jumps in and throws the car into reverse. At that moment, a woman runs out screaming: "You can have the car, just let me have my son." Dave then notices, for the first time, that there is a 5-year-old in a car seat in the back. The woman tries to take the child, but becomes entangled in the seat belt. Dave hits the gas, and the car speeds forward, the child hanging half out the car, and the woman running along side yelling. When the car finally stops, and Dave runs out, the child is dead. Has Dave committed murder? And — for a preview of things to come — if Dave were acting under instructions from a car theft ring, or was a conspirator in such a ring, would the leader of the ring, or Dave's co-conspirators be liable as well?

9. John and Henry conspire to embezzle money from the corporation for whom they work by taking monies that should be used to pay for proper disposition of hazardous wastes, instead dumping the wastes into a river. Allyson is killed by the wastes. Are John and Henry murderers?

EXPLANATIONS

1a. This is the most obvious use of the felony murder doctrine. Ashley is clearly involved in an inherently dangerous felony, the killing is "in furtherance" of the felony, and it occurs during its perpetration. It is also causally linked to the felony. In most jurisdictions this will be a first-degree murder because it is a felony listed in the first-degree murder provision. But we don't need the felony murder doctrine here. Ashley has killed with premeditation (common law) and purposely (MPC).

1b. Ashley may be liable because she killed a pedestrian as she was on her way to commit a robbery. This, however, stretches the limits of the duration doctrine, since the danger here comes simply from Ashley's carrying a weapon; the robbery has not yet "begun" in that sense. That is, suppose that Ashley were not intending to rob the store, but merely carrying an illegal gun, and killed a pedestrian in the same way, because of tripping. Is carrying the gun in a public place sufficiently dangerous to warrant *murder* liability when the gun unexpectedly discharges?

1c. The difficult questions are Examples 1c and 1d, where *someone other*
1d. *than the felon* kills someone else. In Example 1c, the courts are mixed. In Example 1d, virtually all the courts, either in holdings or dicta, are in agreement that Ashley may be held liable. The problem is that no explanation for liability here can be consistent with a finding of no liability in Example 1c: The shooting here is equally not in furtherance of the felony, and it is equally justified (or not) as the shooting in 1c. And even if these inconsistencies are resolved (or ignored), the reason that Ashley is liable under the felony murder doctrine rather than as a "straightforward murderer" is not clear. The Model Penal Code would address the problem as one of cause, not of felony murder. See Chapter 7.

2. This is intended to demonstrate the clearly contrasting case to Example 1a. The typical kind of horrible hypothetical raised by opponents, it employs the broadest statement of the felony murder doctrine to demonstrate its irrationality. The death has occurred "during" the perpetration of "a" felony. The felony is causally related to the death. If the doctrine were not limited in some way, opponents argue, Russ would be guilty not only of embezzlement but of murder. Thus, "the inherently dangerous" requirement is imposed. Without this requirement, Russ might be liable for murder even though he was totally non-negligent with regard to any risk that death would occur. And though it does seem harsh to hold Russ for murder, that argument only urges limitations, not abolition, of the doctrine. Despite the fact that critics have used such horribles over the centuries in attacking the doctrine, they have not pointed to a single appellate, reported, opinion in which the courts have applied the doctrine to such a situation. Under the MPC, Russ is not liable for the death. Only a few felonies will even serve as a possible predicate for felony murder, and embezzlement is not among them.

3. We saw this fact pattern back in Chapter 4 in the context of mens rea

and concluded that Helen had no mens rea with regard to Harry's death. Now, however, we add the doctrine of felony murder. Helen has arguably committed felony murder. Burglary is one of those felonies that most courts have held to be "inherently dangerous" *in the abstract*. Thus, even though she is unarmed and has been extraordinarily careful not to endanger life in committing burglary *as perpetrated*, Helen may be found guilty of felony murder. And in most states this would be first-degree felony murder and death-eligible. It is possible to argue that the death here was not "in furtherance" of the felony, and therefore the application of the felony murder rule is inapt. Under the MPC, there is a presumption in any burglary that the defendant acted with reckless indifference to the value of human life. But the presumption is rebuttable, and Helen would have no difficulty here rebutting that presumption. Moreover, since the passage of the MPC, the Supreme Court has held that it is unconstitutional to put the burden of proof as to any element on the defendant. See Chapter 15.

4. Zeke may be liable for felony murder in some jurisdictions, which have declared drug transactions (or sales of specific drugs) "inherently dangerous" in the abstract. This is a difficult result to accept, since hundreds of thousands of sales are consummated every day with relatively few deaths. Courts have reached differing conclusions. Most find that drug transactions are not, per se, inherently dangerous. Some find no causal relation between the sale and the overdose unless the seller (a) helps administer the fix or (b) watches while the victim administers the fix. But in those situations, the act is not "really" the sale, but the administering or encouraging the administration, of the drug. Moreover, this seems to be applying the "as perpetrated" approach rather than the "in the abstract" approach, and may not need the felony murder doctrine at all to convict. Again, if Zeke knows that Gonzo has overdosed before, Zeke's transfer of so much cocaine at one time might be found by a jury to reflect "a conscious disregard of a risk . . . etc." under the Model Penal Code or the common law, qualifying Zeke for either manslaughter or murder.

5. Keater is probably not guilty of felony murder and probably not even of murder. The felony is not "inherently dangerous" either in the abstract nor as perpetrated. *Even if* a suicide were "foreseeable," the risk is not so great that Keater should be held criminally responsible (civil liability might be another question). And even if all these limitations were somehow avoided, it is hard to see how the deaths are "in furtherance of" the felony. Keater may be a scoundrel but he is not a murderer, even under the felony murder doctrine.

6a. The first problem here is defining what the underlying felony might be. Is it "arson" (almost surely an inherently dangerous felony and a statutorily enunciated basis for first degree felony murder in most states) or is it "insurance fraud" (almost certainly not inherently dangerous in the abstract)? If arson, then under the common law, Larry may be guilty of murder and possibly first-degree murder. There is no requirement, in the harshest articulation of the felony murder doctrine, that the death be foreseeable. Larry's best argument is that the felony has ended, but if the felony is still continuing, he is responsible for the causally related death. Under the MPC, a presumption of recklessness would be established, but Larry could probably rebut that easily unless he knew that the fire would be more dangerous than anyone might expect. See Chapter 7 for a discussion of the causation questions here.

6b. In common law, the victim's negligence was relatively unimportant in any crime and particularly in a felony murder. The only opportunity for Larry here is to argue lack of causation. See Chapter 7.

7. Jethro's method of destroying property may have been sufficiently dangerous ("reckless" or "depraved heart") that he could be convicted of murder even without the felony murder doctrine. However, can the prosecutor avoid having to prove a mens rea by using property destruction as a predicate felony? If the state followed the "as perpetrated" approach in determining whether the felony was dangerous, it might be found to be so. If the state uses the "in the abstract" test, the issue is more difficult because the statute delineates many ways in which one can destroy property. Obviously, "explosions" are dangerous. But is "shredding"? And if burning is covered in "otherwise disposing of" property, should the court consider *only* ways of burning property or should it incorporate *all* (nonburning, nonshredding) methods of destruction (e.g., water damage, car collisions)? Under the Code, since property destruction cannot be a predicate of felony murder, there's no problem.

8. This tragic scene actually occurred in Missouri several years ago. First —is Dave guilty of "straight" murder? He certainly did not "premeditate" the death of the child, and therefore would probably not be guilty of first degree murder in most states. Moreover, he probably did not have "universal malice," or a "depraved mind" under the common law, or "recklessness under circumstances manifesting extreme indifference" under the MPC unless he recognized a real risk to the child. This could be argued either way, but it is at least possible that the entire situation was so confusing at that point that Dave's actions would fall short of this standard.

Can he then be guilty of felony murder? Few statutes articulate larceny as a predicate felony for first degree murder, so the better possibility is second degree. But even here, in most states the felony must be "dangerous" "in the abstract." But larceny—even grand larceny —will not meet this definition. And, given the analysis above, even in those states that allow a "dangerous as perpetrated" standard, Dave must see some risk of death, which is, at the very least, a jury question.

As for the liability of Dave's co-conspirators or accomplices, see Chapters 13 and 14.

9. This question raises, again, defining "the" felony involved. Is the "predicate felony" (a) embezzlement; (b) conspiracy to embezzle; (c) dumping wastes? The first two are almost surely not "inherently dangerous." But the last might be, depending on the precise wording of the statute. (For example, if the statutory violation is "dumping hazardous wastes without a permit," it would not be inherently dangerous, for one could safely dump, but still not have a permit. If the statute prohibited "dangerous dumping of hazardous wastes," however, it might be a predicate felony.)

Manslaughter

Manslaughter is often defined as "an unlawful homicide without malice aforethought." This is then subdivided between "voluntary" and "involuntary" manslaughter, then further explained as follows:

1. Voluntary manslaughter is a killing done "on a sudden" in the "heat of passion" after "adequate provocation."
2. Involuntary manslaughter is either "merely" reckless (but not the result of a "depraved mind") or "criminally negligent" killing.

Voluntary Manslaughter
The Rules of Voluntary Manslaughter

By the middle of the nineteenth century most American courts had come to the conclusion that *only* a killing

1. engendered by an act recognized as "legally adequate provocation" and
2. actually done suddenly, in the heat of passion,

would be reduced to a category of homicide called "voluntary manslaughter," for which the punishment was significantly less than murder.

Unfortunately, the courts were unclear as to why these killings were "reduced." The lack of clarity is itself easily explained. As Justice Holmes said, "the life of the law has not been logic; it has been experience." The Common Law 1 (1881). Manslaughter was a category of homicide created by the judiciary as a way of limiting capital punishment; it was not based on carefully thought-out doctrine.[15] When they did make such an attempt, the

---

15. This explains why provocation only affects murder liability. If *D* is "adequately provoked" by *V* but only breaks his leg, the provocation is irrelevant.

courts articulated two conflicting themes, which even today confuse a serious reader:

1. Voluntary manslaughter was indeed a murder but because of the law's "regard for the frailty of mankind," the punishment was reduced.
2. The defendant killed "in a frenzy" brought on by "sudden provocation" at a time when "reason was dethroned," so there was no mens rea.

The tension in these two explanations is obvious. Under the first, the defendant *is* a murderer because he has intentionally taken human life. Under the second, because the defendant had no mens rea, he is *not* a murderer; indeed, he should perhaps be exonerated. This tension has never been resolved. The Model Penal Code, for example, declares that a killing "which would otherwise be murder" is manslaughter under certain conditions, thus taking the first view. However, even the Code is far from consistent in its explanation.

This failure to explain the rationale of manslaughter has other implications. Thus, even today scholars are unable to agree on whether manslaughter is a "partially excused" or "partially justified" homicide. However, because these issues involve the proper allocation of the burden of proof, they should be resolved. (See Chapter 15.) In addition, this ambiguity creates problems when the defendant, while acting "in the heat of passion," kills the wrong person, either because the actual provoker ducks or because the defendant "flails out" at anyone in the vicinity. If the basis of the reduced liability is that the killing is "partially justified" because the victim in some sense "asked for it" or "had it coming," this rationale clearly is inapplicable to the innocent victim. The dilemma here is avoided if one looks only at the defendant's *conduct* and not the result. If, on the other hand, the rationale is that the defendant's actions are "understandable" because of his loss of control, and therefore "partially excused," the rationale would appear to cover even such a "misaim" case. Some consistency in explanation, however, is necessary if the law is to be fair to all defendants. With this caveat in mind, let us now explore "the doctrines" of the offense.

"Legally Adequate Provocation." People are angered by many things. During that anger they sometimes (a) flail out in despair or (b) take intentional action against the persons they believe responsible for that event. Although the early decisions appeared willing to reduce the punishment of any such killing, by the middle of the nineteenth century courts had limited the kinds of events that would generate such a reduction to the following:[16]

---

16. One of the authors of this book has attempted to show that the common law decisions did not in fact so restrict the juries but treatise writers so construed the decisions, and courts began following those writers rather than the much more liberal, and subjective, decisions. See Singer, The Resurgence of Mens Rea I: Provocation, Emotional Disturbance, and the Model Penal Code, 27 B.C. L. Rev. 243 (1986).

1. a battery, mutual combat, or aggravated assault
2. adultery
3. illegal arrest

We will not speak here of the last of these categories. The first, however, is interesting because of its interplay with the doctrines of self-defense. Initially, the writers and courts spoke of a "tweak on the nose" as being sufficient provocation to warrant reduced punishment if killing ensued: Honor, and not physical disabling, was at stake.[17] A second subcategory involved cases of "mutual combat" undertaken in "chance (or hot) medley." If Jim and John got into a heated barroom debate that escalated from words to fists to weapons, the one who killed the other was held to be a manslaughterer rather than a murderer because the killing was done "on a sudden passion" during a chance occasion. If, however, during the same encounter, Jim tried to "retreat" from the argument and the use of deadly force but found himself pursued by John, whom he then killed, Jim might be acquitted of any homicide because the killing was *"se defendendo."* (See Chapter 16.)

The second category, adultery, is the most interesting. The doctrine was easily stated: If the defendant found his (the defendant was always male) spouse in flagrante delicto and killed either the spouse, or the lover, or both, the killing was manslaughter. One would think that the explanation was obvious: People can and do become outraged in such situations. However, some courts restricted the reduction to instances where the defendant actually *saw* the adultery. No case appears to have actually involved a spouse who walked in on the spouse and lover naked in bed but not actually in flagrante delicto, though some courts came nervously close to restricting the exception to such a case. See, e.g., *State v. John,* 30 N.C. (8 Iredell) 330 (1848), where the husband saw *V* climbing out of the bedroom window and pursued him. The reason for the restriction may be clear; courts did not wish to encourage precipitous action by unduly jealous husbands. However, the restriction was also irrational: Actually jealous husbands who, for example, see their wives in "semi-undress" in the presence of another man may in fact become enraged. To require them to wait until adultery actually occurs seems both unrealistic and unnecessary in assessing the level of their guilt.

At the other extreme of the "adequate provocation" doctrine was an unequivocal rule that words alone could never constitute adequate legal provocation. One court, after specifically concluding that the defendant had in fact killed "in the heat of passion" because of constant taunting by his foreman, nevertheless held the killing to be murder rather than manslaughter because of this doctrine. *Fredo v. State,* 127 Tenn. 376 (1913). Some courts, however, appear to have created an exception to this exception: If the words

---

17. J. Horder, Provocation and Responsibility (1993).

spoken by the victim informed the defendant of an event that, had the defendant witnessed it, would be legally provocative, the words might qualify. However, other courts held that not even a confession of adultery would suffice.

"Heat of Passion." This doctrine reflects one of the original understandings of the reason for the reduction — that the defendant acted in a rage in response to the provocative act. It had a corollary doctrine, that the defendant must not have cooled off, which was then converted into an objective test, that the defendant, even if actually still provoked, must not have had "enough time" to cool off. Again, in an apparent attempt to limit jury sympathy, nineteenth-century courts held that whether enough time had passed for the reasonably prudent person to "cool off" was a question of law (to be decided by the judge). This doctrine also severely penalized "brooders," such as Hamlet. Thus, if *D* finds his wife and her lover in bed and kills them instantly, it is manslaughter. But if *D* does not kill instantly, but broods about the event for several hours (or days) and then lashes out at the spouse, the law did not allow a defense. This is questionable, since it appears to be "rewarding" the person who does not try to control himself, while penalizing one who tries, but fails, to avoid lashing out.

Twentieth-Century Changes in the Doctrines

These restrictive doctrines were criticized as inconsistent and too restrictive. Gradually the courts loosened the rules.

The "Reasonable Man" Test. Adequate legal provocation became anything that could cause the "reasonable man" to act in passion. Quickly, however, this change led to allowing other events to act as provocation, since reasonable people become angry over events other than those listed above at page 172. Today even words, at least words that inform the defendant about events that, if experienced, could otherwise provoke anger, may be sufficient. Thus, confessions of adultery or taunts relating to sexual potency or competency may suffice as provocation. *People v. Berry,* 556 P.2d 777 (Cal. 1976). Recent cases have gone even further. In one case, the House of Lords held that the reasonably prudent person (RPP) was a glue sniffer *if* the reason he became outraged was related to his glue sniffing (in this case, the victim taunted and nagged the defendant about his glue sniffing). *R. v. Morhall,* [1995] 3 W.L.R. 330. The law with regard to racial epithets also seems to be changing, although this has been rather slow, at least in jurisdictions that have not adopted the Model Penal Code's approach (see below).

Similarly, in many jurisdictions the RPP now has many of the physical characteristics and experiences of the defendant. Thus, courts have allowed juries to consider, as part of the reasonable person's make-up, the defendant's age, gender, physical stature, physical disabilities, lack of sleep, and other such factors. Most courts refuse to consider any of the defendant's "psychological" characteristics, fearing that this would allow "hotheads" who do not attempt to control their anger a reduction based on their failure to improve their character. This explanation, however, is unconvincing. Even a hotheaded defendant, after all, will be convicted of manslaughter and be punished for that crime; it may seem excessive to punish the defendant for murder just because he has failed to sufficiently alter his hotheaded nature.[18] English law has almost totally subjectivized the objective standard of the reasonable man. *Director of Public Prosecutions v. Camplin,* [1978] 2 All E.R. 168. See Chapter 4.

(2) The Cooling-Off Period Cools Off. Both as part of the adoption of the RPP test, and as part of a general individualization of the criminal law, the law with regard to the "cooling-off" period has also changed. First, whether the defendant has cooled off or had time to do so is now a question of fact for the jury to resolve. Some modern courts have spoken as well of the "cooled-off person" who has been "rekindled" either by the sight of the victim (initial provoker) or by words, informational or otherwise, spoken by the victim regarding the initial provocation. Thus, if *V* sodomizes *D* and escapes, only to be seen by *D* some days, weeks, or even months later, whereupon *D* immediately kills *V*, there is a greater likelihood today that *D* will be found guilty of manslaughter rather than murder. Cf. *State v. Gounagias,* 88 Wash. 304 (1915). Finally, at least some jurisdictions appear to allow "brooders," whose anger *increases* over time, to plead provocation to reduce the offense to manslaughter.

Critique of Manslaughter Doctrine

In recent years, many writers,[19] particularly feminist philosophers, have attacked both the common law rules of manslaughter and their modern expansion, on the grounds that they (a) were intended to protect violent people (particularly men); (b) indulge violence when the law should be seeking to teach people (particularly men) to control their rages. They also point out that the "adultery" rule was based upon the view of women as property, and that the "insult" rule was based upon a notion of "honor"

---

18. Perhaps the theory here is that *D* has been reckless with regard to whether he might kill, but that should, at least in theory, require some showing that *D* has either killed, or come close to killing, at earlier times. This would require evidence of the extent of his anger and loss of control. Nevertheless, the law is relatively firm on this point.

19. See especially J. Horder, *supra,* n. 17.

similar to that protected by the practice of dueling, hardly a practice to be continued into a new millennium. Supporters of both the older and newer versions of the rules respond that the rules do not — on their face — distinguish between women and men, and that (at least today) many women avail themselves of the doctrines. Moreover, they say, the notion of indulging "human frailty" merely recognizes reality, however unappealing that reality might be, and that to punish persons who act while actually enraged equally with those who act "in cold blood" fails to distinguish between persons of significantly different moral culpabilities. The "manslaughterer" may be morally guilty of not learning how to control (his) passion, but that is not the same level of immorality as purposely "premeditating" and killing. The debate will undoubtedly continue; it has already sharpened the analysis of the criminal law, and its purposes.

Involuntary Manslaughter
Reckless and Negligent Manslaughter

We have already seen that the common law made "depraved heart" killings murder, and that the modern MPC equivalent of that wording is "recklessness under circumstances manifesting extreme indifference to the value of human life." If those circumstances are not present, a reckless killing is not murder but manslaughter. There is as well a parallel to felony murder. Early common law cases spoke of a defendant who, while committing an "unlawful" act, killed someone. The term "unlawful" included not only crimes but torts. Thus, to use an old example, if a roofer throws a beam down from the roof to the street and, in doing so, kills someone, it is manslaughter. However, if the case occurs in a remote area, the death is not manslaughter. Again, the courts and writers were unclear as to the explanation, but it is certainly appropriate to consider the first roofer, but not the second, "reckless."

Serious confusion, however, arose in this area because some courts suggested that the two roofers were (respectively) "negligent" and "nonnegligent" in tortious terms. Thus, the notion grew that a tortiously negligent actor could become liable for manslaughter. This view, however, has been emphatically rejected by virtually all courts, which require a "higher degree of negligence" for criminal liability generally, see Chapter 4, and for homicidal liability in particular. *Fitzgerald v. State*, 112 Ala. 34 (1896); *State v. Weiner*, 41 N.J. 21 (1964).[20]

As noted above in Example 6 at page 157, both courts and juries have

---

20. This may not be the case where the legislature has *explicitly* adopted tortious negligence as a possible predicate for liability. See, e.g., *State v. Williams*, 4 Wash. App. 908 (1971); *State v. Barnett*, 218 S.C. 415 (1951).

had difficulties in assessing the proper response to killings done with automobiles. At least in earlier times, few courts or juries would find a "merely" reckless driver guilty of murder, even if the driver were drunk. (The facts in a case such as *Pears*, cited in that example, were particularly egregious, thus accounting for the result in that case.) And juries were equally reluctant to convict drivers of voluntary manslaughter, apparently on the grounds that many jurors realized that they had driven recklessly or negligently and avoided calamitous results only by chance. Many legislatures responded by either enacting a special crime, "death by vehicle," or providing liability under the existing "involuntary manslaughter" provision. In either case, the penalty was much lower than that of voluntary manslaughter.

In the last ten years or so, however, in reaction against drunk and even nondrunk but highly reckless drivers, juries and courts are evincing a greater willingness to convict such drivers of voluntary manslaughter or even murder. Legislatures have also enacted special statutes making it a new crime to cause death by driving while intoxicated. These statutes demonstrate the responsiveness of law to pressures due to changing perceptions of blameworthiness and dangerousness.

Misdemeanor-Manslaughter

Accidental deaths that occur while the defendant is committing a misdemeanor are sometimes held to be manslaughter. This doctrine acts in the same way as does the felony murder rule. However, courts have not surrounded it with the same limitations and safeguards that they have used in dealing with the felony murder rule, perhaps because there is no possibility of the death penalty. Thus, even misdemeanors that are not "inherently dangerous" in any true sense of that term can be used as the predicate for a manslaughter charge.

The Model Penal Code Approach

Consistent with its general embrace of subjective liability, the Code rejects the rigidity of the common law on heat-of-passion killings. It provides that a "killing which would otherwise be murder" is manslaughter if it is done

> under extreme emotional or mental disturbance [EED] for which there is a reasonable explanation.

Several things should be noted about this provision. By first declaring that the killing would "otherwise" be murder, the Code implicitly adopts the theory that a reduction to manslaughter is not a matter of right, that is, that the defendant's reason was *not* "dethroned" and that he acted "purposefully, knowingly or recklessly" with regard to death. Moreover, there is no "time limit" or "cooling-off" period. Third, *any* impetus for the disturbance is sufficient; it is not limited to "legally adequate provocation." Thus, for example, not only informational words but highly inflammatory taunts (racial, ethnic, or gender epithets), once explicitly excluded from the doctrine of heat of passion, might be covered by the MPC approach. Indeed, there need not even be provocation. If, say, a vehement anti-abortionist were suddenly to kill an abortionist because of a building rage, it is possible that the Code would allow him to plead EED. Similarly, a few years ago a rioter in Los Angeles, outraged by a verdict of acquittal for several white police officers who had beaten a black defendant, chose a white trucker at random and hit him with a brick. Had the victim died (which, fortunately, he did not), it is plausible that the Code would have allowed the rioter to claim EED; it is clear that the common law would not have allowed such a claim. However, a disturbance must still be "extreme"; an event of everyday life would probably not be sufficient.

Ironically, the language of EED, which was expected by the Code drafters to liberate the jury from the rigors of the common law, and send all these cases to the jury, has been interpreted by many courts to require expert witnesses, usually psychiatrists or psychologists, to testify to an "emotional or mental disturbance." Thus, if a defendant is unable (due to any cause, including lack of funds) to put on such evidence, these courts preclude reference in jury instructions to this Code section.

Further, the Code appears to re-inject an objective standard by requiring that the explanation for the disturbance be "reasonable." However, the next sentence of the Code's provision declares that "[t]he reasonableness of such explanation of excuse shall be determined from the viewpoint of a person in the actor's situation under the circumstances as he believes them to be." Thus, the Code both subjectivizes and objectivizes the standard for the reduction to manslaughter. The commentary to the Code *explicitly* refuses to explain what factors (e.g., age, gender, impotency) should be considered as part of the "actor's situation," preferring to leave to the courts the development of that definition.

The Code adopts both prongs of the common law's "involuntary manslaughter" provisions but recasts them in the Code's basic mens rea language. Thus, if a killing is "reckless" (done with a subjective awareness of the risk of death but not under circumstances manifesting extreme indifference to the value of human life), it is manslaughter. If, on the other hand, the killing is done with "criminal negligence" (no actual awareness of the risk but with a gross deviation from the standard of care of an RPP), it is "negligent homicide," which is punished less severely than manslaughter.

Finally, and not surprisingly in light of its views on the felony murder doctrine, the Code rejects entirely the misdemeanor-manslaughter analog.

One possible way to conceptualize the various tests, both common law and modern, with regard to homicides is shown in Table 3.

Table 3. Homicide Under the Common Law and the Model Penal Code*

	Intended Killings	Unintended But Recklessly Risked Killings
	INTENT (+) (**Premeditation, Deliberateness, and Willfulness**)	
MURDER	INTENT *(Purposely or Knowingly)* (**Malice Aforethought**)	RECKLESS (+) *Recklessness under circumstances manifesting extreme indifference to the value of human life* (**Depraved Heart**)
MANSLAUGHTER	INTENT (−) *(Extreme Emotional or Mental Disturbance)* (**Heat of Passion**)	RECKLESS *(Reckless)* (**Culpable Negligence**)
		RECKLESS (−) *(Criminal Negligence)* (**Culpable Negligence**)

* Code: Boldface represents Common Law Language; Italics represents Language of the Penal Code.

EXAMPLES

1a. Papa loved Mama, and Mama loved men (with apologies to Garth Brooks). Papa, a trucker, comes home unexpectedly one night and finds Mama and Neighbor in flagrante delicto. Papa kills Neighbor with the bottle of champagne he had brought to surprise Mama (as Brooks says, "if he was looking to surprise her, he was doing fine"). Manslaughter?

1b. As in the song, Papa finds the house deserted (except for his children) and heads downtown in his semi-tractor trailer truck. He gets to the local motel and, changing from second to first gear, plows through the room in which Mama and Neighbor are cavorting. One or both are killed. Murder or manslaughter?

1c. Same facts as 1b, except that Papa rams his truck into the wrong room, either because (a) the clerk gave him the wrong number; (b) Papa misread the number on the room. What crime(s)?

1d. Papa, depressed by his discovery, and having no clue where Mama is, simply waits at home for her. When she arrives, he asks where she has been, and she responds "I've been with a real man, you chump," at which point Papa hits her with the champagne bottle, killing her.

1e. Suppose that, instead of having intercourse, Mama was having her foot massaged by her (obvious) boyfriend.

2. Mike Douglas, after a particularly hard day at the office, is driving home when he is caught in a traffic jam in mid-August. His air conditioning is out. He has been sitting in 106° weather for one hour with no relief in sight. Just as he sees an opportunity to take an off-ramp, another car, driven by Donny DeVito, cuts him off. Furious and frustrated, Douglas shoots DeVito. Is Mike a murderer?

3a. Marie, an electrician, is called on Super Bowl Sunday, just an hour before kickoff, by Gus, a mechanically inept homeowner, who begs her to come to his house, which has experienced an outage. Expecting the job to take fifteen minutes, Marie accepts it, but once there determines that there is a more serious problem, which *could* result in a fire, although in her judgment the risk is low. Anxious to see the game, she puts in a temporary fix and tells Gus she'll be back tomorrow. Of course, the house burns down during the third quarter, and Gus is killed. Has Marie committed manslaughter?

3b. Same facts except that, in her anxiety over missing the game, Marie simply does not find the latent defect at all.

4. Glen does not know it, but both his taillights are out. Because of this, Linda collides with his car from the rear, and kills Joshua, Glen's passenger. Driving without operative taillights is a strict liability misdemeanor. Is Glen guilty of manslaughter?

5. Hamlet's hunting license has, unknown to him, expired. Using all care, he shoots at a deer but nevertheless kills Polonius, whom he does not know is there. Hunting without a license is a misdemeanor. Manslaughter?

6. Paul was raised by a very religious family. At the age of 8, he attended church four nights a week. By 18, he was in seminary, and by 22, he was an ordained minister. His family always inveighed against abortion. For the first few years of his ministry, Paul preached against abortion on many occasions, but took no further action. As he grew older, however, he first joined, and then led, local and national anti-abortion groups. He participated in numerous sit-ins outside abortion clinics and was frequently arrested. After an abortionist was killed in another state, Paul's fury intensified. He resigned the ministry and devoted himself full-time to anti-abortion activities. Finally, he decided that he could no longer stand on the sidelines. To him, abortionists were committing murder. He purchased a gun and practiced with it every day. After two weeks, he determined to kill the local doctor who performed abortions. Knowing that this was done on Fridays, Paul positioned himself outside the clinic at 6 a.m. and waited. As he sat there, he was nagged by doubts about his course of action, but he convinced himself that it was necessary to save the lives of the unborn. He himself says: "I thought maybe I would feel, y'know, a lot of resolution and that kind of thing, but my

stomach felt like literally a bottomless pit." When the doctor arrived, Paul shot him four times as he stepped from his car. Paul is charged with first-degree murder. What result?

Putting it all together. Let's try a few slightly more complicated ones, which potentially involve all the homicide doctrines. Ready?

7a. Harry takes Hillary out on a date. Intent on having intercourse with her, he obtains some GHB, a colorless odorless drug that is known as the "date rape" drug, which is intended to make Hillary more receptive to Harry's amorous mood. The drug can produce lassitude and a temporary euphoria, and sometimes hallucinations. Unknown to Harry, the drug can also produce unconsciousness if it is even slightly "impure." He asks the bartender, Henry, to put the GHB, which he tells Henry is a harmless substance, in Hillary's drink. If Hillary dies as a result of the drink, what homicidal crime has Harry or Henry committed?

7b. Same facts. Now suppose that the state legislature has recently declared GHB a controlled dangerous substance, whose possession or delivery is a felony. Is there any different answer?

8. At two A.M. on a Sunday morning, Maurice is pulled over by Trooper Ted for speeding through a town, at a speed of 40 miles an hour in a 25 mph zone. As Ted exits his car, Maurice hits the gas, and takes off at 90 miles per hour. Ted follows in "hot pursuit." After 15 minutes, and running two red lights, Maurice collides with a car driven by Joan, containing three young children. All four occupants are killed. Who is guilty of what level of homicide?

EXPLANATIONS

1a. Papa is guilty of manslaughter. This is the classic case of "adequate legal provocation" even under the common law. But the facts as stated could hide an enormous amount of ambiguity. For example: Did Papa see Neighbor's car in the driveway? Did he hear heavy breathing as he approached the bedroom? Suppose Papa had to go to the refrigerator for the champagne, or to his truck for a tire iron? Most discussions of these chestnuts leave out the "ancillary" facts, but they might be enough to suggest either that (1) Papa was not as surprised as he claims; (2) Papa had "some" time to cool off before he killed.

1b. The Brooks song fails to tell us how Papa *knew* the room in which Mama was carrying on; if he had to ask the clerk for this information, there may be less opportunity for reduction. Moreover, Papa may have had time to cool off, either objectively or subjectively, while he was driving to the motel. The unlikeliness of that possibility is what drove the common law to reassess the "cooling-off" rule; indeed, the possibility is that Papa became *more* incensed as he drove. Still, it is clear here that

Papa acted intentionally, albeit still in the heat of passion. Under the Model Penal Code, the passage of time, while one factor, is not determinative of a defendant's inability to have the slaying reduced to manslaughter, as long as he is still acting under the extreme disturbance. Papa might well be eligible under the Code for reduction to manslaughter.

1c. These are misaim cases, and the difference in *reason* for the misaim would seem irrelevant. The question here is whether the law should mitigate Papa's conduct because of *his* mental state ("partial excuse") or preclude mitigation because the *victims* did not "ask for it" ("partial justification").

1d. Under the original common law, Papa has no reduction because words alone are never adequate legal provocation. However, under more recent doctrine and under the Code, this will be a jury question.

1e. Movie buffs will recognize this as the unseen crime committed by the "boss" in Pulp Fiction. The answer under the common law is clear — nothing less than intercourse could be adequate legal provocation. Under the test of the "reasonable person," however, and certainly under the MPC approach, this question might go to the jury.

2.   Under the common law, this is an easy case. Unless DeVito's car has hit Douglas' car (arguably the equivalent of battery), there is no adequate legal provocation. Thus, although Douglas is *really* irate, there is no reduction. This is also the likely result under the Model Penal Code. Even if there is "extreme" mental or emotional disturbance, it is probably not due to a "reasonable explanation" (but the question is closer). After all, most of us have been frustrated by such cutoffs, losses of parking spaces, and so on. Indeed, the phenomenon described here has become so common that in both England and the United States it has a label: "road rage." Still, no reported case reduces the killing from murder to manslaughter.

3a. Marie could be found guilty of manslaughter. Her action here might be characterized as "reckless" under the common law or the MPC, but it is almost certainly not "under circumstances manifesting extreme indifference to human life" or "with a depraved mind." Those tests might be met if Marie had not even put in a temporary fix but had rushed off with no regard for the risks at all. We told you football could be a dangerous game, Marie.

3b. Since Marie did not see the defect, she was not reckless; she did not subjectively perceive and disregard a risk. This is involuntary manslaughter under common law, and, at worst, "negligent homicide" under the Code. Marie's tortiously "unlawful" (though not criminal) failure to repair might activate the common law. Under the Code, the question is whether her failure to see the defect is a "gross" deviation from what a reasonable electrician would see (if not pressured by the big game).

4. Under application of the misdemeanor-manslaughter rule, Glen is guilty of involuntary manslaughter, even if his failure to be aware of the dead taillights is not negligent. The Code rejects this rule and would require proof that Glen's failure to know of the situation was "grossly deviant" from the actions of an RPP.

5. This is not an easy case. Under a rigid application of the misdemeanor-manslaughter rule, Hamlet should be guilty. But unlike Example 4, the failure to have a license has little or no causal relation to the injury; Hamlet has been careful in his hunting. Thus, even under the common law, he should not be found culpable.

6. This is the true story of Paul Hill, who in 1994 shot and killed Dr. Bayard Barrett in Pensacola, Florida. See N.Y. Times, Sept. 24, 1995, sec. 4. Assuming that Paul has no claim of necessity (see Chapter 16) or insanity or diminished capacity (see Chapter 17), he appears to be liable for first-degree murder. He premeditated the crime by purchasing the weapon in advance, practicing with it, and lying in wait for the victim. Under the common law, Paul has no other claims. However, under the Model Penal Code, he may argue that he is guilty only of manslaughter because his killing was committed under "extreme emotional or mental disturbance." The Code, unlike the common law, does not require provocation, much less adequate provocation. Its focus is on the mental state—or lack of it—of one who kills. Arguably, a person in Paul Hill's "situation," as the Code puts it, might argue that his conclusion was reasonable, even though he clearly knew that what he was doing was illegal.

   In fact, Florida has not adopted the MPC, and Paul Hill was found guilty of first-degree murder. Whether or not the MPC would have allowed the jury to consider a reduction to manslaughter in this particular case, the fact pattern illuminates the difference between the common law and the MPC.

7a. Begin by asking whether Harry has committed murder. Harry may be a bad actor, but under the common law, it is unlikely that he had a "depraved heart" with regard to death. Thus, this is probably not murder. And if it were murder, it would not be first degree, since the death was not premeditated. The same result would obtain under the MPC: Harry is not purposeful or knowing with regard to death, and even if he knew that there was *some* risk of death, it would be hard to argue convincingly that he acted under "circumstances manifesting extreme indifference to the value of human life." Under the common law, then, Harry is, at worst, guilty of manslaughter. But not voluntary manslaughter, since this did not occur in the heat of passion brought on by adequate provocation. The common law and the MPC, in slightly different language, would require that Harry exhibit "gross negligence" or "recklessness" in his conduct, which might be appropriate here, depending on Harry's (or the reasonable person's) understanding of GHB's potency.

Henry, not knowing the kind of drug he was distributing, would probably not even be "grossly negligent."

Caveat: in legal theory, Harry and Henry have both committed battery upon Hillary, since they have knowingly caused her to be touched by a drug to which she did not consent. The battery is likely to be a misdemeanor (since no serious bodily harm occurred at a result of the mere touching). If the common law notion of "misdemeanor manslaughter" were applied here, both might be guilty of manslaughter.

This hypothetical is based upon a real case, in which a jury convicted two defendants of involuntary manslaughter. In the actual case, the young men who laced the drinks failed to call emergency help; instead, they argued about what to do when the victim passed out. See New York Times, March 15, 2000.

7b. Is this now a felony murder? The first question would be whether Harry or Henry has committed a felony under the statute. Harry knew that it was a drug. His failure to know that it was a legally proscribed drug is irrelevant. (see Chapter 5 on mistake of law.) Thus, he has committed a felony. But the felony is probably not "inherently dangerous," either in the abstract, as many courts have required, or even as perpetrated here. Thus no felony murder.

But Harry *might* be guilty of felony murder if his drugging of Hillary could be seen as an "attempt" to commit rape (or sexual assault). (See Chapter 9 for a discussion of why this could easily be rape.) Under the common law, most states provide by statute that a death that occurs during the attempt to commit rape will be first degree felony murder. The issue here would be whether Harry has moved sufficiently toward the target crime as to constitute an attempt. For a detailed analysis of that question, see Chapter 12. The short answer is that Harry is probably *not* guilty of attempt under most common law tests, but might well be guilty of attempt under the Model Penal Code. Under the Code, rape (or deviate sexual intercourse) is a predicate crime for which the rebuttable presumption of recklessness arises. Still, Harry can probably rebut that presumption fairly easily.

Henry will *probably* not even be guilty of the felony, since he did not know that he was dealing with a drug which *might* be legally proscribed. If, however, the statute is read as imposing strict liability, or if possessing or distributing any substance is a crime activating the "greater crime" theory (see Chapter 5), then Henry might be responsible for the felony possession. Even then, just as with Harry, this is probably insufficient to warrant felony murder liability.

8. This scene has become all too common in modern America. Many police departments have changed, or are considering changing, their internal rules that govern the circumstances under which high speed pursuit chases are allowed. But do these rules — or their changes — alter our perception of the liability of either Ted or Maurice? Some prosecutors are now beginning to file homicide charges against both the chased and the chaser in such circumstances. See, e.g., New York Times, July 19, 2000, p. B3, where the pursuing officer was killed, and the escapee was charged with manslaughter.

Assuming that Maurice has not committed a felony, either by speeding or by attempting to escape arrest, does he have "malice aforethought"? A fact finder could easily decide that during the 15 minutes, while running red lights, he had a mind "regardless of social duty" — Maurice "must have" adverted to the possibility of injury or death. Maurice, of course, will dispute that—he will argue that he was so scared that his mind was a blank. But that argument also goes to Maurice's liability for voluntary (reckless) homicide: if he argues that he did not advert to death, he cannot be found to be reckless. On this question, he is either potentially guilty of second degree murder, or "only" involuntary manslaughter. Note: In an even more bizarre case, a defendant, pulled over for driving under the influence, ran from the car over a footbridge over the Ohio River. When a pursuing officer fell off the bridge and drowned, the defendant was convicted of "wanton" homicide. See *Robertson v. Comm.*, — Ky. — *(May 19, 2000)*.

What about Ted? Assuming that the police department regulations would allow such a chase, is Ted acting "recklessly" in following regulations? Is the blame to be placed on the department for allowing such a chase? Or should Ted be blamed for following what are obviously disputable regulations? Even if the regulations prohibit chases for "speeders," Ted will surely argue that his police expertise suggested that Maurice was "more than speeding." How should a jury assess that evidence and how should it be weighed in assessing Ted's mens rea? Should the experience of other departments be relevant—admissible— in determining Ted's responsibility here?

9

Rape

Overview

Rape is the taking of sexual intimacy with an unwilling person by force or without consent. Historically, rape was regarded as an offense that could only be committed against a woman not married to the defendant, and it was seen both as a crime of violence against her and as a property crime against her husband or father. Today, the law recognizes that rape can be committed against females and males, and it is viewed both as a crime of violence and as violating an individual's basic right to decide with whom to have sex.

Probably no crime has been more sharply affected by contemporary society's rapidly changing attitudes. Influenced by the newly arrived voices of women in the law, legislatures have recently enacted sweeping changes in the statutory definitions of rape and the evidentiary rules for trying rape cases. That this law reform has been controversial is not surprising. It reflects shifting perceptions about our most intimate human activity, appropriate sexual behavior by males and females, the relative status and power of men and women in society, the proper balance between convicting the guilty but not the innocent, and the legal consequences of the marriage relationship.

A discussion of how the law should define rape and establish procedures for trying rape cases can elicit intense emotional responses. Many people feel strongly that the common law treated women as chattel, keeping them in a subordinate social position. For example, under the common law a wife could not accuse her husband of rape. Furthermore, any crime committed by a married woman (except killing her husband) was deemed to have been coerced by her husband and she could not be punished for it. The common law essentially treated a married woman as totally passive and subject to the will of her husband. Though she may have received some modest advantage from her marriage status, the disadvantages she suffered under the law far outweighed any advantages.

Thus, many critics argue that retaining *any* remnants of the common law, especially the common law of rape, simply preserves women's profoundly disadvantaged legal status. Others, while perhaps agreeing with these criticisms, argue that the common law, including the common law of rape, had some good points that should not be discarded precipitously in the law revision process. They express concern about possible harmful consequences of contemporary law reform, such as increasing the risk that innocent people will be convicted. The discussion is made more complicated by changing social contexts in which acts that are (or can be seen as) rape occur, especially "date rape"; by perceived tensions in the sexual relations between men and women; and by the pressures generated both by biology and culture.

Everyone will undoubtedly approach this subject in light of his or her individual characteristics, experiences, and attitudes. Nevertheless, we should each try to understand the complexity of the issues involved and the different viewpoints others may have.

The Common Law Approach

Definition

The common law defined rape tersely as "carnal knowledge of a woman forcibly and against her will."[1] Rape included only sexual intercourse; it did not include other sex acts such as oral or anal sex or consensual sex with minors. Those acts were usually punished as other crimes. Because of the brevity of the common law rape definition, courts had to explain its terms in greater detail.

Generally, the prosecution had to prove:

1. the defendant had *sexual intercourse* (penetration by the penis of the vulva);
2. with a *woman not his wife;*
3. using *physical force* or the *threat of force;* and
4. *without her consent.*

Rape was a felony at common law and there were no degrees. Like most other common law felonies, rape was punishable by death. The extreme consequences of a rape conviction may have affected both how the common law defined rape and how judges and juries applied the definition.

---

1. 4 William Blackstone, Commentaries on the Law of England 210 (1769).

Spousal Immunity

At common law a man could not rape his wife.[2] Thus, under the doctrine of spousal immunity a husband who forced his wife to have sexual intercourse could not be convicted of rape. Several arguments were put forth to justify this rule:

1. A wife was deemed to have "consented" by marriage to have sexual relations with her husband throughout the course of their marriage.[3]
2. She was considered to be the property of her husband.
3. After marriage both the husband and wife became one person under the law, and neither one retained a separate legal existence.[4]

Force

A major issue for courts was to explain the element of "force or threat of force" in the common law definition of rape. Though case law on the subject is sparse, "force" was generally considered to consist of physical compulsion or violence (beyond that involved in the act of intercourse itself) that effectively subdued the woman. Usually (though not always), such force would result in physical injury to the victim.

Many courts also required that the complainant must have *physically resisted* the defendant before a jury could find he used sufficient force to be convicted of rape. This approach seems to condone the use of force by males in obtaining sexual gratification until or unless the female resists. *If* the female does resist, *then* the male must stop. Moreover, requiring resistance converts what appears to be an element of rape focusing on the defendant's behavior, force, into an inquiry as to how the woman reacted. In these jurisdictions, a woman's refusal to have sex was protected by the law of rape only if she put up physical resistance.

The amount of required resistance varied. Though some courts expected

---

2. This rule only applied to persons who were actually married. It did not apply to couples living together who were not married.

3. Matthew Hale, a seventeenth-century jurist, said: "But the husband cannot be guilty of a rape committed by himself upon his lawful wife, for by their mutual matrimonial consent and contract the wife has given up herself in this kind unto her husband which she cannot retract." 1 Hale, History of the Pleas of the Crown 629 (1778). This marital consent theory emerged in a time when marriage vows themselves (and the conjugal consent implied therefrom) were virtually irrevocable. It is outmoded in contemporary times when changing divorce laws make it much easier to end the marriage relationship.

4. *State v. Smith,* 401 So. 2d 1126 (Fla. 1981) (holding that the unity concept no longer applies in Florida). See also *State v. Smith,* 85 N.J. 193, 426 A.2d 38 (1981), for an excellent overview of this common law doctrine.

the female to have "resisted to the utmost"[5] or "to follow the natural instinct of every proud female,"[6] most jurisdictions required only "reasonable resistance." Even in a jurisdiction that only required reasonable resistance, a woman who submitted when attacked by a stranger rather than risk death or serious injury often could not prove rape because she had not "resisted" her attacker. The common law afforded far too much protection for the rapist who could subdue his victim quickly or choose a less assertive victim.

Requiring substantial physical resistance may have some modest benefits. It makes the complainant's lack of consent abundantly clear to the defendant and may also provide better evidence on whether the sexual act was imposed or consensual. Nonetheless, requiring resistance has been rightly criticized as (1) putting the victim at greater risk of injury because her resistance may escalate the level of violence,[7] and (2) allowing the use of force by the male until or unless the victim physically resists.

Threat of Force

Courts generally did not require proof that the defendant actually used physical force or that the victim resisted if the defendant threatened the victim with serious harm. They did require, however, that the victim's fear of serious harm be reasonable. The threat usually had to be one of death or serious bodily injury to the victim or to a third person. Often the defendant was armed with a deadly weapon and used it to threaten the victim. Under such circumstances resistance would be futile.

Threats of economic harm, damage to reputation, or other nonviolent intimidation usually did not satisfy this element of rape, though the defendant may have committed another crime like extortion. Thus, if a defendant threatened the victim with the loss of her home or damage to her reputation to obtain sexual intimacy, his threat would not satisfy the "threat of force" element of rape.

Consent

If the woman consented to sexual relations, then the defendant could not be convicted of rape. What constituted consent was a factual question for the judge or jury to decide, and it was not always clear. Words or actions clearly manifesting consent were the most obvious means of expressing willingness to have sex. Conversely, words or actions clearly manifesting the

---

5. *State v. Dizon*, 47 Haw. 444, 452, 390 P.2d 759, 764 (1964) (applying a "relaxed" version of the utmost resistance rule).

6. See *State v. Rusk*, 289 Md. 230, 255, 424 A.2d 720 (1981) (Cole, J., dissenting).

7. Law Enforcement Assistance Administration, Battelle Memorial Institute Law and Justice Study Center, Forcible Rape 7 (Prosecutor's Volume 1977).

absence of consent would normally be sufficient to establish that the woman did not consent. Some courts concluded that behavior short of physically fighting back, such as saying "no" or other actions expressing unwillingness to have sex, did not establish the absence of consent. In these cases the requirement of *nonconsent* is effectively transformed into a requirement that the victim *resist*. Defendants successfully argued that the victim had consented even in cases in which the defendant was a stranger or had used force, brutality, or otherwise harmed or intimidated the complainant.

Attacking the Credibility of the Complainant

Often, the only testimony on the question of consent is that of the complainant and the defendant. This is not surprising because sexual acts are usually done in private and, typically, there are no witnesses other than the participants. As a result, rape prosecutions often turn on the participants' testimony (which often is in conflict) and their credibility. In many cases the defense counsel tries to persuade the jury that the complainant had consented by focusing attention on her character and credibility, usually by delving into her past sexual history. The common law generally allowed such cross-examination. Women who claimed that they had been raped could expect to be questioned extensively at the trial on their sexual history.

Legally Ineffective Consent

Over time the common law expanded the definition of rape so that, in a few types of recurring situations, rape occurred even if no force was used. These cases generally involved victims who were considered incapable because of age or incapacity of giving legally effective consent.[8] An early English statute punished intercourse with a female under age 10 as a felony; it did not require proof that it was without her consent. Subsequently, Coke relied on this statute to define rape to include "unlawful and carnal knowledge of . . . a woman child under the age of ten with her will or against her will."[9] The definition of rape was thus expanded to include such cases apparently on the ground that children of such tender years lacked the maturity necessary to comprehend the nature of the sexual act.

The definition of rape was also broadened to include intercourse with a woman who was unconscious or mentally incompetent. Because such

---

8. This concept is similar to the capacity to enter into a legally binding contract or to commit a crime or a tort. The law requires at least a minimal ability to comprehend the nature of the transaction or event and to understand its consequences.

9. 3 Coke, Institutes of the Law of England *60 (1597).

individuals were not aware of what was occurring or did not sufficiently understand the significance of sexual intercourse, they could not legally consent to the act.

Fraud

Someone who obtained sexual intercourse by fraud was not a rapist under the common law, as long as the complainant understood that she was having sexual intercourse. Flattery, promises, or other attempts to manipulate or persuade the female, even if deliberate and untrue, did not establish the crime of rape. These types of cases were considered "fraud in the inducement." This rule could be pressed to the extreme. Someone who shows up at a woman's house in the dark and passes himself off as her lover does not commit rape (even though she was mistaken as to his true identity) because the woman understood that she was having sexual intercourse. Though somewhat controversial, the majority rule today is still that fraud in the inducement does not constitute rape.[10]

If, however, the defendant deceived the woman about the nature of the act, he could be convicted of rape. This was considered "fraud in the *factum*." If a gynecologist told a female patient he needed to insert a medical instrument into her vagina as part of a medical exam, but inserted his penis instead, he could be convicted of rape because the woman was deliberately misled about the nature of the act.[11] If, however, a man falsely pretended to be a doctor and told a woman she had a disease that could best be cured by having intercourse with an anonymous donor who had been injected with a special serum, he could not be convicted of rape because the woman understood that she was having sexual intercourse.[12]

American Common Law

Early American statutes adopted the common law approach to rape, though they varied in their specific definitions. Statutes defined rape in various ways such as "sexual intercourse" with a woman other than one's wife "forcibly," "against her will," or "without her consent." Most American statutes also treated all forms of rape as a single crime for grading purposes and punished them with the same severity.

In summary, the common law defined rape as (1) sexual intercourse by

---

10. See *People v. Evans,* 85 Misc. 2d 1088, 379 N.Y.S.2d 912 (1975).

11. See *People v. Minkowski,* 204 Cal. App. 2d 832, 23 Cal. Rptr. 92 (1962), for a similar fact pattern.

12. *Boro v. Superior Court,* 163 Cal. App. 3d 1224, 210 Cal. Rptr. 122 (1985). But see Falk, Rape by Fraud and Rape by Coercion, 64 Brooklyn L. Rev. 39 (1998).

a man with a woman not his wife (2) by force or threat of force (3) without consent, or (4) with a victim who could not consent because she was unconscious, mentally disabled, or of a young age, or (5) by fraud in the *factum*.

The Actus Reus of Rape

Rape requires a voluntary act by the defendant, though intentional intercourse is seldom in dispute. The prosecution must prove penetration. Occasionally, a defendant might raise the defense of impotence or intoxication. A claim of impotence is generally an evidentiary claim denying penetration, while intoxication usually is relevant to mens rea (did the defendant *know* the woman did not consent) rather than to the actus reus of rape.

The Mens Rea of Rape

The common law did not specify the mens rea of rape. This caused numerous problems. The prosecutor had to prove the defendant *intentionally* had intercourse with a woman he *knew* was not his wife.[13] The prosecution also had to establish the defendant *intentionally* used force or threatened serious physical harm.

The more difficult issue for courts was defining the mens rea toward *consent*. Did the prosecution have to prove the defendant knew or, instead, only that he *should* have known that the woman had not consented? Even if he used force? Or must the woman also resist?

The 1976 *Morgan* case decided in the House of Lords finally resolved this uncertainty in England by requiring the prosecution to establish that the defendant *knew* that the woman had not consented.[14] According to the defendants in this case, the victim's husband convinced them to come to his house and have sex with his wife. He told them not to be surprised if she struggled because she was "kinky" and only enjoyed sex in this way. The defendants entered the husband's home and had sex with his wife even though she resisted them.

The House of Lords concluded that rape was a specific intent crime and that, consequently, intention applied to all of its elements: nonconsensual sexual intercourse. Therefore, it determined that a defendant's *belief* that the

---

13. A man who had intercourse with his wife's twin under the mistaken belief that she was his wife could not be convicted of rape.

14. *Regina v. Morgan*, [1976] A.C. 182.

woman was consenting, even if unreasonable, negates knowledge of non-consent.[15]

Morgan is consistent with a criminal law jurisprudence that puts primary emphasis on punishing the mens rea of the defendant and only punishes someone severely if he knew that he was inflicting a serious harm on another person. It is conceivable that, in some cases of sexual activity, the male honestly but erroneously believes he is engaged in a mutually desired physical act, while the female does not desire to engage in a sexual act and is seriously harmed by it. If, however, the criminal law should be more protective of victims and focus primarily on the harm done rather than on the mens rea with which it was done, the *Morgan* case can be persuasively criticized as favoring fairness to defendants over preventing harm to victims.

The *Morgan* case caused a great deal of controversy because it appeared to most observers that the defendants clearly knew that the victim had not consented. (The House of Lords affirmed the defendants' conviction on the ground that the judge's instructions were harmless error; that is, no miscarriage of justice had occurred because no jury could have concluded that the defendants honestly believed that the complainant had consented.) Critics argued that the case would permit a future defendant to claim his victim was willing to have sex with him, even when the defendant had used force and any reasonable observer would conclude that the victim had clearly manifested her lack of consent. Parliament subsequently enacted a new rape law that only required the prosecution to prove the defendant was *reckless* as to the victim's nonconsent.

The Model Penal Code

The Model Penal Code's revised definition of rape was instrumental in provoking rape law reform throughout the United States. The MPC recognizes that the common law definition of rape created difficult problems of meaning and proof and concludes that the law of rape must be modernized. However, it does not use sex-neutral terms for rape for either the defendant or the victim, and it retains marital immunity for husbands. It also requires prompt complaint and corroboration of the allegation[16] and provides a mistake of age defense.[17] Its underlying policy seems based on the view that

---

15. There is language in the *Morgan* opinion suggesting that "recklessness" is sufficient for conviction. The court said: "[T]he mental element [of rape] is and always has been the intention to commit that act [sexual intercourse] or the *equivalent intention of having intercourse willy-nilly not caring whether the victim consents or not* [emphasis added]."

16. MPC §213.6(4) & (5).

17. MPC §213.6(1).

claims of rape are often groundless and that defendants need more protection, not less.[18] Because the MPC does not sufficiently embody the emerging consensus on how the law of rape should be reformed, most states have not adopted the MPC's proposed definitions for rape.

Nonetheless, the MPC breaks new ground in three important ways:

(1) It expands the behavior that can constitute rape. All forms of sexual penetration of the female by the male, including vaginal, oral, and anal penetration, are considered rape under the MPC.

(2) It provides for degrees of rape. The MPC has both first- and second-degree rape and a new crime, "gross sexual imposition," to distinguish among the more serious and less serious harms. This approach permits both grading and punishment to reflect more accurately the culpability of the offender and the harm done to the victim.

(3) It focuses on the actor's behavior rather than on his internal thought processes. The MPC acknowledges the difficult task often faced by the prosecution in proving the actor knew that the complainant had not consented, especially when, in most cases of rape, there were no witnesses to the event. The MPC's solution is to focus on objective criteria, specifically "upon the objective manifestations of aggression by the actor" rather than trying to decipher his *state of mind* concerning the complainant's *consent*. The essential element of rape in the MPC is the use of *force* or *threat* of serious physical harm by the defendant. *Nonconsent* and *resistance* by the victim *are not* elements of the crime. Thus, the prosecution does not have to prove the defendant *knew* his victim had *not consented* or that the victim had *resisted*. The victim's behavior has evidentiary significance only.

Second-Degree Rape

Section 213.1(1) of the Model Penal Code provides that anyone who compels the victim to have sexual intercourse "by force or by threat of imminent death, serious bodily injury, extreme pain or kidnapping, to be inflicted on anyone" is guilty of basic rape. It is a felony of the second degree.

The MPC elements of rape are

1. *sexual intercourse* (broadly defined)
2. by a *man with a woman not his wife*
3. by *force*, or
4. by *threat* of serious physical harm or kidnapping to the victim or a third person.

---

18. Leigh Bienen, Rape III — National Developments in Rape Reform Legislation, 6 Women's Rts. L. Rev. 170-213 (1980).

Basic rape also includes cases where

1. Without her knowledge the actor uses drugs or other means to substantially impair the woman's ability to appraise or control her conduct or to resist.
2. A male has intercourse with an unconscious female or with one who is under 10 years old.[19]

First-Degree Rape

Basic rape is a second-degree felony (MPC §213.1(1)). However, if the actor inflicts serious bodily harm on anyone or the complainant was not a "voluntary social companion of the actor . . . and had not previously permitted him sexual liberties," the crime is elevated to a felony of the first degree. This definition can make prosecution in "date rape" cases more difficult.

Gross Sexual Imposition

Finally, the Model Penal Code creates a new crime, "gross sexual imposition," which includes intercourse by a male with a female not his wife if he

1. compels her to submit by any threat that would prevent resistance by a woman of *ordinary* resolution; or
2. knows that she is so mentally impaired that she is incapable of appraising the nature of her conduct; or
3. knows that she is unaware that a sexual act is being committed upon her or that she mistakenly believes the actor is her husband.[20]

Element 1 breaks new ground by expanding the type of threat that will support criminal responsibility. Under the common law the threat had to be one of physical violence. The MPC, however, includes nonviolent but nonetheless coercive threats, such as economic loss, provided that the threat would induce a woman of ordinary resolution not to resist. The drafters provided illustrations. Threatening a woman with the loss of her job could support a conviction under this provision. In contrast, a policeman who tells a woman he will not give her a ticket if she has sex with him should not be convicted of gross sexual imposition. This threat is so trivial that a female of ordinary resolution would not be intimidated by it.[21]

---

19. MPC §213.1.

20. MPC §213.1(2).

21. The MPC also creates the crime of *deviate sexual intercourse by force or imposition,* which has virtually the same definitional scheme as rape except that it includes coerced sexual intercourse between an actor and victim of any sex. MPC §213.2.

Modern Rape Statutes

A primary focus of contemporary law reform has been to change the definition of rape. Most modern rape laws, reflecting a concern for gender equality and recognizing that coercive sexual activity between individuals of the same gender occur, are gender-neutral and reach most coerced sexual activity between individuals of the opposite or same gender.

In many new statutes the definition of prohibited conduct has been greatly expanded to encompass, in addition to sexual intercourse, a wider range of sexual acts, such as cunnilingus, fellatio, anal intercourse, and any other intrusion into the body, including those accomplished by the use of objects.[22] Many states have renamed the crime of "rape" as the crime of "criminal sexual conduct" or "sexual assault."[23]

A number of jurisdictions have eliminated the concept of nonconsent entirely from the definition of rape or restrict its use to an affirmative defense. Instead, their statutes use modern definitions of force or the threat of serious bodily harm as the essential definitional elements of rape. The use of these behavioral criteria is intended to shift the fact finders' focus from the internal thought processes of the defendant to his objective conduct.[24] In theory, they also put less emphasis on the complainant's behavior and character.

Though many states retain spousal immunity in some form,[25] some state laws have eliminated or restricted spousal immunity from the definition of rape. Increasingly, legislatures have concluded that, though husbands and wives agree generally by their marriage to have sexual relations with each other, each still retains the right to decide whether to have sex on any particular occasion. Thus, a husband does not have a legal right to demand sex from his wife. More important, these new laws acknowledge that marriage does not entitle the husband to use force or the threat of force against his wife to obtain sex.

Modern laws also reflect changing ideas about the nature of the harm done. Rape is now seen not only as a crime of violence but also as a crime that violates a person's most personal sphere of privacy, thereby inflicting severe and long-lasting psychological damage.[26]

Moreover, society's attitudes toward permissible sexual conduct have

---

22. See, e.g., Mich. Comp. Laws Ann. §750.520a(1) (West 1991).

23. See, e.g., Mich. Comp. Laws. Ann. §750.520b (West 1991); Tex. Penal Code Ann. §22.021 (West 1994) (aggravated sexual assault).

24. At least one state, Washington, may consider rape in the first and second degree and rape of a child to be *strict liability* offenses requiring no mental state with respect to *any* of the elements. *State v. Brown*, 899 P.2d 34 (Wash. 1995); *State v. Chhom*, 911 P.2d 1014 (Wash. 1996).

25. As of 1984 over 40 states apparently retained some form of spousal immunity in rape. *People v. Liberta*, 64 N.Y.2d 152, 474 N.E.2d 567 (1984).

26. See, e.g., Cal. Penal Code §263, which states: "The essential guilt of rape

changed. In the past, the law was unduly protective of aggressive male sexual behavior, tolerating physical assertiveness unless and until the female made it very clear by physical resistance that she did not desire to have sex with the male. Now the law more readily acknowledges that males have no right to use compulsion in sexual relationships. True equality of genders means that the law must protect the right of both men and women to decide with whom they will share sexual intimacy.

Many states have also passed laws limiting the scope of permissible cross-examination of complainants to protect them from being humiliated and having their privacy invaded. Reformers believe that these laws will encourage both the reporting and prosecution of rape cases.

Rape by Force or Threat of Serious Bodily Injury

Force

State statutes vary on how they define the "force" or "threat of force" element of rape. Some statutes do not define "force" at all, leaving it for case law to fill in an operational definition. Most modern laws, however, seek to define more precisely the level of force necessary for rape. In providing a more explicit definition for this element, most courts require the defendant to use physical force that subdues the victim or to threaten death or serious bodily harm to the victim or to a third person.

Additional Force

Most statutory definitions of force require the defendant to use additional force beyond that necessary to accomplish penetration. Several state laws use the term "forcible compulsion," which, though seemingly providing a consistent definition, can have different meanings. For example, New York law defines this term as meaning the use of physical force or a threat of serious harm.[27] It does not take into account the complainant's behavior in determining whether the defendant used "forcible compulsion." Washington law, on the other hand, defines this term as the use of "physical force which overcomes resistance" or a threat of serious harm.[28] The Washington statute

---

consists in the outrage to the person and feelings of the victim of the rape. Any sexual penetration, however slight, is sufficient to complete the crime" (West 1999).

27. See, e.g., N.Y. Penal Law §130.00(8) (West 1997). "Forcible compulsion means to compel by either . . . the use of physical force; or . . . a threat, express or implied, which places a person in fear of immediate death or physical injury to himself, herself, or another person, or in fear that he, she, or another person will immediately be kidnapped."

28. Wash. Rev. Code 9A.44.010(6) (West 2000). "Forcible compulsion means physical force *which overcomes resistance,* or a threat, express or implied, that places

requires fact finders to focus on the behavior of *both* the defendant *and* the complainant.

Focus on the use of force by the defendant may not, as a practical matter, eliminate pressure on the complainant to physically fight back. In the controversial *Berkowitz* case, a Pennsylvania court concluded that a male college student who removed a female student's clothes without *additional* physical force or threats did not use "forcible compulsion," even though the woman said "no" throughout the sexual act.[29] The court held that her *verbal* resistance was relevant to consent but not to whether the defendant used forcible compulsion. Consequently, the court reversed his conviction for rape but reinstated a conviction for indecent assault.

In a somewhat similar case, however, a California court reached the opposite conclusion.[30] In the *Iniquez* case the male defendant had met the victim for the first time earlier that evening. Later, he awakened her while she was sleeping on the sofa in the living room at a friend's house, pulled her pants down, and inserted his penis into her vagina. She did not resist because she was afraid.

The court held that the defendant's conduct satisfied the statutory language of sexual intercourse "accomplished by means of force, violence or fear of immediate and unlawful bodily injury." The *fear* element was met because the woman's fear of bodily injury was reasonable under these circumstances. In California a rape conviction can be obtained even in cases where the defendant does not use additional force and the victim does not resist, provided that the victim honestly and reasonably fears immediate and unlawful bodily injury.

Inherent Force

Some states do not require the defendant to use additional force beyond that necessary to accomplish the proscribed sexual act before he may be convicted of rape.

In New Jersey, sexual assault (a more contemporary term for "rape") could be committed by sexual penetration when the defendant "uses physical force or coercion, but the victim does not sustain severe personal injury."[31] In *State of New Jersey in the Interest of M.T.S.*, the New Jersey Supreme Court

---

a person in fear of death or physical injury to herself or himself or another person, or in fear that she or he or another person will be kidnapped (emphasis added)." This definition requires the victim to resist physical force. *State v. Weisberg*, 65 Wash. App. 721, 829 P.2d 252 (1992).

29. *Commonwealth v. Berkowitz*, 641 A.2d 1161 (Pa. 1994).

30. *People v. Iniquez*, 7 Cal. 4th 847, 872 P.2d 1183, 30 Cal. Rptr. 2d 258 (1994).

31. N.J Stat. Ann. 2C:14-2c(1) (West 1995) (amended, N.J. Stat. Ann. 2C:14-2 (West 2000).

held that "physical force" as used in its statute means "any unauthorized sexual penetration."[32] It does *not* require *additional* physical force.[33] Simply using the amount of force inherently necessary to accomplish sexual penetration is sufficient for conviction unless the defendant reasonably believed that the victim had "freely given affirmative permission." Moreover, the victim is under no obligation to express nonconsent or to have denied permission.

In reaching this conclusion, the court stressed that New Jersey sexual assault laws had been reformed to afford maximum protection for victims and to make it clear sexual assault should be seen primarily as a crime against personal autonomy rather than as a crime of violence.

Nonphysical Force

A few courts have broadened the definition of the force element to include not only physical force or violence but also "moral, psychological or intellectual force used to compel a person to engage in sexual intercourse against the person's will."[34] The respective ages and prior relationship of the defendant and the complainant can be considered.

Other states, however, limit force to a basic meaning of physical compulsion or threat of serious physical harm. In *State v. Thompson*, the court affirmed a trial court's dismissal of an indictment for sexual assault in a case where a high school principal allegedly intimidated a student to have sexual intercourse with him by threatening to prevent her graduation.[35] The court held that "force" must be interpreted as conveying its ordinary and normal meaning of physical compulsion.

Dispensing with the Force Requirement

Some state statutes define rape as nonconsensual intercourse even in the absence of force or threat of force. Thus, sexual intimacy without the *affirmative* manifestation of consent by words or actions is a crime. Usually it is a less serious degree of rape or sexual assault, and spousal immunity often applies.[36] Criminalizing sexual intimacy obtained without affirmative permission affords maximum protection to the right of individuals to decide when and with whom they will share sexual intimacy. This approach, however, may

---

32. 129 N.J. 422, 433, 609 A.2d 1266 (1992).

33. Id., 129 N.J. 422 at 444.

34. *Commonwealth v. Rhodes*, 510 Pa. 537, 555, 510 A.2d 1217, 1226 (1986).

35. 243 Mont. 28, 792 P.2d 1103 (1990).

36. Wis. Stat. §940.225.3 (1996) (third-degree assault); Wash. Rev. Code §9A.44.060 (West 2000) (third-degree rape; spousal immunity applies).

result in the conviction of some defendants who honestly (and perhaps even reasonably) thought the other person was willing to have sex with them.

Threat of Force

Even when the defendant does not actually use force, he still can be convicted of rape if he *threatens* death or serious bodily injury to the victim or to another person.

This element can be confusing. Does the intent of the *speaker* or the perception of the *listener* determine whether the words constitute such a threat? If the mens rea of the defendant is essential for rape, then he can be convicted only if he *intended* to frighten his victim. If fear felt by the complainant establishes the element, then the listener's understanding of his words controls. If it does, must her understanding be reasonable? Most courts require that the victim's fear be reasonable under the circumstances.[37] Other courts, however, have required the prosecution to prove that the defendant intended his words as a threat.[38]

Most states specify that the "threat of force" required for rape must be a threat of physical harm to the victim or a third person that is sufficient to create fear in a reasonable person.[39] But obtaining sex by using other types of threats, such as economic harm or damage to reputation, is often made criminal under state extortion or criminal coercion statutes.

Resistance by the Victim

Most statutes no longer require the complainant to resist, though some still do.[40] Eliminating resistance as an element of rape is seen as decreasing the risk that victims who fight back may suffer greater physical injury than if they remained passive. It also does not make the criminal responsibility of the defendant dependent on the willingness of his victim to offer physical resistance. Otherwise, some defendants might avoid responsibility if they happened to select nonaggressive victims.

As noted above, however, other states still require the defendant to offer some resistance unless threatened with death or serious bodily injury. This requirement raises the question of whether saying "no" satisfies the resistance element.

Some argue that our culture still teaches men that women are often

---

37. See, e.g., *People v. Warren,* 113 Ill. App. 3d 1, 446 N.E.2d 591 (1983).

38. *People v. Evans,* 85 Misc. 2d 1088, 379 N.Y.S.2d 912 (1975).

39. *State v. Rusk,* 289 Md. 230, 424 A.2d 720 (1981).

40. *Satterwhite v. Commonwealth,* 201 Va. 478, 482, 111 S.E.2d 820, 823 (1960); *Goldberg v. State,* 41 Md. App. 58, 68, 395 A.2d 1213, 1218-1219 (1979); *State v. Lima,* 64 Haw. 470, 476-477, 643 P.2d 536, 540 (1982).

ambivalent about whether to have sex and that, even when a woman is saying "no," she really means "yes." Based on this cultural conditioning, some men may *honestly* believe that a woman is not resisting when she says "no" or takes other evasive action.

However, feminists and others argue persuasively that verbal resistance *is* resistance. Unfortunately, courts too often have not regarded verbal resistance as satisfying the resistance requirement.[41] These cases help perpetuate this harmful fallacy.[42]

This controversy poses difficult policy choices for the criminal law. How should the criminal law treat the male who honestly believes that "no" really means "yes"? Should the criminal law punish someone who has no subjective awareness that he might be committing any crime, let alone a serious crime that can result in a long prison term? (Indeed, until not too long ago, rape was a capital offense in many American states.) If so, should it punish him as severely as an actor who does know that his victim does not want to engage in sexual intimacy? The harm done to the victim who does not desire sexual intimacy may be the same in both cases. However, there is a significant difference in moral blameworthiness between someone who does not comprehend the other person is unwilling and one who does.

Others argue that the criminal law is an instrument for social change and that it should be used to help transform the culture. Thus, they argue a woman is raped when she says "no" and the man proceeds to have sex anyway —even if the defendant did not intend to commit rape. If the criminal law gets too far in front of the common social and cultural understanding, however, it runs the risk of using arguably blameless individuals solely as an instrument for the common good. This could violate Kant's command that no one should be used solely as a means to an end. As noted in the *Berkowitz* and *Iniquez* cases discussed above, these questions have not been resolved with finality.

Consent

The modern trend is to eliminate nonconsent as an element in the statutory definition of rape. Nonetheless, consent is still a definitional component or an affirmative defense in a number of states.[43] A few statutes

---

41. *Goldberg v. State,* 41 Md. App. 58, 395 A.2d 1213 (1979).

42. Susan Estrich, Rape, 95 Yale L.J. 1087 (1986).

43. See, e.g., Tex. Penal Code Ann. §22.021 (1994); Cal. Penal Code Ann. §261.6 (West 1999); *People v. Stull,* 127 Mich. App. 14, 338 N.W.2d 403 (1983) (consent is affirmative defense to rape); *Commonwealth v. Hill,* 377 Mass. 59, 385 N.E.2d 253 (1979) (lack of consent is an element of rape); *Goldberg v. State,* 41 Md. App. 58, 395 A.2d 1213 (1979) (consent is an element of rape). Note that the MPC would simply require the defendant to carry the burden of producing evidence on this issue. He would not carry the burden of persuasion. MPC §1.12.

require the prosecution to prove that the defendant knew the complainant did not consent or was negligent as to her consent. Most recent American cases permit a mistake defense but only if the defendant can show he honestly and *reasonably* believed the victim had consented.[44] Other states permit the defendant to establish an affirmative defense by proving he reasonably believed the complainant had consented. Some states provide for degrees of rape with different mental states required for nonconsent, while others have actually made nonconsent a strict liability element. In a strict liability state, the defendant may be convicted of rape if the victim did not consent, even though he honestly and reasonably believed the victim had consented.[45] This is a minority rule, however.

Reformers argue that retaining consent as an element inappropriately focuses the jury's attention on the complainant's behavior rather than on the defendant's behavior. It also allows defendants to claim they believed the complainant had consented in almost any situation, making it too difficult to convict rapists.

Deception

The general rule in most states is that sexual intimacy obtained by deception does not constitute rape.[46] This approach is consistent with the common law, which considered fraud in the factum to be rape but not fraud in the inducement.

Rape in the First Degree

Many state statutes aggravate the crime if, in addition to the use of force or the threat of force, an aggravating circumstance is present. Examples of such a circumstance are commission of another felony, use of a deadly weapon, or the infliction of serious injury on the victim.

Spousal Immunity

Many states still retain the marital exemption for rape in some form.[47] However, the modern trend is to eliminate or restrict marital status as a definitional element or as an affirmative defense. Increasingly, legislatures and

---

44. See, e.g., *State v. Oliver,* 133 N.J. 141, 627 A.2d 144 (1993); *State v. Smith,* 210 Conn. 132, 554 A.2d 713 (1989); *People v. Mayberry,* 15 Cal. 3d 143, 542 P.2d 1337 (1975).

45. *State v. Ascolillo,* 405 Mass. 456, 541 N.E.2d 570 (1989); *State v. Reed,* 479 A.2d 1291 (Me. 1984).

46. *People v. Evans,* 85 Misc. 2d 1088, 379 N.Y.S.2d 912 (1975).

47. See, e.g., *People v. Liberta,* 64 N.Y.2d 152, 474 N.E.2d 567, 485 N.Y.S.2d 207 (1984).

courts are recognizing that a woman does not give irrevocable consent to sexual intimacy to her husband solely by marriage nor does the marriage relationship entitle the husband to use force to obtain sexual intimacy.[48] Nonetheless, in states that have not eliminated this doctrine, a husband who uses force or the threat of force to secure sexual intimacy cannot be convicted of rape, though he may be convicted of assault.

In some states that retain spousal immunity, filing for divorce or living separately will eliminate any claim of spousal immunity,[49] though obtaining a protective order without more may not.

Rape Because No Legally Effective Consent

Most state statutes include within the definition of rape a situation where the defendant does not use force but where he knows, or in some states *should* have known, that the victim is incapable of giving legally effective consent because of physical or mental incapacity. Some states follow the MPC and consider a defendant's belief about the victim's capacity to give legally effective consent as relevant to the mens rea of rape. Others require the defendant to use the affirmative defense of mistake of fact. This approach requires the defendant to carry the burden of persuasion and also to establish that his belief was reasonable.

Nonforcible sexual intimacy with children is often called "statutory rape," though some states are now using more pejorative terms like "rape of a child."[50] The degree usually depends on the age of the victim and sometimes on the age of the defendant.

Summary

Most modern statutes define rape as (1) obtaining sexual intimacy with another (2) by force or threat of force or (3) without legally effective consent due to incapacity. Some states also include nonconsent as an element in the definition or allow the defendant to use a reasonable belief that the complainant consented as an affirmative defense. Rape will be aggravated to the first degree if another harmful act occurs, such as using a deadly weapon,

---

48. *State v. Smith*, 401 So. 2d 1126 (Fla. 1981).

49. *Commonwealth v. Chretien*, 383 Mass. 123, 417 N.E.2d 1203 (1981) (conviction of husband for raping his wife after she had filed for divorce and obtained a judgment nisi upheld even though divorce had not yet become final).

50. Washington now uses this term instead of the term "statutory rape." Wash. Rev. Code 9A.44.073, 9A.44.076, 9A.44.079.

seriously injuring the victim, or committing another felony. Spousal immunity varies with each state.

Evidence Reforms

The Corroboration Requirement

Early common law did not require that the charge of rape be supported by evidence other than the complainant's testimony.[51] Thus, rape prosecutions could be brought and won even if the only evidence presented to the jury was the testimony of the complainant. This rule was consistent with the general common law rule that corroboration was not required for any crime except perjury.[52]

However, in the early part of the twentieth century, a number of states did require corroboration of the complainant's testimony in a rape case. Without some evidence in addition to the complainant's testimony, rape prosecutions were very difficult.

The Model Penal Code also does not allow a defendant to be convicted of rape solely on the testimony of the complainant.[53] There are three primary justifications offered for this rule of evidence: (1) the ease of fabrication and the fear of frequent false charges, (2) the possibility of false conviction because of emotional jury reaction, and (3) the difficulty of disproving a charge of rape.[54] Although these justifications have been cited in case law, the trend among the small minority of states that still have the corroboration requirement is to relax or abolish it.

Critics of the corroboration rule argue that rape victims should be treated like any other crime victims and not be held to a higher standard of credibility. They claim that the rule prevents legitimate prosecutions. Moreover, there is some empirical evidence that contradicts the belief that rape is a charge too easily made and too difficult to disprove.[55] Supporters of the

---

51. See 7 Wigmore, Evidence §2061, at 342 (3d ed. 1940); Note, The Rape Corroboration Requirement, 81 Yale L.J. 1365 (1981).

52. *United States v. Wiley*, 492 F.2d 547 (D.C. Cir. 1974) (J. Bazelon, concurring). See also Note, The Rape Corroboration Requirement: Repeal Not Reform, 81 Yale L.J. 1365 (1981).

53. MPC §213.6, comment at 428-430.

54. "Rape is . . . an accusation easily to be made and hard to be proved, and harder to be defended by the party accused, tho never so innocent." 1 Matthew Hale, The History of the Pleas of the Crown 635 (1778). See also *State v. Byers,* 102 Idaho 159, 627 P.2d 788 (1981); *State v. Cabral,* 410 A.2d 438 (R.I. 1980); *State v. Sheppard,* 569 F.2d 114 (D.C. Cir. 1977). The Rape Corroboration Requirement: Repeal Not Reform, 81 Yale L.J. 1365 (1972).

55. M. Amir, Patterns in Forcible Rape 27-28 (1971) (there is a reluctance to report

rule argue that eliminating the corroboration requirement lessens the protections against convicting an innocent person.

Contrary to the MPC, most states have done away with the corroboration requirement for rape, though a few states still require it in some form.[56] This demonstrates how rapid law reform has been for this crime.

Rape Shield Laws

Until recently, it was common defense strategy in rape cases to attack the credibility of a female complainant by attacking her character.[57] Defense counsel would cross-examine a complainant concerning her past sexual history and reputation, implying that women who had sex outside of marriage were immoral and thus not believable. Defense counsel justified these tactics, arguing that the complainant's past behavior was relevant to determining her behavior during the alleged rape.

Today, many state laws, referred to as "rape shield laws," expressly forbid or severely limit such an inquiry.[58] For example, past consensual sex with the defendant is generally admissible on the issue of consent. Usually, judges must hold a preliminary hearing to rule on whether inquiry by the defense into a complainant's sexual history is relevant and admissible.

These laws prevent people who file rape charges from having their privacy invaded and from being humiliated in court based on matters that are not relevant to their credibility or the issues. Protecting rape victims in this way, in turn, may encourage the reporting and prosecution of rape. Critics are concerned rape shield laws may deprive criminal defendants of their Sixth Amendment right of confrontation.[59]

EXAMPLES

1.   Shortly after her husband left for work early in the morning, Sarah was startled to find Andrew, whom she did not know, in her bedroom where

---

rape); H. Kalven, Jr. & H. Zeisel, The American Jury 249-254 (1966) (juries generally tend to view rape charges with skepticism and suspicion); L. Holstron & A. Burgess, The Victim of Rape: Institutional Reactions 238 (1978) (convictions in the absence of aggravating circumstances are the exception rather than the rule). See also *State v. Byers*, 102 Idaho 159, 627 P.2d 788 (1981); *People v. Rincon-Pineda*, 14 Cal. 3d 864, 123 Cal. Rptr. 119, 538 P.2d 247 (1975).

56. See also *United States v. Wiley*, 492 F.2d 547, 552 (D.C. Cir. 1973) (J. Bazelon, concurring): "Today, thirty-five states have similarly rejected the corroboration requirement for rape."

57. See *State ex rel. Pope v. Superior Court*, 113 Ariz. 22, 545 P.2d 946 (1976).

58. Bienen, Rape III — National Developments in Rape Reform Legislation, 6 Women's Rts. L. Rep. 170 (1980).

59. See generally Tanford & Bocchino, Rape Victim Shield Laws and the Sixth Amendment, 128 U. Pa. L. Rev. 544 (1980).

Sarah had just placed her one-year-old baby in the crib. Andrew, clearly agitated, walked over to the baby's crib and, pointing angrily at the baby, said: "You know what I want. Get on the bed and take off your clothes and no one will get hurt." Frightened and concerned for the safety of her baby, Sarah complied. When Andrew took off his clothes, Sarah, fearing Andrew might be HIV-positive, said to him: "Please use a condom. If you don't have one, I do." Andrew took the condom offered by Sarah and then had intercourse with her.

2. Jane and Tom meet for the first time at a bar and have some drinks. Tom offers to give Jane a ride home. On their way there Jane accepts Tom's invitation to come up to his apartment. After kissing Jane for a while on the couch, Tom starts unbuttoning her blouse:

    a. Jane tells Tom that she does not want to have sex with him. Tom pulls out a knife and says: "If you don't have sex with me, I could get angry." Jane, terrified, says nothing and lets Tom have intercourse with her.

    b. Jane tries to push Tom (who has no weapon) off and says: "I don't want to have sex with you." Tom, calling her a tease, pins her arms and manages to have intercourse with Jane.

    c. Jane, confused by this sudden turn of events, says nothing. Tom lies on top of her, while she does and says nothing, and has intercourse with Jane.

    d. Jane says: "Stop, Tom. I don't want to have sex with you. We just met tonight." Tom replies: "You're right. You don't even know me. Don't you feel foolish coming up here? For all you know, I could be a serial sex killer who preys on women just like you." Though Tom does not intend to frighten Jane, she becomes very frightened after suddenly realizing that what Tom just said could well be true. She moves away from Tom and replies in a faltering voice: "God, you're right. You could be a maniac." Trying to calm the situation and reassure herself, Jane approaches and Tom puts her hands in his hands. Tom, thinking Jane has changed her mind, starts again to undress her. Jane, truly concerned that Tom may be another sex serial killer like Ted Bundy, says nothing while helping Tom take off her clothes. They then have sex.

    e. Tom secretly puts a "roofie" into a drink and offers it to Jane, who wastes little time in finishing it. A "roofie" is the drug, Rohypnol, which is a sedative and muscle relaxant that soon makes a person drowsy and disoriented. Jane feels dizzy, groggy, and unsure of what she is doing. Tom undresses her while she is mumbling words that don't make sense and they have intercourse without any resistance from Jane. When Jane wakes up the next day, she doesn't remember anything.

    f. Jane says to Tom: "I believe you should only have sex with the one you love." Tom replies: "It was love at first sight for me, Jane. I think you are the girl I will marry." Jane, moved by Tom's earnestness, says: "Oh, Tom. I'm so glad you feel that way. Let's make love." They have intercourse and, as Tom leaves that night, he turns to Jane and says: "I don't want to see you again."

g. Jane and Tom go to Jane's apartment rather than to Tom's. After kissing Jane for a while on the couch, Tom starts unbuttoning her blouse. Jane says: "I want you to leave. I expect my boyfriend to come back from a business trip later tonight." Tom leaves. Jane leaves the door unlocked for her boyfriend and then, after turning out the light, goes back to sleep. One hour later Tom enters the apartment, goes into Jane's bedroom, and whispers in her ear: "I can't wait to have sex with you." Thinking it is her boyfriend, Jane pulls him into bed without turning on the light and they have intercourse.

h. Jane and Tom go to Jane's apartment rather than to Tom's. After kissing Jane for a while on the couch, Tom starts unbuttoning her blouse. Jane says: "No. I want you to leave." Tom does. Jane goes to bed and falls asleep, forgetting to lock her apartment door. Several hours later, Tom knowingly enters Jane's bedroom and, seeing Jane asleep, lies on top of her. Jane awakens and is very frightened. Afraid, Jane says nothing and offers no resistance, while Tom has intercourse with her.

3. Richard, age 42, instructed 13-year-old Elizabeth, his daughter, that the Bible commanded a daughter to perform a mother's duties if the mother could not. Elizabeth believed devoutly in the Bible and accepted Richard's teaching on this subject. After several months of stressing her special responsibilities as a daughter to act when her mother could not, Richard went into Elizabeth's room one evening and told her that, because her mother would not have sex with him, Elizabeth must follow the Bible and take on those responsibilities. Without using any physical force other than normally used in the act, Richard undressed and Elizabeth allowed him to have sexual intercourse with her.

4. Mary Kay, a high school history teacher, kept Jamie, a strapping, six-foot mature male 14-year-old student of hers, after school often during the spring semester. Having him serve as her paid student assistant, she groomed him with praise and responsibility. One day after all the other students had left, Mary Kay started to kiss Jamie and then to fondle him. Jamie responded and they had intercourse. They continued the relationship for several months. Mary Kay became pregnant and these events became known. Jamie and Mary Kay insisted that they loved one another and wanted to get married.

5. Demi, a top computer executive, is attracted to Mike, her administrative assistant. Demi and Mike have been working late on a special project the past few weeks. One night Demi asks Mike to have sex with her.

Mike politely declines. Demi tells Mike she will fire him if he does not. Mike, who has just purchased a house and needs his salary, feels he cannot afford to lose his job. They have sex.

6. Dr. Brown, a gynecologist, is about to give his patient, Heather, a vaginal exam. Contrary to professional protocol, he suddenly tells his nurse to leave the examination room on the pretext of locating some test results. Pretending to put on a latex glove, Dr. Brown inserts his bare hand into Heather's vagina and touches it for his own sexual gratification rather than to conduct a proper exam.

7a. Max picks up Roberta, a prostitute, in his van and agrees with her to have sexual intercourse for $100. He gives her a counterfeit bill and has intercourse. The next day Roberta realizes the bill is phony.

7b. Max picks up Roberta, a prostitute, in his van and agrees to have sexual intercourse for $100. Just before having intercourse, Roberta tells Max she wants her money first or she won't have sex. Max, who does not have the $100 and had hoped to tell Roberta this after they had sex, says to Roberta: "I don't have any money." He then physically overpowers Roberta and has sexual intercourse with her.

8. Alan and Bob meet at a gay bar. They decide to go home to Alan's house. Bob agrees to let Alan, who is much bigger than he is, rub his back, though Bob tells Alan: "I only want a back rub; nothing else, understand?" Alan nods and starts to rub Bob's back. Ten minutes later Alan suddenly rolls over on top of Bob and has anal sex with Bob, who unsuccessfully tries to move away.

9. Jo Anne, a heavy crack cocaine user, could not afford to pay cash for her drugs. Instead, she would offer sex in exchange for drugs. Harry, a dealer who has not sold drugs to Jo Anne before but knows of Jo Anne's past sex-for-drugs dealings with other dealers, has sex with Jo Anne. Later, Jo Anne files a rape complaint, alleging Harry forcibly raped her. Harry claims Jo Anne is making a false claim of rape because he did not pay Jo Anne with cocaine for the sex as promised.
   a. At his trial Harry's attorney wants to cross-examine Jo Anne about her past exchange of sex for drugs with other dealers.
   b. At the end of the trial, Harry's lawyer argues that the only proof of rape is Jo Anne's testimony. He asks the judge either to dismiss the case for lack of corroboration or to instruct the jury that there must be evidence in addition to the complainant's testimony to establish the elements of rape.

10. Larry, 32 years old, was Marcia's junior high school history teacher. Marcia, who was 13, had a reputation of sleeping around. She was also barely maintaining the minimum grade point average necessary to stay in school. One day Larry kept Marcia after school and told her he would give her a failing grade if she did not have sexual intercourse with him.

Marcia agreed and they had sex. A few weeks later Marcia reported the incident to the police.

11. Sal and his wife, Carmen, needed a baby-sitter for their two small children. Carmen interviewed Pam, who, though only 14, looked and acted much older. Because of Pam's maturity Carmen hired her to baby-sit the kids. One evening Sal came home early from work and asked Pam to have sex with him. Pam eagerly agreed and they had intercourse. A week later, Pam, angry because Sal would not sleep with her again, reported the incident to the police. Sal was shocked to learn Pam was only 14. She easily looked 18, and Carmen had never told him Pam's age.

EXPLANATIONS

1. This is the paradigm case. Andrew has committed rape under the common law. He had intercourse with a woman not his wife forcibly and without her consent. Andrew could also be convicted of rape under modern statutes. Though he did not actually use physical force to subdue Sarah, he threatened serious physical harm to a third person, Sarah's one-year-old baby. This implied threat should be sufficient for conviction. In some states the fact that Andrew committed a burglary by entering Sarah's house unlawfully to commit rape would aggravate the rape to first degree.

   If the jurisdiction required the victim to resist, Andrew might argue that he thought Sarah consented because she did not even say "no," let alone resist. He would also argue that Sarah's request that he use a condom was further evidence of consent.

   Andrew's defense should not succeed. In many states a victim no longer has to resist the use of force by the defendant. Even states that do require the victim to meet physical force with physical force do not expect physical resistance from a victim who is confronted with a threat of serious physical injury to herself or to a third person. Though Andrew's words did not expressly threaten Sarah's baby, it is clear from the context (an uninvited stranger unlawfully enters a woman's home and points at a vulnerable child using words that demand compliance with sexual demands as the price of not harming the baby) that Andrew was threatening a person other than the victim with serious physical harm.

   Even in states that retain nonconsent as an element of rape, Sarah's acquiescence to intercourse under these facts is very similar to an acceptance of a contract offer under duress. Sarah had no real choice. If she refused, Andrew would seriously harm her young child. Nor would her request that Andrew use a condom establish that Sarah consented or that Andrew believed (or reasonably could have believed) that she had consented to intercourse. In contemporary society it is a reasonable precaution for everyone, especially rape victims who have no knowledge of the rapist's sexual history, to insist on precautions against the spread of serious diseases.

2a. Tom has committed rape. Jane clearly told Tom that she did not want to have sex. Rather than accept her decision about not sharing sexual intimacy with him, Tom threatened her with serious physical harm. Though the common law did and some states still might require Jane to physically resist Tom if he used physical force, most states no longer require the complainant to offer any resistance when confronted with a *threat* of serious physical harm on the view that resistance would be both futile and potentially dangerous.

Tom should not be able to avoid conviction by testifying that he thought Jane had consented to sex. Consent is not an element of rape in many states, and even if it were, his threat of serious physical harm and use of a deadly weapon are very strong evidence that he knew Jane did not consent.

In many states the use of a deadly weapon would aggravate the rape from second degree to first degree because the harm done to the victim also includes fear that her life is in danger.

2b. Tom has committed rape. He has used force to have intercourse with Jane. Even in those states in which consent is an element, Jane has clearly stated that she does not consent to sex and, in addition, has physically resisted.

2c. This is a more difficult case. Some states require that the defendant use force that overcomes physical resistance or threatens the victim with serious physical harm.[60] Tom might not be convicted of rape under this approach because he has, arguably, only used that force normally involved in having intercourse and has not threatened Jane. Moreover, Jane offered no physical or verbal resistance.

Other states consider the defendant's act of nonconsensual sex *by itself* to be rape. Thus, even though Tom might argue that he has not used any force beyond that normally involved in sexual activity, his failure to obtain Jane's *affirmative assent* to sexual intimacy would be rape, though probably of a lesser degree.

If lack of consent is an element, the prosecutor might be able to prove that Tom knew or should have known that Jane did not consent. If consent is an affirmative defense, then Tom would have the burden of establishing that he reasonably believed that Jane had consented.[61]

---

60. See, e.g., *State v. Weisberg,* 65 Wash. App. 721, 829 P.2d 252 (1992).

61. See, e.g., *State v. Camara,* 113 Wash. 2d 631, 781 P.2d 483 (1989) (consent is an affirmative defense to a charge of rape); *People v. Williams,* 841 P.2d 961 (Cal. 1992).

2d. If Tom threatened Jane with death or serious physical injury to have sex with her, then he can be convicted of rape. But did Tom intend merely to state his perception of the obvious, or did he intend his words to intimidate Jane into having sex with him? In those states that define "threat" by the defendant's state of mind, Tom could not be convicted of rape (assuming he did not have this intent). In those states that define threat by whether the victim honestly and reasonably feared death or serious physical injury, Tom might be convicted of rape.

2e. Because of the drug (known on the street as a "date-rape drug"), Jane was incapable of consenting to sexual intimacy. Even though Tom did not use physical force or threaten force and Jane did not resist, she was not "conscious" for the purpose of legally consenting to intercourse. Tom knows this because he slipped the drug into her drink for this very reason. Thus, he can be convicted of rape.

2f. Tom has not used any force or threat. Tom has clearly lied to Jane and misrepresented both his affection for her and his future intentions. But this is not fraud in the factum; Tom has not deceived Jane as to the nature of the sexual act. It may be fraud in the inducement, but the law of rape does not criminalize obtaining sexual intimacy by deception. Jane was still able to make her own decision about sharing sexual intimacy. Thus, Tom has not committed rape. For better or worse, the law of rape does not protect humans from persuasion or seduction, even if it is deliberately dishonest and manipulative.

2g. In most states Tom has not committed rape. He has not used force or threats of physical harm nor was Jane unable, because of incapacity, to give consent. Though mistaken as to her partner's identity, Jane fully understood that she was about to have sexual intercourse, and she has given legally effective consent.

2h. Tom has, arguably, used force or the threat of force by creating a situation in which Jane honestly and reasonably feared bodily harm. Thus, under these circumstances Fred has used an implied threat of force by entering a stranger's bedroom uninvited at night and engaging in intercourse. Many states would not require Jane to resist or even to say "no" in this perilous situation.[62]

3. Whether or not Richard's despicable behavior constitutes rape depends on the law of his state. Some courts have held that coercion is inherent in the parent-child relationship and, therefore, no physical force or threat of force is required to convict a parent of rape.[63] In addition, Richard may also be guilty of statutory rape (nonforcible intercourse with a

---

62. *People v. Iniguez,* 7 Cal. 4th 847, 872 P.2d 1183, 30 Cal. Rptr. 258 (1994).
63. *State v. Eskridge,* 38 Ohio St. 3d 56, 526 N.E.2d 304 (1988).

minor who, because of her age, cannot consent) and incest (intercourse with a close family member). Other courts, however, have held that if the complainant is over the age of majority, even a past pattern of incest will not, by itself, satisfy the force requirement.[64] Here the victim is not over the age of majority, so Richard could be convicted of rape.

4. Mary Kay has committed "statutory rape" — that is, nonforcible intercourse with a minor, who, because of age, cannot give legally effective consent. The degree will depend on the state's particular statute. Mary Kay has not used force, threat of physical harm, or fraud and Jamie was a willing participant. Indeed, they now want to be married. Nonetheless, most states do not permit minors under the age of 15 to give legally effective consent to intercourse.

    Some state laws, following the lead of the MPC, define the crime of statutory rape and its degree by referring to the ages of the victim and of the defendant. In these states consensual sex between individuals close in age is not a crime. This approach will not help Mary Kay; she is significantly older than Jamie.

    A few states, however, have statutory rape laws that only protect females. If Mary Kay and Jamie lived in such a state, Mary Kay could not be convicted of statutory rape. Indeed, when Jamie reaches the requisite age, they can be married.

5. Demi has not committed rape. Rape requires force or the threat of physical injury. Demi has threatened Mike with economic harm, which does not satisfy the force element of rape. However, she may have committed extortion.

6. This scenario is based on the movie, *The Hand That Rocks the Cradle*. Dr. Brown would not have committed rape under the common law because he did not have sexual intercourse with Heather. Whether he could be convicted of rape under contemporary statutes is problematic.

    Most modern statutes cover a broader range of areas protected against penetration (usually including the vagina, anus, and mouth) and the means used (usually including not only the penis but fingers and any other objects used for this purpose). Unlike the common law, modern statutes probably would include the act of digital penetration in the definition of conduct covered by rape.

    However, it would be difficult to convict Dr. Brown under a statute that requires the use of *force* because, arguably, he did not use any force greater than that necessary to accomplish the penetration. Dr. Brown might be convicted of a lesser degree of rape under a statute that only requires *nonconsent* for rape because he inserted his bare hand into

---

64. *State v. Schaim*, 65 Ohio St. 3d 51, 600 N.E.2d 661 (1992); *Commonwealth v. Biggs*, 320 Pa. Super. 265, 467 A.2d 31 (1983).

Heather's vagina without her consent. Heather consented to a professional medical exam, not to an ungloved digital penetration of her vagina by Dr. Brown for his sexual gratification.

7a. Max has not committed rape even though he used fraud to obtain sexual intercourse. His use of counterfeit money may be considered fraud in the inducement because Roberta understood that she was having sexual intercourse for money. Max might have committed fraud or theft (as well as possessing and passing counterfeit money) but he did not commit rape.

7b. Max has committed rape. True, he had hoped to obtain sexual intercourse by fraud. However, when Roberta told him, no money, no sex, she withdrew her consent to sexual intercourse. Max then used physical force to overpower her and have intercourse. The fact that the victim is a prostitute and has regularly exchanged sex for money does not change the nature of the crime. Even though her sexual activity might violate laws on prostitution, Roberta's sexual autonomy is still protected by the law of rape and should be.

8. Alan has committed rape if the state law is gender-neutral and includes anal intercourse with another person by force or threat of serious physical harm. Alan used physical force to accomplish this sex act. If nonconsent is an element of rape, then the prosecution will have to prove that Alan knew that Bob did not consent (or was reckless or negligent as to consent, depending on the statutory language). Bob's initial statement that he only wanted a back rub and his physical resistance to intercourse strongly indicate that Bob did not consent and that Alan knew, or at the very least, should have known this. A few states retain consent as an affirmative defense and require the defendant to establish by a preponderance of the evidence that he honestly and *reasonably* believed that the complainant had consented.[65]

9a. This is a close case under most rape shield laws. This evidence would seriously damage the credibility of the complaining witness by showing that she had engaged in sex for drugs in the past. However, it is relevant to defendant's claim that the complainant consented to have sex and also sheds light on the complainant's motive—that is, she may be filing a rape charge in retaliation for Harry not paying her as promised. This evidence would probably be admitted.[66]

9b. Most states now consider the testimony of a rape victim to be legally sufficient to prove rape and do not require additional corroboration

---

65. *State v. Camara*, 113 Wash. 2d 631, 781 P.2d 483 (1989) (consent, though not mentioned in the rape statute, is an affirmative defense to a charge of rape).

66. *Johnson v. State*, 332 Md. 456, 632 A.2d 152 (1993).

evidence. The jury will be instructed that the prosecution must prove its case beyond a reasonable doubt and will have to decide who is telling the truth.

10. The prosecutor might bring a rape charge if his state is one of the minority jurisdictions that permit nonphysical threats (such as Larry's threat to give Marcia a failing grade) to satisfy the threat of force element. Since Larry's threat did not involve one of physical violence, most jurisdictions would not consider this a case of rape.

    However, the prosecutor could readily bring a statutory rape charge (also called "rape of child" in a few states) because Marcia was clearly under the age of consent, set by many states today at 16. The degree of the charge would depend on Marcia's age and in some states on Larry's age. The law simply considers children and young adolescents as legally incapable of giving consent. Thus, even if Larry might argue that Marcia voluntarily agreed to have sex with him, a statutory rape charge will succeed. In some states this type of threat might also constitute extortion.

11. Sal can be charged with statutory rape. Though Pam was a willing partner, the law protects young people from sexual exploitation by adults. In some states Sal might have a defense of reasonable mistake of fact because his belief that Pam was 18 appears to be reasonable. However, many states do not permit this defense to a charge of statutory rape, while others limit it to cases involving victims of a certain minimum age. Some states provide for degrees depending on the age of the victim.

10

Theft

Overview

Some people always want what the other person has. And they'll do anything to get it: take it, trick the owner into giving it up, hide it, perhaps even destroy the property if they can't have it.

These unhappy facts of life have given rise to one of the most arcane areas of criminal law: property offenses. The doctrines of the various crimes that constitute property offenses—larceny, embezzlement, taking under false pretenses, extortion, and others—are laced with rules and a host of exceptions to the rules. Courts have created fictional devices to reach the "right results" when the rules would not allow such a result. The doctrines also reflect tension between courts and legislatures about the reach of the criminal law and the impact of the death penalty.

There are three "major" property offenses: *larceny, embezzlement,* and *taking under false pretenses.* At the risk of grossly oversimplifying, one might say that the characteristics that distinguish these crimes from each other are as follows:

1. *Larceny* is a taking out of the *possession* of another.
2. *Embezzlement* is the *conversion* to the defendant's use of another's property lawfully obtained.
3. *False pretenses* — unlike the previous two, which are offenses against *possession* — is a taking of *title* by *deceit.*

These simplifications hide a vast array of interlocking and overlapping requirements and fact patterns. The ingenuity of persons who want someone else's property is vast and unlikely to be hemmed in by specific differences among the "elements" of various crimes. Nevertheless, it may help if you keep your eye on these skeletal definitions.

215

The Impact of History[1]

The Death Penalty

Prior to the common law, most legal systems, including both Greek and Roman law, had treated most infringements against property as torts, with only damages as a remedy.[2] In sharp contrast, however, the common law punished larceny with death, as it punished all felonies, until the early part of the nineteenth century.[3] However, many judges, opposed either to the penalty itself or to its imposition for "mere" invasions of property, gave restrictive readings of the "elements" of larceny so as to avoid imposing the death penalty. In the eighteenth century, as the death penalty became more discretionary, the need to restrict the reach of property offenses ebbed, and courts upheld liability in larceny (most notably in *Pear's Case,* infra). And when, in the nineteenth century, the death penalty was removed as a possible penalty for most property offenses unconnected with potential physical violence, courts gave increasingly broad readings to the elements of larceny. Similarly, legislatures enacted a wide range of new statutes proscribing other interferences with property, but not punishable by death.

Protecting Trade vs. Protecting Individualism

The explosion of trade during the fifteenth and sixteenth centuries created the need to protect property entrusted to carriers. The courts were faced with rules of larceny that had been established when most transactions were face-to-face and not national, much less transnational, in scope. Courts and legislatures were anxious to protect burgeoning trade and sometimes created fictions to capture persons who otherwise did not fit within the "elements" of larceny. Thus, the infamous *Carrier's Case,* discussed below, sought to protect merchants who almost by necessity had to "entrust" their property to others.

On the other hand, the "caveat emptor" ideology of the day, that

---

1. No group of crimes so reflects the various tensions in the centuries during which they were developed as do property offenses. For an extraordinary in-depth analysis of the historical development, see J. Hall, Theft, Law and Society (1952).

2. There were some exceptions: Stealing a bather's clothes and theft of livestock were criminally punishable in Rome. Housebreaking and theft at night, which indirectly involved the potential threat to persons, were also treated criminally (under the common law scheme, they would be dealt with as burglary).

3. There is some suggestion that "larceny" was initially (1000-1250 A.D.) limited to forcible takings (what we now call robbery), but the history is somewhat cloudy.

individuals, and not the state, should protect themselves from loss whenever possible, made courts reluctant to broaden the net of the criminal law. For example, in *R. v. Wheatley*, 2 Burr. 1125, 97 Eng. Rep. 746 (1761), the defendant had unquestionably defrauded the victim by asserting that the cask of amber beer that he sold him contained 18 gallons, while in fact it contained only 16. Nevertheless, when the defendant was prosecuted for larceny, the court acquitted. Lord Mansfield held that the defendant had committed no crime: This was "only an inconvenience and injury to a private person, arising from that private person's own negligence and carelessness in not measuring the liquor upon receiving it." Mr. Justice Wilmot concurred, declaring that "it was [the victim's] own indolence and negligence if he did not [measure the beer]." In such an atmosphere, courts were unlikely to protect victims by criminalizing the defendant.[4]

Given these different pressures, it may not be surprising to see courts and legislatures maneuvering, from one fact pattern to another, to mold doctrine to reach the "correct" result. However, such distortions of the "rule of law" inevitably created confusion and intricate, if artificial, distinctions among crimes. It surely would have been better if the courts had created new offenses rather than stretch and distort the definition of larceny. But the history of the law, as Mr. Justice Holmes said, has been experience and not logic. Too bad.

In the nineteenth century, the task of defining and expanding the reach of the criminal law while reducing the impact of the death penalty shifted from courts to the legislatures. In the latter part of our own century, legislatures, abetted by courts, have slowly sought to clarify and rationalize the law of property offenses. The Model Penal Code is one of several such attempts.

Larceny

The "elements" of larceny are easily stated:

1. There must be a *trespassory*
2. *taking*
3. and *asportation*
4. of the *personal property*
5. *of another*

---

4. The case was different, however, when false weights or tokens were used. There, the argument was, the victim *could not* have protected himself against fraud. Statutes punished such "cheating" but not with the death penalty. This limitation is not uniquely English. French law, at least as late as 1952, punished as criminal only elaborate swindling schemes, and mere misrepresentation was not punished. See MPC Commentary, part II, §223.1 n.5, p.130 (1980).

6. with the *intent*
7. to deprive him of it *permanently* (or *for a long period of time*)

Trespass

The first element of larceny limits the crime to acts that violate *possession* of an item. If the defendant has already obtained lawful possession of the property, his later use or conversion cannot be a "trespass" and he has not committed larceny. Thus, if George, with Ralph's permission, borrows Ralph's Maserati, and decides later that he loves the car too much to return it, George may be a dastardly evildoer, but he is not guilty of common law larceny because his initial taking was not a trespass.

That limitation, however, conflicted with the need to protect trade in mid-Renaissance England. In *The Carrier's Case, Anon. v. The Sheriff of London,* 64 Seld. Soc. 30, (1473), a London dealer (call him Henry) had hired the defendant (Jerry) to take some goods from London to Southampton. The goods were inside packages. Jerry got about halfway, broke open the packages, and hid the contents. In a prosecution for larceny, Jerry argued that he had obtained possession of the goods lawfully and consensually and therefore was not guilty of the crime. Jerry *was* right, but he lost anyway. The court announced a new fiction. Jerry, it said, had possession of the packages *qua* packages. Had he simply sold those packages, he would not have "trespassed" on the goods. But since he had *"broken bulk"* of the packages, he had trespassed on the goods inside and hence was guilty of larceny.

The fiction of "breaking bulk" was only the first of many such fictions that the common law courts would create, some favorable to the defendant, some not, in trying to square specific acts with the definition of larceny. A second judicially created fiction was *constructive possession,* which elaborated on the distinction between "custody" and "possession." Usually, we think of anyone who has "dominion" over an item as "possessing" it. However, the courts concluded that a person who had only temporary and extremely limited authorization to use the property had only custody and not possession. This was said to be the case with employees[5] and bailees but not with carriers, apparently because they had authority for larger periods of time than did bailees or employees. Constructive possession remained in the owner, such that a taking by an employee was trespassory.

The doctrine was also used in the case of persons finding lost items. Even if the owner did not know where the item was, he was said to have

---

5. The common law could not be quite so rule-bound. If the employee had "significant" authority, he obtained possession and not mere custody. See *Morgan v. Commonwealth,* 47 S.W.2d 543 (Ky. 1932).

constructive possession of the item. Then, if the finder, *F,* knew, or could suspect, who the owner was, and intended at the time of finding to convert the item, the finding became trespassory.

The constructive possession fiction did not apply to the merchant-deliverer situation nor to a host of other similar (but not identical) relationships. For example, if *A* gives *B* her first edition of Shakespeare, believing *B* to be *C,* an antiques dealer, *B* has obtained possession voluntarily, and his later conversion of the book is not larceny. Similarly, if *D* owes *E* $10 but gives him $100 in error, *E* has not committed larceny of the $90 excess because he obtained it nontrespassorily. *Cooper v. Commonwealth,* 110 Ky. 123 (1901). Now the courts *could* have found *B* and *E* to be "bailees" or, in the alternative, could have concluded that *A* and *D* retained "constructive possession" as well. But they did not, and it was up to legislatures to deal with these situations.

One such exception *was* created by the courts, relatively late, in the infamous *Pear's Case. R. v. Pear,* 168 Eng. Rep. 208 (1779). Pear rented a horse from Victim, intending all the while to take the horse and sell it. Pear argued that his initial taking of the horse was consensual and not trespassory. The court responded by finding that his intent at the initial rental to take the horse vitiated the consensual aspect of the rental and created "larceny by trick." Had Pear formed the intent to take the horse *after* he rented it, it would not be larceny (but *might* be embezzlement) (see infra).

This muddle of rules as to when a trespass does (or does not) occur baffled both courts and prosecutors. And when courts required that the prosecutor indict for the precise crime committed, and prove *that* offense or lose, the stakes were substantial.

Asportation and Taking

Although "taking" and "asportation" seem to describe the same actions, the common law distinguished between them. *Asportation* (a sufficiently clumsy word to justify vilification of the common law courts) occurred only if the defendant actually "moved" the property. Where the property is incapable of being "carried away," such as a house or a heavy object, it may not be the subject of asportation. See Annot., 70 A.L.R.3d 1202 (1976).

The movement need not be far; there are cases holding that even a change of position of two or three inches is sufficient. However, if the item is not moved at all, there is no asportation and hence no larceny. Of course, the courts were always ready to create a fiction if justice required it. Suppose that George "sells" Jamal that red Maserati of Ralph's. George gives Jamal convincing fake copies of title, and Jamal, after depositing $50,000 in George's hand, drives the car away. Even if George has never entered the car, he has "asported" it. The fiction of *innocent agency* turned Jamal into

George's "agent," so that when Jamal took the car, it was "really" George driving it away.[6]

Taking required "caption," defined as exercising *control and dominion* over the property. If the property was not *capable* of being taken, a mere asportation was insufficient. For example, if a clothing store attached a coat to a mannequin by a chain, even if the defendant "moved" (and therefore asported) the coat, his conduct was not a "taking," since the coat could not (short of a blow torch) be removed.

Personal Property

Larceny never applied to real property (possibly because it could never be asported). However, as to items that are "fixtures" on the land, the common law really outdid itself in creating confusion. If Mary Ann trespassed on Celia's land one day, cut down eight cedar trees, and immediately removed the lumber, there was no larceny because the act was seen as affecting not personal property but real property. If, however, Mary Ann got tired after the hewing, went home to relax for an hour or two, and then returned, her subsequent asportation of the downed lumber was *now* larceny, since the trees had become Celia's personal property.[7]

Documents representing either real property or choses in action were not the subject of larceny. The fiction upon which this result rested, that the documents "merged" into the things they represented, may have been helpful in other branches of the law but was a hindrance in criminal law. On the other hand, some *incorporeal* items, such as electricity, *could* be the subject of larceny while others, such as ideas, could not. Thus, when David Ellsberg stole papers from the Pentagon, photocopied them, and publicized them, he was guilty under the common law (if at all) only of the larceny of the value of the paper. The ideas were not items that could be "stolen" under common law larceny.

The common law also held that theft of *services* (as opposed to property) was not larceny. Thus, if Basil hires Joanne to fix his car and then takes off in the repaired auto without paying, Basil has not committed larceny because services are not property and, hence, their "taking" is not criminal.

Finally, the common law distinguished among animals. Not surprisingly, wild animals (*ferrae naturae*) that merely "lived" on a victim's land were not "his," and hence could not be personal property, the subject of larceny. But the law went further: Cows *could* be stolen, but domesticated dogs could

---

6. Not all courts agreed. See *Smith v. State*, 11 Ga. App. 197 (1912) (asportation and hence larceny); *State v. Labrode*, 202 La. 59 (1942) (no larceny). See Annots., 19 A.L.R. 724 (1922); 144 A.L.R. 1383 (1943).

7. It is sometimes explained that if the "trees" are laid on the owner's ground, the "lumber" becomes his property, and the taking is thus from his possession.

not because, while not wild, pets were "base" animals below the law's cognition.

Of Another

It would seem obvious that you cannot "steal" your own property. However, the obvious is never necessarily the legal. Since larceny is a crime *against possession, not ownership,* if Ben loans Greg his putter for a week but then decides in the middle of the week that he wants it back, and simply takes it from Greg's golf bag, Ben *can* be guilty of the larceny of "his" putter. Similarly, if Greg had a lien on the putter, Ben could be guilty of larceny. You can also steal from a thief; although he obviously does not have "title" to his goods, he does have "possession" such that removing his stolen property constitutes larceny.[8]

One aspect of this rule is the effect of a so-called *claim of right.* If George wrongly believes that Stan owes him Stan's red Maserati (for whatever reason) and takes it, George is not guilty of larceny. One way of expressing this rule is to say that a claim of right negates the "specific intent" of larceny. However, as we have already seen (Chapter 4), the specific-general intent distinction is tenuous at best. The better analysis is simply to say that the defendant acting under a claim of right does not "know" that the property belongs to "another," and hence does not meet the culpability requirements with respect to the material elements of the offense. Moreover, consistent with other "specific intent" crimes, any mistake, no matter how unreasonable, will "negate" liability for larceny. Also consistent with those rules, a mistake of law, as well as a mistake of fact, will exculpate.

When the taker has some interest in the property but does not have "full" possession, the common law concluded that a co-owner (partner, spouse, tenant in common) cannot commit larceny from another co-owner. When, however, the partners are in the process of dissolving their relationship, this rule may not always apply.

With Intent

Get ready for another great Latin phrase, *animus furandi.* Under this phrase, the defendant had to "intend" to "deprive" the possessor "permanently" of the item. Suppose that George intends to take what he knows to be Ralph's car but intends to return it within a day or a week. Here the law was somewhat schizophrenic. If George intended to return the same car, then usually there was no larceny. If, however, the property was otherwise

---

8. One suggestion is that this deters thieves from stealing from other thieves. But that would be true only if the second thief *knew* that the possessor was a thief. This seems a stretched explanation.

fungible (such as money), many courts found there *was* larceny, even though Ralph would get "the equivalent" money returned. George had in fact deprived Ralph of the "very" paper that he had taken. That, said the criminal law, was sufficient.

Moreover, George's liability in each instance would depend in part not only on his intent to return the item but on the *reasonableness of his belief that he could do so.* If George was merely wishfully thinking that he could return the same car or even the same amount, it is larceny. Thus, if George intends to use Ralph's car in a demolition derby or even in a stock car race, his ability to return the car in the same condition he takes it is so small that he will be guilty of larceny *even though* his "subjective intent" was not to deprive Ralph of it permanently. In a sense, if George was "reckless" as to his ability to return the property, that was a sufficient basis for liability. Similarly, even in those jurisdictions that would allow George a defense if he intended to return the equivalent amount, if George used the money to gamble on a horse (even a "sure winner"), he would be guilty of larceny. On the other hand, an objectively plausible intent to return the property prevents liability even if some unexpected obstacle prevents an actual return. *Schnectady Varnish Co. v. Automobile Ins. Co.,* 127 Misc. 751 (Sup. Ct. 1926).

To Deprive

The mens rea of larceny is *animus furandi* (intent to steal), not *lucri causa* (because of gain). Although most thieves take property so that they can use the stolen item, that is not required by the definition of larceny. The focus is on *the loss to the possessor,* not the gain to the defendant. Thus, if George, jealous of Stan, takes the Maserati and has it destroyed, it is larceny even though George never expected to retain the car.

Permanently

As already suggested, if George takes Stan's car but only intends to make Stan walk to work for a week and then to return the car, most courts would find that the taking was not larcenous because the intended deprivation was not "permanent." Thus, "borrowing" an item was almost never enough for larceny. Suppose, however, that the defendant knows that the owner needs the item during the time it will be missing? Greg, intending to return it immediately after the tournament is over, takes Ben's favorite putter the night before Ben is to participate in the Masters, or Sheila takes Madeleine's stocks and bonds for a week, knowing that Madeleine will have to declare bankruptcy without them. Some courts began to include in the definition of larceny an intent to deprive of "important" or "economically significant" possession, even if the taker had the purpose to return the property after this usefulness was exhausted.

Injury to aesthetic interests, however, was never included within larceny. If Tom removes Mary's Monets from the wall of her summer house for the one month during which Mary will be there, intending to replace them as soon as Mary leaves, Tom has not committed larceny, even though he has inflicted harm on Mary. Again, suppose that Tom has removed the Monets not to upset Mary but to use as collateral in obtaining a loan. Since Tom's (reasonably achievable) intent is to return these very paintings, it is not larceny.

Contemporaneity

As if all these factors weren't enough to cause apoplexy, the courts further required that the mens rea and the actus reus coincide. Only if, at the time of the taking, D had the requisite mens rea did the taking constitute larceny. Thus, if Greg takes Ben's putter out of his golf bag without Ben's knowledge with every purpose of returning it after ten minutes' practice, but then decides to keep it, Greg has not committed larceny because his intent at the time of the taking was not to deprive Ben of the putter permanently. His later conversion may be immoral, unethical, and even not nice, but it's not larceny.

Here again, however, the common law created new fictions to cover egregious cases. In this instance, courts developed the fiction of *continuing trespass*. Since Greg's original taking was trespassory, the courts concluded that the trespassory nature "continued" as long as Greg had the putter. Therefore, at the time Greg decided to keep it, there was a coincidence of mens rea and actus reus, and Greg could be transported to Australia. But even here, things were complicated. Some courts limited the application of this fictional doctrine to cases where the original taking was not only "trespassory" but done with an immoral, even if not criminal, mens. Thus if, when he picked it up, Greg thought that the putter was his, the taking, though objectively a trespass,[9] was held *not* to be "continuing"; hence, when he later converted it to his own use, the conversion did not transform the original taking into larceny.

Finders

Assume that Alice mislays, or loses, her treasured collection of Nirvana CDs, and John finds them and takes them home. Is this larceny? At first blush, John's taking does not seem to be trespassory, but the common law early established a fiction that lost or mislaid property was still in the constructive possession of the owner. Thus, John's taking was trespassory. However, the law still would not convict John unless:

---

9. In tort, mistake of fact is not a defense to a claim of trespass. It may negate mens rea, but it does not negate the trespassory nature of the taking.

1.   The property bore some indication that it belonged to someone (although it was not necessary that the specific possessor be indicated).
2.   At the time of the finding, John expected and intended to keep it.

Thus, if John finds the CDs, and there is no indication of ownership, he is not guilty of larceny. Even if there is such indication (the owner's mailing label would be nice), it is not larceny if John takes them, intending to return them to Alice, but only later decides to enjoy the music himself (the contemporaneity requirement).

Hasn't this trip through larceny been fun? Every time it looks as though we've got a firm "rule," it turns out squishy. Rules gave way to exceptions, which then became qualified by sub-exceptions, which in turn were changed by fictions to reach a "right" result. And that, as Justice Holmes put it, has been the life of the law.

Embezzlement

Not even all the fictions and exceptions to the general requirements of larceny could meet the needs of society nor the ingenuity of bad-minded folk. Suppose, for example, that Marvin is a bank teller, and Laurel, a depositor, gives him money to deposit for her account. If Marvin puts the money into the till and then removes it for his trip to Rio, he would be guilty of larceny from the bank since the money would first go into possession of the bank (the till), and his later taking would be trespassory. But if Marvin immediately puts the money in his pocket, planning an immediate trip to Rio, it is not larceny. Since Laurel has voluntarily parted with her money, Marvin's initial "taking" is not trespassory from her. And since he has not "tricked" her into giving up her money, *Pear's Case* and the doctrine of larceny by trick are not applicable. Moreover, the bank never possessed the money. Thus, Marvin is not guilty of larceny.

It made little sense to hold Marvin guilty of a crime depending on whether the money physically went into the till. Yet this was exactly the result in the (in)famous *Bazeley's Case*, 168 Eng. Rep. 517 (1799), where Bazeley was acquitted of a larceny charge. Of course, the courts could have established yet another "fiction," for example, that the money remained in the depositor's "constructive possession" until put into the till, but it chose not to do so. The legislature quickly filled this gap by creating the statutory misdemeanor of *embezzlement*.[10] The elements of embezzlement then became

---

10. It has been suggested that common law courts were not prepared to treat as larceners, and thus subject to the death penalty, employees who simply misappropriated property that they received on behalf of their employers. But this seems unlikely, since those same courts treated disloyal employees as guilty of larceny if they misappropriated property given to them by their employers, and indeed erected the new fiction of constructive possession to explain it.

1. a *fraudulent*
2. *conversion*
3. of *property*
4. of *another*
5. by one who is *already in lawful possession* (not mere custody) of it.[11]

The key differences between embezzlement and larceny are (1) an actual conversion must occur; (2) the original taking must *not* be trespassory—that is, the conversion here is *against ownership and not possession.* (Note that it is still necessary to distinguish between "title" and "ownership"; if *title* is misappropriated, it is false pretenses, discussed next.)

Conversion

Conversion requires that the defendant "seriously interfere" with the property — unlike larceny, in which even a movement of a few inches is sufficient to qualify.[12] Like larceny, however, embezzlement does not require that the conversion be for the benefit of the defendant. It can benefit another or in some cases result in little or no gain to anyone, but merely a loss to the owner. Indeed, as in larceny, the focus is on the loss of the owner, not the gain of the thief.

In Lawful Possession

As we have seen, the crime of embezzlement was statutorily enacted to fill the gap in larceny law where possession was initially obtained lawfully; lawful possession is usually the issue in deciding whether the defendant committed larceny or embezzlement. Particularly given the fictions that common law courts had previously created to fill *other* gaps in larceny law, there can be confusion. Thus, an employee may either have possession of property given to him by his employer (and hence be guilty of embezzlement if he converts it) or be only in custody (since his employer retains "constructive possession") and hence be guilty of larceny if he "takes" the property. Thus, if Jim gives John, his employee, $500 in cash, and John heads for Rio, it is fairly clear that this is larceny and not embezzlement, for the "constructive possession" fiction applies. Suppose, however, that Jim gives John a check for $500 and John cashes it, but then takes the proceeds and heads for Rio. Did Jim ever have possession of "the cash," such that John has committed larceny? Or is this a case of embezzlement? Courts differed.

---

11. The initial statute against embezzlement was limited to bank tellers, but subsequent additions to the idea were eventually generalized to include any person who had been "entrusted" with the property in question.

12. In this sense, larceny, which requires only an "intent to deprive" and not an actual deprivation, can be seen as an inchoate offense, while embezzlement is a "result" offense.

Fraud

The requirement that the conversion be "fraudulent" is somewhat misleading, at least if we think of "fraud" in the normal usage of that term, which suggests that at the time he actually got the property, *D* (a) intended to convert it to his own use and/or (b) induced the owner to part with it on the basis of deceit. The term, as used at least in embezzlement statutes, does not necessarily suggest either of these.

As with larceny, embezzlement is said to be a "specific intent" crime, so that a person who converts property under a mistaken claim of right, or with the intent to return the very property he takes, is not guilty of the crime. Also as with larceny, the intent to return the equivalent property is a defense. However, in contrast to larceny, where an intent to return equivalent property that is offered for sale *may* be a defense, embezzlement occurs even with such an intent.

False Pretenses

The common law defined larceny as an offense against possession, and embezzlement as an offense against ownership-possession. Thus, if George persuades Stan to loan him his Maserati for a day, and then converts it to his own use, it is embezzlement if the initial taking was not trespassory. It's larceny by trick if George always intended to convert it. But if the defendant obtained not merely possession of the item but *title* as well, the common law courts held that this was neither larceny nor embezzlement. Thus, if George persuades Stan to *give* him the Maserati so that George can allegedly donate it to a charity, or on the false representation that George needs to sell the car to save his dying mother, George has committed neither of these two crimes. Since, in almost all cases of title passing, possession also passes, the common law courts surely could have held that larceny covered the offense. However, because courts hesitated, for some unclear reason, to create another common law property offense,[13] Parliament stepped in by enacting a statute to plug this loophole and prohibit *obtaining property by false pretenses.* As explained by case law, the offense requires:

1. a *representation*
2. of a *material present or past fact*
3. which the *defendant knows to be false*

---

13. It might be remembered that *Pear's Case,* which created the crime of "larceny by trick," was decided 30 years after the false pretense statute was enacted. Ten years after *Pear's Case* the courts refused to bring embezzlement with the common law larceny crime, thereby impelling Parliament to enact embezzlement statutes.

4. and which he *intends* will and
5. does *cause the victim*
6. to pass *title*
7. of his property

While the requirements of a cause and "property" seem to be fairly straightforward elements, the other elements have created difficulties for the courts.

Representation

The misrepresentation has to be affirmative. The failure to disclose a fact does not constitute common law false pretenses, unless there is a preexisting fiduciary duty between the parties. Thus, if John sells Joe a book labeled "Modern Tax Law," knowing that Joe believes it to be current whereas John knows that the book deals with a repealed Code, John has not obtained the money by false pretenses unless he *affirmatively* tells Joe that the book is "current." His failure to correct Joe's misunderstanding is insufficient.

Present or Past Fact

Although the statutory language contained not even a hint of the limitation, common law courts quickly held that only the representation of a *present or past fact* could be the basis of a conviction of this new crime. If the defendant fraudulently pays the seller with counterfeit money, this is false pretenses for the representation is that the money is valid. If, however, the defendant fraudulently promises the seller that he will pay tomorrow, and does not, this is not false pretenses because the misrepresentation is as to defendant's future intent or acts, and that is a "false promise" and not a present fact.

This distinction is often hard to make. A defendant's (intentionally false) statement that he "will" pay tomorrow could be construed as a misstatement about a present fact, his current state of mind. Moreover, although one hears echoes of the common law's refusal to protect fools, it is not clear why persons who rely on promises about the future are "bigger fools" than those who do not ascertain the accuracy of representations as to present facts.[14] (Or, to put it another way, why persons who deceive using present facts are more dangerous, or more blameworthy, than those who deceive by making promises.)

Supporters of the distinction argue that it is needed to protect legitimate

---

14. Although there apparently was some authority that the lie had to be one calculated to deceive a reasonable man (see *Commonwealth v. Norton*, 93 Mass. 266 (1865)), the modern rule is that the victim's failure to act reasonably is irrelevant.

business deals. Virtually all contracts concern themselves with promises to be performed in the future. Persons often contract with one another with the full expectation of performing in the future. If every failure to perform a contract could be construed as obtaining by false pretenses, business agreements would be undermined. One cannot be sure whether a borrower who has defaulted made a false promise or simply changed his mind about the use of borrowed money (or was simply unable to pay back). If criminal liability were this likely, contracts would become far less prevalent, and commerce would decline.

Those who think that it should be possible to convict on the basis of false promises argue that juries are as capable of deciding this mens rea as they are in other cases. And empirically there appears to be no flood of "bad" prosecutions in jurisdictions that recognize false promises as bases for false pretenses.

Title

The distinguishing factor between false pretenses and the other two offenses we have considered is that *title must pass* at some point to the defendant, whereas in the other two it does not. In many instances, it is clear whether title passes, but some cases are not obvious. Thus, suppose that only part of the title passes, such as when there is a conditional sale induced by false representation. Although full title does not pass until the sale is complete, courts usually conclude that "enough" indices of title have passed to warrant a conviction of false pretenses. On the other hand, if a defendant induces a victim to depart with property for a specific purpose (e.g., to buy a piece of nonexistent land; to give a (fictitious) bribe to a third party), it is held that this is not false pretenses but larceny by trick because title would only pass if the purported goal were actually achieved.

Mens Rea, Knowledge, and Intent to Defraud

Since this crime is limited to representations regarding past or present facts, the prosecution must show not only that the representation was false,[15] but that the defendant knew the falsity of her representation. Although on principle one might be willing to convict a defendant who states facts with

---

15. For some reason, if the defendant believes the representation to be false but it turns out (much to the chagrin of the defendant) to be true, the crime has not been committed. It is *possible* that such a defendant could be convicted of attempting to obtain property by false pretenses, but since there was never a possibility that the fact would be false, such a conclusion is problematic at best. See the discussion of impossibility in Chapter 12.

regard to which she is reckless, the majority view seemed to be that this was not sufficient for liability.

In addition to knowing that the statements she makes are false, the defendant must "intend to defraud." As in larceny and embezzlement, therefore, this "specific intent" requirement is not present if the defendant is acting under a claim of right or intends to return the property.

Puffing and Opinion

The lure of caveat emptor dies hard. Under the common law, no statement as to "value" would be sufficient to find the defendant guilty of false pretenses. This, it was held, was mere opinion (as opposed to fact), and the buyer should be wary of relying on such statements. Similarly, obtaining property by "puffing," exaggerations that are common in the trade, was held not to be sufficient for guilt. Supporters of such restrictions argue that individuals should be required to take some responsibility for their choices, but those in favor of holding "puffers" liable point out that their intent may be no less malicious than those who are less clever about their deceit.

Confusion

All of these conflicting doctrines, exceptions, fine-edged distinctions, and springing fictions gave both courts and prosecutors headaches, particularly in light of the view, held at least by most courts through the early part of this century, that the prosecutor could allege only one such crime in an indictment. If the wrong crime were alleged, there was no remedy except to retry the defendant for the "other" crime. The gossamer lines between larceny and embezzlement, and between false pretenses and larceny by trick, generated severe displeasure with "the system." Thus, if George was convicted of larceny by trick, he could successfully appeal by arguing that he had not intended to convert at the time that he obtained the property. If he was then retried for embezzlement, he could argue that the evidence showed that he *did* intend to convert then, and that he could therefore not be guilty of embezzlement.

During the middle part of this century, state legislatures began attacking these problems, but the attacks were often piecemeal, such as adding a line or two to the larceny statute or embezzlement statute that tried to reach all the various possibilities. Some statutes provided that one who commits embezzlement or false pretenses "shall be deemed guilty of larceny." Still other states allowed the prosecuting attorney to join several counts in one indictment, thus potentially leaving to the jury the job of determining the exact crime that the defendant had committed. However, there was the danger that the jurors would not agree on the crime or, if they did, that an appellate court would find that they selected the wrong one.

Moreover, a number of these statutes seemed wildly untamed. Thus, for example, some statutes penalized as embezzlement a breach of faith, even if there was no expropriation. Other states altered the kinds of property that could be the subject of these crimes, varied the requirements for lost or mislaid property, and so on. In short, there was little uniformity among the statutes.

The Model Penal Code has sought to bring some uniformity to the states. Even here, however, the vagaries of past precedent, ambiguity in statutes, and the ingenuity of defendants still plague the courts. Until and unless we find a way either to be more precise with our language or to allow more flexibility in the process of charging and convicting of crime, the dead hand of the past will continue to govern much of the doctrine of property offenses.

Grading

When larceny was punishable by death, Parliament (and later the states) enacted statutes providing that really trivial (petit) larcenies should be exempted from that punishment. The method used was to assess the value of the goods taken: If the amount was less than 30 pence (the value of one sheep), death was not an available penalty.[16]

Even after the abolition of the death penalty for larceny, American jurisdictions have continued to use the value of goods taken as the demarcation between "grand" and "petty" larceny, with the former obviously being punished more severely. Some states have three or four degrees of larceny, depending on the amount taken. Whether this is a sensible approach is not clear, particularly in cases where the defendant is mistaken as to the amount he intends to (or risks) taking. As discussed in the materials on mistake (Chapter 5), there are instances where such a mistake might be relevant, particularly under the Model Penal Code. Thus, if the defendant *thinks* he is stealing a nickel but the nickel is a valuable coin worth thousands, most jurisdictions would hold that the defendant takes the risk that his crime is greater than he believes (see the discussion in Chapter 6 of the "greater

---

16. The animosity of English juries to the death penalty is reflected in 1 L. Radzin-owicz, History of English Criminal Law and Its Administration (1948), who recites numerous jury verdicts finding the value of goods taken as one pence less than the "death amount." In an intriguing reversion to that time, the current New Jersey statute explicitly provides that the amount of the value of the goods taken shall be fixed by the trier of fact; no guidance is provided by the statute. See N.J. Stat. Ann. 2c:20-2(b)(4).

crime" theory). The Code, however, would make the defendant liable only for the amount he *thought* he was taking. Of course, if the defendant simply decides to take a pocketbook, he probably takes the risk that it will contain the Hope Diamond.

Measuring the value of the goods, of course, is not always easy, particularly where the value of goods changes drastically and quickly, such as futures or works of art. Usually the market value as of the day the item is stolen is used, but there are problems involved in determining both market value and the "time" at which the item was "stolen," particularly in cases of "continuing trespass," which require a "conversion" that occurs principally in the defendant's mind. Problems also occur if the defendant takes several items over a period of time (e.g., a bank teller who embezzles $500 a week for ten weeks), but the courts generally allow aggregation of these amounts *if* they are from the same victim and appear to be part of a "single" plot.[17]

The Model Penal Code

Although several states had preceded it, the Model Penal Code is the leader in the current movement for statutory reform and consolidation of theft crimes. The Code provides for one crime of "theft," which can be committed in a variety of ways, including larceny or embezzlement or false pretenses (the Code also includes extortion, receiving stolen goods, and similar offenses in its general sections on theft). The fine distinctions between the crimes based on the intention of the parties or the victim's understanding and intent have been eliminated; the Code takes the position, reaffirmed by most other modern statutes, that thieves are equally dangerous or culpable and the harm of such crimes equally serious, no matter how caused.

As important as the generic definition is the provision that the prosecution will not be hamstrung if its proofs at trial suggest a different "method" of committing theft than was pled in the indictment; a charge of "theft," without more, will suffice for conviction as long as the actual proof shows that the conduct violated a specific statutory prohibition.

Because it combines all thefts the Code does not require a "taking" or an "asportation." The Code calls "criminologically insignificant" the question of whether the item has been "moved" or not. Instead, the Code requires that the defendant "unlawfully take or exercise unlawful control over" movable property or "unlawfully transfer" immovable property. As the Code commentary puts it: "[T]he critical inquiry is twofold: whether the

---

17. This problem is not unique to theft, of course. If a drug pusher sells ten bags of 1 gram each to a single customer, has he sold 10 grams, or committed ten sales of 1 gram each, assuming that there is a punishment difference?

actor had control of the property, no matter how he got it, and whether the actor's acquisition or use of the property was authorized."

The Code does not require that the defendant intend to deprive "permanently," as the common law did, but it does focus on the deprivation of "economic" value, thereby ignoring the aesthetic or psychological value of items, such as Ben's putter or Mary's Monets. Indeed, since the Code requires that the defendant deprive the victim of the "major portion of the economic value" of the putter, it is not even clear that taking the putter for one golf tournament (even if it is *the* golf tournament) would be sufficient.

A trespass is not needed, and all property, both movable and immovable, is a proper subject of theft. The Code also abolishes the "property" limitations erected by the common law, providing that "anything of value, including real estate, tangible and intangible personal property, contract rights, choses-in-action and other interests in or claims to wealth, admission or transportation tickets, captured or domestic animals, food and drink, electric or other power," are all possible subjects of theft.

In contrast to the common law, the Code's emphasis is on the gain to the defendant rather than the loss to the victim. Actions designed to destroy or damage the tangible property of another are dealt with as "criminal mischief" rather than as theft under the Code. As the commentary puts it: "The provisions against theft contemplate cases where the actor uses the property for his own purposes."

Whether the defendant had the intent at the time of "taking," or formed that intent afterward, is likewise not relevant to the defendant's liability. Not surprisingly, the Code does not limit "deceptive" takings to representations about "past or present facts," and includes all promises as to future action, if not actually fulfilled, as potential grounds of liability. However, reflecting the fear that many good intentions often go awry, the text of the Code expressly warns that a person's intention to deceive shall not be inferred "from the fact *alone*" that he did not fulfill the promise. Finally, the Code allows false promises to be the basis of a charge of theft by deception but continues the common law's reluctance to criminalize those who merely capitalize on others' misimpressions, unless they helped create those impressions or had a fiduciary duty to dispel them.

The Code also rejects the common law rule that one cannot steal from one's spouse, although it does not criminalize the taking of items generally shared, unless the couple has separated.

The Code has a specific provision that broadens the claim of right defense to all theft crimes and that focuses on the way in which a claim negates culpability. The Code also recognizes a claim or right based on a mistake of law as a defense, as well as establishing a defense that the property was for sale as long as the defendant either intended to pay for it promptly or reasonably believed that the owner, if present, would have consented.

Section 223.0 of the Code sets three levels of "theft" — petty misdemeanor (under $50 and as long as there was no threat or breach of a fiduciary obligation), misdemeanor ($50-$500), and third-degree felony (over $500) — and distinguishes punishment on the basis of the types of items stolen.

EXAMPLES

A hint on methodology: First determine which of the three kinds of common law theft the crime may be before deciding whether it meets all of the sub-rules. Probably the best way to do this is to decide what the crime is not. Thus:

1. Did the victim intend to give title? or only possession?

If the former, it can only be false pretenses. If the latter, it can only be either larceny or embezzlement. To decide which of the latter it might be, ask:

2. Did the defendant come into the property lawfully (usually by consent)?

If so, then the offense can only be embezzlement. If not, then it can only be larceny. (*Caveat:* If the consent was obtained by deceit, it can be larceny by trick.)

3. Once you have determined which of the three major offenses it "could" be, *then* explore the intricacies of that offense.

1a. Harry buys the National Enquirer every week from Joe, the neighborhood grocer. This week, discovering to his chagrin that he did not have enough money, Harry took the paper without telling Joe, but intending to pay Joe the next time he visited the store. Has Harry committed any property crime with regard to the paper?

1b. Suppose Harry tells Joe that he's taking the paper, and Joe nods. Afterwards, Harry decides to stiff Joe unless Joe "reminds" him to pay for it.

1c. Same facts, except that Harry knew at the time he took the paper he would not pay for it.

2. Larry asks his neighbor Joan if he can borrow her lawn mower, intending at the time to sell it. He does so.

3. Evelyn and John have been married 15 years. Evelyn has lost $10,000 on the stock market. To pay for her losses, she takes John's Rolex watch and sells it.

4. Jessie, tired and impoverished, but driving a Maserati, pulls into the Ramada Inn, where she signs in. She is not required to give a credit

card imprint. The next morning she leaves without paying as she intended to do all along.

5a. Alexander strolls into Pop's bookstore one day. Picking up the latest Sue Grafton (*L Is for Larceny*), he browses through it. Finding it intriguing enough, he decides to steal it. As he makes his way toward the door, however, he spots Jeremy, who works for the store, looking at him. Fearful that Jeremy has seen him take the book, Alexander replaces it on the shelf, exactly where it was at the start.

5b. Same facts, except that Alexander went to the bookstore with the purpose of taking the Grafton book.

6. Melinda goes to the bank and receives change for her $10 bill. In the middle of the $1 bills, however, there is a $1,000 dollar bill. Melinda keeps the $1,000 bill.

7a. Happy Hennigan, the used car man, knows that the car he is selling Juanita has a defective motor block and will probably run only 500 miles before dying. Assuming that he makes no representations of the fitness of the car, even when asked by Juanita, of what crime is he guilty when he takes her money?

7b. Happy sells Juanita the car above. She knows at the time she buys it, but he does not, that it is a very rare antique auto that, even with a cracked block, is worth $50,000. Has she "stolen" the car and, if so, under what rubric?

8. Martin Miner knows that Billingsley Buyer believes that Miner's mine is valuable. Miner, however, knows it is dry. What offense, if any, if Miner sells it to Buyer?

9a. Bernard, a lawyer, believes that a certain stock will quickly rise in value. He takes several bonds belonging to clients and secures $10,000 from the First National bank, using the bonds as collateral. He buys the stock, which goes up. He makes a $20,000 profit, pays the bank its $10,000, and returns the bonds. Has Bernard committed any property offense?

9b. Same facts, but Bernard leaves an envelope, to be opened in a week if he does not return the money and bonds, explaining his whole scheme and asking for forgiveness. He actually returns both items. What offense?

10. Lloyd, a car mechanic, fixed Bobby's car, for which Bobby has yet to pay him. Bobby has removed the car from Lloyd's garage. One day, Lloyd spots Bobby's new thoroughbred dog. He picks up the dog and sells it to the nearest Poodle Palace, netting $500, which he applies toward Bobby's bill. What crime has Lloyd committed?

11. James has spent all day conversing with Johnnie Walker Black and by now is severely drunk. He fantasizes that Ralph's Maserati belongs to him, and he takes it for a very long drive, never intending to return it.

Neither the police nor Ralph think this is funny. Has James committed larceny?

EXPLANATIONS

1a. First, which kind of crime is this "potentially"? Since Joe didn't know of the taking, he did not intend title to pass. Thus, it cannot be false pretenses. Moreover, since Joe didn't "entrust" the paper to Harry, it is not embezzlement. Thus, if it is anything, it is larceny.

But Harry has probably *not* committed larceny. Because the item was for sale, and Harry did intend to pay for it, he did not have the "animus furandi" required by the law. (This is the American rule: English courts generally see this case as larceny.)

The Model Penal Code has a subsection that deals expressly with items of property "exposed for sale." The section adopts the American view and provides that if a defendant took such an item, "intending to purchase and pay for it promptly, or reasonably believing that the owner, if present would have consented," there is no theft.

1b. Now we seem to have title pass when Joe allows Harry to take the paper. Joe does not expect to see the paper again, so this appears to be a case of false pretenses, if anything. But it is probably not anything. Why? Because at the time he took the paper, Harry lacked the proper mens rea: He didn't intend to deceive Joe.

This might seem to be a case of larceny by trick, as in *Pear's Case.* Here, however, the possession was not trespassory as it was there; Harry did not have the intent to take the paper when he removed it from Joe's store.

Assuming that the "exposure for sale" provision did not exculpate Harry, the MPC would find Harry guilty of unlawful control of the paper without regard to when the "proper mens rea" occurred to Harry.

1c. Since title to the paper passed to Harry with Joe's blessing, this could only be false pretenses — Harry got title by inducing Joe to give him the paper. Under the common law, however, Harry's false promise as to his future payment is insufficient. The (mis)representation must be as to present facts. This would be true even if Harry had the money in his pocket to pay for the newspaper; unless he says, "I don't have enough money, Joe, I'll pay you tomorrow," Harry has committed no common law offense.

Under the Code, a false promise can be sufficient to convict of theft by deceit, so that Harry's precise mental state would be important here.

2. This is not false pretenses since Joan never expected title to pass, nor embezzlement because Larry's intent effectively makes his initial taking

trespassory, much as in *Pear's Case*. Thus, this is larceny by trick and not embezzlement.

Under the MPC, however, the common law distinctions are unimportant. Whether title passed (or was intended to) is irrelevant. Larry's taking is "by deception," and his control is therefore "theft" under the Code.

3. Since Evelyn took the watch without John's permission, it is not a "title" crime. It might be either embezzlement or larceny, but we need not bother with the distinctions between those crimes here since both agreed that spousally owned property could not be the subject of either offense.

    The MPC expressly abolishes the "spousal exception." However, "household belongings or personal effects, or other property normally accessible to both spouses" still cannot be the subject of theft as long as the parties are living together. The watch is a "personal effect" and is "normally accessible to both spouses." Thus, while taking some items from a spouse may now be theft under the Code, Evelyn is probably not going to the slammer.

4. This is obviously not false pretense. There is nothing to which title has passed. Neither is it embezzlement or larceny, since intangible property can't be the basis of these crimes under common law. This has changed in modern statutes and in the MPC, which has a specific provision (§223.7) dealing with "theft of services."

5a. This is not false pretenses since title never passed. Nor can Alexander be guilty of embezzlement. Even if one were to argue that he had lawful possession when he decided to keep the book, that decision is not sufficient: There must a significant interference with ownership (conversion), which is absent here. Has Alexander committed larceny? He has taken and asported the book, although not off the premises of the store. That would suffice for that part of the crime. But did he have the requisite intent when the taking occurred? If not, he is not guilty of larceny. But could he be convicted of *attempted* larceny? See Chapter 12.

    Under the Code, Alexander exercised illegal control over the book as soon as he formed an intent to deprive the bookstore of it, even if it never left the premises. No express requirement of asportation or "taking" is present in the Code, although it is usually difficult to exercise "control" over property unless some physical movement occurs with regard to it.

5b. This *is* larceny; the taking and intent coincide. Larceny in this aspect is really an inchoate crime. Alexander's *intent,* not the actual loss, is the gravamen of the crime.

    Similarly, under the MPC, there is not even a minimum requirement of taking or asportation, and Alexander clearly exercised some unlawful dominion or control over the book.

6. This is not false pretenses because the bank did not intend for title to the $1,000 bill to pass. Nor is it trespassory since Melinda did not know at the time she received the package of bills that there was a $1,000 bill inside. It might be "embezzlement" under current statutes but not under the common law since the common law usually required an "entrusting" of the property, and there was no reliance by the bank on Melinda here.

Some common law courts might find that the $1,000 was still in the "constructive possession" of the bank, although this fiction was usually restricted to employer-employee situations.

Under the MPC, Melinda exercised unlawful control once she realized that she had the $1,000 bill and did not return it to the bank. This is theft by unlawful taking.

7a. Under the common law, Happy's happy. Obviously, Juanita consented to pass title to her money so this could only be false pretenses. But it is not false pretenses because the common law required an affirmative misleading; passive nondisclosure, in the absence of a fiduciary duty, would not suffice. Under modern statutes, however, this may be theft. Even here, however, the question is close. Section 223.3 of the Model Penal Code, for example, requires that the defendant "reinforce" a false impression, and there is no reinforcing here. The only exceptions involve fiduciaries or those who have previously set the false impression.

7b. Again, since Hennigan wished title to the car to pass, unless Juanita has affirmatively represented that she knows that the car is an "old heap" and repressed her expert qualifications, there is no false pretenses. (Of course, if Hennigan wished to replevin the car, he *might* have trouble under *Sherwood v. Walker,* 66 Mich. 568, 33 N.W. 919 (1887), the classic contracts case.)

8. Since title to the mine passed, it can only be false pretenses and not larceny or embezzlement. However, this is not false pretenses under the common law unless Miner has created or reinforced in an affirmative way Buyer's impression: As long as Miner stays silent, it is not illegal.

Even under the MPC, there may be no crime here since Miner has not "created or reinforced" Buyer's impression and does not stand in a fiduciary relationship to Buyer.

9a. As to the bonds, Bernard is not guilty of false pretenses since he never "assumed" title to the bonds. And the possession is not trespassory, unless you consider the constructive possession fiction, which generally required that the employer give the employee the specific property and not merely authority. However, Bernard is guilty of embezzlement; while he didn't take title, he converted the property of which he was lawfully possessed. Even if he didn't personally continue to exercise dominion over the property, his acts were a severe interference with the property rights of the bond owners.

As to the bank loan, Bernard *is* guilty of false pretenses since he took title to the money. Even though he returned the monies and the bonds, this is not relevant. Similarly, Bernard took the monies under false pretenses; that he returned them may mitigate his sentence but not his basic culpability.

9b. Bernard is still guilty of the crimes above. Although he hoped that he would be able to return the items, he took a serious risk that the owners of each of the items, respectively, would lose them. This is sufficient for liability.

10. Lloyd is probably not guilty of larceny under the common law for two reasons. First, dogs were "base animals" and could not be the subject of larceny. Just as important, however, Lloyd has a "claim of right" against Bobby's property. While Lloyd probably does not, under law, have a lien against Bobby's dog, any belief, however, unreasonable, that he does so "negates" Lloyd's specific intent (animus furandi) and exculpates him from larceny liability.

The MPC abolishes the "base animals" limitation of the common law, but it continues the "claim of right" defense. However, under the wording of the Code, the defendant must have an "honest claim of right to the property or service involved." If Lloyd had taken Bobby's car and sold it, the Code would clearly exculpate. But it is not clear whether the claim of right can exist against "equivalent" property. However, the commentary would strongly suggest that an honest belief that he can take any property, not just the original property involved in generating the belief, would exculpate.

11. There are two ways of explaining why James has not committed larceny. First, he was truly unaware that the property belonged to Ralph and therefore did not have the requisite mens rea. In that unfortunate jargon of the common law, he lacked the "specific intent" required for larceny. The other explanation, which is the same explanation in different words, is that his "claim of right," however misguided, is a "defense" to the charge of larceny. In either event, James is exonerated.

The MPC reaches the same result under either the claim of right provision or under the general definitions of culpability. As the commentary to the Code puts it, "The claim-of-right defense . . . can thus be regarded as redundant." However, the Code includes a special section on the claim of right to underscore the point about culpability.

11

Solicitation

Overview

Some people always want someone else to do the dirty work. As with many things in life, this is also true with crime. Some people will try to get others to commit a crime rather than do it themselves.

Solicitation punishes anyone who deliberately encourages someone else to commit a crime. Though in most cases the solicitor will be the one who first thinks of committing a crime, he doesn't have to be. A person is also guilty of solicitation if he eggs on someone who has already decided to commit a crime.

In theory, the ability to punish solicitors is a useful law enforcement device. As with attempt, police can prevent the commission of a more serious crime by arresting the initiator as soon as he has acted with the necessary mens rea to commit a crime. Unlike attempt, however, proximity to the ultimate harm intended is irrelevant. Thus, it makes no difference whether the effort to persuade has been successful or whether the person solicited ever begins to commit the desired crime. Even criminal encouragement doomed to fail from the outset (such as offering money to an undercover police officer to kill someone) will establish solicitation.

Because it can reach so far back in time and space from the crime solicited and because it sets the threshold of crime without *any* concern for prospects for its success, solicitation is the most *inchoate* of *inchoate* crimes. (Who said Latin was a dead language!) Perhaps setting this threshold so early can be justified by the fear that solicitation may give rise to cooperative criminal effort and its special dangers. (Indeed, solicitation has been thought of as an attempt to conspire.) In addition, a solicitor may be a more intelligent and more dangerous criminal because he works through others. However, one can also argue that mere encouragement without agreement by anyone else is not socially dangerous because the resisting will of an independent moral agent stands between the solicitor and the commission of the intended crime.

Solicitation also permits the arrest of people who have shown themselves to be dangerous because they have *acted* with the purpose to cause the commission of a crime. True, the criminal law does not punish for thoughts alone, but solicitors have *spoken* words or engaged in other conduct designed to implement their criminal intent. Thus, solicitation adheres to this basic principle of the criminal law. On the other hand, a solicitor may not be dangerous precisely because he has shown he is unwilling to commit the crime himself or at least alone. He may really be a reluctant lawbreaker. In any event, several purposes of the criminal law, including retribution, rehabilitation, and incapacitation, can be served by convicting solicitors.

Like attempt, solicitation is a relatively recent creation of the common law. It developed during the nineteenth century and covered only solicitation to commit felonies or serious misdemeanors. Generally, solicitation was punished as a misdemeanor. Today, some states limit the crime to solicitation of serious felonies only. Others provide for degrees of solicitation, the various degrees depending on the seriousness of the crime solicited.

The Model Penal Code, however, does not limit the crimes that can be the object of solicitation. Rather, it is an offense to solicit *any* crime, but soliciting someone to commit a "violation" is *not* punishable. In addition, the MPC punishes solicitation as severely as the crime solicited except that the solicitation of a capital offense or first-degree felony is punished as a second-degree felony. (MPC §5.05(1).) This is consistent with the MPC's primary focus on the dangerousness of an offender rather than on how close he actually comes to committing the intended crime.

There are several interesting wrinkles to solicitation, but they are best discussed later.

Definition

The Common Law

The common law defined solicitation in general terms. The defendant must have acted with the specific intent that another person commit a crime and have enticed, advised, incited, ordered, or otherwise encouraged the person to commit a crime. It was not necessary for the person solicited to agree to commit the crime, let alone that the solicited crime be attempted or committed.

Because solicitation sets the threshold of criminality so early, some state statutes require corroboration of the testimony of the person claiming he was solicited. This evidentiary safeguard helps prevent convicting someone based on a misunderstanding or on a false accusation.

The Model Penal Code

Under §5.02 of the MPC a person is guilty of solicitation if, "with the *purpose* of promoting or facilitating its commission he *commands, encourages* or *requests* another person to engage in *specific conduct* that would constitute such crime or an *attempt* to commit such crime or would establish his *complicity* in its commission or attempted commission" (emphasis added). The MPC definition has been influential in shaping state solicitation laws.

The MPC definition is similar to the common law but applies to the solicitation of any crime, not just felonies or serious misdemeanors. Also, unlike the common law, which only applied to the solicitation of another to act as a principal in the first degree (see Chapter 14), the MPC also includes any encouragement that would generate responsibility as an accomplice.

Thus, a typical common law case of solicitation might involve the solicitor asking a hired gunman to kill a particular victim. Here the defendant would be an accomplice (accessory in the second degree) and the gunman would be the principal in the first degree. Under the MPC, if the defendant encouraged the gunman to sell him a weapon with which the defendant himself could kill the victim, the defendant has committed solicitation because he has encouraged the gunman to become an accomplice.

Another Version of Solicitation

Some states have adopted a different definitional approach to solicitation. A defendant must not only encourage another to commit a crime; he must also offer him something of value. This requirement (somewhat similar to the requirement of consideration in contracts) ensures that the defendant is serious about his criminal purpose. It also identifies those cases in which there is an increased probability that the crime solicited will be committed because human nature responds more readily to money than it does to cheerleading.

The Mens Rea of Solicitation

The Common Law

Like attempt, solicitation is a specific intent crime. The defendant must *intend* that the individual solicited commit a crime. The defendant must be serious about encouraging another person actually to commit the solicited crime. If he is merely thinking out loud about the possibility or joking about it, he does not have the mens rea necessary to commit solicitation. As in attempt (see Chapter 12), the defendant must have specific intent as to the conduct, results, and circumstances (including even those that are strict liability in the crime solicited).

The Model Penal Code

Under the MPC, solicitation also requires the highest possible mens rea — purpose. MPC §5.02. Thus, the defendant must desire to encourage all conduct and result elements of the crime solicited and must know or believe that all circumstance elements will be satisfied. (MPC §2.02(2)(a)(ii).) The defendant must also fulfill any additional mens rea elements of the crime solicited.

The Actus Reus of Solicitation

The Common Law

By words or other conduct the defendant must entice, advise, incite, order, or otherwise encourage another person to commit a felony or serious misdemeanor. Speaking is the most common form of actus reus for this crime, but it could also take other forms such as simply being present and applauding or cheering.

If the defendant's "encouraging words" did not, in fact, reach the individual he hoped to encourage, in some jurisdictions he could only be convicted of *attempted* solicitation (pushing the threshold of criminality back even farther).

The Model Penal Code

The defendant must command, encourage, or request another to (a) commit a crime, (b) attempt to commit a crime, or (c) become an accomplice in the commission of or attempt to commit a crime. MPC §5.02(1). As mentioned earlier, the MPC specifically does not require the person solicited to act as a principal. The MPC also punishes as solicitation criminal encouragement that does not actually reach the person solicited, provided it was designed to be communicated. (MPC §5.02(2).)

The Relationship Between Solicitation and Conspiracy

Solicitation is defined solely by the actor's intent and conduct. The response of the person solicited is irrelevant to the crime. In this sense, solicitation is similar to an "offer" in contracts. Whether an offer has been made does not depend on whether there has been an acceptance.

But what if the person solicited does respond to the act of solicitation and agrees to commit the crime solicited? Then, both individuals have entered into a *conspiracy*. (See Chapter 13.) Just as an acceptance to an offer forms a contract, so does acceptance of a solicitation form a conspiracy. (A person, however, cannot be convicted both of solicitation and conspiracy.)

Responsibility for Crime Solicited

Under the general principles of accessorial liability a solicitor will be responsible for any solicited crime that is committed or attempted by the person he solicited. The common law would treat the solicitor as an accessory before the fact. Under modern principles he would be considered an accomplice. (See Chapter 14.)

In states in which the statutory definition of solicitation does not cover certain crimes, a defendant who solicits another person to commit one of these crimes might be charged with an attempt. (Keep in mind that the defendant has not committed solicitation because the solicitation statute does not include the crime he solicited.) It is not clear, however, whether mere solicitation can constitute an attempt; some courts hold that it cannot,[1] while others hold that it can.[2] In any event, a defendant cannot be punished both for solicitation and attempt based on the same conduct.

Solicitation and Immunity for Crime Solicited

Generally speaking, the prosecutor cannot use solicitation to convict someone who could not be convicted of the crime solicited. Thus, a customer who seeks the services of a prostitute cannot be convicted of *soliciting*

---

1. *Gervin v. State*, 212 Tenn. 653, 371 S.W.2d 449 (1963).
2. *Ward v. State*, 528 N.E.2d 52 (Ind. 1988).

prostitution if the prostitution statute only punishes the prostitute's behavior. The law assumes that the legislature did not intend to punish the customer's conduct. To permit the customer's conviction under a general solicitation statute would undermine the public policy clearly reflected in the prostitution statute.

However, there are cases that require an exception to this general policy. For example, at common law a husband could not rape his wife. (See Chapter 9.) If, however, he encouraged another person to rape his wife, the husband could be convicted of solicitation even though he could not have committed rape as a principal in the first degree.

Solicitation and Innocent Agents

Sometimes a defendant may trick an innocent agent into committing a crime. For example, a daughter might substitute poison for the medicine her mother is supposed to take and ask a home caregiver who is ignorant of the switch to administer the fatal "medicine." This is not a case of solicitation because the defendant does not intend that another person knowingly commit a crime. Instead, she is using an innocent agent (i.e., someone who, through no fault of her own, is unaware of the nature of her conduct and who does not intend to commit a crime) as the means to commit murder.

A defendant who activates an innocent agent has committed an *attempt* rather than *solicitation* because she has done her "last act," which was designed to commit the crime. If the innocent agent actually does what the defendant wants her to do, then the defendant is guilty of the crime as a *principal*. (See Chapter 14.)

Impossibility

The Common Law

Legal Impossibility

At common law true legal impossibility is a defense to a charge of solicitation. A person does not commit solicitation by encouraging another to do something that is not a crime. Thus, an individual, who erroneously believes that it is a crime to dispense birth control information on public school property and encourages another person to engage in that conduct, has not committed solicitation because she has not encouraged another person to do anything that is a crime. (See our discussion of legal impossibility in attempt in Chapter 12. The same rules apply here.)

Factual Impossibility

Factual impossibility will seldom occur in cases involving solicitation because the threshold of criminality is set so early that the offense is complete once the defendant has purposefully encouraged another to commit a crime. The law is usually not concerned with how the crime was to be committed or whether it could be committed successfully.

Occasionally in real life (and more frequently in criminal law exams), however, the solicitor is very particular about how he wants the crime committed. And, it turns out, due to facts or conditions unknown to the solicitor, the crime cannot be committed.

The Model Penal Code

As we shall see with attempt (in Chapter 12), the MPC looks unkindly on impossibility. The MPC would not convict the defendant only in cases of true legal impossibility — that is, where there is no law prohibiting the conduct solicited. The prosecutor would not be able to prove that the defendant encouraged another person to commit any particular crime. She could only prove that the defendant had shown a willingness to break the law but not a particular law.

In cases of factual impossibility, the MPC simply assesses the defendant's responsibility based on what he thought the facts were. Recall that the MPC is more concerned with the dangerous attitude of the offender and the need to prevent future crime than actually seeing how close an offender comes to causing harm.

Abandonment

It is unclear whether the common law permitted a change of heart on the solicitor's part to avoid criminal responsibility.[3] At the very least, the solicitor would probably have to communicate his change of heart to the person solicited and perhaps even ensure that the crime was not committed. On the other hand, the common law did not permit the defense of abandonment to an attempt charge, so it might not favor using abandonment as a defense to solicitation.

The MPC expressly provides for the affirmative defense of abandonment to a charge of solicitation. MPC §5.02(3). There are two requirements. First, as in conspiracy (see Chapter 13), the defendant must either persuade the person solicited not to commit the crime or else prevent its commission.

---

3. Evidently, no appellate court has ruled on this question. W. La Fave & A. Scott, Criminal Law 532 (3d ed. 2000).

Second, his renunciation must be "*complete* and *voluntary*." As in attempt, renunciation must be due to a sincere change of heart rather than a discovery that the offense is more difficult to commit than anticipated or that detection is more likely. These are the same requirements for renunciation of an attempt, except that, because another person is involved, the defendant must take steps to prevent that person from committing the offense, thereby stopping what the defendant has put in motion.

From a policy perspective, permitting the defense of renunciation may encourage criminals to break off their planned criminal activity, thereby preventing harm to both the victim and society. The defendant may also not be as dangerous as initially thought if he is willing to change his mind for the right reasons. Several states have adopted the defense of voluntary renunciation by statute.[4]

Solicitation and Law Enforcement

The police often catch criminals by providing them with the opportunity to commit crimes, particularly "victimless crimes" such as drugs, prostitution, and gambling. Thus, undercover officers may solicit prostitutes or try to buy or sell drugs. Much of what law enforcement officers do would be criminal solicitation if done by ordinary citizens. Usually, statutes specifically authorize police officers to engage in conduct that would otherwise constitute solicitation in the interests of detecting criminal activity and arresting criminals. Even in the absence of such a statute, the officers could argue justification for their conduct. (See Chapters 15 and 16.)

Such police activity, however, is not without controversy. Some argue that the police should detect crime, not manufacture it. As we shall see later, defendants often raise the defense of entrapment when caught by this type of police activity. (See Chapter 17.)

Punishment

The Model Penal Code frowns on cumulative punishment of essentially the same conduct. Thus, though a solicitor will be liable as an accomplice for the crimes committed by the person solicited (assuming the person solicited goes forward and commits these crimes), the solicitor cannot be punished both for solicitation and (1) the crime solicited; (2) an attempt by the person solicited; and (3) conspiracy with the person solicited to commit that offense. (MPC §§1.07(1)(a), 1.07(4)(b), and 5.05(3).) Solicitation is a

---

4. W. La Fave, Criminal Law 532 (3d ed. 2000).

lesser included offense to the crime solicited. (MPC §1.07.) Moreover, a person can be convicted of only one Article 5 offense—attempt, solicitation, *or* conspiracy—for conduct designed to culminate in the commission of the same offense.

EXAMPLES

1. It's the final game of the World Series, with bases loaded in the ninth inning, two outs, and the Los Angeles Dodgers leading the New York Yankees 3-2. The last Yankee batter is up, and the count is three balls and two strikes. The Dodger pitcher glares at the batter, goes into his windup, and throws a pitch that to most observers is clearly a ball. But the umpire raises his right hand, calls "Strike 3, you're out," and the Dodgers win the series. A livid Yankee fan yells at the top of his voice: "Kill the umpire!" Can he be charged with solicitation?

2. In the motion picture *Becket,* Henry II, upset with Thomas à Becket's opposition to his expansion of royal jurisdiction, cries out in a drunken stupor: "Will no one rid me of this man?" Subsequently, one of the listeners in fact kills Becket. Did Henry solicit the murder of Thomas à Becket under the common law or the MPC?

3. Liz, a non-drinker, joins Jen, Stephanie, and Megan on the patio of a bar & grill for happy hour. The others each have a couple of drinks. Sipping only water, Liz says: "It would be so easy to 'dine and ditch' — this place is packed." Jen replies: "I have no problem with you all taking off, but I will quietly leave what I owe on the table." After Jen does that, they all get up and casually stroll out to the sidewalk and leave without paying. Can Liz or Jen be charged with any crime?

4. Prof. Zoey, an academic in New Jersey, angry at Prof. Nerd in Illinois for some unforgivable academic put-down, left a message at the Internet address for Mad Max the mad bomber, asking him to send one of his infamous fatal explosive devices to Dr. Nerd. Unknown to Prof. Zoey, Mad Max had already been arrested and sent to prison for mailing such a device to someone else. Only the police read Prof. Zoey's message. Can Prof. Zoey be charged with any crime?

5. Amy desperately wanted the job of her boss, Rebecca. Her only hope was getting Rebecca fired. Amy asked Sam, a seriously mentally ill individual who did not know the difference between right and wrong, to injure Rebecca so that Rebecca could no longer work, and her position would need to be filled (hopefully by Amy). Sam listened to Amy, then got on a bus and left town. Can Amy be convicted of any offense?

6. Fred was drinking at the Spar Tavern with Jose. Jose leaned over to Fred and said, "I've taken enough trash talk from Wilson, who is standing

over there at the bar. I'm going right over there now and hit him upside his head and teach him not to 'dis' me anymore." Fred replied, "That's a great idea. I think Wilson deserves it. Go ahead and unload on him!" Jose got up, went over to Wilson, and taking another look at just how big Wilson really was, decided not to punch him after all. Has Fred committed any crime?

7. Angry because her red Miata was stolen recently and because it was not insured against theft, Harriet asked Ozzie to steal the red Miata she saw parked everyday in the Safeway parking lot far across town. Rather than steal that car, Ozzie, who had already been charged with several car thefts, struck a deal with the police and told them about Harriet. Harriet was arrested. Upon further investigation, it turned out that, unknown to her, the car she wanted Ozzie to steal was actually Harriet's own previously stolen red Miata. Can Harriet be charged with any crime?

8. Yvonne works in a fashionable dress shop in a suburban shopping mall. She craves a great dress in the window but knows she will probably be caught if she takes it without paying for it. So Yvonne asked her good friend Yolanda to shoplift it for her and told her how to do it without getting caught. Yolanda agreed to snatch the dress during the busy Saturday afternoon shopping period.

   Thursday evening Yvonne changed her mind out of true remorse. She called Yolanda to tell her that she did not want Yolanda to go through with the shoplifting plan. Yolanda was not home, however, so Yvonne left a message to this effect on Yolanda's machine. Unfortunately, Yolanda never checked her answering machine and was arrested while she tried to steal the dress that Saturday. Would you charge Yvonne?

EXPLANATIONS

1. If the Yankee fan actually intended to encourage someone else to kill the umpire, then he could be convicted of solicitation—even if no one actually acted on his encouragement. In some states he would be punished just as severely as the individual who actually did kill the umpire. Under the MPC, however, solicitation of a capital offense or a felony in the first degree would be punished as a felony in the second degree. In the context of American sports, however, it is extremely unlikely that any jury (especially a New York City jury!) would conclude that the defendant actually spoke those words with the intent of encouraging someone to kill the umpire. (For a discussion of the fan's liability if someone actually does kill the umpire as a result of the shout, see Chapter 14.)

2. Because solicitation was not fully developed until the late eighteenth century, Henry could not be convicted of solicitation. (Sorry, but we wanted to make sure that you were also paying attention to the history!)

    However, under both late common law and the MPC the analysis would essentially be the same. Did Henry act with the necessary mens rea for solicitation? Did he speak with the *specific intent* or *purpose* of encouraging someone to murder Becket? If he did, then at that moment he committed solicitation even if none of his listeners accepted the challenge. Upon commission of the murder Henry would also become an accessory before the fact under common law or an accomplice under the MPC and would be criminally responsible for murder along with the person solicited. (This assumes that there would be a sheriff foolish enough to arrest and charge Henry!)

3. Liz's statement may have been only an observation made without the aim of encouraging her friends to commit theft. However, since the group acted on her statement and Liz raised no objection, a jury could conclude that her words were said with the *purpose* of encouraging her friends to commit this crime even though Liz, herself, owed nothing and did not commit theft. Jen may argue that she paid her portion of the bill and that this demonstrates she did not approve of such conduct. Furthermore, Jen will argue that Liz came up with the idea and that Liz and Stephanie had already formed their intent to commit the crime. But a jury could find that Jen's words were spoken with the intent to reinforce Liz, Megan, and Stephanie's decision to leave the bar without paying. The prosecution's case against Liz seems stronger than against Jen.

4. Under the common law, Prof. Zoey has committed attempted solicitation. In many states that only require the solicitor to try to encourage someone else to commit a crime by communications designed to reach that person, Prof. Zoey has committed solicitation.

    Under the MPC, Prof. Zoey has committed solicitation because his communication was sent with the purpose of encouraging Mad Max to send his fatal explosive device to Dr. Nerd, and it was designed to reach Max. Prof. Zoey would be punished just as severely as the crime he solicited (probably arson or murder), even though he did not come close to causing either of these serious harms and even though an intervening moral agent (okay, it was only Mad Max) with free will would have to choose to commit a crime. The MPC is concerned with individuals who have demonstrated their dangerous attitude, if not their skill. This is also one of the few times when the criminal law *does* impose responsibility for conduct beyond the last responsible human being.

    Prof. Zoey might try to argue factual impossibility because Max never received his message and, in any event, was otherwise indisposed. This would fail under both the common law and the MPC because Prof. Zoey's responsibility would be assessed based on the facts as *he believed* them to be.

5. Amy deliberately encouraged Sam to commit a serious assault. However, because Sam is legally insane (see Chapter 17), he is not a responsible agent and could not be convicted of the offense solicited (had he committed it). Because Amy has used an "innocent agent," she is guilty of attempted assault under the common law. In effect she has committed her "last act."

    Under the MPC Amy has probably committed solicitation. The MPC focuses on the defendant's attitude rather than on the legal responsibility of the person solicited.

6. When Fred spoke these words with the purpose of reinforcing Jose's resolve to commit the assault, Fred solicited Jose to commit an assault on Wilson under both the common law and the MPC. This is true even though Jose had already formed the intent to commit the assault and even though Jose did not, in fact, commit the solicited crime. A person can commit solicitation even though he did not come up with the idea initially and even though the person solicited changed his mind.

7. Under both the common law and the MPC, Harriet could probably be convicted of solicitation in this case because she encouraged another to engage in conduct with the intent of having him commit a crime. The crime is complete as of that moment. How it was to be done is not the concern under solicitation.

    Harriet might raise the defense of legal impossibility, claiming she could not solicit anyone to steal *her own* property. However, this is really a case of factual impossibility because there is a law against stealing cars. Thus, Harriet's criminal responsibility is determined by the facts as she *believed* them to be.

8. The common law probably did not provide the defense of abandonment so Yvonne has committed the crime of solicitation even though she changed her mind for the right reasons.

    The MPC does authorize the affirmative defense of renunciation, provided that the defendant's decision is voluntary and complete and provided that the defendant either persuades the person solicited not to commit the crime or otherwise prevents the commission of the crime. Unfortunately, Yvonne did neither and therefore could be convicted of solicitation. Unlike an attempt to persuade that can establish solicitation, an attempt to "unpersuade" is not effective in establishing renunciation. Yvonne could have taken other measures such as telling the store owner, but she did not (undoubtedly because she knew she would be fired).

    When Yolanda agreed to steal the dress and Yvonne told Yolanda how to accomplish the theft, Yvonne and Yolanda also committed conspiracy. (See Chapter 13.) When Yolanda attempted to commit the theft of the dress, Yvonne was also responsible for that crime as an accessory before the fact under common law and as an accomplice under the MPC. However, the MPC prevents cumulative punishment for solicitation, conspiracy, and attempt based on essentially the same conduct.

12

Attempt

Overview

Not every criminal succeeds at crime. Some try their best but fail; others may change their mind and stop short of their initially intended goal. Some are even caught before they can complete their crime. *Attempt* punishes offenders who intend to commit a crime (referred to here as the "target" crime) and act to implement that intent, but do not achieve their goal.

Attempt is an important law enforcement tool. Police can prevent crime by arresting an offender before he actually commits his target crime. (This is why attempt is sometimes called an *inchoate* or uncompleted crime.) Attempt also enables the criminal justice system to punish individuals who have acted on their criminal intentions and are dangerous.

Attempt is a crime of recent origin in the common law. Initially, it was usually a misdemeanor. Today, the seriousness of an attempt and its punishment generally depend on the seriousness of the crime attempted. Attempt often carries a lighter penalty than the target crime because the offender has done less harm than a successful criminal. However, except for capital offenses and felonies of the first degree, the Model Penal Code punishes attempt just as severely as the crime attempted because it considers an unsuccessful criminal just as dangerous as a successful one.

If an offender successfully completes the target offense, he cannot also be convicted of an attempt. Attempt is a lesser included offense of the crime attempted and will merge if the prosecution proves the completed offense.

Definition

In general, attempt punishes a defendant because he intended to commit a particular crime and took a significant step to commit it. Most jurisdictions have a single attempt statute phrased in general language that is used to prosecute all attempt crimes. (Otherwise, the legislature would have to enact a separate attempt provision for each substantive crime, creating a much larger and more cumbersome criminal law.) Because this single statutory definition of attempt must be used for so many target crimes, legislatures usually use very broad and abstract language. As a result, many state statutes do not define attempt very carefully, and often courts must interpret these laws to provide a more useful legal definition.

Some state laws make what would ordinarily be considered an attempt into a completed offense. For example, burglary is a form of inchoate crime because it punishes conduct that is preliminary to the commission of the real criminal goal. Thus, a typical burglary statute proscribes "*entering a building* with intent to commit a crime against a person or property therein." Many states push the threshold of criminality back even farther. They prohibit the mere possession of burglar tools, even though the defendant has not used the tools to enter a building, let alone commit a crime against person or property inside. Other statutes define assault as "an attempted battery." Thus, trying to punch someone and missing may be punished as a completed assault rather than an attempted battery.

The Mens Rea of Attempt

The mental state is the intent to commit the target crime. Because attempt does not require successful completion of a crime, the mens rea of attempt is usually more demanding than the mens rea of the crime attempted.

The Actus Reus of Attempt

Criminals often think about committing a crime. They may even take some preparatory steps that will make it easier to commit a crime sometime in the future. Finally, they may actually implement their criminal purpose and begin to commit a crime.

The criminal law does not punish for thoughts alone. (See Chapter 3.) When, however, does a person cross the dividing line between thinking and preparation on the one side, and actually committing an attempt on the other? The definition of the actus reus of attempt draws the line between noncriminal and criminal behavior. Drawing this line early may prevent more crimes and catch more dangerous people, but it may also increase the risk of convicting people who would change their mind. The common law generally drew this line quite late; the MPC draws it much earlier.

The Common Law

Mens Rea

The defendant must have the same state of mind required for conviction of the target offense. Because attempt is a specific intent crime at common law, the defendant must also *intend*

1. to *do the act*
2. to *accomplish the result*
3. *under the same circumstances*

that would be required for conviction of the target offense.

Intend the Act

This specific intent requirement means that a person cannot commit an attempt recklessly or negligently. He must, at the very least, intend the act. Some cases suggest, however, that it is possible to attempt a crime that only requires an act done with recklessness or even negligence. Thus, a person who knows that his car brakes do not work might commit attempted reckless driving if he gets into his parked car and starts it, intending to drive it on the streets. However, because he does not actually drive the car, he cannot be convicted of reckless driving.

Intend the Result

To be convicted of attempting a crime that has a result element, the defendant must intend the result. A defendant who drives his car so dangerously that he kills someone may be convicted of murder or vehicular homicide because his risk-creating behavior has resulted in death. If, however, the same defendant struck the victim while driving in the same reckless way but did not kill him, he cannot be convicted of attempted murder or attempted vehicular homicide because he did not intend the death.

Intend the Circumstances

Likewise, the defendant must know the circumstances of the target offense — even if strict liability applies. Thus, an adult, who had intercourse with a juvenile under the age of 16 erroneously believing she was 18, could be convicted of statutory rape. If, however, the same adult were arrested moments before having intercourse with this juvenile, he could not be convicted of attempted statutory rape because he did not *intend* the juvenile to be under 16.

Actus Reus

Common law definitions of actus reus varied, but generally they required behavior that provided strong evidence of a criminal intent and that came quite close to completing the target offense.

Last Act

The "last act" test is very favorable to the defendant. He must have taken the very last step within his power to commit the target offense.[1] Only after the actor had taken the last step and events were out of his control could the law punish him for attempt. This approach preserves a maximum opportunity for the actor to change his mind (often called *locus penitentiae* or "opportunity to repent"), while also requiring very strong evidence of criminal intent. A professional killer who shoots at his victim intending to kill him has committed the last act. Whether he succeeds is now out of his control.

The Equivocality Test

Some courts and commentators have argued that the actus reus of attempt should *by itself* unquestionably show that the actor is trying to commit a crime.[2] Otherwise, the defendant's behavior is merely "equivocal" — that is, it is consistent with *either* innocent *or* criminal purpose. This test is also quite favorable to defendants. Under this approach the prosecutor may not use any other evidence, such as a confession, a diary, or other statements, to demonstrate that the actor was implementing a criminal design. (This has sometimes been called the "manifest criminality" approach.[3]) Thus, someone who lights a pipe with a match and then drops the match in a haystack in a barn may be simply careless or trying to set the barn on fire. Without additional evidence, it is not clear if he was trying to commit a crime. The equivocality test can be very difficult for the prosecution to satisfy.

Supporters argue that this test maximizes the sphere of liberty in which an individual is free from government interference. Critics claim it damages

---

1. *R. v. Eagleton,* 169 E.R. 826 (1855).
2. *The King v. Barker,* [1924] N.Z.L.R. 865. See also Wis. Stat. Ann. 939.32(3).
3. G. Fletcher, Rethinking Criminal Law (1978).

effective law enforcement and permits dangerous individuals to remain at large because the police can only arrest the actor at the last possible moment because virtually no preparatory act is unequivocal.

Proximity Test

Still other courts used a more flexible definition of actus reus known as the "proximity test." It did not require the defendant to take the last step or to do an unequivocal act before an attempt had been committed. Instead, it allowed the jury to weigh several factors, including the seriousness of the offense, community resentment, and closeness in space and time to completing the crime.[4] This test provided flexibility but also created uncertainty about when an attempt occurred. Some courts required the actor to get physically close to the intended victim or to set in motion a chain of events that created a high probability that the crime would be completed. Other courts have permitted conviction on behavior more remote from the result.

Probable Desistance

Some courts have used the "probable desistance" test. Only an act that would normally be sufficient to result in the commission of a crime "but for" the intervention of some outside person or event is sufficient for the actus reus of attempt.[5] This definition considers whether an ordinary, law-abiding person would probably have changed his mind and broken off from the criminal course of conduct. A terrorist who checked a bag armed with a sophisticated explosive device designed to explode when an airplane reaches 30,000 feet has probably satisfied this test. Although he could still change his mind after checking the bag and warn the authorities, it is unlikely, given the preparation required and his motivation, that he would reconsider.

This test has been criticized because it encourages speculation. How should a jury decide if most law-abiding people would have had a twinge of conscience and stopped? More to the point, a law-abiding citizen does not commit crimes!

In sum, the common law generally required the defendant to engage in behavior that provided strong evidence of his criminal intention and also came close to the commission of the target offense before his conduct satisfied the actus reus requirement of attempt.

---

4. *Commonwealth v. Peaslee,* 177 Mass. 267, 59 N.E. 55 (1901); *People v. Rizzo,* 246 N.Y. 334, 158 N.E. 888 (1927).

5. *Comer v. Bloomfield,* 55 Crim. App. 305 (1971) (Eng.).

The Model Penal Code

Definition

The Model Penal Code definition of attempt is, in sharp contrast to the common law, very specific but also very long and complex. (MPC §5.01.) In general terms, a person commits an attempt under the MPC if, acting with the same state of mind otherwise required for commission of the target offense, he *purposely* does an *act* and *purposely* causes (or believes he will cause) the *result* under the same *circumstances* required by the target offense and he takes a *substantial step* to commit the crime. A "substantial step" is conduct that is "strongly corroborative of [a defendant's] criminal purpose."

Mens Rea

The MPC takes the following approach to the mens rea (i.e., culpability) required for attempt:

Conduct

The MPC requires that the defendant must *purposely* engage in all elements of conduct made criminal by the crime attempted. (§5.01(1)(a).)

Result

The MPC expands the mens rea of attempt slightly beyond the common law approach when causing a particular result is an element of the crime attempted. It permits conviction for attempt if the defendant acted with the purpose or *belief* that his act would cause a particular result. (§5.01.1(1)(b).)

Circumstance

The MPC approach to circumstance is different than that of the common law. Unlike the common law, which required that the defendant *know* all circumstance elements, the MPC provides that, for these elements, the mens rea of the target offense controls. Thus, whatever mens rea toward circumstances is required by the target crime will also be required for an attempt under the MPC. Though the language of the MPC is not as clear as it could be on this point, the commentaries state that the drafters intended this approach, and commentators have agreed.

The statutory rape example given above for the common law would have a different result under the MPC. An adult who intended to have intercourse with a 16-year-old female, erroneously believing she was 18, could be prosecuted for committing attempted statutory rape if arrested just before the act because age is a strict liability circumstance element of the target offense.

Actus Reus

The MPC requires that the actor take a "*substantial step*" before she can be convicted of an attempt. A "substantial step" must be "*strongly corroborative* of the actor's criminal purpose." (MPC §5.01(2).) The MPC emphasizes the dangerousness of the offender based on her criminal determination rather than on how close she is to committing the target offense.

The MPC lists several types of behavior that are *legally sufficient* to prove a substantial step.[6] These include searching for the victim, reconnoitering the crime scene, unlawfully entering a building where the defendant contemplates committing the crime, possessing tools or instruments necessary for committing the crime near the crime scene, or soliciting an innocent agent to do an element of the crime. Unlike the common law, the MPC definition focuses on what the defendant has done rather than what remains to be done. The prosecution also can use evidence other than the substantial step to prove mens rea, including confessions, diaries, and other proof relevant to the actor's state of mind.

In contrast to the common law, the MPC does not require much of an actus reus before a defendant may be convicted of an attempt. Thus, it sets the line between preparation and attempt quite early and expands the authority of the police to nip crime in the bud.

The MPC definition of a "substantial step" has been very influential, and many states have adopted it. Even when the federal or state statutes have not defined the actus reus requirement for attempt, courts often use the MPC approach to interpret the attempt statute in their jurisdiction.[7]

Summary

Mens Rea. Analyze the defendant's mens rea using the following steps:

1. Did she act with the same mens rea required by the crime attempted?
2. *Common law:* Did she also *intend* to commit the *act* and to cause the *result* and intend the same *circumstances* as required by the crime attempted?

---

6. This means that a jury *could* find that the defendant took a "substantial step" based only on this evidence.

7. *United States v. Jackson,* 560 F.2d 112 (2d Cir. 1977); *United States v. Buffington,* 815 F.2d 1292 (9th Cir. 1987).

3.   *MPC:* Did she have

a.   the purpose to do all the *conduct* elements of the target offense?
b.   the purpose to cause the *result* (or believe she would cause the result) of the target offense?
c.   the same mens rea toward the circumstance elements as required by the target offense?

Actus reus. Analyze the defendant's actus reus using the following steps:

1.   *Common law:* Did the defendant's act satisfy the applicable test:
a.   *last act*—did the defendant do everything that he could do and is the result now beyond his control?
b.   *"equivocality test"*—would reasonable people, observing only the defendant's conduct, necessarily conclude that he was trying to commit a crime?
c.   *"proximity test"*—in light of the seriousness of the offense and the scope of possible harm, did the defendant come close in space and time to completing the offense?
d.   *"probable desistance"*—did the defendant's conduct start a chain of causation sufficient to result in the commission of the completed offense unless another person or event would prevent it? Would a law-abiding person likely have changed his mind?
2.   *MPC:* Did the defendant's behavior *strongly corroborate* his criminal purpose? If he searched for his victim, familiarized himself with the crime scene, unlawfully entered a building where he thought he might commit the crime, had special tools essential for committing the crime, or solicited an innocent agent to commit the crime, a jury *could* (but is not required to) find him guilty of an attempt.

Abandonment

The Common Law

The common law did not allow the defense of abandonment. Once a defendant had crossed the line dividing preparation from implementation and had committed an attempt, he could not go back. Of course, if the actus reus test used requires the defendant to be so close to completion before an attempt has occurred, there will probably be no appreciable time left in which to abandon. If, for example, the defendant is guilty of an attempt only after he has pulled the trigger (the last act in his control), he has only a nanosecond to abandon and shout a warning to the victim.

Some states, however, allow a defendant to prove that, though he actually committed an attempt, he subsequently *abandoned* his criminal purpose. The defense is available only if the defendant changed his mind through genuine remorse and not because the risk of arrest or difficulty of committing the crime was greater than anticipated. Though arguably permitting the acquittal of someone who has demonstrated a willingness to engage in criminal conduct, the defense may encourage criminals to change their mind and not complete the crime, saving both the victim and society from more serious harm. Generally, abandonment is an affirmative defense that the defendant must establish by a preponderance of the evidence.

The Model Penal Code

Under the concept of "renunciation," the MPC permits the defendant to introduce evidence that he "abandoned his effort to commit the crime or otherwise prevented its commission, under circumstances manifesting a complete and voluntary renunciation of his criminal purpose." (MPC §5.01(4).) Thus, the defendant must give up his criminal goal or prevent its successful commission. The use of renunciation is strictly limited.

First, the defense is available only when the target offense has a *result* (§5.01(2)) or *circumstance* (§5.01(3)) as a material element. It is not available when *conduct* is the only material element of the target offense because, once the defendant has completed the criminal conduct, the harm has been done and there is nothing for him to abandon. Only outside forces have prevented successful completion of the target offense.

Second, it must be *voluntary*. The defendant must *not* have changed his mind because it was *more difficult* to commit the crime than he originally anticipated.

Third, it must be *complete*. Basically, the defendant must not have decided to wait for a better time or opportunity.

The Code's adoption of an abandonment claim is almost surely the quid pro quo for moving the timeframe of attempt back earlier than the common law tests allowed. Thus, if the defendant intends to rob a bank in one month and reconnoiters it today, he could be convicted of an attempt under the Code (but not under the common law). If we want the defendant to abandon his intent between now and next month, we must provide him with some inducement for doing so. The Code's provision does so.

See Table 4 for a summary of the law of attempt.

Impossibility: Legal, Factual, and Inherent

Despite their best efforts and for reasons beyond their control, criminals sometimes do not commit the crime they set out to commit because — it

Table 4. The Material Elements of Attempt

ATTEMPT — COMMON LAW

Thinking MENS REA	Preparing	Doing ACTUS REUS				
		"Proximity Test" (Close in space and time *or* set forces in motion with high probability of completion)	**"Probable Desistance"** (Law-abiding person would have broken off)	**"Unequivocal Act"** (Clearly manifests criminal purpose)	**"Last Act"** (Beyond *D*'s control)	**Abandonment Not Permitted**
1. Sames mens rea as target offense ±	C R I M I N A L	1. "Strongly corroborates" criminal purpose				T A R G E T
2. Intent to i) do the same act ii) accomplish same result iii) know the same circumstances as target crime						

ATTEMPT — MPC

CULPABILITY		SUBSTANTIAL STEP	Abandonment Permitted If
1. Same culpability as target crime ±	T H R E S H O L D	1. "Strongly corroborates" criminal purpose	1. Voluntary renunciation and 2. Complete renunciation
2. Purposefully engages in conduct ±			C R I M E
3. Purposefully causes result *or* believes result will ensue ±			
4. Same culpability toward circumstances as target offense			

turns out—it was *impossible* to commit the crime. What, if anything, should the criminal law do in such cases? Consider these examples. An individual smuggles a prescription drug into the country thinking it is against the law, but there is no criminal law forbidding the importation of this particular drug. A pickpocket tries to pick someone's pocket, but there is nothing in the victim's pocket. A hunter shoots at a stuffed deer out of hunting season. In *some* cases, the criminal law uses *attempt* to punish the offender. In other cases, using the doctrine of *impossibility*, the criminal law does not punish the actor.[8]

The Common Law

At common law, there were two kinds of impossibility: factual and legal. Legal impossibility was a defense; factual impossibility was not. This means a law student must know the difference. Unfortunately, impossibility is a very complex and confusing area.

Legal Impossibility

Consider a defendant who engages in conduct (such as smuggling a new abortion pill into the United States), thinking it is a crime when, in fact, there is no law making it a crime. This is a case of true legal impossibility under the common law, and the defendant could not be convicted of an attempt. Though the defendant has shown himself willing to break *the* law, he has not broken any *particular* law. Thus, he could not have the mens rea required to attempt a particular offense.

As we saw earlier in the mistake of law section, a belief that conduct is not against the law usually does not excuse behavior if it is a crime. (See Chapter 5.) In legal impossibility, a belief that conduct *is* against the law does not make the conduct criminal if there is no law prohibiting that conduct.

Factual Impossibility

Factual impossibility occurs when the defendant, despite his intentions, could not complete his intended crime because of facts or conditions unknown to him or beyond his control. Thus, a defendant can be convicted of

---

8. One might argue with both logic and irony that *every* attempt is a case of "impossibility" because—for whatever reason—the defendant did not succeed. The concept of "impossibility" is built into "attempt." Many commentators argue that impossibility is of little practical significance in the criminal law. However, other scholars and even some criminal law students find the doctrine a fascinating opportunity to explore the doctrinal logic and policy choices of the criminal law. See Symposium, 5 J. of Cont. Leg. Issues 1-398 (1994).

attempt even though it was factually impossible for him to accomplish his goal.

Consider a defendant who, in violation of a specific statute, tries to sell foreign abortion pills to an undercover police officer and is arrested in a sting operation. After the pills are tested, it turns out that, although the defendant *thought* he was selling the foreign abortion pills, he had been duped by his supplier and had *actually sold* sugar pills. This would be a case of *factual* impossibility. Because of facts unknown to the defendant (the pills were sugar), he did not succeed in selling foreign abortion pills. However, he could be convicted of an *attempt* to sell the proscribed pills.

Analysis

Unfortunately, it is not always easy to tell whether a case is one of legal or factual impossibility, and some courts reach different results in similar cases.

People v. Jaffe[9] is a well-known example of a court's confusion and reluctance to convict someone for trying to commit a crime although, through no fault of his own, he did not succeed. The police, running a "sting" operation, had sold the defendant goods that had at one time been stolen but had since been recovered. The defendant *believed* he was purchasing stolen property. Charged with buying or receiving "any stolen property *knowing* the same to have been stolen" (emphasis added), the defendant was convicted of an *attempt* to commit that crime.

New York's highest court reversed the conviction. It concluded that the defendant could not *know* the property he possessed was stolen if, in fact, it was *no longer* stolen. The court essentially said that the defendant could not *know* something that was not true (even though he *believed* it to be true). Because the defendant could not be prosecuted for *knowingly* "buying or receiving stolen property," the Court held that the defense of *legal* impossibility prevented his conviction for *attempted* buying or receiving property knowing it was stolen.

This case and the reasoning supporting its conclusion have been much criticized. The majority characterized this as a case of *legal* rather than *factual* impossibility because the defendant was mistaken about the legal status of the property; that is, it was no longer stolen. To convict the defendant of the target offense, the prosecution would have to establish that the property was stolen. Thus, this "legal fact" (see Chapter 5) is a circumstance element of the target crime, and the court should have characterized this as a case of factual impossibility.

The confusion generated by the doctrine of impossibility has been made worse by some commentators and some court opinions that determine what

---

9. 185 N.Y. 497, 78 N.E. 169 (1906).

an actor *intended* by what he *did*. Consider a defendant who shoots at a human silhouette behind a window shade intending to kill the person he thinks is standing there. It turns out that there is only a mannequin placed there by the police to create the illusion of a human body. Some commentators (and even some courts) conclude that what the defendant *did* in fact — shoot at a mannequin rather than at a human — is what he *intended* to do. This is a very unusual interpretation of what "intent" means in the criminal law. It equates mens rea with actus reus (he intended what he did) rather than trying to determine what mental activity was occurring in the actor's mind when he performed the actus reus.

The current trend in the criminal law is to focus on what the defendant *thought* he was doing rather than on what it turns out he actually did. If there is no law making what the defendant intended to accomplish a crime, then it will be a case of legal impossibility. Otherwise, most cases of this sort will involve factual impossibility, which is not a defense to attempt. The only question remaining then is whether the defendant's conduct satisfies the actus reus requirement of attempt.

Inherent Impossibility

What, if anything, should be done with an individual who wants to kill her rival for a loved one's affections but uses means that are inherently unlikely to accomplish the intended result — say, sticking pins into a voodoo doll? Though the defendant clearly has a dangerous attitude and has acted to implement her criminal intent, she may seem to some so hopelessly inept as to be more worthy of pity than condemnation and imprisonment. Nonetheless, inherent impossibility was not a defense at common law. Such a defendant's best hope was the common law's demanding actus reus definitions. Many steps taken by a bungling individual might not satisfy them.

The Model Penal Code
Legal Impossibility

Section 5.01 of the MPC requires the actor to intend to do something that is a crime. If he attempts to do something that he thinks is a crime but is not, then he is not guilty of attempt. Thus, legal impossibility is not a true defense under the MPC. Rather, the prosecutor must prove that there is a criminal statute punishing what the defendant intended to accomplish.

Factual Impossibility

Under the MPC factual impossibility is not a defense to attempt. (§5.01.) A defendant is guilty of an attempt if he would have committed the target offense had the facts or conditions been as he *believed* them to be.

Thus, in the *Jaffe* case, the defendant could have been convicted of an attempt to purchase or receive stolen property because he *believed* the property to be stolen, and he would have committed the target offense if his belief were true. Likewise, a defendant, who *believed* his victim to be alive and shot at him to kill, can be convicted of attempted murder even though the victim had already died.[10]

Inherent Impossibility

The MPC does not allow a defense of inherent impossibility. However, it does permit the court to dismiss a prosecution in such a case if the defendant's conduct was so "inherently unlikely to culminate in the commission of a crime that neither such conduct nor the actor presents a public danger." (§5.05(2).) Most such cases are probably disposed of by the prosecutor's exercise of discretion not to prosecute.

Thankfully, the MPC has simplified what had been a very confusing area of the law, and the modern trend is to follow the MPC. Remember, however, that the doctrines of legal and factual impossibility occasionally bedevil prosecutors, defense lawyers, judges, and, yes, law students (especially on criminal law exams!) even today.

Stalking

Legislatures sometimes criminally punish conduct that may appear harmless to most observers. Stalking is a contemporary example of this type of crime. It punishes an actor for repetitive behavior and/or for credible threats that cause the victim to reasonably fear serious bodily harm. Stalking may reach conduct that would not qualify as an attempt. Thus, it permits even earlier intervention by the criminal law. It is similar to "attempt" in stopping preliminary conduct from escalating into more serious violence against the target.

Supporters believe this new crime is necessary because many victims, especially women, are stalked by former spouses, friends, and even strangers who, too often, kill or seriously injure their victims. Eight percent of women and two percent of men are reportedly the victims of stalking sometime in their lives.[11] In 1993 it was estimated that there could be as many as 200,000 stalkers in the United States.[12] Reportedly, 90 percent of all women killed

---

10. *People v. Dlugash,* 41 N.Y.2d 725, 363 N.E.2d 1155 (1977).

11. Tjadean and Thoennes, Stalking in America: Findings from the National Violence Against Women Survey 3 (National Institute of Justice, April 1998).

12. Antistalking Proposals: Hearing on Combating [sic] Stalking and Family Violence Before the Senate Comm. on the Judiciary, 103d Cong., 1st Sess. 3 (1993) (Statement of Sen. Joseph R. Biden, Chairman).

by their husbands or boyfriends were stalked by them before the fatal attack.[13] Other remedies, such as prosecutions for attempt and civil protection orders, have proven ineffective in preventing behavior that creates significant fear and can lead to death or serious injury. Critics are concerned that these laws are too vague (see Chapter 1) or that they punish conduct that is constitutionally protected, including speech.

These statutes punish deliberate and repeated conduct involving visual or physical proximity to the victim (such as following or visually surveilling) or threats that would cause a reasonable person to fear for her safety. Today every state has a stalking law. Most statutes define stalking as the willful, malicious, and repeated following or harassing of another person. Some require the defendant to exhibit threatening behavior *intended* to place the victim in reasonable fear of her safety. This approach allows conviction even if the victim did not feel threatened. Others only require the prosecution to prove that the defendant knew, or *should have known,* that his intentional course of conduct would cause fear of death or serious bodily injury in a reasonable person. This approach allows conviction for *negligence* as to result; that is, even if the defendant did *not intend* to cause such fear. Some stalking statutes exclude behavior that has a legitimate purpose or is constitutionally protected. More recently, these laws have been used to prosecute "electronic" stalking, involving e-mail communications.

Stalking laws enable law enforcement to protect victims from ongoing intimidation. They also codify a specific "inchoate" offense in order to prevent a preliminary course of action from accelerating into more serious injury to the victim.[14]

EXAMPLES

1. Suzy, tired of her marriage, decided to kill her husband, Bob, and collect his life insurance. She purchased a .38 caliber pistol, took shooting lessons, and put the gun in the drawer next to her side of the bed. Pretending she heard a burglar late one evening, she induced Bob to go outside their house to investigate.

   a. Suzy shot Bob in the head, later telling the police she thought he was a burglar. Bob did not die but lived on in a vegetative state.

   b. Suzy loaded her .38 caliber pistol, snuck out the back door, and, unknown to Bob, with finger on the trigger, aimed directly at his heart. She fired but the gun only made a loud noise. Unknown to

---

13. *Id.* at 10. (Statement of Sen. William S. Cohen). Not all stalking is "romantically" motivated. Some stalkers are "persecutory"; that is, they feel their targets have harmed them, either physically or financially. Revenge is their primary motivation. Ronnie B. Harmon et al., Sex and Violence in a Forensic Population of Obsessional Harassers, 4 Psych., Pub. Pol'cy, & L. 236 (1998).

14. Kathleen G. McAnaney, et al. From Imprudence to Crime: Anti-Stalking Law, 68 Notre Dame L. Rev. 819 (1993).

Suzy, she had loaded the gun with blanks, thinking they were real bullets.

c. Suzy loaded her .38 caliber pistol with real bullets, snuck out the back door, and, unknown to Bob, with finger on the trigger, aimed directly at his heart. Suddenly, Suzy became confused and upset. She snuck back inside without being detected, put her gun away, and awaited Bob's return.

2. Max wanted to collect fire insurance on an old tenement building he owns, which contains 25 apartments. Late one evening he spilled gasoline in the basement and set a time-delayed fuse, which erupted into flame at 3:00 a.m. By some miracle most of the tenants escaped the resulting fire without serious harm; however, two tenants were horribly burned and almost died. He is charged with attempted murder.

3. Connor, an inner-city gang member, is selling drugs to a customer on his territorial street corner. As Raphael, a rival gang member, saunters toward him, Connor uses a stolen gun to fire a warning shot over Raphael's head to scare him out of Connor's turf.
    a. Raphael is struck in the head by the bullet and almost dies.
    b. Raphael is struck in the head by the bullet and dies.
    c. What if Connor intends to kill Raphael, but the bullet only grazes Raphael and he dies anyway from a heart attack partially induced by "ecstasy," a street drug Raphael had just taken?

4. During the course of a drug deal in New York City, Paula, thinking Reuben was trying to rip her off by selling her harmless powder as crack cocaine, shot at Reuben intending to kill him. Reuben almost died but eventually recovered. Unknown to Paula, Reuben was an undercover state narcotics officer who was selling her real crack in a "sting" operation in order to then arrest her. In New York first-degree murder includes acting "with intent to cause the death of another person, . . . caus[ing] the death of such person; and . . . the person was a police officer . . . killed in the course of performing his official duties."
    Is Paula guilty of attempted first-degree murder?

5a. Last week Terrence, a law student about to graduate, told Dennis that he is going to "hack" into Sallie Mae's computer system and erase all of his own student loan records so he would not have to repay his humongous debt. That same day Terence visited Internet sites describing basic hacking techniques (including how to penetrate computer security systems and erase files) and downloaded this information. Has Terrence committed an attempt?

5b. Yesterday, Terrence wrote a program that would penetrate Sallie Mae's Internet site security system and obtained the remote access telephone number that would provide him entry into the site. Now?

5c. Earlier today Terrence loaded the hacking program he had written into his computer and dialed the remote access number for Sallie Mae's Internet site. He was met by an unexpected firewall. The system denied Terrence access to his files because he was not using a predesignated computer to access the site. The system posted: "Unauthorized attempt to access system. Please contact administrator" and listed an 800 number for assistance. Terrence quickly exited the system. Now? When?

6. At lunch in a bar Joe, an undercover cop, inquired if Sam could sell him some cocaine. Sam said he would call his suppliers and made several telephone calls. Sam then told Joe he would have a pound of cocaine to sell him at the same bar at 6:00 p.m. that evening. He instructed Joe to return alone at that time with cash. Joe agreed and left the bar. While picking up cocaine from his supplier, Sam was told of a rumor that the FBI was in town with undercover agents trying to set up cocaine buys. Sam gave the cocaine back to his supplier and did not go back to the bar that evening. Sam was arrested three days later and charged with attempted sale of drugs.

7. Noreen needed money for a down payment on a new house. She decided to collect insurance on her wedding ring, a family heirloom insured for $8,000 against theft. She drove to a distant city and sold the ring to a jeweler. Two days later she broke her window from the outside and ransacked her bedroom where she had previously kept the ring. She then called her insurance company and asked what steps she had to take to be paid for the theft of her ring under the policy. The company said it would pay her the $8,000 if she filed a police report and then submitted a claim. Noreen reported to the police that the ring had been stolen.
   a. A few days later, overwhelmed by guilt, she confessed to the police.
   b. The jeweler to whom she sold the ring called her and said he had received a police bulletin describing her ring as stolen property and that he intended to report it to the police. Noreen immediately notified the insurance company that she would not be submitting an insurance claim.

8. Julie, an explosives expert who is angry over Dave's decision to break off their relationship, sneaked over to Dave's house and wired his car so that it would explode when Dave started it the next morning. Later that evening, Dave died of a heart attack. Upon learning of Dave's sudden demise, Julie sneaked over to the car the next evening and removed the explosives.

9. Trevor and Gloria, college freshmen, met briefly during Greek Week. When Trevor asked Gloria for a date, she firmly declined. Trevor then acquired her e-mail address:
   a. The love-struck Trevor sent Gloria three e-mails, professing his undying love. The first stated that he thought of her constantly and could not get her out of his mind. The second stated that he would

do anything to have her. The final one stated that, as he watched her walking to class, he realized she was the only one for him. Gloria, fearful of Trevor's obsession with her and his secret observation, became very fearful of what he might do next. Nervous and apprehensive, Gloria became very jittery and constantly looked over her shoulder whenever she left her room. Has Trevor committed a stalking offense?

b. When Gloria did not react favorably to his "nice" e-mails, Trevor became angry and decided to send some intimidating messages to Gloria as payback. Trevor sent her two anonymous e-mails. One contained lyrics from a contemporary rap song which were sexually explicit and graphically violent. The other contained lyrics about constantly watching a woman who was unaware of the surveillance. Gloria trashed them, thinking a quirky friend with deficient social skills had sent them to her as a joke.

c. After receiving the first set of e-mails, Gloria obtained a restraining order against Trevor ordering him to refrain from all contact with her. Karl, a mutual friend, told Trevor that Gloria was so upset that she had gone to her parents' house, a two-hour drive from campus. Trevor looked up her parents' address and drove to her parents' home with the intention of seriously frightening her. As he approached the house, he circled the block a couple of times and then drove away because he did not want to violate the order. Gloria did not see him. Attempted stalking? Abandonment?

10. A word of caution. This is a controversial example because many people have strongly held views on abortion. This example was derived from a real case, *Planned Parenthood of the Columbia/Willamette, Inc. v. American Coalition of Life Activists*, 41 F. Supp. 2d 1130 (D. Oregon 1999).

   "Life is Right," a pro-life activist group, maintains a Web site at "www.babykillers.org" that lists the names and addresses of doctors in the United States who perform abortions. Some of these doctors have been murdered and their names have been struck through by a red line. After the last two murders Life is Right mailed each remaining doctor on the list a post card that read: "Still killing? Check out "www.babykillers.org"! Can members of Life is Right be convicted of stalking these doctors? If someone who has read the Web site kills one of the doctors, are Life is Right members responsible as accomplices?

11. Quentin loves Cuban cigars. He thinks their importation into the United States is a crime. He purchased several high-priced cigars in Colombia while on a business trip, thinking they were Cuban cigars, and hid them in a secret compartment in his suitcase. A customs inspector discovered the cigars at the airport in Miami.

a. There is a law forbidding the importation of Cuban cigars, but, it turns out, these cigars are from Santo Domingo.

b. These cigars are Cuban, but there is no criminal law forbidding their importation.

c. There is a law forbidding the importation of Cuban cigars, but, unknown to Quentin, these cigars actually are 100 percent marijuana.

EXPLANATIONS

1a. Suzy's purpose was to kill Bob. Because she acted with the purpose to achieve the result element of the target crime, causing the death of another human being, and did the last act necessary to accomplish that result (or took a substantial step under the MPC), Suzy committed attempted murder even though she did not achieve the intended result.

1b. Suzy had the necessary mens rea to commit murder. She intended to kill another human being. She also acted on that criminal purpose by purchasing a gun, becoming proficient in its use, and luring her victim to a scene where she could establish a good cover story explaining the murder as an accident.

Under the common law she took the last step; she actually pulled the trigger of what she thought was a loaded pistol while aiming it at Bob's heart. In addition, her behavior probably satisfies the equivocality test because her course of conduct seems consistent only with a planned murder. (However, because the jury cannot consider any evidence other than her conduct, it could conclude that her behavior was consistent with law-abiding conduct; i.e., she was looking for a burglar and was simply mistaken as to Bob's identity.) Under both the proximity test and probable desistance test, Suzy has committed the actus reus of attempt. She has come very close in time and space to causing the result (proximity test), and she did not break off her criminal course of conduct (probable desistance test).

Under the MPC Suzy took a substantial step that was strongly corroborative of her criminal purpose. She obtained a gun, learned how to use it, lured the victim to the contemplated crime scene, aimed the gun at a vital part of Bob's body, and pulled the trigger.

Suzy might argue impossibility. However, this is simply a case of factual impossibility (unknown to Suzy, the shells were blanks, not bullets), not legal impossibility (there is a law against unlawfully killing another human being). Factual impossibility is no defense at common law. Under the MPC, had the facts been as Suzy believed them to be (i.e., the gun was loaded with bullets, not blanks), Suzy would have committed the target crime (assuming a good aim). Thus, she is guilty of an attempt. The MPC focuses on the defendant's attitude more than on how close she came to actually causing harm.

1c. The same general analysis for mens rea and actus reus used in Example 1b applies here. However, Suzy has not taken the last step (there is still an opportunity to repent and she did), nor is it clear that her conduct satisfies the equivocality test (she could have been looking for a burglar). The prosecution would have a better chance under the proximity test (she stalked her victim and almost pulled the trigger) or probable desistance test (though Suzy did break off her criminal conduct and change her mind, most citizens would not have gone as far as she did). Because murder is a serious crime and most law-abiding citizens would not go through such an elaborate scheme, a jury could convict her under all of these tests except the last-step test. Note how the common law requires the defendant to come very close to actually committing the target offense and also requires strong evidence of criminal intention.

The MPC, however, is more concerned with preventing harm and apprehending dangerous individuals; it is less concerned with waiting until the last possible moment to see if a defendant will actually commit the target offense.

Under the common law there is no defense of abandonment, so Suzy cannot claim she has changed her mind. Under the MPC Suzy can present evidence that she renounced her criminal scheme and did not have the firmness of criminal intention. She also might argue that her renunciation was complete and voluntary because she could easily have carried out the murder as planned. There were no unexpected facts making it more difficult. Suzy would argue that she was filled with remorse and should not be convicted. Her change of heart shows she is not really dangerous. This will be a jury question.

2. Max did not attempt murder even though he acted recklessly with extreme indifference to human life. His purpose was to destroy the building, not to kill people.

Under the common law he did not act with the specific intent as to result—that is, he did not intend to take human life. Thus, he cannot be convicted of attempted murder.

Under the MPC Max also cannot be convicted of attempted murder because he did not act with the purpose of taking human life. (This explanation assumes that Max did not *believe* that people would die. Under the MPC such a belief would satisfy the mens rea for result required for an attempt.)

If a human being had died in the fire, Max could have been convicted of murder under either of two theories: intentional risk creation or felony murder. (See Chapter 8.) However, to convict someone of attempted murder, most jurisdictions and the MPC require that the defendant have acted with the purpose or intent of achieving the result element — that is, taking human life. Even if Max had knowledge that his conduct created a high probability that someone would be killed, he did not commit attempted murder.

Contrary to this clear majority rule, a few jurisdictions have held that a defendant can be convicted of "attempted reckless manslaughter"[15] or "attempted extreme indifference to life murder"[16] even though he did not intend to kill. This minority approach eliminates the traditional requirement for attempt that the defendant must act with the purpose of causing the result element of the target offense. It is sufficient if he intentionally or purposefully does an act either recklessly or with extreme indifference to human life. The rationale is that, when the defendant does an intentional act knowing that it may come very close to killing an innocent victim, he is both blameworthy and dangerous; consequently, attempt liability is appropriate. The facts of this example demonstrate why courts might be persuaded to adopt this approach.

3a. Connor did not commit attempted murder. Even though Raphael almost died as a result of Connor's intentional act, Connor did not act with the *purpose* of killing him. His purpose was to cause his rival to leave Connor's "territory." Thus, under both the common law and the MPC, Connor did not commit attempted murder. Of course, we have posited that Connor's mental state is known. Without such evidence, however, a jury is free to conclude that Connor "intended" the result that he almost caused and to convict him of attempted murder.

3b. Because Connor proximately caused the death of another human being who was not a co-felon during the commission of a felony (the drug sale), Connor could be convicted of felony-murder even though he did not intend to cause Raphael's death. Unlike attempt, which focuses on the actor's mental state or attitude toward causing a particular result, the felony-murder rule imposes homicidal responsibility based primarily on the harm the defendant proximately causes during the commission of a serious crime. (See Chapter 8.)

3c. This is a close one and could go either way. The jury might decide that "ecstasy," the drug voluntarily ingested by Raphael, proximately caused his death and that it was an independent intervening cause. (See Chapter 7.) If so, then Connor can only be convicted of *attempted* murder because, even though his purpose was to kill Raphael, he did not cause that result. While the fright caused by Connor's warning shot may have contributed somewhat to Raphael's death, his death was caused primarily by his own voluntary conduct. Thus, the felony-murder rule would

---

15. *People v. Thomas*, 729 P.2d 972 (Colo. 1986).
16. *People v. Castro*, 657 P.2d 932 (Colo. 1983).

probably not snare Connor. The moral? Don't forget to analyze *both* mens rea and causation on those cagey law school exams!

4. This is a tough one! Paula clearly intended to cause Reuben's death and took a substantial step (and the last step) toward accomplishing her goal. Thus, she can surely be convicted of at least attempted second-degree murder.

    But must the prosecution prove that Paula also intended to kill a police officer in the course of performing his official duties? The prosecution probably could not prove this because Paula would not have knowingly bought drugs from a police officer, nor do any facts indicate that Paula knew Reuben was an undercover police officer.

    Under common law Paula must know all circumstances of the target crime. Because she did not intend to kill a police officer while he was performing his duties, she could not be convicted of attempted first-degree murder even if this circumstance is a strict liability element in the target offense.

    Under the MPC, however, the mens rea toward circumstances of the target offense determines her guilt. If the circumstance that Reuben was a police officer performing his official duties is a strict liability element, then Paula would be guilty of attempted first-degree murder. (Under the MPC, however, it will be a material element.) If, on the other hand, the mens rea of "purpose" or "knowledge" also applies to this circumstance, then she would not be.

5a. Terrence clearly has the mens rea to commit several crimes, including contemporary crimes that prohibit computer hacking and the destruction of computer information as well as traditional crimes like fraud and theft (by not repaying his student loans). His criminal intention can be established by his statement to Dennis and by his gathering information on hacking techniques.

    The more difficult question is whether Terrence is simply in the "preparation" phase or has actually put his plan into "action" by engaging in conduct sufficient to make him guilty of attempt. Under the common law Terrence has surely not yet taken the "last step" since he would have to do much more to accomplish his goal. And his behavior so far (without looking at any other evidence like his remark to Dennis) does not plainly demonstrate that he is going to commit a crime. Thus, it does not satisfy the "equivocality" test.

    Even under the proximity test Terrence has probably not committed an attempt because he has not come close in space or time to actually committing the unauthorized computer entry (let alone destruction of computer information). Under the probable desistance test, he still can change his mind since there are still actions he must take to accomplish his goal. Thus, Terrence has not committed an attempt.

Under the MPC has Terrence taken a "substantial" step? Probably not. His actions appear to be only preparation, acquiring the information necessary to commit the crime at some future time.

5b. Terrence's mens rea is the same as in example 5a. Under the common law he has probably not satisfied the following tests: last step, equivocality, or probable desistance. However, the facts are stronger for the prosecution than in 5a. Terrence would argue that even though he has assembled the "tools and instruments" necessary for committing the crimes on his computer and the computer would be used to carry them out, this location may not be sufficiently "near" the crime scene. However, the prosecutor might argue that Terrence custom designed his "hacking" program to commit these crimes and that the program has no lawful use. Thus, under the MPC he has committed a "substantial step." Ultimately, the jury must determine if this conduct "strongly corroborates a criminal purpose."

5c. Terrence has committed an attempt! He had the necessary mens rea. His actus reus in trying to enter a secure computer site has satisfied all of the common law tests except the "last step" and, perhaps, the equivocality test. Terrence's action would clearly constitute a "substantial step" under the MPC because it confirms his criminal purpose. He used a hacking program, a custom designed criminal instrument, and went (in cyberspace!) to the scene of the contemplated crime, a secure computer system by dialing the remote access number and trying to gain entry.

Under the MPC Terrence might raise the defense of renunciation, arguing that he decided not to commit the offense after all. However, Terrence changed his mind about committing the crime only because he was having difficulty in succeeding and because the chances of being detected had become much higher. He was probably postponing the crime until he could determine how to breach the firewall. Thus, his renunciation is not voluntary and complete. Poor Terrence: criminal punishment and student loans!

6. Sam has the mens rea necessary for conviction of the target offense because he has the purpose of selling drugs to Joe. Under the common law Sam has not taken the last step (though Sam has actually located and bought the drugs, he still must return to the bar to complete the sale). It is also not clear that he has satisfied the proximity test; he is not close in space or time to bringing the drugs to the bar where the sale to Joe would take place. However, his conduct probably satisfies the probable desistance test and, arguably, even the equivocality test because locating and buying illegal drugs are not consistent with innocent behavior. Thus, under some common law tests, Sam has committed an attempt. Under others, he has not and his conduct is still only preparation.

Under the MPC Sam has probably taken a substantial step and has committed an attempt. He actually located a supplier and arranged to pick up and pay for the drugs that he would resell to Joe. This demonstrates that Sam is firm about committing the crime.[17]

Sam might argue, however, that he never came close to actually selling the drugs to Joe. In addition, Sam might argue that, even if he did commit an attempt, he subsequently renounced his plans. The first defense is essentially a denial that he committed the necessary actus reus; it would probably not succeed under some tests. The second defense does not satisfy the elements of renunciation because the only reason Sam decided not to complete the crime is the rumor that Joe might be an undercover officer. Sam has not changed his mind for the right reasons and is simply waiting for a better opportunity.

7a. Noreen has probably not committed attempted fraud (though she may be convicted of filing a false police report). Although she intended to file a false claim of theft, she only engaged in preparatory conduct.

Under the common law she has not taken the last step; she must still submit the claim to the insurance company. Nor is she proximately close to committing fraud. She has ample opportunity to change her mind and has not yet set in motion a chain of events that would lead to her being paid by the insurance company for the "loss" of her ring.

Even under the MPC it is unlikely she has taken a substantial step. Because she needed to actually file the claim before she would collect any money, she could still change her mind and, in fact, she did. And if she has attempted under the Code, she has abandoned.

7b. Just as in Example 7a, Noreen has not committed an attempt. True, she changed her mind only because the chances of succeeding were almost zero. However, her actions would still probably be considered preparation rather than implementation under the analysis in 7a.

8. Julie has committed attempted murder. She purposefully wired Dave's car in order to kill him.

Under the common law she took the last step (though it could be argued that events were not yet beyond her control since she, in fact, did disarm the bomb). Her behavior may also have satisfied the equivocality test because planting a car bomb manifests criminal intent. Under the proximity test, a jury could well find her guilty because she has come close in time and space to committing the target crime, and this is a very serious offense likely to arouse strong community resentment. Though she did change her mind, it was not for the same reasons that would motivate a law-abiding person.

Under the MPC Julie has surely taken a substantial step; planting

---

17. *United States v. Mandujano*, 499 F.2d 370 (5th Cir. 1974).

a car bomb so it would explode when someone started the engine is strongly corroborative of a criminal purpose to kill.

Can Julie raise the defense of impossibility because she could not possibly have killed Dave, who had died during the night? This is not a case of legal impossibility. If the facts had been as Julie thought they were, Dave would have been alive and her plan to kill him would be a crime. Thus, Julie can be convicted of attempted murder.

Julie cannot raise the defense of renunciation. Even though she unwired the car so that no one else would be killed and she probably would not try to kill anyone else, she did not change her mind for the right reasons as required by the MPC. Rotten luck, Julie!

9a. Even though Trevor's three e-mails were willful, they were not malicious and probably not harassing. In addition, Trevor did not intend to place Gloria in fear. Rather, his purpose was to convey his heart-felt emotions. Nonetheless, Gloria became fearful for her physical safety because of the obsessive tone of these unwelcome e-mails. If the state stalking statute defines stalking as repeated behavior *intended* to cause fear of death or serious physical harm, then Trevor did not commit a stalking offense. His intention was not to create such fear; rather, it was to express his sincere love for Gloria. If, however, the state law defines stalking as intentional conduct that the individual *should have known* places a reasonable person in fear of death or serious bodily injury, then Trevor (despite his non-threatening intentions) has committed a stalking offense if Gloria's fearful reactions of serious bodily injury were reasonable.

9b. Gloria is not fearful for her physical safety; yet, Trevor intended to intimidate and harass her and to put her in fear of serious physical harm. Thus, he would clearly be guilty of stalking under a statute that focused on the culpability or attitude of the actor—repeated threatening behavior *intended* to put the victim in fear. However, he might not be guilty under a law that focused on the harm done — intentional conduct the actor knew or *should have known* would cause fear of serious physical harm in a reasonable person — because Gloria was not frightened and, arguably, neither would a reasonable person. If the statute required *both* that the actor intended his conduct to cause fear of serious physical safety and that it did cause such fear, Trevor could not be convicted of stalking.

9c. Trevor seemingly had the mens rea to commit a stalking offense. He located her parents' address and drove to her parents' home with the intent to frighten Gloria. Can he be convicted of attempted stalking? Under the common law Trevor did not take the last step since he did not actually try to contact Gloria; moreover, he also changed his mind about intimidating Gloria. But, under the equivocality and proximity tests, he might be convicted of attempted stalking. Likewise, under the

MPC Trevor could be convicted of attempted stalking. He took a substantial step that strongly corroborated his criminal purpose. He located his victim and drove two hours to come into close proximity to her. Has he renounced his criminal purpose? This is a close case because he broke off his course of conduct to avoid violating the court order, not because of a sincere change of heart. What do you think? Notice how moving back the threshold of criminality in a codified offense such as stalking may allow an "attempt" to occur even earlier.

10. Depending on the specific statutory definition, members of the group may well have committed a stalking offense when they mailed the second postcard to the doctors listed on their Web site. A jury could find that these repeated communications implicitly threatened the doctors by inviting others to use violence to stop them from performing abortions. Consequently, the doctors may reasonably have feared for their lives after receiving these postcards and visiting the Web site. If so, the jury could find that the postcards had been sent to maliciously, repeatedly, and willfully harass and intimidate these doctors to stop them from providing lawful medical services. The defendants would counter that they were engaged in speech protected by the First Amendment and that this use of the stalking statute is unconstitutional because it will chill public debate on an important public issue. As to the potential responsibility of members as accomplices, see example 7 in Chapter 14.

11a. Quentin clearly had the mens rea to commit an attempt, and he took a substantial step to implement that attempt (hiding the cigars in a secret compartment and not declaring them at customs). His actions also satisfy all of the common law tests. For reasons unknown to Quentin, the cigars were not Cuban and could lawfully be imported into the United States.

Under the common law this is a case of factual impossibility, not legal impossibility. There is a law forbidding importation of Cuban cigars into the USA. Quentin intended to engage in conduct that would violate that law, and he took significant action to implement that intent. Though these cigars are not Cuban, Quentin thought they were. Thus, most courts would conclude that Quentin had the purpose to import Cuban cigars and would not allow the defense. However, a minority of courts might conclude that Quentin intended to do what, in fact, he did — import Santo Domingan cigars. This analysis misapprehends the meaning of intent and also equates mens rea with actus rea.

The MPC would also convict Quentin of attempt. It provides that the mens rea toward circumstances required by the target offense will be the mens rea required for an attempt. In this case Quentin has acted with the purpose of importing Cuban cigars. Because this is the highest culpability, it will satisfy whatever mens rea is required by the target offense.

11b. This is a case of true legal impossibility under the common law. There is no statute forbidding the importation of Cuban cigars into the USA. Quentin has shown he is willing to commit a crime and has acted on that willingness, but what he tried to do is not criminal. A belief that one is breaking the law, even when coupled with action to implement that belief, cannot generate criminal responsibility.

Quentin could not be convicted under the MPC either because there is no statute punishing the importation of Cuban cigars.

11c. Quentin can be convicted of attempted importation of Cuban cigars. The analysis of mens rea and actus reus is the same as in Example 11a. This would be a case of factual impossibility under the common law and it would not be a defense. Under the MPC Quentin is also guilty of an attempt because he acted with the same mens rea toward circumstances as required by the target offense.

Whether Quentin can be convicted of possession and/or importation of marijuana depends on whether the applicable statute requires the defendant to know that the substance he possesses or imports is marijuana or whether it is a strict liability element. If it is not a strict liability element, Quentin could raise the defense of mistake of fact under the common law. Under the MPC he could present evidence of his belief to negate the culpability element of the offense. If it is a strict liability element, Quentin is in real trouble!

13

Conspiracy

Overview

Sometimes you can get things done more efficiently by working with others. Criminals have found this form of organization works for them too.

Conspiracy punishes individuals who agree to commit a crime (often called the "target" or "object" crime). Conspiracy, then, responds to the special dangers created by *group criminality:* division of labor, expanded scope of potential harm, mutual encouragement, and greater likelihood the agreed-upon crime — or even future crimes not yet determined or contemplated — will be committed.

Conspiracy is an *inchoate* or unfinished crime because it permits the police to arrest those who have agreed to commit a crime long before they actually carry out their agreement. In fact, conspiracy sets the threshold of criminality much earlier than does attempt.

The early common law did not have a separate crime of conspiracy. It first appeared in a narrow statutory form in the early part of the fourteenth century. By the end of the eighteenth century it had become a common law misdemeanor. Today, every state and the federal government have a conspiracy statute. As both criminal activity and criminal organizations have become more complex and sophisticated in modern society, conspiracy has become a more important law enforcement tool. Federal prosecutors, in particular, rely on conspiracy to prosecute crimes such as drug smuggling, transportation of illegal aliens, and other crimes that require planning and complex coordination of many individuals or groups.

Conspiracy is a powerful weapon for prosecutors. It allows them to take advantage of special procedural and evidentiary rules that increase their prospects for obtaining convictions. Moreover, in many jurisdictions defendants can be punished *both* for conspiracy and for crimes committed in furtherance of the conspiracy. This threat of increased punishment gives prosecutors tremendous leverage in obtaining plea bargains from defendants charged with conspiracy.[1]

Critics complain that the definition of conspiracy is too vague. Historically, there was a great deal of merit to this criticism because common law definitions were very broad. However, contemporary law reforms during the second half of this century have provided narrower and clearer definitions for this crime.[2]

Because the essence of conspiracy is criminal agreement, many definitions of the crime only require an agreement to commit a crime. Critics maintain that contemporary conspiracy definitions set the threshold of crime too early, essentially punishing thoughts rather than conduct. Supporters retort that the early threshold of criminality set by conspiracy is necessary to meet the special dangers posed by collective criminal action.

Definition

At common law and until recently in many states, conspiracy was defined as an agreement of two or more individuals to commit a criminal or unlawful act or a lawful act by unlawful means.[3] No conduct other than the agreement itself was required. (Remember that words alone are a type of conduct that can satisfy the actus reus requirement for a crime. See Chapter 3.) Today many (but not all) statutory definitions of conspiracy do require that at least one conspirator take an *overt act* in furtherance of the conspiracy before the crime is committed.[4] Some states require that one conspirator must take a "substantial act" in furtherance of the conspiracy, pushing the threshold of criminality much closer to the target offense.

---

1. Statistics indicate that conspiracy is one of the most commonly charged crimes in the federal system, though it appears not to be used frequently by state prosecutors. Marcus, Conspiracy: The Criminal Agreement in Theory and Practice, 65 Georgetown L.J. 925, 947-948 (1977).

2. See Johnson, The Unnecessary Crime of Conspiracy, 61 Cal. L. Rev. 1137 (1973).

3. A husband and wife could not commit a conspiracy at common law because a married couple was considered to be one person under the law. This is no longer the law in most jurisdictions.

4. The general federal conspiracy statute, 18 U.S.C. 371, expressly requires proof of an overt act. But the Supreme Court held in *United States v. Shabani*, 513 U.S. 10 (1994), that 21 U.S.C. 846, the federal drug conspiracy statute, which is silent about an overt act, does not require one. The Court concluded that congressional silence concerning an overt act indicates that Congress intended to adopt the common law definition of conspiracy for drug conspiracies.

The Common Law

The common law and early statutory definitions of conspiracy did not limit the object of the agreement to *crimes*. Rather, they included any act that was *unlawful* or *against public policy* or even *lawful* acts committed by *unlawful means*. These open-ended definitions created uncertainty in the criminal law. Criminal responsibility could attach for agreeing to do something with another (such as charging usurious rates of interest[5] or agreeing to bargain for wages as a group[6]) that, if done alone, would not be a crime. In short, common law conspiracy permits conviction for acts that are not expressly made criminal, creating serious risk of ex post facto punishment.

Thus, in the English case *Shaw v. Director of Public Prosecutions*,[7] the defendant's conviction for "conspiracy to corrupt public morals" for agreeing with others to publish a directory for prostitutes was upheld by the House of Lords even though prostitution was not a crime. A statute containing such a broad definitional term would probably be found unconstitutional in the United States as void for vagueness. (See Chapter 1.)

The Model Penal Code

The Model Penal Code, troubled by the expansive definition of conspiracy provided by the common law and by many early-twentieth-century American state statutes, requires that the object of the agreement must be a *crime* for conspiracy to be committed. Most states, though not necessarily using the specific language of the MPC, have followed its policy choice and require that the object of the agreement be a crime.

But beware! Some states still define conspiracy in the old-fashioned sweeping manner. California, for example, defines conspiracy as an agreement of two or more people "[t]o commit any act injurious to the public health, to public morals, ..." Cal. Penal Code §182(a)(5).

Punishment and Grading

The Common Law

At common law, conspiracy, like attempt, merged into the completed substantive offense. Consequently, conspirators could not be punished both for conspiracy and the target offense.

---

5. *Commonwealth v. Donoghue,* 250 Ky. 343, 63 S.W.2d 3, 89 A.L.R. 819 (1933).

6. *People v. Fisher,* 14 Wend. 2 (N.Y. 1835) (union members who organized to raise wages and refused to work until an employee working below union wages was discharged were found guilty of conspiracy against trade and commerce).

7. [1962] A.C. 220 (Eng.).

Today, however, in most jurisdictions conspiracy is a *separate* substantive offense. Unlike solicitation and attempt, conspiracy does not merge with the object crimes. The rationale supporting this antimerger rule is straightforward. Conspiracy criminalizes the act of agreeing to commit a crime and beginning to actually implement that agreement; the target offense punishes the separate behavior of actually committing the offense agreed upon. Thus, generally speaking, conspirators can be (1) convicted of *both* the crime of conspiracy and of target crimes actually committed in furtherance of the conspiracy, and (2) sentenced to consecutive (rather than concurrent) sentences for *both* conspiracy and the target offense.[8]

Conspiracy once was commonly punished with a fixed term without regard to the seriousness of the crime the conspirators planned to commit. Today, however, most jurisdictions either set the punishment at some term less than the object crime or follow the MPC.

The Model Penal Code

The Model Penal Code sets the punishment for conspiracy at the same grade and degree as the most serious object crime, except that a conspiracy to commit a capital offense or a felony of the first degree is punished as a felony of the second degree. MPC §5.05(1). The MPC considers a criminal group to be especially dangerous. Consequently, the deterrent impact of punishment must be harsh to be effective.[9] Critics of this approach argue that, if the conspirators have been arrested *before* they have accomplished their criminal goal, they should be punished *less severely* because they have not done as much harm.

The MPC does not permit conviction for both conspiracy and the target crime except in rare cases. Thus, in effect conspiracy does merge into the target crime under the MPC. MPC §1.07(1)(b). It takes the view that, once a criminal group has committed the object crime, the group's dangerousness

---

8. See *Callanan v. United States,* 364 U.S. 587 (1961) (upholding *consecutive* twelve-year sentences *each* for obstructing commerce by extortion and for conspiracy to commit the same offenses). There is some evidence, however, that defendants convicted of both conspiracy and the target offense are seldom punished for both. Marcus, supra note 1, at 938.

9. Weschler, Jones & Korn, The Treatment of Inchoate Crimes in the Model Penal Code of the American Law Institute: Attempt, Solicitation, and Conspiracy, 61 Colum. L. Rev. 957 (1961). The authors argue that, to the extent that sentencing should focus on the offender's antisocial disposition and the demonstrated need for correction, there is little difference in the required sentences depending on the accomplishment or failure of the plan. Thus, there is no reason to treat conspiracy differently than the completed target offense. However, once sentences reach a certain level, the effectiveness of deterrence declines, so lesser punishment for the most serious crimes (like first-degree crimes) is more economical.

should be measured by the same punishment as provided for the object offense. However, a defendant may be convicted of as many target offenses as are committed in furtherance of the conspiracy whether as perpetrator or an accomplice.

In unusual situations, however, the MPC does permit punishment for both conspiracy and target offenses. If the conspiracy had a goal of committing unspecified future crimes, the MPC permits the government to convict and punish its members for both the conspiracy and any object crimes committed or attempted. MPC §1.07(1)(b). (Note, however, that the MPC does not permit conviction for both conspiracy and an attempt to commit the target crime. MPC §5.05(3).)

The Special Advantages of Conspiracy for Prosecutors

Conspiracy affords prosecutors a number of significant advantages in trying criminal cases. Some of the more important ones are discussed below.

Choice of Venue

The Sixth Amendment to the Constitution provides that an accused has the right to trial "by an impartial jury of the state and district wherein the crime shall have been committed." This important constitutional protection requires the prosecutor to file charges and to try the case where the crime was committed.

The crime of conspiracy, however, is deemed to have been committed in any jurisdiction (or in the federal system in any district) in which any member of the conspiracy committed an act in furtherance of the conspiracy — even an act that was not itself a crime. This rule gives prosecutors, particularly federal prosecutors who often are dealing with conspiracies that they allege span several states, a tremendous tactical advantage. Frequently, there will be more than one such venue where an act connected to the crime has allegedly been committed and where, consequently, the case can be tried.

Joint Trials

Because all members of the conspiracy are considered to have committed the same crime, co-conspirators may be tried together in a single trial. This is far more efficient than having to select a new jury and have a new trial for each defendant. However, joint trials can create serious problems, including "guilt by association." As Justice Jackson said in *Krulewitch v. United States:* "A co-defendant in a conspiracy trial occupies an uneasy seat. There generally will be evidence of wrongdoing by somebody. It is difficult for the individual to make his own case stand on its own merits in the minds of jurors who are ready to believe that birds of a feather are flocked together."[10]

Use of Hearsay Evidence

Hearsay evidence is a statement made by someone who is not actually testifying but is repeated by a testifying witness and offered as stating the truth. Subject to a number of exceptions (many of which you will puzzle over in a course on evidence), the use of "hearsay" to prove something is generally prohibited because the person who made the original statement was not under oath when he made it and cannot be cross-examined in the courtroom. Thus, the truthfulness of the person who actually made the statement cannot be tested adequately.

Under the law of conspiracy, however, each co-conspirator is deemed to have authorized other members of the conspiracy to act and speak on her behalf. Thus, statements that co-conspirators make in furtherance of the conspiracy can be admitted later at trial to prove the defendant entered into a conspiracy.

The logical dilemma posed by this rule is clear: Evidence that is admissible only *if* a conspiracy exists will be admitted to prove that a conspiracy exists! This is a classic case of "bootstrapping."

Should courts first require the prosecutor to use nonhearsay evidence to prove beyond a reasonable doubt that a conspiracy exists before admitting hearsay testimony under the conspiracy exception? This approach, though preserving the logical premise that hearsay is admissible only if there *is* a conspiracy, might seriously hamper prosecutors' effective use of conspiracy. It can also disrupt the presentation of evidence in a coherent chronological sequence.

The Supreme Court resolved this question for the federal courts in *Bourjaily v. United States*.[11] The Court decided that the use of the co-conspirator hearsay exception is a question of evidence to be decided by a judge under the Federal Rules of Evidence. A hearsay statement by a co-conspirator is admissible if the prosecutor, using both nonhearsay evidence *and* hearsay evidence, first proves to the judge's satisfaction by a preponderance of the evidence that a conspiracy exists. The jury may then use the hearsay evidence in determining whether a conspiracy existed. Thus, the jury will usually hear the hearsay evidence before its admissibility is determined. If the judge concludes that the prosecutor has not proven the existence of a conspiracy, the jury will be instructed to disregard this evidence. (This may be like asking the jury not to look at the elephants sitting quietly in the

---

10. 336 U.S. 440, 454 (1949).
11. 483 U.S. 171 (1987).

corner!) Otherwise, jurors may use the hearsay statement in reaching their verdict.

Responsibility for Crimes Committed by Co-Conspirators

The Common Law

Under the "*Pinkerton* rule" (so-called because it was confirmed by the Supreme Court in *Pinkerton v. United States*[12]), each co-conspirator is responsible for

1. any *reasonably foreseeable* crime committed by a co-conspirator
2. in furtherance of the conspiracy.

This rule is an extremely powerful tool in prosecutors' hands.

First, it essentially establishes vicarious liability for every member of a conspiracy for all foreseeable crimes without requiring the government to establish accessorial liability. (See Chapter 14.) The prosecutor does not have to prove that the defendant intended to aid and abet or otherwise facilitate or encourage the commission of these crimes; she only has to prove that they were foreseeable. Under the *Pinkerton* rule each conspirator, by entering into the conspiratorial agreement, authorizes other members of the conspiracy to act as his agent to commit crimes necessary to implement their criminal objective. In turn, each conspirator is responsible for these crimes. The *Pinkerton* rule works like a kind of automatic "cash register" that rings up added punishment for each member of a conspiracy even when, as in the *Pinkerton* case itself, the defendant probably did not know of many of the crimes committed by his co-conspirator and certainly could not have assisted him because the defendant was in prison!

Second, the *Pinkerton* rule establishes vicarious liability based on *negligence*, which is the lowest level of culpability. The prosecutor does not have to prove that the defendant knew or was reckless that his co-conspirator might commit specific crimes in furtherance of the conspiracy. She need only prove that the crimes were *reasonably foreseeable*—that is, that the defendant *should* have anticipated their possible commission. Under the *Pinkerton* rule a conspirator may be convicted on a lower degree of culpability, negligence, than that often required to convict the person who commits the object offense. (See Chapter 4.)

Supporters argue that this rule is necessary so that the masterminds who organize and control sophisticated criminal conspiracies are held responsible for crimes committed by their foot soldiers. Without it, these "generals" would usually be insulated from any criminal responsibility for these target

---

12. 328 U.S. 640 (1946).

crimes. Critics of the rule assert that guilt is personal under our criminal justice system. Imposing punishment for substantive crimes in which the defendant did not participate or assist in some way runs contrary to that fundamental premise.

The *Pinkerton* doctrine can sweep broadly, making members of a conspiracy responsible for serious crimes "not within the originally intended scope of the conspiracy." An example is *United States v. Alvarez*.[13] Here the court affirmed the murder conviction of several members of a drug conspiracy for the death of a federal undercover agent after a proposed drug sale erupted into a gun fight in which the defendants were not personally involved. The court held that, though the murder "was not within the originally intended scope of the conspiracy," it was reasonably foreseeable by the defendants because the deal involved a large volume of drugs with a high value. Relying on this fact, the court concluded that the defendants "*must* have been aware of the *likelihood* that (1) at least some of their number would be carrying weapons, and (2) that deadly force would be used, if necessary, to protect the conspirators' interests" (emphasis added). Moreover, each of the defendants played a significant part in the transaction such as acting as a lookout; introducing the principals and being present during some of the negotiations; or letting the participants use a motel room and translating during some of the negotiations.

The *Pinkerton* rule imposes criminal responsibility on co-conspirators for contingent crimes to which they did not agree but which, under the circumstances, might well be necessary. Thus, the specific terms of the agreement do not set the limit for each member's criminal responsibility.

The Model Penal Code

The MPC rejects the *Pinkerton* rule because the scope of vicarious responsibility theoretically possible under this rule is too broad. Consequently, a co-conspirator must satisfy the MPC elements for accessorial liability (set forth in §2.06), which are more narrow than the common law (see Chapter 14). This means that conspiracy by itself is not a basis for establishing complicity for all reasonably foreseeable substantive offenses committed in furtherance of the conspiracy. Instead, the MPC asks "whether the defendant *solicited* commission of the particular offense or *aided*, or *agreed* or *attempted* to *aid*, in its commission" (emphasis added).[14]

---

13. 755 F.2d 830 (11th Cir. 1985).

14. Model Penal Code and Commentaries, Comment to §2.06(3), at 307 (1985). Under the MPC the act of conspiracy may be used as *evidence* of solicitation or aiding and abetting, but it cannot establish vicarious responsibility as a *matter of law*. Id. at 309.

A number of states, including New York, follow the MPC in rejecting the *Pinkerton* rule.[15]

Federal Sentencing Guidelines Limit the *Pinkerton* Rule

As we have seen, the *Pinkerton* rule is a *substantive* rule of law. It allows all members of the conspiracy to be found guilty for crimes committed by any member of the conspiracy even if the defendant did not assist in any way and did not foresee the particular crime. The federal Sentencing Guidelines, while not limiting the criminal responsibility of co-conspirators, do limit their *punishment* to only those offenses "(i) in furtherance of jointly undertaken criminal activity; and, (ii) reasonably foreseeable in connection with that criminal activity."[16]

Consider this case. The leader of the conspiracy in Tennessee arranged for some of its members to buy heroin in Philadelphia from other members of the conspiracy. Different members then delivered the heroin to customers in Tennessee. A customer died from a heroin overdose after purchasing the drug from a member of the conspiracy. A federal statute provides for a 20-year minimum if "death or serious bodily injury results" from a sale of heroin.

The conspirator who sold the heroin to the customer is clearly eligible for the 20-year minimum sentence. Under *Pinkerton* each member of the conspiracy, including those in Philadelphia, is also responsible for the customer's death. But under the federal Sentencing Guidelines other members of the conspiracy can be given the 20-year mandatory minimum sentence only if the government can prove that the sale was within the scope of the criminal activity the particular defendant agreed to undertake and was reasonably foreseeable by him. Thus, to obtain the 20-year minimum sentence the government must prove that each defendant was part of the distribution chain that led to the customer's death.[17]

Duration

How long does a conspiracy last? By its very nature, conspiracy is an ongoing offense; that is, the parties agree to commit a crime and then usually they must take steps over a period of time to accomplish their criminal

---

15. *People v. McGee,* 49 N.Y.2d 48, 399 N.E.2d 1177 (1979).

16. U.S.S.G. §1B1.3(a)(1)(B), Application Note 2.

17. *United States v. Swiney,* 203 F.3d 397 (2000).

objective. The statute of limitations does not begin to run until the conspiracy terminates.

The Common Law

A conspiracy usually terminates when all of its objectives have been achieved or when all of its members have abandoned all of its objectives.

Extending the Life of a Conspiracy

Prosecutors have been resourceful in trying to extend the life of a conspiracy beyond the accomplishment of its criminal objectives, usually to make full use of the special prosecutorial advantages we discussed earlier. (See pages 285-287, supra.) In *Krulewitch v. United States*,[18] for example, the government argued that conspirators always agree, at least implicitly, to conceal their conspiracy even after they have accomplished its objectives. Relying on the conspiracy hearsay exception, the prosecutors sought to introduce against one conspirator the statement of another conspirator made several months *after* the target offense of the conspiracy had been completed.

The Supreme Court held that such testimony was inadmissible because the conspiracy in this case had terminated once the object crime had been committed. Subsequent case law permits the government to use hearsay testimony made after the normal end of a conspiracy only if it can prove an *express* agreement to conceal the conspiracy or if it can show that ongoing concealment was essential to the conspiracy's success. This type of proof is usually very difficult.[19]

The Model Penal Code

The Model Penal Code considers conspiracy to be a "continuing" crime, beginning when the conspiracy is formed (see the Overview to this chapter) and ending when its criminal objective has been committed or when the agreement has been abandoned by the defendant and those with whom he has conspired. MPC §5.03(7)(a). (Remember, however, that a conspiracy can be charged and prosecuted *immediately* once an agreement and, under some conspiracy statutes, an overt act have been committed. See pages 281-283, supra.) The MPC also presumes abandonment if no conspirator

---

18. 336 U.S. 440 (1949).

19. See *State v. Rivenbark*, 311 Md. 147, 533 A.2d 271 (1987), and cases cited therein.

does an overt act in furtherance of the conspiracy during the applicable statute of limitations.

A conspiracy is terminated for an individual defendant if he abandons the conspiracy by advising his co-conspirators of his abandonment or informing law enforcement of the conspiracy's existence and his participation in it. MPC §5.03(7)(c). (See pages 310-311, infra, for a more complete discussion of this topic.)

Consequences of Termination

As we saw earlier (see pages 285-289, supra), conspiracy affords prosecutors enormous evidentiary, procedural, and substantive advantages, including choice of venue, joint trials, hearsay exception, and responsibility for substantive offenses. How fully prosecutors can exploit these advantages and avoid other legal constraints, such as the statute of limitations, depends in part on how long the conspiracy exists.

The Mens Rea of Conspiracy

The Common Law

Conspiracy is a "specific intent" crime at common law. First, the defendant must *intend* to agree with someone else. Merely approving of or seeking another's participation in a criminal purpose does not satisfy the mental state for conspiracy (though it may trigger criminal responsibility for solicitation (see Chapter 11) or as an accomplice (see Chapter 14)). Second, the defendant must *intend* to commit the offense that is the object of the conspiracy. Thus, the defendant must intend that the group or, at least one member of the group, will commit all elements of the crime agreed on (or, in jurisdictions that have the broader definition of conspiracy, all elements of the acts that are unlawful or against public policy).

Act and Result

Because conspiracy is a specific intent crime, it can require a *higher* mens rea than the crime the parties agree to commit. Recall Example 2 from the attempt materials (see page 268). Change the facts slightly so that Max and Mollie agree to burn down the apartment building in order to collect the insurance, hoping that no one will be injured. If Mollie subsequently sets the time-delayed fuse *and* causes a fire that both destroys the building and causes the death of a tenant, both Max and Mollie could be found guilty of conspiracy to commit arson and guilty of murder under either extreme risk creation or felony murder. Neither, however, is guilty of conspiracy to commit murder because, when they agreed, they did not have the specific intent to cause the death of another human being. Thus, the mens rea requirement for conspiracy can be higher than the mens rea of the crime that is committed as a result of the agreement. If, however, both Max and Mollie had agreed to kill an occupant of the building by setting fire to it, they could be convicted of conspiring to commit murder.

Circumstances

Another interesting question is whether the specific intent requirement of conspiracy includes the circumstance elements of the target crime. Put differently, must the government prove that the defendants intended the circumstance elements of the target crime or must it only prove the same mens rea toward a circumstance element for conspiracy as that required for conviction of the target offense?

This question was raised in *United States v. Feola*.[20] In that case several defendants agreed to sell heroin to prospective purchasers. Being overly ambitious (and perhaps a little lazy), they planned to pass off powdered sugar (no kidding!) as heroin, hoping to "rip off" the purchasers. If the purchasers discovered that the "heroin" was fake, the defendants had agreed to simply take their money by armed force.

Unfortunately for the defendants and unknown to them, their naive "buyers" were actually undercover federal narcotics officers. During the course of this bungled sale, one of the defendants assaulted one of the buyers without knowing he was a federal officer. Subsequently, all the defendants were charged with and convicted of both assault on a federal officer and of *conspiring* to assault a federal officer while engaged in the performance of his official duties.

The Second Circuit reversed the conspiracy convictions, holding that, although the substantive offense did not require intent as to the victim's status as a federal law officer, the federal conspiracy statute did.[21] The court held that the government must prove that the conspirators *intended* to assault a person they knew was a federal officer while engaged in the performance of his official duties because conspiracy is a specific intent offense. Failure to require such proof would expand the terms of their original agreement beyond those agreed to by the conspirators. Because the defendants did not know that their victims were federal officers, they could not intend to assault them while they were performing their official duties.

The Supreme Court reversed and affirmed the conspiracy convictions,

---

20. 420 U.S. 671 (1975).
21. *United States v. Alsondo*, 486 F.2d 1339 (2d Cir. 1973).

holding that the federal conspiracy statute only requires the prosecutor to establish the same mens rea toward this circumstance element (i.e., the victim was a federal officer performing his official duties) as that required for conviction of the substantive crime.[22] By disregarding the generally accepted understanding that conspiracy is a "specific intent" crime, this case establishes that the federal conspiracy statute does not require any higher proof toward a circumstance element of the agreed-upon crime than that required for conviction of that crime.

The Model Penal Code

The MPC is not as precise on the mens rea or culpability elements as one might expect. Section 5.03 states only that the agreement must have been made "with the purpose of promoting or facilitating" the commission of a crime.

Conduct and Result

However, the Commentaries to §5.03 state that the MPC requires *purpose* as to the conduct and result elements to establish conspiracy *regardless* of what the substantive crime requires. Thus, if the target offense is the sale of narcotics, the defendant must act with the purpose of promoting or facilitating the sale of narcotics. Likewise, the Commentaries state that, if the target offense is defined in terms of a prohibited result (such as homicide, which requires the death of a human being), the MPC requires that the defendant must act with the purpose of promoting or facilitating that result.

However, consider the following case. Suppose that a defendant conspires to sell what he thinks is heroin but is actually crack cocaine. The sale of heroin is punishable by a five-year sentence, and the sale of crack cocaine is punishable by a ten-year sentence. Conspiracy is punishable by a term one-half as long as the target offense of the conspiracy. If the defendant is arrested and convicted of conspiracy, what is his sentence?

Under *Feola* whether the defendant could be punished for conspiring to sell crack cocaine would depend on whether the substantive offense required him to act with the purpose of selling crack cocaine. Obviously, he could not have this purpose on these facts because he thought he was selling heroin.

According to the MPC Commentaries, however, the prosecution would have to prove that the defendant acted with the purpose of conspiring to sell crack cocaine regardless of what the target offense required. This approach

---

22. *United States v. Feola,* 420 U.S. 671 (1975). A good argument can be made that the federal status of the officers is not a circumstance element of the offense but only a jurisdictional element. See Chapter 4.

in effect requires the prosecution to prove "specific intent" for conspiracy even though it might not be required for the target offense.

Circumstances

Section 5.03 is also silent concerning what culpability toward circumstances is required. The Commentaries add that the conspiracy provision "does not attempt to solve the problem by explicit formulation."[23] Rather, the MPC concluded that the matter was best resolved by the courts.

If "purpose" toward circumstances is required to convict for conspiracy, then under §2.02(2)(a)(ii) knowledge or belief that the circumstance exists is sufficient. This is so because §2.02(2)(a)(ii), the general culpability provision in the MPC, provides that "purposely" with respect to circumstances is satisfied if the defendant "is aware of the existence of such circumstances or he believes or hopes they exist."

The Corrupt Motive Doctrine

In *People v. Powell,*[24] an 1875 case, the New York Court of Appeals reversed a conspiracy conviction of election officials who, truly thinking it was in the best interests of the state to save money, agreed not to advertise for election bids even though they were required to do so by law. The court held that, in addition to showing an intent to agree and an intent to accomplish an agreed-upon objective, the prosecutor must also show a "corrupt motive" or, put more simply, an intent to break the law. The court said: "The agreement must have been entered into with an evil purpose, as distinguished from a purpose simply to do the act prohibited, in ignorance of the prohibition. This is implied in the *meaning* of the word conspiracy" (emphasis added).[25] The court limited its holding to cases where the object of the agreement was not immoral and where the defendants were ignorant of the law. Nonetheless, the *Powell* case has come to stand for the proposition that a conspiracy must be committed, as the Supreme Court said in *Feola,* with a "corrupt motive or a motive to do wrong."[26] When the target crime is a *malum in se* offense or "clearly wrong in itself,"[27] the Supreme Court noted it will be easy to demonstrate a corrupt motive. When (as in the *Powell* case), the target offense is a *malum prohibitum* or regulatory offense, the *Powell* doctrine serves to protect individuals from being convicted of con-

---

23. Model Penal Code and Commentaries, Comment to §5.03, at 413 (1985).
24. 63 N.Y. 88 (1875).
25. Id. at 92.
26. 420 U.S. 671, 691 (1975).
27. Id.

spiracy simply because they *agreed* to do an act that, unknown to them, was a regulatory offense.

The "corrupt motive" doctrine makes some sense if conspiracy is considered to mean a criminal agreement — that is, a conscious decision by a group to commit an act they know is criminal. If, on the other hand, it simply means a group decision to engage in conduct that is criminal, then the doctrine is less convincing. Generally speaking, ignorance of the law is no excuse, and there seems nothing special about the crime of conspiracy that would require providing this special defense.

In support of the *Powell* doctrine, one might argue (at least where the parties are ignorant of the law and a regulatory offense is involved) that the parties may well discover their contemplated conduct is against the law and change their plans before committing the target offense. Thus, the inchoate or unfinished crime rationale of conspiracy does not require conviction in such cases. On the other hand, the policy choices that regulatory offenses pose for the criminal law are probably best faced when these laws are enacted. This includes deciding whether awareness that the criminal law forbids their behavior should be required for conviction. Group activity does not create a special problem that needs a special defense.

The Supreme Court in *Feola* did not consider whether the corrupt motive requirement embodied in the *Powell* case required reversal of the defendants' conviction for assaulting a federal officer because the defendants, in fact, had agreed to commit an assault, which they knew to be a wrongful and criminal act. Thus, they should not have been surprised to find themselves being prosecuted for a crime. Their only surprise (other than the obvious one that they inadvertently tried to rip off law enforcement agents) was that they were being tried in a federal court rather than a state court and faced harsher penalties than normally provided under a general assault statute.

Though traces of the corrupt motive doctrine can sometimes be found in cases, most contemporary courts and commentators do not consider it to be part of conspiracy law because it effectively creates a limited ignorance of the law defense for the crime of conspiracy.

The MPC, together with most recent state law revisions, reject the *Powell* doctrine, concluding that the mens rea requirements of the target offense, including regulatory offenses, and the public policies reflected therein should control.[28] As noted in Chapter 5, the MPC generally rejects both ignorance of the law or a mistake of law defense unless relevant to culpability or a material element of the specific statute. Concert of action should not provide a special ignorance of the law defense when it is not

---

28. Note, Conspiracy: Statutory Reform Since the Model Penal Code, 75 Colum. L. Rev. 1122, 1131 n.48 (1975).

available for the substantive offense.[29] The Supreme Court, though not specifically overruling the corrupt motive doctrine in *Feola*, certainly did not seem fond of it.

The Crimmins *Doctrine*

In *United States v. Crimmins,* a 1941 opinion written by Judge Learned Hand, the Second Circuit reversed a conviction for conspiracy to transport stolen securities in interstate commerce because the government had failed to prove that Crimmins *knew* the bonds had moved across state lines.[30] Even though the court assumed that this knowledge would not be essential for a conviction of the substantive offense, it concluded the defendant could not agree to an element of the substantive offense if he did not know of its existence. Judge Hand was concerned that convicting an individual under a *federal* conspiracy statute when he was unaware of facts that would alert him to the federal implications of his actions would enlarge the agreement beyond the terms originally understood by the parties. This holding has generated a line of cases that hold that the prosecution must prove that the defendant actually knew of the facts that gave rise to federal law enforcement interests.

To justify his holding, Judge Hand used the now famous "traffic light" analogy. He argued that, although a defendant can be convicted of running a traffic light he was unaware of, he cannot be found guilty of *conspiring* to run a traffic light if he did not know there was a traffic light in the first instance. In logical terms, Judge Hand's analogy assumes that knowledge of *material* facts is essential for an agreement to engage in conduct that includes those facts.

The Supreme Court in *Feola* noted that Judge Hand's traffic light analogy raised the public policy question of "whether it is fair to punish parties to an agreement to engage intentionally in apparently innocent conduct where the unintended result of engaging in that conduct is the violation of a criminal statute."[31] The Court concluded that the *Feola* case did not require it to decide this question. Instead, it determined that parties can be convicted of conspiracy to commit a crime if they knew of the material facts involved in the wrongful conduct; they did not have to know those facts that would give rise to federal jurisdiction. The defendants in *Feola* knew that they were agreeing to commit an assault. However, they did not know the status of their victim nor that they could be prosecuted in a federal court and face federal penalties. Recasting the "traffic light" analogy as suggested by the government, the majority said that the *Feola* case is more like agreeing

---

29. Model Penal Code and Commentaries, Comment to §5.03, at 417-418 (1985).
30. 123 F.2d 271 (2d Cir. 1941).
31. 420 U.S. 671, 690-691 (1975).

to run a red light without realizing it is on an Indian reservation and, therefore, can be prosecuted in the federal system.[32] The basic criminal nature of the conduct they had agreed to had not changed; they were only ignorant of a *jurisdictional element* that affected the choice of forums. Though the Supreme Court has not explicitly rejected the *Crimmins* doctrine, it has clearly indicated that, as long as the parties agree to engage in conduct that constitutes a *malum in se* crime, the government can convict them of violating the federal conspiracy statute even when they did not know facts that would sustain a federal law enforcement interest.

Purpose or Knowledge When Providing Goods and Services

A special mens rea problem occurs when one of the alleged parties to the conspiracy provides goods and services, such as a telephone answering service for prostitutes or ingredients for the manufacture of illegal goods. Can the supplier be convicted of conspiracy solely because he *knows* his goods or services are being used for a criminal goal? Or must the prosecutor prove that the defendant provided the goods or services with the *purpose* to advance the criminal object? Cases reach contrary conclusions, but the majority rule appears to be that purpose is required for a conspiracy conviction.

Case Law

In *People v. Lauria*[33] the government charged the owner of a telephone answering service and three prostitutes with conspiracy to commit prostitution. Lauria, the owner of the answering service, readily admitted that he knew some of his customers used his answering service for prostitution. However, he denied that he intended to further their criminal business. The court held that the government must prove intent; mere knowledge was insufficient. The court went on to explain that a jury may infer intent from knowledge, especially where the defendant has a "stake in the venture." A stake in the venture, in turn, may be established by showing that (1) the defendant charged excessive prices; (2) there is no legitimate use for the goods or services (e.g., selling gambling equipment in a state that does not allow gambling); or (3) the volume of defendant's business with the buyer

---

32. Of course, in recasting the traffic light analogy to take place on an Indian reservation, the Court created a fact pattern in which there is little doubt but that the situs of the conduct is solely jurisdictional. This may beg the question of when a fact is a material element or only a jurisdictional element.

33. 251 Cal. App. 2d 471, 59 Cal. Rptr. 628 (1967).

is grossly disproportionate to any legitimate demand for his goods or services or constitutes a substantial percentage of the defendant's business.[34]

In *People v. Roy*, a companion case with very similar facts to *Lauria*, the court upheld liability because there was evidence the answering service operator actively participated in the prostitution business by arranging the sharing of customers by two prostitutes who used the service. The court concluded that this constituted "promotion of a criminal enterprise."[35]

Requiring *purpose* rather than *knowledge* maximizes the freedom of businesses to pursue their individual economic gain rather than imposing a more demanding duty on them to prevent their products or services from being used to commit crime. It is also consistent with the criminal law's general policy not to look beyond the last responsible moral agent. The purchaser of the goods and services must still decide whether she will use them to commit a crime.

On the other hand, some courts consider knowledge that another will use the provider's goods or services to commit a crime is sufficient to impose criminal liability for conspiracy, especially when a serious crime, such as a felony, is involved. Even the *Lauria* court in dictum indicated that it might hold that knowledge rather than purpose is sufficient to convict of conspiracy when a serious crime such as kidnapping or the distribution of heroin is involved.[36] Critics respond that this rule is too burdensome on businesses and that, in most cases, the purchaser will simply obtain the goods or services from someone else who will not know of their intended use. Others argue that causation—simply being a link in a chain of events that enables someone to commit a serious crime — is not the gravamen of conspiracy. Rather, conspiracy requires a purposeful union of wills with the intent to accomplish a crime.

The Model Penal Code

The Model Penal Code requires that a provider of goods or services must have "the purpose of promoting or facilitating" the commission of the crime. Mere knowledge that his services or goods are being used by another to commit a crime will not satisfy this culpability requirement. MPC §5.03.[37]

Note: Whether a person who provides goods or services to someone he knows will use them to commit a crime can be convicted as an accomplice or for criminal facilitation under the MPC raises the same general issue! See Chapter 14.

---

34. *Direct Sales Co. v. United States*, 319 U.S. 703 (1943).
35. 59 Cal. Rptr. 636, 641 (1967).
36. 251 Cal. App. 2d 471, 480, 59 Cal. Rptr. 628 (1967).
37. Model Penal Code and Commentaries, Comment to §5.03, at 404 (1985).

The Actus Reus of Conspiracy

Agreement

The Common Law

The actus reus of conspiracy at common law was an *agreement* between *two or more parties* to commit a criminal or an unlawful act or a lawful act by unlawful means. An "overt act" in furtherance of the conspiracy was *not* required.

Though a conspiracy may involve an express agreement, perhaps by words or letters, in which the parties explicitly communicate their accord, it can also be indirect. What is required is a shared determination to accomplish a goal that is punished by the applicable conspiracy statute. The parties do not have to know all of its details, but they do have to know its basic purpose.

A person can become a party to a conspiracy without knowing the exact identity of all of its members or without having direct dealings with them. One can also join a conspiracy *after* its initial formation. However, the late-arriver, though guilty of conspiracy, is not responsible for substantive offenses committed by her co-conspirators in furtherance of the conspiracy *before* she joined. Thus, the *Pinkerton* rule is not retroactive.[38] (See pages 287-288, supra.)

The difficult question is not *what* must be proven — an agreement — but *how* it can be proven. Parties to a conspiracy might well discuss their plans in some detail and orally agree to the important points. Typically, however, when three people decide to rob a bank, they usually do not sign a "Bank Robbery Contract" and have it notarized — perhaps because they can't write or, more likely, because they fear such incriminating evidence may come back to haunt them at trial. Thus, prosecutors are unlikely to obtain a written document that embodies the terms of the agreement or its signatories. Unless one of the conspirators later turns state's evidence and becomes a witness for the prosecution or, better yet, law enforcement has the good fortune of obtaining a warrant and placing an electronic recording device where the parties entered into their agreement, it is usually difficult for the prosecution to present direct evidence of the agreement.

The law accommodates this difficulty by letting prosecutors use indirect evidence to prove the existence of a conspiracy. This evidence often consists of aiding and abetting or coordinated action by the parties from which the jury is asked to infer a *prior* agreement. The logic of such evidence is that group conduct is usually the result of a prior agreement. Neither aiding and abetting nor concerted action, however, necessarily establish a prior agree-

---

38. *United States v. Blackmon,* 839 F.2d 900 (2d Cir. 1988).

ment because one can assist another in committing a crime without such an agreement. (See *State v. Tally,* page 301, infra.) Moreover, proving a prior agreement from a later criminal act runs the risk of collapsing the substantive offense into the prior criminal agreement.

Permitting proof of an agreement by circumstantial evidence, though necessary, requires careful implementation so that it does not seriously weaken the due process protection afforded criminal defendants. As one commentator has cautioned: "[I]n their zeal to emphasize that the agreement need not be proved directly, the courts sometimes neglect to say that it need be proved at all."[39] Ensuring that the prosecution establishes the agreement by sufficient probative evidence is especially important because the "conspiracy doctrine comes closest to making a state of mind the occasion for preventive action against those who threaten society but who have come nowhere near carrying out the threat."[40]

In some cases the evidence of agreement is quite minimal. For example, in *United States v. Alvarez,*[41] government undercover agents agreed to purchase from two conspirators marijuana to be flown into Florida from South America. Speaking in Spanish near the proposed off-loading site, the agents asked the two about Alvarez, the person driving their truck They replied that he would be at the site when the marijuana would be off-loaded. One agent turned to Alvarez and asked if he would be at the site to help off-load. Alvarez nodded his head indicating "yes," smiled, and asked the DEA agent if he was going to be on the plane when it arrived to unload the marijuana. After some further conversation with the original two conspirators concerning the details of the plane's arrival and unloading, they and Alvarez were arrested and charged with conspiracy to import drugs into the United States.

A three-judge panel initially reversed Alvarez's conviction for conspiracy, holding that this evidence was insufficient to establish that the defendant had joined in an agreement to import drugs. The court noted that a defendant "does not join in a conspiracy merely by participating in a substantive offense, or by association with persons who are members of the conspiracy."[42] The court was concerned that Alvarez's expressed willingness to assist in the commission of the conspiracy's target offense was also used to establish that he had previously joined the agreement to commit that offense.

Subsequently, an en banc decision[43] of the Fifth Circuit reversed the

---

39. Note, Developments in the Law — Criminal Conspiracy, 72 Harv. L. Rev. 920, 933 (1959).

40. Goldstein, Conspiracy to Defraud the United States, 68 Yale L.J. 405, 406 (1959).

41. 610 F.2d 1250 (5th Cir. 1980), conviction affd., 625 F.2d 1196 (1980) (en banc).

42. 610 F.2d at 1255.

43. An en banc opinion is one in which all sitting members of the Circuit Court of

panel decision and affirmed the conviction. It noted that a conspirator can join a conspiracy after its initial inception. Moreover, Alvarez knew criminal activity was planned and that a conspiracy had been formed to import drugs and unload them at this site. There was also direct evidence that Alvarez planned to help unload the drugs; a jury could infer from this fact that he must have agreed at an earlier time to help unload. Alternatively, in assuring the others that he would help unload, a jury could find that Alvarez was doing an act to further the conspiracy. Consequently, there was sufficient evidence from which a jury could find that Alvarez had intentionally joined the conspiracy.

The Model Penal Code

The Model Penal Code takes the same basic approach as the common law; agreement is the core concept of conspiracy. The MPC provides a more thorough definition to include two types of agreement: (1) the defendant or another co-conspirator will commit, attempt to commit, or solicit a crime, or (2) the defendant agrees with another to aid him in the planning or commission of a crime, an attempt to commit it, or its solicitation. Under the MPC a person is guilty of conspiracy if he agrees (a) with other persons that any one of them will commit, attempt, or solicit a crime, or (b) to be an accessory to the crime by facilitating its commission. MPC §5.03(1)(a)(b). Note, however, that aid *without agreement* does not constitute conspiracy under the MPC.

In *State v. Tally*,[44] the defendant tried to aid murderers by preventing the delivery of a warning telegram to the victim. He would not be guilty of committing conspiracy under the MPC because there was no agreement or concert of action between Tally and the others. Tally could be convicted of aiding and abetting but not conspiracy. Otherwise, anyone who aided and abetted could be convicted of conspiracy and subjected to the broad vicarious liability and additional punishment for conspiracy. Most states have adopted this approach.

Overt Act
In General

Unlike the common law, which only required an agreement for the actus reus of conspiracy, most modern statutes also require that *one member* of the

---

Appeals for the particular circuit participate. In the initial *Alvarez* decision, three judges participated.

44. 102 Ala. 25, 15 So. 722 (1894). See Chapter 14 for a more detailed account of this case.

conspiracy commit an *overt act* in furtherance of the conspiracy for the crime to be committed.[45] The overt act demonstrates that the conspiracy has gone beyond the purely "mental state" and has reached the implementation stage. However, the overt act can be an act that, by itself, would be lawful and innocent such as renting a van or buying a ladder. It does not have to be an act that would come anywhere near satisfying the actus reus of attempt, such as an "unequivocal act" or a "substantial step." A few states do require that at least one member of the conspiracy must take a "substantial step" in furtherance of the conspiracy.[46] This usually has the same meaning as it does in attempt—an act that "strongly corroborates the actor's criminal purpose." (See Chapter 12.)

The Model Penal Code

The Model Penal Code only requires that the defendant or any other party to the conspiracy must commit an overt act if the substantive offense is relatively minor—that is, a felony of the third degree or a misdemeanor. If the substantive offense is serious, a felony of the first or second degree, no overt act in furtherance of the conspiracy is required. MPC §5.03(5). When a serious crime is the object of the agreement, the MPC essentially adopts the common law actus reus requirement that the act of agreeing is itself the actus reus of conspiracy. The MPC concludes that the act of agreeing is "concrete and unambiguous." Thus, there is much less danger of incorrectly interpreting innocent or equivocal behavior as criminal conduct. Also, the act of combining wills makes it more likely, both psychologically and practically, that the target offense will be committed.[47]

The Scope of the Agreement or How Many Conspiracies?

Perhaps the two most perplexing questions to be resolved in conspiracy cases are (1) how many conspiracies are there? and (2) who is a party to which conspiracy? The answers to these two questions are extremely important because they determine a number of other significant legal issues,

---

45. Sometimes conspiracy statutes can vary within a jurisdiction. The general federal conspiracy statute, 18 U.S.C. 371, expressly requires an overt act. However, 21 U.S.C. 846, the federal drug conspiracy statute, does not. *United States v. Shabani*, 513 U.S. 10 (1994).

46. See, e.g., Maine Rev. Stat. Ann. tit. 17-A (West 1983), §151.4; Wash. Rev. Code Ann. §9A.28.040 (West 2000).

47. Model Penal Code and Commentaries, Comment to §5.03, at 388 (1985).

including choice of venue, propriety of a joint trial, admissibility of hearsay testimony, satisfaction of the overt act requirement, and liability for any substantive offense committed in furtherance of the conspiracy.

However, setting forth the black letter law is much easier than applying it, as the case law makes clear. The law of conspiracy permits the fact finder to convict only those individuals who have entered into the same agreement. Yet, as we saw earlier, there is seldom tidy evidence available clearly establishing who those parties are. To the contrary, there is often a large cast of characters involved in committing a number of similar crimes. Often, individual members of the cast deal directly with some characters but not with others. Unfortunately, the case law has developed some rather primitive analytic approaches to ascertaining who is a member of a particular conspiracy.

Single Agreement with Multiple Criminal Objectives

One agreement establishes one conspiracy, even though there may be several criminal objectives of that agreement.[48] Thus, if *A*, *B*, and *C* agree to rob one bank each day for the next five days, there is only one conspiracy — even though the conspirators have agreed to commit five robberies. If there are multiple agreements, however, then there are multiple conspiracies even if each has only a single criminal objective. So if *A*, *B*, and *C* agree to rob a bank and do so and then, elated with their success, agree to rob another bank, there are two conspiracies.

Single or Multiple Agreements?
The Wheel and Spokes Approach

In *Kotteakos v. United States*,[49] the government charged and convicted 32 defendants of participating in a *single* conspiracy with Simon Brown. The evidence showed that over a period of time each of the defendants and Brown had fraudulently obtained loans to be insured by a federal agency. The defendants, on the other hand, claimed that each of them had formed a separate conspiracy with Brown but not with each other. Thus, there were a number of distinct conspiracies rather than one large one.[50]

---

48. *Braverman v. United States*, 317 U.S. 49 (1942).

49. 328 U.S. 750 (1946).

50. "As the Government puts it, the pattern was 'that of separate spokes meeting at a common center' though, we may add, without the rim of the wheel to enclose the spokes." Id. at 755.

Needless to say, all the defendants had a tremendous stake in how this question was resolved. Under the government's view each of the 32 defendants could be punished under the *Pinkerton* rule for each of the fraudulent loans obtained by the others. Under the defendants' view Brown could be found guilty on 32 separate counts of conspiracy, each with one co-conspirator.

The Supreme Court determined that, though these defendants committed similar crimes with the same individual, Brown, there was no connection or relationship between the defendants. The pattern of their behavior looked like many spokes of a wheel with a common center (Brown) but without a common rim. Thus, the Court held that there were a number of conspiracies rather than a single conspiracy.

Therefore, committing the same type of crime with a common participant is not necessarily sufficient to establish a single agreement. In *Kotteakos* there was no interdependence or even communication among the defendants; they did not depend on one another for their individual success. Nor was there any division of labor or other cooperation that facilitated a common goal.

In contrast to *Kotteakos* is *Interstate Circuit, Inc. v. United States*.[51] A manager of Interstate, a chain of theaters, sent a letter to each of eight movie distributors (who together controlled 75 percent of the first-run film market in the country), with copies to the others, demanding that theaters charge a minimum price and not permit first-run movies to be shown on a double feature with another feature film as a condition of Interstate's continued showing of their movies. Subsequently, each distributor complied with Interstate's terms.

The trial court found that the distributors had agreed with one another and with Interstate to fix prices in violation of the Sherman Antitrust Act because each of the distributors knew that the others had received the letter and because concerted action of all was necessary for the price-fixing to be effective. The Supreme Court upheld the convictions, concluding: "It is elementary that an unlawful conspiracy may be and often is formed without simultaneous action or *agreement* on the part of the conspirators" (emphasis added).[52]

This case comes perilously close to *dispensing* with the need to prove an agreement rather than letting the government use circumstantial evidence to establish an agreement. It also demonstrates how the loose definition of conspiracy often applied in antitrust cases poses the risk of being applied in more traditional criminal cases. Finally, the case establishes that co-conspira-

---

51. 306 U.S. 208 (1939).
52. Id. at 227.

tors can enter into a criminal agreement by concerted action alone if they have the necessary knowledge.

The Chain Approach

Blumenthal v. United States[53] involved a scheme whereby an unknown owner sent shipments of liquor to Weiss and Goldsmith. In turn, Weiss and Goldsmith agreed with three other defendants (Feigenbaum, Blumenthal, and Abel) that these three would sell the liquor to various taverns at prices exceeding the ceiling set by law. There was no evidence that these three defendants knew of the unknown owner or of his part in the plan. Nonetheless, the Supreme Court affirmed the trial court's finding there was only one conspiracy including all six individuals.

The Court concluded the case was not like *Kotteakos,* saying:

> The scheme was in fact the same scheme; the salesmen knew or *must have known* that others unknown to them were sharing in so large a project; and it hardly can be sufficient to relieve them [of responsibility] that they did not know, when they joined the scheme, who those people were or exactly the parts they were playing in carrying out the common design and object of all. By their separate agreements, if such they were, they became parties to the larger common plan, joined together by their knowledge of its essential features and broad scope, though not of its exact limits, and by their common single goal [emphasis added].[54]

The Court analogized each of the defendants as links in a common chain, each essential to the ultimate task of selling the liquor at illegal prices. Where there is a common objective that, because of complexity, magnitude, or other factors, requires the attributes of collective criminal behavior, courts are more likely to find a single conspiracy rather than a number of conspiracies.

However, not all behavior that initially looks like the result of a single agreement will support that finding. In the Woody Allen movie, *Take the Money and Run,* two groups of would-be bank robbers enter a bank at the same time, each trying to rob it. An observer seeing this scene might well conclude that, because all of the robbers enter the bank and start to rob it at about the same time, everyone is a party to the same agreement and, therefore, there is one conspiracy. However, the two groups soon start arguing with each other about who was there first and which one has the "right" to rob the bank. But as unrealistic and farcical as this example is, this additional evidence establishes that there were two conspiracies at work here, each with a different membership.

---

53. 332 U.S. 539 (1947).
54. Id. at 558.

Wheel and Chain Conspiracies

United States v. Bruno involved a complicated drug-smuggling operation involving four groups.[55] One group imported the drugs into the country and sold them to middlemen, who in turn distributed them to two groups of retailers, one in New York and one in Louisiana. The government charged them all with one conspiracy. The defendants claimed that there were at least three conspiracies: one between the importers and the middlemen; another between the middlemen and the New York retailers; and a third between the middlemen and the Louisiana retailers. Though there was no evidence of communication or cooperation between the two retail groups in New York and Louisiana or between these groups and the importers, the court affirmed the finding of a single conspiracy involving all four groups. It found that the importers knew that the middlemen must in turn sell to retailers and, conversely, the retailers must have known their distributor bought from an importer. Thus, everyone could be found to have embarked on a common venture whose success depended on the participation of all.

The Model Penal Code

In General. Under the Model Penal Code the identity and scope of a conspiracy is determined by the combined operation of §5.03(1), (2), and (3). The MPC adopts a *unilateral* approach to conspiracy. It looks at each individual defendant and asks with *whom did she agree* to commit a *common criminal objective.* MPC §5.03(1). If the defendant knows that a person with whom she has conspired to commit a crime has also agreed with a third person to commit the *same* crime, then the defendant has agreed with both of them. MPC §5.03(2). Thus, the MPC determines the scope of a conspiracy for *each* defendant by asking with whom each defendant agreed to commit the same target offense. This approach, based on personal culpability and shared criminal objectives, can result in different conclusions for each defendant.

The MPC also provides that each person has entered into a single conspiracy even if there are multiple criminal objectives as long as the "crimes are the object of the same agreement or continuous conspiratorial relationship." MPC §5.03(3).

The Wheel and Chain Approach. The MPC would require a different analytic approach in the *Bruno* case and could produce a different result. In that case there were two distinct crimes: importing drugs and selling drugs. As to each defendant the MPC asks whether and with whom did he conspire to commit *each* of these crimes. Only if *both* of these crimes were the object of the same agreement or conspiratorial relationship among *all* parties would

---

55. 105 F.2d 921 (2d Cir.), revd. on other grounds, 308 U.S. 287 (1939).

there be a single conspiracy. As the Commentaries note, "it would be possible to find . . . that the smugglers conspired to commit the illegal sales of the retailers, but that the retailers did not conspire to commit the importing of the smugglers."[56]

When applying the MPC, look at each possible conspirator *individually*. Decide with whom she has agreed to commit a specific crime or crimes. This will determine what conspiracy charge may be brought against her.

Whatever the applicable law, you will find it very useful to actually outline the relationship of the various actors in analyzing both a real life situation and a criminal law exam question. Simply characterizing the group as a "wheel with (or without) a rim" or as a "chain" does not necessarily provide the correct answer, though this will help provide a picture of the actors and their roles. Instead, keep in mind this fundamental question: Who agreed to carry out the common criminal goal? This question, in turn, is often answered by a functional analysis of the group. Even if they did not know of each other's identity, did each know of the others' existence? Was each person useful in accomplishing a common goal? Did the success of the venture depend on each of them carrying out their task successfully? Was there communication and cooperation between or among the parties? Were the other characteristics of group criminality present: a division of labor, specialization, reinforcement of wills?

Parties to a Conspiracy

The Common Law's Bilateral Approach

The common law required an agreement between two or more guilty persons. This approach has been called the "bilateral approach" to conspiracy. The logic of requiring at least two guilty parties for a conspiracy (sometimes called the "plurality" requirement) is inherent in the meaning of agreement. Usually, it takes two people to "agree."

Thus, at common law if a defendant agreed to commit a crime with a legally insane person or with an undercover police officer who did not intend to commit the substantive offense, there was no agreement between two or more guilty individuals, and, thus, no conspiracy. Though prosecutors have occasionally tried to convict the defendant of attempted conspiracy in such cases, most courts have not been very sympathetic. In their view, solicitation is the proper charge. (See Chapter 11.) The federal courts have adopted the bilateral approach to conspiracy.[57]

Contemporary statutes that adopt the bilateral approach will often use

---

56. Model Penal Code and Commentaries, Comment to §5.03, at 427-428 (1985).
57. *United States v. Escobar de Bright*, 742 F.2d 1196 (9th Cir. 1984).

definitional terms like that used by California. Its statute begins with "If two or more persons conspire. . . ."[58] So be on the look-out for definitional terms that require at least two persons to agree or to conspire because they often indicate the jurisdiction has adopted the bilateral approach.

The bilateral approach to conspiracy makes sense if conspiracy is viewed primarily as a crime that strikes at bona fide group criminal activity. If the defendant has agreed with an undercover police officer to commit a crime, there is no genuine criminal collaboration at work and the special dangers of a group are not present. (Indeed, in such a case law enforcement is well positioned to ensure that the criminal objective is *never* going to be achieved.) However, the plurality requirement can be overly broad. A defendant who agrees with a mentally disabled individual to commit a crime has formed a genuine collaborative criminal effort. Though the mentally disabled individual might subsequently be found "not guilty by reason of insanity," he could still contribute significant intelligence, effort, and encouragement to achieving the criminal objective of the agreement.

In jurisdictions that have adopted the bilateral approach the prosecutor must prove that two or more persons have agreed to commit a crime. Under the common law rule requiring consistency in a verdict, if all but one of the charged conspirators are acquitted in the same trial, the conviction of the remaining conspirator must be reversed. The rationale is that the jury verdict establishes that there was only one guilty party to the conspiracy and the common law requires at least two. If, however, one of the alleged co-conspirators has fled the jurisdiction and cannot be brought to trial, the prosecutor can still convict the remaining co-conspirator, provided he proves there was an agreement between two or more persons to commit a crime.

The bilateral approach can be criticized when considering conspiracy as an *inchoate* crime. Police cannot intervene early and convict someone of conspiracy unless there are two or more culpable individuals. This is true even though an individual has clearly demonstrated her dangerousness and might subsequently find a truly willing and able partner in crime. Instead, the police can arrest her for solicitation, which has a relatively light punishment (see Chapter 11). Or, they can wait until the defendant has moved much closer to the target offense and actually commits an attempt. The bilateral approach thus seems to conflict with the inchoate *rationale* of conspiracy—to prevent crime at its earliest stages.

The Model Penal Code's Unilateral Approach

The Model Penal Code departs from the bilateral approach of the common law. Instead, it permits conviction of any person who "agrees" with

---

58. Cal. Penal Code tit. 7, ch. 8, §182(a) (West 1999).

another person to commit a crime. MPC §5.03(1)(a) and (b). Thus, the MPC would convict a defendant who has agreed to commit a crime with someone who could not be convicted, such as a diplomat or a legally insane individual, or with someone who has no real intention to commit a crime, such as an undercover police officer. In this sense, the MPC imposes responsibility on a defendant who *believes* he has agreed with another person to commit a crime. A defendant who agreed with another to commit a murder could be convicted of conspiracy to commit murder even if the evidence showed that his co-conspirator never intended to participate in the murder but merely feigned agreement while cooperating with the police.[59]

Under the inchoate or unfinished crime part of conspiracy's rationale, the MPC assesses each individual's culpability based on his individual mental state and conduct. Its definition of conspiracy does not require an agreement between at least two guilty parties. MPC §5.03(1). Consequently, the MPC does not require the same "answer" for each party; indeed, it accepts that its analytic approach may generate a different result for each party, depending on his individual culpability and conduct.

Section 5.04(1)(b) explicitly states that it is no defense that the person with whom the defendant conspired is irresponsible or has immunity from conviction. Under the MPC the result is the same in the case of a co-conspirator who does not really intend to commit the crime, such as an undercover police officer. The MPC is not concerned with whether a truly criminal group forms or whether it has a good chance of succeeding. Rather, it is concerned with convicting a culpable individual who has provided "unequivocal evidence of a firm purpose to commit a crime."[60]

Critics of the MPC argue that its unilateral approach (1) departs without justification from the well-settled law of conspiracy and its group crime rationale, which requires actual collaborative effort; (2) invites police to "manufacture" crime by encouraging police agents to enter into unilateral conspiracies; and (3) is unnecessary because solicitation and attempt are adequate to protect the public from the perceived dangerousness of a unilateral conspirator, at least when an undercover police agent is the only other party.[61]

Some commentators support the MPC's unilateral approach. By way of a contracts analogy, they argue that a mental reservation by one party to an express acceptance of an offer (such as an undercover police officer would surely have in agreeing to commit a crime) should not prevent a judge or jury from finding an "agreement." Rather, the court *should* find that there is an agreement in such cases and then decide whether the police agent has a valid defense to the charge, such as statutory privilege or necessity, or

---

59. *State v. St. Christopher,* 305 Minn. 226, 232 N.W.2d 798 (1975).

60. Model Penal Code and Commentaries, Comment to §5.04, at 400 (1985).

61. Burgman, Unilateral Conspiracy: Three Critical Perspectives, 29 DePaul L. Rev. 75 (1979).

whether the defendant has a defense of entrapment (see Chapter 17). Making police officers run the risk of being found to be co-conspirators if they do not have a valid defense or of having entrapped the defendant might make them think more carefully about their proper role in detecting crime.

Abandonment

The Common Law

The common law does not allow the defense of abandonment to conspiracy. The crime of conspiracy is complete with the agreement and no subsequent act can exonerate the actors. As in attempt, once the actors have crossed the threshold of criminality, they cannot go back.

The Model Penal Code

The Model Penal Code does allow this defense to conspiracy and calls it "renunciation." It is a limited affirmative defense and there are two stringent requirements: (1) the defendant must have "thwarted the success of the conspiracy," and (2) the abandonment must be "complete and voluntary." MPC §5.03(6). (Remember that under the MPC the defendant has the burden of producing evidence to support an affirmative defense, but the prosecution has the burden of persuasion. MPC §1.12.) Ordinarily, informing law enforcement officials in a timely manner is considered sufficient; simply withdrawing from the conspiracy is not. However, if such notice fails to thwart the success of the conspiracy because it is too late or because the police simply fail, then the defense of renunciation will not prevail. It will, however, start the running of the statute of limitations under §5.03(7)(c) for that defendant.[62]

Also, as in attempt (see Chapter 12), the defendant must have made his decision for the "right" reasons. It is ineffective if he changed his mind because the chances of detection became greater or he wanted to wait for a more opportune time or place.

The MPC permits this defense because (a) effective renunciation demonstrates a lack of firm criminal determination and thus of dangerousness,

---

62. Model Penal Code and Commentaries, Comment to §5.03, at 458 (1985). Contrary to the position taken by the MPC Commentaries, some states *will* permit the defense of renunciation if the actor has given timely notice but the police, nonetheless, fail to prevent the conspiracy from succeeding. Id. at 459. See, e.g., Ark. Code Ann. §5-3-405(2)(B) (Michie 1987); Hawaii Rev. Stat. tit. 37, §705-530(3).

and (b) the law should create incentives for individuals to call off their criminal plans.

Most recent state criminal law revisions have followed the MPC in creating the defense of renunciation. A majority of those states that have adopted the renunciation defense place the burden of proving it on the defendant.

Withdrawal

The Common Law

This defense is available to co-conspirators in a number of jurisdictions.[63] Giving reasonably adequate notice to *all* co-conspirators that one no longer intends to take part in the criminal plan in time for the other conspirators to abandon the conspiracy is usually sufficient to establish withdrawal. This defense permits a conspirator to avoid criminal responsibility for *future* crimes. Unlike the MPC defense of renunciation, the common law defense of withdrawal does not "undo" the offense of conspiracy or the withdrawing conspirator's responsibility for any substantive crimes *already* committed. However, withdrawal does start the running of the statute of limitations and limits the admissibility of co-conspirator statements and actions occurring after withdrawal.

The Model Penal Code

The MPC also provides this defense. MPC §5.03(7)(c). To be effective the actor must either advise his co-conspirators that he is no longer involved or inform law enforcement of the conspiracy and his involvement in it.[64]

For a comparison of conspiracy under the common law and the Model Penal Code, see Table 5.

Impossibility

Impossibility in conspiracy cases does not occur very often. However, just in case a clever law professor thinks it should occur on your exam, here is an explanation!

---

63. See, e.g., *Hyde v. United States,* 225 U.S. 347 (1912).

64. Federal courts also permit the defense of withdrawal. It is generally established if the defendant takes affirmative acts inconsistent with the conspiracy's goal and takes reasonable steps to communicate his abandonment to his co-conspirators. *United States v. United States Gypsum Co.,* 438 U.S. 422, 464-465 (1978).

Table 5. Comparison of Conspiracy Under the Common Law and the Model Penal Code.

Common Law	Model Penal Code
Rationale: inchoate crime & group liability	*Rationale:* Treated *solely* as inchoate crime
"Unlawful Act" may be object of conspiracy	Only a "Crime" may be object of conspiracy
No Overt Act required	Overt Act required except for first- and second-degree felonies
Does *not* merge with Target Offense	Merges with Target Offense unless criminal objectives go beyond particular offenses
Specific Intent required for all *material* elements	"Purpose" required for *conduct* and *result* elements; unclear if "purpose" required for *circumstance* elements
Pinkerton rule adopted	*Pinkerton* rule rejected; accomplice liability required
No Renunciation (No Abandonment)	Renunciation permitted
Withdrawal permitted	Withdrawal permitted

Legal Impossibility

If the parties agree to commit an act they *believe* is a crime or is covered by the applicable conspiracy statute but is not, they cannot be convicted of conspiracy. Just as in attempt (see Chapter 12), the actors' belief that they are breaking the law cannot generate criminal responsibility when there is no law proscribing their conduct. Though the group has shown themselves willing to break *the* law, they have not managed to plan behavior that breaks a *specific* law. The principle of legality limits the power of the state to punish in such cases.

Moreover, the group does not pose any special dangers to socially protected interests, though it may be argued that it may eventually shift its aim to conduct covered by the law of conspiracy, and corrective action is appropriate. However, this is a general problem in cases of legal impossibility and probably should be dealt with on a uniform and consistent basis rather than being adjusted on a crime-specific basis.

Factual Impossibility

Factual impossibility in attempt involved cases where the defendant tried to implement her criminal mens rea but, for some reason beyond her control, could not. In conspiracy, however, the crime is completed as of the moment there is an agreement or, in some jurisdictions, as of the moment an overt act in furtherance of the conspiracy is done by any member of the conspiracy. Thus, it is possible that the substantive offense can still be committed.

Consider this case. *A* and *B* agree to kill *C* while *C* sleeps, and *A* buys a gun in furtherance of that agreement. Two days later, unknown to *A* and *B*, *C* dies in his sleep of a heart attack several hours before *B* shoots to kill *C* as he apparently sleeps. *A* and *B* can be convicted of *conspiracy to murder C* even though (a) in some jurisdictions shooting at *C* would be considered a case of *legal impossibility* and, therefore, *B* would not be guilty of attempted murder; (b) under the MPC and in those jurisdictions that consider this *factual impossibility,* *B* would only be guilty of *attempted murder* because he *thought* *C* was still alive. *A* and *B* cannot use the impossibility of accomplishing the goal of their conspiracy as a defense to the charge of conspiracy to commit murder. Both have demonstrated their dangerousness by entering into an agreement and acting on it. Even if *C* died right after *A* and *B* committed the crime of conspiracy, and *A* and *B* took no further acts because they learned of *C*'s death, *A* and *B* could be convicted of conspiracy to murder *C*.

The only tricky case arises when parties agree to commit a crime in a particular way and, on those facts, the substantive offense could not be complete. Suppose Jody and Jenny agree to steal the red Miata in the Safeway parking lot but are then arrested. Can they be convicted of conspiracy when the car they agreed to steal was actually Jody's car? This is the strongest case for a claim of impossibility. However, the trend today, particularly under the MPC, is to assess the actors' culpability based on the facts as they believed them to be. In all probability, both Jody and Jenny would be convicted of conspiracy to commit theft.

Wharton's Rule

The Common Law

Some crimes logically require the participation of two individuals. Common law crimes such as adultery or dueling, for example, require two participants, as do some contemporary crimes. For example, the sale of drugs requires both a seller and a buyer. When the substantive offense requires concert of action between two people to accomplish a common criminal goal, it necessarily requires agreement. Wharton's rule (named after a legal scholar who analyzed this problem) says that conspiracy cannot be used to criminalize the agreement that is a logically required component of the substantive offense.

The rule, generally accepted by most courts, prevents the use of conspiracy to pile up more punishment on conduct that is already punished by the substantive offense. Moreover, when only the two necessary parties are involved, there is no additional threat posed by this particular group that is not already anticipated and punished by the substantive offense.

On the other hand, the rule defeats the use of conspiracy to punish conduct that has not yet resulted in the commission of the target crime. Consequently, only attempt may be used. Attempt requires the parties to come closer to committing the offense than does the crime of conspiracy. By eliminating the availability of conspiracy when only two parties are logically required for commission of the target offense, Wharton's rule decreases the usefulness of conspiracy as a preventive measure to reach inchoate or unfinished crimes.

There are exceptions to this rule. The "third party" exception provides that conspiracy may be used when *more* than the two parties logically required to commit the target offense are involved. The rationale is that the addition of a third (or more) person does, in fact, enhance the dangers of group criminal activity. This type of line-drawing can be criticized as highly formalistic and perhaps even unrealistic. However, it does provide a "bright line" for courts and prosecutors and may also serve as a deterrent to keep the size of criminal groups to the number of individuals necessarily required to commit the substantive offense.

In *Iannelli v. United States*,[65] the Supreme Court treated Wharton's rule as a presumption to be applied by courts in the absence of contrary legislative intent. When legislative intent does indicate that conspiracy may also be charged in addition to the substantive offense, Wharton's rule does not bar its use.[66]

Some courts also hold that Wharton's rule is inapplicable when the substantive offense requires the participation of two culpable parties but does not specify any punishment for one of them.[67] For example, Wharton's rule would not preclude a charge of conspiracy to sell intoxicating liquor when the law punished only the seller but not the buyer.[68]

The Model Penal Code

The MPC rejects Wharton's rule. Instead, it provides that a person who could not be convicted of the substantive offense or as an accomplice to the substantive offense may not be convicted of conspiracy to commit that offense. MPC §5.04(2). Under the MPC's unilateral approach to conspiracy, immunity for one defendant under this section does not prevent conviction of another co-conspirator.

---

65. 420 U.S. 770 (1975).
66. Comment, An Analysis of Wharton's Rule, 71 Nw. U.L. Rev. 547 (1977).
67. *United States v. Previte*, 648 F.2d 73 (1st Cir. 1981).
68. *Vannata v. United States*, 289 F. 424, 428 (2d Cir. 1923).

Immunity for Substantive Offense

The Common Law

Another common law rule, based on inferred legislative intent, prevents the prosecutor from using conspiracy to punish the conduct of an individual whose participation in the substantive offense is logically required but whose behavior is not made criminal by that offense. In *Gebardi v. United States,*[69] the Supreme Court reversed a woman's conviction for conspiracy to violate the Mann Act. This statute prohibited the transportation of a woman across state lines for immoral purposes. However, it only punished the individual who transported the female; it did not punish *her* conduct. To permit the use of conspiracy to punish the agreement of the female who is necessarily included in the proscribed act but whom the legislature decided not to punish would undermine the public policy of the statute.

The Model Penal Code

The Model Penal Code states that, unless otherwise provided in a criminal statute, a person cannot be convicted of conspiracy if she could not be guilty of the substantive offense either (a) under the definition of the substantive offense, or (b) as an accomplice to its commission under the MPC's definition of accomplice. MPC §5.04(2) (incorporating by reference MPC §2.06(5) and 2.06(6)(a)). Under the MPC's accomplice section, an individual cannot be convicted as an accomplice if she is the victim of the conduct or if her participation is "inevitably incident to its commission." The *Gebardi* case would come out the same way under the MPC. The prostitute's conduct is "inevitably incident" to a violation of the Mann Act. Similarly, in a statutory rape case the prosecutor cannot use conspiracy to convict the underage participant because the substantive offense considers her to be the "victim" protected by the statute. To permit a conspiracy conviction in such cases would undermine the legislature's intent and the public policy of the specific criminal law.

EXAMPLES

1a. Heather and Penelope are having lunch at the Brass Rail, a posh watering hole for the upscale and trendy. Bemoaning the high price of the cocaine they consume in rather large quantities and the resulting crimp in their lifestyle, Heather turns to Penelope and says: "Why don't we

---

69. 287 U.S. 112 (1932).

sell the stuff ourselves? That way we can make enough money to buy and use as much as we want and have enough money left over to indulge ourselves." Penelope, sipping her champagne slowly, finally says: "That is a great idea. Let's do it! I know where we can get crack cocaine in volume and on credit. I will call my friend tomorrow and make the arrangements. We are on our way to crack independence!" Heather and Penelope then lift their glasses to toast their arrangement, saying in unison: "To our new business!"

1b. The next day, Penelope calls Rachel, her cocaine supplier, on the telephone to arrange for the purchase of a large amount of cocaine on credit, but she is not in.

1c. It turns out Heather is an undercover police officer who, after telling her superior officers, arrests Penelope. Penelope utters the immortal words: "Et tu, Heather!"

1d. Heather is *not* a police informant. Two days later, Penelope reaches Rachel, her supplier, and tells Rachel: "My friend and I want to purchase a large amount of cocaine on credit in order to sell it at retail."

Rachel, having done her undergraduate degree in economics at a famous mid-Western urban school, is always looking to expand her market share. She decides this is a great idea and tells Penelope she will furnish Penelope with 2 kilos on credit and that Penelope can get another 2 kilos from her under the same terms after Penelope has paid for the first 2 kilos. The next day Rachel delivers the cocaine to Penelope's apartment after telling Penelope how much she owes and when she expects both Penelope and "her friend" to repay her.

Over the next two weeks Penelope sells most of the cocaine in five separate sales while Heather is away on vacation. Unfortunately for Penelope, the last sale she makes is to Pat, an undercover police officer. Pat tries to arrest Penelope, who pulls a gun and shoots and wounds Pat. Other officers arrive almost immediately and subdue and arrest Penelope.

Heather, Penelope, and Rachel are all arrested. The prosecutor charges all three of them with a single conspiracy, four counts of selling drugs, one count of an attempted sale, and one count of assaulting a police officer while in performance of her duties. Heather and Rachel's lawyers object.

How many conspiracies are there and who are parties?

What charges can be brought as a result of Penelope's shooting Pat, the federal undercover police officer?

1e. In prosecuting Heather, Penelope, and Rachel for conspiracy, the prosecution seeks to introduce the statement of Penelope to Rachel ("My friend and I want to purchase a large amount of cocaine on credit in order to sell it at retail") to establish that Heather was a member of the conspiracy. Assuming for the moment that Rachel is prepared to testify as to what Penelope told her, is this statement admissible to establish that Penelope and Heather had entered into a conspiracy to purchase and sell drugs?

2. Susan, Kelly, and Cathy have smuggled cocaine into Florida from various Caribbean islands using the same modus operandi. They charter a small plane at rates well above market, use different disguises during each trip, fly at night, fly low to avoid detection, and depart from destinations known to be drug sources.

   Recently, they chartered a small plane owned and piloted by Norm to fly them to the islands and then to fly them back to Florida. Although they did not explicitly tell Norm that they were using these trips to transport drugs into the USA, they told Norm all the other details of their previous trips. In addition, they paid Norm $3,000 more than his normal fee and used obvious disguises for each trip. On the fifth flight Norm and the ladies were arrested in Florida and charged with a conspiracy to smuggle drugs into the USA.

   a. Can Norm be convicted of conspiring with Susan, Kelly, and Cathy to illegally transport cocaine into the United States?

   b. If so, can Norm be convicted on the smuggling counts for the trips the ladies made prior to his involvement?

3a. Jay is being held in an old rural county jail. Late one afternoon, Rhonda, his girlfriend, visits Jay and tells him that she and Joe, his best friend, are going to bust him out that night. (Rhonda does not tell him they do not intend to leave any witnesses.) Jay says: "Great! I knew I could count on both of you." At about 3:00 a.m. the next morning Rhonda and Joe ring the jail's night bell and are admitted by Doug, the night jailer. While Joe distracts the guards, Rhonda walks up behind Doug and kills him. Unfortunately, Rhonda and Joe cannot find the keys to Jay's cell, so they flee. The next day they are both apprehended. Is Jay responsible for the murder of Doug?

3b. Same facts except that, as Joe and Rhonda enter the jail, Jay sees Rhonda pointing a gun at Doug's head. Jay screams to her: "Put the gun down. Don't shoot him!" Rhonda ignores Jay and kills Doug.

4. Stan told Gary, a federal undercover narcotics agent, that Stan's friend, Stella, occasionally drives to Mexico, purchases heroin, and smuggles it into California where she resells it. He also told Gary that he thought Stella would probably drive with Gary to Mexico where they could pick up heroin and bring it back to California for resale at a hefty profit. Gary contacted Stella and they decided to drive to Mexico together, buy the heroin, and bring it back to California. They were stopped while driving back across the border. Can Stan *and* Stella be convicted of conspiracy to transport heroin into the United States?

5. Al Falfa, a retail seller of farm chemicals, sold several large batches of ammonium nitrate, a fertilizer generally known to be a key ingredient in homemade terrorist bombs, to Jed, a young man in his 20s with very short hair and dressed in an army surplus camouflage uniform. Al Falfa knew Jed did not own a farm but did own a very small house with a small yard. He also knew that Jed belonged to a militant "people's militia" that advocated extreme antigovernment views. After the first sale, Al Falfa said to Jed: "You know this is far too much to use on your lawn. If you use all of it, you'll surely kill it." Jed replied: "I am not going to use it on my lawn. As a former army explosives expert I know how to use this stuff in some unusual ways. It's not the lawn I'm going to kill. Its time we showed them government folks we mean business!" Jed loaded the fertilizer onto his large pick-up truck and left. Jed subsequently returned to make several more large purchases. Al Falfa, content with making more than half of his annual sales of this product to a single customer at his usual price, did not take any further action.

   One week later a huge explosion destroyed the federal building in a nearby city killing over 20 children in an on-site day care center and over 50 federal workers. Jed was arrested shortly thereafter and experts have determined that he used the fertilizer that he purchased from Al Falfa to make the bomb. Can the government convict Al Falfa of entering into a conspiracy with Jed?

6. Tom and Dave run into Linda at a bar. They have a few drinks and then decide to walk to a different bar nearby. While they walk along, Tom suggests a short-cut through an alley. Linda and Dave agree. Once they are in the alley, Tom grabs Linda and rapes her. While Tom is raping Linda, Dave pulls a garbage can in front of them so that no one can see from the street what Tom is doing. Did Tom and Dave conspire to rape Linda?

7. Sherrie and Bill Green agreed with Dr. Feelgood to exchange stolen goods for amphetamines. The Greens would steal household goods and bring them to Dr. Feelgood, who would then write a prescription for them for amphetamines. Eventually, the Greens and Dr. Feelgood were arrested and charged with conspiracy to unlawfully dispense controlled substances. Dr. Feelgood's lawyer argued that laypersons cannot conspire to illegally dispense prescription drugs because laypersons are not authorized to prescribe them. Is Dr. Feelgood's lawyer correct?

8. Lisa, Jane, and Mark learn that Lisa's elderly uncle keeps his life savings under his mattress. They agree to break into his home, kill him, and take the money. Lisa buys a gun and delivers it to Mark.
   a. Lisa, on the way to meet Mark and Jane at her uncle's home, is overcome by guilt and fond memories of her uncle. She decides she cannot go through with the plan. Instead, she catches a plane to San

Francisco. Shortly thereafter, Mark and Jane break into the uncle's house, kill him, and steal his money.

b. Lisa meets Mark and Jane at her uncle's house as planned. Overcome by guilt and fond memories of her uncle, she turns to Jane and Mark and says: "I can't go through with this. I want nothing more to do with this crazy idea." She then leaves Mark and Jane who, nonetheless, break into her uncle's house, kill him, and steal his money.

c. Overcome by guilt and fond memories while on the way to meet Mark and Jane at her uncle's house, Lisa calls her uncle to warn him of the impending crimes. Unfortunately, his telephone is busy. Mark and Jane break into the uncle's house, kill him, and steal his money.

d. Overcome by guilt and fond memories while on the way to meet Mark and Jane at her uncle's house, Lisa calls the police and tells them of the planned crime. The police dispatch a patrol car, which arrives in time to arrest Mark and Jane before they can break into the uncle's house.

9. Ralph and Andrew agree to burglarize the home of Judy, Andrew's aunt, because Andrew knows Judy keeps a lot of cash under her mattress. Ralph then buys a gun to use in the burglary. Several days later, Ralph and Andrew break into Judy's home knowing she is away at church. Unfortunately, Judy comes home early and recognizes Andrew so Ralph shoots and kills her. Both Ralph and Andrew agree to keep the burglary and the killing secret.

Later that night, Andrew tells Esther, his girlfriend: "Take this gun that Ralph used in a burglary and murder we committed earlier today and throw it in the river." Esther does this.

Fearing Esther may talk, Andrew beats her for several months to keep her quiet. Finally, Esther goes to the police and tells them about the burglary and murder. The police put an electronic recording device on Esther, and Andrew makes several statements incriminating Ralph and himself to Esther, which are recorded.

To prove the conspiracy between Ralph and Andrew, can the prosecutor use at trial:

a. the statement Andrew made to Esther telling her to throw the gun into the river?

b. the recorded statements made recently to Esther?

EXPLANATIONS

1a. Heather and Penelope agreed to commit at least two crimes, (1) the purchase and (2) the subsequent sale of drugs. Under the common law and the MPC (because the substantive crimes that are the object of the agreement are serious felonies), Heather and Penelope committed one conspiracy once they entered into the criminal agreement (even though it had two target crimes). In many jurisdictions, however, one of the parties must commit an overt act in furtherance of the conspiracy in addition to the agreement before the elements of conspiracy are satisfied. In these jurisdictions Heather and Penelope have not committed conspiracy until one of them does an overt act to implement their agreement.

1b. Even in those jurisdictions that require an overt act, both Heather and Penelope can be convicted of conspiracy because Penelope acted to implement their criminal agreement by calling her supplier in an attempt to secure drugs on credit. Even though it is an innocent act that does not provide strong evidence of criminal intent and even though it did not move the conspiracy any further along the path of implementation, making the telephone call at least demonstrates that the conspiracy has moved beyond intention to action. The defendants will argue that, because Penelope did not actually talk to Rachel, the telephone call should not be considered an "overt act in furtherance of the conspiracy." This argument will probably not succeed. Unlike attempt, there is no requirement that the overt act come close to committing the target offense or even strongly corroborate the actors' criminal purpose. Thus, both Heather and Penelope can be convicted of conspiracy.

This particular example illustrates that the "overt act" requirement for conspiracy often does not provide very strong evidence establishing either firmness of criminal intention or significant implementation of the criminal plan.

1c. In this example Heather does not have the mens rea necessary to commit conspiracy because she is a police officer. In those states that have retained the common law's bilateral theory of conspiracy, Penelope could not be convicted of conspiracy because the crime requires at least two culpable parties. Because Heather is a police officer, there is no true collaborative criminal enterprise at work and the special dangers of a criminal group are not present. The prosecutor might consider charging Penelope with solicitation; however, Heather, not Penelope, originated the criminal scheme. Thus, Penelope cannot be convicted of encouraging Heather to commit a crime. Nor will attempted conspiracy succeed; to permit this strategy to work would undercut the bilateral theory of conspiracy and its plurality requirement. Finally, Penelope cannot be convicted either of attempted possession or sale of crack cocaine. The Bad News? Penelope has lost a good friend! The Good News? Penelope probably cannot be convicted of any crime.

Under the MPC, however, Penelope *could* be convicted of conspiracy. She did agree with Heather to commit a crime; under the unilateral theory of conspiracy adopted by the MPC, she is guilty of this crime. The MPC focuses on the culpability and conduct of each individual and her dangerousness. It does not require that a genuine criminal group be actually at work.

1d. *Number of conspiracies and parties.* Rachel, the supplier, would argue that she agreed to sell cocaine to Penelope and did so. Thus, in her view she can only be convicted of the sale, not of agreeing to sell. She would claim that Wharton's rule precludes her conviction when the participation of two parties is necessary to commit the crime (as in the sale of drugs that require a seller and a buyer). The government would respond that, even if Wharton's rule might normally apply, Rachel knew that there was a third party involved because Penelope told her about her friend. Thus, the *third-party exception* would defeat Wharton's rule, and Rachel can be convicted for both the prior criminal agreement and committing the crime that is the object of that agreement.

The government will also argue that this is a "chain" conspiracy. Though Rachel did not know who Penelope's friend was, she knew there was a friend who would help sell the cocaine and be jointly responsible for paying for it. Thus, she knew the essential elements of the scheme. Finally, the government will argue that Rachel had a "stake in Heather's and Penelope's venture" to sell crack cocaine because Rachel sold the drugs on credit and also entered into an ongoing business relationship, promising to sell additional drugs on the same favorable terms. Unless Heather and Penelope succeeded in selling the cocaine, Rachel might not get paid. The government will probably succeed in charging and proving a single conspiracy.

If it does, then Rachel is responsible under the *Pinkerton* rule for all of the retail sales Penelope made because they were foreseeable crimes. Heather is also responsible for these sales under the *Pinkerton* rule even though she was on vacation when Penelope made the sales and did not aid and abet those crimes. The *Pinkerton* rule effectively attributes criminal responsibility for foreseeable crimes in furtherance of the conspiracy committed by other co-conspirators without requiring proof that would satisfy the elements of accomplice liability.

The federal Sentencing Guidelines limit *punishment* more narrowly than the *Pinkerton* rule. If this is a federal prosecution, the United States attorney must prove that these five separate sales were "in furtherance of jointly undertaken criminal activity" and were "reasonably foreseeable in connection with that criminal activity." The guidelines probably do not help Rachel. She provided 2 kilos to Penelope with the understanding that Penelope would sell them and that she (Rachel) would then provide additional cocaine. Thus, Rachel and Penelope have agreed to jointly undertaken criminal activity and these sales were reasonably foreseeable criminal acts implementing that agreement. Moreover, Rachel, as the supplier, is a part of the distribution chain for the cocaine sold. Heather has a stronger case for not being punished for sales that occurred while she was on vacation. It appears that Penelope, not Heather, initiated joint criminal activity with Rachel since she made the initial contact with Rachel and arranged for Rachel to deliver the initial 2 kilos of cocaine. It is not clear whether Heather was present or on vacation while all of this activity took place. In addition, Heather was seemingly not part of the distribution chain. Without additional evidence, it appears that Heather would benefit from the federal Sentencing Guidelines and could not be punished for these five separate sales.

The MPC focuses on each individual and analyzes with whom each agreed and to what purpose. The government might still succeed in establishing that this is a single conspiracy with three parties. Heather did not know who Rachel was, but she did know that Penelope had a friend who would supply the cocaine on credit. Thus, Heather has arguably authorized Penelope to enter into an agreement with Rachel on her behalf. Likewise, Rachel knows that Penelope has a "friend" (though she does not know her identity) and that the friend will help Penelope sell the drugs and be responsible for paying for them.

Unlike the *Pinkerton* rule, however, both Rachel and Heather might not be responsible under the MPC for the five retail sales that Penelope made since the government will have a difficult time establishing the elements of accomplice liability (especially "purpose" rather than "knowledge") as required by the MPC.

The assault on Pat. Penelope is clearly guilty of assaulting Pat, an undercover police officer, while in the performance of her duties. The more difficult question is whether Heather and Rachel can be charged with this crime by virtue of being co-conspirators with Penelope. On these facts neither Heather nor Rachel expressly agreed that Penelope should use deadly force if necessary to resist arrest. Nor is there any indication that Heather or Rachel knew, or should have known, that Penelope was armed or would use deadly force to resist arrest. The amount and value of the cocaine involved in the sale were not large. Neither Heather nor Rachel was present during the sale or played a major role in the attempted sale. Thus, it is unlikely that a jury would conclude that, under these circumstances, Heather or Rachel should have foreseen that Penelope would use deadly force to resist arrest.

1e. Under the conspiracy exception to the hearsay rule, a statement by one conspirator implicating another conspirator is admissible in federal courts, provided the prosecutor proves by a preponderance of the evidence (including the contested statement itself) that a conspiracy involving these individuals exist. If the judge so finds, Penelope's statement to Rachel about her "friend" is admissible.

2. A jury could infer that, though Norm did not actually know he was transporting cocaine into the United States, he nonetheless knew he was

participating with others in illegal drug smuggling and that he intended to join and participate in the conspiracy. Norm was paid more than his usual fee, made several trips at night while flying low to and from destinations known as sources for drugs, and knew his clients used various disguises. He also knew that they had done this before. A conspirator does not have to know all the details of a conspiracy as long as he knows its essentials and intends to participate in the conspiracy.

Though Norm may have joined a conspiracy "in progress," so to speak, he is not liable for any substantive offense committed by his co-conspirators *prior* to his becoming a co-conspirator. The *Pinkerton* rule does not impose responsibility for foreseeable crimes committed before a co-conspirator joins the conspiracy.

3a.   Rhonda and Joe obviously formed a conspiracy to break Jay out of jail and each of them is responsible for the murders committed by Rhonda because they had expressly agreed to kill all witnesses. Even under the MPC Joe would be responsible for the guard's death because he aided Rhonda by distracting Doug.

The prosecutor would argue that Jay joined the conspiracy the afternoon when Rhonda visited him and outlined the general plan. But did Jay agree to kill the guard? Can he be held accountable for Doug's murder when he did not know of the planned killing and was a completely passive agent unable to control the behavior of either Rhonda or Joe?

The prosecutor will argue that Jay is also responsible for these murders under the *Pinkerton* rule because it was reasonably foreseeable that deadly force might be necessary to accomplish the general plan. Consequently, Jay can be charged with Doug's murder. Under the MPC the prosecutor must prove that Jay is an accessory to the murder because he solicited this *particular* crime or aided or agreed to aid or attempted to aid in its commission murder. Without more evidence, this will be difficult — but not impossible — to prove.

3b.   Under these facts, Jay might still be responsible for Doug's murder under the *Pinkerton* rule. Though he tried to prevent Doug's murder, the prosecutor could still try to establish that this crime was foreseeable and in furtherance of the conspiracy. Under the MPC it will be very difficult to prove that Jay, who was confined to a cell, is responsible for the murder. Not only did he not assist or try to assist in any way; he actually tried to prevent the crime. Thus, he is not an accessory to Doug's murder.

4.   Without additional evidence it would be difficult to prove that Stella and Stan had previously agreed to transport heroin into the USA. It seems more likely that Stan was simply telling Gary about Stella's past

drug smuggling. This is particularly true since it was Gary who contacted Stella and made specific arrangements. Thus, it would be very difficult to convict Stan and Stella of conspiring together to transport heroin into the USA.

Whether Stella can be convicted of conspiracy to transport heroin into the USA depends on whether the federal law embraces the unilateral or bilateral theory of conspiracy. The prevailing view is that it adopts the bilateral theory; thus, Stella cannot be convicted of conspiring with Gary, an undercover federal drug agent, who did not have the necessary mens rea to commit the object crime. Stella can be convicted of an attempt to transport heroin into the USA, but she cannot be convicted of conspiracy.

5. Most cases require the government to prove a provider of goods or services acted with the *purpose* of furthering the criminal objective; mere *knowledge* is not enough. The cases hold, however, that a vendor can be convicted of conspiracy if he has a "stake in the criminal venture." The first question is whether Al Falfa knew that Jed was going to use the fertilizer for a criminal purpose. This is a close question. Given recent events like the bombing of the World Trade Center in New York City and the Federal Building in Oklahoma City, most sellers of this type of fertilizer probably know it can be used to make powerful homemade bombs. Assuming that Al Falfa did know that Jed would use the fertilizer to make a bomb, can the government prove purpose? Al Falfa sold more than half of his supply to this customer who did not appear to use it for its intended use. He also knew that Jed was a former army explosives expert and a member of a group whose political views were very extreme. However, he did not sell the product at an inflated price and it is possible that Jed did have some legitimate use for the purchase unknown to Al Falfa. It will be a jury question whether Al Falfa had a "stake in the venture" and acted with the purpose of furthering the criminal objective. The facts of this example may be less persuasive than the facts in Example 2 in establishing that a vendor of goods or services acted with the "purpose" of furthering the criminal objective and thereby entered into a conspiracy.

Should "knowledge" suffice, at least when the harm to be avoided is so serious? Some commentators argue that knowledge should suffice — at least in cases like this. They would use the criminal law to impose a duty on a seller of goods or services to take rather modest measures (such as not selling) in order to prevent such serious harm. Though some jurisdictions would convict if the seller of goods or services had *knowledge* of the purchaser's criminal objective (particularly if a serious crime is involved), the MPC requires the government to prove that Al Falfa acted with *purpose*.

6.   Probably not. To find a conspiracy, there must be evidence of a prior agreement that reflects a shared criminal purpose. An agreement does not require an express act of communication; a jury may infer the existence of a prior agreement from concerted activity. Nonetheless, on these facts, it appears that Tom's rape of Linda was a spur of the moment decision that was not the result of a prior agreement with Dave. Obviously, Tom can be convicted of rape. Because Dave has seemingly acted with the purpose of facilitating Tom's crime, Dave has aided and abetted the rape and can therefore be convicted and punished as an accomplice. Neither Tom nor Dave would probably be convicted and punished for the separate crime of conspiracy.

7.   This argument is clever but will fail. This is a variation of a defense of "legal impossibility." However, a person can be guilty of conspiring to commit a crime even if he could not commit the substantive crime himself. It is sufficient where persons knowingly participate in a conspiracy to have one conspirator who is capable of committing the offense do so. This is also not a case where an individual who is immune from conviction for committing the substantive offense is being convicted by the use of conspiracy.

8a.   *The common law.* The common law does not recognize the defense of *abandonment*. Thus, Lisa is guilty of conspiracy. Just as in attempt, a defendant who crosses the "threshold of criminality" cannot go back under the common law.

       However, the common law does permit a conspirator to *withdraw* from a conspiracy by clearly indicating to all of her co-conspirators that she is no longer associated with the conspiracy. This communication must be made in a manner that would inform a reasonable person of her intent to withdraw and must be made in time for all co-conspirators to abandon the conspiracy. Because Lisa merely did not show up at the intended crime scene, she did not meet the requirements for withdrawal. She can be convicted of conspiracy and, under the *Pinkerton* rule, of the target offenses because she did not communicate her withdrawal to all of her co-conspirators in a timely manner.

       The Model Penal Code. The MPC does permit the defense of *renunciation*. To be effective the defendant must have "thwarted the success of the conspiracy" and must have completely and voluntarily renounced the criminal purpose. Lisa has not satisfied either of these two elements. She did not inform her co-conspirators of her firm intention to renounce the conspiracy, nor has she tried to prevent the commission of the target crimes. Thus, she can be convicted of conspiracy.

       Lisa has also not satisfied the MPC's requirements for *withdrawal*. She neither advised her co-conspirators of her intention to abandon the conspiracy nor did she inform law enforcement authorities of the conspiracy or her involvement in it. MPC §5.03(7)(c). Thus, Lisa can also be convicted of the substantive offenses. She obtained the murder weapon with the purpose of its being used in the crime. Consequently, she is an accomplice of the target offenses.

8b. *The common law.* Because the common law does not permit the defense of abandonment, the analysis here results in the same answer as in 7a. Lisa can be convicted of conspiracy even though she has communicated her intention not to participate any further in the criminal conduct.

However, the common law does permit a co-conspirator to withdraw from a conspiracy, thereby terminating her liability for any crimes committed by her co-conspirators after her withdrawal. Because she has conveyed to all of her co-conspirators her intention to withdraw from the conspiracy in time for them to abandon the target offenses, Lisa will not be responsible under the *Pinkerton* rule for the subsequent murder, burglary, and theft committed by Mark and Jane.

The Model Penal Code. Under the MPC, Lisa has successfully withdrawn from the conspiracy because she has advised all of her co-conspirators that she will have no further involvement in the criminal plan and leaves them. Thus, Lisa is not responsible for crimes committed *after* her withdrawal.

However, Lisa has not met the tough requirements for renunciation under the MPC. She has not thwarted the success of conspiracy as required by §5.03(6). Consequently, she may be convicted of conspiracy but not of the target offenses.

8c. *The common law.* Under the common law, Lisa cannot abandon the conspiracy; thus, she is guilty of conspiracy. In this hypothetical, Lisa has not communicated to her co-conspirators her firm intention to withdraw from the conspiracy. Thus, her vain attempt to thwart the target offense is of no benefit to her. She can also be convicted of the target offenses.

The Model Penal Code. Under the MPC the result is the same. Lisa neither communicated her intention to withdraw nor thwarted the success of the conspiracy. Too little, too late!

8d. *The common law.* Again, there is no defense of abandonment under the common law to conspiracy. Lisa can be convicted of conspiracy.

It is not clear that she has withdrawn under the common law because she did not communicate to her co-conspirators her firm intention to withdraw in a timely manner. Timely police intervention prevented Mark and Jane from committing the target offenses; however, depending on the facts, they may have attempted the substantive offenses. Lisa may be responsible for any attempt but not for the target offenses that were not committed.

The Model Penal Code. Under the MPC Lisa has successfully

thwarted the commission of the target offenses in a manner that reflects a complete and voluntary renunciation of criminal purpose. Thus, she may succeed in using the defense of renunciation, thus cutting off liability *both* for the conspiracy and for any attempts.

9a. Most jurisdictions hold that only statements made before and up to completion of the target offenses are admissible against co-conspirators. This usually includes any statements made during acts of concealment performed before the conspiracy finally achieves its main objective. These acts can include, for example, dividing the proceeds of the crime, selling stolen property, or persuading an insurance company that a property that had been burned in an arson was destroyed accidentally.

There are only two exceptions to this general rule. The prosecutor must prove either an express agreement to conceal the conspiracy or that silence was an essential element of the conspiracy.

The government can probably use the statement Andrew made to Esther right after the burglary to prove a conspiracy between Ralph and Andrew. This is a close case but the conspiracy hearsay exception would probably include statements made while disposing of an instrumentality of the crime shortly after its commission.

9b. Probably not. Here Andrew's statements to Esther were made well after the object of the conspiracy, the burglary and the killing, were successfully completed. The conspirators had probably spent the money already and there is no indication that further silence was necessary to accomplish their goals. In addition, there is no express agreement to conceal the conspiracy made at the time the parties entered into the conspiracy.

One can imagine a case in which statements made well after the initial target offense had been complete could, nonetheless, be admitted to establish the conspiracy. Take a case in which a securities trader for a bank in New York City agrees with his supervisor to bilk his firm of millions of dollars by reporting phony currency trades and phony profits. They further agree that concealment of the phony trades is essential to prevent the scheme from becoming known. Statements discussing the cover-up made by either of the two conspirators even long after the phony trades have been made will probably be admissible for two reasons. First, the co-conspirators expressly agreed to cover up the conspiracy for as long as necessary. Second, the cover-up is essential to prevent subsequent detection and prosecution.

14

Complicity

Overview

A leading actor or actress often has a supporting cast who assist in one way or another in the leading player's performance. Likewise, criminals are often assisted by others in the commission of crime.

Complicity is a broad doctrine that imposes criminal responsibility on individuals for a crime committed by someone else, usually because these secondary actors have intentionally helped or encouraged the primary actor to commit the crime. However, complicity also imposes responsibility based on other criminal law doctrines such as conspiracy.

In this chapter we will focus on a form of complicity called *accessorial* or *accomplice* liability. In general, individuals who help another person to commit a crime are *accessories* or *accomplices* to that crime and are also responsible for its commission. Frequently, statutes and case law will use terms like "aid, abet, encourage, assist, advise, solicit, or procure" to describe the various kinds of conduct that can generate accomplice liability. Throughout this chapter we will call individuals who help another to commit a crime through such activities "accomplices."

There are two ways of helping someone else commit a crime:

1. Physical Aid. The defendant can physically help another person commit a crime. For example, he might obtain the gun used by the primary actor in the bank robbery. Or he may actually be present at the crime and help with its commission, perhaps by acting as a lookout or by driving the getaway car.

2. Psychological Aid. The defendant can encourage or reinforce the primary actor's decision to commit a crime. For example, she may urge a fellow gang member to shoot a rival gang member who has shown her disrespect.

Note two interesting aspects of accomplice liability. First, it is a form of *group criminality*. It will necessarily involve at least two individuals — a primary actor (*P*) and a secondary actor, the accomplice (*A*), who is helping or encouraging *P*. Second, although the accomplice is held accountable because of his own voluntary act and mens rea, his guilt is based on the commission of a crime by *P*. Thus, *A*'s guilt is *derivative: A*'s liability is dependent on *P*'s committing a crime or a criminal act.[1] The accomplice will usually be guilty of the same crime committed by the primary actor. Conversely, if *P* does *not* commit a crime, the accomplice cannot be convicted at common law because of the absence of a "guilty principal." (As we shall see, the Model Penal Code does not require a guilty principal.)

Complicity can actually be a very expansive doctrine, making individuals responsible for crimes committed by others that they did not expressly aid or encourage. As we saw in Chapter 13, the *Pinkerton* rule in conspiracy makes every co-conspirator responsible for all reasonably foreseeable crimes committed by other members in furtherance of the conspiracy. This is a very broad type of complicity. It does not require any co-conspirator actually to aid or encourage the specific crime committed by a co-conspirator. Likewise, felony murder makes all members of the joint venture responsible for a murder committed by a joint venturer in furtherance of the felony even though they might not have helped commit the murder or encouraged another to commit it.

In this chapter, we will focus on the more narrow type of complicity that requires the individual to actually encourage or help with *P*'s crime.

The Rationale of Accomplice Liability

As we saw in Chapter 7, the criminal law usually does not look beyond the last responsible human agent in determining causation.[2] Thus, the person who actually pulls the trigger in a homicide is normally responsible for the crime of murder.

Should other individuals who helped with the crime, perhaps by providing the murder weapon or encouraging the shooter to kill the victim, also be held responsible for the murder? If so, why? After all, the shooter has free will; he could always have decided *not* to pull the trigger. Moreover, *A* did not engage in the conduct that actually constituted the crime of homicide. Why hold him responsible for what someone else did?

Causation is not the basis of accomplice liability. Though *A* may

---

1. Kadish, Complicity, Cause and Blame: A Study in the Interpretation of Doctrine, 73 Cal. L. Rev. 323, 337-338 (1985).
2. *Stephenson v. State*, 205 Ind. 141, 179 N.E. 633 (1932).

influence P to act, the law assumes that P's criminal act is volitional and not physically caused by A's encouragement or assistance.[3] Indeed, A may have actually played a very minor role in helping P commit the crime, and P may have committed the crime even if A had not encouraged him. Thus, one may be found guilty as an accomplice even though his actions do not satisfy "but for" causation.

Accomplice liability differs from the law's general approach to human causation. Accomplice liability *does* look beyond the last responsible human agent and makes others also responsible for P's criminal act. This extended reach of accomplice liability is justified because A, by her actions and her state of mind, has chosen to *adopt* P's criminal act as her own. By encouraging or helping another commit a crime, she has extended her will to embrace the actions of another.[4] P's criminal act is now also *her* criminal act. Moreover, in intentionally helping another to commit a crime, she has demonstrated by her own state of mind and by her own action that she is a socially dangerous individual.

In making A also responsible for the crime committed by P, accomplice liability might appear to contradict the general assumption in our criminal system that guilt must be personal. However, accomplice liability still requires proof of mens rea and a voluntary act for A. Thus, A's guilt *is* personal.

Accomplice liability has been criticized on several grounds. First, it may extend the net of criminal responsibility too wide, punishing truly peripheral actors who did not play a significant role in causing harm. Second, it may punish a defendant more for her attitude than for the significance of her actions. Third, because the modern trend is to punish accessories just as harshly as principals, punishment may not be proportional to the defendant's moral guilt. All accessories, including those who play very minor roles or whose help or encouragement may not have been needed, will be *punished the same* as those who actually commit the object offense. In short, standby actors can be treated as if they actually played leading roles.

Definitions

The Common Law

The common law used fairly precise terms to describe individuals who could be responsible for crimes committed by others.[5]

---

3. Kadish, supra note 1, 73 Cal. L. Rev. 323 (1985).

4. Id. at 355.

5. We have modified the basic definitional terms provided by Blackstone at 4 Blackstone, Commentaries, ch. 3, 33-39.

Principles and Accessories. Principal in the first degree (*P-1*) is the individual who (1) personally commits the crime or (2) uses an innocent agent to commit a crime. Thus, the professional killer who actually commits homicide by shooting and killing the victim is a *P-1*. An individual can also be guilty as a *P-1* if he uses an innocent agent to commit a crime.

Innocent agent is someone who (1) commits a criminal act but (2) lacks capacity to commit a crime or the mens rea for the crime and (3) is fooled or forced to commit the criminal act. An innocent agent is usually a person, but it can also be an animal or an inanimate object (such as a computer programmed to destroy files). A drug dealer who deceives a teenager into delivering drugs by telling him it is medicine has used an innocent agent to commit a crime. Or a dolphin trained to attach a magnetic explosive device to a boat that then explodes and kills the passengers would be an innocent agent. Both have committed a criminal act, but neither would be considered to have committed a crime.

The actus reus of the person delivering the drugs will be combined with the dealer's mens rea to impose liability on the dealer as *P-1* for the crime of delivering drugs. Likewise, the actus reus of the dolphin will be combined with the mens rea of *P-1* to impose liability on *P-1* for murder. Similarly, someone who is forced by another at gunpoint to commit a crime is an innocent agent; the coercer is guilty as a *P-1*.

Note that when someone uses an innocent agent to commit a crime, the law considers him a principal in the first degree and not an accomplice. The act of an innocent agent is not considered the act of the agent but rather the principal's act.

Principal in the second degree (*P-2*) is the individual who intentionally helps or encourages *P-1* to commit the crime and is actually present at the crime scene or is constructively present (i.e., near enough to assist *P-1* if needed). *P-2* could be the lookout who alerts the shooter to the victim's imminent arrival or the driver of the getaway car.

Accessory before the fact (*A-BTF*) is someone who intentionally helps *P-1* *beforehand,* perhaps by obtaining the murder weapon or by encouraging *P-1* to commit the murder, but is *not present* or *nearby* when *P-1* commits the crime.

Accessory after the fact (*A-ATF*) is someone who, though not part of the planning or commission of the crime committed by *P-1,* intentionally renders aid *after* the crime. For example, he may furnish plane tickets to help *P-1* escape or destroy evidence or hide the fruits of the crime. An *A-ATF* obstructs justice by making it more difficult to apprehend and convict the other parties to the crime. At common law husbands and wives could not be *A-ATF*s. Because of the marital relationship, they were expected to aid each other and therefore had an excuse if they did.

Misprision of Felony. Individuals who, knowing that a felony had been committed, did not report it to authorities could be convicted of misprison of felony. No state has upheld a conviction for this crime since 1878.[6] More recently, however, several states have enacted statutes that punish the failure to report serious crimes.[7]

A federal law enacted in 1908, 18 U.S.C. §4, makes misprision of felony a crime. However, it has been interpreted to require active concealment. A person cannot be convicted for simply not reporting the crime.[8]

Treason. All parties to treason were treated as principals.

Misdemeanors. All parties to a misdemeanor were treated as principals, though it was not a crime to be an *A-ATF* to a misdemeanor.

The Model Penal Code

Principals and Accessories Before the Fact. The MPC abandons the common law's definitions of principals and accessories. It considers *all* actors, except those involved *after* the commission of the crime, as equals. Thus, §2.06 spells out the responsibility of principals in the first and second degree as well as accessories before the fact. The MPC provides a separate crime to cover the conduct of accessories after the fact.[9]

Section 2.06(1) provides that a defendant is guilty of any offense "committed by his own conduct" — that is, by his own voluntary act and mens rea. An actor is also guilty of offenses "committed by the conduct of another for which he is legally accountable."

Under §2.06(2) an actor is "legally accountable" for the conduct of another when:

(a) *P* uses an "innocent agent" or "irresponsible person" (e.g., a legally insane agent[10]) to engage in the criminal conduct. For example, *P* could deceive or force someone else to steal property.

(b) The legislature has enacted a special law making one person liable for the conduct of another. For example, some jurisdictions have enacted vicarious liability statutes based on an employer-employee relationship. This MPC provision allows the legislature to enact broader rules of responsibility for the conduct of another beyond that allowed in subsection (c).

(c) The actor is an *accomplice* of another. Accomplice liability is the basis for imposing criminal responsibility for the conduct of another in most cases.

---

6. See Frankel, Criminal Omissions: A Legal Microcosm, 11 Wayne L. Rev. 367, 417 n.170 (1965).

7. Mass. Gen. Laws Ann. ch. 268, §40 (West 2000); Wash. Rev. Code Ann. §9.69.100 (West 2000).

8. *United States v. Johnson*, 546 F.2d 1225 (5th Cir. 1977).

9. See offenses provided in MPC Article 242.

10. For more on legal insanity, see Chapter 17.

Section 2.06(3) then spells out when someone is an accomplice:

(i) If the defendant solicits another to commit a crime, then the defendant is also responsible for the crime committed by the person solicited.[11]

(ii) If the person "aids or agrees or *attempts* to aid" another in planning or committing a crime, he is responsible for the crime committed by the other person. Note that this section makes an attempt to *aid* (but not an attempt to *solicit* under (i) above) just as culpable as successfully aiding. The MPC thus expands liability for accomplice liability beyond what the common law would impose.

(iii) If the person has a duty to prevent *P*'s crime but fails to act, then he is responsible for the crime committed by *P*.

Accessories After the Fact. The MPC does not use the common law term "accomplice after the fact." Section 242.3 (Hindering Apprehension or Prosecution) is the primary offense covering the conduct of those previously considered *A-ATF*s.

For a summary of terms and definitions used by both the common law and the MPC to describe accomplice liability, see Table 6.

Procedural Consequences of Classification

The Common Law

Venue. At common law *P-1* and *P-2* could only be tried in the jurisdiction where the crime was committed. *A-BTF* could only be tried in a jurisdiction where she provided assistance.

Pleadings and Proof. A defendant charged as a *P-1* could still be convicted even if the evidence established that she was actually a *P-2*. The converse was also true; a defendant charged as a *P-2* could be convicted if the evidence established that she was actually a *P-1*.

However if a defendant was charged as either a *P-1* or *P-2*, but the evidence established that she was an *A-BTF* or vice versa, a variance between the pleading and the proof was not allowed, and the defendant could not be convicted.

The Requirement of a Guilty Principal. Even though an *A-BTF* and a *P-1* could be tried together, *A-BTF* could not be convicted unless *P-1* was convicted first. A formal finding of *P-1*'s guilt had to be made before the

---

11. For more on solicitation, see Chapter 11.

Table 6. Accomplice Liability

COMMON LAW

T-1 Before *Target Crime* ***Accessory Before the Fact*** *(ABTF)*	*T-2* During *Target Crime* ***Principal 1st Degree*** *(P-1)*	*T-3* After *Target Crime* ***Accessory After the Fact*** *(AATF)*
1. Helps or encourages *P-1* to commit Target Crime *BUT* 2. Is not present at or near crime scene	1. Personally commits Target Crime *OR* 2. Uses Innocent Agent to commit Target Crime ***Innocent Agent*** 1. commits criminal act; but 2. lacks capacity or mens rea for crime; and 3. is fooled or forced to commit criminal act ***Principal 2d Degree*** *(P-2)* 1. Helps or encourages *P-1* to commit Target Crime *AND* 2. Is at or near crime scene	1. Helps P-1, P-2, or *ABTF after* Target Crime

---

MODEL PENAL CODE

T-1 Before *Target Crime* ***Principal***	*T-2* During *Target Crime* ***Principal***	*T-3* After *Target Crime*
1. Solicits another to commit a crime, which is then committed by person solicited *OR* 2. Aids, agrees, or attempts to aid another in planning a crime who then commits the crime *OR* 3. Having a legal duty to prevent the commission of the crime, fails to do so	1. Personally commits Target Crime *OR* 2. Uses Innocent or Irresponsible Person ***Principal*** 1. Aids, agrees, or attempts to aid another in committing a crime	1. Hindering apprehension or prosecution. See MPC §242.3

---

guilt of *A-BTF* could be considered. This stringent rule, designed in part to limit the death penalty, was applied even in those cases where *P-1* was guilty but could not be prosecuted for reasons unrelated to guilt or innocence — for example, because *P-1* enjoyed diplomatic immunity.

This approach was not followed in prosecutions of *P-1* and *P-2*. They could be prosecuted in any sequence and an acquittal of one did not affect the guilt of the other.

The Model Penal Code

The MPC, as well as most jurisdictions today, do not have the complex procedural rules that the common law had.

Venue. Section 1.03(d) of the MPC provides that an accomplice can be prosecuted in the same place where *P* committed the offense or where the accomplice provided aid.

Pleadings and Proof. The MPC does not cover variance between the pleadings and proof. The generally applicable procedural rules would apply, and there are no special rules for each specific type of accomplice.

The Requirement of a Guilty Principal. Section 2.06(7) does not require the prior conviction of *P*. The evidence must only prove that an offense was committed by *P* and that *A* was an accomplice to that crime; what happened to *P* is simply not relevant to *A*'s guilt.

Contemporary Law

Most jurisdictions treat *P-1, P-2,* and *A-BTF* by statute as "principals." Thus, they are all considered equally responsible for the crime committed by *P-1.* Only *A-ATF* is treated differently.

Principals and Accessories. Most states now call all parties who committed the crime or provided assistance either before or during its commission *principals.* (Note, however, that many courts and commentators still use the term "principal" to describe the primary actor (*P-1*) and "accomplice" or "accessory" to describe the supporting actors (*P-2* and *A-BTF*). These terms help clarify the respective roles the actors played in the crime, but they generally do not affect their legal responsibility.) We also will continue to use the terms "principal" (*P*) to describe the primary actor and "accomplice" (*A*) to describe the secondary or supporting actor.

Generally, the procedural consequences of the common law classifications have also been abolished. Thus, for example, an accomplice can be tried and convicted even though the primary actor has fled the jurisdiction or has died. Nonetheless, some states still retain the old common law definitions and some of the procedural consequences.

Accessories After the Fact. Most states now treat individuals who provide aid *after* the commission of a crime less harshly than those actually involved in its planning or commission. These after-the-fact helpers are usually convicted of a different crime, often called "rendering criminal assistance," "criminal facilitation," or some variation.

Elements of Accessorial Responsibility

Mens Rea

There are two kinds of mens rea generally required for accomplice responsibility.

The Mens Rea of the Crime Aided

The Common Law. *A* must act with at least the same mens rea or culpability required for conviction of the offense committed by *P*.[12] If the object offense requires a specific intent, *A* must act with that same intent. If the object crime requires only recklessness or negligence as to result, it is sufficient if *A* acts with the same mens rea toward result as is required by the object offense.

The Model Penal Code. The MPC would also require that *A* act with at least the same culpability or mens rea of the crime being aided.

The Mens Rea to Be an Accomplice: Purpose or Intent to Aid the Principal's Criminal Action

The Common Law. In addition, an accomplice must want to help someone else commit a crime.

Conduct. Most jurisdictions require the accomplice to act with the *purpose* or *intent* to encourage or assist in the conduct element of a crime. Suppose *A* yelled the following at *V*, who was about to be shot by *P*: "Take off your hat and die like a man." *P*, understanding these words as encouragement to kill *V*, shoots and kills *V*. Though *A*'s words may have had the *effect* of encouraging *P* to shoot *V*, *A* would not be guilty under accomplice liability unless he spoke those words with the *intent* of encouraging *P* to

---

12. Kadish, supra note 1, at 349.

engage in that conduct.[13] Likewise, unintentional assistance does not result in responsibility as an accomplice.

Requiring the highest level of mens rea or culpability for conduct makes sense because, as we saw, the actus reus of accomplice liability can be quite minimal; that is, one does not have to provide very much help or encouragement to become an accomplice. In this sense, accessorial liability may punish more for bad attitude than for bad behavior!

Recklessness or Negligence as to Result. Though cases are split, the general rule is that *A* must act with the same mens rea toward result as is required to convict *P* of the object crime. Consider *A* who aids *P* in the commission of stealing a car, perhaps standing lookout while *P* hot-wires the car, and then jumps into the car while *P*, the driver, speeds away. What if *P* hits and seriously injures a victim? If *P* may be convicted of the crime of vehicular assault based on proof of recklessness toward injuring another, then *A* also may be convicted of being an accomplice to that offense *if* the prosecution can show *A* also acted with recklessness toward this result.

Strict Liability. If *A* assists *P* in committing a strict liability offense, can *A* be convicted as an accomplice? In theory, the answer should be yes. After all, *A* acted with the purpose of aiding *P* engage in conduct that constituted the offense.

However, some courts find the reach of strict liability through the doctrine of complicity to be unfair. In *Johnson v. Youden*, [1950] 1 K.B. 544, the court affirmed the dismissal of an indictment against solicitors (English lawyers), charging them with aiding their client in selling a house at an unlawful price, which was a strict liability offense. The court concluded that *A* could not be convicted as an accomplice to a strict liability offense unless he "knows the facts that constitute an offense." Because the defendants did not know all of the facts, they could not be convicted.

The Model Penal Code. To be an accomplice the actor must act with the "purpose of promoting or facilitating the commission of an offense." (§2.06(3)(a). This rule needs careful analysis.

Conduct. The accomplice must have as her *purpose* that *P* will engage in the conduct elements of the object crime. Knowledge as to *P*'s conduct is an insufficient basis for responsibility under the MPC.

Circumstances. Though it is not clear from the language of the MPC itself, the Commentaries indicate that the drafters intended to let the courts decide whether purpose as to circumstances is required for conviction or simply the same *culpability or mens rea* toward circumstances as is required for the object crime.[14] Courts that demand *purpose* as to circumstances may require a *higher* culpability for the accomplice than might be required for *P*.

---

13. *Hicks v. United States,* 150 U.S. 442 (1893).

14. Model Penal Code and Commentaries, Comment to §2.06, at 311 n.37 (1985). "There is deliberate ambiguity as to whether the purpose requirement extends to

Result. The MPC requires the same culpability or mens rea toward result as would be required for conviction of *P* for the object offense. §2.06(4).

Knowledge That Another Intends to Commit a Crime

Some courts hold that furnishing assistance to someone that the defendant knows is intending to commit a crime is sufficient for accomplice responsibility, particularly if the object crime is very serious. Thus, in *United States v. Fountain*,[15] a prison inmate who furnished a knife to another inmate knowing it would be used to attack a guard was convicted of aiding and abetting murder. Judge Posner concluded that the use of the criminal law to deter individuals from helping others they *know* intend to commit *serious* crimes is justified. Nonetheless, many courts take the MPC approach and require purpose or intent rather than knowledge for accomplice responsibility.

Providers of Goods and Services

As we saw in conspiracy,[16] a troublesome question of mens rea arises when someone provides innocuous goods and services to another she knows will use them to commit a crime. Can someone who provides large quantities of sugar at prices higher than usual to another she knows will use it to make illegal liquor be convicted as an accomplice?

The Common Law. Some earlier cases held that providing goods or services with knowledge that another intended to use them to commit a crime established accomplice liability.[17] However, most jurisdictions permit conviction only if the prosecutor can prove that the defendant acted with a *purpose* to aid.[18] The prosecutor has to demonstrate that the defendant had a "stake in the venture" — for example, the provider's success or profits depended on helping *P* successfully commit the object offense or the provider has a psychological involvement in *P*'s success. This analysis focuses both on the materiality of the aid provided to *P* as well as the profit the provider

---

circumstance elements of the contemplated offense or whether, as in the case of attempts, the policy of the substantive offense on this point should control. . . . The result, therefore, is that the actor must have a purpose with respect to the proscribed conduct or the proscribed result, with his attitude towards the circumstances to be left to resolution by the courts."

15. 768 F.2d 790 (7th Cir. 1985).

16. See Chapter 13.

17. *Jindra v. United States,* 69 F.2d 429 (5th Cir. 1934).

18. *United States v. Peoni,* 100 F.2d 401 (2d Cir. 1938).

realizes. Many jurisdictions permit the jury to use the defendant's knowledge that P intends to commit a crime, together with other evidence such as excess volume or profits, to find that A acted with the requisite purpose.

The Model Penal Code. The Model Penal Code also requires the prosecution to prove that the actor had the "purpose of promoting or facilitating" the commission of the crime. §2.06(3).

A few commentators argue that those who supply legitimate goods and services in normal quantities and at market price have no duty to intervene to prevent the harm P intends to commit. In their view the criminal law only requires each of us not to personally harm others. Absent a specific legal duty in civil law, we have no duty in the course of our everyday lives to prevent someone else from committing a harmful act.[19] This analysis turns on characterizing furnishing goods with knowledge as an "omission" rather than as a voluntary act. (See Chapter 3.)

Some states have responded to this difficult question by statutorily creating the less serious crime of criminal facilitation. These laws punish someone who *knowingly* provides another with significant aid used to commit a serious crime. The punishment provided is usually less than that provided for the crime committed by P. *Purpose* to aid is still required to convict D as an accomplice. Under a criminal facilitation statute, the defendant in *Fountain*, supra, could only be found guilty of criminal facilitation rather than accomplice liability.

Liability for Unintended Crimes Committed by the Principal

The Common Law. In theory, the mens rea element of accomplice liability clearly suggests that an accomplice should only be held responsible for the *specific acts* of P that he intended to aid. This approach, used in early cases, would limit A's responsibility to those crimes he had, through the mens rea of intent, adopted as his own acts. This limiting principle made sense because, as we just saw, accomplice liability is very broad and can be extended to very minor actors who may not even satisfy "but for" causation.

A number of recent cases, however, have expanded A's liability beyond this limit to include those acts that A should have "reasonably foreseen" or that were a "natural and probable consequence" of the offense that A intended to aid. This approach is very similar to the rule in conspiracy that

---

19. G. Fletcher, Rethinking Criminal Law 676 (1978).

all co-conspirators are liable for all reasonably foreseeable crimes committed by other co-conspirators in furtherance of the conspiracy.[20]

Imposing liability on A for "reasonably foreseeable" crimes committed by P may make sense in cases where there is a high probability of an additional crime being committed. But how is such probability determined? A helps P enter a residence at night so P can steal jewelry. P, while inside, assaults the homeowner who has come to investigate the noise. Should A be held responsible for P's assault? Both A and P were undoubtedly hoping there would be no assault. Thus, it is hard to conclude that A intended to assist or encourage P to commit an assault. Is P's assault "a natural and probable consequence" of committing a residential burglary in the evening? On what basis should a jury decide this issue?

More recently, courts have supported an even broader extension of accomplice liability to encompass those crimes committed by P that A has "naturally, probably and foreseeably put in motion."[21] This approach has been used to impose liability when P killed V rather than roughing him up to get information (as A expressly told him), thereby defeating A's goal.[22] It has also been used even when A tried to stop P from killing someone because V was not their intended victim.[23]

Justifications for holding A responsible not only for the crime A intended to aid, but also for any other reasonably foreseeable crime committed by P, are based on A's causal role in bringing about these crimes. However, this overlooks the fact that accomplice liability does not require that A's assistance be very significant before liability attaches. Indeed, the MPC includes "attempts" at aiding as sufficient. Thus, even an unsuccessful role in causing another to commit a crime will trigger accomplice liability. This expansive approach to accomplice liability primarily punishes attitude rather than acts that cause harm.

Just as in conspiracy, then, some jurisdictions are imposing criminal responsibility on accomplices if P commits an unintended or unplanned crime, including one clearly not sought by A, provided that it was reasonably foreseeable.[24] This approach essentially makes the accomplice responsible for his *negligence* — that is, he *should* have foreseen that P may have committed crimes other than those A intended to aid. Convicting A on this low mens rea is ironic in that the prosecution may have to prove a higher degree of

---

20. See Chapter 13.
21. *People v. Luparello*, 187 Ca. App. 3d 410, 439, 231 Cal. Rptr. 832, 849 (1986).
22. Id.
23. *People v. Brigham*, 216 Cal. App. 3d 1039, 265 Cal. Rptr. 486 (1989).
24. See, e.g., *People v. Luparello*, supra note 21.

culpability to convict *P.* It also inflicts punishment that is disproportionate to *A*'s mental state.

Courts that enlarge accomplice liability based on foreseeability may be using a *causal* analysis to expand the mens rea of accessorial liability. Or, to put it differently, what *P does* is what *A should have been aware* might happen. There is also the risk that tort law's concept of reasonable foreseeability may be imported into the criminal law.

The Model Penal Code. The MPC does not permit responsibility to be imposed on *A* because of negligence toward unanticipated crimes committed by *P.* Thus, *A* cannot be convicted of crimes that were the "natural and probable consequence" of the crime *A* did intend to assist. Instead, the MPC's culpability requirements for the conduct and result elements (discussed above) must be met.

Actus Reus

The actus reus element of accomplice responsibility includes a broad range of conduct. Descriptive words such as "aid, abet, counsel," and so on that are used in various statutes to describe the actus reus of accessorial liability can be broken down into the following general categories of conduct.

Actual Assistance

In general, there are two primary kinds of conduct that will satisfy this requirement: actually helping in a *physical* sense (providing the murder weapon, acting as lookout, or driving the getaway car) or assisting in a *psychological* sense by reinforcing the will of *P* (encouraging *P* to commit the crime either before or during its actual commission).

Usually, it will not be too difficult to establish this actus reus element. If *A* holds the victim while *P* punches him or steadies the ladder while *P* climbs in the second story of the home, there will be strong evidence of actus reus. So, too, if *A* yells at *P* while *P* is assaulting *V*: "Kick him again; he's still moving!"

But what if *A* is simply present while *P* commits an offense? Is the mere act of "being there" sufficient to constitute the actus reus for accomplice liability? This conduct is ambiguous. Nonetheless, presence during the commission of a crime by another *is* legally sufficient to constitute the actus reus provided *P knows A* is there to render encouragement or to help if necessary. If, however, *P* does not understand that *A* will assist if needed, then a person's mere presence with knowledge that *P* is committing a crime does not satisfy the actus reus requirement. In addition, yelling words of encouragement at

P is insufficient if P does not hear them.[25] (But note that the MPC would consider an attempt at aiding and abetting sufficient for responsibility.)

Omission

The Common Law. The actus reus requirement can also be satisfied by an omission, provided A has a legal duty to act. Thus, a police officer who stands by and watches P attack and rape V in a bar has satisfied the actus reus requirement. This is a classic case of a failure to act when there is a legal duty to act generating criminal responsibility.

The Model Penal Code. The Model Penal Code also takes this approach. A person who has a legal duty to prevent the commission of the offense is responsible for that offense if he "fails to make proper effort" to prevent it. MPC §2.06(3)(a)(iii). The passive police officer observing a rape would also be liable under the MPC.

How Much Aid Is Enough?

Perhaps the most difficult question is how much aid is enough to become an accomplice? Short answer: any aid! This compact summary obviously needs some explanation.

The Common Law. There can be instances in which A renders aid to P, but it really is not very helpful. Nonetheless, courts generally will find A guilty if his help was useful in any way to P. Thus, in *Wilcox v. Jeffery,* the defendant was found guilty of aiding and abetting an American jazz musician play unlawfully in England because A attended a concert along with hundreds of others in the audience and later wrote about the concert in a magazine.[26] Of course, the musician would have performed whether or not A was present or wrote about his concert. Here, there is accomplice liability without *any* meaningful causal connection between A's presence and P's crime.

In *State ex. rel. Attorney General v. Tally,* the court impeached Judge Tally for sending a telegram trying to prevent the delivery of another telegram sent earlier that warned the intended murder victim of his peril. In considering when the action of an accomplice will impose responsibility, the court said: "If the aid in homicide can be shown to have put the deceased at a disadvantage, to have deprived him of a *single chance* of life, but for which he would have had, he who furnishes such aid is guilty though it can

---

25. Kadish, supra note 1, at 358-359.
26. *Wilcox v. Jeffery,* King's Bench Division, [1951] 1 All E.R. 464.

not be known or shown that the dead man, in the absence thereof, would have availed himself of the chance."[27] Note that it is not necessary for *P* to know that *A* is assisting him before *A* can be found guilty of accessorial responsibility. In the *Tally* case the principals did not know that the judge had sent the telegram in order to help them kill their victim. Nonetheless, *A* will still be guilty as long as his aid had some minimal effect on *P*'s being able to commit the crime.

In some cases the offered assistance will have no impact at all on *P*'s commission of the crime. Suppose that in the *Tally* case the telegram operator had simply delivered the warning telegram while tearing up Tally's telegram. Or if *A* shouts words of encouragement to *P* to commit a crime, but *P* is deaf and cannot hear *A*. As long as the aid is completely ineffective or *P* does not know that any encouragement is being given (thus leaving *P* unaware that anyone is encouraging him to commit the crime), most courts will probably not find accomplice liability.

The Model Penal Code. The Model Penal Code takes a broader approach. It considers any effort at aiding, even if ineffective or unknown to *P*, as satisfying the actus reus requirement of accessorial liability. The MPC does this by providing that a person is an accomplice of another if she "aids or agrees or *attempts* to aid such other person in planning or committing" the crime. MPC §2.06(3)(a)(ii) (emphasis added). Thus, an "attempt" at providing aid is sufficient for accomplice responsibility even if it is unsuccessful. The term "attempt" most likely has the same meaning here as it does under §5.01. And, as you recall from our discussion of attempt in Chapter 12, the MPC requires that the actor's conduct "strongly corroborate the actor's criminal purpose" (§5.01(2)).

The MPC thus converts the question of how much aid is enough from a substantive element into an evidentiary element — that is, has the accomplice done enough to persuade a jury that he acted with the *purpose* of aiding in the commission of the crime, even if he wasn't helpful at all?

Immunity from Conviction

The Common Law. Accomplice liability cannot be used to convict an individual whose behavior is not punished by the substantive law. For example, statutory rape laws make it a crime to have sexual intercourse with a minor because minors lack the maturity necessary to give legally effective consent.[28] A prosecutor cannot charge a minor who encouraged the defendant to have sexual intercourse with liability as an accomplice to statutory

---

27. *State ex. rel. Attorney General v. Tally, Judge,* 102 Ala. 25, 15 So. 722, 739 (1894) (emphasis added).
28. See Chapter 9.

rape. Because she is a victim in need of protection, the substantive law of statutory rape does not punish the minor. Permitting her to be convicted as an accomplice would undermine the legislative policy expressed in the substantive offense. (This same limitation applies to conspiracy. *Gebardi v. United States*, 287 U.S. 112 (1932). See Chapter 13.)

The Model Penal Code. The MPC takes the same approach. Under §2.06(6)(a) a person cannot be an accomplice if he is "a victim of that offense." Thus, an underage minor could not be convicted under the MPC of being an accomplice to a principal charged with statutory rape.

Conduct Necessarily Part of the Crime

What if the legislature has only punished one party to a criminal transaction that necessarily involves another person? Can the other party be convicted as an accomplice?

The Common Law. Courts generally have said no. Again, using accomplice liability in such cases would undermine the policy of the substantive offense. Thus, a customer who hires a prostitute cannot be convicted as an accomplice to prostitution if the substantive law of prostitution does not punish his behavior. Prostitution necessarily involves a customer and a provider. If the legislature had wanted to punish both parties, it readily could have done so.

The Model Penal Code. Section 2.06(6)(b) provides the same result. An individual cannot be convicted of being an accomplice if "the offense is so defined that *his conduct* is *inevitably incident* to its commission" (emphasis added).

Legal Incapacity to Commit Substantive Crime

Occasionally, only an individual with certain attributes can commit a crime. Under common law a husband could not rape his wife,[29] but he could be guilty of raping his wife if he acted as an accomplice.

In *Regina v. Cogan and Leak*, [1976] 1 Q.B. 217 (Eng.), Leak, the husband, persuaded Cogan to have sexual intercourse with Leak's wife by incorrectly telling him that his wife consented to have sex with him. Cogan was acquitted of rape, based on *Morgan*, because he did not intend to have intercourse without consent. Leak argued that *he* could not be convicted because he was the victim's *husband*. The court disagreed, concluding that Leak had used Cogan as an innocent agent. Therefore, while Leak could not

---

29. See Chapter 9.

be convicted as aider and abettor to Cogan as originally charged, his guilt as a principal had been clearly established and his conviction was upheld. This case demonstrates that courts will not allow individuals to hide behind their own legal incapacity to commit a crime if they use others to accomplish it.

The Common Law. In the infamous *Morgan* case,[30] for example, the husband could have been convicted as an accomplice to rape either for encouraging others to rape his wife or (if you believed the defendants) for using innocent agents to rape her. The husband would be held liable even though *he* could not have been guilty as *P* if he had forcibly had sexual intercourse with his wife.

The Model Penal Code. The MPC follows this approach also. Under §2.06(5) a defendant who was herself legally incapable of committing a particular crime may become an accomplice if she helps someone who is legally capable of committing the offense.

The Relationship Between Principal and Accessories

The Common Law

The Requirement of a Guilty Principal

As noted at the outset, accomplice responsibility is *derivative*. *A* is legally responsible for the crimes committed by *P* that *A* aided or (in some jurisdictions) that were a natural and probable consequence of the crime *A* aided. Thus, complicity is a means of attributing the criminal responsibility of *P* to *A*. This means that there *must* be a guilty *P;* without a guilty *P*, there can be no guilty *A*. (Of course, if *P* is convicted of an *attempt* rather than the completed offense, *A* can be convicted of being an accomplice to that attempt.)

At common law the acquittal of *P*, for whatever reason, precluded the conviction of *A* as a principal in the second degree or as an accomplice. (There is an occasional exception to this principle. See our discussion of *Cogan*, supra.) Even if *P* did commit the crime and *A* fully intended to aid *P* in its commission, *A* could not be convicted if *P* was acquitted. This was true even if *P*'s defense was personal, such as diplomatic immunity, or if *P* had an excuse, such as legal insanity. The requirement of a guilty *P* can benefit

---

30. *Regina v. Morgan*, House of Lords, [1976] A.C. 182. See discussion of this case in Chapter 9.

A in fortuitous ways that are unrelated to *A*'s moral culpability. Nonetheless, some jurisdictions still retain the requirement of a guilty principal.

The Pretending Principal

Can *A* be convicted if *P* does not have the mens rea necessary for conviction? No. Thus, in *State v. Hayes*,[31] *P*, related to the store owner, entered the store in an apparent burglary. However, *P* had no intention of stealing the goods inside. He only went through with this charade to secure *A*'s conviction. Because *P* was acting as a citizen decoy, he did not have the mens rea necessary for burglary and larceny. Consequently, *A*'s conviction as an accomplice on these charges had to be reversed for lack of a "guilty principal" even though *A*'s moral culpability and need for punishment were apparent.

Some courts and commentators, however, have indicated their dislike for this rule.[32] In *Vaden v. State*,[33] the Alaska Supreme Court upheld the conviction of a pilot for aiding an undercover agent to shoot foxes illegally from the pilot's airplane. The majority held that the undercover agent's actions were not justified under a public authority defense. Thus, there was a "guilty" (though unprosecuted) *P*. The majority also said in dicta that, even if the defense were valid, it was *personal* to *P*, and *A* could therefore be convicted. This approach is inconsistent with traditional common law rules. The acquittal of *P*, even under a personal defense, would have precluded the conviction of *A* at common law.

Differences in Degree of Culpability Between Principal and Accomplice

There is no clear consensus among jurisdictions as to whether *A* can only be convicted of the same crime as *P* was convicted or whether *A* could be convicted of a *greater* offense. Put differently, does the level of *P*'s responsibility establish the upper limit of *A*'s responsibility?

Consider a case in which Iago (*A*) with cool deliberation provokes Othello (*P*), through false information, to kill *V. P* might be able to prove that he did not premeditate or that he acted in the heat of passion. *A*, on the other hand, could not. Can *A* be convicted of a more serious crime than *P*? Or consider the *Richards* case in which a wife hired two men to beat her husband severely enough to be hospitalized; they, however, merely roughed

---

31. 105 Mo. 76, 16 S.W. 514 (1891).
32. Kadish, supra note 1, at 381; Fletcher, supra note 19, at 664-667.
33. 768 P.2d 1102 (Alaska 1989).

him up without serious injury. Can *A*, the wife, be guilty of a more serious assault charge than either *P*?[34]

At common law, *A* was convicted of the same offense as *P* unless the crime was homicide. Because murder and manslaughter were considered different forms of the same offense,[35] *A* in the homicide case above could be convicted of murder even though *P* had been convicted of manslaughter. In the *Richards* case, however, the court held that the accomplice could not be convicted of a more serious assault charge than that for which the *P*s were convicted.

Today, some jurisdictions have changed the common law approach and permit *A* to be convicted of a more serious offense than *P*.[36] This approach allows the law to assess the moral culpability of each party according to his or her *individual* mens rea.

Withdrawal of Aid

Under the common law, *A* could avoid criminal responsibility if she withdrew her aid before *P* committed the offense. Similarly to the requirements of withdrawal in conspiracy,[37] *A* must (1) inform *P* not to commit the offense and (2) do everything possible to render ineffective any aid she has already given.

If *A* had encouraged *P* to commit the crime, she must try to discourage *P*. If *A* had provided physical assistance of some sort, she must try to render it useless. *A* must take these steps in sufficient time to prevent *P* from committing the crime. *A*'s efforts can satisfy the required elements of withdrawal even if *P* independently decides to commit the crime anyway without *A*'s help.

The Model Penal Code
The Requirement of a Guilty Principal

The MPC *seemingly* does not require the conviction of *P* for *A* to be guilty, *provided P* has engaged in the *conduct* required by the commission of the object crime or by an attempt to commit it. This is true regardless of the basis of *P*'s acquittal.

This is the result reached if "conduct" in §2.06(1) refers *only* to *A* assisting *P* to engage in conduct sufficient to constitute the offense (or an

---

34. *Regina v. Richards,* [1974] Q.B. 776.

35. See Chapter 8.

36. *Regina v. Howe,* [1987] 1 All E.R. 771, 799. However, the House of Lords in dicta indicated that *Regina v. Richards,* supra note 34, was wrongly decided.

37. See Chapter 13.

attempt) and does *not* refer to the mens rea with which *P* engaged in the conduct or to *P*'s guilt for having engaged in the conduct. Put more simply, §2.06(1) makes *A* responsible for *P*'s conduct and for *A*'s mens rea or culpability. This reading is consistent with the MPC's focus on each individual's moral culpability. A contrary reading of this section is possible, however. If a court did not accept the approach we outline, it might well require a guilty *P* before *A* could be convicted.

There is a more difficult question. What, if any, responsibility does *A* have if *A* "aids" *P* to commit a crime, but *P* does not engage in conduct sufficient to constitute the crime or even an attempt to commit the crime? Section 5.01(3) covers this situation. It considers *A*'s conduct to be an "attempt" to commit the object crime, not *attempted* aiding and abetting.

The Pretending Principal

For the reasons explained in the previous section, a pretending *P* does not affect responsibility under the MPC. Thus, an *A* who assists a *P* who cannot be convicted (because he lacks mens rea or has a personal excuse, for example) can still be convicted under §2.06(1).

Differences in Degree of Culpability Between Principal and Accomplice

Under the MPC an accomplice is graded based on the *conduct* committed by *P* and the *culpability* of *A*. Thus, the MPC readily allows differential punishment for *P* and *A*.

Withdrawal of Aid

Section 2.06(6)(c) permits an accomplice to withdraw previously provided assistance and thereby avoid criminal responsibility already incurred. To accomplish an effective withdrawal, *A* must terminate his complicity before *P* commits the offense and do any one of the following: (i) completely deprive the aid of its effectiveness, or (ii) give timely warning to the police, or (iii) otherwise make a "proper effort to prevent the commission of the crime."

EXAMPLES

Whom would you charge? With what crime? Why? Who is an accomplice, principal, or accessory?

1a. Linda robs a bank while Brad drives the getaway car.

1b. Linda enters a bank to rob it. She turns to Clara, a kindly elderly lady, and says: "Would you deliver this note to my boyfriend? He is the teller behind that first window. I don't want to get him in trouble for conducting personal business during banking hours." Clara gladly delivered the folded note to the teller. The teller opened and read it: "I have a gun and will use it. Put all the money in a bag and have this lady give it to me." He complied and gave the bag to Clara, asking her to return it to the person who gave her the note. Clara, not suspecting anything, took the bag and gave it to Linda, who promptly left the bank with the cash.

1c.   Linda enters the bank to rob it and points her gun at Olga, a bank customer, saying: "Get all the cash from the tellers and put it in a bag for me or else you're dead meat!" Olga does this and hands Linda the bag with all the cash in it. Linda then runs out the door with the cash.

1d.   Same facts as Example 1c except that, after Olga hands Linda the bag, Linda hits the bank guard over the head with her gun to immobilize him. Two days later the guard dies from massive internal bleeding in the brain.

1e.   Linda and Brad are married. Unknown to Brad, Linda robs a bank by herself and comes home with a lot of money. She tells Brad of her accomplishment and asks him to throw the gun she used in the robbery in a deep lake. Brad gladly disposes of the gun as requested.

2.   Dan tells Laura, his wife, that he is going out to rob a grocery store on the other side of town. Laura shouts out as Dan is leaving: "Be sure to bring back a bottle of milk while you are at it." Dan robs the grocery store and brings back a half-gallon of milk.

3.   While driving along the highway with Tara in the passenger seat, Jennifer spotted Bob, her fiance, several car lengths ahead of her. She speeded up to wave at him. Bob, recognizing Jennifer in the car behind him, waited until she almost caught up to him and then sped away. Jennifer then increased her speed so she could catch up to Bob once more. Again, Bob, smiling, waited until Jennifer almost caught up to him and then increased his speed even more. This game of "cat and mouse" continued as each car increased their respective speeds. Bob and Jennifer were both laughing out loud when, suddenly, Jennifer, traveling well above the speed limit, lost control and hit a tree. Tara died instantly. Jennifer was charged with vehicular homicide. Is Bob liable as an accomplice? (Remember this scenario from Chapter 7?)

4.   Frank and Mark went to an ATM to get cash. Frank used his ATM card to withdraw $40. After Frank inadvertently pushed the "Enter" button a second time, the machine gave him $80, but his account only reflected a $40 deduction. Frank said: "WOW! Two for one! I asked for $40 and got $80 and my account is down only $40. You can't beat that. I mistakenly pushed the 'enter' button a second time." Mark, until then

unaware of what had happened, inserted his card and, instead of withdrawing $50 as planned, withdrew $400. He pushed the "Enter" button a second time. The machine gave him $800, while his account only reflected a $400 deduction. Frank and Mark then returned to their dormitory and told Chris all about this magical machine. Chris went to the ATM and withdrew $1,000. It gave him $2,000, while his account only reflected a $1,000 deduction. Is Frank, Mark, or Chris responsible for any crimes committed by each other?

5a. Lydia covets a painting at the local museum. She persuades Bruno, a guard at the museum, to leave a window in the ladies' room unlocked so that she can enter the museum during the night and steal the painting. That evening Bruno leaves the window unlocked. While on her way to the window, Lydia discovers that a door has been inadvertently left open by a museum employee. Lydia enters through the door, steals the painting, and leaves.

5b. Bruno was angry at the museum for making him stand up during his day shift. One day he saw Anthony creeping slowly toward a famous small painting on display at the museum. Strongly suspecting that Anthony intended to steal the picture and hoping to get back at his boss, Bruno took an unscheduled "coffee break" to make it easier for Anthony. Anthony, unaware that Bruno had left the room, took the painting from the wall and quickly left the museum.

6. Eric and Ian are students at Columbia, a large suburban high school. They sell drugs to a number of students. Pat, a friend, often buys drugs from them. Eric and Ian know that Pat's father is an avid gun collector and that Pat has access to his father's large gun collection. Eric and Ian have frequently told Pat that they want to get their hands on guns like those his father owns so they can kill all the "jocks" and "punks" at their school. One day Eric and Ian offer Pat a very large amount of cocaine in exchange for borrowing several semi-automatic guns and a lot of ammunition from Pat. Pat knows something is brewing because Eric and Ian never make deals — they always make him pay top dollar for his drugs. Nevertheless, Pat agrees to loan them the guns and ammo in exchange for the drugs because he is not worried for his safety — after all, he is not a jock or a punk. To be extra safe, Pat decides he won't go to school until the guns are returned. The next day Eric and Ian open fire in the school cafeteria with the guns and ammo they borrowed from Pat. Ten students are killed and many more are wounded. Is Pat guilty as an accomplice of these murders and attempted murders?

7. SISTER OF FORTUNE magazine, compiled and published solely by Amanda Ashwood, recently ran an advertisement in its classified ad section, which read: "Do you need help PERMANENTLY ridding your

life of battering boyfriends? Just call Tammy the Terminator at 1-800-MRCNARRY." One week later the body of a battering boyfriend was found. Two weeks later Tammy confessed to this murder-for-hire homicide, telling the police that Leslie, her client, found her and hired her through this ad. The prosecutor wants your advice (ignoring any constitutional law or corporate law issues) on whether she can prosecute Amanda as an accomplice. Please advise.

8. Pedro's wife, Maria, recently left him for Jose. Pedro, upset and angry, discussed his situation with his close friend, Al. Pedro told Al he was so mad, he could kill Jose. Al replied: "The man who stole Maria deserves to die. Your honor will be upheld and you will feel much better. If you are a real man, you must do it."

    a. That evening Pedro grabs his pistol from his closet but cannot bring himself to leave his house. Nothing further happens.

    b. Same facts, except that Pedro leaves his house and kills Jose.

    c. Same facts, except that Pedro leaves his house and kills Jose and Maria.

    d. Same facts, except that Al gives Pedro a loaded gun and says: "Here, my friend. This is for your honor." That evening Pedro kills Jose and Maria.

    e. Same facts as in 8d except that later that afternoon Al decides that killing Jose is wrong. Al calls Pedro and tells him in strong language that killing Jose is wrong and will not solve anything. Pedro says he will think it over. Later that night Pedro uses the gun Al gave him and kills Jose.

    f. Pedro uses his own gun to kill Jose and later goes to Al's house (who does not know that Maria has left Pedro to run off with Jose) and says: "I have just killed the man who stole my wife with this gun. Get rid of it immediately." Al has already heard news reports that say that Pedro is the prime suspect but that the murder will probably not be solved unless the murder weapon is recovered. Al takes the gun Pedro gave him to a garbage dump where it is soon covered over with several tons of new garbage.

    g. Same facts as in the first paragraph of this example except that Pedro tells Al that he has placed a bomb in Jose's home set to explode at 9:00 p.m. Al replies that Maria and Jose will be at a movie at that time. Pedro says: "I know that. I just want to scare them. Maybe Maria will come back to me." Al decides that scaring Maria and Jose is not enough. At 8:30 Al calls Jose at the movie theater and tells him his house has been broken into. Jose and Maria immediately leave the theater and return to Jose's house. The bomb explodes while they are there, killing both of them.

9. "Sharkie" specializes in lending money at illegal interest rates to individuals with terrible credit records. He tells Thug, one of his collection

agents, to "do what you have to do to collect the money from Sam but, remember, I want my money." Thug, not being terribly bright, uses his fists a bit too much on Sam trying to persuade Sam to pay the money he owes Sharkie. Sam dies from the beating.

10. Tiny regularly visits an exotic dancing club. The local prostitution law makes it a criminal offense for exotic dancers to make physical contact with a customer in exchange for money.

One evening Tiny becomes extremely frustrated with the law and offers Candy, a dancer, $100 for a lap dance. Candy agrees and does a lap dance while seated on Tiny's lap. An undercover police officer immediately arrests both. Subsequently, the prosecutor charges Tiny as an accomplice to Candy's act of prostitution.

EXPLANATIONS

1a. Brad intentionally provided assistance to Linda while she committed the bank robbery. Thus, Brad is an accomplice and could be held liable as such for the crime of bank robbery committed by Linda. At common law, Brad would be a principal in the second degree because he was present and actually rendering assistance while Linda, the principal in the first degree, was committing a crime.

Under the MPC and most modern statutes, Brad would be considered a principal and would be convicted as such for the crime of bank robbery because he purposefully rendered aid to one he knew was committing this crime.

1b. Although Clara assisted Linda in robbing the bank by delivering the note to the teller and then delivering the cash to Linda, Clara had no intention to assist Linda in the commission of a crime. Clara is an "innocent agent" who, while trying to be helpful, has been deceived as to what she is doing.

1c. Olga assisted Linda to commit the bank robbery by gathering up the cash and putting it in a bag for her. However, Olga did so only because she was threatened with imminent deadly force. Olga would have a successful defense of duress (see Chapter 16) and, thus, would be an innocent agent. She could not be convicted as an accomplice.

1d. Linda could be convicted under a felony murder/murder charge in most states. Olga also may be in trouble unless this jurisdiction allows the defense of duress to a murder charge, including felony murder. Most jurisdictions would probably allow Olga to use this defense. If not, then Olga might be held liable under the law as an accomplice.

The point here is that liability as an accomplice can depend on other legal doctrines such as duress. If the alleged accomplice has a defense in cases where she intentionally rendered aid, then she cannot be held guilty as an accomplice. If that defense fails, however, she then may be convicted as an accomplice. (*Note:* A really clever defense attorney might argue that Olga did not act with "purpose" to take the money by threat of deadly force. But that evidence may be relevant only to "motive.")

1e. At common law Brad would not be liable as an accessory after the fact. Both husband and wife were expected to help each other avoid conviction if a spouse committed a crime.

In most jurisdictions today Brad would be convicted of rendering criminal assistance or criminal facilitation. There is no defense for a spouse or relative who knowingly helps someone who has committed a crime avoid apprehension or conviction. Some jurisdictions, however, will reduce the degree of the offense if a spouse or relative is involved and only provides certain kinds of assistance.

2. The general rule is that *any* encouragement is sufficient even though the principal would have committed the crime anyway. If the jury finds that Laura's statement was intended to encourage Dan to commit the crime and had any impact on the principal, it would be legally sufficient to convict Laura as an accomplice. See *State v. Helmenstein*, 163 N.W.2d 85 (N.D. 1968).

3. Jennifer is clearly a principal in the first degree at common law and is a principal under the MPC.

In many jurisdictions Bob could be charged as an accomplice in the vehicular homicide of Tara for intentionally encouraging Jennifer to drive well over the speed limit by initiating and continuing to play this dangerous game. Granted, Bob did not verbally communicate with Jennifer to egg her on, and Jennifer was the last responsible moral agent who could have slowed down at any time and avoided this tragedy. However, the law of accomplice liability does not require significant encouragement nor does it require "but for" causation as required elements for liability. Thus, Bob can be convicted as an accomplice and could receive the same sentence as Jennifer.

4. Frank, Mark, and Chris is each responsible for his own withdrawal and each may face a criminal charge of theft if they do not return the extra cash or tell the bank. (See Chapter 10.) Frank and Mark were both present when the other obtained the extra cash. Generally, being present with the knowledge that someone else is committing a crime is not sufficient for accomplice liability unless the individual is there for the *purpose* of encouraging a crime or unless the principal knows that the individual is willing to help if necessary. Here Mark did not know what Frank had done until after Frank had obtained the extra cash. Thus, Mark is clearly not responsible for any crime Frank may have committed. Frank, however, told Mark what happened and provided Mark with essential knowledge about how to obtain extra cash. Mark, relying on that information, increased his withdrawal significantly and also received

a double payment. But did Frank tell Mark what happened and provide him with vital information on how to obtain an extra payout with the *intent* to encourage Mark to commit a crime? If the prosecution can prove that Frank did have this purpose, then Frank could be convicted as an accomplice and would also be responsible for Mark's crime. In most jurisdictions merely providing useful information without intent to encourage another person's committing a crime does not suffice for accomplice responsibility. The MPC also requires *purpose*. This will be a close case. The same analysis applies to Frank and Mark's responsibility for Chris's crime. It may be easier for the prosecution to prove that they did act with the purpose of encouraging Chris to commit a crime because they sought him out and provided the information necessary to improperly obtain extra cash. What do you think the result should be?

5a. Bruno would argue that his aid to Lydia—leaving the window unlocked—was completely ineffective; consequently, he cannot be convicted of being an accomplice. This argument would probably be successful. The prosecutor may have a fall-back theory, however. By telling Lydia he would leave the window open, Bruno may have encouraged Lydia to commit the burglary and theft. Thus, these words by themselves might be considered legally sufficient assistance to convict Bruno of being an accomplice.

At common law doing something that did not help *P-1* in any way to commit the offense was an insufficient actus reus for accomplice liability. Under the MPC, however, Bruno has clearly "attempted" to render assistance; consequently, under §2.06(3)(a)(i) he can be convicted as a principal even though he did not provide any useful assistance. (This assumes that leaving the window open meets the MPC's definition of "substantial step" by "strongly corroborating" the actor's criminal purpose.) The MPC focuses more on the actor's attitude rather than on whether his help was useful.

Of course, the prosecutor may also be able to establish a conspiracy to commit burglary and theft if she can show that Bruno and Lydia had entered into an agreement to commit a crime and one of them took an overt act in furtherance of the conspiracy. If this argument proves successful, Bruno would be liable for the crimes of burglary and theft committed by Lydia in a jurisdiction that follows the *Pinkerton* rule.

5b. Bruno can be convicted of being an accomplice to Anthony's theft of the painting. This is a case of omission or failure to act when there is a legal duty to prevent another person from committing a crime. As a security guard Bruno had a civil legal duty by virtue of his employment contract to take reasonable steps within his power to prevent the theft of the picture. Instead, Bruno left the room with the purpose of making it easier for Anthony to commit the crime.

Note that Bruno is an accomplice even though Anthony did not realize that he was being assisted in committing the crime. There is no requirement that the principal know he is being assisted to commit the object offense, though this is generally the case.

6. This example is based loosely on the Littleton, Colorado high-school massacre. The tragedy really makes one think about what culpability should be required for accomplice liability.

Pat loaned his father's semi-automatic weapons and a large amount of ammunition to Eric and Ian. The prosecutor could probably prove Pat *knew* they intended to use them to kill fellow students at their high school. Eric and Ian had often told Pat they wanted to use his father's guns to kill certain students. Pat also knew something big was up because Eric and Ian had never let him swap for drugs; they always insisted on cold cash. Finally, Pat avoided the crime scene precisely because of what he expected would happen.

Nonetheless, without additional evidence, it would be difficult to prove that Pat loaned his father's automatic weapons with the *purpose* of assisting or encouraging their crimes. Pat would argue that his purpose was simply to obtain drugs and that he was indifferent as to what Eric and Ian did with the weapons and ammunition. Because Pat was able to obtain a large amount of drugs without paying for them—only by loaning these dangerous items—the prosecutor could argue that Pat had a "stake in the venture" and thus did act with purpose to assist Eric and Ian. The MPC and a number of jurisdictions would not convict Pat as an accomplice unless the prosecutor could prove Pat acted with such purpose.

Other jurisdictions, however, would convict Pat if he had had *knowledge* that the guns and ammunition he loaned his friends would be used to commit a *serious* crime. Criminal conviction and punishment of such "enablers" is necessary to deter them and others like them from providing such aid. A much stronger case can be made that Pat had such knowledge.

In some states Pat could be convicted of criminal facilitation because he knowingly provided significant aid, the weapons and ammunition, to someone he knew (or, in some states, had reason to know) intended to commit a serious crime. In this case Pat would be punished less severely than Eric and Ian.

7. Amanda provided vital information about how to hire a professional killer to interested consumers. Most jurisdictions and the MPC would require the prosecution to prove that Amanda acted with the *purpose* of assisting another person to commit a crime. Some courts would hold an actor guilty as an accomplice if she provided assistance to someone she *knows* intends to commit a *serious* crime. (See the *Fountain* case,

supra.) The prosecutor would point out that this information could only be used to assist someone in committing a serious crime; it had no lawful purpose. Moreover, the language in the advertisement was very clear about the ultimate criminal purpose for which Tammy would be hired. Amanda would counter that she did not know that Tammy, let alone Leslie, presently intended to commit a crime. Thus, she could not have acted with the necessary mens rea. What would you tell the prosecutor?

8a. Because Pedro has not committed any crime, there is no guilty principal. At common law Al could not be convicted as an accomplice. Under the MPC the result is the same; Al cannot be convicted as an accomplice because Pedro has not engaged in the conduct required to commit the object crime or an attempt to commit it.

8b. Al is guilty as an accomplice because he has provided psychological reinforcement to Pedro to commit murder and the principal committed that very crime. Because there is a guilty principal, Al would be convicted under both the common law and the MPC.

An interesting question here is whether Al might be guilty of a greater crime than the principal. Pedro might have a heat of passion or related defense (though unlikely); Al would not. If Pedro is convicted of manslaughter, can Al be convicted of premeditated murder? At common law the accomplice's liability is generally limited by that of the principal's unless the crime is murder. Thus, Al can be convicted of a more serious offense than Pedro. If a crime other than homicide were involved, such as assault, the general rule is that the accomplice cannot be convicted of a more serious crime than the principal.

Under the MPC and the law of some jurisdictions, the liability of the accomplice is measured by *his* culpability together with the conduct of the principal. Consequently, Al could be convicted of a more serious degree of homicide. This is true even for less serious crimes than homicide.

8c. This is a tricky one. Al only encouraged Pedro to kill Jose; he did not encourage him to kill Maria. Thus, Al did not intend to assist Pedro in the particular criminal action of killing his wife. The MPC and many jurisdictions would require that the accomplice act with the purpose or intent of encouraging the specific criminal conduct of the principal. Negligence toward other crimes committed by the principal is not a sufficient basis for accomplice liability. Thus, Al would not be guilty as an accomplice for Pedro's murder of Maria in these jurisdictions.

However, some jurisdictions are expanding accomplice liability to include crimes committed by the principal that were a "natural or probable consequence" of the offense the accomplice intended to aid or that should have been "reasonably foreseen." A prosecutor could argue that Al should have foreseen that a jealous husband might well kill his wife as well as her lover. (Unfortunately, this argument may reinforce the law's acceptance that male violence in intimate relationships is understandable and should be condoned or at least partially excused.) Or a prosecutor could argue that the accomplice has set in motion forces that might readily lead to this particular consequence. Convicting Al as an accomplice for the murder of Maria would be possible in these jurisdictions.

8d. The only difference here is that Al actually provided physical assistance as well as psychological reinforcement. The analysis of Al's criminal responsibility here is the same as in Explanations 8b and 8c above. Evidence of the actus reus required for assistance is stronger.

8e. By telephoning Pedro and telling him not to kill Jose, Al has clearly withdrawn the psychological encouragement to commit murder he had given Pedro earlier in the day. Thus, his telephone call to Pedro is an effective withdrawal of aid previously furnished. However, Al also gave Pedro a loaded gun to use in killing Jose. Al has not rendered *that* aid ineffective. Thus, under common law Al would still be liable as an accomplice.

The MPC is also very demanding before withdrawal will be legally effective. Al has not completely removed the effectiveness of his aid (providing the loaded gun). Al should have gone to Pedro's home and taken back the gun. Nor did Al call the police. A jury might conclude that Al has made a "proper effort" to prevent the commission of the crime, but more likely Al will be convicted because he did not take sufficient steps to prevent the commission of the crime.

8f. Al is clearly an accomplice after the fact at common law because he has intentionally disposed of a weapon that he knows has been used in a homicide, making it difficult, if not impossible, for the police to gather essential evidence for investigation and prosecution.

Under the MPC and many modern statutes, Al would be guilty of criminal facilitation or rendering criminal assistance. The degree of punishment often depends on the severity of the crime committed by the principal. The liability of the person rendering aid after the crime has been committed usually is not affected by the subsequent acquittal of the principal. The essence of this crime is obstructing justice by aiding flight, preventing apprehension, or destroying or concealing evidence.

8g. This is an extremely difficult problem (even for us, if that is any consolation). Pedro only intended to scare Jose and Maria; he did not intend to kill them. Al did not intend to help Pedro accomplish that goal. Instead, Al decided to kill Jose and Maria. Thus, Al is a principal in a homicide charge. Granted that Pedro might be liable as a principal under a separate felony murder theory, is he guilty as an accomplice to Al's murder? Probably not because Pedro did not act with the purpose to assist Al commit a homicide. Indeed, Pedro did not know that Al intended to commit any crime.

9. Thug is surely guilty of homicide, either "serious bodily injury" murder or manslaughter in the first or second degree. But is Sharkie also guilty as an accomplice? Sharkie did not want Sam killed because Sam's death means Sharkie will *not* get his money back. Thus, Sharkie did not intend that Thug engage in the criminal action that caused Sam's death. Because Sharkie did not have this necessary mens rea, many jurisdictions, including those that follow the MPC, would not convict Sharkie as an accomplice to Thug's crime of manslaughter.

    Some courts, however, are now holding the accomplice responsible for crimes committed by the principal if *P*'s crime was reasonably foreseeable or if *A* has set in motion a chain of events and *P*'s crime was a "natural and probable result" of this chain. In these jurisdictions Sharkie might be convicted as an accomplice to Thug's crime of manslaughter.

10. The criminal law in this jurisdiction prohibits exotic dancers from making physical contact with patrons in exchange for money. It does not punish the customer who pays for the dance. By doing a lap dance in exchange for money, Candy has clearly violated the law.

    Can the prosecutor convict Tiny as an accomplice? After all, he initiated Candy's crime and gave very strong encouragement to her by paying her $100. Nonetheless, the charge should be dismissed. The substantive law here punishes only the conduct of one party even though the crime necessarily requires participation by two parties. A court will conclude that the legislature, in not punishing the conduct of one party essential to the commission of the crime, did not intend to impose criminal responsibility on that party. To permit a prosecutor to use accomplice liability to punish that very same conduct will subvert legislative intent.

15

Defenses:
An Initial Survey

Overview

Caution. You are about to enter difficult waters. Much of the material in this chapter — and in the subsequent two chapters as well — concerns highly controversial, very unsettled questions in the criminal law. We will do our best to guide you through this maze, but you must always keep in mind that the issues addressed here are new to the law and are in constant flux.d

The materials concern the place of "defenses" in the criminal law. One might think that, after several hundred years, the criminal law might have settled these issues, but that is not the case. First, the theory of criminal liability has been shifting in the past two hundred years; learning and understanding have altered. Consequently, the question of which claims are "defenses" has changed. This area is under rapid challenge today as new "scientific" claims about responsibility (and the lack of responsibility) are being heard frequently. Second, the notion that defenses can be categorized as either excuse or justification, which is the primary topic in Chapter 15, is new to Anglo-Saxon jurisprudence. Although at one time the common law recognized the distinction in the area of self-defense, there never was a full-blown theory to support it. Today, commentators are beginning to suggest the adoption of such a distinction, which has many practical, as well as theoretical, implications, particularly for the question of burden of proof. It was only in 1970 that the Supreme Court decided *In re Winship*, 397 U.S. 358, which held that the prosecution had the burden of proof on "all facts necessary to constitute the crime." But the distinction between the "burden of production" and the "burden of proof," upon which *Winship* rests, was not fully understood by common law courts — particularly common law courts dealing with criminal cases — until very recently. They tended to use the terms interchangeably. See Fletcher, Two Types of Legal Rules: A Comparative Study of Burden of Persuasion Practices in Criminal Cases, 77 Yale L.J. 886 (1968). Finally, the role of presumptions and the question of their constitutionality have only recently come under examination by the United States Supreme Court.

In short, the law is in flux here. There are some guideposts that will help you — and us — in this exploration, but don't be surprised if you feel very uncertain after this is all over. Many of us feel the same way. (On the other hand, there is more adventure and thrill of discovery where some things are unknown.) You may reasonably ask why these questions haven't been settled decades, or at least weeks, ago. The answer may be historical — courts and lawyers simply hadn't thought about these questions in the terms we now employ. Certainly, for example, the *constitutional* analysis would not have been possible fifty, much less two hundred, years ago.

With that said, let us provide at least a small road map. Chapter 15 investigates what we *mean* when we say that D has a "defense." Does a defense relate to an element of the crime? And, if so, how? On what issues, if not "defenses," may the state require the defendant to carry the burden of proof? And by what procedural mechanisms or labels may it do that? Chapters 16 and 17 investigate specific kinds of defensive claims. Chapter 16 looks at many claims that may be classified as "justifications," while Chapter 17 considers claims of "excuse." Throughout those two chapters, however, we will refer back to the issues raised in Chapter 15. They are all of the same cloth.

Affirmative Defenses and Element Negations

Not everything a defendant says in an adversarial setting is a "defense." If a defendant in a tort case denies an allegation of negligence by saying that the light was green when he went through it, he is not raising a "defense" but challenging the very heart of the plaintiff's case. On the other hand, there are "true" defenses in civil law. Demonstrating that the case was not brought within the time allowed by the statute of limitations, for example, is an *affirmative defense* upon which the defendant carries the burden. Whether there are similar affirmative defenses in the criminal law upon which the defendant may be required to carry the burden of proof is a matter of vigorous debate.[1]

---

1. G. Fletcher, Rethinking Criminal Law (1978). This is not a problem in England. In *D.P.P. v. Woolmington,* [1935] A.C. 481, the House of Lords declared that the prosecution holds the burden of proof in all aspects of the case. But see Tanovich,

In criminal cases, some claims that we initially think of as defenses actually go to the heart of the prosecution's case. Just as in the color-of-the-light issue above, a criminal defendant who claims that he was in Cleveland when the killing occurred in Poughkeepsie is *not* raising a defense. He is challenging a critical aspect of the prosecutor's case—that it was *D* who was present at the crime. We call this kind of claim a *failure of proof* or an *element negation* defense because it argues that the prosecution has failed to prove even its prima facie case. Robinson, Criminal Law Defenses: A Systematic Analysis, 82 Colum. L. Rev. 190 (1982).

Are all defenses "element negations"? Surely in the early common law that argument could be made. Virtually all defenses concerned whether the defendant should be punished as an "immoral actor" (traditional mens rea) and, if so, how severely. In that sense, all defenses were element negations.

Most modern criminal law analysts, however, would reject that approach. They would argue that *Winship* has held that the prosecution must prove beyond a doubt *only* "every fact necessary to constitute the crime." This language seems equal to the term "element" as used in both the common law and the Model Penal Code (see Chapter 4). These analysts would then argue that some affirmative defenses, at least, do not negate such elements or facts.

The accuracy of this statement requires a careful analysis of what "elements" are and when they are negated. It also requires an exploration of the "offense-defense" distinction and interpretation of some recent, and controversial, decisions of the United States Supreme Court. Let us begin. But remember our warning—this is very difficult going.

Legislative Clarity and the Offense-Defense Distinction

Let's begin with the "easy" case. Consider the following two statutes:

1. "Unauthorized possession of A is a crime."
2. "Possession of A, unless authorized, is a crime."

Obviously, authorization (or its absence) is relevant. In which of these statutes, however, must the *state* prove that the defendant "lacked" authority? In which must the *defendant* establish that he acted "with" authority? Does either statute clearly tell us?

Courts have relied on maxims of statutory construction to resolve these issues. But as we have already seen in other contexts, none of these maxims solve the conundrum. Professor Robinson has argued that "whether a defense is a failure of proof defense or an offense modification may depend on

---

The Unravelling of the Golden Thread: The Supreme Court's Compromise of the Presumption of Innocence, [1993] Crim. L.Q. 194.

the form in which it is drafted." Robinson, supra, at 203. But Professor Glanville Williams has responded that this is a purely verbal and formal distinction: "The definitional elements are those that we choose to pick out from all the elements expressed in the rules relating to the offense."[2]

Williams' point is essentially that legislatures have an obligation to be clear (see the discussion of the legality principle in Chapter 1) and the legislature *could* have made the statute clearer on this point. *If* they wished the defendant to carry the burden of demonstrating authorization, the statute could have been written as follows:

3. "Possession of A is a crime. If the defendant shows authorization for the possession, there is no criminal liability."

There will *always* be a way in which the legislature could have phrased a statute so as to make clear on whom it intended to place the burden of proving an issue. An ambiguous statute should be construed to narrow the reach of the criminal law, thus requiring legislatures to reenact the statute in a clearer way (see the discussion of the rule of lenity in Chapter 1). Therefore, a salutary rule of interpreting criminal statutes might be "Unless the legislation *expressly* uses the form, 'X is a defense that must be proved by the defendant,' all claims relevant to guilt must be proved by the prosecution."

The Common Law and Affirmative Defenses

The statutory interpretation case described above, involving a statute that establishes both a rule and an exception to the rule somewhere in the same text, is known as the *exception problem*. But it only illustrates the larger question: When are claims true "defenses" such that the defendant may be required to carry the risk of nonpersuasion? Healy, Proof and Policy: No Golden Threads, [1987] Crim. L. Rev. 355; Williams, The Logic of "Exceptions," 47 Cambridge L.J. 261 (1988).

The common law recognized certain specified claims, which it called "affirmative defenses," by which the defendant could avoid criminal liability. Among these were self-defense, necessity, duress, insanity, infancy, and others. The term "defense" and the subsequent placement of the burden of proof, however, have caused significant confusion among American courts. There is substantial disagreement as to the *reason* why defensive claims are even relevant to the criminal law. Thus, for example: Does a claim that the defendant was duressed challenge the mens rea (or actus reus) of the crime?

---

2. Williams, Offenses and Defenses, 2 Legal Stud. 233 (1982); Williams, The Logic of "Exceptions," 47 Cambridge L.J. 261 (1988).

Or is such a claim irrelevant to either of these two elements? Some would argue that no "insane" person can have mens rea, even if he can "intend" his acts *and* those acts' consequences. Others would argue that many, if not all, insane persons intend an act and therefore *are* guilty of crime, *even if* they are insane.

Both court opinions and treatise writers have been notoriously opaque about the relationship between all these defensive claims and mens rea. It does seem clear that at least at one time mens rea entailed moral as well as legal guilt (see Chapter 4). This suggests that each of these claims *did* then directly challenge the prosecution's case. If that ever was the law, the argument is much harder to make now since statutes have adopted mental state words (statutory mens rea) that do not, on their face, entail an additional moral culpability (traditional mens rea).

Supreme Court Confusion

The Supreme Court has confronted this question several times in the past twenty-five years and has given somewhat contradictory answers. In *Mullaney v. Wilbur,* 421 U.S. 684 (1975), the defendant was charged with killing a victim who made a sexual advance toward him. The defendant, while admitting the killing, argued that it was done "in the heat of passion" and thereby was not murder but manslaughter (see Chapter 8). The trial court instructed the jury that, to obtain a verdict of manslaughter, the defendant had the burden of proving that the killing was in the heat of passion. However, the court also instructed the jury that to prove murder, the state had the burden of proving malice, and that under Maine law heat of passion negated malice. The defendant appealed his murder conviction, arguing that, since heat of passion was the "negation" of a "fact necessary to constitute murder" (malice aforethought), the state was in essence requiring the defendant to disprove that element. The defendant argued that this violated *Winship.* The Maine Supreme Judicial Court did not address the defendant's claim directly but instead held that under Maine law, there was only one general crime of "felonious homicide," which did not require a showing of malice aforethought. Instead, said the state court, the presence of malice aforethought or of heat of passion was used only in deciding which "kind" of felonious homicide was involved. Thus, heat of passion did not negate an element of the crime of felonious homicide, and *Winship* was not involved.

The United States Supreme Court reversed the conviction[3] and ap-

---

3. The Court affirmed the granting of a writ of habeas corpus, which had been issued by a federal district court on the grounds that the conviction violated *Winship.* The procedural steps of *Mullaney,* while perhaps critical to a "realistic" understanding of the opinion, will not be discussed here.

peared to expand on *Winship*. The Court seemed to hold that any fact that could affect either the offense for which the defendant was convicted *or* the sentence he might receive would fall within *Winship*'s requirements. The Court explained that this reading of *Winship* was necessary lest state legislatures and courts "rewrite" crimes to include only "minimal" elements, making defendants "disprove" everything else that might be relevant.

Two years later, however, the Court appeared to retreat significantly from *Mullaney*. The defendant in *Patterson v. New York*, 432 U.S. 197 (1977), like the defendant in *Mullaney*, was charged with a homicide which he argued was committed in the "heat of passion." New York's statute on murder, however, required proof of only three facts: (1) a human death (2) caused by (3) an intentional act of the defendant. New York's statute did not speak in terms of "heat of passion" or "malice aforethought." It *did* speak of "extreme emotional or mental disturbance" (EED), a phrase taken directly from the Model Penal Code (see Chapter 8). The statute explicitly put on the defendant the burden of proving EED to reduce the charge from murder to manslaughter.

The defendant's argument that the statute was invalid under *Mullaney* seemed impregnable. The state had explicitly placed the burden on him to show a factor that would reduce his punishment and "lower" the crime of which he would be convicted. Moreover, EED seemed like a mere rephrasing of "heat of passion." The Court, however, found that, in contrast to the Maine court's interpretation of that state's felonious homicide crime, New York did *not* say that extreme emotional or mental disturbance "negated" intent, the "mens rea" element of murder under New York law. Thus, said the Court, *Winship* was not violated.

It is difficult at first (or even second) blush to reconcile these two cases. The *effect* of EED in New York, like heat of passion in Maine, was to convict the defendant of a lesser crime and to reduce the punishment involved. But a closer reading of *Patterson* suggests that two things were critical to the decision. First, the New York legislature had explicitly stated that EED did *not* negate the mens rea requirements for murder, in contrast to the statement of the trial court in *Mullaney* that in Maine heat of passion negated mens rea. The power to decide what elements were "negated" by what conditions was, within broad constitutional limits, said the Court, to be determined by the states and not by the United States Supreme Court. In this light, *Mullaney* had *not* held that heat of passion negated malice aforethought, but only that *if* Maine said it did so, then Maine's prosecutors had to disprove heat of passion.

Second, the Court was substantially impressed by the good faith of the New York legislature. It noted that EED was not, like "heat of passion," a narrow, objectivized test that allowed only a few defendants to reduce their liability to manslaughter (see Chapter 8). It was a much broader, more subjective, approach to liability. The Court appeared to wish to encourage this kind of broadening of the subjective approach to criminal liability. It expressed concern that putting the burden on the prosecution to disprove broad "defenses" would chill such reforms. Its specific citations to the Model Penal Code, both as the source of New York's EED language and in general, support this view.

The next relevant decision is *McMillan v. Pennsylvania,* 477 U.S. 79 (1986). The defendants[4] in *McMillan* were convicted of a variety of different crimes, each of which carried a potential sentence of 0-20 years. Before trial, the prosecution gave notice that, at sentencing, it intended to prove that, in addition to committing the crime, the defendant had "visibly possessed a firearm." Under the applicable statute, such a finding required the imposition of a minimum term of five years. The trial court refused to consider such evidence. The trial court held that since this factor increased the minimum sentence, it was necessary, after *Mullaney,* for the prosecutor to prove it beyond a reasonable doubt and at trial, rather than by a preponderance at sentencing. It therefore had held that the statute allowing proof by a preponderance at sentencing was unconstitutional. Essentially, this meant that "visible firearm" was an element of the crime.

The United States Supreme Court disagreed, pointing out that the minimum sentence required (five years) was well within the range to which the judge could have sentenced the defendant even without a firearm. There was therefore no proof that the judge would have relied on the visible firearm to impose a five-year sentence.[5] Moreover, said the Court, the legislative history of the statute indicated that the Pennsylvania legislature had not sought to evade *Winship* by "redefining" the crimes involved. Thus, it was apparent that the legislature was not seeking to prejudice the defendant.

Montana v. Egelhoff, 518 U.S. 37 (1996) appeared to confirm *McMillan* and *Patterson*'s deference to the states. There, the Court held that a statute declaring intoxication to be irrelevant to mens rea was constitutional. (See Chapter 17 for a discussion of the intoxication doctrine.) Although not dealing directly with the burden of proof issue, the Court's analysis suggests that (1) common law history and (2) current legislative views will be important factors in deciding whether a state can constitutionally abolish a defense (as in *Egelhoff*) or put the burden of proof on the defendant. Thus, if a statute has previously required the prosecutor to prove elements A, B, and C to convict, but now is rewritten to require only proof of A and B, with "non-C" as a defense, the presumption will be that the legislature has been attempting to manipulate earlier law. If, however, the common law allowed

---

4. There were several unrelated cases joined in *McMillan*. For purposes of simplification, we will treat the case as though it involved only one defendant.

5. One of the trial judges, however, had indicated that, except for the statutorily mandated term of five years minimum, he would have sentenced the defendant to a two-year maximum sentence.

"non-C" only as a defense, or if many state legislatures have so decided, *Egelhoff* suggests that this is constitutional.

In June 2000, shortly before this edition went to press, the United States Supreme Court decided *Apprendi v. New Jersey,* —U.S. — (2000), holding that a defendant whose maximum sentence may be increased on the basis of a statutory fact (e.g., motive for carrying a weapon) has a Sixth Amendment right to have the jury decide that question, and to require the prosecution to convince them beyond a reasonable doubt of its existence. On its face, *Apprendi* does not affect affirmative defenses at all, since juries already decide these questions. But at least some states require defendants to prove such defenses. Obviously, since a defendant who is acquitted (say on the grounds of necessity) will not be sentenced at all, his "maximum sentence" will be increased if he does not prove necessity. To require him to prove necessity thus seems to conflict with *Apprendi.* Moreover, in its rather short opinion, the Court cited *Mullaney* approvingly, and directly disapproved of *McMillan,* treating them as dealing with the same issue. This suggests that we may now be where we seemed to be after *Mullaney*— that the Constitution requires the state to disprove all "affirmative defenses" once properly raised. On the other hand, the *Apprendi* Court did not cite, much less discuss, *Egelhoff,* which would allow the state to eliminate totally from the definition of a crime an "affirmative defense"—which would clearly have the effect of increasing the potential maximum sentence of some defendants. Stay tuned—perhaps by the next edition (but almost certainly not before your exam in criminal law—sorry) the Court will have clarified this series of cases.

The limits to which a legislature might constitutionally reduce the "elements" of a crime, and put the burden of "reducing" the level of punishment upon the defendant by showing other "facts," are still not clear. Justice Powell, who wrote the majority opinion in *Mullaney,* gave a hypothetical in his dissent in *Patterson.* Could a legislature, he asked, define and punish as murder any physical contact with a person who thereupon died, and then put upon the defendant the burden of showing that he acted without mens rea? Powell, and probably most of us, would say no. But upon what basis? Some writers have suggested that the answer lies in the notion of proportionality, that the state may not disproportionately punish what it defines as a crime. Allen, The Restoration of *In re Winship:* A Comment on Burdens of Persuasion in Criminal Cases After *Patterson v. New York,* 76 Mich. L. Rev. 30 (1977). Thus, even if having had contact with a person who thereafter dies might be defined as "a" crime, it would be disproportionate to define (or punish) it as murder. This gives some guidance, but not much; the Supreme Court's decisions on proportionality with regard to penalties have been as confusing and conflicting as its opinions in the area of "elements" itself. *Solem v. Helm,* 463 U.S. 277 (1984); *Harmelin v. Michigan,* 501 U.S. 957 (1991).

Another possible indicator seems to be history. Has the legislature shifted to the defendant a fact upon which, historically, the state has carried the burden? The difficulty with *this* approach is (a) the historical record on many of these questions is not clear, since common law courts often used the terms "burden of proof" and "burden of persuasion" interchangeably; (b) the arguments concerning the relation of a defense to mens rea in the nineteenth century, when mens rea included not only "statutory" but "traditional" mens rea as well (see Chapter 4), may be different than the arguments now, when mens rea is often initially limited to "statutory" mens rea.

The Model Penal Code

With a few, very clearly enunciated, exceptions, the Code puts on the prosecution the burden of proving *any* element and disproving any "defense." However, the Code's approach is indirect. Section 1.12(2)(a) provides that the prosecutor need not disprove an affirmative defense "unless there is evidence supporting such defense." When there *is* such evidence, the prosecution must bear the burden. Section 1.13(9)(c) of the Code also provides that an element includes any factors or explanations that "negatives an excuse or justification" for the defendant's act. Neither "excuse" nor "justification," however, is defined in the Code. The prosecution will carry the burden on all issues, except those explicitly left to the defendant. See, e.g., MPC §2.13 (entrapment); MPC §2.04(3)(b) (reasonable reliance on official advice).

Presumptions

In addition to general affirmative defenses, another procedural device by which the state may attempt to shift the burden of proof to the defendant is to establish a *presumption*. Civil law employs many different kinds of presumptions. Some are "irrebuttable"—no matter what proof the opposing party wishes to present, the law will "presume" the fact against her. For example, the common law presumed that a child born to a married woman was the child of the husband. No contrary facts, such as that the husband was infertile or that he had been absent for a year, were admissible to rebut the presumption. This was a policy decision. The courts did not wish to inquire into the private lives of married couples, nor did they wish to label children as "illegitimate" unless they could not avoid it.

Other presumptions are established for other reasons. Some are based on common sense and experience. The law presumes that a letter dropped in a government mail box was delivered. In the vast majority of cases, when a letter is sent, it actually arrives (this rule was created during the days of the Pony Express when it was usually true; some skeptics would question its factual accuracy today). By applying this "presumption," we move the litigation forward. Since, in our common experience, most letters are delivered, we require the defendant to show that our common experience should not be applied to the specific facts of this specific case. It would be needlessly time-consuming to require the plaintiff to show that the letter was delivered.

Finally, some presumptions, such as res ipsa loquitur, seem to be devices by which we "smoke out" the opposing party (usually the defendant) to tell us what he knows about the event. Res ipsa was first applied when there was little or no discovery, and a defendant, merely by stonewalling, could effectively prevent the plaintiff from proving his case. *Byrne v. Boadle,* 159 Eng. Rep. 299 (1863).

We usually speak of this process as *presuming* fact B (delivery of the letter) from the *basic* (or *predicate*) fact A (posting of the letter), and require that there be *some* connection between facts A and B. This may be graphically illustrated as follows:

$$(Predicate) \ A \rightarrow B \ (Presumed)$$

There is considerable uncertainty, even in civil cases, as to the procedural importance of presumptions. While all agree that most presumptions are rebuttable, the question of who has to rebut, and to what degree, is contested. Some courts and writers argue that a presumption, at least one based on common experience, should always shift the burden of disproof to the defendant. Morgan, Basic Problems of Evidence (1963). Others argue that most presumptions are simply "smoking out" devices and should disappear entirely if the defendant comes forward with as much evidence as he has. Thayer, A Preliminary Treatise on Evidence at the Common Law (1898).

These rules may be more easily understood as applied. If you see puddles in the street after you've been in a building for hours, you are likely to conclude that it has rained, although you didn't see it rain. Why? Because "in the vast majority of cases" puddles in the streets come from rain. A statutory declaration that "puddles on the street presumes rain" is probably commonsensical: proof of the predicate fact A (puddles) leads to the conclusion that it has rained (B). Someone else may later tell you that the water was from some other source (e.g., a street cleaner, an overturned water truck), but you *start* from the premise, based on common experience, that *if* there are puddles, it is highly *likely* that it rained. Indeed, in the absence of other suggestions, you are likely to conclude beyond a reasonable doubt that it rained.

These same considerations may apply to criminal cases. Suppose, for example, that statutes prohibit the possession of certain drugs *only* if they have been imported into the United States. An instruction to the jury that, if the prosecution proves the drug to be heroin, it can be presumed that it was imported unless the defendant brings on some evidence to the contrary is probably constitutional because virtually no heroin is produced in the United States. On the other hand, that same instruction applied to marijuana is probably invalid because much marijuana (even if not over 50 percent) is homegrown. The United States Supreme Court so held in *Leary v. United States*, 395 U.S. 6 (1969).

May the criminal law also employ presumptions as to "elements" of the offense? Clearly, establishing a "conclusive" presumption against the defendant would conflict with the requirement that the prosecution carry the burden on every element. *In re Winship*, 397 U.S. 358 (1970) (see Chapter 1). But what about lesser, "rebuttable" presumptions? Could a presumption shift to the defendant the burden of disproving an element? And what of those presumptions that try to "smoke out" the defendant, or don't require but merely "allow" the jury to reach conclusions?

In earlier centuries, the criminal law employed many such presumptions. Thus, a defendant was "presumed" sane. A person who used a deadly weapon in killing another was "presumed" to have "malice aforethought" (or, in a variation of this presumption, to "intend" the death). Even more broadly, defendants were said to be "presumed" to "intend the natural and probable consequences of their acts." Some of these presumptions were established not only because, factually, they might be commonsensical, but also because defendants were not only not required to testify but were precluded from doing so. Thus, mens rea "had to be" presumed from facts proved by the prosecution.

Constitutional Aspects of Presumptions

Modern analysis suggests the need for reevaluation of the law relating to presumptions. Since most people are "sane" within the meaning of the criminal law, that presumption may still be valid (although there may be other objections to placing the burden of "disproof" on the defendant). (See Chapter 17.) But other presumptions may be suspect.

Careful scrutiny suggests ambiguities in the wording of some other presumptions that compel us to reject them. One such ambiguity is in the term "act." What is the "natural and probable consequence" of firing a gun at a person? Statistically, roughly 10 percent of all persons injured by firearms die. Therefore, to presume that a defendant using a firearm intended the "natural and probable consequence" of death is at least factually questionable, if "probable" means anything more than 10 percent likelihood. *Certainly* our own intuition tells us that hunters, for example, do not "intend" the death of a person when they shoot in a direction in which a person happens to appear, or that persons who kill another while mishandling firearms do not "intend" that death. On the other hand, if a defendant holds a .357 Magnum to the head of a victim and pulls the trigger six times, a "presumption" that she intended death to occur is probably both accurate (and unnecessary).

In *Allen v. Ulster County Court*, 442 U.S. 140 (1979), and *Sandstrom v. Montana*, 442 U.S. 510 (1979), the Supreme Court divided such devices into "mandatory" presumptions and "permissive" inferences. Presumptions that actually shift the burden of proof on such elements — or could be misconstrued by the jury as doing so — are unconstitutional. Devices that only shift the burden of going forward on an element, however, are constitutional, *if* there was a connection between A (the predicate fact) and B (the presumed fact).

The *degree* of the relation between A and B that would be necessary to allow the presumption to survive a constitutionality challenge would depend on the exact instructions given by the judge to the jury. If the judge instructed the jurors that, if they found A, the defendant had the burden of going forward on B, the connection between A and B would have to be *beyond a reasonable doubt (mandatory presumption)*. If, however, the judge did not instruct the jury on this matter but simply allowed the prosecutor to get the case to the jury, or was *very* clear that the inference was permissive, not requiring rebuttal by the defendant, the "real life" connection would have to be merely *more likely than not (permissive inference)*.

In other words, the validity of any presumption depends on the specificity with which the underlying items are defined. The Supreme Court's opinion in *Allen* reflects this insight. Four defendants, including a young minor in the passenger seat of a borrowed car, were stopped on the New York State Thruway by a state trooper, who testified that he saw guns protruding from the minor's purse. Upholding the conviction of the other three defendants for possession of these guns, the Court allowed the use of a statutory "presumption" that all persons in a car are in possession of a firearm found therein. But it did so only after noting that the instruction to the jurors had emphasized that they should consider *all* the facts, including the age of the minor, the fact that the defendants had all driven several hundred miles, and that the trooper had seen some furtive movements just before he approached the car. In such circumstances, said the court, the law could reasonably allow the jury to find that the other three defendants knew of the guns and possessed them. Moreover, the instruction stressed that the jurors need not rely on any such presumption, and that they were the sole deciders of fact.[6]

---

6. Justice Powell dissented in *Allen*. While agreeing with the majority that *if* the jury had found that the guns were where the trooper said they were, the presumption would be valid, he argued that the jury might have relied on the presumption ("anywhere in the car") and not made specific findings as to where the guns actually were. Thus, he argued, the majority's opinion was flawed by its assumption that the jury had not relied on the presumption. But Powell's fear, while obviously a serious concern, is undercut by the verdict in *Allen* itself, since the jury acquitted the defendants of possessing both firearms and drugs that were in the trunk of the car. Had the jury relied solely on the presumption (which did not differentiate among areas of the car), it would have convicted on all counts.

In *Sandstrom,* the Court considered one other problem relating to jury instructions: Although the jury instruction in that case was consistent with the black letter of *Allen,*[7] the Court concluded that it could have been misunderstood by the jury to impose on the defendant a burden to "disprove" the presumption. This reemphasized the point of *Allen* that jury instructions must be very clear and should not tread close to the line of suggesting a shifting of the persuasion burden.

This approach of looking at the jury instructions makes eminent sense: Even if a *statutory* presumption is stated in absolute terms (proof of A means that the jury *must* find B), if the trial judge refuses to instruct in such terms, the jury's deliberations are not affected because the jury will never hear nor see the statute. Similarly, if the statutory presumption is exceedingly permissive ("if the jury finds A, it may, but need not under any circumstances, conclude B"), a judicial instruction that "if you find A, you *must* find B unless defendant convinces you beyond a reasonable doubt of non-B" would run afoul of *Winship.*

The thrust of these cases is that presumptions are on weak ground as we enter the twenty-first century, and that they are likely to be valid only if (1) the link between A and B is very strong and (2) the judge's instructions so weaken the "mandatory" nature of the "presumption" and make it so fact-specific to the case at hand that it is no longer an abstract proposition.

The Model Penal Code

The Code does not recognize mandatory presumptions, preferring instead that the legislature explicitly place the burden of production or persuasion on the defendant. (As already noted, the Code itself establishes only a small handful of such claims.) On the other hand, §1.12(b) allows the court to instruct the jury that it may (not must) use a permissive inference on its way to finding the presumed fact.

Excuse and Justification:
The Debate and Confusion

The Distinction Drawn

Another possible way to discuss claims such as insanity or duress, is to distinguish between excuses or justifications. For example, Schmidlap has just

---

7. A cynic might suggest that the Court took this approach in *Sandstrom* because the trial court, confronted by a defense attorney who cited *Mullaney,* explicitly told him to "tell that to the Supreme Court" and instructed the jury in a way clearly contrary to *Winship.* The Montana Supreme Court, in an effort to save the instruction, interpreted it as a permissive inference.

purposely parked next to a fire hydrant. When asked why he did so, he replies either:

1. "I had to. I was taking my injured baby to the hospital to save his life."
2. "I had to. The Martians told me to do it."

In the first response, Schmidlap is said to be *justifying* his action. He is claiming that, although the act appears illegal, he violated the law in order to achieve a greater good — saving the life of his child. His claim is that his act is *not* wrongful; he argues that we should implicitly recognize that some violations of statutes may be not wrongful if a greater good is served. His decision to violate the law may be seen as praiseworthy.

In the second response, Schmidlap is obviously irrational. We recognize that he should never have done what he did (it was wrong), but because of some personal disability (in this case what the law calls "insanity") he claims that he should not be punished for what is otherwise a wrongful act. His claim is not one of justification but of *excuse*. It is often said that justification focuses on the *act*, whereas excuse focuses on the *actor*.

In some cases, it is clear that the defendant is claiming only justification. Thus, if Martha, the state executioner, cold-bloodedly and premeditatedly injects George with a lethal dose of poison, her killing is not merely excused but praiseworthy. The state wanted, indeed ordered, her to carry out the killing. Killings in war are similarly said to be justified.

The Distinction Questioned

Some courts and writers argue that many, indeed most, acts sought to be excused or justified are sufficiently morally problematic as to not be "clearly" wrongful or not. Consider, for example, the following hypothetical:[8] Gary sees Ingrid, a two-year old, pointing a gun (which Gary knows to possess a hair trigger) directly at the temple of Henrietta. Gary concludes that the *only* way to save Henrietta's life is to shoot Ingrid. If he indeed kills Ingrid, it is difficult to say that Gary's act was morally praiseworthy and hence justified. On the other hand, his act was not "wrong," and he should not be blamed for acting under the circumstances. To "merely" excuse Gary suggests that he did something wrong, for which he would usually be blamed, if not punished. At best it was a tragic choice, which we should tolerate.

Critics of the distinction also argue that, if academics cannot resolve difficult cases, juries may also be unable to do so. There would be no benefit in asking them to decide whether, for example, Gary's shooting was justified or excused, as long as all agreed that he should not be punished. To the

---

8. Dressler, New Thoughts About the Concept of Justification in the Criminal Law: A Critique of Fletcher's Thinking and Rethinking, 32 UCLA L. Rev. 61, 84-85 (1984).

argument that verdicts should reflect jurors' resolution of this issue, critics ask what happens if the jury splits 8-4 on which of these explanations is the "better" one?[9]

We shall more fully explore the difficulties of determining whether a claim is a justification or excuse as we explore each individually. However, it should be noted that arguments exist that, except for insanity, which clearly only raises an excuse, all the major defenses — self-defense, necessity, duress — can sound in either justification or excuse, depending on the precise facts of the case.

Procedural Implications of the Distinctions

These debates may appear to be "academic" in the pejorative sense: the musings of tweed-coated law professors with nothing better to do after having pummeled and confused first-year law students. Yet, the allocation of the burden of proof *could* depend on whether a claim goes to justification or excuse. Moreover, since justified acts are "right," they cannot be resisted by others; excused acts, however, are wrong and can be resisted. Similarly, one may assist a justified actor but not an excused one.[10]

The Burden of Proof Problem

No matter how narrowly one reads *In re Winship*,[11] due process requires the state to show that a crime has been committed. A claim of justification essentially denies that a crime has been committed. Under this analysis, the prosecution must *disprove* any justificatory claim. On the other hand, excuses appear to acknowledge that a crime has been committed but argue that the defendant should not be punished because of something unique to her. Since the excuse does *not* deny the crime, it is unclear whether *Winship* would require the prosecution to disprove the excuse as well.

For example, the United States Supreme Court has held that the state may put on the defendant the burden of proving he killed in self-defense. *Martin v. Ohio*, 480 U.S. 228 (1987). The Court's opinion, however, did not consider whether self-defense is a justification or an excuse, a difference

---

9. Some writers have argued that the practical problems are worth confronting because in the absence of a jury verdict explicitly concluding that an acquitted defendant was "only" excused, nonjurors may conclude that the jury found her to be justified. Still, these writers would have to educate not only the nonjurors but many academics as well.

10. This, at least, is the claim. But if an actor mistakenly believes the circumstances to be such that his act is justified, he *may* be able to claim an excuse. See below.

11. Discussed, supra, Chapter 1.

that might undermine the decision. The Court's failure to distinguish between excused and justified self-defense is even more striking because the common law drew precisely such a distinction. See Chapter 16.

The Abolition Problem

The issues go even deeper: A claim that does not go to whether a crime has been committed could simply be ignored by the state altogether. Thus, as discussed in Chapter 17, all "excuses" could theoretically be abolished. Indeed, three state legislatures recently have attempted to "abolish" the "special defense" of insanity. If insanity is an excuse, this legislation would appear to be constitutional. Moreover, *Egelhoff* (supra, pages 367-368) supports this view as well.

The Assistance and Resistance Problem

It seems self-evident that George (a condemned criminal) could not kill Martha (the executioner) and claim self-defense. The doctrinal explanation is that Martha's act was *justified* and hence cannot be resisted. Nor can Alexander help George, since George's act was unjustified. But Amelia *can* help Martha resist George's escape attempt because her act was justified.

On the other hand, Schmidlap's insanity defense does not make his act "right"; it merely establishes a reason for not punishing him. If Hermione assisted him in parking, and assuming she is not similarly obeying Martian instructions, she has no insanity claim. She cannot claim an excuse either directly or derivatively. Similarly, if Herman tried to throw Schmidlap out of the space and injured him, his resistance is acceptable because Schmidlap's act was not justified.

Unknowing Justification: "The *Dadson* Problem"

A conundrum surrounding justification is whether the actor who is objectively justified must know that he is justified in order to successfully claim justification. The issue arose in a real case, *R. v. Dadson*, [1850] 4 Cox C.C. 358. Defendant, seeing *V* fleeing from a house with a bundle in his hand, shot *V*. Under the common law this was a crime because deadly force could not be used to prevent a misdemeanor. As it turned out, however, unknown to *D*, *V* had already been twice convicted of similar acts, and thus his third try was a felony under the law. Under the then-existing common law, using deadly force to prevent a felony was justified. This meant, in turn, that *D*'s shooting was objectively justified. Nevertheless, the court held that *D* was culpable if he did not know the facts (i.e., *V*'s prior two misdemeanor convictions), which would otherwise have justified his using deadly force.

The theoretical problem generated by this decision and situation is provocative. Under the theory of justification, an act is justified if, on balance, D did the "right" thing — that is, he prevented more social harm than he cause. Dadson did that. Therefore, no crime occurred. But others argue that a defendant who believes he is committing a crime should be punished because he has demonstrated (1) a bad character and (2) a criminal choice. The analogs to other areas — impossible attempts, for example (see Chapter 12) — are manifest. Unfortunately, the law here is no clearer than it is there.[12]

Another way to slice this pie is to ask how many facts we know when we ask whether a defendant is justified. Do we know *all* the facts or only those known to the defendant at the time? Dadson's act was, given *all* the facts, justified. But given only the facts known to him before he shot, it was not justified. Similarly, suppose that Rowanda, believing a fire threatens an entire town, destroys Martin's house as a firebreak. Unknown to her, the wind was about to change and the town was safe. Her act will be justified if we look at the act from her perspective. But if we consider all the facts, including the change of wind, she has not objectively chosen the "lesser evil," since, given the direction of the wind, Martin's house would *not* have burned down. Is she justified? Excused? Or neither?

The debate over these matters goes to the heart of the purposes of the criminal sanction. As we go through each "defense" claim in Chapters 16 and 17, keep in mind these generic issues.

EXAMPLES

1. On a very hot summer night Alan, a homeless person, breaks into the house of Beatrice, whom he knows to be away for the week. He is

---

12. For a recent review of the problem, see Christopher, Unknowing Justification and the Logical Necessity of the *Dadson* Principle in Self-Defense, 15 Ox. J. Leg. Stud. 229 (1995) (cataloging the position of courts and academics). One of the hypotheticals used in discussing this problem involves D, who is a patient in a hospital. D has decided to kill N, her nurse, the next time he comes in. Unknown to D, N has decided to kill D. If D shoots N before N can inject D with a poison, is D's act justified since it turns out that N was about to use illegal deadly force? The hypothetical divided academics for years, but Christopher makes the (now self-evident) point that both actors are in exactly the same posture, and that the puzzle was created only because the question was always framed from D's point of view. Christopher points out that N is in exactly the same position: He is being threatened (unknown to him) by deadly force from D. Because two people cannot both be justified in a setting, and because the two people here are in exactly the same situation, Christopher argues that no person can be unknowingly justified in a self-defense setting. Even if that conclusion is sound, however, it is unclear whether this would bar a Dadson, who is not in a reciprocal setting, from being justified.

prosecuted for "burglary," which is defined as "the breaking and entering of the dwelling house of another," punishable by a mandatory five years in prison. The statute further provides, however, that if the defendant proves he did not intend to commit a felony therein, the penalty shall be no more than two years in prison. Alan claims that he only wanted to sleep in an air-conditioned place, and there is no evidence that he took, or even attempted to take, any items in the house. Can the state make Alan bear this burden?

2. Ronald kills his mother, who is dying of terminal cancer and has asked him to assist her to die. He is prosecuted for first-degree murder, but the statute provides that "whoever proves, beyond a reasonable doubt, that he has committed murder in order to alleviate the pain and suffering of a person within two degrees of consanguinity shall be guilty of merciful murder, punishable by 25 years (rather than death)." Can the state make Ronald prove these facts?

3. Lionel lends his car to Hampton. Six weeks later, Lionel receives in the mail a ticket for $500 for parking near a water hydrant on the day Hampton borrowed the car. The statute, after defining "illegal parking," provides that "the owner of an illegally parked car is responsible for the fine, unless he can prove that he was not driving it that day, and otherwise did not exercise control over it." May the state thus make Lionel prove "noncontrol"?

4a. Claudius Hamlet's checkbook showed he had balance of $5,000. Just before leaving with his wife, Gertrude, on a six-month vacation to Nepal, he wrote a check of $3,500 as payment to a roofer. Unhappily, unknown to him, Gertrude had written another check on the same account for $1,800. As they stepped off the plane six months later, they were arrested for fraud. The relevant statute provides that anyone "who overdraws on his bank account" is presumed to intend to defraud the payee. In their mailbox are three notices from the bank indicating the overdraft. At the trial, the judge instructs the jury of the statutory presumption. Can they successfully attack this instruction if they are convicted?

4b. Same facts, except that the statute provides that "intent is presumed if the overdrawn check is not made good within 30 days after the payor has been notified by the bank of the overdraft."

4c. Same facts, except that the Hamlets are prosecuted under a statute that provides that "writing a check on an account with insufficient funds is a felony, unless the defendant proves that he was unaware of the insufficiency."

5. Arthur kills Guinevere, thinking that she is a gigantic snake about to crush him to death. He is charged with "intentionally killing another human being." At the trial, he raises a claim of insanity. The judge

instructs the jury that "every person is presumed sane, and the defendant has the burden of proving to you that he is insane." Is the instruction correct? Constitutionally sound?

EXPLANATIONS

1. This is difficult. Under the common law, burglary was defined as requiring an intent to commit a felony in the house. It thus appears that the legislature has taken one of the elements of this common law offense and turned it into a "defense," violating both *Patterson* and *Mullaney*. But would five years in prison be constitutionally disproportionate to the mere offense of breaking and entering a dwelling home, if there were no intent to commit a felony there? The example could be made even more difficult if the penalty for burglary was 1-5, such that even a *real* burglar could be punished less than Alan. Then the state would be giving Alan a break by reducing his exposure by three years, but not necessarily treating him as "less dangerous" than a "real" burglar.

2. Certainly. Ronald has premeditated the killing and hence has committed first-degree murder under the statute. Notwithstanding the arguments that one who kills in such circumstances lacks the mens rea necessary for murder (or even manslaughter), the common law has rejected such arguments. Thus, the state here has given Ronald a "bonus" beyond that which the common law would allow. Consistent with *Patterson*, the state may circumscribe such a defense by placing upon the defendant the burden of proving it. Under the Code, the issue is not so clear. Such "exceptions" seem like excuses that, pursuant to §1.13(9), must be "disproved" by the state once reasonably raised by the defendant.

3. This problem raises yet another possible argument about affirmative defenses — that the state may require a defendant to prove a "defense" in cases where it need not provide the defense at all. The alleged reason is that the "greater includes the lesser." Since the state could abolish the defense of "noncontrol," it can place the burden of its proof upon the defendant. This, of course, assumes that the state *can* constitutionally prohibit such parking without requiring any showing of actus reus or mens rea. Since this is a "malum prohibitum" offense (see Chapter 6), the state probably could erect such a statute. Thus, it probably can put the burden on the defendant to show noncontrol.

4a. This is a trick question. It may well depend on what *else* the jury was told. After *Allen*, the complete instructions to the jury are critical. And it would appear that the instruction established a "mandatory presumption," which the jury could interpret as shifting either the burden of proof or the burden of production. *If* the jury understood the instruction as shifting the burden of proof, then it violates *Sandstrom*. But even if the jury understood the instruction as only shifting the burden of production, Claudius and Gertrude are probably okay. After all, many people make "innocent" mistakes about their checkbook balances whether as to large (as here) or small amounts. It is not even "more likely than not," much less "beyond a reasonable doubt," that such people intend to defraud their payees. The presumption is therefore empirically invalid.

4b. This change in the statutory language may have dire consequences for the Hamlets. Surely it is true that *many* people who innocently write such a check, after being informed of the overdraft, make up the difference immediately. And the statute goes further. It allows a 30-day grace period, just in case (as here) there was an error in the keeping of the accounts. Thus, the presumed fact (fraudulent intent) does seem to flow from the predicate fact (failure to make up the deficit within 30 days) in at least *many* cases. This may be sufficient to meet the "beyond a reasonable doubt" test enunciated in *Allen*. While, in the way we have worded the question, it may seem that the Hamlets are "innocent," a jury could certainly infer negligence, or even recklessness, from their failure to provide measures to take care of these matters should they arise. Of course, the Hamlets may in fact rebut the statutory presumption by producing evidence of nonculpability.

4c. We have now moved from presumptions to "affirmative defenses." Does this change the analysis? There is at least some suggestion in *Patterson* that it might. After all, if the legislature *could* punish mere "overdrafting" (and it probably could), then it would seem within its powers to make "lack of fraudulent intent" a defense. This demonstrates the fragility of the line, which seems to be drawn by the cases, between presumptions and affirmative defenses. Since, as suggested in the text, there appear to be few limits (under a theory of proportionality) to the state's ability to punish almost any act with almost any punishment, drafting this statute as an affirmative defense may abolish the possible constitutionality infirmity when it was cast as a presumption.

5. This problem raises many of the intricacies of elements, defenses, and statutory interpretation. Does "intentionally" modify "human being"? If so, then Arthur is not guilty, for Arthur did not know he was killing a human. If the statute does so require, then Arthur's insanity is not even relevant. His mental state, if believed by the jury, means that he has not committed the crime. If, however, the statute is read as only requiring that Arthur intend to "kill," the issue of the relevance of sanity is raised. First, as an affirmative defense: Does insanity "negate" mens rea in the sense of "blameworthiness"? If so, then insanity is an "element negation," and the burden cannot be placed on the defendant to negate an element. But suppose that "intentionally" does not require "blame-

worthiness" but is only a "statutory mens rea." Can one act intentionally although insane? Most psychiatrists and many lay people would say yes. Many defendants *even though insane* shoot persons they know to be human beings (e.g., upon being told to do so by God). If these acts are "intentional," then insanity *can* be construed as an affirmative defense. Second, if one treats this as a question of presumption, the question appears to be whether the "presumption" of sanity is proper. Under *Allen,* the test for a proper "mandatory" presumption is whether the presumed fact (sanity) flows beyond a reasonable doubt from the proved fact (Arthur is a person). It may well be that the vast bulk of the population is (legally, if not psychiatrically) sane. Thus, the presumption seems valid.

The Code, in this specific example, makes clear that the prosecution carries the burden of proof on the issue of sanity once properly raised by the defendant. But the Code's generic treatment of all "issues," whether denominated element negations, excuses, or justifications, as "elements" avoids the problems otherwise present in this problem.

16

Acts in Emergency: Justification vs. Excuse

Overview

Donald, charged by a raging bull, hits it with Victoria's Ming vase, destroying the vase but diverting the bull. Is Donald guilty of intentional damage to Victoria's property? Martina tells Ken that unless Ken steals Joan's lawn mower, Martina will kill him. If Ken does so, is he guilty of larceny? Suppose the threat is not to kill Ken but to destroy his Mercedes. What then? Finally, Ebenezer sees Marley coming at him with what appears to Ebenezer to be a machine gun. May Ebenezer pull out a pistol and shoot Marley, or must he wait until Marley himself actually shoots?

In each of these situations, the defendant is faced with a situation in which a decision must be made instantly. Rather than labeling all three such acts as "emergency decisions" and treating them similarly, the common law created separate doctrines that, while similar, have been treated differently with somewhat different rules. Thus, Donald would have to argue that he acted in "necessity" (choosing the lesser of two evils). Ken, in either of the examples, would have to argue "duress." Finally, Ebenezer would claim neither of these defenses but "self-defense." In assessing these doctrines do not lose sight that each of them involves emergent action.[1]

Some writers argue that the unifying theme of these claims, rather than emergency, is whether they are excused or justified. As suggested immediately

---

1. Elliott, Necessity, Duress and Self-Defense, [1989] Crim. L. Rev. 611; Colvin, Exculpatory Defenses in Criminal Law, 10 Oxford J. Legal Stud. 381 (1990).

below, and again in the sections dealing with each separate claim, however, the difficulty with this view is that neither the writers nor the courts agree on which of these claims sound in justification and which in excuse. Although the "emergency" explanation is just as controversial, it seems to capture more readily the psychological assessment of the actor — her mens rea — and is therefore embraced in this chapter.

Common Requirements, Common Problems

The *essence* of these three claims is that the defendant

a. is acting under *extraordinary pressure,*
b. from which there is (or appears to him to be) no *reasonable escape,*
c. to do something that *involves injury to his or another's person or property,* and that, in the absence of the emergency, would clearly be criminal (although the defendant may not recognize or know that).

Excused or Justified? Or Both?

Legal writers (and the courts, to the extent they discuss the theoretical problems) are divided over whether a defendant who claims duress, necessity, or self-defense is "justified" or "excused." Some argue that a defendant who acts in extremis *always* does the correct thing and therefore is always justified. They maintain this position even if the defendant turns out to be objectively wrong, and there is in reality no threat. Other writers suggest that some actors in emergency are justified, while others, including the mistaken actor, must be considered "excused" rather than "justified."[2]

A retributivist would argue that anyone who succumbs in these terrifying situations is not morally blameworthy for doing so and should not be

---

2. Another way of describing the struggle over whether duress and necessity are excuses or justifications is to ask whether duress and necessity defeat responsibility in strict liability cases. If excuses "lower" or "negate" the defendant's mens rea, then a claim based on excuse should not avoid responsibility for strict liability offenses because the defendant's mens rea is irrelevant. For example, if speeding is a strict liability offense, a person who speeds either (a) at the point of a gun or (b) to save the life of a passenger should still be guilty because the "crime" requires no mens rea that can be negated by an excuse. In fact, both cases (which seldom discuss the underlying reasoning) and commentators reach mixed results. The English Law Revision Commission, for example, concluded that not even the speeding driver should be exculpated and decided, therefore, to recommend the abandonment of the doctrine of necessity. That position, however, has not been adopted by the English courts.

punished. Many utilitarians might agree in this result, claiming that most individuals will inevitably succumb to the terror of the moment rather than worry about criminal punishment in the future. Consequently, punishment in such cases would be futile.[3]

Actus Reus, Mens Rea, or Both? Or Neither?

Actus Reus

Some theorists argue that the defendant who acts under such pressure does not meet even the primary requirement for criminal responsibility—a voluntary act (see Chapter 3). One who kills another while a gun is aimed at his own head is not "really" acting voluntarily, the argument goes. The law has rejected this nonvoluntary act argument. As is often said, the defendant may be faced with a hard choice, but it is a choice nonetheless.

Mens Rea

Somewhat more plausibly, a defendant who "chooses" to kill when faced with such dangers may be argued to have no mens rea. After all, who has a "mens" at all when a gun is aimed at his temple or that of his spouse or child? The argument is that the defendant's mind is "blank," not only metaphorically but literally. This argument is more persuasive if one adopts the broad (traditional), sense of mens rea (see Chapter 4) that the defendant must act in a culpable, blameworthy way. Even if one uses the narrow (statutory) meaning of mens rea (see Chapter 4), there are at least some instances when a plausible argument can be made that the defendant did not "intend" or "purpose" death. The mountain climber who cuts the rope below him to save himself from being plunged into the canyon, thereby sending a fellow climber into a deep abyss, may hope and pray that his falling colleague is saved. And a person who, trembling, shoots another in self-defense, all the while saying "Please just go away—don't make me shoot you," might well argue that it was not his "conscious object to cause death." Nor does a bank teller who hands over money at the point of a gun necessarily have the mens rea for larceny/robbery, that is, to intend to permanently deprive the owner of his money; he probably hopes the robber will be caught instantly. Indeed, in some emergency situations it is plausible that the defendant is not even *reckless* with regard to the risk of criminal harm. Simply put, he never subjectively thought about this risk because he was consumed only

---

3. On the other hand, Sir James Stephen, a prominent utilitarian, argued that it is exactly when human nature is most vulnerable to the almost irresistible threat of death that the punishment threatened by the law must be the greatest. It is precisely in such situations, he argued, that a counterbalancing motivation for not committing a crime is most needed.

by a concern for his own safety. In such a case, the defendant really *is* arguing that there was no mens rea, even in the narrow sense, as to the result.

However, the argument is less tenable in other factual settings. The defendant who, under duress, destroys a car or severely assaults an innocent victim may not "want" to inflict the injury but surely foresees the unlikelihood of putting things back together again later on. Far too often the use of generic terms, such as "intent" or "mens rea," may conceal important factual differences within the assumed scenarios each writer or court tacitly posits when discussing these issues. Thus, it is more accurate to say that *some* persons in extremis have statutory mens rea, while others do not.

Why Punish?

Whether actors who see themselves as acting in necessity can be deterred is uncertain. Some persons thrust into a situation in which death seems imminent are unlikely to be intimidated by a threat of later punishment (including death) if they survive. Perhaps the only deterrent effect here is to reduce precipitous action — that is, to require the defendants to hold off until the "very last minute."[4] However, the dilemma is that almost every defendant in such situations believes that "the final" minute has arrived. Thus, the difficult question is whether the defendant's belief that the threat is imminent must be reasonable.

Mistaken Justifications

Perhaps no problem vexes the doctrinal approach to either justification or excuse like that of mistake. The first enigma is whether a mistake as to facts which (if true) would justify an act, reduce that act to an excuse, or whether the act remains justified. The second dilemma is what the result should be when the mistake is honestly held, but unreasonable.

The first problem arises because there is still disagreement among commentators (and hence among courts) as to WHY an act is justified. Consider: Jane pulls out a gun and aims it at Joe, who kills her. If Jane is an actual aggressor, some social benefit has occurred, for reasons we will explore more thoroughly in the self-defense section. But suppose that Jane only *seemed* to be an aggressor — that the gun was unloaded or not a real gun, or that she

---

4. One therefore might explain the opinion in *Dudley and Stephens,* infra, as arguing that taking the life of an innocent is never justified because it is never actually necessary. As Justice Cardozo put it, "Who shall know when the masts and sails of rescue may emerge out of the fog?" B. Cardozo, Law and Literature 113 (1931). Indeed, one could argue in *Dudley* itself that the four should have waited until one of them died. This argument would then turn on whether the men believed that, if they had waited, the remaining three (whoever they were) would have been so weakened as to make nourishment unavailing. If this were then the case, one could analyze it as a mistake as to a justification, discussed in the text below.

had previously announced to others that she was only trying to scare Joe. Jane then is, at worst, a practical joker who deceived Joe into believing her purported threat. Jane's death is NOT a real benefit to the world—it would have been better for Joe to have been actually scared than for Jane to be dead. Is Joe's act nevertheless justified? Those who believe that an act is justified ONLY if there is actual resulting social benefit deny that Joe's act is justified. This view assesses Joe's act "ex post" — AFTER the results are known. Another way to put this is that "we" view Joe's act from the viewpoint of an omniscient observer — knowing that Jane is only kidding. To these writers, Joe is, at best, excused, and never justified.

Another view, however, is that Joe's ACT should be judged "ex ante" — BEFORE we know what the true facts are, and (rather than from an omniscient viewpoint) from Joe's viewpoint. From that view, Joe is justified, because under the facts as he saw them, he is doing social good—dispatching a killer, and saving an innocent life (his). The focus is on Joe's ACT, and not on the results of that act as they turn out.

Mistake—Honest, or Reasonable?

The second part of the puzzle relating to all mistaken justifications, unsurprisingly, is whether a mistake — whether counted either as an excuse or a justification — must be reasonable. Suppose that Joe was not only mistaken, but that his mistake was an unreasonable one: no one would have taken the water pistol which Jane was brandishing for a gun. But Joe honestly believed it was a real gun. Should Joe lose his claim of defense? Or does his mistake reduce what would otherwise be a justifiable act to a wrongful (but excused) one? And if so, what does that do to Jeffrey (who helped him)?

All courts hold that a *reasonable* mistake as to a justification will continue to hold the act justifiable. But what about the *unreasonable mistake?* Here the courts are in conflict. Some hold that an unreasonably mistaken person loses all claims of defense and is to be punished as though he made no mistake at all. Others hold that an unreasonable mistake reduces liability (i.e. partially excuses) but does not exonerate. Still others conclude that even an unreasonably mistaken person should be liable only for criminal negligence.[5] In our earlier terms, Joe does not seem seriously morally blameworthy (although perhaps his negligence in not being reasonable carries some moral opprobrium), nor in need of incapacitation. He might, however, benefit from treatment, and others like him might be deterred into acting more carefully.

---

5. Price, Faultless Mistake of Fact: Justification or Excuse, 12 Crim. Just. Ethics 14 (1993); Alexander, Inculpatory and Exculpatory Mistakes and the Fact/Law Distinction: An Essay in Memory of Myke Bayles, 12 Law and Philosophy 33 (1993); Simester, Mistakes in Defence, 12 Oxford J. Leg. Stud. 295 (1991); Byrd, Wrong-doing and Attribution: Implications Beyond the Justification-Excuse Distinction, 33 Wayne L. Rev. 1289 (1987).

Duress

The common law normally does not expect most of us to be heroes—that is, to die willingly or to suffer serious bodily harm—if we can avoid this fate by doing what someone else demands of us, even if that means committing what would otherwise be a crime. So long as the pressure was great and there was no obvious escape, a defendant who acted under duress from another human being is exculpated. The one exception, discussed in more detail below, is homicide. Not even the threat of immediate death will allow (justify or excuse) the killing of a person the duressed person knows to be "innocent." Instead, the duressed person is required to sacrifice her own life.

The Doctrines of Duress

As a general matter, the common law required the following elements for a claim of duress:

1. a *well-founded fear,* generated by
2. a *threat from a human being* of
3. an *imminent* (or "immediate")
4. *serious bodily harm or death*
5. to *himself* (or sometimes to a near relative)
6. *not of his own doing*

Personal Injury

Under this restriction no threat to property, no matter how severe when compared to the injury threatened, will sustain a duress claim. For example, if Bob helps Alex embezzle $1,000 from Bob's employer because Alex threatens to destroy the Mona Lisa or a $10 million building unless Bob helps him, Bob cannot claim duress. If he has any useful claim at all, it may be one of "necessity" rather than duress (see below). Unless there is a doctrinal or moral imperative for disallowing the claim under one rubric but allowing it under another, *D should* be able to submit his claim to the jury regardless of its formal label.

"Imminence"

Determining whether a threat of harm is "imminent" is quite difficult as we will see in the discussion on self-defense.

Regina v. Hudson and Taylor, [1971] All E.R. 248, presents an interesting case testing the soundness of the "imminence" requirement. The defendants, key witnesses at the criminal trial of *X,* committed perjury at the trial by failing to identify *X* as the perpetrator of another crime because they were told by *X*'s friends that they would be beaten if they told the truth. However, they were not told when the beating would occur, arguably rendering the threatened injury not "imminent." Nevertheless, the appellate court held that the question of imminence was one of fact, not law. If the jury found the defendants' will was overborne, they could properly claim duress.

An argument can be made that the defendants should have made use of official protection, particularly since the crime itself (perjury) occurred in court. Had they done so, the argument goes, the police would have protected them and they would not have had to commit perjury. See, e.g., *State v. Dunn*, 243 Kan. 414, (1988); *Dunn v. Roberts*, 768 F. Supp. 1442 (D. Kan. 1991), aff'd, 963 F.2d 308 (10th Cir. 1992). See also *People v. Romero*, 10 Cal. App. 4th 1150 (1992). This contention certainly has an appeal. Why let someone commit a crime if they could have avoided the threatened harm by going to the police? Nonetheless, requiring the threat to be imminent raises other serious questions (as we shall see again shortly in self-defense cases involving the battered woman defense): (1) to what extent should the trial investigate the actual ability of the police to protect someone like the defendants, and (2) should the defendants' responsibility depend on their subjective belief?

Reasonableness of Fear

The common law generally provides an answer to the last question. (Well, at last!!!!) Under the common law only a reasonable fear is sufficient to sustain a claim of duress. Thus, if Hans pointed at Stephi what Stephi unreasonably believes is a real gun, but what is obviously a water pistol and threatened to kill her "instantly" unless she stole *V*'s wallet, Stephi has no claim of duress to a charge of theft because the threat is not well grounded and the fear is unreasonable.

Because the law requires the actor's fear to meet an objective standard, it should come as no surprise that to meet an objective standard the law also requires a defendant's belief that the police cannot protect her be reasonable. As with all other instances of objectivization, however, this requirement has the undesirable effect of criminalizing a person who, in the maelstrom of circumstances, acts unreasonably but does not intend to act criminally.

To "Himself"

The common law appears initially to have limited duress to cases where the defendant personally was threatened. Threats to strangers, and even to spouse and children, were insufficient. These limits have now been discarded by most states.

Creating Conditions of Duress

Another restriction on the availability of the claim is that the defendant must not have been "responsible" for the threat. If *D* knowingly joins a violent gang and later commits a crime under threat of immediate death from fellow gang members, he will not be permitted to claim duress.

Of course, the law may seek to deter people from joining such gangs, but a good case can be made that disallowing duress in such a case is disproportionate to the defendant's blameworthiness. One may wish to punish someone for his knowing membership in the gang, but to punish him for a serious crime when he actually was duressed may be unfair. At the very least, there should be a causal link between *D*'s joining the gang and *D*'s crime. If *D* had actually heard of other inductees being required to commit criminal acts in order to be accepted and joined the gang anyway, then disallowing duress would be logically related to the defendant's moral culpability.

A subcategory of duress, which may raise the problem of creating one's own exculpatory conditions, is the duty to obey superior officers. In wartime, officers sometimes issue commands that are palpably illegal, such as ordering a subordinate to shoot an innocent civilian without trial. Can the subordinate who obeys that command claim duress, or has he "created his own conditions" by entering the armed forces? Should it matter whether he volunteered or was drafted? International law is clear on this matter — the subordinate must refuse to obey a "clearly" illegal order, even if it jeopardizes his own life to do so. The common law was less clear, and the Model Penal Code has a special provision on precisely this situation.

Wives and Duress

Historically, when a wife committed a criminal act with her husband, she was presumed by the law to have been coerced and therefore not culpable. Although that doctrine has been abolished at common law, in recent years battered spouses have argued that they committed crimes with their husbands not because they were threatened with immediate harm but either because they (1) feared future harm or (2) were incapable of resisting the pressure their spouses created.

Duress and Homicide

Under the common law, a defendant could not claim duress if he killed a victim. Instead, he was required to sacrifice himself to the threatener. The English House of Lords, in two cases in the 1970s, appeared to reconsider the rule, distinguishing between those who (under threat of death) actually killed the victim and those who merely aided in the killing. See *Director of*

Public Prosecutions v. Lynch [1975] 2 W.L.R. 641 and *Abbott v. Queen* [1977] 3 W.L.R. 462. The House ultimately concluded that this distinction was illogical, and inconsistent with history, and reinstated the old common law rule barring the use of duress to anyone involved in a killing.

Besides the uneasiness exhibited in these cases, critics of the rule argue that it is unfair to the duressed actor to deny categorically the defense in this one crime, since many reasonable persons would kill another rather than die themselves (or have significant others killed). They argue, also, that it is illogical to allow the defense to attempted murder, or aggravated assault, where the victim does not in fact die, but to disallow it when the victim actually dies. Nevertheless, the experiment in England seems to have ended, and most common law courts continue to apply the rule (but see the Model Penal Code, discussed later).

The Guilt of the Duressor: A Note

Just in case you're wondering (or forgot about the innocent pawn doctrine), the person who threatens the defendant in a case of duress is always going to be guilty of the crime, whether or not the actual perpetrator has a duress claim. The criminal law may be weird, but it's not stupid. See Chapter 14.

The Rationale of Duress

There is no agreement on the rationale of duress. From a utilitarian viewpoint a person faced with the prospect of imminent death is not likely to be deterred by the state's threat of future punishment, even if it includes possible execution. Similarly, such a person is not morally culpable for committing a harmful act, even if in hindsight we would prefer that she had chosen to be subjected to the threatened harm.

Some writers argue that duress is a justification rather than an excuse, but the consensus is to the contrary. The argument that duress sounds in justification is fairly straightforward. Under the common law only a threat of death or serious bodily harm will sustain a claim of duress. Since duress was not allowed in homicide cases, under the common law the defendant's act is almost surely less harmful than the harm with which he was threatened. Put simply, the defense will generally result in choosing the lesser harm, which is the essence of a justification.

If duress were expanded by making it available in homicide cases and by not restricting it to cases in which the actor was threatened with death or serious bodily harm, it would more clearly be an excuse. Such an expansion would recognize that defendants who act in such situations lack moral culpability. Simply put, people threatened with what they perceive as serious threats simply do not have the "vicious will" that criminal penalties require.

By expanding duress in this manner, we would occasionally exonerate individuals who inflict more harm than they prevent. This could occur only if duress is seen as an excuse and is not limited by its justificatory aspects, which generally require the choice of lesser evils.

The Model Penal Code

The Model Penal Code retains the common law requirement that the threat be one of personal injury rather than property damage. But the MPC allows a threat of "unlawful force" to support duress, thus allowing the threat of minor physical harm.

The Code has changed the common law of duress in several ways. It subtly varies the common law's requirement of reasonableness by requiring that the threat involved would have similarly affected a "person of reasonable firmness *in the defendant's situation*" (emphasis added). For example, if the defendant is unusually vulnerable (e.g., a hemophiliac) or has a particular fear of a particular injury (an ice skater who fears breaking her knees), this may be part of the "situation." Whether other factors such as extreme cowardice would qualify is less clear.

The MPC otherwise rejects most of the specific limitations imposed by the common law. Thus, (1) duress is a valid claim in all prosecutions, including homicide; (2) there is no restriction to "imminent harm"; (3) if the threat is to a third person, there is no requirement that the person be a relative, or even an acquaintance, of the defendant.

The Code also abolishes the "husband-wife" rules of duress. MPC §2.09(3).

Like the common law, the Code disallows the defense in certain cases. The Code does not allow a defendant to claim duress if he *recklessly* placed himself in the position where he could be duressed. Thus, if he joined a gang of known terrorists, the defendant cannot claim duress even if he is charged with a crime requiring knowledge or purpose. In contrast, he has a claim of duress except to a charge requiring negligence. This is in clear contrast to the requirements of necessity discussed below.

Necessity

The Doctrines of Necessity

The claim of necessity and the restrictions on it essentially replicate the claim of duress. There must be

1. a *threat* of
2. *imminent injury* to the person or property

3. for which there are *no (reasonable) alternatives* except the commission of the crime;
4. the *defendant's acts must prevent an equal or more serious harm;*
5. the defendant *must not have created the conditions of his own dilemma.*

In early common law decisions, this threat had to emanate from natural forces and not from human beings. That requirement, however, has been eased or abrogated in most jurisdictions.

"Necessity" is also referred to as a "choice of evils" claim. Someone (usually the defendant) is threatened with serious harm and chooses (to the extent that one chooses in such a situation) to inflict harm in a way that would otherwise be deemed criminal. If the harm the defendant actually inflicts is less than that which would have occurred had he not acted, a social benefit has occurred, notwithstanding that the harm inflicted would otherwise be criminally proscribed. He has chosen the "lesser evil." Thus, if Elvira purposely burns down Josh's barn to act as a firebreak, which prevents the fire from destroying the town, the town has a net benefit. What would otherwise be arson is no longer criminal.

Many of the problems discussed in the duress section apply here as well. For example, it is not clear what "imminent" means in this context. Similarly, the question of what alternatives are relevant and must be considered (thereby rendering the threatened harm "nonimminent") is uncertain. Blackstone argued that a starving person could not claim necessity for stealing bread because in eighteenth-century England there was always help and food for the starving.

Duress vs. Necessity

Two major differences with duress are apparent. First, necessity does not require a threat of death or serious bodily harm. As long as the defendant actually inflicts less harm than he was threatened with, the claim of necessity can be made. Thus, if Trump lashes his $500,000 yacht to a dock in a fierce storm, thereby doing $500 worth of damage to the dock, he has a defense to the criminal charge of intentional destruction of property.[6]

Second, while necessity requires a weighing of the injury inflicted with the injury threatened, there is no inherent reason to restrict necessity to threats against life or person. This means that necessity may serve as a "default" claim for some cases where duress cannot apply. Thus, Bob, who helped Alex embezzle money from Bob's employer rather than have Alex destroy the Mona Lisa (see above), has no claim of duress. But he might

---

6. Of course, as every torts student knows, Trump may still have to pay the dock owner damages for the loss. See *Vincent v. Lake Erie Transp. Co.*, 109 Minn. 456, 124 N.W. 221 (1910).

have a claim of necessity, depending on how the jury balances the employer's money against the loss of a valuable piece of art.

Necessity and Homicide

As already discussed, duress was simply not allowed as a claim when the duressed person had killed a person he knew to be innocent, no matter how severe the conditions under which the killing occurred. It is not as clear whether necessity could be asserted in homicide cases. However, the most famous necessity case involving such a claim seemed to establish that, at least in English law, the answer is no.

In *Regina v. Dudley and Stephens,* 14 Q.B.D. 273 (1884), four men were cast adrift in a lifeboat in the Atlantic Ocean when the boat on which they had been sailing sank. After 19 days of subsisting on two small cans of turnips and a small turtle, the two defendants killed one of the other two, whom they selected because he was (a) the youngest; (b) the only one without family; and (c) the weakest/sickest. (The fourth seaman refused to participate in the killing.) The three survived by eating the corpse.

The court, while acknowledging that it was establishing a moral rule that no one could follow, refused to allow the two defendants the claim of necessity. It concluded that knowingly taking innocent life could never be allowed by the law. In this sense the *Dudley and Stephens* limitation replicates that initially placed on duress.

However, the limitation may not hold where it is "fate" that decides the victim. In *Dudley,* as noted above, the victim was apparently chosen because he was the youngest, had no family, and was the weakest. On the other hand, in *United States v. Holmes,* 26 F. Cas. 360 (C.C.E.D. Pa. 1842), an almost identical case, an American court had suggested that, if lots were chosen to select the victim, the claim might be recognized. Similarly, in a hypothetical often used by law professors, if several mountaineers suddenly find themselves hanging over a crevasse, with the rope threatening to break from the excessive load, the topmost may cut the rope holding the ones below, since fate decided the "obvious" victims. Or consider this case: If in order to save 100 houses and their occupants from a flooding river, someone breaks a dike that would result in the destruction of three houses and the death of their five occupants, the principle of necessity would appear to apply.

Creating Conditions of Necessity

As with duress, if the defendant "created the conditions of his own necessity," the common law denied the claim. The point is just as ambiguous here as it was there. For example in *Dudley and Stephens,* it is not clear why the yacht sank. Suppose it was due to some negligence (or even recklessness) by Dudley (or Stephens). Should that alone preclude the claim for a much different event that occurred much later in time? On the other hand, suppose that the starving condition of the lifeboat occupants was due to reckless consumption of the foodstuffs they had. What if, for example, on the first day in the lifeboat they had eaten four large hams, which otherwise could have been used to feed them for three weeks? (Does this sound familiar? Does the term "proximate cause" spring to mind? If not, see Chapter 3. If so, see it anyway.)

Excuse or Justification?

As with duress, the question arises whether necessity is an "excuse" or a "justification." The court in *Dudley and Stephens* framed it only as a justification, but in a recent decision the Canadian Supreme Court held that necessity could only be an excuse and never a justification. *Perka v. The Queen,* 13 D.L.R. (4th) 1 (1984). The answer may be that it can be either. That is the answer that some foreign legal systems have given. German Penal Code §§34 & 35 (1975); Swedish Penal Code ch. 24, §§4 & 5 (1963).

Neither the question nor the answer is academic. A justificatory claim would have to demonstrate that the defendant actually achieved, or intended to achieve, a "greater good" (or lesser harm) than he committed. In contrast, an excuse claim would argue that the defendant was not morally blameworthy in choosing, in extremely severe and pressing circumstances, a path that at the time looked reasonable, even if it (a) was not in fact reasonable and (b) did not result in a "greater good."

The justificatory analysis suffers from a number of problems, not the least of which is that it may be construed to support a quantification approach. Thus, in *Dudley* Lord Coleridge resisted a quantification analysis because it would allow Dudley and Stephens to claim necessity if they then killed Brooks (the fourth passenger) and then allow Dudley to kill Stephens (or vice versa). Calculating net gain (or loss) in this manner would, according to Coleridge, allow one survivor to justify the killing of three other people. Consequently, Coleridge rejected the plea of necessity.

Coleridge, however, was wrong on two grounds. First, the surviving sailor of the four would claim not that he killed three to save one, but that he killed three rather than allow all four to die. Second, such manipulation of the quantification approach is undesirable. The real question should be whether a person acting under such extreme pressure can be held morally culpable if he "capitulates" to those pressures. That's why we have juries.

The Problem of Imminence and Democracy

The difficulties of defining when a threat is imminent arises in cases of necessity as well as in duress. However, there is also another problem that, though not unique to necessity situations, occurs more frequently in such cases than in duress situations.

Many recent attempts to invoke necessity have involved civil disobedience in one form or another. Thus, sit-in demonstrators at nuclear plants or abortion clinics, patients using prohibited drugs to ease the pain, or to stop the progress of a disease, or public health advocates distributing clean needles to drug addicts in an effort to prevent the spread of AIDS have recently claimed necessity when charged with crimes arising out of their acts of civil disobedience. Some juries have acquitted in these cases. Appellate courts, however, have almost unanimously rejected the claims on two grounds: (1) the threatened injury was not "imminent" enough or (2) the legislature (or in the abortion cases, the Constitution) had already weighed the conflicting policies and resolved them against the disobedients. The defendants could have participated in the political process to alter public policy but chose not to. Consequently, their claim that breaking the law to protest public policy was justified by necessity was rejected.

Jury nullification can undermine the rationale adopted by courts. For that reason, perhaps, appellate courts have generally held that it is not reversible error to preclude evidence of defendants' beliefs from being introduced at trial. Keeping such evidence from the jury effectively prevents it from knowing why the defendants acted as they did, thereby reducing the possibility of nullification on such claims.

The Model Penal Code

The Code recognizes a claim of necessity or "lesser evils," which it calls "justification." MPC §3.02. *D* must believe that his conduct is necessary to avoid harm to himself or others and that the harm to be avoided by committing a "criminal" act is greater than that sought to be avoided by the criminal law. The Code rejects most common law restrictions on the claim, preferring instead simply to allow the jury to weigh all the factors involved in a particular situation. Thus, the Code's provision (a) does not require that the actual infliction of the harm be "imminent"; (b) does not distinguish between threats from human versus nonhuman forces; and (c) does not restrict the claim to instances involving a threat of death or serious bodily harm. The Code appears to resolve the "democracy" problem by requiring that the claim be allowed only if the harm "sought to be prevented" "outweighs" the harm that the law broken seeks to prevent. The decision as to this balance is apparently one of law to be made by the judge, who will ostensibly consider the political apparatus available in cases of civil disobedience.

In contrast to its section on duress, which made that claim unavailable if the defendant had recklessly created the conditions of the threat, the Code provides that if the defendant has been reckless or negligent in placing himself in the position where the necessity occurred, he may still raise the claim in all instances where he is charged with a purposeful or knowing crime. However, he may be prosecuted for a reckless or negligent crime. Thus, a defendant will be treated differently under the Code, depending on whether he has a claim of duress or necessity. Someone who has been reckless in creating a duress situation will be guilty of murder, while a defendant who has been reckless in creating a necessitous homicide situation will be guilty only of manslaughter.

Finally, to make clear the relation between necessity and duress, the *duress* section of the Code explicitly provides that §2.09 does not, by negative implication, limit any defense that would be available under §3.02. See §2.09(4).

EXAMPLES

In which of the following can the defendant(s) claim a justification or excuse of duress or necessity?

1a. Boris and his wife, Natasha, are sitting in their car at a traffic light when they are suddenly confronted by six men wearing ski masks and armed with machine guns, who "hijack" the car. Three miles later, the men kidnap a police officer and handcuff him. They then force Natasha to drive to a remote spot, where the terrorists order Natasha to hold the officer still while Boris shoots him in the head. The men threaten to kill Boris, Natasha, and their two children unless the two comply. Natasha holds the officer, but Boris, after firing three wild shots, faints. The men then order Natasha to shoot the officer while they hold him. She does so.

1b. Suppose, instead, that Boris and Natasha are kidnapped and told to help rob a bank by holding open the bags into which the money is put. During the robbery one of the original robbers accidentally shoots and kills a teller.

2. Alvin tells Van Cliburn (a famous concert pianist) that unless Van helps him extort money from Sylvia, Alvin will break his fingers so that Cliburn can never play the piano again. Van helps Alvin and is charged as an accomplice.

3. Darrell, a bank executive, has spent the last twenty years of his life writing his version of the great American novel. He has only one copy of the manuscript, which is now 98 percent complete. Douglas steals the one existing hard copy of the manuscript and erases the original from the hard drive. He tells Darrell that he will destroy the piece unless Darrell gives Doug the combination to the bank vault. Darrell, after much agony, complies and is charged with theft.

4. Jonathan, the head of a dedicated right-to-life organization known for using violence, tells Bruce, the secretary of an abortionist, that unless

Bruce gives Jonathan the key to the office so that Jonathan can destroy the equipment in the office, he will kill Bruce "when you least expect it, sometime in the next month, or the next year, or whenever." Bruce complies.

5.   Horace, a nurse at the local hospital, has spent the last three years ministering to those in the last stages of AIDS. Distraught by what he has seen, he steals hypodermics and syringes from the hospital and distributes them to heroin and cocaine addicts in an attempt to reduce the spread of AIDS. He is prosecuted for (1) larceny; (2) distribution of drug paraphernalia.

6.   Jerry, the head of a group dedicated to reducing cancer, purchases in a foreign country a drug that is supposed to retard the spread of the disease in those diagnosed to have it, and to reduce the pain of those already in the last stages. He smuggles the drug into the country, and (1) gives some of it to Janet, who is only days away from death; (2) gives some of it to Marty, who has just been diagnosed as having leukemia. Jerry is prosecuted for (a) one count of smuggling the drug into the country, and (b) two counts of distributing an unauthorized drug.

7.   Despite adverse weather predictions and warnings from several knowledgeable climbers, Edmund Hillary tries to scale K2, a mountain in the Himalayas, with a crew of four. All are tied together, with Hillary at one end. The weather is indeed terrible (even worse than forecast), and the five fall into a crevasse. Hillary cuts the rope that holds three of the other four, and they die.

8.   While driving down the street at a legal rate of speed, Clara is suddenly beset by a mob screaming at her and clearly intending serious bodily harm. The streets are blocked, and she drives on the sidewalk, in desperation, seeking an avenue of escape. She is arrested and charged with driving on a sidewalk.

9.   Gottfried is driving to Pittsburgh in a car that has failed to pass environmental and safety inspection four times. In the middle of this drive, he stops at a rest stop. As he gets back into the car, Himmelfarb, an escaped convict, comes up, points a gun to his head, and says, "Drive to Pittsburgh." Gottfried complies. He is charged with (1) driving an unsafe car; (2) assisting Himmelfarb's escape.

10.   Jack, an accountant, is ordered by Gertrude, his boss, to fraudulently increase the billings for customers by 30 percent; she tells him he will be fired unless he complies. Unknown to Gertrude, Jack has a daughter who will die unless she obtains a liver transplant in the next week. If Jack is fired, he will not have sufficient funds to pay for the transplant. Jack complies. Has Jack committed fraud?

11. Reread the case of Paul Hill in Chapter 8, Example 6, at page 171. Consider that case in the context of this chapter.

EXPLANATIONS

1a. The threat here is obviously serious enough to constitute duress: It is a threat of death or serious bodily harm that would make any person reasonably fear that it will be carried out in the immediate future. The threat to the children, however, might not be "imminent" enough under common law. If the threat had only been to the children, the original doctrine of the common law *might* have barred the use of the threat at all, which sometimes required that it be to the defendant personally. Most courts, however, would now allow a jury to consider the threat. Nevertheless, under the common law neither Boris nor Natasha would be able to assert the issue since they are charged with homicide. The Model Penal Code would allow both to claim duress. Some states have found a "compromise" position by allowing defendants to reduce their liability to manslaughter. E.g., N.J.S.A. 2C:2-9.

There is one other possibility. Since the threat was to kill four people, and only one was killed, Boris and Natasha might have a choice-of-evils (necessity) claim. This depends on whether the common law would have allowed the claim in a homicide case, notwithstanding *Dudley and Stephens* (remember—there three were saved although one was killed). Moreover (although this is an arcane rule), some courts still restrict necessity to those cases in which a force of nature posed the threat. Since the threat here is human, that doctrinal restriction would have been sufficient to preclude a claim of necessity.[7]

1b. This death falls under the felony murder rule. (Go back to Chapter 8 if this sounds only vaguely familiar.) Can duress be a defense to *felony* murder, even if not to "regular" murder? Most courts have said yes. Whether this would be true if it were one of the duressed who accidentally killed the teller is unclear.

2. There are two issues here. First, is this "serious bodily harm"? If so, then

---

7. Arcane though it might be, this qualification on necessity was followed by some courts in the well-known early "prison escape" cases. Here, inmate Brutus would threaten inmate Wally with homosexual rape. Wally would jump the wall. When caught and charged with escape, he'd claim duress or necessity. But duress was unavailable because Brutus didn't order Wally to escape (indeed, that was the last thing that Brutus wanted). And necessity was unavailable because the source of the threat was human, not a force of nature (although rapists might sometimes metaphorically be so labeled). Thankfully, the courts ultimately jettisoned the restrictions of the two doctrines, at least in these cases. See Gardner, The Defense of Necessity and the Right to Escape from Prison: A Step Towards Incarceration Free from Sexual Assault, 49 S. Cal. L. Rev. 110 (1975).

is there any meaning to the word "serious"? (This doesn't mean that broken fingers don't hurt, but if the word means anything, surely this is a dubious application.) Under the MPC, however, the threat is "unlawful force," and thus sufficient to qualify. Second, if we assume that this is serious bodily harm, would a person of "reasonable firmness" have resisted the threat and accepted the broken fingers? This is obviously a difficult question. That is what juries are for.

Assume, however, that a jury would conclude that a "usual" person would prefer broken fingers to having Sylvia suffer extortion. What, then, of the Model Code's restriction that the defendant's "situation" must be considered? Is the fact that Van Cliburn is a concert pianist whose career will be ended part of his "situation"? Again, the issue is difficult. And we can make it more difficult. Assume, for the moment, that a concert pianist of reasonable firmness would not help the extortion. Or change the threat to Sylvia from extortion to rape. How does one balance these interests and assess these threats and interests?

3.   Even if a reasonable person in Darrell's position would give the key to Douglas, the common law would not allow Darrell a claim of duress to a charge of being an accomplice, since the threat is not one of serious bodily harm or death. The Model Penal Code would similarly disallow the claim and for the same reason. Poor Darrell. We told you to always have a backup copy.

Wait, Darrell! Don't pack for prison yet! Even if you don't have a claim of duress, you might have a claim, at least under the MPC and possibly even under common law, of necessity. If the jury felt that your decision was the "right" one — that is, balancing all the interests, the lesser of two evils — you might be exonerated.

Now think about that for a moment. If duress is an "excuse," how could a rational criminal law system declare an act not excusable but yet justifiable? Does this make you wonder about all these issues again? (It should.)

4.   Under the common law, the threat must be one of "imminent" violence if the defendant is to be able to use the plea. A vague threat such as the one here has divided the courts over whether there is such a plea. In *State v. Toscano*, 74 N.J. 421 (1977), a case of threats of unspecified future injury, the Court adopted the rationale of the Model Penal Code that duress was a question of fact for the jury rather than a question of law for the judge.

5.   The claim here must be one of necessity. Yet the threat of death is surely remote for most of those who received the needles: Even if some of them were to become afflicted with the disease, their deaths are not "imminent." Moreover, from an objective viewpoint, Horace has alternatives, including those of the usual political process. Indeed, a number of cities in the United States and elsewhere have adopted policies of

distributing needles to addicts, with precisely the objective Horace seeks. Therefore, Horace should be admonished to use those processes. On the other hand, Horace may seek to assert an "excuse" version of necessity; given his personal anguish over the plight of those with AIDS, he was subjectively unable to weigh carefully such arguments and honestly believed he was doing the "right thing." But will this defense work for the theft? Probably not, since Horace could have bought the syringes. The case also asks whether, in assessing the weight of the defendant's actions against the crime committed, one should weigh the crime "in the abstract" (larceny) or in the context of the facts (larceny of needles from a hospital with distribution in mind). Horace will not have a defense under the common law but would have a possible defense under the Model Penal Code.

6. Here, in distinction to Example 5, we have specific persons whom Jerry seeks to help, and specific facts as to the precise harm being alleviated. Both Janet and Marty are facing death "soon." Indeed, Janet seems doomed, while Marty may be able to be saved for some very long period of time. Thus, under an objective standard, we must weigh Janet's short-term "comfort" against Jerry's clear violation of the law. Marty, on the other hand, provides a possible case of life-saving treatment. Yet these very distinctions cause trouble in weighing the results: There seems no "need" to minister to Janet, who will die soon. And as for Marty, other "acceptable" treatments may or may not prove just as helpful as Jerry's. Thus, on one side or the other, Jerry may lose any claim to necessitous action. One way to treat these events is to assess not the "actual" necessity of Jerry's act but to ask whether, even if Jerry is "wrong," he is "acting in the maelstrom of events" such that his judgment does not reflect moral culpability. This analysis might qualify him for an "excuse."[8]

7. Under the common law, if *Dudley and Stephens* is the rule, Hillary would have no defense to a homicide. Even if *Dudley* is not the clear rule, he has (at least) negligently placed himself in the situation of peril and loses all claim of necessity. Under the Model Penal Code, however, Hillary would have a defense to prosecutions for purposeful and knowing murder, and possibly even reckless murder, but almost surely not for reckless manslaughter or negligent homicide.

8. This case poses the same dilemma as that of the prison escape cases.

---

8. Another possible way to confront the issues in both Examples 5 and 6 is to avoid them, to argue that in all cases of civil disobedience the only proper "claim" that a defendant has is to accept the consequences of his intentional conduct. He must suffer the criminal penalties in order to demonstrate the immorality of the regime or the law to which he objects. Thus, those who sit in to protest civil rights infringements or abortions or the proliferation of nuclear power plants could be denied the claim of necessity/justification solely as a definitional matter.

Clara has no claim of duress, since the mob did not want her to escape. On the other hand, under the earlier common law, she has no claim of necessity since the force is not a teleological one. Some courts have created a claim that they have called "duress of circumstance" to reach this case, while others have simply left the case to the jury on the issue of "responsibility." Some writers have urged rejection of any such "situational duress" claim, lest it swallow all concepts of free will and moral culpability; yet, this may show a lack of faith in the jury's ability to weigh these intricate and difficult moral issues.

9.   This appears to be primarily a problem of causation rather than of duress. If Gottfried were charged with aiding Himmelfarb's escape, he could easily claim duress. But what if he is charged with driving an unsafe vehicle? It is not clear that Himmelfarb's threat induced him to drive to Pittsburgh; he was already on the way. Moreover, even if that were not a problem, it is not clear that duress *could* be used as a claim in what may be a strict liability crime. If it goes to mens rea, duress is probably *not* allowable since strict liability offenses do not require mens rea.

10. This problem raises the issue of immediacy since it is *possible* that the hospital would perform the operation in any event. But leaving that aside, the problem really raises the issue of whether the duressor has to know that her threat endangers life. If Jack did not have a dying daughter, he would be unable to claim duress since the threat of losing one's job has not been recognized by the law in a duress context. However, here he knows that the threat is one to life but Gertrude does not. Does the threat then meet the common law's requirements of "death or serious bodily harm"? All the policy reasons for allowing a claim suggest that it should be so considered. But the common law was often very restrictive and hewed closely to doctrine. On the other hand, Jack may be able to claim necessity in any event.

11. In the actual case, Hill was precluded by the court, as a matter of law, from raising the plea of necessity. The court concluded that under the United States Constitution fetuses were not "human beings," and Hill could not therefore argue that his shooting was justified by the need to save lives. Had the doctor been planning to kill "human beings," Hill might have had a claim of necessity. But even then he would face two further hurdles: (1) whether their deaths were "imminent" since Dr. Brittan had not even entered the clinic; (2) whether a killer can claim necessity.

Notice that these problems exist as well under the Model Penal Code, which requires not only that the defendant believe his act is necessary but that the court determine that a jury could find that he has in fact (and law) done the "right thing." If this were not the case, all terrorists might successfully plead necessity. Indeed, in *Dudley*, Lord

Chief Justice Coleridge quotes from Milton's *Paradise Lost* that the devil, in explaining his temptation of Eve, claimed necessity — "the tyrant's plea." On the other hand, Paul Hill is, in his own eyes, not acting immorally. And he is certainly not the "bad actor" that a paid assassin is. How should the law differentiate between these two?

Self-Defense

The claim of self-defense was one of the first recognized by the common law. Definitions and restrictions on its use were slow in coming, and over the centuries there has been much confusion in its application. Although courts and scholars are unanimous that self-defense should be recognized as a claim, there is substantial uncertainty about why this is so. From these disagreements come disagreements on the conditions under which self-defense may properly be claimed, and the degree to which the law should use a subjective standard by which the claim is to be judged.

A utilitarian might argue that failure to recognize a claim of self-defense would be pointless, since, as with other acts done under threat of death, the law's threat of punishment in the future is unlikely to deter an actor who believes he must act or die now. As Justice Holmes once said, "Detached reflection cannot be expected in the presence of an uplifted knife." Other utilitarian explanations, sounding in partial or total justification, would posit that (a) the defendant-slayer did the right thing, and (b) by initiating an aggressive (or deadly) attack, the victim-initial aggressor "asked for" the response and lost his right not to be injured or killed. Additionally, allowing victims of aggressive attacks to respond with proportionate force may deter future aggression.

A retributivist would argue that innocent victims of aggressive attacks are not immoral actors and cannot be seen as "blameworthy" when they respond to such attacks. Moreover, people who are or believe they are suddenly threatened by death may not think clearly. Unlike Holmes, who argued that a threat of punishment *could not* change a human response to a threat of death, the retributivist would care only that the defendant *did not* reflect, even if others could be made to do so. To paraphrase Holmes (above), "Detached reflection *is usually not present* in the presence of an uplifted knife," or more particularly, "This defendant did not reflect in the presence of an uplifted knife, and that is not morally blameworthy."

Still another, morally based, explanation is that the defendant has a right to autonomy, which she cannot be made to surrender even if she must kill to enforce that right. Thus, even if the defendant could avoid injury to the aggressor by retreating, we authenticate her right not to have her "space" and autonomy infringed.

The Rules of Self-Defense

Self-defense mimics other in extremis claims, requiring

1. a *threat* of
2. "*imminent,*" *unlawful,*
3. *(serious) bodily harm,*[9]
4. to which there are, or appear to be, *no available alternatives* to the defendant except the use of force

Some courts add a fifth requirement:

5. *nonculpability* on the part of the defendant in *bringing about the situation*

Imminence; No Alternatives

The essence of self-defense is that it "sounds in necessity." Like that claim, self-defense usually demands that the defendant take any and all escape routes available before taking human life.

Preemptive Strikes

In most states a claim of self-defense requires that the harm threatened be "imminent." If Mike threatens to kill Harry "the next time I see your ugly face," or tells Harry to "get out of town by sundown or else," Harry has alternatives to killing Mike. He can leave the territory, obtain police protection, try to persuade Mike to recant, or hope that Mike will reconsider (or die). However, some jurisdictions recognize that those who engage in "preemptive strikes" may be acting properly or at least excusably in some circumstances. *Carico v. Commonwealth,* 70 Ky. 124 (1870).

To Retreat or Not to Retreat, That Is the Dilemma

Although often stated as a separate "rule" of self-defense, the requirement that the defendant "retreat" before using deadly force is really a rewording of the imminence/no alternative requirement of the common law. Unhappily, that history has been confused almost beyond comprehension

---

9. When the defendant uses deadly force, the threat must be of serious bodily harm or death and not merely harm. Thus, if *A* threatens to slap *B,* *B* may not kill *A,* even if that is the only way to avoid the slap. Generally, the rules regarding the use of nondeadly force parallel those for the use of deadly force. The text focuses on the use of deadly force.

and is no closer to resolution now than it was 150 years ago, when the courts first made the wrong turn. To understand the current chaos of the doctrine, a short historical review is helpful.

The common law of the eighteenth century recognized two kinds of claims that we now combine under the heading of self-defense: (1) prevention of felony and (2) homicide se defendendo. The distinction worked as follows: If John Mouse, while walking peacefully down the street, was suddenly affronted by a "murderous assault" by Jim Godzilla ("your money or your life"), Mouse's killing of Godzilla was a justifiable *prevention of felony*. If, on the other hand, Mouse and Godzilla were friends who engaged in a friendly argument that escalated into mutual combat, during which Mouse killed Godzilla on the spot, Mouse was guilty of manslaughter "in chaud [chance] medley"(see Chapter 8). *If,* however, Mouse "retreated" from the site of the dispute and ran "to the wall," with Godzilla pursuing, and only then killed Godzilla, the killing was *"se defendendo,"* and Mouse was "excused" (not justified). In one sense, this looked like a "prevention of felony" killing. However, since Mouse had played a part in creating the situation in which deadly force became "necessary," the state leveled a severe "civil sanction," the forfeiture of all Mouse's property to the state.

The retreat requirement applied only to homicides se defendendo and not to "prevention of felony" slayings. In the mid-nineteenth century, however, American courts, possibly because of the abolition of the forfeiture sanction, jumbled the requirement, applying it either to *all* killings or to none. Thus, in some states retreat was *always* required, even of the obviously innocent victim of an aggressive, murderous attack, while in other states it was said that "no true man" (the actual language of some courts) would ever retreat in the face of an attack, even if he had helped create that situation.

A full "retreat" or "no retreat" rule would have at least established a bright line. However, in those states that *did* require retreat, exceptions were soon created. The courts held that the slayer need not retreat in, or from, his own home (no doubt a residue of the "home as castle" view). Unable, however, to articulate why this exception applied only to homes, some courts then expanded the exception to places "like" homes, in which a person *should* feel, and should be able to feel, secure — offices, private clubs, cars, and so on. At the same time, other courts, uncomfortable with the doctrine that allowed the (by hypothesis) otherwise unnecessary taking of life, restricted the application of the exception by severely redefining "home" to include (a) only the curtilage and not the entire residential "lot"; (b) only the house and not even the curtilage; (c) only the interior of the actual house and not even the porch. *State v. Bonano*, 284 A.2d 345 (N.J. 1971). Other problems occur: Must a co-tenant or co-owner retreat if the aggressor is the other tenant/owner? What relationships might apply here?

Today, the retreat doctrine is an incomprehensible muddle, even in those states that formally adhere to it. In most states that require retreat, it is seen as a free-standing, independent criterion. Where it is required, a person who does not retreat loses the entire claim of self-defense, whatever other facts exist to dilute his moral culpability. Much more sensible is the position, espoused by Justice Holmes 75 years ago, that the failure to retreat should be one factor considered in the entire assessment of the defendant's response to the threat. *Brown v. United States*, 256 U.S. 335, 343 (1921).

Proportionality and Subjectivity

Consistent with an attempt to limit the use of deadly force, self-defense doctrine has generally required that the defendant use no more force than "necessary" to repel the aggressor. Whether deadly force is "necessary," however, depends on a number of factors relating to the victim and the defendant. If, for example, Maury (the defendant) is 5′3″ and weighs 120 lbs, and Rocky (the threatener-aggressor) is 6′4″ and weighs 240 lbs, it may be "necessary" for Maury to use deadly force to prevent Rocky from carrying out a threat to "beat Maury to a pulp." If, however, the sizes are reversed, Maury's claim to self-defense, much less to the use of deadly force, is suspect.

Similarly, in a jurisdiction requiring retreat, the respective ability of each actor to escape may be relevant. If Egmont the track star is accosted in the open street, he may be required to try to outrun Theodore to a point of safety. (The precise aspects of retreat are discussed above). If, however, the threat occurs in a moving train, the relative running talents of the two are less important. ("You can run, but you can't hide" in a train.)

This raises the general issue, already discussed in many other contexts, of the extent to which the actual characteristics of the defendant or victim are relevant in the case. As in other areas, the decisions are mixed.

In *State v. Wanrow*, 559 P.2d 548 (Wash. 1976), the defendant was a 5′4″ woman on crutches who shot and killed an unarmed, drunk 6′2″ man who had not overtly threatened her, but who she ostensibly believed had threatened to molest her child, who was asleep only a few feet away. The relative size, weight, and mobility of the defendant and the victim were clearly relevant facts under existing law. *Wanrow* broke new ground, however, by holding that a jury could find that women, as a group, are socialized *not* to use intermediate force against aggressors, particularly aggressor males. Thus, if Sid hit Wally in the nose, Wally "would probably" react by hitting Sid back or wrestling Sid to the ground. But if Sid hit Henrietta in the nose, Henrietta (the court implied) would only either submit (to further force) or employ deadly force. Thus, proportionality had to be assessed from the viewpoint of a defendant with the characteristics, at least the gender characteristics, of the defendant. At the same time, the court suggested, but did not hold, that the concept was not limited to gender. If a male defendant could demonstrate that he, individually or as a member of a culture, had not been taught how to use intermediate force, the claim would be similarly available.[10]

The problem here, as in other areas where the law begins to "subjectivize" an objective standard, is finding the stopping point. Courts had long recognized, as suggested above, that the respective sizes of the defendant and the victim were relevant. However, it is not clear whether the victim's and the defendant's ages (for example) are similarly relevant. Similar problems arise when considering defendant's reading habits, his own actual past experiences (suppose the defendant has been assaulted before), or his understanding of others' experiences (suppose he knows someone who has been assaulted or has read about people who have been). In the (in)famous case of the "subway shooter," Bernhard Goetz, the New York Court of Appeals, while saying it adhered to an objective standard, held that most of these latter characteristics should be considered by the jury in assessing the reasonableness of Goetz's reaction when confronted in the subway by several youths who appeared to him to be threatening to rob him. *People v. Goetz*, 497 N.E.2d 41 (N.Y. 1986).

Mistake and Reasonableness

We have already seen that the law puzzles over the effect of mistake in any alleged necessitous situation. In self-defense cases, the defendant could be mistaken in his belief that he is about to be attacked, or about the need to use deadly force to repel the attack, or in his belief that retreat is not likely to be successful. Suppose, however, that (1) his belief is wrong; (2) his belief is not only wrong but unreasonable. The traditional classroom hypothetical is one where B and C become involved in a heated argument over the respective lifetime batting averages of Ty Cobb and Pete Rose, leading B to shout, "I've had enough of your lying, you SOB; I'll make sure you don't make that mistake any more," while reaching into his coat pocket. C, fearing that B will pull out a gun, kills B instantly. Inside B's coat pocket is the encyclopedia of baseball but no weapon.

The early common law allowed the mistake defense to any person who

---

10. *Wanrow* is difficult to interpret. The trial court had precluded evidence that the defendant's Indian culture also militated against the use of deadly force. The Washington Supreme Court said only that it could not hold that this was an abuse of discretion. This certainly implies that it would have been within the discretion of the judge to admit such evidence. If so, then the implication is that *any* source that led the defendant (even a male) generically to abandon the use of intermediate force would be relevant and admissible.

honestly believed that he was the victim of an aggressive attack even if that belief was unreasonable.[11] Therefore, *C* in the above hypothetical would be exculpated. In the mid-nineteenth century, however, many American courts adopted the rule that a defendant who killed in the mistaken belief that he was the victim of a deadly attack would entirely lose the defense if the mistake was unreasonable. This "all or nothing" approach appears to be the current rule in the majority of jurisdictions. Its advocates argue that, as in all other claims, defendants who act unreasonably should not be exculpated. Moreover, they contend, this rule will make persons who are or perceive themselves to be threatened act more cautiously before using any deadly force.

These arguments seem misguided. If a defendant honestly believes she is threatened now with death, she is certainly unlikely to be deterred from self-defense by the threat of future state punishment. Moreover, even if she is culpable in not taking more time to assess the situation, it seems excessive to punish her equally with a killer who makes no such exculpatory claim at all. The harshness of the "all or nothing" approach has led many courts to create an intermediate position dubbed "imperfect self-defense,"[12] under which an unreasonable but honestly held belief would reduce the killing to manslaughter.

Another problem, never addressed by the courts who used the reasonableness standard, is that unless jurors are instructed to the contrary, it is at least possible that they will assume that the term "reasonableness" reflects the normal "tort" standard of the reasonable person. Thus, although the courts have struggled to make clear that criminal negligence is "more than" mere tort negligence (see Chapter 4), the latter objective standard sneaks in through the back door of this, and other, defenses relying on reasonableness.

The recent spate of cases in which police, who ostensibly have received special training NOT to react precipitously, appear to have used excessive force, often very quickly, killing someone who turns out to be an innocent victim, pointedly raises the issue. On the one hand, police should generally be held to a "higher standard" of care[13] than non-police. In torts, we sometimes employ the "superreasonable" person test when the defendant has special skills or training in particular settings. On the other hand, one

---

11. See Singer, The Resurgence of Mens Rea II: Honest but Unreasonable Mistake of Fact in Self-Defense, 28 B.C. L. Rev. 459 (1987). Cf. Giles, Self-Defense and Mistake: A Way Forward, 53 Mod. L. Rev. 187 (1990); Simester, Mistakes in Defence, 12 Oxford J. Leg. Stud. 295 (1991).

12. Some states, such as North Carolina, use this same term differently, thereby adding confusion to any generalized discussion of this (and other topics). See, e.g., State v. Norman, 378 S.E.2d 8 (N.C. 1989).

13. Of course here, as in tort, this can be rephrased to require the "ordinary" care used by a person with "extraordinary" skills. The point is the same, however worded.

reason the law recognizes self-defense and other emergency claims is that we do NOT expect reasonability in the face of what is perceived as a threat of death, again a rule recognized in torts. The question becomes even more pointed when charges of racism are added. Allowing the victim's race, and the defendant's views regarding members of the victim's race, to be considered as one of the "circumstances" in assessing reasonableness appears to endorse a "reasonable bigot" test. But failing to allow its use ignores what many might argue are the background facts of the lives of many police officers. And, let us not forget, in most instances the question will be whether the officer has acted in a "criminally" negligent manner, not "merely" negligently. These are thorny questions.

The Position of the "Aggressor"; Withdrawal

The rules articulated above apply to the innocent victim of an aggressive attack. The aggressor cannot claim their protection as *long as the initial aggression has not ended*. Thus, if *A* attacks *B* with deadly force, and *B* responds with similar force, *A* cannot claim self-defense when he injures or kills *B*, since *A* began the "episode." However, if *A* makes clear to *B* that he "withdraws" from the initial aggression, the right to self-defense returns to *A,* and *B* is now the "aggressor." *A* can make his withdrawal clear by (1) stating that he is withdrawing and/or (2) physically removing himself from the immediate area. This position reflects the common law, described above, which required retreat during a "chance encounter" that had escalated to the use of deadly force. The retreat itself was surely evidence that the retreater wished to "withdraw" from the fight.

However, the issue can become complex when *B* either does not, or cannot, understand *A*'s intent to withdraw or is (reasonably) dubious about *A*'s professed new pacifism. Thus, in some cases the courts have held that *A* may have so disoriented or terrified *B* that *B*'s failure to comprehend *A*'s attempt to stop the fight is *A*'s "fault," and therefore *A* cannot avail himself of the self-defense claim. Similarly, if *B* believes that *A*'s withdrawal is merely a ploy, and not seriously undertaken, *B* has an obvious right to continue to use defensive force, thus making *A*'s claim less potent.

The "Not Unlawful" Aggressor

Another way of articulating this aspect of self-defense is to say that defensive force can only be used against "unlawful" force. Suppose, however, that the "aggressor's" force is not "unlawful," although wrong? For example, suppose that Henrietta, loping down the sidewalk, suddenly sees Mary's car coming at her? Mary is having a seizure (see the *Decina* case in Chapter 3), and hence is not acting "unlawfully"; indeed, she is not even acting. Can Henrietta use force—including deadly force—to prevent the car from hitting her? Or suppose that she is attacked by Bugs, whom she knows to be insane? If Bugs were to kill Henrietta, his use of force would be excused (trust us; see Chapter 17). Does that mean that it is not "unlawful," such that Henrietta cannot defend herself? These questions keep academics awake at night. The courts, using common sense, allow Henrietta to defend herself.

The Battered Wives Cases: A Challenge to the Doctrines

Virtually every aspect of the claim to self-defense has been challenged in cases involving battered wives[14] who have killed their husbands in what are called "nonconfrontational" settings.[15] The challenging fact pattern often involves a husband who, over many years, has continuously beaten and abused his wife. He beats her again and falls asleep. Often, he threatens her with resumptions of the beating when he awakes; in other cases, she believes (reasonably?) that the beating will resume, even though he has said nothing in particular about this. She kills him while he sleeps. The issues raised in these cases have required courts to rethink the rules of self-defense. Even where the decisions have not altered these rules, the process of examination itself has proved illuminating.

The major doctrinal issue posed by the sleeping spouse cases is the meaning of "imminent." This, in turn, has two doctrinal components. First, if the husband is asleep, it may be hard to see any threat to injure the wife when he awakes as constituting an "imminent" threat such that the spouse has "no" alternatives left. Second, it may be argued that his sleeping puts an end to the entire episode. Several courts have held, often in the face of vigorous dissent, that when the abusive husband goes to sleep, the battering episode has terminated. See *State v. Norman*, 324 N.C. 253 (1989); *State v. Stewart*, 763 P.2d 572 (Kan. 1988). Thus, even if the battered wife *reasonably* believes that the battering will continue when the husband awakes, *she* becomes the "aggressor" against the sleeping husband and cannot avail

---

14. This term will be used generically here. It includes battered women who are *not* married to the batterer at the time of the killing (although many were married to him at an earlier time) *and* battered children. It also includes battered husbands and beating victims in same-sex relationships.

15. Most cases involving battered wives involve actual confrontation and are thus governed by "normal" self-defense rules. Maguigan, Battered Women and Self-Defense: Myths and Misconceptions in Current Reform Proposals, 140 U. Pa. L. Rev. 379 (1991).

herself of the self-defense claim at all. In short, these killings are perceived as preemptive strikes and, no matter how "reasonable," are disallowed.[16]

Prosecutors in these cases contend that the threat was not imminent because the defendants could simply leave their house, or their husbands, or both. These defendants have sought to explain why they did not do so. They often point out that when in the past they have left, their spouses have simply followed them, beaten them, and "recaptured" them. This, of course, does not explain why they did not *then* leave.

To meet this issue, battered wives have relied on what has been termed "battered wife syndrome," a cycle of "learned helplessness" aggravated by the so-called "Cinderella complex." The latter is said to convince the wives that it is they, not the husbands, who are to blame for the beatings; if they were simply better wives, the husbands would not beat them. The "learned helplessness" factor argues that, over a period of cycles involving beatings, reconciliation, and growing tension, the wives have come to believe that there *is* no escape. Thus, a mixture of fear and guilt persuades these women to submit to intolerable abuse.

Most courts now admit evidence of battered wife syndrome. It is on the second prong of the defense that the problem is currently focused. In arguing that there were no realistic alternatives to the killing, battered wives often point to a history of inadequate protection by police and other governmental agencies.[17] Two objections to such evidence are raised: (1) it may distract the jury from the killing at hand to the *general* question of police response; (2) no matter how accurate a picture of governmental response the evidence may cast, it cannot generate a justification for the wife, who "should have" tried those avenues (or retreated) once more before taking life. The surre-buttal to the first point is that if the system has in fact failed to protect a person who has, by default, taken the law into her own hands, it *should* be subjected to such scrutiny. Fairness to the defendant, the argument goes,

---

16. Additionally, the issue of whether the wife has to retreat has hung in the background because, unlike the aggressor who pursues the defendant to her home, *both* parties in this case have a claim not to retreat. Although as a matter of logic this should be irrelevant (since the husband has no right to use illegal force against his wife, even in the home), it appears to have bothered some courts.

17. The term "police" here is used generically to characterize all governmental response. Thus, for example, battered women often argue that there are few governmental shelters to which they can retreat, and that their spouses have often ignored, without penalty, court orders forbidding further contact. The statistics on these matters, while in dispute in any given jurisdiction, certainly have borne out the complaints that at least in the past governmental response to fears, and even beatings, of wives has been slow and sporadic at best. While governmental authorities now seem to be much more sensitive to such concerns, there is still good reason to believe that the system has much left to do. See Tracy Chapman's song, "Last Night I Heard the Screaming."

demands no less, and the community as a whole should be made aware of these failings. As to the second objection, it merely restates the subjective-objective question of necessity.

These two questions then become intertwined with the question of subjective versus objective testing. If the defendant in a self-defense case is wrong (actually or normatively) about her assessment of the need for using deadly force to extricate herself from the perceived threat, it is unclear whether that belief must be reasonable or whether it is enough that the defendant actually believed it to be necessary. And if the "reasonable person" is the test, what characteristics of the defendant are to be used in making the assessment? Clearly, if the battering and the "syndrome" are part of the reasonable person's background, then the test is one of the reasonably battered woman who suffers from learned helplessness.

Conclusion: Need for a General Rethinking

In a number of jurisdictions in the United States, the doctrine of self-defense has become a set of "doctrines" and "mini-requirements" that unduly narrow the focus of the claim and often are in conflict with each other. The better approach is simply to ask whether the defendant was the target of an aggressive, deadly attack and (honestly? reasonably?) believed that there were no reasonable alternatives to the use of deadly force.

Doctrinal Problems of Self-Defense
The Mens Rea of Self-Defense

Kant and Bentham become involved in a heated discussion about retribution and utilitarianism. Bentham grabs a bottle of beer, breaks it, and walks menacingly toward Kant, saying "I'll kill you, you retributivist, you." Kant pulls out a knife and says, "Don't come any closer. Just let me be. I don't want to be hurt." Bentham lunges at Kant, who stabs Bentham. Bentham dies.

We normally think of this typical scenario of self-defense as demonstrating an intentional death that *A* wishes to explain by referring to self-defense. But it can be argued that the killing was not intentional. Rather, Kant's *intent* (purpose) was to escape, without any clear reference to the possibility of killing Bentham. Catholic doctrine, for example, uses this analysis to explain self-defense.[18] More difficult is the issue of whether *A* was highly *reckless* ("under circumstance manifesting extreme indifference to the value of hu-

---

18. F. Spinagle, The Catechism Explained 388 (1961).

man life" in the words of the MPC, or manifesting a "depraved heart" in the common law language) as to B's death. A jury could surely find that a person in A's position *did* consciously disregard such a risk, but it could just as easily find that A didn't consciously think about the consequences to B at all.

The issue here is whether a claim of self-defense is really a claim negating the mens rea of the crime. If so, then the prosecution must carry the burden of proof on this issue, once properly raised (see Chapter 15).[19] At one level, the question goes to what we have already called "statutory mens rea." At another level, however, the question involves what we have called "traditional" mens rea. (See Chapter 4 for both these terms.) Thus, even if a jury concludes that Kant "intended" or was "reckless" as to Bentham's death or serious bodily harm, it might well find that Kant was not "evil" or "malevolent" because of the exigent circumstances under which Kant operated. As already discussed this sense of mens rea has somewhat disappeared from criminal law, but analysis should consider its impact. See Pilsbury, The Meaning of Deserved Punishment: An Essay on Choice, Character, and Responsibility, 67 Ind. L.J. 719 (1992).

Justification or Excuse?

"Creating the Conditions of Self-Defense": Excusable vs. Justifiable Self-Defense. Rejecting the common law's line between "justified" killings in self-defense and those that were "necessitated" only because of the defendant's earlier actions, modern courts and most writers treat self-defense only as a "justification." Current doctrine either ignores the defendant's participation in the events leading up to the necessitous killing or makes the defendant liable only if he was negligent (or reckless) in those events. This, however, seems to miss the common law's kernel of insight that those who "create the conditions of their own defense claims" should not be fully exonerated.

Defense of Others

If Yitzhak sees Yassir "beating up" Clyde, Yitzhak may come to Clyde's defense. He may use force to defend another to the same extent that he may

---

19. Most states place on the prosecution the burden of proof in self-defense. In *Martin v. Ohio*, 480 U.S. 228 (1987), however, the Supreme Court held that placing the burden of proof on the defendant did not violate the United States Constitution. The Court's opinion did not consider the question of whether self-defense is "usually" a justification, as many academic analysts have suggested. Nor did the Court refer to, much less discuss, the historic difference between excused and justified self-defense. Many attorneys — and courts — may be unfamiliar with the analytic framework of justification/excuse.

protect himself. This result can be understood by many of the explanations surrounding self-defense. For example, Yassir, the aggressor, has "given up" his right not to be assaulted.

But suppose Yitzhak is mistaken, and Yassir is (a) responding — legitimately — to Clyde's initial aggression or (b) a police officer arresting Clyde. Should Yitzhak be liable for assault on Yassir? Here, states are divided on what result should obtain. On the one hand, we applaud Yitzhak's humanitarianism. On the other, Yitzhak has been an "officious intermeddler" — indeed, a vigilante. Early common law punished Yitzhak on the ground that he could only use as much force as Clyde could. This was known as the "alter ego" rule. Most courts — and the Model Penal Code — have now decided to encourage reasonable intervention and would exculpate Yitzhak.

The Model Penal Code

The Code adopts many of the changes wrought by American courts in the nineteenth and twentieth centuries. Under §3.04, retreat is required before deadly force may be used, but only where the defendant "*knows* he may retreat in *complete* safety" (emphasis added). This may totally undercut the retreat requirement; in an age of guns and other such weapons, it is the rare case where the defendant "knows" (in contrast to believes or hopes) that he may retreat in "complete" safety. The Code, however, broadens the notion of "imminence" and also enlarges the notion of when an "occasion" occurs or ends.

Similarly, the Code's initial sections on self-defense consistently describe the actual defendant's honest belief as sufficient to allow the claim. Section 3.09, however, dilutes this view by allowing prosecution for manslaughter or negligent homicide if the defendant has been reckless or negligent, respectively, in reaching a mistaken belief. Thus, on this issue the Code is much more subjective than those courts adopting the "all or nothing" approach with regard to the self-defense claim but only slightly more subjective than those endorsing the "imperfect self-defense" doctrine.

EXAMPLES

In which of the following can the defendant(s) claim self-defense?

1a. Hubert is walking down the street when he is confronted by Lyndon, who pulls a knife, drags Hubert into an alley, and demands money. Hubert pulls out an Uzi and kills Lyndon.

1b. Same facts, except that Hubert has no Uzi, but instead wrestles the knife away from Lyndon and then stabs him to death.

2. Quincy is mowing his lawn one day when his neighbor, Ralph, comes over, shovel in hand. "Your dog has ruined my azaleas again, Quincy,"

he shouts, and swings the shovel madly at Quincy. Quincy drops the mower, grabs a pitchfork, and kills Ralph.

3a. Jack, a famous movie actor, is driving on a major road when Bert's car pulls in front. Enraged because he believes he has been "cut off," Jack follows Bert's car to the next intersection, where both cars stop for a red light. Jack leaps out of his car with a golf club in his hand, and begins screaming at Bert, "I'll kill you, you S.O.B." He then begins smashing Bert's car. Bert jumps out of his car and wrestles Jack to the ground, breaking two of Jack's fingers.

3b. Bert also grabs the golf club and flings it into nearby bushes, hits Jack, runs to his car, and attempts to lock the door. Jack pulls Bert out and hits him several times in the face with his fists.

3c. Bert thereupon pulls out a knife and confronts Jack with it. Jack backs up and runs for his car. Bert follows, Jack finds another golf club, and hits Bert once, killing him.

4. Lyle, 14 years old, has been beaten by his father at least once every two months since the time he was 7. One night three days before his junior high school graduation, Lyle and his father have another run-in, but his father is on the way to work. "You won't live to see graduation," says his father as he leaves. That night Lyle is unable to sleep. The next morning he goes to school but leaves at 11:00 to return home, where he picks up his father's shotgun and loads it. At 3:00 that afternoon, his father walks through the front door, and Lyle empties both barrels, killing him instantly.

5. Leonard, 5 foot 3 inches, and weighing 135 pounds, is walking down a dark street at 2:00 a.m. Suddenly, as he turns a corner, he is confronted by a man who asks him for a light. As Leonard fumbles for a match, the stranger says "Well, maybe you can help me with something else," and puts his hand inside his pocket. Leonard shoots him instantly. At trial, the prosecutor shows that the stranger was reaching for a street map. Leonard seeks to introduce evidence that (a) five years ago he was attacked by a stranger and severely beaten; (b) his best friend was recently mugged in this same area; (c) the stranger vaguely resembled the drawing, which had appeared in a number of local newspapers and which Leonard had seen at least five times, of a suspected robber, whose robberies, however, had occurred in another section of the city. Leonard also seeks to introduce evidence that (d) the victim was 6 foot 6 inches, weighed 268 pounds, and was redheaded; (e) defendant has always had a dread fear of redheaded men; (f) the stranger was wearing a raincoat but it had not rained for three days and the temperature at the time of their encounter was 65°. Which, if any, of these pieces of evidence bears on defendant's liability and is therefore admissible?

EXPLANATIONS

1a. This is the classic case of self-defense. Hubert is the innocent victim of an unprovoked felonious attack. He is clearly justified in killing Lyndon. Even in a jurisdiction requiring retreat, there is no apparent way for Hubert to retreat safely.

1b. Now the facts have changed. Hubert *was* under deadly attack. But when he wrestles the knife away from Lyndon, the situation may be different than in Example 1. Since Hubert now has the knife, it is at least arguable that he could have retreated. On the other hand, Hubert might reasonably conclude (particularly in emergency conditions) that Lyndon would continue the pursuit, perhaps with another deadly weapon, unless Hubert stopped him now.

2. Even in a jurisdiction that requires retreat, Quincy is on his own property, thereby apparently nullifying the requirement. Some courts, however, have restricted the "castle" exception to the house. Since Quincy is not in his house, he might lose the exception. If he could have ducked into the house, he may be required to do so in some jurisdictions. If Ralph had not swung the shovel at Quincy, we would have the issue of whether Ralph intended to hurt Quincy (as opposed to his dog) and also whether Quincy's perception that Ralph was threatening him was reasonable. See the next example.

3a. These facts show the ambiguity in many altercations. Although Jack's words carry a threat of serious bodily harm or death, his actions belie them. He has used force against Bert's property but not against Bert. Yet he has threatened Bert's person. If Bert used deadly force, it might be deemed excessive. On the other hand, it is not clear whether the force that Bert used could be characterized as deadly force. Whether Bert could *reasonably* fear serious bodily harm may be one for the jury.

3b. Since Jack was the initial aggressor, he cannot respond to Bert's use of force. Moreover, it appears that Bert has attempted to withdraw.

3c. Bert's use of a knife may change this into a new encounter. Even though Jack used his golf club on Bert's car, he did not aim for Bert's head or other vital parts. Therefore, Jack was not threatening or using deadly force. Bert's reaction, however, does constitute deadly force, and Jack may respond to it accordingly. In a jurisdiction generally requiring retreat, however, Jack may have to retreat, since Bert may not obviously have the ability to pursue, catch, and stab Jack if he runs away. These factual questions and Jack's (reasonable) assessment of his chance of successful retreat will be for the jury.

4. These facts are very close to those of an actual case, *State v. Janes,* 64 Wash. App. 134 (1992). The questions raised include whether the father's words constituted an "imminent threat" of serious bodily harm

or death, whether Lyle had alternatives other than killing, and whether he could reasonably believe those alternatives to be futile. All these issues could be used to determine whether the killing was "justified" self-defense. Still another issue that might be raised is whether Lyle had to retreat even if his father intended to beat him. Although he lives in the house, it is not, as a matter of property law, "his" house.

Assuming for a moment that the killing is not justified, one other issue is whether Lyle could be excused: whether, notwithstanding the "intentionality" of Lyle's acts, the obvious stress under which he operated suggests that he is not as blameworthy as other "intentional" killers. If not, he might have his liability reduced to manslaughter. See Chapter 8.

5.   The question obviously deals with the extent to which the reasonable man has characteristics of the defendant. As suggested in the example, these questions usually arise during evidentiary rulings. If the jurisdiction allows the comparison, then the evidence is admissible; if not, then the evidence is excluded. The stranger's resemblance to the robber is likely to be admissible even in a jurisdiction using the objective test, since a "reasonable person" might be aware of the drawings and therefore might be more justifiably afraid of someone with this resemblance. The dress of the victim is likely to be admissible because it goes to whether Leonard's fears were reasonable (contrast cases involving a person wearing a three-piece suit and one where the stranger is wearing a leather jacket and a set of brass knuckles). The two crime incidents are unlikely to be admitted in many jurisdictions because they do not go to what the "reasonable man" (as opposed to Leonard) might draw from them. The long-standing paranoia is almost certainly not admissible since "reasonable people" are not paranoid. All the information is admissible in a jurisdiction that allows a claim if the defendant "honestly" believed himself to be in danger.

Defense of Property and Habitat

Most people work hard to acquire their property and want to keep it safe from others. We have laws, such as those against theft, to help safeguard our property, but the law also allows people to use force if necessary to prevent others from taking or destroying their property.

Even more important, most people want to be safe in their homes. The maxim, "A man's home is his castle," though sexist by contemporary standards, recognizes that threats to our physical safety while we are in our homes commonly cause fierce fear and resentment. That is why we have laws against burglary and trespass. Again, however, the law also allows people the use of force, including deadly force in some cases, to defend themselves in their homes if they reasonably appear to be threatened.

Using force can involve harming those who want to take our property or harm us in our homes. It can also create a risk that innocent people will be hurt. Thus, the law must balance the need to forcibly defend property and personal security, on the one hand, and the need to protect lives and safety on the other. The law prefers the value of human life (including that of the thief) to that of property. It does this by only permitting the use of nondeadly force to defend property, thereby ensuring that human life is not taken merely to save property. However, the law also prefers the value of innocent human life over the lives of aggressors who threaten innocent life. Thus, the law permits the use of deadly force in some cases to defend habitation.

Use of force to defend property or habitation is justified under the law because the owner's superior claims to possession and personal security are considered more important than the aggressor's bodily safety. Because the individual must act under tremendous pressure in an emergency situation, the law permits him to resort to self-help by using force against thieves and aggressors.

The Common Law

A defendant has a legal right to use nondeadly force when he has an honest and reasonable belief that it is necessary to protect real or personal property in his possession from imminent unlawful taking, damage, dispossession, or trespass. He may also use nondeadly force to reenter real property or to recover personal property immediately after it has been taken. However, as described below, there are limits on this right to use nondeadly force.

Other Lawful Means Available

Force may not be used if there is time to use other lawful measures, such as calling the police. Consistent with other defenses and excuses grounded in necessity, this rule avoids the possibility of physical harm to someone unless it is really required.

Warning

If he can do so without risk to himself or his property, an individual must warn the aggressor to stop unless it is clear the warning would be useless.

Deadly Force Not Permitted

A person may not use deadly force solely to protect property. This rule is based on the value judgment that human life is worth more than property.

Personal Property. An individual may use *nondeadly* force to protect personal property from imminent unlawful taking or destruction. If the property owner is then met with what reasonably appears to be deadly force by the thief, the owner may respond with deadly force in self-defense. The thief's resort to deadly force has changed the situation from the defense of property to the defense of human life, and the rules of self-defense now apply.

Conversely, if the property owner uses *deadly* force when the thief does not appear to be using it, the thief then has the right to use deadly force in self-defense because the property owner has exceeded his legal privilege to use force. (See the discussion of self-defense above at pages 403-410.)

Real Property. In contrast to the rules governing the use of force to defend personal property, the common law is somewhat more permissive in authorizing the use of deadly force to defend real property.

Defense of Dwelling. One early English case held that deadly force could be used to prevent forcible entry into a dwelling, provided a warning had been given not to enter. Most jurisdictions, however, no longer follow this rule.

Today most jurisdictions allow the use of deadly force to prevent forcible entry into a dwelling only if the occupant has a reasonable belief that the intruder intends to commit a felony inside. The occupant can use deadly force in these circumstances because the balance of interests has changed dramatically. Now there is a threat of imminent harm both to property and to human life.

Mechanical Devices. Most jurisdictions do not permit the use of deadly mechanical devices, such as spring guns, to protect property. These devices operate automatically even when the occupant is not there. They pose serious risk of harm to innocent people, such as firefighters, and also activate deadly force when the occupant's life is not in jeopardy.

A few jurisdictions permit the use of these deadly devices, but only if the defendant would have been privileged to use deadly force if he were there. If a firefighter responding to an alarm at the dwelling is killed or injured, the occupant is strictly liable for the unlawful use of deadly force.

Some jurisdictions will permit the use of *nondeadly* devices, such as electric fences, provided proper warning is posted.

Mistakes. Most jurisdictions allow the use of force, including deadly force, if the occupant reasonably believes that the elements of the privilege exist. If, however, the defendant is *negligent* in forming his belief, his use of force is unlawful.

The Model Penal Code

The MPC also permits the use of nondeadly force to defend real or personal property.

Initial Aggression

Section 3.06(1)(a) permits a person to use nondeadly force (i) to defend against an entry into, or trespass against, her real property, or (ii) to prevent another from taking her personal property when she believes it is immediately required to prevent it. The actor must believe the land or personal property is in her possession or in another's possession for whom she is acting. Section 3.06(2) defines "possession."

Retaking Property

Section 3.06(1)(b) allows individuals forcibly to reenter land or to retake personal property taken by another. The actor must believe that the other person does not have lawful title to the property and that she (or the person for whom she is acting) is entitled to possession.

The actor must also satisfy two additional requirements: (i) she uses force immediately or in "fresh pursuit," or (ii) the actor believes she is using force against someone who has no claim of right to possession and that, in cases involving real property, it would impose an exceptional hardship to wait for a court order before reentry.

Use of Force

Somewhat begrudgingly, the MPC authorizes the use of force to defend or retake property. The balance of §3.06 imposes limitations on the use of force otherwise authorized by that section. Some of the more important limitations are indicated below.

Request to Desist. The actor must first request the aggressor to stop, unless the actor believes that the request would be useless or dangerous or that substantial harm will be done to the property before the request can be made.

Risk of Serious Bodily Injury. Force, even if otherwise justified, cannot be used if the actor knows it may expose the aggressor to serious bodily injury.

Use of Deadly Force. The actor can use deadly force only if (a) she believes she is defending her dwelling against someone with no claim of right to possession, or (b) the aggressor is committing a serious crime and has used or threatened deadly force, or (c) the actor's use of nondeadly force would expose her (or someone else in her presence) to substantial danger of serious bodily injury.

Use of Mechanical Devices. Use of mechanical devices to protect property is permitted, provided they do not threaten death or serious bodily harm, are reasonable, and either are customarily used or a warning is given.

EXAMPLES

1. Maria Rodriguez owns a holiday condominium in Kansas City. She stays at the condo periodically and keeps her irreplaceable collection of twelfth- and thirteenth-century Mayan and Aztec jewelry from Latin America there. Last year two attempts were made to break in; they almost succeeded. The condo cannot be made more resistant to break-ins and the jewelry cannot be insured. One night Maria wakes up and hears a burglar in the kitchen. She grabs the .38 pistol under her pillow, quietly enters the kitchen, and shoots the burglar, killing him. Was Maria's use of deadly force lawful?

2a. Afraid to leave her invaluable jewelry at the condo without effective protection, Maria wants to use a deadly cobra snake as a "watch dog." She would place it in a very secure box that could only be released electronically if a door or window to her condo is opened. Advise Maria.

2b. Would your advice be different if Maria said she would post easily recognized warnings — "Do Not Enter Without Permission: Deadly Cobra Inside" — on the outside of her condo?

3. Finally, Maria decides she must put her rare jewelry in a bank safe-deposit box. She loads it into her large purse and drives downtown. While walking to the bank, a large man tries to snatch her purse by grabbing onto it and trying to pull it from her. Maria desperately hangs on. The man yells, "Let go. I'm not going to hurt you. All I want is your purse." With her free hand Maria manages to free her .38 pistol from her pocket and shoots the purse-snatcher, killing him instantly. As prosecutor, would you charge Maria with murder?

EXPLANATIONS

1. As an occupant in lawful possession of a dwelling, Maria may use deadly force against an aggressor only if she reasonably believes he intends to commit a felony against person or property therein. The difficulty here is that there are no facts indicating what the dead aggressor intended once inside. The defense will argue that a homeowner should not have to make further inquiry to ascertain the aggressor's intentions because that would only put Maria at greater disadvantage and increase her danger. Moreover, it is reasonable to infer that the intruder had a felonious purpose in mind when entering Maria's condo.

    Though this is a close case, a jury would probably find Maria was justified in using deadly force to defend herself and her dwelling from the intruder.

    The MPC takes substantially the same approach as the common law. Maria would have to persuade the jury that she reasonably believed the aggressor was committing a serious crime or that, without recourse to deadly force, she risked serious bodily injury. Again, the jury would probably agree with her.

2a. Hopefully, you immediately told Maria that she may be criminally liable for using a deadly cobra as a mechanical watch dog. Neither the common law nor the MPC authorizes the use of deadly devices to defend property, including a dwelling. The fact that this deadly device is also defending extremely valuable personal property does not make a difference. Human life, even that of a criminal, is considered more valuable than property. Thus, tell Maria to immediately take her killer cobra back to the pet store for a refund. Otherwise, she may be charged with a serious crime such as homicide or assault if the cobra is released during a break-in. You might also point out that her slinky sleuth also presents serious risk to innocent people like firefighters or caretakers who might be forced to enter the condo in an emergency.

2b. Posting warning signs would not relieve Maria of criminal responsibility. Neither the common law nor the MPC permits the use of deadly force to protect unoccupied dwellings or personal property located there. The MPC permits the use of unusual mechanical devices to protect real or personal property if adequate notice is given, but only if they do not pose a substantial risk of serious bodily harm.

Posting warnings does not relieve Maria of responsibility for using a *deadly* mechanical device to defend her property. Most jurisdictions prohibit the use of such devices. The MPC allows the use of nondeadly devices if they are customary (like razor-sharp wire around a warehouse) or if notice is posted. It does not allow the use of deadly mechanical devices under any circumstances.

3. Maria is not entitled to use deadly force to defend her personal property from a thief even though it is very valuable and, in this case, is not insured. Thus, she is guilty of homicide. Maria might claim that she reasonably feared death or great bodily harm at the hands of the thief, but he was unarmed and told her he would not hurt her and that he only wanted to steal her property.

Use of Force

Trained police forces are a modern development. Before they were established, citizens often had to make arrests and bring those suspected of committing crimes to the public authorities. The common law developed special rules governing the use of force by peace officers and citizens to apprehend criminal suspects and to prevent their escape.

Because citizens, as well as police, may also need to prevent others from committing crime, the law authorizes both police officers and citizens to use force to stop crime. Again, the common law distinguishes between the use of *nondeadly force* and *deadly force* and between the authority of *police* and of the *citizen* to use either kind of force.

To complicate matters, both police and citizens can be mistaken about whether a crime has been committed and whether the person they suspect has indeed committed it. Police and citizens may also be mistaken about whether a crime is in progress or whether the person they suspect is *attempting* to commit it. Thus, the law must strike a delicate balance between allowing police and citizens to arrest criminals and to prevent crimes, while also protecting innocent people who may be mistakenly suspected of committing crimes.

Arrest

The Common Law

The common law permits both peace officers and citizens to use force, including deadly force in certain cases, to arrest individuals suspected of committing a crime. The common law distinguishes between the use of force by the police and by private citizens and between the use of nondeadly and deadly force. Not surprisingly, the common law provides broader authority for peace officers to use force than it does for citizens.

Police Authority to Arrest. At common law police can arrest a suspect if they have a warrant for his arrest. They may arrest someone without a warrant if they have reasonable grounds to believe that the suspect has committed a felony or if the suspect commits a misdemeanor in their presence. Today, most jurisdictions have enacted statutes that explicitly confer this same scope of arrest authority on police officers.

Nondeadly Force. Police can use nondeadly force when they reasonably believe it necessary to make a lawful arrest for any crime, including a felony or a misdemeanor. Apprehension of criminal suspects is considered more important than the risk of bodily injury that can occur when nondeadly force is used to make an arrest or prevent escape. Note that the police need only have reasonable grounds for believing that the suspect committed a crime. Their use of force under these circumstances is permitted even if it turns out that no crime was committed or that the suspect did not commit it.

Deadly Force. Police can use deadly force if they reasonably believe it is necessary to prevent a felon from escaping arrest. Deadly force cannot be used to prevent the escape of a misdemeanant.

Some jurisdictions impose more restrictive limits on the use of deadly force, authorizing it only when the police reasonably believe that the felon trying to escape arrest is dangerous. The officer must reasonably believe the fleeing felon is armed or has committed a serious crime dangerous to life, such as murder. This approach limits the possible taking of life to cases in which the felon, if not apprehended, may pose a future risk to human life.

Constitutional Limits. The Supreme Court has narrowed the common law authority of police to apprehend criminal suspects. The Court held that it is an unreasonable seizure of a person in violation of the Fourth Amendment for the police to use deadly force to apprehend a fleeing felon unless (i) deadly force is necessary to prevent escape; (ii) if practical, a warning is given; and (iii) the officer has probable cause (essentially the same as "reasonable grounds" at common law) to believe the felon poses a serious threat of death or serious bodily injury to others if he is not apprehended. *Tennessee v. Garner,* 471 U.S. 1 (1985). Risking the life of a dangerous felony suspect is justified in this situation in order to prevent risking the loss of innocent life.

There are sound reasons for not allowing the police to use deadly force to apprehend a criminal suspect who is not reasonably believed to be dangerous to human life. Killing a nondangerous, unarmed suspect effectively deprives him of his due process right to a trial to determine his guilt or innocence and to be punished according to law. The police officer, in effect, becomes prosecutor, judge, and jury. Moreover, killing the suspect imposes a much harsher punishment than could be imposed for the crime he is suspected of committing unless it is a capital offense.

Self-Defense. If met with forcible resistance while trying to apprehend a criminal suspect, the police are entitled to use force in self-defense, including deadly force, if they reasonably fear imminent death or serious bodily injury. (See pages 403-410.)

Private Citizens. The common law gives citizens authority to make arrests for any felony or for a misdemeanor involving breach of the peace occurring in their presence, provided (i) the offense was committed and (ii) the citizen reasonably believes the suspect committed the felony. The actual commission of the offense is a strict liability element. If no crime occurred, then a citizen who uses force to arrest or prevent flight of a criminal suspect is criminally responsible even if her belief was reasonable.

Thus, while a police officer may use force even when no crime has been committed provided he has probable cause to believe it has occurred, a private citizen will be criminally liable for the use of force in such circumstances.

Assisting the Police. A private citizen asked to help police officers stands in their shoes. The citizen can assert any defense that the officer can assert, whether the citizen uses nondeadly or deadly force.

Nondeadly Force. Private citizens acting on their own may use nondeadly force only when they reasonably believe it necessary to arrest someone for a felony that was actually committed. If the felony was not committed, the private citizen is strictly liable for her use of force.

Deadly Force. The authority of a private person acting alone to use deadly force to apprehend a felon is more narrow than that of a police officer. A citizen may use deadly force when she reasonably believes it is necessary to arrest a person who has actually committed a felony (and perhaps only a dangerous felony). If the person did not commit the felony, a private citizen using deadly force is strictly liable. Thus, unlike a police officer, a private citizen uses deadly force to apprehend a felon at her own peril.

The Model Penal Code

Use of Force in Law Enforcement. Section 3.07 authorizes the use of force when the actor is making (or assisting in making) an arrest and believes it is immediately necessary to effect a lawful arrest.

Limitations. This section limits the privilege as follows:

Nondeadly Force. Force is not justified unless the actor informs the person, if feasible, why he is being arrested and, if the arrest is made under a warrant, the warrant is valid or believed to be valid.

Deadly Force. Deadly force is not justified in making an arrest unless (a) the arrest is for a felony; (b) the person is a peace officer or assisting someone she believes is a peace officer; (c) the actor believes there is no substantial risk to innocent people; and (d) the actor believes the suspect committed a crime involving the use or threat of deadly force or there is a substantial risk the person will cause death or serious bodily injury if apprehension is delayed.

Note that (1) *all* four elements must be satisfied before deadly force can be used, and (2) a *private citizen* cannot use deadly force to arrest a felony suspect unless she believes she is assisting a police officer. Note also that §3.09(2) of the MPC allows an actor to be prosecuted for an offense requiring proof of recklessness or negligence if she was reckless or negligent in forming the beliefs required for justification under §§3.03 to 3.08. Thus, if the actor was reckless or negligent in forming the beliefs set forth in (b), (c), or (d) above, she can be prosecuted for any applicable offense requiring those culpability states.

Preventing Crime
The Common Law

Nondeadly Force. Individuals may use nondeadly force if they reasonably believe a misdemeanor is being committed. Deadly force is never permitted to prevent a misdemeanor. Preventing a minor crime is simply not worth the loss of human life that can occur when deadly force is used.

Deadly Force. There are two views on the lawful use of deadly force to prevent commission of felony.

Any Felony. Some jurisdictions allow both police officers and private citizens to use deadly force when they reasonably believe it is necessary to prevent the commission of *any* felony. Because it includes *all* felonies, this broad rule accepts the possible loss of life that deadly force may cause in order to prevent crimes that, though serious, do not necessarily pose danger to human life.

The balance of interests struck by this rule is even more remarkable because a *reasonable belief* is sufficient to justify the use of deadly force. Thus, human life may be taken even though the person killed may not actually have intended to commit any offense. For example, a citizen who shoots and kills a stranger he reasonably mistakes to be stealing the citizen's expensive mountain bike could not be convicted of homicide.

Dangerous Felony. Some jurisdictions only allow the use of deadly force to prevent the commission of felonies dangerous to human life. This appears to be the modern approach.

The Model Penal Code

Section 3.07(5) authorizes the use of force when the actor believes it is immediately necessary to prevent suicide or serious self-injury, a crime involving or threatening bodily harm, damage to property, or a breach of the peace subject to these two limitations contained in §§3.05(a)(i) and (ii):

(i) Other limitations on the use of force contained in the MPC apply even though the person against whom force is used is committing a crime.

(ii) *Deadly* force is not justified unless the actor believes: (a) there is a substantial risk the person will cause death or serious bodily injury to another if he is not prevented from committing the crime and there is no substantial risk of injuring innocent people; or (b) use of deadly force is necessary to suppress a riot or mutiny after the rioters (or mutineers) have been ordered to disperse and warned that deadly force will be used if they do not.

EXAMPLES

1. Rex is working alone at the grocery store late Friday evening. He notices Ruth, a suspicious woman who is quite small and wearing a long coat, loitering in the corner. He sees that a plainclothes police officer buying some milk has also noticed her. Suddenly, Ruth pulls a rifle out from under her long coat and, though having a great deal of trouble holding the weapon steady, points it in Rex's direction, saying, "Give me all the money in the cash register." The plainclothes officer, realizing what is going on, moves carefully toward her. Seconds after Rex has given Ruth all the money in the register, the officer lunges at the woman, knocking the rifle from her hands. She escapes his grasp and runs out into the parking lot.

a. Rex picks up her rifle, aims it at Ruth and shoots, killing her instantly.

b. The plainclothes officer aims his service revolver at the legs of the fleeing suspect in order to wound her and fires. Unfortunately, the bullet strikes Ruth in the head, killing her instantly.

As prosecutor, would you conclude that either Rex or the officer were justified in using deadly force?

2. Several young boys are playing basketball on a Saturday afternoon in an apartment complex. Julio thinks they are making too much noise, so he takes the basketball away from them and takes it to his apartment. Eric, one of the boys, runs to his dad, Hector, and tells him what Julio did. Hector starts walking toward Julio's apartment. Julio, seeing Hector coming, closes his front door. Rather than knocking, Hector simply opens the unlocked front door and walks into Julio's apartment intending to discuss the incident with him. Julio shoots Hector in the chest with a double-barrel shotgun, killing him instantly as he enters the apartment. Murder or a justified killing? Your call, district attorney.

3. Juan is driving a truck loaded with illegal immigrants on a highway near San Diego. Officers Smith and Wesson spot the truck and suspect Juan is violating immigration laws. They turn on the siren and pursue Juan. Juan speeds up. After a very dangerous chase at high speeds, Juan pulls over and stops the truck. Most of the occupants (all illegal immigrants whom Juan was smuggling into the country) flee. Officers Smith and Wesson pull up and see Juan running away from the truck and give chase. Smith yells, "Stop! Police!" Juan ignores the warning and continues to flee. Smith finally catches Juan and tackles him. Juan is sitting passively on the ground when Officer Wesson arrives on the scene and starts beating Juan severely about the head and shoulders with his baton. Can Officer Wesson be charged with assault?

EXPLANATIONS

1a. Rex is not preventing a crime. The suspect has broken off her criminal enterprise and is fleeing. Thus, Rex's privilege to use deadly force must be analyzed under the law of arrest, not crime prevention.

Under the common law a private person can use deadly force to apprehend a fleeing felon, provided a felony was committed. Here Rex shot at someone who had, in fact, committed a felony. Thus, his use of deadly force to apprehend the woman is justified and he may not be convicted of any crime.

The MPC does not allow a private person acting alone to use deadly force to apprehend a felon, even one who might pose a danger to life if not apprehended. Was Rex acting alone? Or can he persuade the fact finder that he was actually assisting a police officer? Did the police officer ask for assistance? Ruth was committing a felony, so that element is met. But Rex must also show (i) he believed there was no substantial risk to innocent people; (ii) the suspect committed a crime involving the threat of deadly force; and (iii) the suspect is dangerous if not apprehended. He could probably prove the first two elements. But was Ruth dangerous if not apprehended? This is a close case on the facts and could go either way.

1b. Under the common law a police officer may also use deadly force to apprehend someone he has reasonable grounds to believe committed a felony. Because he may act on "reasonable grounds," a police officer has more authority to use deadly force than a private citizen who acts at his peril that a felony has been committed.

The MPC limits police use of *deadly force* to arrest in the same manner as it limits private actors. Thus, the same analysis applies to the undercover police officer as we applied to Rex (except, of course, there is no dispute that the officer is a "peace officer" within the meaning of the MPC).

Tennessee v. Garner, 471 U.S. 1 (1985), imposes more stringent limits on the use of deadly force by police officers to arrest a fleeing suspect than the common law did. Police officers cannot use deadly force to apprehend a fleeing felon unless (1) deadly force is necessary to prevent the escape, and (2) the officer has probable cause to believe that the person has committed a felony and is dangerous to human life if not apprehended.

This is a close case. Could the officer have run after the fleeing suspect and used nondeadly force to prevent her escape, or was deadly force necessary? Does the officer have probable cause to believe the suspect poses a danger to human life if not apprehended? True, Ruth used deadly force in an attempt to commit a felony, and the officer saw this with his own eyes. But the suspect could barely lift the weapon and use it effectively. Moreover, the rifle was knocked from her arms; thus, she was no longer armed. Would a reasonable police officer believe the suspect is dangerous if not apprehended immediately?

2. Julio will claim that the common law allows him to use deadly force to prevent the commission of *any* felony. Julio will argue that Hector, by entering Julio's dwelling without permission, was committing the felony of first-degree criminal trespass and that Julio was justified in killing Hector. The prosecution will counter that the felony was complete and that Julio was no longer justified in using deadly force to *prevent* the felony. Julio will respond that he shot Hector as Hector was committing the felony by entering his apartment without permission. Interesting issue!

In those jurisdictions that have adopted the broad common law rule governing the use of deadly force to prevent the commission of *any* felony, Julio will probably prevail unless the jury concludes the felony was already over when Julio shot Hector.

Ironically, this common law rule governing the use of deadly force to prevent felonies provides broader authority than does the law of self-defense. It is unlikely that Julio would be able to succeed with a claim of self-defense because he did not reasonably fear imminent death or serious bodily harm. To take a human life merely to prevent such a minor felony seems uncivilized in modern times. Because so many felonies were capital offenses at early common law, the rule did not seem so harsh then.

If, however, the jurisdiction limits the use of deadly force to prevent the commission only of felonies that are dangerous to human life, Julio may not be privileged to use deadly force to prevent the commission of felonious trespass. Under the majority view today, Julio would not be privileged to use deadly force to prevent this nondangerous felony.

Under the MPC Julio would not be authorized to use deadly force because he did not believe he was preventing the commission of a felony that posed serious risk to human life.

3. Under the common law police officers may use nondeadly force when they reasonably believe it necessary to make a lawful arrest for any crime. Under the MPC and under *Tennessee v. Garner* police may use nondeadly force to apprehend someone they reasonably suspect of committing a crime after giving a warning (if feasible).

Here Officer Smith's tackling Juan was lawful because Smith had reason to believe that Juan had committed a crime and Juan would not surrender even after being warned to stop and surrender. Officer Wesson's beating of Juan, however, is not lawful. Juan was already in police custody when Wesson arrived on the scene. Wesson's use of the police baton to beat Juan was probably intended as retaliation for fleeing and causing risk of death or injury during the police chase.

Officer Wesson is in deep trouble, especially if a local TV news helicopter catches the whole incident on tape and broadcasts it.

17

Defenses Based on Individual Characteristics

Overview

The criminal law generally assumes that most people have common mental and psychological capabilities sufficient to hold them responsible for the crimes they commit. But the criminal law does provide limited opportunities for a defendant to avoid or lessen his responsibility by demonstrating that one or more of his important human capacities was significantly impaired when he committed the criminal act.

Defenses such as insanity, infancy, intoxication, and diminished capacity are among the more important of these opportunities. These doctrines permit a defendant to claim that it would be unjust to punish him at all or as severely as a normal person because of his unusual limitations. They are fundamentally different from defenses like self-defense or necessity, which claim the defendant did the "right thing" in the situation. The defenses discussed in this chapter acknowledge that the defendant did not do the "right thing" but that, nonetheless, other policy considerations require that he be treated differently. For this reason many courts and scholars describe these defenses as "excuses" rather than "justifications."

The defense of entrapment is somewhat unusual. It claims that the defendant did not "really" act with the same bad attitude as a criminal. It is also aimed at making sure the police do not "manufacture" crime.

Insanity

As we saw earlier, the criminal law assumes people know the law and have free will.[1] Their abilities to know and to choose (or, put in psychological terms, their cognitive and volitional capacities) are bedrock premises of criminal responsibility and underlie all philosophical theories of punishment.[2] Utilitarians expect the threat of punishment to influence behavior because people know they will be punished for breaking the law and will decide not to. Retributivists punish because defendants have chosen to commit a criminal act and have thereby earned their just deserts.[3]

Consequently, the criminal law generally does not ask whether a defendant knows if his conduct violates the law or finds it difficult to obey the law. Criminal law doctrine condones cognitive or volitional failure as an excuse in only a very few and well-defined instances.

For example, mistake of law is one situation in which the law may excuse the defendant if her belief about an act's legality was incorrect. However, that is a very narrow exception and difficult to establish. The common law did not permit the defense at all, and the MPC permits it only under stringent conditions. Likewise, duress is an example of when an individual will be excused because he does not make a free choice to commit a crime. But, again, the elements for a successful duress defense are quite demanding (see Chapter 16).

Legal insanity is an excuse that also permits inquiry into a defendant's capacity to know the law or to exercise free will. It focuses on the individual's personal characteristics rather than the situation in which she acts. There are two primary insanity defenses used by various jurisdictions in the United States: the *M'Naghten* test[4] and the Model Penal Code test.[5] Depending on the applicable legal test, a person is legally insane and not responsible for a crime if, as a result of mental illness, her cognitive or volitional capacity was seriously impaired when she committed the offense.

The rationale of the insanity defense is complex. Most supporters argue that it is vital to maintaining the moral foundation of criminal law.[6] Punishing a seriously disturbed person, who through no fault of her own, is simply unable to comprehend the immorality of her conduct or to obey the law, is pointless and cruel. These individuals can be sent to a secure mental health

---

1. See *United State v. Barker,* 514 F.2d 208 (D.C. Cir. 1975) (Bazelon, J., dissenting).
2. J. Feinberg, What Is So Special About Mental Illness, in Doing and Deserving: Essays in the Theory of Responsibility (1970).
3. Hart, The Aims of the Criminal Law, 23 Law & Contemp. Problems 401 (1958).
4. *M'Naghten's Case,* 101 Cl. & F. 200, 8 Eng. Rep. 718 (H.L. 1843).
5. See §4.01 (Mental Disease or Defect Excluding Responsibility).
6. Bonnie, The Moral Basis of the Insanity Defense, 69 A.B.A.J. 194 (1983).

facility to be treated. When they are no longer mentally ill or dangerous, they will be released.

The insanity test rests on three crucial assumptions. First, mental illness (sometimes called "mental disorder") exists and is beyond the control of the afflicted person. Second, this illness interferes with important psychological functions. Third, this impaired functioning significantly impairs an individual's ability to understand and direct her behavior. In sum, the insanity defense assumes there is a causal connection between the existence of mental illness and the individual's criminal conduct.

Though the insanity defense has been recognized since the early 1500s,[7] today it is extremely controversial. As we shall see, high-profile cases involving the insanity defense receive broad media coverage. Insanity acquittals often provoke public outrage and evoke powerful agitation for the reform or abolition of the defense and for changing the manner in which the insanity test is litigated.[8] Legal insanity sharply focuses the tension in the criminal law between ensuring community safety and doing justice to the individual.

The Relevance of Mental Illness in the Criminal Justice System

The mental illness of a defendant is relevant for different purposes in the criminal justice system. Before considering the insanity defense in depth, it is important to note the relevance of mental illness in several other situations.

Competency to Stand Trial

Our adversarial system of criminal justice assumes a contest between two parties: a prosecutor seeking to obtain a conviction and a self-interested defendant seeking to obtain an acquittal. Because the defendant is often the primary source of useful information for his own defense and because he has a constitutional right to make many significant decisions in the criminal justice system, including whether to plead guilty, to conduct his own defense, or to assert an insanity defense, he must be capable of meaningful participation in his own defense. Competency to stand trial ensures that a defendant can perform these vital roles and that the system will work as intended.

Both the common law and the Constitution require that a criminal defendant be competent to stand trial.[9] The Supreme Court has stated the test of competency to stand trial as follows: "[T]he test must be whether

---

7. N. Walker, Crime and Insanity in England 24-26 (1968).

8. See J. Q. La Fond & Mary L. Durham, Back to the Asylum: The Future of Mental Health Law and Policy in the United States (1992).

9. *Medina v. California*, 505 U.S. 437 (1992).

[the defendant] has sufficient present ability to consult with his lawyer with a reasonable degree of rational understanding—and whether he has a rational as well as factual understanding of the proceedings against him."[10]

The MPC also requires that a defendant must be competent before he can be tried. Section 4.04 states: "No person who as a result of mental disease or defect lacks the capacity to understand the proceedings against him or to assist in his own defense shall be tried, convicted or sentenced for the commission of an offense so long as such incapacity endures."

In assessing the competency of a criminal defendant to stand trial, the relevant time frame is his *current* mental status at the time of trial. Mental health professionals must evaluate the defendant and determine if he suffers from a mental illness that prevents him from understanding the significance of a criminal trial, including the role of the prosecutor, judge, jury, and defense counsel, and from being helpful in his own defense.

Burden of Proof. The common law assumed a criminal defendant was competent to stand trial unless some evidence indicated he was not. Historical analysis of British and American common law does not firmly establish whether the prosecution or the defendant carried the burden of persuasion on the defendant's competency to stand trial.[11] The Supreme Court has held that it is constitutional to impose this burden of proof on a defendant by a preponderance of the evidence,[12] but not by clear and convincing evidence.[13]

Disposition of an Incompetent Defendant. If a defendant is so mentally ill that he does not understand what a criminal trial is and cannot assist in his own defense, he may not be tried. Instead, the government may release him if he is charged with a minor offense or commit him to a mental health facility where he may be treated to restore his competency to stand trial. Different states have enacted statutes specifying how long a person may be committed before he must be released if not brought to trial. However, the Constitution requires that if it becomes clear the defendant will *never* become competent to stand trial, he must be civilly committed under other commitment laws or be released.[14]

Transfer from Prison to a Psychiatric Hospital

Some convicted defendants may become mentally ill while serving their prison terms. The state may transfer them to a mental health facility for

---

10. *Dusky v. United States,* 362 U.S. 402 (1960).
11. *Medina v. California,* 505 U.S. 437 (1992).
12. *Medina v. California,* 505 U.S. (1992).
13. *Cooper v. Oklahoma,* 517 U.S. 348 (1996).
14. *Jackson v. Indiana,* 406 U.S. 715 (1972).

appropriate treatment, but the inmate must be provided adequate procedural due process to determine if he is presently mentally ill.[15]

Release from Confinement

A person found not guilty by reason of insanity (NGRI) may be committed to a secure mental health facility indefinitely, even beyond the maximum term for which she could have been sentenced if found guilty.[16] The government may use commitment standards and procedures that are somewhat different from those used to civilly commit mentally ill individuals. A defendant initially found NGRI must be released if she is no longer mentally ill or dangerous.[17]

Execution Pursuant to a Sentence of Death

Both the common law and the Constitution prohibit the execution of an individual sentenced to death if, at the time the death sentence is to be carried out, he is mentally ill and does not comprehend why he will be executed. This ensures that the individual understands the retributive purpose of his execution and will not view his death as pointless and cruel. It also ensures that he can assist in any appellate proceedings.[18]

The Insanity Defense

The defense of insanity is litigated at the criminal trial. The relevant time frame for the inquiry is the defendant's mental status at the time of the alleged offense. Thus, the assessment is retrospective.

In preparing for the trial a mental health expert representing the government and one representing the defense may evaluate the defendant prior to trial. Based on a wide variety of information, such as the defendant's mental health history, his account of the crime, the facts and circumstances surrounding the crime, and psychological and medical testing, these experts will form an opinion as to the defendant's mental status at the time of the crime and whether it satisfies the elements of the insanity test used in their jurisdiction.

---

15. *Vitek v. Jones,* 445 U.S. 480 (1980).
16. *Jones v. United States,* 463 U.S. 354 (1983).
17. *Foucha v. Louisiana,* 504 U.S. 71 (1992).
18. *Ford v. Wainwright,* 477 U.S. 399 (1986).

The *M'Naghten* Test

First announced by the House of Lords in 1843, the *M'Naghten* test excuses a defendant from criminal responsibility if, at the time of the crime, he was "labouring under such a defect of reason, from disease of the mind, as not to know the nature and quality of the act he was doing; or, if he did know it, that he did not know he was doing what was wrong."[19] In modern times the test has been slightly modified; it no longer requires a "defect of reason."[20] Under the *M'Naghten* test a criminal defendant cannot be convicted if, as a result of mental illness at the time of the crime, he did not know what he was doing or that it was wrong.

In sum, mental illness must have virtually nullified the actor's cognitive capacity so that he was unable to exercise the moral understanding of normal persons. Without a rational ability to recognize and evaluate the moral issues raised by his behavior, the criminal law could not influence him.

The Meaning of Mental Illness. Most mental health professionals have interpreted the *M'Naghten* test as requiring the defendant to be out of touch with reality and not accurately perceiving the world around him.[21] For example, he may be hearing voices that command him to commit harmful acts. Or he may be acting under a delusional belief system, such as a belief that secret agents are out to kill him or that he is a significant historical person like Christ. These impairments can make it very difficult for the defendant to comprehend reality accurately and to evaluate the appropriateness of his conduct. Consequently, individuals with these impairments may engage in inappropriate and even criminal behavior.

The Meaning of "Wrong." A major controversy surrounding the *M'Naghten* test is whether the term "wrong" refers to awareness of an act's criminality or that it is morally wrong. And, if it means "moral wrong," should the defendant's personal moral beliefs or society's morality control? A mentally ill person may know that an act is against the law and even that society considers the act wrong. However, should he be punished for committing an act that, according to his own delusional sense of morality, is not wrong? Arguably, this person is not deserving of punishment because he did not choose to do wrong as he saw things. Nor could he be deterred if he thought he was doing the right thing.

American courts are split on this question. Some will hold a mentally ill

---

19. *M'Naghten's Case,* 101 Cl. & F. 200, 8 Eng. Rep. 718 (H.L. 1843).

20. See H. Fingarette, The Meaning of Criminal Insanity (1972).

21. Many mental health professionals would probably require an individual to suffer from an axis 1 diagnosis under the Diagnostic and Statistical Manual of Mental Disorders (4th ed. 1994).

defendant responsible if he knew his actions were against the law. This approach is consistent with the general rule that ignorance of the law is no excuse. However, it may ignore the serious and pronounced difficulty the defendant has in rationally taking that knowledge into account in deciding whether to act. Some states will excuse a defendant if, because of serious mental illness, he believed he had received a direct command from God to commit the harmful act.[22]

The Irresistible Impulse Test

A few jurisdictions added to the *M'Naghten* test by also permitting legal insanity to apply to cases in which mental illness produced an "irresistible impulse" to act. This component, which adds severe volitional impairment to the insanity test, is generally satisfied if the defendant persuades a judge or jury that he would have committed the crime even if a policeman were at his side at the time.[23] Needless to say, it is a difficult test to satisfy.

The Model Penal Code Test

During the 1950s, the *M'Naghten* test was severely criticized by psychiatrists, judges, and legal scholars because it excused only those individuals who lacked cognitive ability. These experts argued that legal insanity should also excuse those who could not control their behavior. Additionally, the *M'Naghten* test required *total* impairment. Finally, it did not take into account new psychiatric knowledge about human behavior.[24]

Influenced by these criticisms and the emergence of rehabilitation as the primary goal of the criminal justice system, the American Law Institute proposed a new insanity test in the Model Penal Code. It provides in part that

> (1) [a] person is not responsible for criminal conduct if at the time of such conduct as a result of mental disease or defect he lacks substantial capacity either to appreciate the criminality [wrongfulness] of his conduct or to conform his conduct to the requirements of law.[25]

The MPC test expands the test of legal insanity significantly. First, it expands the kinds of psychological impairments that can excuse a defendant; now, *volitional* as well as *cognitive* disability qualifies. Second, the MPC test does not require *total* impairment; instead, if a person "lacks *substantial*

---

22. *State v. Cameron,* 100 Wash. 2d 520, 674 P.2d 650 (1983).

23. See *United States v. Kunak,* 17 C.M.R. 346 (Ct. Mil. App. 1954).

24. For a thorough judicial critique of the *M'Naghten* test, see *United States v. Freeman,* 357 F.2d 606, 618-622 (1966).

25. MPC §4.01 (Mental Disease or Defect Excluding Responsibility).

capacity," he may be excused. Third, it expands the scope of relevant testimony by mental health professionals. Some psychiatrists had criticized the *M'Naghten* test because it required them to commit professional "perjury" in the courtroom in order to present evidence they considered relevant to criminal responsibility.[26]

This test is considered "modern" in that it is more in keeping with supposedly new knowledge about human behavior. Unlike *M'Naghten*, it accepts that some mentally ill individuals may understand that their conduct is wrong but cannot control their behavior. Thus, they cannot be deterred nor have they chosen to do wrong.

The Meaning of Mental Disease or Defect. The MPC does not define "mental disease or defect" other than to provide that these terms "do not include an abnormality manifested only by repeated criminal or otherwise antisocial conduct." This caveat was added to ensure that someone could not claim he was mentally ill just because he had an extensive criminal history. Therefore, it excludes psychopathic or sociopathic personalities as such individuals were generally known when the MPC was adopted.[27]

Expanding the Meaning of Mental Illness. Many mental health professionals have applied the MPC terms more broadly to include recently recognized diagnoses of mental disorder, particularly those that identify volitional impairment. Thus, as new mental disorders are recognized as appropriate for treatment, the MPC test permits them to be used to establish legal insanity.

The Meaning of "Appreciate." The MPC test's use of "appreciate" rather than "know" suggests that "purely verbal knowledge" that an act is wrong will not suffice to find a defendant legally sane. Rather, the defendant must have a deeper understanding of its wrongfulness. The MPC and Commentaries said: "The use of 'appreciate' rather than 'know' conveys a broader sense of understanding than simple cognition."[28] Unfortunately, the Commentaries do not suggest just what that "broader sense" means.

The Meaning of "Substantial." The MPC test does not require complete inability to know or to choose. Instead, a person may be legally insane if his impairment is "substantial." This determination may require the fact finder to make a value judgment in light of the evidence.

---

26. Diamond, Criminal Responsibility of the Mentally Ill, 14 Stanford L. Rev. 59, 60-61 (1961).

27. Today, this definition would probably exclude individuals with an "antisocial personality disorder," a diagnosis based primarily on an extensive history of getting into trouble with the law. Diagnostic and Statistical Manual of Mental Disorders 645-650 (4th ed. 1994).

28. Model Penal Code and Commentaries, vol. 2 at 169 (1985).

Criticisms. There are two primary objections to the MPC test. First, it may provide too much room for experts to recognize new kinds of mental illness that can excuse individuals from criminal responsibility. Second, many critics claim that mental health experts cannot determine with reasonable accuracy an individual's capacity for self-control or measure the extent of that impairment. As the American Psychiatric Association noted in recommending the adoption of a more restrictive version of the *M'Naghten* test for legal insanity, "the line between an irresistible impulse and an impulse not resisted is probably no sharper than that between twilight and dusk."[29]

The Federal Insanity Test

Before John Hinckley tried to assassinate President Reagan in 1981, all but one federal court of appeal used the MPC test for legal insanity. In 1984, after Hinckley's subsequent acquittal by reason of insanity, Congress enacted a new insanity test that must be used in all federal prosecutions. In part 18 U.S.C. provides:

Section 17. Insanity Defense

(a) *Affirmative Defense.* It is an affirmative defense to a prosecution under any federal statute that, at the time of the commission of the acts constituting the offense, the defendant, as a result of a severe mental disease or defect, was unable to appreciate the nature and quality or the wrongfulness of his acts. Mental disease or defect does not otherwise constitute a defense.[30]

This new insanity test is arguably tougher than even the *M'Naghten* test adopted more than a century ago. The defendant must now suffer from a "severe" mental disease or defect.

Reform of the Insanity Defense
Substantive Changes

Before John Hinckley's acquittal by reason of insanity, every jurisdiction in the United States provided the defense of legal insanity. All but one federal court used the MPC test of insanity as did more than half the states.[31] By 1990, however, three states, Idaho, Montana, and Utah, had abolished the

---

29. American Psychiatric Association Statement on the Insanity Defense 11 (Washington, D.C., 1982).

30. Comprehensive Crime Control Act of 1984 (Insanity Defense Reform Act), P.L. No. 98-473, ch. IV.

31. La Fond & Durham, supra note 8, at 36.

insanity defense entirely.[32] Eight other states have abandoned the MPC test and gone back to *M'Naghten* or a tougher version.

Procedural Changes

As of 1978 twenty-seven states and all federal courts required the government to prove beyond a reasonable doubt that a criminal defendant was sane, once the defendant had produced some evidence establishing legal insanity.[33]

By 1985 thirty-five states and the District of Columbia required defendants to prove insanity by a preponderance of the evidence. Arizona requires the defendant to establish this defense by "clear and convincing" evidence.[34] In 1984 Congress also imposed this same burden of persuasion on federal criminal defendants. In most jurisdictions the defendant must now carry the burden of persuasion, and doubt is resolved in favor of responsibility.

Insanity Defense Myths and Facts

The insanity defense has been under heavy attack recently. The public becomes upset when individuals who intentionally engaged in harmful conduct are acquitted by reason of insanity. There are also common misconceptions about the use and consequences of this defense.

The insanity defense is not used very often. Criminal defendants use the insanity defense in less than 1 or 2 percent of all American criminal cases. When plead, the defense is usually not successful; only about one-third of insanity pleas succeed. Moreover, the defense is not used only by those charged with serious crimes such as murder. Defendants found NGRI have been charged with a wide variety of crimes, including felonies and misdemeanors. Minor property crimes are common among those found NGRI. Successful NGRIs are no more dangerous than criminals; they have re-arrest rates comparable to convicted felons.[35]

There is also risk in pleading insanity. NGRI defendants who successfully plead the insanity defense often spend significantly longer time in

---

32. Kansas abolished the insanity defense effective January 1, 1996. Rosen, Insanity Denied: Abolition of the Insanity Defense in Kansas, 8 Kan. J.L. & Pub. Policy 253 (1999).

33. Comment, Recent Changes in the Criminal Law: The Federal Insanity Defense, 46 La. L. Rev. 337 (1985).

34. Ariz. Rev. Stat. Ann. §13-502(c) (West 2000).

35. See La Fond & Durham, Cognitive Dissonance: Have Insanity Defense and Civil Commitment Reforms Made a Difference?, 39 Villanova L. Rev. 71 (1994).

confinement for serious offenses than defendants convicted of a similar offense.[36]

The Guilty but Mentally Ill Defense
Historical Origin

In 1975 Michigan enacted a guilty but mentally ill defense (GBMI). At least 14 states have enacted the defense since then.[37]

Jury Options

The GBMI defense permits a jury to find a defendant who raises the insanity defense "guilty but mentally ill" rather than NGRI. In a few states that have abolished the insanity defense, the defendant may still raise a GBMI defense.[38] A GBMI verdict determines that the defendant is responsible for committing the crime but also recognizes that she was mentally ill at the time.

Dispositional Consequences

The dispositional consequences of a GBMI verdict vary. Usually, a GBMI defendant may be sentenced to prison for up to the maximum authorized term. This keeps her under the control of the criminal justice system and ensures her confinement for a definite period of time. In some states a verdict of GBMI requires a mental health evaluation of the defendant to determine if she needs treatment.

In a few states a defendant found GBMI cannot be sentenced to imprisonment unless the trial judge specifically finds that the defendant was not suffering from a mental disease that rendered her unable to appreciate the criminality of her conduct or to conform her conduct to the requirements of law.[39] This approach effectively moves the issues raised by the insanity defense from the jury's consideration at the guilt phase to the judge's determination at sentencing. In other states, a GBMI verdict does not have

---

36. Steadman, Empirical Research on the Insanity Defense, 477 Annals Am. Acad., Pol. & Soc. Sci. 58 (1985).

37. McGinley & Pasewark, National Survey of the Frequency and Success of the Insanity Plea and Alternate Pleas, 17 J. Psychiatry & L. 205 (1989).

38. Montana takes this approach. See *State v. Korell*, 690 P.2d 992 (1984).

39. Id.

any legal consequences for the defendant.[40] A defendant found GBMI may be sentenced to death.[41]

Arguments Pro and Con

Supporters argue that the defense enhances public safety by permitting dangerous mentally ill individuals to be confined in prison rather than prematurely released from mental health facilities. Critics claim that the GBMI defense requires the jury to consider an issue that is not relevant to guilt, sentencing, or release. Critics also claim that the GBMI defense confuses the jury and invites compromise verdicts, thereby allowing juries to avoid the difficult question of whether a mentally ill offender should be held criminally responsible.

The Empirical Consequences of the GBMI Defense

The GBMI defense was enacted to encourage juries not to find defendants NGRI. However, the impact of the GBMI defense on the insanity defense is mixed. It has not made much difference in the frequency of NGRI verdicts in Michigan. In Illinois the number of NGRI verdicts actually increased following enactment of the GBMI defense but declined in Georgia. On balance, the GBMI defense does not seem to have achieved its goal of decreasing the number of successful insanity defenses.[42]

On the other hand, research indicates that GBMI offenders are more likely to go to prison, to receive life sentences, and to receive longer sentences for the same crime than normal offenders.[43] Thus, defendants found GBMI may be treated as both "bad" and "mad."

EXAMPLES

1. Jason, who lives with his father and stepmother, is 22 years old and has suffered from serious schizophrenia for several years. Jason comes in and out of touch with reality. Often he does not recognize where he is, what day it is, or who is around him. In addition, he is deeply religious and

---

40. *See* Slobogin, The Guilty but Mentally Ill Verdict: An Idea Whose Time Should Not Have Come, 53 Geo. Wash. L. Rev. 494 (1985).

41. *Harris v. State*, 499 N.E. 723 (Ind. 1986); *People v. Crews*, 122 Ill. 2d 266, 522 N.E. 1167 (1988).

42. La Fond & Durham, supra note 8, at 138-139.

43. Callaghan et al., Measuring the Effects of the Guilty but Mentally Ill (GBMI) Verdict, 16 Law & Human Behavior 447, 452 (1992).

reads the Bible often. He has been committed to the state psychiatric hospital on several occasions because of his irrational, delusional, and frightening behavior, though he has never actually harmed anyone.

a. One day he is sure he sees the devil himself come into his bedroom to take away his soul. In fact his stepmother has come into his bedroom and simply asked him to go to the store for her. Jason, fearing for his salvation, grabs the devil by the throat and strangles him until he no longer moves. A few hours later his father comes home and discovers his wife dead on the floor and Jason praying. Jason looks up and says, "I have just slain the devil." He returns to his prayers.

   Presently, Jason is in touch with reality after taking psychotropic drugs. He is horrified by what he did because he loved his stepmother very much. He understands in general terms what a trial is, the role of the various participants, and what he is charged with. When asked about this event, however, Jason only remembers attacking the devil who was trying to take away his soul.

b. One day Jason hears the voice of God commanding him to slay his stepmother because she is in league with the devil and must be destroyed as evil incarnate. Even though he knows that killing a human being is against the law, Jason obeys the divine command and strangles his stepmother to death, exclaiming "Hallelujah, Lord" throughout the episode.

c. One day Jason decides, based on his reading of the Bible, that his stepmother is a religious heretic who, according to his reading of scripture, must die for her sins. Jason strangles his stepmother to death.

d. Peter Salli is 22 years old and has suffered from serious paranoid schizophrenia for several years. He is an extremely devout Catholic. Believing for the past five years that a worldwide conspiracy is out to destroy the Catholic Church, Peter feels he is God's chosen defender of Catholicism from these conspiratorial forces. Acting more strangely than ever, Peter buys an automatic weapon and a large amount of ammunition. He also locates the addresses of several abortion clinics in his area.

   Shortly thereafter, Peter enters two separate abortion clinics, screaming, "Abortion is wrong! You should pray the rosary and stop this killing!" Peter then kills two clinic staff members and wounds several others. He flees and is apprehended while trying to avoid detection.

   Is the insanity defense available in any of these examples?

2. Sybil is 22 and suffers from Dissociative Identity Disorder (DID). Physically and sexually abused by her mother during childhood, she has

developed several different identities to cope with this stress. Each of these identities is a well-integrated personality (with its own pattern of perceiving, relating to, and thinking about the environment and one's self) within the primary or "host" personality. Each personality may at various times take full control of the individual's behavior.

One of Sybil's alter egos, Bridget, is particularly troubling to Sybil's psychiatrist because Bridget is a pyromaniac, always setting fires. In fact, the psychiatrist has forced Gilda, another personality or alter ego, to stop smoking. The doctor does not want to risk that Bridget will emerge and find matches on Sybil's person. Sybil, the host personality, does not smoke.

Much to her psychiatrist's dismay, Sybil is finally charged with arson for burning down a garage. Sybil, the host personality, doesn't recall the event at all. When the government psychiatrist talks to Bridget, she admits that she set the fire on purpose. "I knew it was against the law, but it looks cool!" Bridget is not remorseful about this act, and she understands that Sybil will go to prison.

As prosecutor, you must decide whom to charge and whether you can convict Sybil for what Bridget did.

3. Lucky bets on the horses. Lucky bets on the dogs. Lucky bets on football games. Lucky bets on everything — and usually loses! Lucky is a compulsive gambler, unable to stop his excessive and destructive betting.

In fact, he has been diagnosed as suffering from "pathological gambling disorder," a disorder of impulse control recognized in 1980 by the mental health professions in the Diagnostic and Statistical Manual of Mental Disorders published by the American Psychiatric Association. These individuals have an overwhelming urge to gamble, and their compulsive gambling disrupts their family and work life. They always think the next bet is the "grand slam" that will finally put them ahead.

Lucky knows. He owes his bookie so much that he secretly embezzled money from his job to place the grand slam bet. When he lost again, he wore a mask and robbed a bank to get money for his next bet. Arrested shortly thereafter, Lucky is charged with gambling, embezzling, and armed robbery. Can he plead insanity?

4. Cassandra, mother of Becky, a 2-year-old, and Ben, a 3-three-year-old, has suffered from severe depression for the past several years. From time to time she would slip into periods of complete despair. Deeply religious, Cassandra has sought solace in prayer. Convinced that the world is hopelessly evil and sinful, she decides that her children should be spared any more time in the devil's den of earthly life. Instead, they will be better off going immediately to heaven to be with their Lord and God and enjoy the goodness of heaven. Cassandra takes her children to the Golden Gate bridge and, after kissing them goodbye and telling them

that she will soon see them in heaven, throws Becky and Ben off the bridge. They die.

When questioned by the police, Cassandra said, "I knew it was against the law and that people would not approve. But I was so sad and I thought the world was unbearably bad. I wanted them to be in heaven. Now that I feel better, I am sorry for what I did."

Cassandra has been charged with two counts of premeditated murder. She pleads insanity. Will she succeed?

EXPLANATIONS

1a. Jason suffers from a serious mental disorder, schizophrenia, which causes significant distortions in perception and thinking. His medical history provides persuasive evidence of his long-standing illness.

Jason is competent to stand trial. He understands the nature of the charges and has a present ability to consult with his attorney with a reasonable degree of rational understanding. Though his factual recall is obviously incorrect in some important ways, he can recall what he thought he was doing and why he was doing it. A trial judge is likely to find Jason competent to stand trial on the murder charge.

This is a REAL DIFFICULT case! It is not clear that the government can prove the mens rea of murder beyond a reasonable doubt. After all, Jason may not have intended to kill *another human being*. Rather, as a result of mental illness he may honestly have believed he was killing the "devil." Thus, the prosecutor's only alternative may be to seek involuntary civil commitment of Jason to a mental health facility where he will be confined and receive treatment until he is no longer mentally ill or dangerous.

If the jury does find the mens rea and actus reus of murder, then whether the state has an insanity defense becomes important. Under the *M'Naghten* test, Jason would be found not guilty by reason of insanity. As a result of his mental illness, Jason did not, at the time of the crime, understand the nature of his act, let alone that it was wrong. He actually perceived himself to be slaying the devil. Because he did not realize he was killing a human being, there was no reason for him even to consider if what he was doing might be against the law or morally wrong. On the contrary, Jason undoubtedly thought he was doing the right thing. Punishing Jason will not deter others like him nor has he earned punishment by choosing to do a wrongful act. Jason will be confined in a secure mental health facility until he is no longer mentally ill or dangerous.

Under the MPC test, Jason would also be found NGRI. As a result of mental disease or defect, Jason lacked substantial capacity either to appreciate that his conduct was wrong or to obey the law by not killing someone he thought was the devil. Again, most purposes of punishment would not be served by convicting Jason.

In a GBMI state, the jury could simply find Jason "guilty but mentally ill" rather than insane. This verdict establishes that the defendant committed a voluntary act with the required mens rea or culpability. In most states the verdict has no significance. The defendant may be sentenced to prison for the maximum term and even sentenced to death for a capital offense. In a few states he will automatically be evaluated to see if he needs treatment. If he does, he may be sent to a mental health facility for treatment, and minimum sentences may be waived under certain circumstances.

Because some of these different outcomes may be possible in states that have adopted the GBMI defense, we will not repeat them for the rest of this section of Examples and Explanations.

1b. Though suffering from a serious mental illness, Jason knows that he is killing his stepmother. He also knows that killing another human being is against the law. In a number of jurisdictions Jason would be held responsible for his acts and found guilty if he knew that his conduct was against the law. Some utilitarians would support this result, arguing that, because he knew he would be punished, Jason (and those like him) are deterrable. Some retributivists might argue that Jason chose to break the law and thus deserves his punishment.

Other jurisdictions permit a divine command exception and will not punish a mentally ill person who commits a harmful act thinking he is obeying a command from God. Not only is such persons' ability to know in a relevant way disturbed; they may even be acting under duress. After all, one does not disobey a command from God lightly!

Some utilitarians would agree that many disturbed individuals would do what they thought God told them to do, regardless of the criminal law. Thus, it is very difficult to change their behavior even by a threat of incarceration. Some retributivists would also agree, concluding that these unfortunate individuals simply do not have the necessary ability to make a rational moral choice and, therefore, do not deserve punishment.

In the few states that have abolished the insanity defense, the only issues to be litigated at trial are the defendant's actus reus and mens rea. The defendant's mental illness might be relevant to his mens rea at the time of the crime. It will not be admitted to establish a claim of legal insanity.

1c. This is a more difficult case. In many ways Jason is very much as he was in Examples 1a and 1b. However, in this example his acts are based on a delusional religious belief system; he does not act because of a divine command. Some jurisdictions would permit conviction in this case even though it is not clear whether Jason is deterrable or has made a meaningful choice to do wrong.

1d. The defense will claim that, at the time of the killings, Peter suffered from a pronounced mental illness that made him perceive the world in a very distorted way. His perception of persecution may have put him in a very defensive position toward the world in general and in a state of constant vigilance.

Peter's perception of persecution, though grossly incorrect, may also have led him to believe he was acting in justifiable self-defense. This is an interesting question. Even if Peter's view of the threat was correct, he would not be justified in using deadly force because there is no threat of death or serious bodily injury. In this case there is a good argument that Peter's response to his perception was inappropriate, even conceding his distorted view of the world. The insanity defense, however, does not require that the defendant's action be lawful if the facts were as the defendant thought them to be. His inability to gauge reality may also impair his ability to morally evaluate possible courses of action.

In a *M'Naghten* jurisdiction the defense will assert that Peter's delusional sense of persecution, both of his church and of himself, left him unable to know that his act was wrong. This will be a close case, but if Peter knew that his conduct was against the law, he might be convicted. A jury may conclude that he is just like a conscientious objector who chooses to place his value system above society's and to disregard the criminal law. Or it may find Peter NGRI, concluding that Peter does not possess sufficient rationality to make a meaningful moral choice.

The result would not necessarily be any clearer in a jurisdiction that used the MPC test. This test lets the defense argue that, as a result of mental disease or defect, Peter lacked substantial capacity either to appreciate the criminality of his conduct or to conform his conduct to the requirements of law. The word "appreciate" may require a better understanding than simply "knowing" his conduct was wrong. It may also include some genuine emotional grasp.

The prosecutor will retort that Peter may have been mentally ill, but he knew his act was against the law. She will claim that there is no evidence of compulsion in this case: no divine command, no delusional religious beliefs that killing, even in the defense of one's church, is appropriate. Moreover, there is abundant evidence of planning, preparation, and attempt to avoid detection and apprehension. Thus, she will argue that Peter should be convicted.

You call it!

2. Now this is an interesting case! If one of the personalities within an individual suffering from DID knows what she is doing and appreciates

that the conduct is criminal, can the "host" or "dominant" personality be held accountable for the actions of this other "alter" personality?

One federal district court said no. The host personality must appreciate the wrongfulness of the conduct that is under the control of the alter personality. The court held that the insanity defense must be presented to the jury, even though the "acting" personality was *not* insane at the time of the offense.[44] Thus, Sybil cannot be found guilty of the crime committed by Bridget because Sybil did not know what Bridget was doing or that it was wrong. The fact that Bridget, an alter ego, did know what she was doing and that it was wrong will not impose criminal responsibility on Sybil. Criminal responsibility depends on the mental status of the host personality.

Note, however, that some jurisdictions take a contrary approach and assess responsibility on the personality that is in control at that time[45] or refuse to recognize the defense altogether.[46] In jurisdictions that focus on the personality in control, the defense might prevail with an insanity defense if it uses the ALI test. Pyromania is a recognized impulse control disorder that substantially interferes with an individual's capacity to obey the law. Thus, "Bridget" may be successful pleading insanity.

3. In a *M'Naghten* jurisdiction Lucky is out of luck. There is no evidence that he did not know what he was doing when he embezzled from his employer or robbed the bank, or that he did not know that these actions were wrong. To avoid apprehension, he tried to keep these crimes secret or his identity unknown. Thus, he would not succeed with a *M'Naghten* insanity defense.

In a jurisdiction that used the MPC test, Lucky just might get lucky. He suffers from "pathological gambling disorder." This impulse-control disorder substantially interferes with Lucky's capacity to "conform his conduct to the requirements of the law." Thus, he might be successful in using the MPC insanity defense to all charges, including not only the gambling charge, which is a "symptom" of his disorder, but also to the other two charges involving crimes against property and persons committed to support his compulsive conduct.[47]

Defendants with a diagnosis of compulsive gambling have successfully used the MPC insanity defense to a charge of writing bad checks[48]

---

44. *United States v. Denny-Shaffer,* 2 F.3d 999 (10th Cir. 1993).

45. See, e.g., *State v. Grimsley,* 3 Ohio App. 3d 265, 444 N.E.2d 1071 (1982); *Kirkland v. State,* 166 Ga. App. 478, 304 S.E.2d 561 (1983).

46. *State v. Greene,* 984 P.2d 1024 (Wash. 1999).

47. See McGarry, *Pathological Gambling: A New Insanity Defense,* 11 Bull. Am. Acad. Psychiatry & L. 301 (1983).

48. *State v. Campanaro,* Nos. 632-679, 1309-1379, 514-580 & 707-789 (Superior Court of New Jersey Crim. Div., Union County, 1980).

and to a charge of first-degree larceny.[49] Other defendants have used the defense to charges like forgery, embezzlement, and armed bank robbery.[50] Some were successful; others were not.

4. At the time of her crime Cassandra suffered from severe depression, a mental disorder that severely affected her emotions. Nonetheless, in a *M'Naghten* jurisdiction Cassandra would probably be convicted of murder. She knew what she was doing and that it was against the law and against society's morality. She did not act as a result of divine command. The defense might argue that the word "know" in the *M'Naghten* test must include some emotional appreciation of the wrongfulness of her conduct, but most courts would not agree. Thus, she would probably be convicted on the charges.

    Cassandra has a better chance of succeeding in a MPC jurisdiction. Arguably, as a result of mental disease or defect her capacity to "appreciate" the criminality of her conduct was substantially impaired. However, this depends on what a jury determines "appreciate" to require. It might decide that her severe depression prevented her from truly grasping the legal and moral significance of her conduct. In the alternative, it might conclude that she understood that her action was against the law and social morality and that this basic comprehension is sufficient for criminal responsibility. It does not appear that Cassandra's ability to control her conduct was impaired. In fact, she made a very deliberate choice to act. Despite the greater leeway provided by the MPC test, Cassandra would probably be convicted of murder.

    What do you think the verdict should be? Why?

Infancy

Young children can commit harmful acts ranging from simple mischief, like setting off a firecracker in a mailbox, to serious havoc, like killing another person. Should they be held criminally responsible for such conduct?

The criminal law ordinarily requires more than harmful conduct before it will impose blame and punishment. In addition to requiring mens rea, the criminal law will not blame and punish individuals who are so very different from ordinary people that they are incapable of understanding the moral significance of their behavior.

Most young children do not have the intelligence, judgment, emotional maturity, and moral capacity to make the rational choices the criminal law requires. For this reason the law does not hold very young children criminally

---

49. *State v. Lafferty,* No. 44359 (Connecticut Superior Court, June 5, 1981). But see *United States v. Lyons,* 731 F.2d 243, 245 (5th Cir. 1982).

50. See McGarry, supra note 47, and cases cited therein.

responsible even for behavior designed to cause serious harm. This is accomplished by providing the defense of "infancy."

On the other hand, every "child" eventually becomes an "adult" and becomes responsible for his or her behavior. The criminal law has taken different approaches to determining when a child can no longer assert the infancy defense and may be held criminally accountable for his behavior.

The Common Law

At very early common law infancy was seemingly not a defense to a criminal prosecution. Instead, a young offender usually was pardoned for his crime.[51]

Over time, however, the common law developed the defense of infancy, which could be used to excuse children for crimes they had committed. The common law used chronological age at the time of the crime to determine when a child could be held criminally responsible.

Under Age 7

By the early fourteenth century a child under the age of 7 was considered not to have the capacity to commit a crime. He was considered incapable of forming the mens rea necessary to commit a crime and was also considered undeterred by the threat of punishment. The common law used a conclusive presumption—that anyone under age 7 was incapable of committing a crime — to preclude criminal responsibility. The prosecutor could not in fact introduce evidence that a particular child under age 7 had the mental capacity and moral sensibility necessary for making rational choices sufficient to justify criminal blame and punishment.

Between Ages 7 and 14

Children between the ages of 7 and 14 were presumed incapable of committing a crime, but this presumption was not conclusive. It could be overcome by evidence establishing that the child understood what he was doing and that it was wrong. (Note the similarity of this test to the *M'Naghten* test for legal insanity. See pages 436-437.) The prosecutor carried the burdens of production and persuasion, the latter probably beyond a reasonable doubt.

---

51. Kean, The History of the Criminal Liability of Children, 53 L.Q. Rev. 364 (1937).

Over Age 14

Children over the age of 14 were considered capable of committing crimes and could be tried as adult offenders unless insane.

The Model Penal Code

The Model Penal Code takes a very different approach to the age when children can be held fully responsible under the criminal law for criminal conduct. Section 4.10 provides a defense of "immaturity." Simply put, no one under the age of 16 can be tried and convicted of a crime. Children who are age 16 or 17 at the time of the crime can be tried in the juvenile court or, if the juvenile court waives jurisdiction over the offender and consents, in an adult court. Interestingly, the MPC does not establish a juvenile court system. It simply assumes that this system exists.

Contemporary Law

Juvenile Court Jurisdiction

All states have established juvenile court systems. They handle most cases involving children who engage in conduct that would be a crime if committed by an adult. Such conduct is often defined by statute as "delinquency."[52]

Most juvenile court laws do not set a minimum age for jurisdiction over delinquency cases, though they usually set under 18 as the maximum age of their jurisdiction. Thus, unless the state follows the common law approach, children under age 7 can be adjudged delinquent.

Juvenile courts were initially concerned primarily with the welfare of the child. Rehabilitation was their primary goal. Young offenders were channeled out of the adult criminal justice system and placed in special juvenile facilities designed to change their antisocial behavior and to restore them as productive members of society. Consequently, inquiry into a child's capacity to commit a crime was not considered relevant in a juvenile court proceeding.

Currently, many state legislatures have concluded that rehabilitation is not effective and that society needs to be protected from violent juvenile offenders. They have revised their juvenile court laws to emphasize responsibility rather than rehabilitation.[53]

Juvenile court laws generally permit judges to waive or decline jurisdiction (often based on the offender's age and on the seriousness of the crime)

---

52. Juvenile courts also deal with other kinds of cases involving young people, including children in need of supervision and the termination of parental rights.

53. Walkover, The Infancy Defense in the New Juvenile Court, 31 UCLA L. Rev. 503 (1984); Ainsworth, Re-Imagining Childhood and Reconstructing the Legal Order: The Case for Abolishing the Juvenile Court, 69 N.C.L. Rev. 1083 (1991).

if the best interests of the child or the public require. If the juvenile court declines to assert its jurisdiction, the defendant will be charged and tried as an adult offender in the regular criminal court system. If convicted, he will be sentenced to adult penal institutions and can serve the same sentences as adult offenders.

Criminal Responsibility

Many states follow some version of the common law. Their statutes set a minimum age of criminal responsibility, often 7 or 8 years old at the time of the crime. Children under the specified age are conclusively presumed incapable of committing a crime.

Some states, however, do not set a minimum chronological age. Instead, they presume young children under a specified age, such as 14 in California,[54] are incapable of committing a crime unless the state can prove the child knew what she was doing and that it was wrong. This approach focuses on the "mental age" of the child rather than her physical age.

In most states older children, often between 7 or 8 and 12, 13, or 14 (depending on the specific statute), are *presumed* incapable of committing a crime. However, the prosecutor may introduce evidence that a young defendant within this age group understood the nature of her conduct and that it was wrong. If the prosecution carries the burden of persuasion on these issues, the child is considered to have sufficient mental and moral capacity to make rational choices sufficient for criminal responsibility. Consequently, she can be tried as an adult offender, usually subject to the juvenile court's declining its jurisdiction. If convicted, she can be punished just as severely as an adult offender.

In response to the growing number of juvenile offenders committing "adult crimes" at younger ages, many legislatures have lowered or eliminated the minimum age at which a juvenile can be tried as an adult. The empirical research supports this perceived trend of more juveniles committing more violent offenses. In 1994 persons under the age of 18 accounted for 11 percent of the willful killings cleared by law enforcement authorities nationally.[55] Additionally, in 1990 there was a 27 percent increase over 1980 figures for juveniles arrested for violent crimes, and three out of four juveniles used guns to commit those crimes.[56]

---

54. Cal. Pen. Code §26 (West 1999).

55. Federal Bureau of Investigations, U.S. Dept. of Justice, Uniform Crime Report 279 (1994).

56. Federal Bureau of Investigations, U.S. Dept. of Justice, Uniform Crime Report 410 (1992). However, the rate of juvenile violent crime fell slightly in 1995 for the first time in almost a decade, and in that same year the rate of homicide by juveniles decreased for the second year in a row, down by 15.2 percent. "After a Decade, Juvenile Crime Begins to Drop," N.Y. Times, Aug. 9, 1996, at A1.

EXAMPLE

Lem, aged 6, Ben, aged 7, and Jamal, aged 9, enter a neighbor's house to steal a tricycle while the parents are shopping. While in the house, Lem seeks out Matt, a six-month-old baby, lying in a crib. He drags Matt out of the crib and drops him on the floor. He then kicks him repeatedly in the stomach and head, inflicting very serious injuries. He and the other two boys flee the house with the tricycle when they hear Gabriel, the 13-year-old babysitter, waking up from a nap in the bedroom. Gabriel sees Lem leaving Matt's bedroom.

Matt is taken to the hospital where he is on life-support systems for several weeks. He eventually recovers but suffers serious long-term brain damage.

The prosecutor has witnesses who will testify that Lem had threatened to kill Matt because he did not like "the way Matt's parents look at me." Gabriel will also testify that, shortly after the incident, Lem threatened to burn down Gabriel's house if he told the police about seeing Lem in Matt's house that day.

Can the prosecutor charge Lem with aggravated assault and have him tried in an adult court? Or must Lem be tried in the juvenile justice system?

EXPLANATION

In most states Lem could not be held criminally responsible for his attack on Matt. Because he was 6 years old at the time of the crime, Lem would be conclusively presumed incapable of committing a crime. Lem could probably be tried as a juvenile offender; he could not be tried and convicted as an adult for a criminal offense.

Some states, however, do not set any minimum age of responsibility. Instead, they permit the prosecutor to introduce evidence that the defendant knew what he was doing and that it was wrong. Here the prosecutor might be able to prove that Lem had a motive to commit the crime and that the attack on Matt was premeditated and intentional. Moreover, Gabriel's testimony might also establish that Lem knew that his behavior was wrong. By threatening Gabriel, Lem was trying to avoid detection. This indicates that Lem knew that attacking Matt was wrong. Lem might be tried for attempted murder in the first degree, subject to the juvenile court's jurisdiction in this state.

Whether Ben and Jamal can be tried and convicted for burglary and theft of the tricycle will be decided by the same analysis. Because Ben was 7 and Jamal was 9 when they went into Matt's house and stole the tricycle, it is more likely that the prosecutor would be able to try both as adults.

If successful in persuading a court that any of these young children should be tried as adult offenders, the prosecutor would also have to persuade the court that the defendants are competent to stand trial.[57] She would have to show that they understand the charges against them and the nature of the proceedings and that they could assist their attorneys.

Under the Model Penal Code all of the defendants would have a valid defense of "immaturity" because they were under 16 years old at the time of the crime. Thus, none of the defendants could be tried and convicted of any crime. Instead, they would be dealt with in the juvenile court system.

Intoxication

From time immemorial most societies have enjoyed alcoholic beverages, but alcohol can change the way many people behave. It can loosen social and moral inhibitions, impair physical performance, and cloud judgment. Studies have consistently demonstrated a high correlation between alcohol consumption and crime.[58] Precisely because it may increase the frequency of harmful behavior, alcohol consumption poses special problems for the criminal law.

Early common law treated the inebriated offender and the sober offender in the same way. Intoxication was not relevant to criminal responsibility. Late common law modified this approach, permitting evidence of intoxication to reduce criminal responsibility for some crimes.

Except for occasional experiments with prohibition, contemporary criminal law has generally recognized that alcohol is a widely used and, some might argue, socially useful beverage. Because alcohol can seriously impair mental and physical abilities, however, the criminal law must impose its behavioral expectations on those who use it. The criminal law has developed doctrines that take into account the fact of intoxication in assessing responsibility but do not completely excuse crimes committed by people simply because they were intoxicated.

The law distinguishes between "voluntary intoxication" and "involuntary intoxication." *Voluntary intoxication* refers to individuals who know, or

---

57. See pages 433-434 for a discussion of competency to stand trial.

58. One study showed that 64 percent of 882 felons arrested in a two-year period in Cincinnati were intoxicated. A four-year study of 588 homicide cases in Philadelphia indicated that one or both parties had been drinking in 64 percent of the cases. Moore, Legal Responsibility and Chronic Alcoholism, 122 Am. J. Psychiatry 748, 753 (1966). Some studies indicate that as many as half of all homicides are committed by intoxicated offenders. See, e.g., Third Special Report to the U.S. Congress on Alcohol and Health from the Secretary of Health, Education and Welfare 64 (1978). A study by the Drug Use Forecasting System found that from 53 percent to 79 percent of men arrested in twelve major cities tested positive for illegal drug use. Even excluding those who tested positive for marijuana, the results still ranged from 25 percent to 74 percent. "Crime Study Finds Recent Drug Use in Most Arrested," *N.Y. Times*, Jan. 22, 1988, §A, at 1, col. 6.

should know, that the substance they are consuming (e.g., alcohol, drugs, medication) is likely to produce intoxicating effects. *Involuntary intoxication* refers either to consuming such substances without realizing it or to an unanticipated and unforeseen response to these substances. This is treated differently from voluntary intoxication.

Frequently, the criminal law has struck an imperfect compromise. It holds voluntarily intoxicated offenders responsible but often allows them to be convicted and punished less severely than sober offenders. Not everyone is satisfied with this approach. The impact alcohol consumption should have on criminal responsibility remains a controversial subject.

The advent of drug use has complicated matters even more. Drugs can have many of the same consequences on behavioral controls as alcohol. In addition, some drugs are hallucinogenic and can severely distort the user's perceptions of reality.

In the common law tradition, courts generally analogized drug use to alcohol in deciding how the criminal law should respond to drugs. Because drug use is today much less socially accepted than drinking, the criminal law is less tolerant of those who commit crimes while under the influence of drugs. In our discussion here we include intoxication caused by alcohol, drug use, or prescription medicine unless otherwise indicated.

Intoxication as an Element

Many criminal laws forbid the use of intoxicating substances under certain circumstances. Thus, laws criminalize certain activity while intoxicated, such as driving while under the influence of alcohol or drugs. In these cases proof of intoxication is an element of the crime.[59] Hence, the prosecutor is allowed to introduce such evidence to establish a necessary element of her case. These cases are governed by ordinary criminal law rules governing proof of crime. The defendant may deny using intoxicating substances or, in the alternative, concede their use but maintain they did not adversely affect his mental or physical capabilities.

The Relevance of Voluntary Intoxication to Mens Rea or Culpability
The Common Law

Early common law held the intoxicated defendant to the same standard of responsibility as the sober defendant. Hale wrote that the intoxicated defendant "shall have no privilege by this voluntarily contracted madness,

---

59. Many modern statutes criminalize drivers who operate a motor vehicle with a specified amount of alcohol in their blood. These statutes do not require any proof of intoxication.

but shall have the same judgement as if he were in his right senses."[60] Indeed, some commentators stated the law viewed intoxication "as an *aggravation* of the offense, rather than an excuse for any criminal misbehavior" (emphasis added).[61] This approach was also adopted in early American common law, and evidence of intoxication was not admitted in criminal trials.

During the nineteenth century, however, English courts modified this hard-line approach and permitted defendants to introduce evidence of voluntary intoxication in criminal trials. American courts followed suit, but judges did not want intoxicated offenders to avoid all criminal responsibility so they created "specific intent" crimes and admitted this evidence only when those crimes were charged (see Chapter 4). Such evidence was not admitted in "general intent" crimes. By the end of the nineteenth century most American jurisdictions allowed evidence of intoxication to be considered in determining whether the defendant was capable of forming the specific intent to commit the charged offense.[62] Thus, an intoxicated defendant, charged with assault with intent to commit rape, could present evidence of his intoxication to show that, because he was drunk, he thought the victim had consented and consequently he did not intend to rape her. If, however, he simply intended to assault the victim, he could not introduce evidence of intoxication to negate the elements of assault because assault is a "general intent" crime.

A defendant might argue that he would not have committed either crime if he were sober. Thus, his moral claim is that he is really being punished for getting drunk.[63] This is a plausible claim. Many people do things when intoxicated that they would not dream of doing while sober. However, the common law concluded that the act of getting drunk was itself a culpable act. By drinking the defendant was "reckless" as to the effect alcohol might have on him.[64] Moral blameworthiness could at least be attributed to his decision to drink despite realizing the impact alcohol can have.

Limiting evidence of voluntary intoxication to specific intent offenses is criticized as arbitrary and illogical. If alcohol consumption is logically relevant to the presence or absence of mens rea (or, as we called it earlier, to "element negation," see Chapter 4), then it should be admissible *whenever* it tends to

---

60. 1 M. Hale, Pleas of the Crown *32-33.

61. 4 W. Blackstone, Commentaries *25-26.

62. Hall, Intoxication and Criminal Responsibility, 57 Harv. L. Rev. 1045 (1944).

63. There is some evidence that courts would not permit the defendant to introduce evidence of voluntary intoxication if he had formed his criminal intent *before* drinking and had consumed alcohol solely to summon up courage to commit the offense. *Roberts v. Michigan,* 19 Mich. 401 (1870).

64. Of course, the legislature could enact a law that punished the act of getting drunk more severely precisely because of this risk. A defendant could then be charged with this offense rather than a crime involving recklessness or negligence. However, this approach has been rejected.

show the defendant did not act with the culpability required for commission of the charged offense. Critics point out that excluding relevant and probative evidence of mens rea simply because a court has characterized the charged offense as one of "general intent" defies both logic and experience. Indeed, this doctrine creates pressure on courts to characterize a crime as one of "general intent" precisely so that evidence of intoxication will *not* be admissible to negate an element of the charged offense. See *People v. Hood,* 1 Cal. 3d 444, 462 P.2d 370 (1969). Policy concerns may override the logic of mens rea in such cases.

Supporters point out that the "specific intent only" approach ensures that the intoxicated defendant will usually be convicted of *some* crime because most specific intent offenses have lesser included general intent crimes. To allow evidence of intoxication in *every* case might lead to not convicting the intoxicated defendant of *any* crime. This result would be intolerable to most people. Individuals might simply put themselves beyond the reach of the criminal law by drinking and then committing their crimes while drunk. Public safety could be seriously damaged.

Thus, the common law eventually compromised. In specific intent crimes, which were usually punished more severely than general intent crimes, the intoxicated individual would "get a break." By introducing evidence of voluntary intoxication, he might reduce the seriousness of the conviction. However, he would usually not walk out of the courtroom a free man simply because he was drunk. In most cases there was a general intent crime that covered his harmful behavior.

Note that under the later common law voluntary intoxication is not a defense. Rather, it is a doctrine that permits the defendant to introduce evidence to negate an element. Thus, the prosecution does not have the burden of proving the defendant was not intoxicated nor does the defendant have the burden of proving voluntary intoxication. (Of course, the prosecutor still must prove the required mens rea.) However, the defendant will have the burden of producing evidence of voluntary intoxication if the jury is to consider it.

In *Montana v. Egelhoff,* 518 U.S. 37 (1996), the Supreme Court held that a Montana statute that precludes the jury from considering evidence of voluntary intoxication in determining the existence of any mental state that is an element of the charged crime does not violate due process. The Court concluded that the respondent did not carry his burden of showing that the more recent common law allowing such evidence was "so deeply rooted at the time of the Fourteenth Amendment (or perhaps has become so deeply rooted since) as to be a fundamental principle which that Amendment enshrined."[65] Nine other states currently take the same basic approach as Montana.

---

65. 518 U.S. 37 at 2019.

The Model Penal Code

The Model Penal Code provides more precise definitions than the common law did. *Intoxication* means a "disturbance of mental or physical capabilities resulting from the introduction of substances into the body." MPC §2.08(5)(a). *Self-induced intoxication* means taking substances one knows, or should know, have a tendency to cause intoxication unless taken pursuant to medical advice or when one would otherwise have a valid defense to a charge of crime, such as duress. Although the MPC does not use the term *involuntary intoxication,* it recognizes intoxication that is "not self-induced." *Pathological intoxication* means intoxication that is grossly excessive given the amount of intoxicant the actor consumed and assuming that she did not know of her special susceptibility.

Section 2.08 allows the defendant to introduce evidence of self-induced intoxication whenever it "negatives an element of the offense." Evidence of intoxication is admissible but only if the crime requires proof of intention, purpose, or knowledge. Section 2.08(2) excludes such evidence if the offense requires recklessness, and the actor is unaware of a risk he would have been aware of had he been sober. People now know the impact alcohol and other intoxicating substances can have on human behavior. Drinking or taking drugs in the face of this knowledge is treated as the moral equivalent of being reckless (and negligent) about risk.

Thus, a defendant charged with "knowingly entering the house of another" could present evidence of voluntary intoxication to establish that he thought he was breaking into his own house. Such evidence would negate the element of "knowingly entering the house of *another*" (emphasis added). The MPC is intended to be more permissive than the common law because it does not exclude such evidence in "general intent" crimes.[66] Instead, it allows it in whenever it is logically relevant to the presence or absence of an element, except for recklessness or negligence. The MPC approach may lead to an outright acquittal, depending on the crime charged and its lesser included offenses.

The Relevance of Voluntary Intoxication to Defenses

Many defenses require the actor to perceive his situation reasonably and to respond to it reasonably. What, if any, impact should voluntary intoxication have on defenses?

---

66. If, however, crimes requiring "purpose, intent, and knowledge" are considered to be the functional equivalent of the common law's "specific intent crimes," then the MPC produces virtually the same result as the common law.

Voluntary intoxication is not a defense. In fact, it often makes it more difficult for the defendant to prevail when he does present a defense because most defenses require the defendant to act as a reasonable person would in the situation. Several examples will illustrate this point. In many jurisdictions a defendant who claims self-defense must *reasonably* believe that he is in imminent danger of death or serious bodily injury (see Chapter 16). If voluntary intoxication causes him to perceive such a threat when a sober individual would not, then the defense will fail. Likewise, voluntary manslaughter requires that the defendant acted in the "heat of passion upon *reasonable* provocation" (see Chapter 8). As already noted, the act of becoming voluntarily intoxicated is itself considered a kind of recklessness and negligence. Finally, the mistake of fact defense usually requires the defendant's mistake to be reasonable. Voluntary intoxication usually precludes this. Thus, voluntary intoxication undercuts most defenses because, in most cases, the defendant is held to the standard of a reasonable *sober* person.

There may be some limited exceptions. In jurisdictions that consider "fighting words" to be legally sufficient provocation (see Chapter 8), voluntary intoxication may be relevant if the provoking words relate to the defendant's condition of being intoxicated. For example, using words that demean an alcoholic and his condition of voluntary intoxication might be considered legally adequate provocation in some jurisdictions. (Even here, however, the defendant may be held to the standard of the reasonable alcoholic.) Generally speaking, however, the criminal law will hold an actor who is voluntarily intoxicated to the standard of the reasonably sober person when the actor asserts a defense.

Involuntary Intoxication

People can also become involuntarily intoxicated. Thus, someone may drink a beverage without having the slightest inkling that it contains alcohol or other inebriating substances. Or someone may have an extremely unusual reaction to prescription drugs. The common law permitted defendants to introduce such evidence as an affirmative defense, regardless of the crime charged, to establish the defense of involuntary intoxication.[67]

The defendant must prove that he unwittingly consumed an intoxicating substance (or that he took medication and had a highly unlikely and unforeseeable reaction) that produced the same symptoms as required by the *M'Naghten* test of legal insanity; that is, he did not know what he was doing or that it was wrong. (See pages 436-437.) Since the defendant was not at fault in becoming intoxicated, fairness requires the defendant to have an opportunity to present this defense in *all* cases. Because involuntary intoxi-

---

67. Reported cases of involuntary intoxication are extremely rare.

cation can be used for all criminal charges, it is broader than voluntary intoxication, which is generally limited to specific intent offenses at common law or to negate intent, purpose, or knowledge under the MPC.

However, the involuntary intoxication defense requires the defendant to establish that the involuntary intoxication caused very severe impairment of his cognitive ability. This seems unfair considering that the defendant was not to blame for consuming the substance or for not appreciating the risk of such an unusual reaction.

The Relevance of Voluntary Intoxication to Actus Reus

Defendants have also sought to introduce evidence of intoxication to show that they did not commit a voluntary act. The common law excluded this evidence because voluntary intoxication does not undermine the exercise of free will in human behavior.

It is possible, however, to argue that a defendant was so intoxicated that he could not have physically performed an act. Thus, if the defendant had passed out from drinking too much alcohol or using drugs, he could introduce this evidence to show that he could not have committed the voluntary act of the charged offense.

Alcoholism and Insanity

The Supreme Court has held that the constitutional prohibition on cruel and unusual punishment contained in the Eighth Amendment does not preclude punishing someone for appearing drunk in a public place even though the defendant claimed that, as an alcoholic, he could not control his drinking. *Powell v. Texas*, 392 U.S. 514 (1968). Though the Court has implicitly held that one cannot be punished for having the *status* of a chronic alcoholic, *Robinson v. California*, 370 U.S. 660 (1962), the Court concluded in *Powell* that a defendant may still be punished for conduct involving the use of alcohol if the behavior is not a symptom of the disease of alcoholism.

The Court noted that there was no medical consensus on whether alcoholism compelled a person to drink, thereby destroying an individual's free will. It therefore refused to strike down such laws as unconstitutional, preferring instead to permit states to experiment.

In some cases heavy consumption of alcohol over an extended period can actually cause organic brain damage. A person suffering from this condition may actually raise the defense of legal insanity if his condition has become "settled" or "fixed" and results in the same cognitive or volitional impairments recognized by the insanity test used in the jurisdiction. (See pages 435-439.) Many such individuals suffer from delirium tremens, which can cause hallucinations. These individuals may raise the defense of insanity even if they were not intoxicated at the time of the crime.

It is not unusual to find that mental illness causally contributes to voluntary intoxication. Many people have the dual diagnosis of "mentally ill" and "substance abuser." The defenses of legal insanity and voluntary intoxication are available to these individuals in appropriate cases.

The Model Penal Code permits a defendant to introduce evidence of intoxication that is "not self-induced" (e.g., someone spiked the nonalcoholic punch) or "pathological" (e.g., someone has a very unusual reaction to prescribed medication for the first time) to negate recklessness. MPC §2.08(2).

It also permits the defendant to introduce this evidence to establish the special affirmative defense provided in §2.08(4). The defendant must prove by a preponderance of the evidence that, as a result of either involuntary or pathological intoxication, she lacked substantial capacity either to appreciate the criminality of her act or to conform her conduct to the requirements of law. (This is almost the same as the MPC's insanity defense but here is caused by intoxication that is "pathological" or is not "self-induced" rather than by a mental disease or defect. See pages 437-438. It is not an insanity defense because §2.08(3) states that "intoxication does not, in itself, constitute mental disease within the meaning of §4.01.") If established, this affirmative defense will excuse the defendant from criminal responsibility even if the prosecutor has proven all the elements of the charged offense.

EXAMPLES

1. Bo is drinking heavily in a bar. He meets Amanda, who also is drinking, and they dance and drink for several hours. Bo asks her if she would like to come to his apartment. Amanda readily agrees. At his apartment, they have several more drinks. Then . . .
   a. Bo undresses Amanda and is about to have intercourse with her when she begins screaming. An off-duty police officer, hearing her cry, bursts through the door and arrests Bo for assault with intent to rape Amanda.
   b. Same facts except the police officer does not hear Amanda's scream until after Bo has sexual intercourse with Amanda. He bursts through the door and arrests Bo for rape.
   c. Bo starts to undress Amanda, intending to have sex with her. Sometime later, he is awakened by an off-duty police officer who bursts through the door and arrests him for attempting to rape Amanda. Bo denies he ever initiated sexual intercourse, claiming he had passed out.

   Can Bo introduce evidence of his voluntary intoxication?

2a. Paul is at a party. Melissa offers him a Cuban cigar, which was illegally imported into this country. Unknown to Paul, it contains marijuana. After smoking the cigar, Paul becomes giddy and hyperactive. He goes to the adjacent house and opens the door without knocking. He then goes inside and invites "everyone to come join the party." The neighbors, an elderly couple, are not amused. They have Paul arrested and charged with criminal trespass.

2b. Paul is at a party. Melissa offers him a marijuana cigarette, which, unknown to Paul, contains "angel dust." Paul smokes the cigarette and has a psychotic-like reaction. Believing Melissa to be Satan, he savagely beats her. He is arrested and charged with aggravated assault. Can he introduce evidence that he smoked a marijuana cigarette or that it was laced with "angel dust"?

3. Brent and Teresa had been dating for over a year, but had recently broken up. Extremely upset, Brent followed Teresa in his car after seeing her at a club. Brent had been drinking and was driving aggressively. Afraid, Teresa returned to the club to get help. She told the doorman about Brent. He came outside and asked Brent to leave. Brent drove straight into Teresa's car. He was charged with DUI and with the intentional destruction of another's property. Brent argues that he was unable to control his vehicle because of his intoxication and that his collision with Teresa's car was an accident. Does it matter if this state does not allow evidence of voluntary intoxication to negate a mens rea element?

4. Tubby drank incessantly. He was always arrested for being drunk in public and other nuisance crimes. Finally, Tubby drank so much, he suffered organic brain damage. He began to hallucinate and to imagine terrible creatures were attacking him while he slept. One evening a police officer tried to wake him after he had fallen asleep on a park bench; Tubby attacked the police officer, mistaking him for a giant spider. Can Tubby introduce this evidence in his trial on third-degree assault for attacking a police officer while in the performance of his duties?

EXPLANATIONS

1a. Because assault with intent to rape is a "specific intent" crime, later common law would allow Bo to introduce evidence of his drinking throughout the evening to prove that he thought Amanda had consented to have sexual intercourse with him. If believed by the jury, Bo would not be convicted of "assault with intent to rape" because his voluntary intoxication prevented him from acting with the "specific intent" of raping Amanda. He did *not intend* to have sexual intercourse with a female *without her consent*. He might be charged with a lesser included offense like assault, however, if it is one of "general intent."

The MPC would also allow Bo to present evidence of his voluntary intoxication that is logically relevant to negating any element of the charged offense. Thus, if the statute required that he "*knowingly* have intercourse without consent," evidence of his voluntary intoxication may negate "knowingly." If, however, a rape statute in this jurisdiction made *recklessness* with regard to consent an element of the crime, the MPC would not permit Bo to use this evidence to negate such recklessness. By drinking so much, Bo decreased his ability to evaluate the risk that Amanda did not consent. The act of drinking is sufficiently blameworthy to satisfy the requirement of recklessness in the rape statute.

1b. In many jurisdictions rape is considered a "general intent" offense. Thus, the common law would not allow Bo to introduce evidence of voluntary intoxication to negate the mens rea of rape. This may seem unfair to the defendant (though not to the victim who has been subjected to unwanted intercourse). After all, Bo's mental state was the same in both Examples 1a and 1b. Though influenced by the alcohol, Bo thought Amanda had consented to sexual intercourse in both cases. Yet, simply because a court has decided rape is a "general intent" crime, he will not be allowed to introduce evidence of voluntary intoxication in 1b.

Under the MPC, however, the analysis is essentially the same as in Example 1a. Bo could introduce this evidence if it tended to negate any element of the charged crime. If the rape statute requires the defendant to have acted intentionally, purposefully, or knowingly with respect to any element, then this evidence is admissible.

1c. Bo could introduce this evidence under both the common law and the MPC. The common law would let him argue that the evidence established he could not physically have performed the act of intercourse because he was unconscious. Likewise, the MPC would let him introduce the evidence because it is relevant to an "element" of the charged offense. He would argue that he could not, and therefore did not, engage in the voluntary act of sexual intercourse.

2a. Though Paul probably knew that the cigar was illegally imported, he had no idea it contained a prohibited substance or drug that could cause intoxication. If this were a case of *voluntary* intoxication, under the common law Paul could use this evidence if he was charged with a specific intent crime. Criminal trespass, however, is probably not a specific intent offense. Thus, he probably cannot use this evidence to negate the element of "knowingly" entering another's house without permission. The MPC would allow Paul to use evidence of self-induced intoxication to negate any element of a charged offense. Paul would argue that this evidence negates that he "knowingly" (a) entered another person's house (b) without permission.

Unfortunately, this is more likely a case of *involuntary* intoxication.

Paul had no idea he was consuming a substance that would, or was likely, to cause intoxication. To succeed under common law, he would have to prove that the marijuana made him unable to know what he was doing or that it was wrong. Paul probably did know that he was going into someone else's house and that he did not have permission. Thus, he would probably be convicted. Only if he was "really out of it" would he be acquitted. This is unjust. Ironically, Paul is probably in a better position under *voluntary* intoxication than he is under *involuntary* intoxication.

2b. This is a complicated case because it is, arguably, a case of both voluntary and involuntary intoxication. Paul knew that he was committing a crime — that is, smoking marijuana, an intoxicating substance. However, he did not know, or have reason to know, that he was consuming a far more powerful mind- and mood-altering drug. (See Chapter 6 for a review of the "greater crime" doctrine.)

Under common law Paul can use evidence of *voluntary* intoxication to negate specific intent. If the aggravated assault statute proscribes an assault "with intent to inflict serious bodily injury" or other such language, it is probably a specific intent offense. If the court considered this a case of voluntary intoxication, Paul would be allowed to introduce this evidence to negate that specific intent. However, he could not use it in a general intent crime. Most likely, a general intent charge of assault is a lesser included offense, and the jury could not consider this evidence on that charge.

Under the MPC, however, Paul can use evidence of self-induced intoxication to negate any element of the charged crime except recklessness and negligence. Because a jury could consider this evidence on all charges, Paul has a better chance under the MPC than under common law.

If the jury considers this a case of *involuntary* intoxication, then both under common law and the MPC Paul can introduce this evidence to show that he did not know what he was doing (he thought he was attacking the devil) or that it was wrong. Thus, he may be better using involuntary intoxication as a defense. The problem, of course, is that the judge may rule that this is a case of voluntary intoxication because Paul knew that he was taking an illegal substance; therefore, he consciously disregarded the risk that he might consume another illegal substance.

3. If the state follows the Montana approach and excludes evidence of voluntary intoxication in determining mens rea or a culpability element (unless intoxication is an element of the charged offense), it will be much easier for the prosecutor to persuade a jury that Brent did, in fact, *intend* to damage Teresa's car. The jury could likely infer "intent" based on his

conduct leading up to the incident without being allowed to consider the effect of his alcohol consumption on his judgment, perception, and motor skills. If, however, the state allows evidence of voluntary intoxication on the issue of mens rea or culpability, then Brent could introduce evidence of his drinking just prior to the event to support his claim that his collision with Teresa's car was accidental rather than intentional.

Ironically, even in a state that excludes evidence of voluntary intoxication on mens rea or culpability, the prosecutor could introduce evidence of Brent's drinking to prove that he was "driving under the influence" of alcohol because intoxication is an element of the charged offense. Thus, in some states the prosecution could use this evidence to convict Brent of the DUI charge, while preventing Brent from using the same evidence to negate the mens rea of the intentional destruction of property charge. Is this consistent, logical, or fair?

4. Under the common law Tubby could not introduce this evidence to negate mens rea because he is not charged with a specific intent offense. Because Tubby's extended drinking has actually caused organic brain damage with resulting impairment in his cognitive abilities, he may now also have a defense of legal insanity. Depending on the jurisdiction, this might be a successful defense, though it may also lead to mandatory commitment in a mental health facility if the jury finds Tubby "not guilty by reason of insanity."

Under the MPC Tubby could introduce this evidence if it negatives an element of the crime, including recklessness. Because Tubby was intoxicated and did not know that he was attacking a police officer while in the performance of his duties, this evidence should be admissible and Tubby may be acquitted.

However, the MPC would not allow Tubby to raise the special affirmative defense of intoxication because his intoxication was self-induced. He may still have a defense of legal insanity if experts conclude that organic brain damage caused by excessive alcohol consumption is properly characterized as a "mental disease or defect" as used in the MPC.

Diminished Capacity

The diminished capacity defense permits a more subjective inquiry into the blameworthiness of criminal defendants. The fact finder can take into account certain characteristics of the defendant, including mental illness and voluntary intoxication, in determining the degree of the crime committed. Courts initially developed this doctrine to ameliorate the restrictiveness of the *M'Naghten* insanity test, to avoid imposing capital punishment on mentally disabled killers, and to individualize judgments of criminal responsibility. See Arenella, The Diminished Capacity and Diminished Responsibility Defenses: Two Children of a Doomed Marriage, 77 Colum. L. Rev. 827 (1977). Today, the diminished capacity defense also includes voluntary intoxication in many jurisdictions. See pages 455-459.

Despite its relatively young history, the diminished capacity defense has proven confusing and troublesome to courts, scholars, and law students alike. There are several reasons for this chaos. First, there are several versions of the defense, each with a fundamentally different conceptual basis. Second, it is not really a "defense" at all. Third, it may permit a broad range of expert testimony to be introduced that, arguably, is not relevant in determining criminal responsibility under the law.

There have been three primary versions of this defense: (1) the "diminished responsibility" defense used in Great Britain, (2) the "diminished capacity" defense used in California, and (3) the "diminished capacity" defense that is still used in a large number of jurisdictions today.

A Brief History

The best way to understand this confusing area is to look at each of these versions.

The British Version: Diminished Responsibility

The diminished responsibility defense was a creation of Scottish common law. See *HM Advocate v. Dingwall,* [1867] J.C. 466 (Scot). In 1957 Great Britain enacted the defense in statutory form when capital punishment was still used in premeditated murder cases.[68] Under the British statute a defendant could introduce evidence showing that, though not legally insane, he was nevertheless mentally disturbed at the time of the offense. If the jury found that mental retardation or mental illness "substantially impaired the [defendant's] mental responsibility" for the crime, it could find him guilty of manslaughter, even though the prosecution had actually proved all the elements of premeditated murder. Thus, mentally ill defendants who were not legally insane could avoid execution. In essence the British doctrine of "diminished responsibility" is really a form of mitigation in punishment.

The California Version

The California Supreme Court developed its version of the diminished capacity defense primarily to soften the perceived rigidity of the *M'Naghten*

---

68. The Homicide Act of 1957, 5 & 6 Eliz. II, ch. II, §2(1).

insanity defense. If a mentally ill offender was not found insane, he was held fully accountable under the criminal law. Initially, the California Court simply permitted mental health experts to testify that the defendant could not entertain the mens rea required for conviction of the charged offense. Thus, expert testimony could now be admitted not only on the insanity defense but also on the material element of mens rea or culpability. *People v. Wells*, 33 Cal. 2d 330 (1949).

In subsequent cases, however, the California Supreme Court began to use the diminished capacity defense to *redefine* the mens rea elements of homicide in California law. In *People v. Wolff*, 61 Cal. 2d 795, 394 P.2d 959 (1964), the court reversed the first-degree murder conviction of a schizophrenic 15-year-old who had planned and deliberately carried out the killing of his mother so he could realize his sexual fantasies of murder and rape. The court agreed that the jury had properly rejected his insanity defense under the *M'Naghten* test because the defendant knew that his acts were against the law. Nonetheless, it held that the undisputed psychiatric evidence admitted at trial established that the defendant was mentally ill and, consequently, could not "maturely and meaningfully reflect upon the gravity" of his contemplated act. The court thereupon reduced his conviction to second-degree murder.[69]

Later, in *People v. Conley*, 64 Cal. 2d 310 (1964), the court decided that the defendant was entitled to introduce evidence of mental illness and voluntary intoxication to reduce a charge of first-degree murder to voluntary manslaughter. The court concluded that such evidence could establish that the defendant did not act with "malice aforethought" because he was "unable to comprehend his duty to govern his actions in accord with the duty imposed by law."[70]

Then, in 1974 the California court held in *People v. Poddar* that "[i]f it is established that an accused, because he suffered a diminished capacity, was . . . *unable to act in accordance with the law*," he could only be convicted of manslaughter.[71] Under California's ever-expanding diminished capacity defense, volitional as well as cognitive impairment caused by mental illness could negate the "malice aforethought" necessary for conviction of both first- and second-degree murder.

The California Supreme Court had used the diminished capacity defense to infuse new meaning into the statutory elements for homicide. In so doing, the court had effectively created a "mini-insanity" defense. See Morse, Undiminished Confusion in Diminished Capacity, 75 J. Crim. L. & Criminology 1 (1984). It had changed homicide's mens rea terms from simple descriptive terms describing planning, motive, and manner of killing into normative

---

69. 61 Cal. 2d 795, 821, 394 P.2d 959, 975, 40 Cal. Rptr. 271, 287 (1964).

70. 64 Cal. 2d 310, 322, 411 P.2d 911, 49 Cal. Rptr. 271 (1964).

71. 10 Cal. 3d 750, 758, 518 P.2d 342, 348 (1974) (emphasis added).

terms requiring both subjective awareness of wrongdoing and ability to obey the law.[72]

The California approach enhanced the law's ability to take into account an individual's characteristics in assessing criminal responsibility. On the other hand, it was virtually impossible to apply the doctrine consistently and with an even hand. Juries returned different verdicts in very similar cases.[73] Moreover, once psychiatric evidence was admitted to negate mens rea in homicide cases, it became virtually impossible to exclude it in cases involving other crimes, such as burglary.[74] If a defendant was successful in using the diminished capacity defense, he would be convicted of a lesser included offense or, if there was no such offense, he would simply be acquitted and released immediately. Initially, the California Supreme Court tried to limit the availability of the defense to "specific intent" offenses,[75] but the court eventually permitted the defense to introduce any evidence seemingly relevant to the presence or absence of statutory mens rea.[76]

In 1978 Dan White, a former member of the San Francisco Board of Supervisors, shot and killed Mayor George Moscone, the popular mayor of the city, and Harvey Milk, a member of the Board of Supervisors, in what appeared to be a well-planned and calculated murder motivated by revenge. He was charged with two counts of first-degree murder. The jury accepted White's diminished capacity defense that, because of mental problems aggravated by erratic junk food binges, he did not act with "malice aforethought." It convicted him of voluntary manslaughter. The public was outraged. The verdict in this high-profile case, in which the claim of diminished capacity was quickly dubbed the "twinkie defense" by its critics, provided strong impetus for changing the law. In 1982 the defense of diminished capacity was abolished by public initiative.[77]

The Rule of Evidence Approach

The simplest version of the diminished capacity defense is best understood as a rule of evidence. If evidence logically tends to establish or negate a mental state of the charged offense, then either the defendant or the government may introduce such evidence for the jury's consideration on the issue of mens rea. If a defendant's mental illness prevented him from acting

---

72. G. Fletcher, Rethinking Criminal Law 250-259 (1978).

73. Note, A Punishment Rationale for Diminished Capacity, 18 UCLA L. Rev. 561 (1971).

74. *People v. Wetmore,* 22 Cal. 3d 318, 583 P.2d 1308 (1978).

75. See *People v. Hood,* 1 Cal. 3d 444, 462 P.2d 370 (1969).

76. *People v. Wetmore,* 22 Cal. 3d 318, 583 P.2d 1308 (1978).

77. Cal. Pen. Code §25(a) (West 1999).

with "premeditation," "intent," or whatever mental state is required for conviction, he may introduce expert testimony to establish that he did not have the necessary mens rea.

The form in which expert testimony is permitted can vary. In most jurisdictions the expert will simply express an opinion as to whether the defendant, because of his mental disability, did or did not have the mental state of the charged offense. In other jurisdictions the expert will testify as to whether the defendant, because of his mental disability, had the "capacity" to form this mental state. Note that, regardless of the form or content of the experts' opinions, the prosecution still must prove beyond a reasonable doubt that the defendant had the mens rea required for conviction.

Thus, a person suffering from an emotional disorder such as bipolar disorder (manic-depression) that causes him to become very exhilarated and excited might introduce psychiatric testimony that he did not have the mental state necessary for fraud or theft though he paid for a large purchase of clothing with a worthless check. The expert might conclude that, because of his mental condition, the defendant believed he had the money in his account or could readily get it in time to cover the check.

The rule of evidence version of the diminished capacity defense is still widely used in many jurisdictions. There is a strong argument that a defendant has a constitutional right to use evidence of mental illness if it is relevant to the presence or absence of mens rea.[78] Most federal courts and about half the states permit the use of psychiatric evidence when it is relevant to the mens rea of a specific intent crime. Some jurisdictions permit its use whenever it is relevant to the mens rea of *any* crime,[79] while others limit it to first-degree murder.

Increasingly, however, many jurisdictions are concluding that psychiatric evidence should not be admitted on mens rea at all either because it is not relevant to mens rea or because it is too confusing for juries.[80] In these jurisdictions, mental illness that does not satisfy legal insanity will not be considered in determining guilt or innocence.

The Model Penal Code

The Model Penal Code essentially adopts the rule of evidence approach and permits psychiatric evidence to be admitted whenever it is relevant to

---

78. See, e.g., *United States v. Pholot,* 827 F.2d 889 (3d Cir. 1987) (holding that the Federal Insanity Defense Reform Act of 1984 did not prevent defendants from using psychiatric evidence if relevant to the mens rea).

79. See, e.g., *United States v. Cameron,* 907 F.2d 1051 (10th Cir. 1990); *People v. Saille,* 54 Cal. 3d 1103, 820 P.2d 588 (1991).

80. See, e.g., *State v. Bouwman,* 328 N.W.2d 703 (Minn. 1982); *State v. Wilcox,* 70 Ohio St. 2d 182, 436 N.E.2d 523 (1982).

negate the mens rea of *any* crime: "Evidence that the defendant suffered from a mental disease or defect is admissible whenever it is relevant to prove that the defendant did or did not have a state of mind which is an element of the offense." §4.02(1).

The MPC concluded that psychiatric evidence should be treated just like any other relevant evidence. It argued: "If states of mind are accorded legal significance, psychiatric evidence should be admissible whenever relevant to prove or disprove their existence to the same extent as any other relevant evidence." If a defendant successfully used the diminished capacity defense to be acquitted of all charges, public safety could be adequately protected by involuntary civil commitment. See Model Penal Code and Commentaries, Comment to §4.02, at 219 (1985).

Summary

The diminished capacity defense today is best understood as a rule of evidence rather than a "defense." The doctrine simply permits courts to admit the opinions of mental health experts as evidence in a criminal trial if their testimony is relevant to the presence or absence of mens rea. Though such evidence has the potential for confusing juries and creating expert domination, it can in appropriate cases be relevant and useful to the jury's task of determining whether the defendant acted with the culpability required for conviction.

EXAMPLES

1a. Bertrand's, wife, Lisu, recently divorced Bertrand, but he desperately wants to get back together. He has called her numerous times to no avail.

Bertrand suffers from a minimal brain dysfunction with an associated explosive personality disorder with paranoid features. Minimal brain dysfunction is a biochemical imbalance in the brain that prevents Bertrand from maintaining control over his emotional impulses, especially in stressful situations.

Finally, Bertrand visits Lisu at home, unannounced. She is very upset at Bertrand for his untimely visit and does not want to let him into the house, but finally does. She tries to explain that they cannot reconcile but he will not listen. When the discussion turns into a verbal fight, she tells him he is a "loser, incompetent, and sexually inadequate." Bertrand becomes extremely angry and upset. He grabs Lisu and indescribable violence ensues. Lisu ends up in the hospital in critical condition for her injuries. The prosecution charges Bertrand with attempted murder.

Bertrand seeks to present the testimony of a psychiatrist concerning his mental condition. The prosecution moves to exclude the evidence as irrelevant to legal insanity or to any other issue. Should the trial judge permit Bertrand to present the testimony of the psychiatrist, and, if so, on what issues?

1b. Same facts as above, except Bertrand's rage is caused by his drunkenness and not a minimal brain dysfunction. What about evidence he was drunk?

2. Linky has been plagued with a "passive aggressive personality" and "passive dependent personality" all his life. His dominating and over-bearing father has humiliated and embarrassed him since he was a young boy. Finally, at 18 Linky decides to strike back. He pays Frank $500 to steal his father's pride and joy, a '69 Ford Mustang. Linky calls Frank and meets with him to tell Frank dates and times when his father will be out of town. He also tells Frank to make sure he (Linky) isn't connected to the theft.

   Linky, empowered and liberated by this assertive act, feels fantastic after paying Frank to steal his father's car. He has "finally fought back." Linky moves out of his father's house, gets a job, and finds a girlfriend. Deciding that he no longer wants his father's car stolen, he telephones Frank and calls it off. Unfortunately, Frank is an undercover police officer. Linky is arrested and charged with conspiracy to steal a car. (This jurisdiction has adopted the unilateral approach to conspiracy. See Chapter 14).

   A defense psychiatrist testifies at trial that, at the conscious level, Linky wanted his father's car to be stolen. But what Linky *really intended* at a subconscious level was finally to take control of his life by acting forcefully against the single overpowering person who had been controlling and dominating his life. The expert concludes that, in reality, Linky did not intend to commit a crime; he *intended* to obtain his psychological freedom by the act of hiring Frank to commit a crime. The fact that Linky called off the job after obtaining that psychological freedom is proof of what he "actually" intended.

EXPLANATIONS

1a. Although Bertrand suffers from a "minimal brain dysfunction," it probably does not prevent Bertrand from understanding the nature or quality of his act or that it was wrong to strike Lisu. Under the *M'Naghten* test, he is not legally insane.

   If the jurisdiction used the MPC insanity test, Bertrand could introduce the testimony of a mental health expert to show that, at the time of the offense, he suffered from a mental disorder that substantially impaired his ability to conform his conduct to the requirements of the law. If the jury agreed, he might be found not guilty by reason of insanity.

But if the jury does not find Bertrand legally insane, it might still be able to consider the expert testimony in determining whether Bertrand intended to kill Lisu if the jurisdiction permits the diminished capacity defense.

Because of the very serious injuries Lisu suffered, a jury might reasonably conclude that Bertrand intended to kill her rather than just to assault her. Thus, a jury might well convict him of attempted murder. Under the diminished capacity defense Bertrand could introduce the expert's testimony on the mens rea. He would argue that his minimal brain dysfunction prevented him from forming the necessary mens rea for attempted murder; that is, he did not intend to cause Lisu's death. Rather, he was angry, stressed, and upset, and his brain dysfunction made him unable to control his impulses of rage. The testimony would help the jury understand that, though he may have intended seriously to hurt Lisu, Bertrand did not want to kill her. Even if this defense is successful on the mens rea element of attempted murder, Bertrand will not be fully acquitted. Rather, he will probably be convicted of a less serious crime, such as assault.

This example illustrates an important point. Evidence concerning the defendant's mental condition at the time of the crime may be admissible on *both* the defense of legal insanity (particularly if the MPC test is used) and on the presence of mens rea if a diminished capacity defense is allowed.

1b. Whether Bertrand might be convicted of assault rather than attempted murder depends on whether this jurisdiction permits voluntary intoxication to support a diminished capacity defense.

Most states permit the defendant to present evidence of voluntary intoxication to negate intent or knowledge. (Usually, evidence of voluntary intoxication is *not* permitted to negate recklessness because voluntarily becoming intoxicated is itself considered a reckless act.) In such a jurisdiction Bertrand might be convicted of assault rather than attempted murder if a jury decided that, because he was drunk, Bertrand did not intend to kill Lisu.

Other jurisdictions hold voluntarily intoxicated individuals to the same standard of criminal responsibility as sober actors and do not permit a defendant to introduce evidence that he was drunk at the time of the crime. These jurisdictions assume everyone knows that excessive use of alcohol impairs perception, judgment, and volitional faculties. Bertrand must also be aware that alcohol will affect his mental faculties. The criminal law attributes moral responsibility to the defendant because he voluntarily drank and became intoxicated. As one court noted: "The moral blameworthiness lies in the voluntary impairment of one's mental faculties with knowledge that the resulting condition is a source of potential danger to others."[81]

Therefore, some jurisdictions do not permit defendants under a "diminished capacity" defense to introduce evidence of voluntary intoxication to negate mens rea.

2. Although Linky suffers from diagnosed psychological disorders, he will not prevail on his insanity defense whether under the *M'Naghten* or the MPC tests. He understood the nature of the act and that it was wrong. He also could control his behavior as evidenced by his first hiring and then firing Frank to do the job.

Linky would also argue "diminished capacity" if this jurisdiction permitted this defense. He would claim that his mental illness prevented him from forming the mental state required for conviction of conspiracy or solicitation. However, mens rea elements like "intent" and "knowledge" do not require awareness of the unconscious influences that may influence a person's decision to commit a crime. They only require awareness of the behavior that constitutes the crime. Put simply, these criminal mental states only require that a person is aware of *what* he is doing; they do not require awareness of *why* he may be doing it.

Linky has acted purposefully. He *intended* to come to an agreement with Frank and *intended* that Frank would commit a crime. Expert evidence on possible psychological reasons why Linky undertook this criminal enterprise will not be admitted under a diminished capacity defense because it is not relevant to the presence or absence of the mental states required for either conspiracy or solicitation. The defense may be able to use this evidence at sentencing.

Entrapment

Not all crimes are reported to the police, particularly so-called "victimless crimes." These crimes usually involve willing participants engaged in activities that appear to involve no "real" victim. Prostitution, selling or purchasing drugs, and gambling are common examples of "victimless" crimes.

Because there is usually no incentive for the participants to notify the police when they commit these crimes, effective law enforcement often requires undercover police to engage in these criminal acts in order to detect and apprehend those who do. Thus, a police officer may buy crack cocaine to gather sufficient evidence to charge and convict drug dealers.

This active involvement by the police in what would otherwise clearly be criminal activity if there were no legal authority for them to do so raises

---

81. *Hendershott v. People*, 653 P.2d 385, 396 (Colo. 1982).

difficult public policy questions. After all, the role of the police is to detect and solve crime, not to manufacture crimes or to induce law-abiding citizens to commit them.

Entrapment is a defense that attempts to strike the balance between proper police undercover investigation and detection of crime and inappropriate police instigation of crime. The defense focuses both on (1) what the police did and (2) the defendant's predisposition to commit the crime. Because of this dual concern, the entrapment defense may be seen either as a rule of criminal procedure regulating police investigatory conduct or as a denial of true mens rea, claiming that the defendant did not really choose to commit a crime.

In some jurisdictions entrapment is an affirmative defense. The defendant must produce evidence supporting the defense and must also establish it by a preponderance of the evidence. In other jurisdictions the defendant has the burden of production, but the prosecution must establish that the defendant was predisposed to commit the offense. If successful, a claim of entrapment bars prosecution.

The History of the Entrapment Defense

American common law generally did not provide the defense of entrapment. As long as the defendant committed a crime, the police role in providing him with the opportunity to do so was simply not relevant to his guilt or innocence.

The primary impetus for recognizing this defense came from federal courts. In 1932 the Supreme Court held in *Sorrells v. United States,* 287 U.S. 435, that the defendant should have been allowed to use the entrapment defense to a charge of selling liquor to a government agent in violation of Prohibition laws. After refusing to sell liquor to the agent despite several requests, the defendant finally relented and sold him some. The Court defined the defense as follows: "Entrapment is the conception and planning of an offense by an officer, and his procurement of its commission by one who would not have perpetrated it except for the trickery, persuasion, or fraud of the officer."

One argument offered to support the entrapment defense is that of presumed legislative intent. Simply put, the legislature did not intend that enforcement of a criminal law should ensnare otherwise innocent people caught by abusive government inducement. (Of course, the legislature was silent on this question. This is really a classic judicial stratagem for reaching a decision based primarily on public policy grounds.)

Another rationale supporting the defense is to deter improper police conduct. The government will not be allowed to obtain a conviction if police investigatory methods improperly fabricated criminal activity. Thus, the defense is available only if law enforcement officials or their agents, such as informants, *induce*—rather than merely enable—the defendant to commit the crime.

The defense to federal crimes announced in *Sorrells* is not required by the Constitution. Nonetheless, today all states have adopted this defense, though there are two different approaches.

The Defense Today
The Subjective Approach

This two-step approach, used by federal courts and a majority of state courts, focuses both on the *nature of the police conduct* and on the *defendant's predisposition* to commit the offense.

The first requirement is that government conduct induce the commission of the crime. There is, as the *Sorrells* Court noted, a fine line between merely affording an opportunity to an "unwary criminal" to commit a crime and actually inducing an "unwary innocent" to commit a crime.[82]

The second requirement is that the defendant not be predisposed to commit the crime. This element shifts the analysis from what the government did to the character and criminal history of the defendant. It allows the government to argue that it was simply providing an opportunity for an "unwary criminal" to take the bait and commit a crime.

In *Jacobson v. United States,* 503 U.S. 540 (1992), the Supreme Court limited somewhat the targeting of criminal suspects. The defendant had subscribed to a magazine featuring nude pictures of boys under 18. After passage of a federal law criminalizing child pornography, the defendant stopped ordering the magazine. Government agents continually sent him material in the mail, including literature from a fake lobbying organization advocating repeal of the law and criticizing government censorship. The agents then sent him information for ordering magazines with titles indicating that they contained erotic pictures of young boys. Twenty-six months after receiving these various mailings, the defendant placed one order for two magazines that contained pornographic materials. After a controlled delivery to the defendant, he was arrested, charged, and convicted of possessing child pornography.

The majority held that the government had to establish that the defendant was predisposed to commit the crime and that *his predisposition was not the product of government conduct.* Because the defendant had never before

---

82. As a matter of causation, the criminal law usually does not look beyond the last causal agent. Yet, the defense of entrapment effectively permits the defendant to argue that the government "caused" him to commit the crime.

ordered illegal material, the Court ruled as a matter of law that the government had not established this element.

Because the subjective approach allows the government to show that the defendant was predisposed to commit the crime, some critics believe this approach encourages the police to declare "open season" on individuals with a criminal history and to use any imaginable inducement to obtain their conviction. Using the defense is risky. A defendant's past criminal history usually becomes fair game, running the substantial risk of prejudicing the jury. And, in some states, the defendant must admit committing the crime.

The Objective Approach

This approach, adopted in the Model Penal Code and a minority of states, looks primarily at what the government did and assesses what its impact would be on normally law-abiding people. It is less concerned with the criminal attitude or history of a particular offender than with controlling police conduct.

Under §2.13 of the MPC the defense is established if a government agent, in order to gather evidence that a crime has been committed, "induces or encourages another person to engage [in an offense] either by (a) making knowingly false representations designed to induce the belief that such conduct is not prohibited; or (b) employing methods of persuasion or inducement which create a substantial risk that such an offense will be committed by persons other than those who are ready to commit it." The defendant's predispositions are irrelevant.

Because the MPC defense is phrased in general terms, its application depends on the facts of each case. Frequent entreaties over time despite initial refusals, continuing appeals to sympathy, promises of excessive profit, or other persuasive stratagems that might induce law-abiding individuals to commit a crime will support the claim. However, the MPC does not permit the claim of entrapment when "causing or threatening bodily injury" to someone other than the individual inducing the crime is an element of the charged offense.

Because the objective approach to entrapment focuses on whether the police behavior was appropriate and not on the characteristics of the offender, this formulation can be seen as an attempt to oversee how the police do their job. By creating disincentives for inappropriate police conduct, this substantive criminal law defense serves the same general purpose as a rule of criminal procedure, much like the *Miranda* exclusionary rule.

Critics of the objective approach point out that it is good police work to target individuals with a known criminal history. And, they add, it may take special inducements to persuade an experienced and savvy criminal to commit a crime.

Due Process

So far the Supreme Court has not held that constitutional due process requires the defense of entrapment. Thus, both Congress and other jurisdictions are free to do away with the defense.

Nonetheless, several Supreme Court cases suggest that, at least in cases involving outrageous police conduct, the Constitution *may* require the availability of the defense.[83] In *Russell,* a government informer had supplied the defendant with an indispensable ingredient (which was extremely difficult to obtain) for manufacturing methamphetamine ("speed"). In *Hampton* the defendant obtained heroin from a government informant and then sold it to a government agent. Though the Court upheld convictions in both cases, five Justices indicated that, in some cases of extremely outrageous government conduct, due process might require dismissal of the charges.[84]

EXAMPLES

1a. Linda, a prostitute, sees a man and asks if he needs a date. The man replies that Linda looks nice, but that he does not know if he can afford a date. Linda says that "a date" would only cost him $50, and they can have sex in her car parked just around the corner. The man then arrests Linda for soliciting prostitution.

1b. Linda occasionally engages in prostitution to raise extra money. One night she is walking home from a party, not intending to engage in prostitution. A man approaches Linda and asks her how much it would cost to have sex. Linda says she is not interested and keeps walking. The man follows her and says he will give her $1,000 to have sex with him in his car. Linda stops, thinks about it for a minute, and then agrees. The man, an undercover police officer, arrests her for prostitution.

Will the defense of entrapment succeed in either of these cases?

2. Lucy, a heroin addict, recently lost her job. Though she has saved some money, it is quickly running out. Unable to find her normal dealer, Lucy approaches someone else and asks to buy some heroin. The man says he will give her twice the amount if she will have sex with him in his car. Knowing she is short of cash and needs a fix, Lucy agrees. He arrests her for prostitution. Entrapment?

3. Al, a local car dealer, has a reputation for selling cars at a good price but

---

83. *United States v. Russell,* 411 U.S. 423 (1973); *United States v. Hampton,* 425 U.S. 484 (1976).

84. At least one lower federal appellate court has held that the Constitution requires reversal of a conviction when government conduct was so outrageous as to violate due process. *United States v. Twigg,* 588 F.2d 373 (3d Cir. 1978). This is a minority view.

only if buyers pay in cash or cash equivalents. Maria tells Al that she is a commodities broker and wants to buy a Jeep Cherokee for cash. Al tells her she can pay $9,000 in cash and the rest in bank checks under $10,000 each. He says she must obtain cashier checks just under $10,000 from several banks for the rest of the purchase price because, under federal law, the bank must report any transaction involving $10,000 or more to the government. Maria agrees.

A few days later she shows up to purchase the Cherokee with $9,000 cash and two bank checks for $9,900 each. Before signing the papers, Maria tells Al, "I really appreciate your telling me how to do this deal. In fact, I am a drug dealer and it's been difficult for me to spend the money I earn from dealing drugs without tipping off the cops." Al smiles and says, "Where there's a will, there is a way." After all the papers are signed, Maria arrests Al, who is subsequently charged with conducting a financial transaction involving property represented to be the proceeds of an illegal activity. Guilty or entrapped?

4a. An FBI agent poses as an Arab sheik and twice attempts to bribe a congressman. Both times the congressman rejects the bribes, telling the sheik, "This is neither the time nor the place. I need a place I am certain is secure so that I can't be caught." The "sheik" then arranges to meet the congressman in a hotel room. After the congressman hugs the sheik to make sure he is not "wired" with electronic recording devices, the congressman accepts the bribe. The event is recorded by secret cameras and microphones in the hotel room. Does the congressman have an entrapment claim?

4b. An FBI agent poses as an Arab sheik and twice attempts to bribe a congressman. Both times the congressman rejects the bribes, asserting they are unethical and illegal. On the third attempt the sheik says, "I fully understand your reasons for not accepting money. Will you accept a new kidney from my country for your daughter who, I understand, will die soon unless she gets a new kidney?" The congressman, knowing this is true, reluctantly agrees. The "sheik" then arrests him for accepting a bribe.

5. Shawn occasionally sells small amounts of marijuana to his friends. Oprah, a recent acquaintance, approaches Shawn and asks to buy some marijuana to relieve the pain she feels from her cancer. Shawn sympathizes with her plight, but declines. A week later, Oprah pleads with Shawn, saying her pain is getting worse. Again, Shawn declines. Finally, Oprah calls him on the telephone and, pretending to scream in agony, says: "For the love of God, sell me some marijuana. You're my only hope to ease my pain." Shawn, feeling sorry for Oprah and her suffering, sells her some marijuana. The next day he is arrested. Any defense?

6. Rashwana, pretending to be a battered wife whose husband often beats

her severely, approaches Msumo and describes a powerful but false history of the violence she has suffered. Rashwana begs Msumo to kill her husband and offers him $4,000 for the job. Msumo, feeling sorry for Rashwana, agrees. He is then arrested for conspiracy to commit murder. Entrapment?

7. Pete's Trucking has suffered great losses from thefts of valuable cargoes carried on his trucks. Seeking to find out the culprit, Pete arranges to have some particularly valuable fur coats shipped on each of his drivers' trucks. Jose's truck is selected to be the first. The furs are not packed in secure boxes nor is there any of the usual paperwork. Jose has never stolen a dime in his life. In fact, another driver has actually done all the stealing. Jose, who earns the minimum wage and has a family of seven children to support, suddenly realizes the golden opportunity that has presented itself. He stops the truck en route and off-loads the furs into his house, intending to sell them and use the money to support his poor family. Pete, who has been following Jose's truck from a distance, sees this and calls the police immediately. Jose is arrested and charged with theft. The prosecution moves to bar the defense of entrapment. Why?

EXPLANATIONS

1a. This is an easy case. The defendant approached the officer, initiated the discussion about sex for money, and provided a place for the crime. The government did no more than present an opportunity for an "unwary criminal" to commit a crime. In a jurisdiction adopting the subjective approach, the government could produce evidence of Linda's predisposition to commit prostitution, including any past convictions. Even under the objective approach, which focuses on the impact police conduct would have on a law-abiding citizen, Linda would not be successful. Ordinary citizens would not agree to commit an act of prostitution under these circumstances, so there is no risk of trapping the "unwary innocent."

1b. This case is more complicated. Under both the subjective and objective approaches the police instigated this criminal activity. The subjective approach looks not only at what the police did but also at the defendant's predisposition. Linda's past prostitution supports the prosecution's claim that she was predisposed to criminal activity even before the police embarked on the undercover operation. Here the police officer initiated the criminal venture by asking Linda if she would commit prostitution.

Yet, Linda initially declined the offer. Only when the undercover officer offered an extremely high payment did she agree. Even though the police conduct was extremely persuasive, a judge or jury could well find that Linda was predisposed to commit prostitution if the price was right, thereby defeating her claim of entrapment.

The objective approach looks at what the police did and determines whether a reasonable law-abiding person would commit the offense. Under this approach Linda's past history of occasional prostitution would be irrelevant. Nonetheless, even an offer of $1,000 would probably not induce a law-abiding citizen to commit an act of prostitution. Linda might well be convicted even under the objective approach.

2. Poor Lucy. Of course, she initiated a drug purchase; there can be little doubt about her predisposition to commit that crime. However, it was the undercover police officer who instigated prostitution. Moreover, he took advantage of her addiction. He offered her heroin — something she needed more desperately than money.

There is no evidence indicating that Lucy was predisposed to commit prostitution. More important, the undercover officer used her addiction as a powerful incentive to induce Lucy to agree to prostitution. Is this appropriate police conduct? Is it entrapment? You decide.

3. Al would argue that the government entrapped him by providing an indispensable element of the offense — the cash and the checks represented to be proceeds of illegal activity. He would also point out that the government agent went beyond mere investigation to gather evidence of ongoing crime. She actually created the crime for which Al was charged.

The prosecution would argue that Al clearly was predisposed to commit other crimes because he actually told the undercover agent how to avoid the $10,000 cash transaction-reporting law. All the police did was to provide Al an opportunity to commit a different crime; they offered no unusual incentives. In a similar case the court concluded that the police conduct was not improper and dismissed the defense. See *United States v. Jensen*, 69 F.3d 906 (8th Cir. 1995).

4a. No. He rejected the bribe the first two times only because he was concerned about getting caught. When he thought he was in a secure place (even checking out the sheik for electronic surveillance), he readily accepted the bribe. Although the government did offer the bribe several times, this conduct did not reach a "level of outrageousness" sufficient to bar the prosecution. See *United States v. Kelly*, 707 F.2d 1460 (D.C. Cir. 1983).

4b. Wow! The congressman has not previously indicated a predisposition to accept the bribe. In fact, he actually refused it on ethical grounds (though he did not inform law enforcement officials of the attempted bribe). But an offer to save the life of your child is a very powerful inducement to which even a law-abiding citizen might succumb. You are the judge. How are you going to rule, using either test?

5. Clearly, the government initiated this criminal act by having Oprah ask Shawn to sell her marijuana. And there appears to be some basis for targeting Shawn as someone who occasionally sells marijuana. However, Shawn consistently refused to sell marijuana to Oprah until she appeared to be in extremely severe pain. The jury might well conclude that such callous manipulation of human sympathy for another suffering human being is so outrageous that the charge should be dismissed.

6. The government initiated this criminal activity and there is no basis for thinking Msumo was predisposed to commit a crime. Moreover, any law-abiding citizen might be sympathetic to Rashwana's plight. None-theless, entrapment is not available if an element of the charge includes inflicting bodily injury on another. Thus, Msumo cannot use this de-fense.

7. Entrapment is available only if the government is involved. Because Pete is a private citizen, Jose will not be able to raise this defense.

New Excuses: The Future Is Upon Us

What is the future of excuses in the criminal law? Defense attorneys increasingly suggest that the law should recognize new claims of defense. These claims appear to raise the same questions of free will, "lessened choice," and nonblameworthy character raised by existing excuses. The restrictions placed on such claims are increasingly attacked as dubious. Fur-thermore, supporters of this broadening trend point out that forcing a defendant to "squeeze" his new claim into preexisting categories of excuse, rather than simply allowing juries to consider the claim on its face, both trivializes the claim and results in possible unfairness to defendants. Thus, for example, women who have claimed either battered wife or premenstrual syndrome have to distort the doctrines of insanity or self-defense or provo-cation. And even if they are successful, they will face either civil commitment (on the basis of an insanity claim) or some (though lessened) incarceration. Since proponents of these new claims believe that these actors should be totally exonerated, they contend that the law's reluctance to widen its excul-patory net is unprincipled and unfair.[85]

To some, these new claims seem like nothing more than the last straw that an obviously guilty defendant will grasp. They characterize these claims as the "defense du jour" and talk about the "abuse excuse." Indeed, Professor

---

85. There is sometimes a claim of discrimination as well. Supporters of the "battered wife" syndrome contend that the current rules of self-defense are based on a male stereotype of a stranger-to-stranger encounter and do not consider long-standing relationships as relevant to the doctrinal factors. See Chapter 16.

Alan Dershowitz, highly critical of most of these claims, has listed over 50 such claims that have allegedly been made by defendants in criminal cases.[86] Although many of the excuses listed by Dershowitz have been rejected both by courts as a matter of law and by juries on resolution of fact, the argument he makes cannot be dismissed offhandedly.

Opponents of liberalizing the law of defensive claims have more than just precedent on their side. They aver that many of these new claims are based upon "junk science," and that there is no compelling evidence yet that these new findings show that criminal behavior is "caused" by such excuses. Moreover, to the extent that there is *some* evidence that such behavior is "influenced," opponents argue that it is the responsibility of an individual of good character to resist that influence, no matter how strong. Finally, some opponents argue eloquently that such claims will undermine the very premise of the criminal law, that of free will, and thus decimate the very concept of blameworthiness. *Even if* the claims are true, these persons argue, the criminal law must proceed *as if* they were not, for to admit them is to erode the very foundation of criminal liability.[87]

Proponents contend that the law *should* be responsive to such evidence and reject the "parade of horribles" argument. They maintain that judges and juries can filter the relevant claims from the frivolous. The essence of criminal responsibility, they argue, requires the law to examine *any* claim that a defendant's power of control was undermined. After all, that is why we have juries, as Professor Williams has declared:

> Once it is recognized that excuses are based on notions of justice, and show the law's consideration for the defendant's predicament in particular circumstances, it becomes obvious that the list of excuses need not be regarded as closed. [The Theory of Excuses, 1982 Crim. L. Rev. 732, 741-742.]

This question is often dealt with as one of the general rules of evidence. Usually, defendants will need, or certainly want, the testimony of an "expert" on the alleged excuse and its effects. A decade ago this might have been very difficult. Until very recently, most courts, following the lead of *Frye v. United States*, 293 F. 1013 (D. Cir. 1923), severely restricted the instances where expert testimony was allowed. In *Daubert v. Merrell Dow Pharmaceuticals, Inc.*, 509 U.S. 579 (1993), however, the United States Supreme Court adopted a more generous rule for federal civil cases. Many state courts seem to be adopting a *Daubert*-like standard as well. Whether this trend will be followed in criminal cases is uncertain.

---

86. The Abuse Excuse (1994). See also J. Wilson, Moral Judgment (1997); Turk, Abuses and Syndromes: Excuses or Justifications?, 18 Whittier L. Rev. 901 (1997). But see Singer, No Excuse for a Law Professor, 6 Crim. L. Forum 121 (1995).

87. E.g., Justice Weintraub, concurring in *State v. Sikora*, 44 N.J. 453 (1965); Lord Simon in *Lynch v. Director of Public Prosecutions*, [1975] 1 All E.R. 913.

We will not discuss the merits or demerits of any of the new claims. Instead, we will simply catalog a few of the more persistent claims. How these will be treated by the courts in the coming years is highly uncertain. The struggle between empirical claims and criminal law's assumptions of free will will be fought in many of these battlegrounds.

It is always dangerous—even under the best of circumstances and with a great deal of information—to try to "categorize" anything. This is certainly true of the new claims. The lines suggested here are tentative. Thus, most "psychological" defense claims described below may later be treated as physiological in nature, if research increasingly indicates these conditions to be physiologically based.[88] Nevertheless, we shall make the attempt, in part because there may be similar issues surrounding one type of claim that do not surround others.

Physiologically (Biologically) Based Excuses for Criminality

At least since Ceaseare Lombroso claimed to be able to determine a person's propensity for crime by feeling the bumps on his head,[89] both scientists and laymen have hoped that they could find a connection between biology and criminal behavior. After all, such persons might be "treatable," or if nontreatable, they could be incapacitated. In the early 1900s in this country and others, belief in such a biological connection led a number of state legislatures to enact statutes providing for the mandatory sterilization of criminals. Only after Hitler's "final solution" were these statutes repealed.[90]

Still, the search continues for a biological "cause" of crime, as controversial now as ever,[91] and again attacked on grounds that it supports racism.

---

88. For example, some geneticists now claim that there is good evidence that schizophrenia, a "psychologically based" claim already recognized under the common law "insanity" test, is really chromosomally and genetically influenced, if not determined.

89. C. Lombroso, Crime: Its Causes and Remedies (1911).

90. The United States Supreme Court considered the constitutionality of these statutes only once, in *Skinner v. Oklahoma ex rel. Williamson,* 316 U.S. 535 (1942). The Court found the statute unconstitutional on equal protection grounds: it did not sterilize *enough* criminals. Since, in *Buck v. Bell,* 274 U.S. 200 (1927), the Court had upheld a mandatory sterilization statute involving the mentally ill against an equal protection challenge, it is not clear what the Court might have done in the criminal context had the Oklahoma statute punished *all* thieves with sterilization.

91. In 1993 the National Institutes of Health funded a conference to assess the current status of the investigation of the link between biology and crime, but withdrew the funds after public outcry. Two years later, however, the Institutes refunded the conference, which was held in late 1995. Science, Sept. 29, 1995, at p.1808; N.Y. Times, Sept. 20, 1995, at sec. C, p.8.

The XYY Chromosome Affair[92]

Only one alleged genetic link to criminality has ever reached the appellate courts of this country. In the 1960s, researchers announced that they had discovered that a vastly disproportionate percentage of prison inmates had "an extra" Y chromosome. The suggestion was that, since the Y chromosome is what makes a fetus a male (each fetus has two sex chromosomes, at least one of which is an X; if the other is also an X, the fetus is a female), the "extra" Y chromosome must "add to" the "maleness" of the individual. Since crime — and particularly violent crime — is mostly a male activity, the argument was that this extra Y chromosome "caused" (or at least strongly influenced) the violence. Since no individual can control his genetic makeup, it was argued that XYY men who committed crime could not be blamed for those acts because they could not have done differently. Before the courts were confronted with potentially hundreds of such cases,[93] the methodology of the research was thrown into disrepute. However, the issue raised by the experience will not merely survive but will certainly be raised again as biology purports to find more physical links to specific kinds of behavior. The law will inevitably have to confront the question: What *should* the criminal law do if a genetic link, of some reasonable strength, is shown to "cause" specific conduct? See Dreyfuss & Nelkin, The Jurisprudence of Genetics, 45 Vand. L. Rev. 313 (1992). See also Coffey, The Genetic Defense: Excuse or Explanation?, 35 Wm. & Mary L. Rev. 353 (1993); Friedland, The Criminal Law Implications of the Human Genome Project: Reimagining a Genetically Oriented Criminal Justice System, 86 Ky. L.J. 303 (1997-98).

Premenstrual Syndrome (PMS)

Premenstrual syndrome[94] is another biological condition alleged to affect behavior. While many women experience cramps, nausea, and other (often severe) discomfort just before their menstruation, the term PMS has always been restricted to the small percentage (about 2-3 percent) who suffer such agony and pain that they sometimes become severely violent.

Women who have raised this claim have been forced to fit it into existing categories of defenses recognized by the common law—for example, insanity, provocation, diminished responsibility. Provocation is unavailable, however,

---

92. See Burke, The "XYY" Syndrome: Genetics, Behavior and the Law, 46 Den. L.J. 261 (1969).

93. At least one American court rejected the XYY chromosome argument. *Millard v. State*, 8 Md. App. 419 (1970). Because then-existing (and probably current) criminal law had no niche for the claim, the defendant argued that he was "insane" under the *M'Naghten* rules.

94. The literature on PMS is massive. See Note, 24 Wash. L.J. 54 (1984), for a typical commentary on the issue and citing (unreported) cases.

because the victim may have done *nothing* provocative at all. The variations of insanity are usually not available because PMS is not considered to be a mental disease and because it is not permanent. In 1994, however, the American Psychiatric Association (APA) added premenstrual dysphoric disorder (PMDD), a severe form of premenstrual syndrome, to the list of depressive disorders in its Diagnostic and Statistical Manual (DSM-IV). The definition applies to a small percentage (2-6 percent) of women. The DSM expressly states that its classifications are not to be used in nonpsychiatric settings (e.g., in court), but lawyers have consistently relied on its authority in other types of cases in the past. This might mean that (1) other women will be excluded from claiming PMS; (2) women who claim PMDD will be treated as suffering from a mental illness, with possible commitment after a successful defense. It is not clear that this is a sound approach. See Solomon, Premenstrual Syndrome: The Debate Surrounding Criminal Defense, 54 Md. L. Rev. 571 (1995).

As with some of the other claims considered here, PMS raises other intriguing questions. For example, there are alleged "treatments" for the serious forms of PMS. Could a woman who fails or refuses to undergo such treatment lose the claim, on the basis of omission, much as did Decina (see Chapter 3 at page 37)? How would such an argument take into consideration the fact that some of these treatments have potentially long-run, serious side-effects? Would a "choice of evils" analysis apply here in determining whether the woman who refused such treatments had acted "reasonably"? Is reasonableness the standard? And, if so, would that reasonableness be judged by the standard of (1) the reasonable woman; (2) the reasonable woman with PMS; or (3) the reasonable woman with PMS who feared such side-effects (a) reasonably; (b) unreasonably? These questions may be precluded by the recognition of PMDD as a mental disorder, but perhaps not. After all, many women who do not fit the PMDD profile may still wish to argue that they were affected by PMS. There is no a priori reason why they should be prohibited from raising the facts just because the APA has declared some other women to be suffering from a mental illness.

Other Physiologically Based Claims

There is no end to the possible claims, but we list several more: hypoglycemia,[95] Alzheimer's disease,[96] neurotoxic damage,[97] and testosterone overload.[98]

---

95. See *Regina v. Quick*, [1973] 3 W.L.R. 26 (Ct. of Crim. App.).

96. See Cohen, Old Age as a Criminal Defense, 21 Crim. L. Bull. 5 (1985).

97. See Note, The Sevin Made Me Do It: Mental Non-responsibility and the Neurotoxic Damage Defense, 14 Va. Envtl. L.J. 151 (1994).

98. Within the past few years, researchers have concluded that testosterone, a hormone found in much greater concentration in men than in women, does in fact

Psychologically Based Excuses
Brainwashing

Many of the new claims of psychological causation and defense, diminished capacity, pathological behavior, post-traumatic stress disorder, temporary insanity, and the like have already been considered in the section on insanity. At least one claim does not quite fit the usual psychiatric mode: brainwashing.[99] This phenomenon was first detected by studies of prisoners of war, but it became a criminal law issue in the bizarre case of Patty Hearst. As usual, truth is stranger than fiction.

Patty Hearst was an heiress to a fortune. By all accounts, she had little concern for political issues, much less for violent politics. Ms. Hearst was kidnapped by a militant group of terrorists in California, who demanded that her father take certain social measures (such as distributing free food to thousands of hungry poor people in several California cities). Months later, Ms. Hearst appeared, dressed in black and carrying a machine gun, assisting the terrorists in robbing a California bank. She was arrested about a year later in San Francisco. When booked, she gave her name as Tanya, and her occupation as "revolutionary." (Not even Danielle Steele could concoct such a plot. But it all happened.)

At trial, Hearst (as she now called herself again) argued that it was not "she" but "Tanya" who had robbed the bank. During her captivity, she argued, she had been not merely tortured but indoctrinated. She had "become" another person, Tanya, and remained so until "deprogrammed" after her arrest.

The jury rejected Hearst's claim, but the judge allowed it to be presented. Clearly, it raises almost primordial questions. (1) When is a person "herself"? (2) Can that person "change" under psychological pressure and then revert back when the pressure is removed?[100] (3) "Who" is punished

---

affect "aggressive" behavior. See, e.g., Sullivan, the HE Hormone, N.Y. Times Magazine, April 2, 2000, p.46. While this may echo the "XYY" syndrome, the research seems much more methodologically sound. Whether the "influence" is sufficient to warrant consideration by courts is unclear.

99. See Delgado, Ascription of Criminal States of Mind: Toward a Defense Theory for the Coercively Persuaded ("Brainwashed") Defendant, 63 Minn. L. Rev. 1 (1978); Dressler, Professor Delgado's "Brainwashing" Defense: Courting a Deterministic Legal System, 63 Minn. L. Rev. 335 (1979). Note that even Dressler's title poses the philosophical question—to what extent would recognition of such a claim "court" a deterministic view of human behavior (and how would the criminal law deal with such a view)?

100. Hearst had been out of the clutches of her captives for at least nine months before her arrest; police had destroyed the terrorist-robbers' hideout and killed virtually everyone there. Hearst had already disappeared before that event. She explained that merely being "away from" the terrorists was insufficient to allow "regression" back to her "real self"; it required professional assistance that was only available after her arrest.

—the previous "person" or that person's "mind" (which, by hypothesis, no longer exists)? (4) To what degree would an acceptance of the claim weaken the criminal law's moral stature? Some of these questions may also be raised in other contexts—for example, in dealing with "multiple personalities." But brainwashing raises all of them.

Mob Mentality

In a very famous (but not officially reported) incident, Damien Williams, a black resident of Los Angeles, joined a mob of rioters who were outraged by a jury verdict acquitting several white police officers charged with unlawfully beating a black man. The mob stopped a truck and its white driver, pulled him from the cab, and began beating him. Williams picked up a brick and hit the driver. Fortunately, the driver survived, but Williams was charged with attempted murder, aggravated assault, and several other offenses. At trial, Williams argued (among other things) that he had no intent to injure, much less kill, the driver, but that he was simply "swept up" in the emotions of the moment. The jury acquitted him of the most serious of these charges. Had the driver died, it is possible that Williams might have argued, at least under the Model Penal Code, that he was suffering from an "extreme emotional disturbance" that would lower his homicide from murder to manslaughter. However, the jury obviously sympathized with Williams' claim that he had been "caused" to act the way he did by influences beyond his power to control.

Sociologically Based Claims

Many of the claims listed and criticized by Professor Dershowitz, while ultimately going to the defendant's blameworthiness, are currently cast in terms of "syndromes" uncovered by sociologists, anthropologists, or others who study human behavior. Many of these seek to "explain" criminal behavior in terms of the defendant's past experiences. In particular, they point to "abuses" of one sort or another, psychological, physical, sexual, that he suffered. Again, categorizing is both dangerous and simplistic. Nonetheless, one could distinguish between claims that these abuses led directly to criminality and those that argue that the abuse made the defendant more sensitive to indicia of imminent abuse.

Criminogenic Causes: Rotten Social Background

Certainly one of the more controversial claims, still not raised in court, has been the suggestion that persons raised in ghetto-like environments become hardened to the pain that crime inflicts on its victims and are therefore less "blameworthy" when they inflict such injury. Delgado, "Rotten Social Background": Should the Criminal Law Recognize a Defense of Severe Environmental Deprivation? 3 Law & Inequality 9 (1985). Further, the argument runs, deprivation itself "creates" a "propensity to commit crimes." This is *not* merely an argument that poor people, or those living in a ghetto, are more likely to steal than people who are not poor — everyone likes material goods. It is, rather, that the constant deprivation affects the ability of the actor to assess the moral weight of his claim to goods (or bodily integrity) versus that of the "owner" of those goods.

Urban Survival Syndrome and Black Rage

Although conceptually distinct, these two claims are suggested along with Rotten Social Background as fertile fields for defenses. The first argues that persons in tense urban settings (much like battered women) are more sensitive to, and therefore more able to comprehend than others, "signs" that suggest violence is imminent. See Liggins, Urban Survival Syndrome: Novel Concept or Recognized Defense?, 23 Am. J. Trial Advoc. 215 (1999). It has been rejected in the several cases thus far raising it, but that does not mean that it won't be raised (or accepted) in another case in the future. The second — possibly a variant of heat of passion — argues that minorities, especially blacks, have so long been the victims of discrimination that their anger simply "erupts" against whites who are ostensibly unoffending, but who are seen as exemplars of the oppressing group. See W. Grier & P. Cobbs, Black Rage (1968) and E. Cose, The Rage of a Privileged Class (1993); Goldklang, Post Traumatic Stress Disorder and Black Rage: Clinical Validity, Criminal Responsibility, 5 Va. J. Soc. Pol'y & L. 213 (1997); Snierson, Black Rage and the Criminal Law: A Principled Approach to a Polarized Debate, 143 U. Pa. L. Rev. 2251. This claim has been raised — and rejected — in several unreported cases.

"Abuse Excuses"

Most of these new claims find their source in abuse suffered at an earlier time. One argument is that this abuse "explodes" in an episode (or episodes) of violence that the actor is unable to control, and that, because of earlier experiences, the defendant is more capable of discerning imminent danger than the "normal" defendant. This group includes battered wife or child syndrome. The first group generates a claim of "no voluntary act." The second group tends to coalesce in arguments that these acts are justified (or excused) self-defense (see Chapter 16) or that the criminal law's notion of mens rea should be more subjectivized. In each instance, these claims require (or need) expert testimony to support the contention; in many cases, courts have rejected the testimony and, hence, the claim.

Recap

Many of these claims may seem to raise issues involving, either directly or by analogy, "diminished capacity," discussed above (pages 465-473), but it is not clear that the claims involve underlying *mental* incapacities. This is particularly true with genetically or sociologically based claims. Moreover, such a limit might preclude the reference of such defenses to "general intent" crimes. Finally, it is not obvious that these defendants could, or should, be subject to preventive detention, as now occurs with many who raise diminished capacity.

It is easy to dismiss these claims as Dershowitz and many others do. But these claims touch directly the clash between the criminal law's assumption of free will and the scientific, determining view that much human behavior is caused by physical or physiological factors we cannot control. How the criminal law responds to such claims, both specifically and generally, may become one measure of how evenhanded and fair it is. It is not necessarily an exaggeration to say that how the criminal law deals with such claims in the next century may well decide whether it continues to carry the moral weight it has always sought.

EXAMPLES

1. Jim lived near a former uranium mine. His family's well and the foundation of their house were built with uranium rock. One day Hank insulted Jim, who went back to his house — a walk of several miles — and returned with a shotgun. He thereupon killed Hank. Indicted for first-degree murder, Jim seeks to introduce evidence that his exposure to uranium caused organic brain damage and an inability to premeditate. What should the judge do?

2. Frank is a landscape gardener and has been exposed to pesticides for fifteen years. Charged with first-degree murder, he seeks to introduce evidence that his exposure affected his mens rea. What result?

3. Lyle and Erik walked into the living room of their parents' home one night and shot both parents with a barrage of weapons. They seek to introduce evidence that they were sexually abused by their father as children. Should the evidence be admitted?

EXPLANATIONS

1. This is a real case, reported in the Virginia Environmental Law Journal (supra note 97). The judge admitted the evidence, and the jury, apparently on a basis of diminished capacity, found the defendant guilty of second- rather than first-degree murder. Note that there was evidence of "organic" brain disease. This is *not* necessarily a "disease of the mind"

as required by *M'Naghten* (see pages 436-437). Note also that in this case, unlike others, there is no evidence that the defendant knew of possible neurological damage and ignored it.

2.   This too is a real case, *Commonwealth v. Garabedian*, 503 N.E.2d 1290 (Mass. 1987). The trial court admitted the evidence, but the jury rejected the claim. The defendant argued that his toxicalogical intoxication was *involuntary,* in the sense that he was unaware of the impact of the chemicals on his nervous (control) system. Many of these "toxicological damage" cases involve such a claim. Indeed, a defendant who is asked why he did not seek treatment or refrain from further exposure is likely to argue that the earlier exposure diminished or removed his capacity for self-assessment. In this regard, the claim is akin to insanity.

3.   This is the famous Menendez brothers trial. At the first trial the evidence was admitted. Separate juries, deliberating the fate of each brother, were unable to reach verdicts. The evidence was argued as relevant for either of several points: (a) the past abuse created a rage against their father that suddenly "exploded" into a killing spree; (b) the past abuse made them sensitive to "little signs" that their father was displeased with them and might abuse them again; (c) the past abuse, combined with this sensitivity, made them able to discern, through "little signs," that their father (abetted by the mother) was about to kill them to prevent them from revealing the past abuse, and therefore went to a self-defense claim. The court admitted the evidence for at least the third purpose. At retrial, this evidence was barred, and both brothers were convicted.

Table of Selected Cases

Index